A Companion to African Philosophy

Blackwell Companions to Philosophy

This outstanding student reference series offers a comprehensive and authoritative survey of philosophy as a whole. Written by today's leading philosophers, each volume provides lucid and engaging coverage of the key figures, terms, topics, and problems of the field. Taken together, the volumes provide the ideal basis for course use, representing an unparalleled work of reference for students and specialists alike.

A Companion to African Philosophy

Edited by

Kwasi Wiredu

Advisory editors:

William E. Abraham, Abiola Irele,

and

Ifeanyi A. Menkiti

Blackwell Publishing

BLACKWELL PUBLISHING
350 Main Street, Malden, MA 02148-5020, USA
9600 Garsington Road, Oxford OX4 2DQ, UK
550 Swanston Street, Carlton, Victoria 3053, Australia

The right of Kwasi Wiredu to be identified as the Author of the Editorial Material in this Work has been asserted in accordance with the UK Copyright, Designs, and Patents Act 1988.

First published 2004 by Blackwell Publishing Ltd
First published in paperback 2006

1   2006

Library of Congress Cataloging-in-Publication Data

A companion to African philosophy / edited by Kwasi Wiredu.
    p. cm.
Includes bibliographical references and index.
  ISBN 0-631-20751-1 (alk. paper)
  1. Philosophy, African.   I. Wiredu, Kwasi.

B5305.C66 2004
199'.6 — dc21

                                        2003005561

ISBN-13: 978-0-631-20751-1 (alk. paper)
ISBN-13: 978-1-4051-4567-1 (paperback)
ISBN-10: 1-4051-4567-6 (paperback)

A catalogue record for this title is available from the British Library.

Set in 10/12.5 Photina
by Kolam Information Services Pvt. Ltd, Pondicherry, India
Printed and bound in the United Kingdom
by TJ International, Padstow, Cornwall

The publisher's policy is to use permanent paper from mills that operate a sustainable forestry policy, and which has been manufactured from pulp processed using acid-free and elementary chlorine-free practices. Furthermore, the publisher ensures that the text paper and cover board used have met acceptable environmental accreditation standards.

For further information on
Blackwell Publishing, visit our website:
www.blackwellpublishing.com

Contents

*To the memory of Cheikh Anta Diop and Alexis Kagame,
departed leaders of Contemporary African Philosophy,
and of our lamented colleagues John Arthur,
Peter Bodunrin, Didier Kaphagawani, Benjamin Oguah,
Henry Odera Oruka, and John Olu Sodipo.*

Contributors

William E. Abraham was born in Lagos, Nigeria, of Ghanaian parents, and educated in Ghana and Great Britain. He has taught in various universities, including Oxford, Ghana, Stanford, and California, and has held fellowships including at All Souls College, Oxford, Rockefeller, and the Stanford Hoover Institution. Now an emeritus professor, his principal publications include *The Mind of Africa*, articles on African philosophy and culture, on Leibniz, and on topics and figures in Greek philosophy. He has also held civic positions, including the chairmanship of national committees or commissions of inquiry, and membership of the first Presidential Commission of Ghana.

Born in Ghana, **Kofi Agawu** is Professor of Music at Princeton University. He earned his M.M. from King's College, London (1978) and Ph.D. from Stanford (1982). He has taught at King's College London, Duke, Cornell, and Yale. His books include *Playing with Signs: A Semiotic Interpretation of Classic Music* (1991), *African Rhythm: A Northern Ewe Perspective* (1995), and *Representing African Music: Postcolonial Notes, Queries, Positions* (2003). He received the Dent Medal from the Royal Musical Association in 1992 and an Outstanding Publication Award from the Society for Music Theory in 1994. He was elected Fellow of the Ghana Academy of Arts and Sciences in 2000.

Until recently the Charles H. Carswell Professor of Afro-American Studies and of Philosophy at Harvard University, **Anthony Kwame Appiah** is the Laurance S. Rockefeller University Professor of Philosophy at Princeton University. He was born in Ghana and studied at Cambridge University (UK) and Yale. He has taught at the Universities of Ghana, Yale, Cornell, and Duke. He has done work in the philosophy of mind, language and logic and in African philosophy and the philosophy of culture and politics. His books include *Necessary Questions*, *In My Father's House: Africa in the Philosophy of Culture*, and *Color Conscious: The Political Morality of Race* (with Amy Gutmann).

John Ayotunde (Tunde) Isola Bewaji, Visiting Scholar, University of Botswana, is a senior lecturer at the University of the West Indies, Mona. He was born in Esa-Oke, Nigeria, studied philosophy at the Universities of Ife and Ibadan, and has taught at the University of Ife, Ogun State University, Nigeria, and the University of Botswana. He was awarded the T. T. Solaru Prize in 1979 and won a Rhodes Visiting Scholarship in 1991. He was founding President of the International Society for African Philosophy and Studies, co-editor of *Quest, African Philosophy* and *Africana Philosophy*. His publications include *Beauty and Culture* and numerous articles.

A. G. A. Bello is a senior lecturer in philosophy at the University of Ibadan. He was born in Bibiani, Ghana, of Nigerian parentage. He did his undergraduate studies at the University of Karachi, Pakistan, and took his Ph.D. from the University of Ibadan. He has research interests in Islamic philosophy, African philosophy, and logic. His publications include *Introduction to Logic* (2000), "Moral Discourse in the Qur'an" (*Muslim Education Quarterly*, 18(2), 2001), and "Towards a History of African Philosophy" (*Ibadan Journal of Humanistic Studies*, No. 8, 1998).

Jean-Godefroy Bidima is Professor of Philosophy at the Institut d'Ethique du Centre Hosp, Universitaire St Louis, and Directeur de Programme at the Collège International de Philosophie, Paris. A Cameroonian, he studied at the Universities of Yaoundé and Sorbonne and has held Fellowships in Germany. He has been Visiting Professor in Bayreuth. His books include: *Théorie critique et modernité négro-africaine: de l'école de Francfort à la "Docta Spes africana"*, *La Philosophie négro-africaine*, *L'Art négro-africain*, and *La Palabre: une juridiction de la parole*. He has edited some books and published many articles.

Until recently **George Carew** taught philosophy at Spelman College, Atlanta. He is now a missionary of the United Methodist Church in Africa. Born in Sierra Leone, he studied philosophy at Westmar College, Iowa and gained his Master's from Howard and his Ph.D. from the University of Connecticut. He has taught in Fourah Bay College, Sierra Leone, and has been Visiting Professor at the University of Connecticut. He has also been Sierra Leone's ambassador to the USA. His publications include "Myths, Symbols and other Life-Worlds: The Limits of Empiricism," in Floistad (ed.), *Contemporary Philosophy*, and "Transitional Democracy," in Yeager Hudson (ed.), *Studies in Social and Political Theory*.

Francis M. Deng is Research Professor of International Politics, Law, and Society at Johns Hopkins' SAIS and Director of the Center for Displacement Studies. Born in the Sudan, he holds a B.A. from Khartoum University and a J.S.D. from Yale. Previously he was Sudan's ambassador to the USA and Minister of Foreign Affairs. He has held senior fellowships at the Wilson Center, the United States Institute of Peace, and the Brookings Institution. He was Distinguished Professor of Political Science at CUNY in 2001–2. He has written more than 20 books, including *The Dinka of the Sudan* (1972), *Dinka Cosmology* (1980), and (with William Zartman) *A Strategic Vision for Africa* (2002).

Souleymane Bachir Diagne is Professor of Philosophy at Northwestern University, Evanston. He was born in Saint-Louis, Senegal, and studied at the Ecole Normale Supérieure and at the University of Sorbonne in Paris. He taught for 20 years at the Cheikh Anta Diop University of Dakar, Senegal. His books include *Boole,* *l'oiseau de nuit en plein jour* (1989), *Islam et société ouverte: la fidélité et le mouvement dans la pensée de Muhammad Iqbal* (2001), and *100 mots pour dire l'islam* (2002). He has published articles in the history of philosophy, history of logic, Islamic philosophy, and African philosophy.

Pieter Duvenage was born in Pretoria, South Africa, and studied philosophy and communication theory in South Africa and Germany. He is currently Associate Professor in the Department of Communication at Rand Africaans University, Johannesburg. He was previously a Professor of Philosophy at the University of the North in South Africa. He has published various articles on hermeneutics, Critical Theory, postmodernism, and South African intellectual history. His book *Habermas and Aesthetics* is published by Polity (2003).

Segun Gbadegesin was born in Nigeria. He holds a B.Sc. from the University of Ife, Nigeria, now Obafemi Awolowo University, and an M.A. and a Ph.D. from the University of Wisconsin-Madison. He is currently Professor at Howard University's Department of Philosophy, which he has chaired for several years. He was previously Head of the Philosophy Department at Obafemi Awolowo University. He has been Visiting Professor at Wisconsin-Madison and Colgate. His publications include *African Philosophy: Traditional Yoruba Philosophy and Contemporary African Realities* (1991) and a great number of articles, including "Current Trends and Perspectives in African Philosophy," in Deutsch and Bontekoe (eds.), *Blackwell Companion to World Philosophies* (1997).

Barry Hallen is Professor of Philosophy at Morehouse College, Atlanta, Georgia, USA. He was born in Chicago, Illinois, and studied at Carleton College and Boston University. He has taught at the University of Lagos and Obafemi Awolowo University, Nigeria, and is Fellow of the W. E. B. Du Bois Institute, Harvard University. His books include *Knowledge, Belief, and Witchcraft* (1997), *The Good, the Bad, and the Beautiful* (2000), and *A Short History of African Philosophy* (2002). He has published articles in aesthetics, African philosophy, epistemology, and ethics.

Paulin J. Hountondji was born in Abidjan. He is Professor of Philosophy at the University of Cotonou and Director of the African Center for Advanced Studies in Porto-Novo (Benin). His publications include *African Philosophy, Myth and Reality* (1997), *The Struggle for Meaning: Reflections on Philosophy, Culture and Democracy in Africa* (2002), and other books and articles mainly in French. From 1998 to 2002 he was Vice-President of the International Council for Philosophy and Humanistic Studies (CIPSH) and is currently Vice-President of the Council for the Development of Social Science Research in Africa (CODESRIA).

Samuel O. Imbo is Associate Professor of Philosophy and Director of the African American Studies Program at Hamline University in St. Paul, Minnesota. He was born in Kenya and studied at the University of Nairobi and at Purdue University where he took his Ph.D. in 1995. He is author of *An Introduction to African Philosophy* (1998) and *Oral Traditions as Philosophy: Okot p'Bitek's Legacy for African Philosophy* (2002). In addition to his research and teaching interests in Africana philosophy, he has contributed book chapters on communitarianism and on cyber-space.

Liboire Kagabo is Professor of Philosophy at the University of Burundi in Bujum-bura. He was born in Kigarama, Burundi in 1947. He studied modern literature at the University of Butare (Rwanda), philosophy in Fribourg (Switzerland) and Lou-vain-La-Neuve, Belgium, and theology at Fribourg and Bujumbura. He has pub-lished many articles in African philosophy, especially in ethics and the philosophy of values, including "La Problématique des valeurs au Burundi," "Democracy and Civil Society in Africa," and "Quest for Paradigm in the Philosophy of Values in Africa."

Kibujjo M. Kalumba is Associate Professor of Philosophy at Ball State University in Muncie, Indiana. He was born at Mpigi, Uganda, and educated at Katigondo Seminary, Uganda, St Francis Seminary, Milwaukee, Wisconsin and Indiana Uni-versity, Bloomington. He has co-edited, with Parker English, *African Philosophy: A Classical Approach* (1996), and published several articles in African philosophy and social philosophy, including "The Political Philosophy of Nelson Mandela: A Primer" (*Journal of Social Philosophy*, 26(3), 1995).

Didier Njirayamanda Kaphagawani was Professor of Philosophy and Vice-Prin-cipal of Chancellor College, University of Malawi. He was born in Malawi and had his undergraduate education at the University of Malawi and his graduate educa-tion at Belfast University. He had specialist interest in Leibniz, and wrote a book on him entitled *Leibniz on Freedom and Determinism in Relation to Aquinas and Molina* (1999). He also had research interests in African metaphysics and epistemology. His articles include "Themes in Chewa Epistemology," in Coetzee and Roux (eds.), *African Philosophy Reader* (1998). To our deep mortification, Kaphagawani passed away in 2000 not long after completing his chapter for this volume.

Teodros Kiros is a philosopher and writer. Currently a Du Bois Fellow and Associ-ate in Residence at Harvard University, he has published extensively in journals. He received his M.A. and Ph.D. from Kent State University. He is editor and writer at large for the newspaper, *Ethiopian Reporter* and a columnist for *Somerville Journal*. He has published six books. His *Self-Construction and the Formation of Human Values* won the Harrington Book Award. His most recent books are *Explorations in African Political Thought*, and his forthcoming *Zara Yacob, a Seventeenth-Century Philosopher of Modernity*.

Safro Kwame is an Associate Professor of Philosophy at Lincoln University, Penn-sylvania. He was born and raised in Ghana and educated at the Universities of Ghana and Cincinnati. He holds two doctorates from Ghana and Cincinnati. His areas of specialization are metaphysics and moral and political philosophy. His current areas of research include African philosophy and the philosophy of com-puters. His publications include *Readings in African Philosophy: An Akan Collection* (1995) and "African Philosophy: An Overview" (*Philosophy Now*, 28 (August/Sep-tember) 2000). His website is located at <http://www.lincoln.edu/philosophy/kwame>.

D. A. Masolo is Professor of Philosophy at the University of Louisville, Kentucky (USA). He was born in Alego, Kenya, and studied at the Gregorian University in Rome, Italy, gaining his Ph.D. in 1980. He previously taught philosophy at the University of Nairobi and at Antioch College in Yellow Springs, Ohio (USA). He has held academic fellowships at several other universities. His books include *African Philosophy in Search of Identity* (1994) and *African Philosophy as Cultural Inquiry*, co-edited with Ivan Karp (2000). He has published articles in comparative philosophy, philosophy and society, and African philosophy.

Born in Mombasa, Kenya, **Ali A. Mazrui** is Albert Schweitzer Professor and Director of the Institute of Global Cultural Studies, State University of New York at Binghamton. He obtained his B.A. from Manchester University (UK), his M.A. from Columbia, and his Ph.D. from Oxford. He is Senior Scholar in Africana Studies at Cornell. He has been a Visiting Scholar at Oxford, Stanford, and Harvard, and has published more than 20 books and hundreds of articles. He is best known internationally for his television series, *The Africans: A Triple Heritage* (1986). His latest book is *Africa and Other Civilizations* (2002). He has been Dean at Makerere University, Uganda, and Research Professor at the University of Jos, Nigeria. He is now Albert Luthuli Professor-at-Large at Jos.

Ifeanyi A. Menkiti was born in Ontsha, Nigeria. He studied at Pomona College. He holds an M.S. from Columbia, an M.A. from New York University, and a Ph.D. from Harvard where John Rawls supervised his doctoral dissertation. He has been Professor of Philosophy at Wellesley College since 1973. His publications include "Person and Community in African Traditional Thought," "Normative Instability as Source of Africa's Political Disorder," "Philosophy and the State in Africa: Some Rawlsian Considerations," and "The Resentment of Injustice: Some Consequences of Institutional Racism." He is also author of two collections of poetry: *Affirmations* (1971) and *The Jubilation of Falling Bodies* (1978).

Mabogo P. More is currently Associate Professor of Philosophy at the University of Durban-Westville, South Africa. Born in Johannesburg, South Africa, he studied at the University of the North, University of South Africa, and Indiana University (USA). He has taught philosophy at the University of the North (South Africa) and has held academic fellowships in Britain and the USA. He has published articles on African philosophy, social philosophy, and political philosophy in a number of academic journals such as *South African Journal of Philosophy*, *Dialogue and Universalism*, *Quest*, *Alternation*, *Theoria*, *African Journal of Political Science*.

John Murungi is Professor of Philosophy at Towson University, Towson, Maryland. He was born in Kenya, and studied at Beloit College and at Pennsylvania State University. He also studied Law at the Law School of the University of Maryland, Baltimore, where he received his JD (1986). He is co-editor of two books, *Transformations of Urban and Sub-Urban Landscapes* (2001) and *Tensional Landscapes* (2002). He has published articles in the philosophy of art, African philosophy, and existential and phenomenological philosophy, and is currently doing research in African jurisprudence and in the philosophy of geography.

Nkiru Nzegwu is Associate Professor of Philosophy in the Department of Africana Studies at Binghamton University, New York State. She has published extensively in the areas of gender studies, African philosophy, African art, and aesthetics. She has edited two books on African art: *Issues in Contemporary African Art* (1998) and *Contemporary Textures: Multidimensionality in Nigerian Art* (1999). She is the founder of the online educational portal, africaresource.com, and its academic journals, notably, *West Africa Review, Ijele: Art eJournal of the African World, JENdA: A Journal of Culture and African Women Studies, Journal on African Philosophy* and others.

Théophile Obenga is Professor and Chair of African Studies at San Francisco State University, where he teaches Egyptian language and African civilizations. He was born in Brazzaville, Congo, and studied at the University of Bordeaux and Sorbonne, the University of Pittsburgh (USA), and Geneva University. He earned his Ph.D. at Montpellier University (France). He has taught at Temple University (USA), Brazzaville, Abidjan (Ivory Coast), Libreville (Gabon), Bangui (Central Africa Republic), and Lubumbashi (Congo, formerly Zaire). He is a member of the French Association of Egyptology (Collège de France, Paris). His books include *African Philosophy during the Pharaonic Period* (1990) and *Egyptian Geometry* (1995).

Victor Ocaya was born in Uganda and studied at Makerere University. Until recently he was Senior Lecturer in Philosophy at the University of Botswana, Gaboroni. He previously taught philosophy at Makerere and at the University of Zambia. His research interests are in African philosophy, epistemology, critical thinking and, most particularly, logic. He has made a special study of logic in Acholi, his mother tongue. Since his M.A dissertation on this subject, he has continued to deepen his results.

Olusegun Oladipo is Senior Lecturer in Philosophy at the University of Ibadan, Nigeria, where he studied and has been teaching since 1984. Among his publications are *The Idea of African Philosophy* (1992) and *Philosophy and the African Experience: The Contributions of Kwasi Wiredu* (1996), as well as articles, including: "The Commitment of the African Philosopher" (*Journal of Philosophical Research*, XX1, 1996), "Emerging Issues in African Philosophy" (*International Philosophical Quarterly*, XXXVIII(1) 1998), and "Knowledge and the African Renaissance" (*Philosophia Africana*, 4(1) 2001).

Formerly T. Wistar Brown Professor of Philosophy at Haverford College (Pennsylvania), **Lucius T. Outlaw, Jr.** is Professor of Philosophy and Director of the African American Studies Program at Vanderbilt University. He works on Africana philosophy, Marx, social and political philosophy, and the history of Western philosophy. Born in Starkville, Mississippi, he studied at Fisk University and at Boston College, gaining his Ph.D. in 1972. Recent essays have been published in *Philosophical Forum, Journal of Social Philosophy, Man and World, Graduate Faculty Philosophy Journal, The Journal of Ethics*, and a number of anthologies. His book, *On Race and Philosophy*, was published by Routledge.

Eritrean by origin, **Tsenay Serequeberhan** secured his Ph.D. at Boston College in 1988. He is a teacher of philosophy whose work is focused on African/Africana and

Continental philosophy. He has taught at Boston College, the University of Massachusetts (Boston), Hampshire College, Brown University, and Simmons College, and is now Associate Professor of Philosophy at Morgan State University. He is author of *African Philosophy: The Essential Readings* (1991), *The Hermeneutics of African Philosophy* (1994), *Our Heritage* (2000), and numerous papers. He is currently working on a book-length manuscript, *Contested Memory: The Icons of the Occidental Tradition.*

Claude Sumner ("Canadian by birth, Ethiopian by choice") is Professor of Philosophy at Addis Ababa University. He was born in Saskatoon, Saskatchewan, Canada in 1919 and studied philosophy, theology and linguistics in Canada. He has resided in Addis Ababa since 1953, when he was invited to the University. He has written 56 books, including *The Philosophy of Man* (3 vols.), *Ethiopian Philosophy* (5 vols.), and *Classical Ethiopian Philosophy* (1994). He has organized two Pan-African Conferences on African Philosophy and has published more than 200 articles. More than 350 articles, reviews, theses, and dissertations have been published on his work.

Olúfémi Táíwò is Director of the Global African Studies Program and Professor of Philosophy and Global African Studies at Seattle University. He was born in Ibadan, Nigeria, and studied at the Ôbafçmi Awolôwô University, Nigeria and the University of Toronto, Canada. He has taught at Ôbafçmi Awolôwô University, Loyola University, Chicago, the University of Virginia, Charlottesville, and the Institut für Afrikastudien, Universität Bayreuth, Germany, and has received fellowships from the Rockefeller and Ford Foundations and the Getty Senior Grant Program. He is author of *Legal Naturalism: A Marxist Theory of Law* (1996). His numerous articles include "Exorcising Hegel's Ghost: Africa's Challenge to Philosophy" (*African Studies Quarterly*, 1(4), 1997).

Godfrey B. Tangwa was born in Shisong, Nso', in Cameroon and studied in Cameroon and Nigeria, gaining his Ph.D. at Ibadan in 1984. He has taught philosophy at the University of Ife, Nigeria, and is currently Associate Professor of Philosophy at the University of Yaoundé 1, Cameroon. He is a current member of the Board of Directors of the International Association of Bioethics (IAB) and a founding executive member of the Pan-African Bioethics Initiative (PABIN). Recent publications include "Traditional African Perception of a Person: Some Implications for Bioethics" (*Hastings Center Report*, 30(5), 2000) and "The HIV/AIDS Pandemic, African Traditional Values and the Search for a Vaccine in Africa" (*Journal of Medicine and Philosophy*, 27(2), 2002).

Joe Teffo is currently the Professorial Assistant to the Vice-Chancellor of the University of the North, South Africa. He was previously Professor and Head of the Department of Philosophy there. He was born in South Africa and studied in South Africa and Belgium (Katholike Universiteit Leuven). He has been President of the Philosophical Association of South Africa. His publications include "The Other in African Experience" (1996), "Science, Religious Pluralism and the African Experience" (1997), and, with Abraham Roux, "Themes in African Metaphysics," in Coetzee and Roux (eds.), *Philosophy from Africa: A Text with Readings* (2002).

Pieter Boele van Hensbroek was born in the Netherlands. He studied philosophy at the University of Groningen where he is currently Research Coordinator at the

Center for Development Studies and lecturer in the Faculty of Philosophy. He has taught at several institutions, including the University of Zambia. His publications include *Political Discourses in African Thought: 1860 to the Present* (1999) and a number of articles on cultural citizenship, ideology, culturalism, and the philosophy of the social sciences. He was co-founder, in 1987, of the African Journal of Philosophy *QUEST*, and its managing editor until 2001.

Mourad Wahba is Professor Emeritus of Philosophy at Ain Shams University, Egypt. He has been a member of the Steering Committee of the International Federation of Philosophical Societies (FISP). He is also Founder and Honorary President of the Afro-Asian Philosophical Association (AAPA) and President of the Averroes and Enlightenment International Association. His publications include *The System of Kant, The System of Bergson, Dictionary of Philosophy*, and, more recently, *Love as the Foundation of Moral Education and Character Development* (1995) and *Averroes and the Enlightenment* (1996), jointly edited with Mona Abousenna. He is a Humanist Laureate of the International Academy of Humanists.

Edward Wamala was born in Uganda. He received his M.A. in New Delhi University, India, and his Ph.D. in Makerere in 1999. He currently lectures in philosophy at Makerere University, Uganda. His research interests are in African philosophy, the philosophy of development, and political philosophy. His publications include "The Socio-Political Philosophy of Traditional Buganda Society: Breaks and Continuity into the Present," in Dalfovo et al., *The Foundations of Social Life: Ugandan Philosophical Studies*, vol. I (1992) and "Cultural Elements in Social Reconstruction in Africa" (same series, vol. II).

Nicolas de Warren who translated Jean-Godefroy Bidima's chapter in this volume, is Assistant Professor of Philosophy at Wellesley College. He studied in Paris, Heidelberg, and Boston, and his interests include German idealism, phenomenology, and hermeneutics. He has published articles on Husserlian phenomenology and Descartes, and is currently writing a study of Brentano's peculiar brand of Aristotelianism.

Ajume H. Wingo was born in Nso, Cameroon. He studied at the Universities of Yaoundé (Cameroon), California (Berkeley), and Wisconsin-Madison, where he took his Ph.D. in 1997. He is Assistant Professor of Philosophy and Senior Fellow at the McCormack Institute's Center for Democracy and Development, University of Massachusetts, Boston. He is a Fellow at the Harvard Du Bois Institute. He has published many articles on African politics and aesthetics and is the author of *Veil Politics in Liberal Democratic States* (2003). He is currently working on a book titled *The Citizen*.

Kwasi Wiredu is Professor of Philosophy at the University of South Florida. He was born in Ghana and studied at the University of Ghana and Oxford. He was for many years Professor and Head of the Department of Philosophy at the University of Ghana. He has been Visiting Professor at the University of Ibadan (Nigeria), UCLA, Richmond, Carleton College, and Duke, and has held fellowships at the Wilson Center, Washington DC and The National Humanities Center, North Carolina. His publications include *Philosophy and An African Culture* (1980) and *Cultural Universals and Particulars: An African Perspective* (1996).

Preface

This volume is intended to be a comprehensive anthology of essays on the history of African philosophy, ancient, medieval, modern, and contemporary, and on all the main branches of the discipline, including logic, epistemology, metaphysics, aesthetics, ethics, and politics. The chapters are nearly all new. They have been written in such a way as to be reflective, enlightening, and useful to both students and scholars. Methodological concerns as manifested in contemporary controversies among African philosophers on the proper relations between the traditional and the modern in their discipline have been addressed. But pride of place belongs to substantive issues of philosophy as these have occupied the African mind in communal conceptions and individualized cogitations.

Accordingly, this text will not only serve as a companion to a main text in a course in African philosophy; it can also serve as the principal text at the graduate as well as the undergraduate level. The reader will therefore find ample bibliographies appended to most chapters. But this is not their only rationale. The discipline itself, of contemporary African philosophy, is in a phase of intense postcolonial reconstruction, which manifests itself in print in many different ways. The availability of relevant literature must therefore be a welcome aid to the curious. But even to the incurious outside of Africa, who are still often frankly taken by surprise by the mention of *African* philosophy, such notification of availability might well occasion the beginning of curiosity. Teachers newly embarked upon courses in African philosophy will also be empowered by the same circumstance. They will find that the Introduction to this volume was designed with their basic needs, though not only that, in mind.

It is a pleasure to specify my own helpers. My thanks go first to Professors Abraham, Irele, and Menkiti for their help as advisory editors. Thanks go next to all the contributors for their contributions. The call of the *Companion* often diverted them from pressing pursuits. Last, but most lasting of all, my thanks go to Barry Hallen for helping me with this work in every conceivable way from conception to completion. His lengthy survey of contemporary Anglophone philosophy (see chapter 6), which, more than any of the entries, gives this work the stamp of a *companion*, is only a sign of the lengths to which he has gone to bring help to me in various ways. To be sure, without him, that survey would most likely have taken a committee of at least five scholars.

In a class of its own is my indebtedness to Blackwell's technical staff. Without the initiative of Steve Smith, Blackwell's philosophy editor, in concert with inputs from Professor Tommy Lott, the project would never have started. And without the combination of patience and purposefulness on the part of his colleagues at Blackwell, Beth Remmes, Nirit Simon, and Sarah Dancy, it would never have been completed. The completion was also facilitated by the extraordinary collegiality of Professor Lewis Gordon through whom I had access to the facilities of the Department of Africana Studies when I was Visiting Scholar at Brown University in the summer of 2002.

Kwasi Wiredu

Introduction: African Philosophy in Our Time

KWASI WIREDU

The Postcolonial Situation

A principal driving force in postcolonial African philosophy has been a quest for self-definition. It was therefore quite appropriate that Masolo entitled his history of contemporary African philosophy, the first full-length history of the discipline in English, *African Philosophy in Search of Identity*. This search is part of a general postcolonial soul-searching in Africa. Because the colonialists and related personnel perceived African culture as inferior in at least some important respects, colonialism included a systematic program of de-Africanization. The most unmistakable example, perhaps, of this pattern of activity was in the sphere of religion, where mighty efforts were made by the missionaries to save African souls perceived to be caught up in the darkness of "paganism." But, at least, it did seem to them that Africans had something somewhat similar to religion, and some of them actually wrote books on African religion and even, in some cases, mentioned that subject in their university teaching.

The position was markedly different as regards African philosophy. Philosophy departments tended not to develop the impression that there was any such thing. I graduated from the University of Ghana in 1958 after at least five years of under-graduate study. In all those years I was not once exposed to the concept of African philosophy. J. B. Danquah's *The Akan Doctrine of God*, subtitled *A Fragment of Gold Coast Ethics*, had been published in 1945. Yet for all the information that was made available at the Department of Philosophy, that would have remained a secret to me if I hadn't made acquaintance with it in my own private reading in secondary school. I do not now remember what else in the literature relevant to African philosophy I knew by the time of graduation (1958) either by the grace of God or by the play of accident, except for the bare title of Radin's *Primitive Man as Philosopher*. However, when I ran across or stumbled over it, the word "primitive" in the title put me off, and I stayed away from its pages until a long time after graduation.

I do not say these things with the slightest intention of casting aspersions on my teachers. They were hired to teach my schoolmates and me Western philosophy, and they did that well. I remember them with the fondest feelings, not only because they gave us good mental training, but also because they were good men. In any case, at the time in question, although there was a lot to research, there was little to teach. The reason for bringing up these things is that they give some idea of the kind of academic and pedagogic situation that faced the first wave of post-independence African teachers of philosophy. Ghana won independence from Britain in 1957. Independence for other African countries followed in rapid succession. In 1960 alone, 16 African countries became independent. Thus by the mid-1960s there were significant numbers of post-independence African academics in various universities throughout Africa. African Studies became a very visible feature of university life in Africa, now with the participation of Africans in leadership positions. Certain African disciplines made immediate progress, as, for example, African history and also African literature, in which there were early manifestations of creative genius.

In African philosophy the situation was somewhat more imponderable. Unlike the disciplines just mentioned, African philosophy was usually non-existent in university departments of philosophy. If the post-independence African philosophers did not start with an absolute *tabula rasa*, it was because some relevant materials were available in the departments of anthropology and in those concerned with the study of religions. We may note examples like Evans-Pritchard (1937); Forde (1954); Herskovits (1938); Rattray (1923); and Smith (1950). African philosophers are beholden to these authors among others for a certain amount of preliminary data. But due to no fault of these authors, the works in question have tended to foster models of exposition in African philosophy that have been the source of considerable controversy. The troublesome features of these models were the following.

First, they were narrative and interpretative but, as a rule, not evaluative except indirectly. Their main aim was to explain, largely to foreigners, how Africans lived by their *ideas*. Their philosophical relevance was due to the fact that some of these were fundamental ideas regarding such topics as God, mind, time, causality, destiny, freedom, and the good. In the field of religion, the evaluative element in these accounts of African thought, which were generally (though not universally) written by Christian authors, consisted in the presumption, carried by immanent implication rather than explicit assertion, that if an African idea proved to be irreducibly incompatible with a Christian one, it was due for correction in the interests of salvation. In anthropology, indications as to where validity or truth might lie often came in the form of explanations of how given African modes of thought deviated from those of the researchers concerned. Nevertheless, as far as their basic intent was concerned, the texts were intended to be informative rather than speculative. Investigations into the validity or soundness of the ideas were no intrinsic part of the objectives of the researches.

Second, the accounts in question attributed ideas to whole African peoples, sometimes even to the entire African race. Information was, of course, collected from individual "informants." But interest lay in the beliefs of the communities to which the individuals belonged and not in the thinking of the individual "informants." The case of Griaule's *Conversations with Ogotemmeli* (1965), in which exposure was given to a named individual of an African society, is an (apparent) exception that proves the rule. Wittingly or unwittingly, the impression seems to have been created of unanimity of belief among African peoples. Underlying this whole situation was the fact that the African ideas under study in the present context usually existed in an oral rather than a written tradition of thought. The best way of gaining information about those ideas seemed to be by interviewing living repositories of African world views and also piecing together information embedded in proverbs, folktales, funeral dirges, ethical maxims, and the like.

When, by the force of historical circumstances, African teachers of African philosophy found themselves relying on works of the kind just described, that reliance soon bred, in many instances, unmistakable affinities of approach. Thus, in the hands of some African philosophers, African philosophy was becoming hard to distinguish from a sort of informal anthropology. An important difference between the resulting literature and its precolonial antecedents was that the African philosophers concerned wrote in a nationalistic spirit that brooked no nonsense about the possibility of philosophical error within African traditional thinking. The ground of dismay in the minds of other African philosophers with this development consisted in the conviction that philosophy is not just a narrative, but also an evaluative enterprise, the latter being an essential aspect of the discipline. On this view, philosophers should not content themselves with just informing others of the ideas entertained by their communities; they should also concern themselves with figuring out, for their own enlightenment and, perhaps, that of others, what in them is true, if any, and what is false, if any. Sometimes associated with this conviction has been the opinion that philosophizing is such an individualized activity that it is not plausible to suppose that whole cultures could have a common philosophy. There has also been the suggestion that without writing you don't really have philosophy, for the discipline must go hand in hand with science, and without writing you do not have science.

Paulin Hountondji

The person in whose writings all these reservations about the anthropology-like approach in African philosophy have been united, which for convenience we may call traditionalist, is the French-speaking African philosopher Paulin Hountondji. Among Francophone African philosophers, he is the one who has had the most impact on philosophical discussions in the world of Anglophone African philosophy. The best-known presentation of his views is in his *African Philosophy: Myth and Reality* (1996). He has, along with some Francophone African philosophers, used the word "ethnophilosophy" as a kind of negative characterization of what I have called here the traditionalist approach to African philosophy. The controversy that Hountondji's critique of ethnophilosophy has precipitated has constituted quite a large part of the concerns of contemporary African philosophy. That controversy may be studied in quite a few books. I mention the following almost at random: Appiah (1989: ch. 8); Appiah (1992: ch. 5); Gbadegesin (1991: ch. 1); Gyekye (1987: chs. 1–3); also see the preface to the revised edition; Kwame (1995: Introduction, chs. 1, 2, and 5); Makinde (1988: chs. 1–3); Masolo (1994: chs. 2, 3, and 7); Mosley (1995); Oladipo (1992); Oruka (1990a); Serequeberhan (1991);

3

Sogolo (1992: ch. 1); Wiredu (1980: chs. 1–4); and Wright (1984: chs. 1–5 and 8). In this controversy, Hountondji's dialectical resilience has been much on display. But he has not been averse to revision. In his contribution to the present volume (see chapter 44), he adds extension to revision by demonstrating how the scope of his critique of ethnophilosophy may be extended to comprehend the need to marshal our indigenous resources of knowledge as a basis of scientific development.

Since I myself am often grouped together with Hountondji as belonging to the anti-ethnophilosophy school, I might take the opportunity both to acknowledge the basic correctness of the classification and to point out, however, that my own reservations about the traditionalist approach are more limited than Hountondji's. I have no objection, in principle, to attributing a philosophy to a whole people, at certain levels of generality. Nor, although I am all for a scientific orientation in philosophy, do I define philosophy in such close intimacy with science as Houn-tondji does. My main unhappiness with the traditionalist approach derives from its insufficiently critical stance. Just as there was an element of implied evaluation in the accounts of African thought offered by the anthropologists and specialists in religion, there is an evaluation implicit in traditionalist accounts. The difference is only that whereas in the former case, particularly, where the authors concerned were Western scholars, the evaluations tended, *by and large*, to be negative, in the latter they have uniformly tended to be positive. In itself, that is no problem. But there are, among traditionalists, as hinted above, clear indications of impatience with any suggestion, on the part of an African philosopher, that philosophical fallibility might possibly be encountered in the thought of our ancestors or that there might be some aspect of an African culture that could be less than ideal from a philosophical point of view.

Traditionalists have tended, furthermore, to restrict the concerns of modern Afri-can philosophy to issues having some connection with traditional African thought and culture. But the modern world presents intellectual challenges which may not all admit of such a derivation, and to abstain from involvement with them on the grounds of a non-African origination is unlikely to prove a blessing to Africa in the modern world. Should it occur to anyone to liberalize the restriction by requiring, not that everything in modern African philosophy must have a connection with traditional Africa but only that it should bear some relevance to Africa, it can be shown that the new restriction is vacuous, for what makes Africa modern must include her ability to domesticate any useful modern resources of knowledge and reflection not already to hand. This is, of course, without prejudice to the need for a proper sense of African priorities. On any judicious reckoning, such priorities will include a careful study of African traditional thought. Thus one can be both sympa-thetic to traditional (not necessarily traditionalist) thinking and sensitive to the imperatives of modern existence. (See A. G. A. Bello's forthright discussion of meth-odological controversies in African philosophy in this volume, chapter 18.)

Indeed, what to do with modern issues and resources of philosophical thinking not directly originating from Africa is one of the two main topics around which the controversy on the question of African philosophy has revolved, explicitly or impli-citly. The other topic is, of course, what to do with our inheritance of traditional philosophy. Among Africans, there has not, contrary to copious appearances, been any question as to whether there is any such thing as African philosophy, but rather how best African philosophy may be done. The question whether African philosophy exists, taken *simpliciter*, has always, in my opinion, been an absurd question. Any group of bipeds that are barely rational will have to have some general conceptions about such things as, for example, what is meant by saying that a person is virtuous or the opposite. It would be an extreme step indeed to deny to the traditional African mind any tendency of a philosophical kind. Certainly, Hountondji does not take that step. He concedes at least that "we Africans can probably today recover philosophical fragments from our oral literature" (1996: 106). On the other hand, if we do not include in our philosophical program, *in addition to* the study of our traditional philosophy, the investigation of modern issues not dictated by traditionalist prepossessions, then the question whether there is a modern tradition of African philosophy would continue to have at least a prima facie relevance.

The Study of African Traditional Philosophy

But let us reflect for a moment on the study of African traditional philosophy. As already noted, there is a conflict between the traditionalist and the anti-ethnophilosophical approach, in regard, for example, to the need for a critical evaluation. But there is a prior question as to how the traditional thought-contents are to be discovered. One historic claim to such discovery was Father Placide Tempels's *Bantu Philosophy* (1959). Tempels was a Belgian missionary belonging to the Catholic faith, who ministered unto the Baluba of present-day Zaire (see Barry Hallen's survey of contemporary Anglophone African philosophy in this volume, chapter 6). Tempels formed the impression, which in the circles in which he moved was quite revolutionary, that those African peoples actually had a coherent philosophy and that it governed their day-to-day living. Not, of course, that he thought much of the validity of the Bantu philosophy. "No doubt," he remarked, "anyone can show the error of their reasoning, but it must none the less be admitted that their notions are based on reason" (p. 77). He wrote the book to prove this revolutionary point and to equip fellow missionaries with an insight into the thinking of the Bantu accurate enough to facilitate their conversion to the truths of the Christian message.

Tempels's book, which was actually published in the present English translation by a group of African intellectuals in Paris, was received with considerable enthusiasm among some African scholars and others of the generation of Senghor. Senghor was the first post-independence President of the West African State of Senegal, a man of many parts, who was responsible for elaborating the philosophy of Negritude to which we shall return below. That philosophy fell into disrepute, however, among Francophone African philosophers roughly of the generation of Hountondji, such as Marcien Towa and Fabien Eboussi-Boulaga, and has been one of the principal objects of attack in the critique of ethnophilosophy. Another principal target of anti-ethnophilosophy has been Alexis Kagame's linguistic studies of Bantu thought.

In connection with Kagame, whose principal works, as far as I know, have not been translated into English, an extremely important question arises, namely, to

5

what extent do the characteristics of a natural language give any indications as to the philosophical thinking of the people who speak it? Kagame (see chapter 16 by Liboire Kagabo in this volume) thought that the Bantu languages were fairly revealing in this respect, and he has been criticized quite considerably on this count. But the constraints of language on philosophical thinking are notorious in the Western tradition. Witness, for example, Bertrand Russell's animadversion with respect to the metaphysical notion of substance that "A great book can be written showing the influence of syntax on philosophy; in such a book the author could trace the influence of the subject-predicate structure of sentences upon European thought, more particularly, in this matter of substance" (1946: 225). Another book could be devoted to the influence of the superabundance of abstract nouns on European philosophies. Whatever the truth in this matter, it is plain that, although language may not necessarily lead to the discovery of truths about reality, it can lead to the discovery of some truths about the thought of an individual or a group about reality. Language is, in fact, an essential resource in the discovery of the philosophy embedded in an oral tradition not just in a lexicographical, but also in a deep conceptual sense. It goes without saying, of course, that caution is necessary in any recourse to language in this matter. Attention to the language issue is evident in the following pieces of writing in African philosophy: Bello (1990); Gyekye (1987: ch. 11); Masolo (1994); Sogolo (1992: ch. 1, sect. 3); and Wiredu (1996a: chs. 7 and 8). In this volume, considerations of language assume an evident importance in A. G. A. Bello's "Some Methodological Controversies in African Philosophy" (chapter 18), Victor Ocaya's "Logic in the Acholi Language" (chapter 20), and Barry Hallen's "Yoruba Moral Epistemology" (chapter 21).

To return to Senghor, his Negritude is, of course, a philosophy of black identity. Senghor argued that black people had a particular way of knowing, determined by their psychophysiology, which may be described as knowing by participation. In contrast to Western ways of knowing, which, he said, analyzes the object, breaking it into pieces, so to speak, African cognition proceeded by embracing the object. He actually once said approvingly, in a lecture in Nigeria in the 1960s, that this cognitive procedure "con-fused" objects rather than breaking them down; which raised anxieties among some African intellectuals that this came a little too close to making non-hyphenated confusion a congenital trait of the African psyche. To the Francophone critics of ethnophilosophy, indeed, the mere postulating of a peculiarly African mentality was obnoxious enough.

It is an interesting fact that keenness on the critique of ethnophilosophy has not been as much in evidence among Anglophone African philosophers as among their Francophone counterparts. (On philosophical thought in Francophone Africa generally, see Abiola Irele's (1995) magisterial survey. Among Anglophone African philosophers, the study of communal African philosophies has not evoked any concerted outcry, and works such as Abraham (1962), Danquah (1944) or Idowu (1962) remain highly esteemed, and rightly so. If Mbiti (1990) has been greeted with considerable criticism, it has been mainly because of certain specific things, such as its claim that Africans cannot conceive of a future extending beyond two years, to which we will return below. In fact, the study of traditional communal philosophies is a time-honored branch of African philosophy, with antecedents in the work of such historic thinkers as Edward Blyden, Africanus Horton, and Mensah Sarbah. These thinkers are discussed briefly by Pieter Boele van Hensbroek in the present volume in "Some Nineteenth-Century African Political Thinkers" (chapter 4) and at more length in his book *Political Discourses in African Thought 1860 to the Present* (1999). More recent works of high standing in the tradition of Abraham, Danquah, and Idowu are Gbadegesin (1991) and Gyekye (1987).

A notable fact about the books by Abraham, Danquah, Idowu, Gbadegesin, and Gyekye is that they undertake detailed and in-depth exposition, analysis, and interpretation of the traditional philosophies of specific African peoples of whose languages the authors have at least a first-hand knowledge. Also they eschew unrestrained generalizations about the traditional philosophies of the entire continent. In one chapter, indeed, Gyekye ventures some continental generalizations, but he is at pains to tender his evidence (1987: ch. 12).

The peak of such methodological circumspection is reached in Hallen and Sodipo (1997). In this work Hallen and his late co-author Sodipo study, among other things, the epistemological thought of the Yoruba of Nigeria in close collegial collaboration with traditional specialists in Yoruba medicine, language, and culture. Their inferences and interpretations are based on copious quotations from the discourse of the traditional thinkers in question, who remain unnamed at their own express request. The significance of the methodology of the two authors goes beyond mere circumspection. It is a definite departure from the old procedure – which elicited data from "informants," veritable informational servants – about African traditional thought. In the present method, traditional thinkers are brought into the enterprise of expounding and elucidating the traditional thought of an African people as authorities commanding respect in their own right. Hallen's "Yoruba Moral Epistemology" (chapter 21 in this volume) and, on a greater scale, his *The Good, the Bad and the Beautiful: Discourse about Values in Yoruba Culture* (2000) are continuing fruits of that program of meticulous research.

One of the most remarkable results of the investigation under discussion is the finding that Yoruba discourse lays down more stringent conditions for knowledge (or more strictly, what corresponds to knowledge in the Yoruba language) than is apparent in English or, generally, Anglo-American speech. In English-speaking philosophy it seems to be generally accepted that somebody may be said to know something, provided that she believes it, and it is true, and the belief is justified in some appropriate way. By the way, the need for not just a justification, but also one of an appropriate type, was pressed upon the attention of contemporary Anglo-American epistemologists by Edmund Gettier, in a three-page article entitled "Is Justified True Belief Knowledge?" (1963). The control that those three pages have exercised on recent epistemology has been, to say the least, tremendous.

On the showing of Hallen and Sodipo and their traditional Yoruba colleagues, a further condition would seem to be indicated, namely, that the prospective knower must have an eye-witness acquaintance with what is claimed to be known. This difference in English and Yoruba discourse about knowledge does not seem to be a matter that can be reconciled by mere verbal readjustments; it reflects different valuations of cognitive data. Interestingly, the language of the Akans (of Ghana) does not seem to carry any eye-witness imperative in its concept of knowledge;

which must reinforce the need for caution in the generalized attribution of philosophical persuasions to the entirety of the African race.

A project in some ways akin to that of Hallen and Sodipo, but quite distinct, was pursued by Henry Odera Oruka (of treasured memory) in Kenya. In his research into what he called "sage philosophy," he sought out individuals among traditional Kenyans who were reputed for wisdom and noted for their independence from foreign influences, and held (and recorded) long question-and-answer sessions with them. In these encounters the sages expressed their views about various topics, such as the existence and nature of God, freedom, justice, equality, and so on. Oruka (1990b) published translations of these discussions together with the names and even pictures of the sages concerned.

Already, this marks a difference between Oruka's project and that of Hallen and Sodipo. But a deeper difference is that Oruka's traditional collaborators, especially those among them that he called philosophic sages, expressed their own personal views and were sometimes quite critical of the communal thought of their society. For example, some of them avowed atheism, contrary to the widespread impression that traditional Africans are universally religious. Oruka's work in this area confirms a belief which the present writer, for one, has entertained right from the beginning, that among our traditional peoples there are original philosophers from whom we may have something to learn. The work on "sage philosophy" was not the only contribution that Oruka, who died prematurely in 1996, made to contemporary African philosophy; but for that in particular we are all eternally indebted to him. (For further discussion of the sage philosophy project, see Kibujjo M. Kalumba, "Sage Philosophy: Its Methodology, Results, Significance, and Future," chapter 19 in this volume.)

A point, which is obvious once you think about it, but which is easily overlooked, is that African traditional philosophy is not coextensive with African communal philosophy, for traditional thought, as is apparent from the immediately preceding remarks, has an individualized component. Moreover, a communal philosophy is, in any case, a kind of historical précis of the excogitations of individual philosophic thinkers, usually, though not invariably, of unknown identity. Some of these would, inevitably, have had views that did not conform to previously received notions. There are, for example, in some of the deliverances of Akan talking drums some cosmological paradoxes, which, in my opinion, suggest pantheistic views quite at variance with the commonplace theism of Akan communal thinking (see Wiredu 1996a: 119–21). Looked at in this way the study of traditional philosophy becomes more multifaceted than hitherto.

Mbiti and Time in Africa

Controversy is one of the marks of vitality in philosophy. In contemporary African philosophy controversy has tended to be more *about* traditional African philosophy itself than *in* it. Among the issues that have invoked discussions of the latter category, pride of place belongs to the debate about the question of "the African conception of time." This circumstance is thanks to Mbiti's treatment of the subject in his *African Religions and Philosophy* (1990). The issue concerns his claims as to the shortness of African prevision. In an exceedingly interesting discussion of what he called the African conception of time, Mbiti asserted that, for Africans, time is a composition of events, those that have happened, those that are now happening and those that are about to happen, longest two years hence. What has not yet happened or is not happening or has no likelihood of immediate occurrence falls into the category of what he calls "No-time." But if something will inevitably happen within the recurrent rhythm of nature, then it belongs to "potential time" (ibid. 16).

In spite of the window into the infinite future that his quaint notion of "potential time" seemed to open up for the African mentality, Mbiti held that the African conception of the future is so circumscribed by this overall notion of time that "any meaningful event in the future must be so immediate and certain that people have almost experienced it. Therefore, if the event is remote, say, beyond *two* years from now . . . then *it cannot be conceived*, it cannot be spoken of" (ibid. 21). He adds:

> In traditional African thought there is no concept of history moving "forward" towards a future climax, or towards the end of the world. *Since the future does not exist beyond a few months*, the future cannot be expected to usher in a golden age . . . The notion of a messianic hope, or a final destruction of the world, has no place in the traditional concept of history. *So Africans have no "belief in progress," the idea that the development of human activities and achievements move from a low to a higher degree. The people neither plan for a distant future* nor "build castles in the air." (ibid. 23; italics added)

On display in this quotation are the true, the false, and the doubtful in equal measures. There is some truth here, for neither tidings of a future golden age nor forebodings of an eventual cosmic cataclysm are heard of in accounts of African life and thought. Moreover, to say that Africans do not build castles in the air is to pay them a compliment that some, though perhaps not all, Africans, surely, deserve. But to suggest that Africans do not traditionally plan for a distant future is to debit them with an incapacity that some of them at least do not deserve. How could the great empire-builders of African history have accomplished such objectives in total innocence of long-term planning? In this respect, then, what we have from Mbiti here is the opposite of *the true*. As it happens, moreover, Mbiti himself, in a moment of inconsistency, declares, in effect, that he is aware that Africans can "act, plan, and live . . . knowing that, for example, their ten-year-old child will be getting married one day (though it does not matter whether this occurs after another ten or fifteen years" (ibid. 28).

As for the claim that Africans have no belief in progress, it is at best doubtful. Nor is it absolutely clear what the belief in question amounts to exactly. In any case, it is the view that Africans traditionally had no conception of the future beyond two years that has scandalized Mbiti's African critics. Among the numerous discussions of this matter one might mention the following: Alfa (1988); Appiah (1984); Gyekye (1987: ch. 11, sec. 2); Masolo (1994: ch. 5); Oruka (1990a: 8, 9); Parratt (1977); and Wiredu (1996b). See also Hallen's "Contemporary Anglophone African Philosophy" (chapter 6 in this volume). Of these, only Parratt is sympathetic to Mbiti. All these discussions, except Hallen's and Wiredu's, came before the second edition of Mbiti's book. In the new edition (1990) Mbiti reacted to the hue and cry, but retracted nothing. On the contrary, he added remarks, such as the last quotation above, that made the original confusion even more confounded.

Yet, Mbiti's basic claim that time, for traditional Africans, is a "composition" of events is extremely interesting metaphysically, and is worthy of investigation independently of his problematic inferences from it. This view has a basic similarity to Leibniz's conception of time as nothing but an ordering of events. Two questions arise immediately. Is the attribution correct? And is its content valid? Gyekye (1987: ch. 11, sec. 2) powerfully disputes the accuracy of the attribution, as far as Akan thought at least is concerned, and seems to perceive in that system of thought an absolutist conception of time not altogether unlike Newton's. According to Gyekye, "In Akan philosophy time is regarded as a concrete reality" (ibid. 170). Time "is held to have an objective metaphysical existence, so that even if there were no changes, processes, and events, time would still be real" (ibid. 171). This is not altogether unlike Newton's absolutist conception of time as something which "of itself and from its own nature flows equably without relation to anything external." Newton famously opposed this conception to Leibniz's relational view of time in a controversy in the history of Western philosophy that was as important as it was undignified. Neither giant has run out of followers, nor does the corresponding issue in African philosophy resemble one that allows of easy resolution. The apparent parallelism here between African and Western philosophies of time demonstrates nothing, perhaps, beyond the fact that dissimilar cultures may sometimes be faced with similar metaphysical options.

It must be acknowledged that the issues here, not only in regard to the validity of the absolutist or the relational conception of time, but also in regard to the accuracy of ascribing the one or the other to the Akans or their thinkers, are unusually subtle. As to the latter, the following reason might, perhaps, incline one to attribute a relational or "compositional" conception of time à la Mbiti to the Akans. The concept of existence, as it functions even at the pre-philosophical level of Akan discourse, is spatial, or even locative. To exist is to *wo ho*, that is, to be there at some place. (In support of this conceptual claim about the Akan language, see Gyekye 1987: 179.) Given this understanding of existence, it would be deeply paradoxical to speak of time as existing, for it would then have to be at some place. And, whether or not the Akans, notwithstanding any resulting incoherence, entertain an absolutist conception of time, it seems that a spatial conception of existence is not compatible with such a conception of time. Thus if the spatial conception of existence is sound, one option in the ontological elucidation of time is ruled out. But is that conception of existence plausible? Considering the widespread reverberations that such a conception is bound to have in any system of thought, this question should challenge the most earnest attention of all inquirers into the traditional philosophy of the Akans and various other African peoples. If Alexis Kagame (1976) is right, the particle *ho* is, interestingly, used in Bantu languages to perform the same semantic function as *ho* in Akan. The Bantu, according to him, express "exists," by *liho* or *baho*, which means "is there" or "is at that place." (Kagame, Rwandese philosopher, poet, and linguist, is discussed by Liboire Kagabo in this volume – see chapter 16.)

A defense of the spatial conception of existence on independent grounds, that is, by means of considerations that do not rely on the peculiarities of one language or culture as opposed to any other, does not strike me as an impossibility, but it is not a priority here. Our motive here is to illustrate how the study of African traditional philosophy is apt to precipitate issues of the most direct contemporary pertinence.

Contemporary African Philosophy as Comparative Philosophy

Contemporary work in African philosophy has a certain richness deriving from its unavoidably comparative character. This is due to the interesting fact that contemporary African philosophers belong to two cultural traditions, the African and the Western. This can be an advantage, because working in more than one tradition can broaden your mind by acquainting you with a multiplicity of fundamentally different conceptual options. But it is also a problem, because African philosophers came to be situated within the Western tradition through the historical adversity of colonization.

Now, in colonial times, as previously noted, African philosophy was generally not investigated in philosophy departments in Africa. It was left to departments of religion and anthropology, usually staffed by foreign scholars, to study African thought as best they could. Unsurprisingly, the resulting literature often reflected the uncritical employment of foreign categories of thought.

Taken together, the circumstances noted define the following imperatives of research for contemporary African philosophers. There is the need, first, to bring out the true character of African traditional philosophy by means of conceptual clarification and reconstruction and, second, to try to find out what is living or fit to be resurrected in the tradition. To this might be added any insights that might be available from the foreign traditions of philosophy with which Africa has become associated by the force of historical circumstances. Of course, other traditions too can be quarried with the same motive, the shortness of time being the only constraint. At any rate, these imperatives have informed my own research efforts.

In talking of the uncritical use of foreign categories in the exposition of African thought, one is thinking of such categories of thought as are embodied in the distinctions between the spiritual and the physical, the natural and the supernatural, the religious and the secular, the mystical and the non-mystical, or, by way of substantives, between substance and attribute, mind and matter, truth and fact, etc. As I have argued in various places (see, for example, Wiredu 1996a: ch. 7), it is questionable whether any of these distinctions corresponds to anything, at least in Akan thought. A noteworthy fact, then, about the colonial accounts of African thought is that although the authors often thought that they were explaining the differences between African ways of thought and those of their cultures, they usually were, in fact, unwittingly assimilating African thought to that of their culture, because they routinely formulated those accounts in terms of their own conceptual frameworks.

11

The Question of Relativism

If one has been used to thinking exclusively in languages in which such concepts as the ones in question are embedded, it is likely to sound strange to hear it suggested that they are not applicable in the thought of some peoples. But this is exactly why exposure to such ways of thought can broaden the human mind. They challenge one to rethink the fundamental categories of one's way of thinking. This remark assumes that it is possible to evaluate categories of thought across cultures; it assumes, in other words, that conceptual relativism is false. Relativism in this sense is the view that the soundness, or even intelligibility, of any set of categories of thought is relative to its time, place, or context of origin. And this relativity is intended to exclude the possibility of critical evaluation from the standpoint of another time, place, or context. Relativism is, in itself, an issue of great interest. In contemporary African philosophy it is an unavoidable one. The most obvious argument against it is based on the empirically verifiable biological unity of the human species. A subsidiary premise is to be found in the actual fact of cross-cultural communication among the peoples of the world, in spite of the well-known difficulties of inter-cultural translation. (On both counts see Wiredu 1996a: chs. 2 and 3.) In truth, any contemporary African philosopher or, indeed, any teacher or researcher in African philosophy, because of the historically engendered cultural duality noted above, is a walking refutation of relativism.

The notion of the cross-cultural evaluation of thought implies the universality, at some levels, of some canons of thought. Such an idea is nothing short of anathema to many traditionalists, for they are apt to suspect that African philosophy might thereby become subordinated to Western philosophy. Accordingly, in such circles "universalist," especially as applied to a fellow African, is a term of reproof. It is not clear that traditionalists wish to commit themselves to an unlimited relativism. That would generate quite an unlimited inconsistency, for, in expounding African traditional philosophy, they do not hesitate, either on behalf of their communities or of themselves or both, to make universal claims, such, for example, as that every human being comes to the world with a destiny apportioned to them by God. This is, most assuredly, not intended to be true only of Akans or Yorubas, but of all human beings everywhere. And, obviously, it would be high-handed to advance a claim about all humankind, and then withhold from those not belonging to one's epistemic circle the right of philosophical comment. Anybody who consciously tries to avoid such arbitrariness by total abstention from universal claims will quickly find herself compelled to abandon philosophy in favor of some non-dialogical employment.

Yet in certain specific cases some form of relativism seems operative in traditionalist protestations. Suppose, for example, that someone were to comment that empirical evidence is lacking for the proposition that our ancestors are alive and kicking in some region adjoining the world of mortals. Such a person would be liable to be met with the complaint that she is inadmissibly importing Western canons of reasoning into a domain of African discourse that has suitable canons of its own.

12

Actually, in this debate the traditionalists have sometimes had some foreign aid. One recalls, for example, Peter Winch (1964), in which he criticized Evans-Pritchard (1934) for saying that the Azande belief that spiritistic forces can influence rainfall is not in accord with objective reality. (I use the word "spiritistic" here as an adjective formed from the word "spirits." The plural use of "spirit" often refers to semi-physical entities such as ghosts and other such apparitions. I reserve the word "spiritual" for the Cartesian concept of a non-extended substance, whatever that means.) To return to Winch, his own view was that "what is real and what is unreal shows itself in the sense that language has" (1964: 82). Evans-Pritchard was thus trying, "on the contrary, to work with a conception of reality which is not determined by its actual use in language" (ibid.). The implication seems to be that the phenomenon of rain being brought on by pro-spiritistic incantations is a reality determined by Azande usage. (One wishes that one could count on such usage in times of major drought in Africa.) Although, on the question of relativism, Winch himself was unhappy to be called a relativist, his doctrine seems to be exactly such as to encourage relativistic talk. Whether this is the case or not, there is no doubt that many African philosophers seem to regard relativism as an avenue to philosophical self-respect. Barry Hallen is, therefore, right, whether or not one agrees with him as to details, in devoting a lot of attention to the question of relativism in his tremendous essay in this volume (chapter 6).

But what, one might ask, is wrong with relativistic talk? A preliminary answer is, "It depends." Suppose relativism is understood to mean that what is right, true, valid, intelligible, is *relative* to culture. This immediately invites the question, "What do you mean by 'relative' in this context?" One answer is that to say of a concept that it is intelligible, or of a proposition that it is true, or of an argument that it is valid is to say nothing more nor less than that it is used or accepted within a given culture on the basis of criteria operative therein. The same applies, *mutatis mutandis*, to judgments of right and wrong: The entire meaning of the comment that an action is right is taken to be that it is approved of by some culture under consideration. This is normative relativism, with a cultural scope. It does not actually follow from this thesis that different cultures employ different criteria in their thinking. It might, for all that is contained in normative relativism, just happen that all the peoples of the earth use the same criteria with respect to some issues of thought or conduct. But it is easy to see that where different peoples differ, there can be no dialogue, if normative relativism is right. Under this dispensation, the most that a potential disputant can do is to point out that some proposition accepted in his culture is not accepted in another culture or vice versa. And that would be an end of the matter, as far as intercultural communication is concerned. (It might, however, be the beginning of less benign forms of interaction, such as war.) The infelicities of normative relativism are legion – I have discussed some of them in detail in "Canons of Conceptualization" (1993) and "Knowledge, Truth and Fallibility" (1995) – but the fact alone that it is incompatible with intercultural dialogue in conditions of diversity is a sufficient *reductio ad absurdum* of the theory.

However, relativity to culture can have another connotation. It might mean simply that the ways in which certain aspects of life and reality have actually been conceptualized and evaluated are relative to culture. Assuming relevant diversity,

13

this means that certain concepts and values are not universal among the different cultures of the world. This might be called descriptive relativism. It notices difference; it does not canonize it. It leaves open the possibility of dialogue among cultures. Some, including me, might not want to call this relativism unless a suitable rider is attached, but the intellectual state of affairs referred to is of the last consequence. Intellectual relations between cultures have sometimes been marred by the forced universalization of the modes of thought of a colonizing culture. This is exactly what happened in the Western colonization of Africa. Accordingly, pointing out the lack of universality in certain modes of conceptualization in Western philosophy could be a first step in the clarification of an African mode of thought. Another step would, of course, still await being taken, and that is the comparative evaluation of both the African and the Western conceptions.

Hallen and Sodipo (1997) have argued that the English word "know" does not translate unproblematically into Yoruba, since *"mo,"* the nearest Yoruba approximation, still requires eyewitness acquaintance. This implies that the degree of value attached to eyewitness cognition is variable among cultures. But whether one degree of valuation is better than another in relation to some shared human imperative or not remains an open question. Similarly, as mentioned above, I have argued that the modes of conceptualization embodied in such distinctions as that between the physical and the spiritual, the natural and the supernatural, are not universal to human thought, since they are absent from Akan thought (see Wiredu 1996a). I have also suggested, as a separate point, that those distinctions can be shown to be incoherent on *independent* grounds, though the arguments need to be set forth more fully than so far. Such kinds of African-illustrated limits to the supposed universality of certain Western modes of thinking are more appropriate than cases such as the Azande belief in extra-scientific rainmaking, which is discussed by Evans-Pritchard and Winch. The reason is simple. Belief in extra-scientific rainmaking is not peculiar to Africa; it has been known in Europe (and other parts of the world). The wonder is why Evans-Pritchard and Winch saw it as an African problem. More generally, contra-scientific, spiritistic beliefs are not met with in Africa alone. They are routine in much Western thought. In Christianity they are even foundational.

Conceptual Decolonization

At all events, it is with regard to the more abstract concepts just mentioned that we need to be most alert to the effects, on African thought, of the premature universalization of certain Western modes of thought that came along with European colonialism and evangelism. As matters stand now, concepts such as the physical, the spiritual, the natural, and the supernatural lie at the deepest reaches of our thought about life and reality – and I am referring to most of us African philosophers. For that very reason, they are apt to be taken for granted. Suppose they should turn out not to be coherent within an African conceptual framework. That circumstance should lead, in the first place, to a re-examination of the resources of that African framework of thought and, in the second place, to a critical review of the concepts concerned in their own original European conceptual setting. However the exercise

14

turns out, the results should hold two kinds of benefit. To an African, it should bring freedom from any subjection to a colonial mentality in relation to the intellectual issue on hand. To a Westerner, who, on observing the disputing of so fundamental an array of Western categories of thought, takes the opportunity to review them critically, it should bring the satisfaction of having implemented the precept of one of the most illustrious of his spiritual ancestors, who said that the unexamined life is not worth living.

But let us return to the decolonizing effect. What is in play here is what might be called conceptual decolonization. It consists in an African's divesting his thought of all modes of conceptualization emanating from the colonial past that cannot stand the test of due reflection. This divesture does not mean automatically repudiating every mode of thought having a colonial provenance. That would be absurd beyond description. What it calls for is the reviewing of any such thought materials in the light of indigenous categories, as a first step, and, as a second, evaluating them on independent grounds. Of the indigenous categories of thought one can take appropriate cognizance by simply trying to think matters through in the vernacular. To do this, however, requires a conscious and deliberate effort, because if you are trained in philosophy exclusively in a second language, it tends to become your first language of abstract meditation. If, upon such a review, some Africans should become confirmed exponents of some Western mode of thought, they would, of course, be within their rational rights. The considerations leading to the sought-after intellectual liberation merely enlarge our options, they do not decide them. For example, if an African Christian, on critically examining his faith in the light of renewed attention to his indigenous conceptual framework by way of his own language and culture, decides that there are good reasons to retain the faith in Christ, philosophy cannot demand any more than that of him. Due reflection, to be sure, could also lead to atheism. No matter. After all, atheists were not unknown in African traditional society. For example, some of Oruka's traditional sages were atheists. To return to the African Christian: there is one thing he cannot do in the face of the imperative of due reflection. He cannot say that he entertains his preference for the Christian faith over the African one by faith. Since the question is "Why go with faith A rather than faith B?" such an answer would only manifest a brazen resolve to persist in the unexamined life.

The need for conceptual decolonization in African philosophy is pervasive. Only a few of the concepts that cry for a decolonized treatment have been mentioned. To them might be added the following list:

Reality, Being, Existence, Object, Entity, Substance, Property, Quality, Truth, Fact, Opinion, Belief, Knowledge, Faith, Doubt, Certainty, Statement, Proposition, Sentence, Idea, Mind, Soul, Spirit, Thought, Sensation, Matter, Ego, Self, Person, Individuality, Community, Subjectivity, Objectivity, Cause, Chance, Reason, Explanation, Meaning, Freedom, Responsibility, Punishment, Democracy, Justice, God, World, Universe, Nature, Supernature, Space, Time, Nothingness, Creation, Life, Death, Afterlife, Morality, Religion. (Wiredu 1996a: 137)

In regard to all these, the simple experiment of trying to think various issues through in an African vernacular is likely to generate second thoughts about a lot of notions that have seemed intelligible or even plausible when viewed within the framework of some Western system of thought. (I have discussed various issues from a decolonizing standpoint in ibid. chs. 5–11. See, alternatively, Oladipo 1995.) Of all the areas of African philosophy, the need for conceptual decolonization is perhaps greatest in that of religion. In the present volume (see chapter 27), Oladipo engages in the exercise of conceptual decolonization to good effect. The most impressive antecedent in conceptual decolonization is to be found in p'Bitek (1970). Bitek, one of Africa's best writers was, in my opinion, also one of her best philosophers. He is the subject of Samuel O. Imbo's contribution to this volume – see chapter 28.

The Concept of a Person

The study of African traditional philosophy provides many opportunities for conceptual decolonization. Approached from this standpoint, it can be quite enlightening to both Africans and non-Africans in furnishing concrete embodiments of categories of thought alternative to some Western ones. African traditional philosophies are, perhaps, richest in ethics and metaphysics. In these areas of inquiry the concept of God and the nature of human personality are the dominant issues. Concerning the concept of God, see chapter 27 in this volume, by Oladipo. The concept of a person is probably the topic that has evoked the most interesting discussions. There is a basic similarity in the conceptions of a person to be found in the traditional thought of many of the peoples of Africa. (See in this connection the late Kaphagawani's contribution to this volume, chapter 25.) A human being is held to consist of a variable number of elements, one of which typically might be called the life principle, that is, that in a person whose presence makes him alive and whose absence makes him dead. This is sometimes called in English "the soul," but that is incorrect, because in English-speaking philosophy the word "soul," which is used to refer to a kind of entity, is often used interchangeably with the word "mind." But I do not know of any African thought system in which mind is conceived as an entity rather than as a capacity, namely, the capacity to think. The life principle, then, being a kind of entity, cannot be identical with the mind.

This, however, is a claim of interpretation, and, as in all philosophy, has been subject to controversy. As far as Akan is concerned, some of its interpreters, such as Gyekye, my good friend and former colleague at the University of Ghana, have defended the identification of the life principle (in Akan the *okra*) with the soul. He has argued lucidly for his position in his *Essay on African Philosophical Thought* (1987: ch. 6). For my part, I have sought to clarify my interpretation in various writings (see, especially, Wiredu 1987). A simple consideration I have urged in this connection is that mind – *adwene* in Akan – is never mentioned in any enumeration of the entities that unite to constitute a person. If mind were thought of as an entity, this omission would be totally inexplicable. Elsewhere (for example, in Wiredu 1996a: 121–3), I have given a less simple reason why the *okra* (the life principle) cannot be interpreted as being identical with the soul: In Western discourse, the soul is usually conceived as an immaterial entity. Such a conception is, however,

16

inadmissible within any known Akan conceptual scheme. The reason is that exist-ence in the Akan language is intrinsically locative, as we saw in an earlier connec-tion. To exist is to *wo ho*, i.e., to be at some place. Since the soul, being supposedly an immaterial entity by definition, does not occupy space, it is highly implausible to suppose that such a leading idea of Akan thought as the *okra* could be equated with the soul.

To return to the inventory of the constituents of human personality, the other constituents of a person additional to the *okra* are even harder to characterize in English. There is what might be called the individuality principle, something in a person that is supposed to be responsible for the unique impression that he or she communicates to others. And there is also an element that is thought of as the basis of lineage or clan identity. Various subtle issues of a metaphysical character arise in the discussion of these elements of human personality. (See chapter 25 in this volume.)

However, from a more strictly traditional standpoint, ethical issues are more im-portant than metaphysical ones in the characterization of human personality. A person is perceived as definable only in terms of membership in a society. This is a consequence of the communalistic character of African society. Right from the be-ginning of socialization one is brought up to develop such strong bonds with large kinship units that one comes to see oneself as necessarily bound up with a commu-nity. (Recently, communitarianism has been much in the news in Anglo-American philosophy. It is, however, not quite the same thing as communitarianism in African culture. Dismas Masolo clarifies the differences in chapter 40 of this volume.)

Existentially, the link between the African individual and his large kinship affili-ations manifests itself as a combination of obligations and matching rights. The concept of a person, not surprisingly, becomes essentially normative: A person is not just a certain biological entity with a certain psycho-physical endowment, but, rather, a being of this kind who has shown a basic willingness and ability to fulfill his or her obligations in the community. Personhood, on this showing, is something of an achievement. It is only comparatively recently that attention has been called, in contemporary African philosophy, to this normative character of the traditional African concept of a person. In anthropology, however, Meyer Fortes, in the 1940s, noted (1987) the normative dimensions of the concept of a person among the Tallensi of Northern Ghana and other African peoples. In contemporary African philosophy the *locus classicus* of the normative conception of a person is Ifeanyi Menkiti's "Person and Community in African Traditional Thought" (1984). My views regarding the normative conception of a person are in substantial agreement with Menkiti's (see Wiredu 1992b; see also Wiredu 1992a). Criticisms of the nor-mative concept of a person, as expounded by Menkiti, were offered by Gyekye (1992). Later, Gyekye returns to the subject (1997: ch. 4), now agreeing in principle with the normative conception, but disputing certain aspects of Menkiti's elaboration of the idea. Menkiti, for his part, pursues further aspects of the norma-tive conception of a person in chapter 24 of this volume. The *dialectic*, for sure, is at work in our midst, and we can anticipate a synthesis.

There are some normative hints in the concept of a person in English-speaking discourse. But they are quite peripheral in comparison with the normative dimension of the African conception of a person, which is part of its very connotation. To note the contrast is, of course, not to prove validity either way. What it does is to challenge cross-cultural evaluation. So much work for the future!

Morality

Talking of the *normative* concept of a person brings us naturally to the subject of morality. In its narrowest sense, morality is universal. Dishonesty is bad, by definition, everywhere – China, Africa, Europe, America, etc. In this sense, morality is the harmonization of the interests of the individual with the interests of the community from a standpoint of empathetic impartiality, a fragile endowment of the human psyche. Nevertheless, we can legitimately speak of African ethics or European or American or Chinese ethics. That refers to the systems of local rules or customs by which a particular society regulates human relations. Confusion sometimes occurs because the words "ethics" or "morality" are frequently used now with the first sense, now with the second, without due notice.

With respect to ethics in the broad sense, it is easy to understand from what we said in the previous section that African ethics would be of a communalistic kind. A communalist ethic is one in which the interests of the individual are placed in a reciprocal adjustment with the interests of others in the community with reference to many specific circumstances of life and beyond the call of pure morality. Communalistic rules of conduct are a clear extension of the imperatives of pure morality. Since both are defined in terms of human interests, the African ethic might be called humanistic, as opposed to supernaturalistic. This contradicts the widely received notion that in Africa morality logically depends upon religion. A number of contemporary studies of traditional African philosophies of morals converge on this point. (See Gbadegesin 1991: 67–8; Gyekye 1987: ch. 8; Kudadjie 1976; and Wiredu 1991; also see chapter 31 in this volume: J. A. I. Bewaji, "Ethics and Morality in Yoruba Culture.")

Africa's Philosopher Kings

It is remarkable that the most substantive body of African philosophical literature in early post-independence Africa was produced by the first wave of post-independence leaders, notably, Nkrumah of Ghana, Sekou Toure of Guinea, Senghor of Senegal, Nyerere of Tanzania, and Kaunda of Zambia. That was in response to the challenges of national reconstruction in the 1960s and 1970s. In a relatively short time many of them produced political philosophies that reflected their understanding of their own cultural heritage in combination sometimes with their appreciation of certain elements of the political thought of the West. That Western input usually, though not always, came from the thought of Marx and Lenin. This combination was known as African socialism. Whether of a Marxist tendency or not, the African part of the intellectual construct always consisted of the construal of African communalism, of which mention was made above, as either an incipient or an idyllic form of socialism. Those of a Marxist persuasion, such as Nkrumah and Sekou Toure, argued that the socialist potential of traditional African communalism could only be brought to fruition through an infusion of Marxist dialectics. That socialism was the form of social organization best suited to the circumstances of Africa was taken to be proven by its assumed cultural authenticity and its supposed moral merits. The same conviction underlay the socialist faith of those like Nyerere and Kaunda who found Marxism unattractive. (Senghor's position in this matter of Marxism was quite ambiguous. He seems to have found aspects of Marxism highly intriguing intellectually, but he was hardly addicted to it ideologically.) All the resulting varieties of socialist experiments, however, brought little salvation to Africa, and one wonders what Plato would have thought of such philosopher kings. Nevertheless, their intellectual legacy demands a philosophical study. One recent such study can be found in Gyekye 1997: ch. 5. Among other things, Gyekye develops a considerable critique of the construal of traditional African communalism as a form of socialism. In "Post-Independence African Political Philosophy" (see chapter 17 in this volume), Olúfémi Táíwò too takes the legacy seriously, though not uncritically. (See also Gbadegesin 1991: ch. 7, and Wiredu 1998.)

The Question of Violence

A question that exercised the philosopher kings a great deal was the question of violence. If anything, it is now of a more grievous urgency than before. Previously, this question arose in two connections. First, those cognizant of the Marxist doctrine of the class struggle as a mode of struggle for socialism were moved to consider whether that mode of struggle was necessary in the conditions of Africa. Mixed feelings were apparent. Second, the question of the legitimacy of violence arose in regard to the struggle for independence from colonialism and also for liberation from white-settler minority rule in Africa. Here, most African thinkers affirmed the legitimacy of armed struggle, though with varying degrees of anguish, ranging from zero in the case of Franz Fanon to a very high degree of agonized soul-searching in the case of Kaunda.

The liberation struggles are now all won, but the philosophical problem of violence remains in Africa and everywhere else. Armed conflicts are raging in various parts of the world. In Africa one has to deal both emotionally and intellectually with the spate of military coups that have afflicted political life since the mid-1960s or so, not to talk of the variety of ethnic conflicts in which lives have been lost on an unspeakable scale. Much of the problem, in my opinion, is due to the kind of democracy being sought to be implemented in Africa. Trying to imitate majoritarian democracy in the conditions of Africa's ethnic stratification, which, at best, is what is being done, is a tragic experiment from which Africa can hardly expect anything but the opposite of salvation. Everything seems to indicate the necessity for fresh thinking about democracy in Africa. Of course, social problems hardly ever arise from single causes, and it will always be rational to explore additional possible causes and solutions.

Certainly the problem of violence in Africa seems somewhat more straightforward in the context of the anti-colonial struggles than it does now. Still, writings on the subject raise questions of continuing interest. Fanon's *The Wretched of the Earth* (1978) continues to be a strong incentive to reflection. The same applies to Kenneth D. Kaunda's *The Riddle of Violence* (1980). Kaunda's earnest reflections on the "riddle" of violence have an eloquence and a poignancy that are not widely recognized. The following publications, with the exception of Oruka's book, deal in one way or another with anti-colonial violence: Axelsen (1984: 237, 239–40); Fashina (1989); Mazrui (1978); Serequeberhan (1994); Wiredu (1986). The late Oruka's *Punishment and Terrorism in Africa* (1976) was concerned also with the use in Africa of state violence against citizens. Ali A. Mazrui's "Nationalism, Ethnicity, and Violence" (chapter 39 in this volume) is an even broader study of violence with both continental African and international ramifications. It is, perhaps, not too far-fetched to see the Truth and Reconciliation Commission of South Africa as, among other things, an approach to the problem of violence. The thinking underlying it sought a mutual balancing of the imperatives of truth, justice, and reconciliation in circumstances in which a single-minded fixation on justice would predictably have generated violence of unpredictable consequences. Pieter Duvenage grapples with the underlying issues in "The Politics of Memory and Forgetting After Apartheid" (chapter 42 in this volume).

The Question of Democracy

A connection was indicated between violence and democracy in Africa in the last section. That alone is a reason for a concentrated interest in the subject of democracy. But there are even more direct reasons for such a concernment. It is not lost on too many people that one has a natural right of democratic representation. As Francis M. Deng makes clear in his contribution to this volume (chapter 41, "Human Rights in the African Context"), this was not lost on traditional Africans either. The question naturally arises as to what is the most suitable form of democracy for Africa. It is becoming increasingly clear that the multiparty system of politics that is currently being operated in Africa, though, of course, better than the accursed one-party dictatorships of a few years ago, does not necessarily ensure a suitable form of democracy. There are, therefore, currently, some attempts to think out possible alternative embodiments of democracy. It is being remembered that in many parts of traditional Africa, decision by consensus in the governing councils ensured a veritable democracy without any analogue of the present-day system of parties. The problem in contemporary Africa is how to devise a system that, unlike the one-party regimes of the recent past, fully recognizes the right of free political association, and yet does not rely upon a party-based majoritarianism in the formation of government. It is arguable that only some such system can peacefully accommodate the complicated ethnic composition of most contemporary African states. In regard to this problem of democracy and good government, there is still a good deal of conceptual ground-clearing to be done by the philosophers. An issue that cries out for elucidation is whether any decision procedure not based on the principle of consensus could possibly ensure substantive representation for the people. The concept of a party itself is one that calls for a careful scrutiny in any philosophical examination of the relation between democracy and the party system. These are but a few of the conceptual as well as practical issues that African philosophy needs to confront. The enterprise, if successful, might conceivably yield benefits beyond the borders of Africa. I have discussed elsewhere (2001) some issues of this kind; see also Gyekye 1997: ch. 4. My earlier discussion of democracy and consensus (1996a: ch. 14; see also chs. 12 and 23), evoked a response from Emmanuel Eze (1997). Ernest Wamba-dia-Wamba, at any rate in his pre-guerrilla phase, had some interesting ideas in the direction of a non-adversarial form of democracy in Africa (1996).

The controversy that raged in Africa from the 1960s to the early 1990s as to whether the one-party system of statecraft is compatible with democracy is also relevant to the issue of democracy and consensus. This controversy may be studied in Mutiso and Rohio (1975): see Part VII: chs. 1 (Busia – contra), 2 (Sithole – more or less neutral), 3 (Busia), 4 (Kaunda – pro), 5 (Nyerere – pro), 6 (Nyerere), 7 (Sekou Toure – pro), and 11 (Ben Yahmed – ambiguous). This particular debate has been eclipsed by the recent establishment of multiparty constitutions (against the designs of resident dictators) in many parts of Africa with the help of international forces. The demise of the one-party system in Africa must remain unlamented. But there is an associated question that needs to be explored philosophically. The question is whether there might not be a non-party form of democracy based on consensus, which is more in harmony with most African indigenous traditions, and more suited to Africa's contemporary conditions. Indeed, it is a legitimate question, of interest to all humankind, whether a non-party, consensual system of democracy would not be a better form of democracy than the multiparty variety. But in Africa at the present time it is a question that has a life-and-death urgency. Note that a conceptual issue of considerable general interest arises here, namely, whether democracy, by its very meaning, entails a multiparty polity. Not much attention, however, has been given to this question, either in its African particularity or in its general applicability.

The question of democracy and the party system, by the way, provides an example of how conceptual issues in philosophy can have practical, normative consequences. For example, if it should turn out that democracy does not conceptually entail a party system, the demand for parties as a necessary condition of democracy, which some Western financial authorities have made a condition of help, may begin to seem less than well considered.

There are fully four articles on democracy included in this volume, contributed by Edward Wamala (chapter 35), Joe Teffo (chapter 36), Ajume H. Wingo (chapter 37), and George Carew (chapter 38). Together they constitute a quantum jump in the philosophical literature, quantitatively as well as qualitatively. Philosophy may yet assume its practical responsibilities in Africa. Ultimately, that may be all the rationale it has anywhere in the world.

Dimensions of African Philosophy

The foregoing should give a sense of some of the dimensions of African philosophy. There is the dimension of the traditional. This is multifaceted not only because, as we saw, it has a communal as well as an individualized component, but also because it has multifarious media of expression. Access to it can be gained through "communal proverbs, maxims, tales, myths, lyrics, poetry, art motifs and the like" (Wiredu 1996a: 114). Art motifs are in some ways approximations to writing. In some ways, indeed, they may have a vividness of message that a piece of writing may not approximate. In terms of profundity, this is even truer of some of the deliverances of African talking drums, which communicate abstract reflections through riddles and paradoxes in the very midst of music and dance (ibid. 15ff.).

This last observation brings us to the intimate connection between philosophy and art, music, and dance in African society. This volume is indebted to Kofi Agawu (chapter 32, "Aesthetic Inquiry and the Music of Africa"), Nkiru Nzegwu (chapter 33, "Art and Community: A Social Conception of Beauty and Individuality"), and Ajume H. Wingo (chapter 34, "The Many-Layered Aesthetics of African Art") for bringing this home to the reader.

To the dimension of the traditional, obviously, is to be added that of the contemporary. This is an evolving or, more strictly, an escalating tradition of thought and talk by way of books, journals, classroom teaching, and conferences. A good indication of this dimension is writ large in Barry Hallen's survey of contemporary Anglophone African philosophy (chapter 6 in this volume). In truth, every contribution in this volume is evidence of work in contemporary African philosophy. But it might be convenient to group together here those more concerned with making a point than with noting a traditional one. Additionally, we might note here those that mainly discuss contemporary efforts at philosophic thinking. Such contributions need not, of course, be devoid of all allusion to traditional sources. Proceeding almost in random order, we note Jean-Godefroy Bidima's reflective survey (chapter 46) of philosophy and literature in Francophone Africa. Engaged with literature and philosophy also, but in an Anglophone direction, is Anthony Kwame Appiah's "African Philosophy and African Literature" (chapter 45). The intersection of philosophy and literature in Africa is more important than the space available to it here. It deserves a whole volume to itself. As for the rest of the contributions in the present category, it is sufficient barely to mention some of them to get an idea of their scope and variety. We have Victor Ocaya, "Logic in the Acholi Language" (chapter 20); Olúfémi Táíwò, "Ifá: An Account of a Divination System and Some Concluding Epistemological Questions" (chapter 22); Segun Gbadegesin, "Toward a Theory of Destiny" (chapter 23); Safro Kwame, "Quasi-Materialism: A Contemporary African Philosophy of Mind" (chapter 26); Souleymane Bachir Diagne, "Islam in Africa: Examining the Notion of an African Identity within the Islamic World" (chapter 29); Godfrey B. Tangwa, "Some African Reflections on Biomedical and Environmental Ethics" (chapter 30); J. A. I. Bewaji, "Ethics and Morality in Yoruba Culture" (chapter 31); and John Murungi, "The Question of an African Jurisprudence: Some Hermeneutic Reflections" (chapter 43). Paulin J. Hountondji's "Knowledge as a Development Issue" (chapter 44), though already mentioned in an earlier connection, deserves to be mentioned here again on account of the extraordinary importance of the "capitalization" of indigenous knowledge systems advocated therein. It should be easy also to recognize contributions mentioned in earlier connections that belong here. At the least, all the contributions dealing with music and art belong here. So too do all those in the sections on relativism, democracy, Africa's philosopher kings, violence, and conceptual decolonization. Nor can one forget the contributions on individual contemporary thinkers.

A contribution to this volume that deserves special mention is Lucius T. Outlaw's "Africana Philosophy: Origins and Prospects" (chapter 5). By Outlaw's definition, Africana philosophy is philosophy by and in the interests of black peoples. This, evidently, encompasses both African philosophy and philosophy as cultivated by all peoples of African descent in the diaspora. (The diaspora qualification is necessary, by the way, since otherwise, in light of well-known archeological discoveries, the definition would cover all the peoples of the entire world.) As philosophy is an essentially collaborative enterprise, this concept should open up, in the imagination at least, vistas of cooperation between the Africans of Africa and the Africans of the diaspora. Historically, that kind of interaction has been an objective fact of blessed consequences. The most effective and influential African liberation leaders, such as Leopold Senghor, Nnamdi Azikiwe, Kwame Nkrumah, Jomo Kenyatta, owed much of their inspiration, at the level of philosophy and ideology, to figures of the diaspora, such as Aime Cesaire, Marcus Garvey, W. E. B. Du Bois, Alain Locke, and others. In the converse of this flow of influence, Nkrumah had considerable impact on the struggles of the peoples of the diaspora. Masolo brings out the first direction of influence with particular clarity (1994: ch. 1). And van Hensbroek explores the workings of the same flow of influence on the ground in Africa in the nineteenth century (1999; see also this volume, chapter 4). There is little doubt that in our own time more interchanges among all the worlds of Africana philosophy will yield, to say the least, non-trivial results. Lucius Outlaw has been responsible for much of what has been done so far in this area of endeavor.

It remains to take note of the historical dimension of African philosophy. Théophile Obenga's authoritative chapter on ancient Egyptian philosophy (chapter 1 in this volume) is a highly informative exposition of philosophical thought in a historically all-important part of ancient Africa. Similarly informative is Masolo's survey of African philosophers in the Greco-Roman era (chapter 2). The philosophers in question – unsung ones apart – are Origen (AD 185–253), Clement (AD c.150–c.215), Tertullian (AD c.155–c.240), Augustine (AD 354–430), and Cyprian (AD 200–58). An interesting question arises at once. These thinkers were Africans and were responsible for a considerable body of thought. But did that formation of thought constitute an African philosophy? This question poses a problem at all because these philosophers, though African, thought and wrote within the context of a Western tradition. Granted. But, in this respect, how different are they from contemporary African philosophers? The answer is not as simple as one might, at first sight, have supposed. Every point of differentiation turns out to be a matter of degree rather than of kind. Contemporary African philosophers too, especially if they are Christians, are in no wise innocent of Western influence. Perhaps the greater difference is that the psyche of a contemporary African philosopher is shaped by an African culture and imbued with a commitment to it. But, for example, Augustine's consciousness was not untouched by his African roots, and it is speculated that some of his views were conditioned by that circumstance. In the final analysis, it is the degree of dedication to the advancement of an African tradition of thought that must make the difference. Whether this is so or not, it seems clear that, if the thought of Augustine, as also of the others mentioned along with him, were to become a subject of sustained and prolonged interest among contemporary African philosophers, it would *ipso facto* become part of African philosophy in a quite stout sense.

The philosopher Anton Wilhelm Amo (1703–58), discussed in this volume by William E. Abraham and Kwasi Wiredu (chapters 11 and 12), is somewhat like St Augustine, but, if anything, closer to home. Born in Axim, Ghana, he was raised in Germany and academically trained there. He was productive philosophically within the traditions of German philosophy operative at his time. But his commitment to Africa was explicit and repeated. He returned to Ghana and remained there until the end of his days. His work invites African exploration.

By comparison with either Augustine or Amo, the place of Zera Yacob and Walda Heywat in African philosophy is totally unmistakable. It has been known for a long time that Ethiopia has a remarkable tradition of written philosophy. But it is only comparatively recently that the literature has become easily available. The enabler has been Claude Sumner of Addis Ababa University, "Canadian by birth, Ethiopian by choice." He has produced countless publications about Ethiopian philosophy (see, e.g., 1974, 1976/8). His most accessible book is aptly titled *Classical Ethiopian Philosophy* (1994). His essay in this volume (see chapter 9) is nicely complemented by Teodros Kiros's contribution (chapter 10).

Bearing interesting similarities to the status of the thought of the African philosophers of the Greco-Roman era and that of classical Ethiopian philosophy is the tradition of Islamic philosophy in East and West Africa. Souleymane Bachir Diagne's contribution, "Precolonial African Philosophy in Arabic" (chapter 3), is quite a groundbreaking account of that tradition. Its affinity with the tradition of Tertullian, Augustine, and others consists in the fact that both are assimilations of religious philosophies emanating from abroad. But one gets the distinct impression of a strong African self-consciousness among, for example, the West African Islamic philosophers. That is impressive enough. But, according to Diagne, they sometimes, at least in the north of Nigeria, wrote philosophy in Hausa, their vernacular. This would seem to suggest that, in the matter of African purposefulness, they sometimes went beyond at least most contemporary African philosophers who write exclusively in some metropolitan language. The scholarly world is indebted to John. O Hunwick and Rex Sean O'Fahey for (in Diagne's apt word) "exhuming" Arabic texts in East and West Africa and getting them translated and published. Diagne notes that two out of the six volumes projected in these two authors' program of publication on Arabic literature of Africa have been published (1994/1995). What has come out already enlarges our idea of the historical dimension of African philosophy.

When all the dimensions surveyed above are viewed together, our conception of African philosophy in our time must be even more amply enlarged. With that enlargement must come a legitimate excitement about future possibilities.

References

Abraham, W. E. (1962) *The Mind of Africa* (Chicago: Chicago University Press).

Alfa, Samuel Audu (1988) *The African Philosophical Concept of Time and its Metaphysical and Epistemological Ramifications*, Ph.D. dissertation, Drew University (Ann Arbor, Michigan: University Microfilms International, 1990).

Appiah, Kwame Anthony (1989) *Necessary Questions: An Introduction to Philosophy* (Englewood Cliffs, NJ: Prentice-Hall).

Appiah, Kwame Anthony (1984) "Strictures on Structures: The Prospects of a Structuralist Poetics of African Fiction," in Henry Louis Gates, *Black Literature and Literary Theory* (New York: Methuen).

Appiah, Anthony Kwame (1992) *In My Father's House: Africa in the Philosophy of Culture* (New York: Oxford University Press).

Axelsen, Diana (1984) "Philosophical Justifications for Contemporary African Social and Political Values and Strategies," in Richard A. Wright (ed.), *African Philosophy: An Introduction*, 3rd edn. (New York: University Press of America).

Bello, A. G. A. (1990) "Philosophy and an African Language," *Quest: An International African Journal of Philosophy*, 4(2), December.

p'Bitek, Okot (1970) *African Religions in Western Scholarship* (Nairobi, Kenya: East African Literature Bureau).

Danquah, J. B. (1944) *The Akan Doctrine of God* (London: Frank Cass; 2nd edn., 1968).

Evans-Pritchard, E. E. P. (1934) "Levy Bruhl's Theory of Primitive Mentality," *Bulletin of the Faculty of Arts*, University of Egypt.

Evans-Pritchard, E. E. P. (1937) *Witchcraft and Magic among the Azande* (Oxford: Oxford University Press; abridged edn. 1976).

Eze, Emmanuel Chukwudi (1997) "Democracy or Consensus: A Response to Wiredu," in Emmanuel Chukwudi Eze (ed.), *Postcolonial African Philosophy* (Cambridge, MA: Blackwell Publishers).

Fanon, Frantz (1978) *The Wretched of the Earth* (London: Penguin Books).

Fashina, Oladipo (1989) "Frantz Fanon and the Ethical Justification of Anti-Colonial Violence," *Social Theory and Practice*, 15(2).

Forde, Daryll (1954) *African Worlds: Studies in the Cosmological Ideas and Social Values of African Peoples* (Oxford: Oxford University Press; repr. New York, 1968).

Fortes, Meyer (1987) *Religion, Morality and the Person: Essays on Tallensi Religion*, ed. Jack Goody (New York: Cambridge University Press).

Gbadegesin, Segun (1991) *African Philosophy: Traditional Yoruba Philosophy and Contemporary African Realities* (New York: Peter Lang).

Gettier, Edmund (1963) "Is Justified True Belief Knowledge?" *Analysis*, 23.

Griaule, Marcel (1965) *Conversations with Ogotemmeli* (Oxford: Oxford University Press).

Gyekye, Kwame (1987) *An Essay on African Philosophical Thought* (New York: Cambridge University Press; 2nd rev. edn., Philadelphia: Temple University Press, 1995).

Gyekye, Kwame (1992) "Person and Community in Akan Thought," in Kwasi Wiredu and Kwame Gyekye (eds.), *Person and Community: Ghanaian Philosophical Studies, I* (Washington, DC: Council for Research in Values and Philosophy).

Gyekye, Kwame (1997) *Tradition and Modernity: Philosophical Reflections on the African Experience* (New York: Oxford University Press).

Hallen, Barry (2000) *The Good, the Bad and the Beautiful: Discourse about Values in Yoruba Culture* (Bloomington: Indiana University Press).

Hallen, Barry and Sodipo, J. Olubi (1997) *Knowledge, Belief and Witchcraft: Analytic Experiments in African Philosophy*, rev. edn. (Stanford: Stanford University Press).

Herskovits, M. J. (1938) *Dahomey, An Ancient West African Kingdom* (New York: J. August).

Hountondji, Paulin (1996) *African Philosophy: Myth and Reality*, 2nd edn. (Bloomington: Indiana University Press; first published in French 1976).

Hunwick, John O. and O'Fahey, Rex Sean (1994/1995) *Arabic Literature of Africa* (Leiden: E. J. Brill).

Idowu, E. Bolaji (1962) *Olodumare: God in Yoruba Belief* (London: Longman).

Irele, Abiola (1995) "Contemporary Thought in French Speaking Africa," in Albert G. Mosley (ed.), *African Philosophy: Selected Readings* (Englewood Cliffs, NJ: Prentice-Hall).

Kagame, Alexis (1976) "The Empirical Apperception of Time and the Conception of History in Bantu Thought," in Paul Ricoeur (ed.), *Cultures and Time* (Paris: UNESCO).

Kaunda, Kenneth D. (1980) *The Riddle of Violence* (London: Collins).

Kudadjie, J. N. (1976) "Does Religion Determine Morality in African Societies?" in J. S. Pobee (ed.), *Religion in a Pluralistic Society* (Leiden: E. J. Brill).

Kwame, Safro (1995) *Readings in African Philosophy: An Akan Collection* (New York: University Press of America).

Makinde, M. Akin (1988) *African Philosophy, Culture and Traditional Medicine* (Athens, Ohio: Ohio University Center for International Studies).

Masolo, D. A. (1994) *African Philosophy in Search of Identity* (Bloomington: Indiana University Press).

Mazrui, Ali (1978) "Mahatma Gandhi and Black Nationalism," in idem, *Political Values and the Educated Class in Africa* (London: Heinemann).

Mbiti, John S. (1990) *African Religions and Philosophy*, 2nd edn. (London: Heinemann; 1st edn. 1969).

Menkiti, Ifeanyi (1984) "Person and Community in African Traditional Thought," in Richard A. Wright (ed.), *African Philosophy: An Introduction*, 3rd edn. (New York: University Press of America).

Mosley, Albert G. (1995) *African Philosophy: Selected Readings* (Englewood Cliffs, NJ: Prentice-Hall).

Mutiso, Gideon-Cyrus M. and Rohio, S. W. (1975) *Readings in African Political Thought* (London: Heinemann Educational Books).

Oladipo, Olusegun (1992) *The Idea of African Philosophy* (Ibadan, Nigeria: Molecular Press).

Oladipo, Olusegun (1995) *Conceptual Decolonization in African Philosophy: Four Essays by Kwasi Wiredu* (Ibadan, Nigeria: Hope Publications).

Oruka, Henry Odera (1976) *Punishment and Terrorism in Africa* (Nairobi, Kenya: East Africa Literature Bureau).

Oruka, Henry Odera (1990a) *Trends in Contemporary African Philosophy* (Nairobi, Kenya: Shirikon Publishers).

Oruka, Henry Odera (1990b) *Sage Philosophy and the Modern Debate on African Philosophy* (Leiden: Brill Publishers).

Parratt, John (1977) "Time in Traditional African Thought," *Religion*, 7.

Rattray, R. S. (1923) *Ashanti* (Oxford: Oxford University Press).

Russell, Bertrand (1946) *A History of Western Philosophy* (London: George Allen and Unwin).

Serequeberhan, Tsenay (ed.) (1991) *African Philosophy: The Essential Readings* (New York: Paragon House).

Serequeberhan, Tsenay (1994) *The Hermeneutics of African Philosophy* (New York: Routledge).

Smith, Edwin (ed.) (1950) *African Ideas of God: A Symposium* (London: Edinburgh House Press).

Sogolo, Godwin S. (1992) *Foundations of African Philosophy* (Ibadan, Nigeria: University of Ibadan Press).

Sumner, Claude (1974, 1976/8) *Ethiopian Philosophy* (Addis Ababa: Central Printing Press; Addis Ababa University Press).

Sumner, Claude (1994) *Classical Ethiopian Philosophy* (Los Angeles: Adey Publishing Company).

Tempels, Placide (1959) *Bantu Philosophy* (Paris: Presence Africaine).

van Hensbroek, Pieter Boele (1999) *Political Discourses in African Thought 1860 to the Present* (London: Praeger).

Wamba-dia-Wamba, Ernest (1996) "Beyond Elite Politics of Democracy in Africa," *Quest, Philosophical Discussions: An International African Journal of Philosophy*, 10(2).

Winch, Peter (1964) "Understanding a Primitive Society," *American Philosophical Quarterly*, 1 (repr. in Bryan R. Wilson (ed.), *Rationality* (Oxford: Blackwell, 1974), p. 82).

Wiredu, Kwasi (1980) *Philosophy and an African Culture* (London: Cambridge University Press).

Wiredu, Kwasi (1986) "The Question of Violence in Contemporary African Thought," *Praxis International*, 6(3).

Wiredu, Kwasi (1987) "The Concept of Mind with Particular Reference to the Language and Thought of the Akans of Ghana," in G. Floistad (ed.), *Contemporary Philosophy: A New Survey*. Vol. 5: *African Philosophy* (Dordrecht: Martinus Nijhoff Publishers; Boston: Kluwer Academic).

Wiredu, Kwasi (1991) "Morality and Religion in Akan Thought," in Norm Allen, Jr., *African American Humanism: An Anthology* (New York: Prometheus Books).

Wiredu, Kwasi (1992a) "African Concept of Personhood," in Harley E. Flack and Edmond D. Pellegrino (eds.), *African American Perspectives on Biomedical Ethics* (Georgetown University Press).

Wiredu, Kwasi (1992b) "Moral Foundations of African Culture," in Kwasi Wiredu and Kwame Gyekye (eds.), *Person and Community: Ghanaian Philosophical Studies*, I (Washington, DC: The Council for Research in Values and Philosophy).

Wiredu, Kwasi (1993) "Canons of Conceptualization," *The Monist*, 76(4).

Wiredu, Kwasi (1995) "Knowledge, Truth and Fallibility," in I. Kucuradi and R. S. Cohen (eds.), *The Concept of Knowledge* (Boston: Kluwer Academic).

Wiredu, Kwasi (1996a) *Cultural Universals and Particulars: An African Perspective* (Bloomington, Indiana: Indiana University Press).

Wiredu, Kwasi (1996b) "Time and African Thought," in D. Tiemersma and H. A. F. Oosterling (eds.), *Time and Temporality in Intercultural Perspective* (Atlanta: Rodopi).

Wiredu, Kwasi (1998) "African Philosophy: Anglophone," in the *Routledge Encyclopedia of Philosophy, 1998* (London: Routledge).

Wiredu, Kwasi (2001) "Democracy by Consensus: Some Conceptual Considerations," *Philosophical Papers*, 30(3).

Wright, Richard A. (1984) *African Philosophy: An Introduction*, 3rd edn. (New York: University Press of America; 1st edn. 1977).

Part I

HISTORY

1

Egypt: Ancient History of African Philosophy

THÉOPHILE OBENGA

The Problem

It is a mere prejudice to believe that the philosophical epoch of humanity begins first among the Greeks in the fifth century BC. This prejudice implies that other ancient people did not engage in speculative thought. Undoubtedly, speculative thought transcends experience, but it always attempts to explain, interpret, and unify it in order to systematize it. Speculative thought, using aphorisms, allusions, metaphors, negative or positive methods, and dialectics, can be oral or written, and it is necessarily connected with the problems of life. Thus philosophy can be defined as "systematic reflective thinking on life" (Yu-lan 1976: 16).

The spirit of Chinese philosophy, Indian philosophy, African philosophy, European philosophy, and Maya philosophy can differ greatly in their treatment of a subject, but philosophy always deals with human knowledge, and the elevation of the mind. The *future philosophy of the world* must then take into account the great speculative systems of all humanity.

Therefore, there is an urgent need to gain some acquaintance with the traditions of African philosophy from the remote times to the contemporary era. I am going to try to present the ancient history of African philosophy by bringing into focus the speculative thought of ancient Egypt.

Method

African philosophy as a historical fact must be understood within a historical frame. The origin, evolution, and development of African philosophy follow the streams and currents of African history. The long history of African philosophy has shown connections with other continents, chiefly with Europe, since the Graeco-Roman world. In remote times African philosophy was mainly located in the Nile Valley, that is, in Kemet or ancient Egypt, and in Kush (Napata-Meroe). Philosophy flourished in Egypt from about 3400 BC to 343 BC and in Kush (also known as Nubia or Ethiopia by the Greeks) from about 1000 BC to 625 BC.

31

The task of the historian of philosophy requires valid methods for clarifying the ideas, concepts, and speculations of the philosophers of the past, and to push their theories to their ultimate conclusion in order to show their effectiveness. But the historian of philosophy is himself to some extent a philosopher, because his work is not only a mere historical investigation, but also a creative one. The historian of philosophy thinks about the ideas and theories of the past. Thus the analytical and critical methods of history undergo mutations to become a productive method of philosophy.

The Question of Ancient Egypt

The question of the ancient Egypt connection with the rest of Black Africa was opened to an intensive discussion involving opposing points of view in 1974 during an international symposium organized by the United Nations Educational, Scientific and Cultural Organization (UNESCO) held in Cairo and Aswan. Present were more than 20 of the best Egyptologists in the world. All the outstanding scholars and specialists at the Cairo symposium, although they took opposing sides about other items, came, in spite of that, to agreement regarding the following significant points.

First, Egyptian language as revealed in hieroglyphic, hieratic, and demotic writings, and Coptic, that is, the old Egyptian language in its latest developments, as written in the Greek-Coptic script, and modern African languages, as spoken nowadays in Black Africa, constitute the same linguistic community broken into several parts. Comparative grammar and the method of internal reconstruction allow scholars to reconstruct certain features of the language spoken by the original, unseparated community, on the basis of corresponding features of the descent languages. The comparative method in historical linguistics is still a valid method for defining change and determining earlier forms of two or more related languages to prove their precise relationship. Technically speaking, no scholar, using the method of internal reconstruction, has proved objectively that the Semitic, Egyptian, and Berber languages are descended from a common ancestor. The so-called "Afro-Asiatic family," or "Chamito-Semitic family," which has gained wide circulation, has no scientific foundation at all. There is no proof of an "Afro-Asiatic historical grammar." One may recall here what Immanuel Kant (1724–1804) called "the prejudice of the prestige of the multitude," that is to say, the supposition that what everyone says must be true. In the human sciences "scientific" circles often make claims not based on any objectively verifiable grounds but rather just on this kind of prejudice.

Second, ancient Egypt was a flourishing ancient kingdom of Northeast Africa, located in the Nile Valley, nowise in "Asia Minor" or in the "Near East." The Egyptian civilization of the Pharaonic period (3400–343 BC) was intrinsically, that is, in its essential nature, an African civilization, on account of its spirit, character, behavior, culture, thought, and deep feeling.

As we know, Georg Wilhelm Friedrich Hegel (1770–1831), who was not a historian, but a great philosopher, stated in his lectures delivered in the winter of

1830–1 on the philosophical history of the world: "Africa is no historical part of the world; it has no movement or development to exhibit.... *Egypt ... does not belong to the African Spirit*" (1956: 99; emphasis mine). This view of the Hegelian philosophy of history has become almost a common opinion and an academic paradigm in Western historiography. A great culture or civilization cannot be produced by African (Black) people. Moreover, African people have never made any kind of contribution to world history. Even some brilliant African minds still accept as true Hegel's incongruous statement. In modern times the primary document concerning the "question" of the ancient Egyptian connection with the rest of Black Africa was, until the Cairo symposium, Hegel's *Philosophy of History*. Thus, it took one century and 44 years, from Hegel (1830) to the Cairo symposium (1974), to change the paradigm installed by the German philosopher. The Cairo symposium was, then, a turning point in African historiography and philosophy.

Ancient Egyptian Concepts of "Philosophy"

It was said above that philosophy could be defined as systematic reflective thinking on life. There is not a single philosophy that could be excogitated except in relation to life, society, existence, and universe. Even abstract reasoning about the condition or quality of being nothing ("Nothingness") still deals with something in the universe, since the universe is the totality of all that is. Human beings always need to discern what is real, true, right, or lasting. Such insight is wisdom, because understanding what is true, right, or lasting necessarily elevates the mind. This is why "philosophy" was understood by the Greeks as "love of wisdom," and "philosopher" as "lover of wisdom." To philosophize was not just to speculate about life and reflect on nature, but also to be engaged with love, intense desire, and strong enthusiasm in the investigation of causes underlying reality in order to build up a system of values by which society may live.

Philosophy is more important in its essential function than in its mere methodology as a critical or analytical inquiry into the nature of things. The basic notion of philosophy in ancient Egypt referred precisely to the synthesis of all learning and also to the pursuit of wisdom and moral and spiritual perfection. Philosophy in the ancient times of Pharaonic Egypt was, then, a kind of pedagogy fielding the wise teachings (*sebayit*) of the old sages, who were scholars, priests, and officials or statesmen at the same time.

Indeed, the verb *rekh* (written with the hieroglyphic signs of "mouth," "placenta," and "papyrus rolled up, tied and sealed") means "to know" or "to be aware of" but also "to learn." Human beings know by learning, that is, through experience or conditioning, schooling or study. The word *rekh* (when written with the hieroglyph of a seated man) means "wise man," that is, a learned man, an erudite, a philosopher. Thus the concept *rekhet* (written with the hieroglyph for abstract notions) means "knowledge," "science," in the sense of "philosophy," that is, inquiry into the nature of things (*khet*) based on accurate knowledge (*rekhet*) and good (*nefer*) judgment (*upi*). The word *upi* means "to judge," "to discern," that is,

33

"to dissect." The cognate word *upet* means "specification," "judgment," and *upset* means "specify," that is, give the details of something.

In the Egyptian language "wisdom" and "prudence" are expressed by the same word: *sat* (the hieroglyphic determinative is very characteristic; it is of a man with hand to mouth). Indeed, to be wise (*sai*) is to be prudent (*sai*); it is to be almost "silent," that is, sagacious in handling matters, and exercising good judgment. Wisdom and prudence imply knowledge (*rekhet*) and the awareness of the principles of moral conduct and sociable behavior. The wise man (*rekh* or *sai*) grasps in his mind with clarity and certainty what is known distinctively to him.

The wise man or woman, of course, loves truth (*maat*). He or she is shrewd, marked by a keen awareness and a penetrating intelligence, because he or she has received formal instruction. In the Egyptian language, the word *seba* (written with the symbol of a "star") means, "to teach," suggesting methodological teaching and an arduous learning process, such as at school. To teach (*seba*) is to open the door (*seba*) to the mind of the pupil (*seba*) in order to bring in light, as from a star (*seba*). Egyptian concepts concerning the topic under consideration are precise:

Seba: "to teach"
at seba: "school," literally "house of teaching." (A famous school director was Kemhu, who lived during the 13th Dynasty, 1782–1650 BC. His statue from Abydos is now in the Egyptian Museum at Cairo.)
seba, also *sebaty*: "pupil"
sebayit: "written teaching," "instruction," "wisdom," also "pedagogy," that is, the art of bringing pupils from darkness to light in intellectual and spiritual life
tep-heseb: "correct method"

This last methodological concept, *tep-heseb*, occurs in the very title of a scientific text, the so-called "Rhind Mathematical Papyrus," copied by the scribe and teacher Ahmes in about 1650 BC from writings dating from about 200 years earlier (see Gillings 1972).

From the concepts clearly defined above, it is obvious that Egyptian thinking created the terminology for the formulation of a system of abstract thought by using a graphic and concrete symbolism. Egyptian thinking was graphic and abstract at the same time. Pictures were used as symbols of thought. The tangible signs, pictures, and symbols were related to ideas and meanings. They were, in fact, semiotic structures. The Egyptians did develop a kind of semiology by studying the relationship between signs and pictures, using material objects to represent something invisible or abstract. This is not to say that the Egyptian philosophers thought "in" graphic and concrete terms. They made use of graphic and concrete forms to think abstractions. This may seem quaint for the modern mind, because of the alphabetical system of writing. In fact, semiotic structures in hieroglyphic signs were a fine equipment for precise abstract thinking. And the earliest abstract terms for expressing transcendental ideas known in the history of philosophy appear among the Egyptians of the Pyramid Age, that is, during the Old Kingdom

(2686–2181 BC). One is referring to ideas, such as the goodness of God (*nefer netcher*), moral obligation, and high ideals of social equity (*maat*). Notable also are the ideas of human kingship (*nesyt*) and of the concept of the Supreme Principle, or God (*Ra*), symbolized by the sun.

The First Definition of a "Philosopher" in World History

The ancient Egyptians meant by *rekh* or *sai* a "wise human being" or "philosopher." It was not just a question of words. Two thousand years ago in ancient Egypt, without a doubt, the "inscription of Antef" gave the first clear and distinct statement conveying the fundamental meaning of a "philosopher." This is a demonstrable fact. The German Egyptologist Hellmut Brunner translates the "inscription of Antef," which gives the definition of a "philosopher," as follows:

> [He is the one] whose heart is informed about these things which would be otherwise ignored, the one who is clear-sighted when he is deep into a problem, the one who is moderate in his actions, who penetrates ancient writings, whose advice is [sought] to unravel complications, who is really wise, who instructed his own heart, who stays awake at night as he looks for the right paths, who surpasses what he accomplished yesterday, who is wiser than a sage, who brought himself to wisdom, who asks for advice and sees to it that he is asked advice. (*Inscription of Antef*, 12th Dynasty, 1991–1782 BC)

The heart *ib*, also *haty*, in the Egyptian language was conceived as the seat of thoughts and emotions. The word for heart also meant "mind," "understanding," and "intelligence." Reason, emotion, spirit, mind, and body were not conceived as separate antithetical entities. Matter and spirit were not opposites in conflict. Thus, in their inquiries philosophers can draw on all the resources of their being, including reason and feeling. In this way they can expect to achieve fulfillment.

The reference to being deep into a problem indicates that philosophical thinking is a critical undertaking. Philosophy is not concerned with what is apparent, obvious, shallow, or insignificant. Thinking deep means dealing with substantial issues. And what a philosopher does in life, he must do within reasonable limits, not at all being subject to radical or extreme views. A philosopher champions moderate views or judgments, as he or she loves truth (*maat*).

A great philosophical and scientific tradition existed in ancient Egypt. The philosopher was regarded as one who could penetrate ancient writings and avail himself of the instructions available therein. These works constituted a philosophical tradition, that is, a set of teachings (*sebayit*) viewed as a coherent body of precedents influencing the present. The history of philosophy was thus already a system of philosophy. Imhotep, Hor-Djed-Ef, Kagemni, and Ptah-Hotep in the Old Kingdom (2686–2181 BC) built the first philosophical tradition in world history. Their wisdom or philosophy did them credit, because a thousand years after they had passed away they were still remembered with reverence:

>Books of wisdom (i.e. philosophy) were their pyramids,
>And the pen was their child...
>Is there anyone here like Hor-Djed-Ef?
>Is there another like Imhotep?
>They are gone and forgotten,
>But their names through their writings cause them to be remembered.
>
>(*Papyrus Beatty* IV, Verso)

Imhotep was grand vizier to King Djoser (2668–2649 BC), 3rd Dynasty. He was also high priest at Heliopolis, the main city of the Sun-God, *Ra*. He designed, as chief architect, the step-pyramid at Saqqara, which is the first construction in hewn stone in world history. Hor-Djed-Ef was a royal prince, son of Khufu (2589–2566 BC), 4th Dynasty. He was connected with the greatest pyramid of Giza.

Women too were involved in the intellectual, scientific, and philosophical tradition. Lady Peseshet was the first woman doctor of medicine in world history. She lived during the 4th Dynasty or the early 5th Dynasty (2584 or 2465 BC). Her titles indeed included *imyt-r swnwwt*, that is, "the lady director of lady physicians." She was also a funerary priestess.

On the ancient Egyptian model, philosophers are not just critical analysts, scholarly minds able to read ancient texts. They must also be prepared to ask for advice and look for the right paths. In addition, they must surpass their own performance by conducting the investigation of causes underlying reality always in a detailed and accurate manner. But beyond this, the philosopher must betake himself to wisdom, that is, to what is true, right, and useful to the community. Thus, for ancient Egypt, philosophy implies the critical building of knowledge, intellectual penetration, and profundity, but also, and perhaps above all, modesty and moderation, humility, and an endless desire for perfection. This is wisdom and still a valid conception of philosophy today.

Hieroglyphic Signs and Philosophy

Plotinus (205–70 AD), Egyptian-born Roman philosopher and writer who founded Neoplatonism, wrote during the third century AD that the "Egyptian sages showed their consummate science by using symbolic signs.... Thus, each hieroglyph constituted a sort of science of wisdom." On this showing, Plotinus considered hieroglyphs to be a writing system that recorded real things and ideas without confusion. Apparently, hieroglyphs have no hidden and impenetrable mysteries. What hieroglyphs disclose is of unique interest in the intellectual history of humanity. There are more than 800 hieroglyphic signs; they describe all the classes and categories of beings and things held by creation. Hieroglyphs are the complete and systematized conceptualization of all that is; they are an all-embracing knowledge of reality. Egyptian hieroglyphs express the universe, as it is known and as it exists; they mean, refer to, the totality of things. It is because of the universe that there are hieroglyphs. In a sense, all things are hieroglyphs, and hieroglyphs are all things. This is why it was impossible for the Egyptians to conceive the idea of non-existence in the sense of the absence of the existent. Since the universe is beauty, abundance, plentitude, diversity, harmony, and unity, hieroglyphs reproduce by drawings all these manifestations of the universe.

Everything is in hieroglyphs, such as, in random order, man and his occupations, woman and her activities, deities, mammals, birds, amphibious animals, reptiles, fish, insects, plants, trees, sky, earth, mountains, water, buildings, ships, domestic and funerary furniture, temple furniture and sacred emblems, crowns, dress, staves, warfare, hunting, butchery, agriculture, crafts and professions, rope, fiber, baskets, bags, vessels of stone, earthenware, cakes, writing, games, music, geometrical figures, etc. Hieroglyphs, being about reality in all its diversity, also feature abstract concepts, such as spirituality, consciousness, love, sexuality, happiness, beauty, ugliness, rites, eloquence, loyalty, sovereignty, joy, life, power, birth, death, immortality, motion, wind, knowledge, silence, wisdom, flame, light, day, night, darkness, fear, alteration, smell, perfume, truth, justice, etc.

The hieroglyphic script is a most complete semiotic system – complete, that is, systematic, and comprehending everything in the universe. Studying the Egyptian hieroglyphic script is like being in communication with all that exists. The discipline of Egyptology involves the learning of the Egyptian system of writing. Egyptian hieroglyphic writing is found everywhere: on temple walls and columns, tombs, sacred monuments, and so forth. Painted inscriptions do exist, illustrating the aesthetic sensibilities of the Egyptian scribes. Egyptian writing reached its full development around 3200 BC, and thereafter remained fundamentally unchanged for a period of 3,000 years.

The universal human need for communication and self-expression was graphically crystallized in the Egyptian script, which sought to represent the form of the universe itself. This is impressive from both a semantical and a philosophical standpoint. Africans, at all events, must study the Egyptian language and script.

The Dynamic Character of Egyptian Thinking on "Existence"

Verbs expressing existence are not static but dynamic in Egyptian philosophy. They are basically verbs of movement, stressing duration and referring to moments of time. Verbs like "to exist," "to be," "to be stable, enduring," and "to become" were dominant in Egyptian speculation about life and the existence of the universe.

The verb wnn (unen): "to exist," "to be"

The verb *wnn (unen)*, written with the hieroglyphic sign of the long-eared desert hare, means "to exist," "to be." This verb expresses being or existence in a full-blooded sense. Originally, it meant perhaps "to move," "to run." To be a true being, something always has to be moving or running. Therefore, non-being is not.

This means that existence excludes illusion, delusion, and mere sense impression. Existence is the prodigious dynamic of all being. The synthesis of rest (*hotep*) and movement (*shemet*) is the entirety of being, and it is unalterable and indestructible like the divine life. The concept of "existence" is closely related to that of "eternity,"

37

that is, the manner of being of that which may be called the perfect (*nefer*), that is, the god *Ra*. *Ra* is the highest being, imperishable, eternal, possessing full reality, that is, power, beauty, truth, perfection, and goodness.

"To exist" as duration is also a dynamic process referring to any point of time. This is why one and the same sentence can be understood in a past, present or future sense, according to the particular context and the intention of the text. For example, the sentence *wnn pt wnn. t hr. i (unen pet unen. etj kher. i)* means:

"The sky existed when you were with me" (Past)
"The sky exists, and you are with me" (Present)
"So long as heaven shall exist, you shall exist with me" (Future)
(*Urkunden des aegyptischen Altertums*, IV, 348, 9)

Existence, whether absolute or relative to some situation, is always a dynamic process. The name given to the resurrected god Osiris (Usire) was *Wnn-nfr* (*Unen-nefer*) meaning "He who is continually happy," or "He whose life was regenerated." Here, the verb *wnn* (*unen*) "to exist," "to be," evokes the immortality of Osiris, who died and was reborn. The main goal of human life (*ankh*) was to come to exist as a good (*nefer*) divine being in order to become Osiris, that is, immortal and eternal. The distinction between "being" and "non-being" was only a "semantical" distinction. It had no ontological significance in Egyptian philosophy.

The verb d d (djed) *"to be stable," "enduring"*

Columns in the temple stand; that is, they are stable (*djed*). But standing is viewed as the result of a rising. The "standing" of the columns in a temple is not a static image, because the mind is always thinking of the firmness and stability of the columns as a process. Indeed, movement is conceived to be carried from the earth to the sky through columns. This means that humanity, by building civilization and spirituality on earth, must reach up to the world of Truth (*maat*) and eternity (*djet*). The "being" of a column as it stands (*djed*) in its stability (*djedet*) is, in fact, analogous to the cosmos itself. So, indeed, is the entire temple. The hardness of a column is a revealing reality because truth (*maat*) constitutes the real (*maa*) being of the column.

By the art of the sculptor, a statue (*tut*) is not something "static," as it is perceived to be in Western thought. A statue is a living image (*tut ankh*), a real (*maa*) becoming. Indeed, to carve (*se-ankh*) is to make life (*ankh*) itself as a real thing. A statue comes to be a power; it is the localized existence of the power (*ka*) of someone. King Tut-ankh-Amon and his golden statues are all of them "living (*ankh*) images (*tut*) of Amon," "an imaged life of Amon." Everything described as durative (*djed*) is, in fact, a dynamic expression of life, and a manifestation of truth itself. Beauty (*nefer*) is not just an aesthetic category, but also the manifestation of a transcendental force.

The pillar (*djed*) projected eternal life because it was a symbol of Osiris. As a matter of fact, the Nile was but the source and visible symbol of that fertility of which Osiris was the exemplification.

The verb hpr (kheper) *"to become"*

The notions "learn" (*rekh*), "ignore" (*khem*), and "love" (*mer*) imply continuity, but "know," "not know," and "wish" are regarded in Egyptian grammar as definitive occurrences resulting from "having learnt," "failed to learn," "conceived a wish." Thus, as in some examples noted above, basically the same grammatical form is used to express the continuity of a contemporaneous occurrence and the pastness of a past occurrence.

Actually, at the beginning of the 12th Dynasty (1991–1782 BC) the two verbs *wnn (unen)* ("be") and *kheper* ("become") were used with a past reference and also with a future or prospective reference. The following clause is an example of the first usage: *iret kheperu neb mery. ef kheper im. ef* ("the making (*iret*) of all changes (*kheperu neb*) in which (*im. ef*) one may wish (*mery. ef*) to be involved (*kheper*)") (*Urk*, V. 4).

We must then devote special attention to this verb *kheper* not only because it occurs very frequently in the Egyptian texts, but also because the grammatical points discussed above are concentrated in this verb. The verb *kheper* expresses being or existence in all its possibilities. It thus means both "becoming" and "effecting." Included also in the meaning of the verb are the ideas of cause and effect. It is in this sense of the verb that the creator says to himself, "I exist, and in me possibilities become existents" (*kheper.i kheper kheperu*). The existent exists because of the existence of the creator. The existence (*kheperu*) of the creator manifests (*kheper*) itself as "becoming" and "effecting."

There is no genesis, but co-genesis, in the sense that the existent exists by the simple fact of its inner nature. Coming into being by itself (*kheper. ef djes. ef*), the existent brings out, at the same time, the entirety of existence. The one and the many are interlaced by the same dynamic power of the existent. One implication of this is that "matter" and "spirit" are two aspects of the same reality. Try to deal with "matter" without "spirit," and what you have is incomplete, because "matter" and "spirit" do not just lie side by side. They are inextricably connected together.

As an intransitive verb, *kheper* means "come into being," "change into," "occur," "happen," "be effective," also "go by," "be past," always with the idea of continuity. *Kheper* also means, as noted earlier, "to exist," "to be." As a transitive verb it means "bring out."

The dynamic character of *kheper* is generally clear. Its connotation contains the unity of being, becoming, and effecting. Within it, the gap between becoming and being is closed by virtue of "effecting." In the universe everything is full of power (*ka*) and effectiveness (*kheper*). The *ka* is the dynamic essence of each existence or being in the universe.

We can understand now the dynamic character of the ancient Egyptian conception of the world. Things do not have the fixity and inflexibility that we believe they have. Things are changeable and in motion on the earth, in the sky, under water, etc. The earth and the sky themselves move.

The Egyptian Conception of the Universe

Because of the dynamic nature of its thinking on "existence" and the universal semiology of the hieroglyphs, Egyptian philosophy was of a solar and cosmic orientation. The material sun was known as *Ra*, that is, the "sun-god." Many deities were associated in some way with the sun-god *Ra*, such as *Ra-Atum*, the creator; *Khepri*, a winged beetle or scarab rising in the east; *Horus*, the son of *Ra*; *Hor-akhty*, the *Horus* of the two Horizons; *Amon-Ra*, the god Amon of Thebes solarized.

In the beginning the sun-god as *Atum* or *Ra-Atum* had appeared from primeval waters known as *nun* by his own power of self-development. Note that "spirit" is thought of here as a self-development of "matter." The sun-god begat *Shu*, the wind, and *Te fnut*, the first woman. Of these two were born *Geb*, the earth-god, and *Nut*, the goddess of the sky, whose children were the two brothers *Osiris* and *Seth*, and the sisters *Isis* and *Nephthys*. *Osiris* and *Isis* will give birth to *Horus*, the dynastic divine falcon. The Pharaoh himself assumed the title "Son of Ra" (*sa-Ra*) from the 5th Dynasty (2498–2345 BC) onward. *Maat*, the goddess of Truth or Righteousness, was a daughter of *Ra* (*sat-Ra*). The conception of Truth and Right occupied a prominent place in thought about *Aton*, a solar deity. *Hathor*, the goddess of beauty, love, dance, and music, was the "eye of *Ra*." The pyramid was the chief symbol of the sun-god *Ra*. It was believed to help the Pharaoh in his transition from the earthly to the celestial realm.

In the philosophy of the ancient Egyptians these elements of myth and cosmogony contain their basic ideas about the world.

The modern European mind conceives of "chaos" and "cosmos" as antithetical concepts. Chaos is defined as a disorderly mass, a jumble that existed before the ordered universe, the cosmos. On the other hand, for the Egyptian mind, there is no such thing as chaos in this sense. In the beginning there was primordial space and time, the *Nun*, from which the sun-god *Ra* emerged by his own energy to start the existence of all beings. *Nun*, the primeval flood or water, was a god, existing before the sky came forth (*kheper*), before the earth came forth, before humans came forth, before the multitude of gods were born, and before death came forth (*Pyramid Texts*, §§1466–8).

The sun-god's life-giving power brought forth (*kheper*) all in existence, and his creative power continues to bring forth (*kheper*) life and force even in "inanimate" things. This life-giving power of *Ra* is the constant source of life and sustenance. *Ra* is present on earth as a beneficent power; the Pharaoh, son of *Ra*, expresses his own consciousness of the god's presence by performing rituals in the temple.

In Egyptian philosophy, therefore, *Nun* is the primordial element that existed prior to creation and *Ra* the source of life and rationality. These cosmological concepts are original with the ancient Egyptians.

The Universe as an Endless Boundary

The word *djeru (drw)* means: "boundary," "limit," "end." The "universe" is self-contained, that is to say, it is its own boundary. The "universe" is, then, endless because it has no boundaries; it is its own limit. This is why the word *djeru (djer)* means also "the all," "the universe." The expression *neb-er-djer* means "Lord of All," that is, Lord of the universe, an endless boundary.

The Universe as an Endless Totality

Being without a boundary within itself, the "universe" (*tem*) is complete (*tem*), that is, entire and all-comprehending (*tem*). Because the "universe" is all-comprehending, it is a totality. The expression *neb tem* also means "Lord of All," that is, Lord of the universe, the totality of all that is. The "Creator of All" is named *kema tem*, that is, he who created (*kema*) everything, entire, complete, and sound.

Being total (*tem*), the universe has, in fact, no limit, except its own totality. The boundary (*djer*) of the universe is its totality (*tem*). All is then *djer* or *tem*, also *djer* and *tem*. Constituting the whole, the universe is entire, but its entirety is limited by the universe itself; that is, the universe is an endless totality.

Egyptian Logic

Logic designates a specific branch of philosophy that deals with the study of the principles of reasoning. The quality or condition of being rational – that is, having or exercising the ability to reason – is rationality. In the history of Western philosophy, rationality has often been blended with philosophy itself, so that philosophy and rationality have become merged into one, namely, rationalism. Much Western philosophy, from Aristotle (384–322 BC) to Ludwig Wittgenstein (1889–1951), is deeply rooted in the notion that reason, rather than emotion, sense experience, authority, or spiritual experience, provides the only valid basis for action, and is the prime source of knowledge and spiritual truth. Other civilizations are usually judged by the criteria of this Western rationalistic attitude.

If, as Descartes (1596–1650) remarked, good sense or reason is equally distributed among all human beings, it is then unjustified to believe that some groups of the human race are deficient in logic or point-device reasoning. The so-called "native" or "primitive mind" is but a racist prejudice, based on the belief that a particular human population or race is superior to others.

When Egyptian mathematics, for example, are not smattered or studied superficially, one can find that Egyptian mathematicians dealt rationally with the problems. Indeed, the Egyptians made use of logic as a tool of precision in constructing and developing their mathematics. In geometry – that is, the mathematics of the properties, measurement, and relationships of points, lines, angles, surfaces, and solids or three-dimensional figures – all the problems were arranged in a clear and consistent manner. There is always a *logical coherence* among the parts of a problem. The basic structure of a problem always consisted of the following parts:

1 *tep*: The Given Problem. This is the precise enunciation of the problem to be solved, with elucidatory examples.
2 *mi djed en. Ek*: Literally, "if one says to you that." This is the stage of *definition*, where everything is made clear and distinct, and all the relevant terms are

explicitly and precisely defined. The expression *mi djed* means "according to that which is said," that is, the process of reasoning is to be addressed to a precisely formulated problem.

3 *peter* or *pety*. Literally, this means "What?" In Egyptian grammar *ptr (peter)* stands at the beginning of questions with the function of eliciting a logical predicate (Gardiner 1957: 406, §497). A question is an expression of inquiry that invites a reply or solution. At this stage, then, the student is directly required to ponder and analyze (*ptr (peter)*) the problem under examination.

4 *iret mi kheper*: Correct Procedure. This is the stage of demonstration, that is, the mental process of showing something to be true by reasoning and computation from initial data. The process of calculating is based on a careful set of mathematical formulas.

5 *rekhet. ef pw*: The Solution. This is knowledge (*rekhet*) found, and grasped in the mind with clarity or certainty. The solution is regarded as true beyond doubt. The student has shown the requisite know-how, that is, the knowledge and skill required to do something correctly. The solution is evident, thanks to the demonstration by a dependable logical procedure.

6 *seshemet, seshmet*: Examination of the Proof. This is the review of the whole body of evidence or premises and rules that determine the validity of a solution. Such an examination of a logical proof always leads to a further conceptual generalization. Thus the ancient Egyptians had the technique of forming concepts inductively.

7 *gemi. ek nefer*: Literally, "You have found good." This is the concluding stage. To be able to do something, and find it correctly done, means that it was done as it should be done. To find (*gemi*) is to obtain by intellectual effort, and bring oneself to a mental awareness of what is correct, precise, perfect (*nefer*). To arrive at a *logical* conclusion and find that the conclusion withstands critical scrutiny is an achievement in the art of deduction. The adverb *nefer* ("well") implies that the solution is convincing, so that a contradiction is impossible. The concluding observations are mainly confirmatory. Nevertheless, the rigor of the entire process is evident in the method, and the result is objectively known in all truth.

The Being and Essence of the Cosmos and of Humans

How did the cosmos come to be? What is the fundamental nature of a human being? These philosophical questions deal with the being and essence of the cosmos and of humans. It is, then, of importance to turn our attention now to ancient Egyptian thinking concerning these questions. The Egyptians conceived the origin of the universe and all things in it as an *evolution*, but also as a physical *emanation* of the divine power.

Genesis or "Creation" as an Evolution

The Nile and the sun are the two phenomena that dominated the Egyptian intellectual and spiritual life from the earliest times. However, long before the Nile and the sun came into existence, there was, in Egyptian cosmogony, the primeval *Nun*, an ethereal substance that existed before all else. It was from this original substance that *Ra-Atum* originated. *Nun* is a dense and opaque substance, neither transparent nor translucent, impenetrable by light. But, with the appearance in it of *Ra-Atum*, there comes light and spirit. *Ra-Atum* has within itself a force, a power of nature. Thanks to this power of nature, gods and goddesses, heaven and earth, animals and human beings gradually will come into existence. *There is no God standing at the beginning as a conscious and moral personality, and as creator of heaven and earth.*

Nun itself is an uncreated fluid or substance ("primeval water"). But the world and all things in it are brought into being out of *Nun*. The created comes gradually from the uncreated. Contrary to the usual supposition, here "spirit" comes out of "matter." *Nun*, a physical substance, and *Ra-Atum*, an intellectual and spiritual force, are different, with opposite properties, but complementary to each other. *Nun* can be described as *being*, and *Ra-Atum* as movement. The complementarity of "matter" and "spirit" clearly illustrates the unity of opposites in various processes within the universe. Nevertheless, there is an epistemological problem of the greatest difficulty.

As noted above, the historical development of the universe, in ancient Egyptian cosmogony, goes back to *Nun* as the original "matter" and *Ra-Atum* as the first "form" from which other forms are made or developed. This is an evolution, that is to say, a natural process in which something changes into a different more complex or better form. In the present case what we have is a process of cosmic evolution, and the fundamental elements may be grouped as follows:

1   *Nun*, the primordial "waters" existing prior to the emergence of the creator-god; *Huh*, the boundless stretches of primordial formlessness; *Kuk*, darkness, and *Amon*, "the hidden," representing the intangibility and imperceptibility of pre-creation existence.
2   *Ra-Atum*, the self-emanating creator-god from *Nun*. In the Book of Genesis (Old Testament) the creator-god existed alongside chaos. The earth was chaos, waste, and void (*weha' arets hayetha thohû wabhohû*, in Hebrew). By contrast, *Atum* was alone in *Nun*; *Atum* was *Ra* in his very first appearance, a king in full glory (*kha*), one who existed before *Shu* had even lifted heaven from earth. *Atum* means "everything," and it means also "nothing." *Atum* is what is finished, completed, and perfected. It means both all-inclusiveness and emptiness.
3   *Geb* and *Nut*, earth and sky. These represent the created things of this world, whether divine, cosmic, human, animal, vegetal, or mineral.

Genesis or "Creation" as a Physical Emanation from the Divine Power

The qualities of the creator-gods (*Atum, Ra, Ptah*) are: might (*bau*), radiance (*hedjut*), prosperity (*udjau*), victory (*nakhtu*), wealth (*useru*), plenty (*asha*), sanctity (*djoseru*), readiness (*aperu*), creativity (*iri*), intelligence (*ib*), adornment (*djeba*), and stability (*djedet*). These qualities appear also with the *ka*, "spirit," at royal birth (Brugsch 1968: 996ff.). Because of all these qualities, the creator-god is able to bring a new being into existence by the act of naming it. The name is a thing of individuality and power; the act of uttering a new name is an act of creation.

In the text *Memphite Philosophy* (a mutilated stela now in the British Museum, London, no. 797, formerly no. 135), we find clearly articulated a broad philosophical system about the nature of the universe, emphasizing the divine *word* that brought forth the world. Creation is explained strictly in physical terms. Creation is an act of thought (*hatiu*) which came into the heart (*ib*) of a god and the commanding utterance (*udjet-medu*) which brought that thought into reality. This creation by thought and utterance is like a physical emanation from God himself.

The divine word is treasured in ancient Egypt because of its sensible nature and its enormous power. The divine word is clearly the ever-active divine power proceeding out of the mouth of the divinity. The divine word appeared in Egypt as a corporeal emanation from the creator-god:

> It was he who made every work, every handicraft, which the hands make, the going of the feet, the movement of every limb, according to his command, through the thought of the heart that came forth from the tongue. (British Museum, stela no. 797, trans. James H. Breasted, 1912)

A pair of related attributes of the creator-god, which were themselves personified as deities, were *Hu*, "authoritative utterance," or the commanding speech which brings a situation into being, and *Sia*, "perception," the cognitive reception of an object, idea, or situation. Perception in this dynamic sense and authoritative utterance were together the ongoing creative principles of the universe which involved the heart (*ib*), which conceived thoughts (*hatiu*), and the tongue (*nes*), which produced the command (*udjet-medu*).

The world is first an idea conceived in the "heart," i.e. mind, of the divinity. All things first existed in the thought of the god, and then assumed objective reality by the utterance of the "tongue." The utterance of the thought in the form of a divine "let it be done" brought forth the world. This Egyptian conception of creation by thought and word was stated many centuries before the Logos doctrine of the New Testament, which has it that "In the beginning was the Word, and the Word was with God, and the Word was God."

The Egyptian Conception of Immortality

According to the Egyptian conception of the origin of the universe (by evolution or divine emanation), everything is in eternal movement: gods and goddesses, human beings, nature, and the world. The totality of existence is *kheper*, that is, transformation and becoming through time and space. All sources of being and life (*ankh*) are in God, the only true one (*maat*). Egyptian thought made the greatest achievements in the fields of philosophy (wisdom) and science, i.e. astronomy, medicine, architecture. But spirituality ("religion") and morals were not neglected. In all these fields the Egyptians sought truth and certainty through rational inquiry. They combined the capacity for logical reasoning with deep psychological understanding.

Harmony, and self-control, movement, life, deep emotion, power: this is the Egyptian way. Human beings were conceived as being ennobled with spiritual entities such as *ka*, "spiritual essence," *ba*, "the soul," i.e. the power to make the dead a "mighty one," and *akh*, a spiritual equipment for greatness. The idea of a life beyond the grave – that is, the belief in the immortality of the soul and the resuscitation of the body – was first explicitly expressed among the ancient Egyptians. It is evident that the Egyptians had developed a psychology of the dead for the first time in human history. Mortuary priests and priestesses knew from a study of manuals the right rituals and procedures for reconstituting, one by one, the faculties of the dead, so that they will be able to live again in the hereafter. For the Egyptians, death was a kind of process of self-consciousness in which humans attain an identification with the gods whose reaction is summed up as "One of us comes to us" (*Pyramid Texts*, pyramid of Mer-en-Ra, 6th Dynasty).

The celestial and mortuary teachings on the Kingdom of the dead and teachings on moral values in the affairs of living human beings were never separated in ancient Egypt. This is why the earliest chapter in the moral development of human society is to be found in Egypt, "a chapter marking perhaps the most important fundamental step in the evolution of civilization" (Breasted 1972: 165–6).

The Metaphysical Problem of "Evil"

In the beginning, the creation was *neferu*, that is, "perfection," "beauty," and "goodness." The *ka* or spirit of the universe was nothing but good. How then can it become evil?

When an individual being, god or goddess, human being, animal, or tree, comes into existence, a certain *ka* ("soul," "spirit," "essence") is inherent in him or her or it. This *ka* makes a being what he, she, or it is and constitutes his, her, or its nature or personality. Hence, "human nature" is simply the *ka* of humanity that is inherent in each individual. The *ka* was thought to be a person's god, sometimes godhead in general, and sometimes a specific god (*netcher*; Coptic *nute*, *nuti*). The *ka* is, then, the divine force within humans that governs their behavior. How then can it be evil?

Egyptian women and men were beings possessed of value in themselves. Eternal life was the great goal. Spiritual and mental vigor was very deep. How then can there be evil?

A remarkable text gives four good things the supreme God did in order to silence evil:

1 The creator made Wind, i.e. life equally available to all humans.
2 Water being a crucial factor in the formation of the Nile Valley, an assurance of equal access to water meant basic equality of opportunity.
3 All humans are created equal ("I made every human like his or her fellow"). This means that the creator had not intended that humans do evil.
4 The final good deed of the supreme God was to call human attention to the kingdom of the dead, the region of eternal life and to the god-worship and rituals that must be performed in order to attain that immortality.

In full, the verse on the third good deed of the supreme God runs as follows:

> I made every human like his fellow.
> I did not command that they might do evil,
> But it was their hearts that violated what I had said.
> That is (the third) of the deeds.
> (Adriaan de Buck, *CoffinTexts*, VII, 1130: 461–5)

It is clear that humans are the flock of God. He made heaven and earth so as to satisfy their desires and wishes. He made the breath of life for their nostrils. Humans are God's image fashioned out of the divine body. Plants and animals, fowl and fish, were made in order to nourish human beings. How then can there be evil?

Evil comes from humans themselves. Their own hearts (*haty*, "heart," *hatiu*, "thoughts," *ib*, "heart," "mind," "understanding," "intelligence," "will") have devised wrong. Social inequality is no part of God's plan. Equality is a divine dispensation, but wrongdoing is a human act. Human beings must bear the responsibility for the latter alone.

Evil is not a divine principle in the world. The origin of evil is to be found within the nature of human beings themselves. Human nature (*ka*) is good, but the first thing in life is consciousness (*ib*). The mind (*ib*) can have various activities, such as thinking and feeling, but to think and feel well depends on consciousness. In human beings the principle of humanity, righteousness, propriety, and wisdom belongs to consciousness. Human beings can distinguish between what is right and wrong, thanks to their consciousness. They are capable of having commiseration, forgiveness, and also of being ashamed of wrongdoing. The flame of a candle depends on how the candle has received the rich tallow that gives light. The flame is the *ka*, but the tallow that really gives light is the human mind and its consciousness (*ib*). For all these reasons, education (*seba*) is very necessary.

Maat, the Keystone of Egyptian Philosophy

Ancient Egyptian society lasted almost 35 centuries. During this long span of time, there was no social discrimination between men and women, no human servitude or slavery, no detention in jails, and no capital punishment. This was possible because of *Maat*, the keystone of the Egyptian philosophy.

Symbolism of Maat

The goddess *Maat*, wearing a tall ostrich feather upon her head as her symbol, was called the daughter of *Ra*, or the eye of *Ra*. She was also known as lady of the heavens, queen of the earth, mistress of the underworld, and mistress of all gods. Ritual scenes depict Egyptian kings presenting a statuette of *Maat* to the gods as a supreme gift.

Maat *as the Embodiment of Perfect Virtue*

Maa basically means "the real," "reality," that is, that which is genuine and authentic as opposed to artificial or spurious. *Maat* is reality as a whole, that is, the totality of all things possessing actuality, existence, or essence. *Maat* is that which exists objectively. In fact, *Maat* is that which has necessary and not just contingent existence. This is why *Maat* is everywhere and pervades all creation (*er-djer*). It means also that *Maat* is pertinent to all the spheres of reality, the divine or sacred, the cosmic, the physical, the political, and the familial. In short, *Maat* is an exhaustive and comprehensive concept.

This inclusiveness makes it an orderly and aesthetically coherent whole; which is why *Maat* also means the orderliness of the totality of existence. Accordingly, everything in the universe that is real and orderly is the expression or manifestation of *Maat*.

In particular, when in society human beings conduct themselves in the proper way or perform in the correct way, they are manifesting *Maat*. Hence these other meanings of *Maat*, as "truth," "justice," "righteousness," "rightness." *Maat* is the highest conception of physical and moral law known to the ancient Egyptians. Thus it is that the goddess *Maat* was the personification of law, order, rule, truth, right, righteousness, canon, justice, straightforwardness, integrity, uprightness, conscientiousness, and perfection. Egyptian civilization was built upon this very inclusive concept, with its great fecundity of meaning. However, to talk *Maat* is of no use, if it is not practiced. In truth, *Maat* is a way of life and spirituality.

Maat *is more than Ethics or Moral Philosophy*

The Pharaonic state was organized according to the political principles of *Maat*. Because of this, people did not live in what Thomas Hobbes (1588–1679) called "the state of nature." In philosophy, ethics designates moral philosophy, that is, the principles of right conduct theorized as a system of moral values. But *Maat* can be understood as a transcendental moral philosophy, because it is already divine. *Maat* has nothing to do with what is called in Western philosophy "moral values," "ethics," "imperatives," etc. A Pharaoh was not a "political animal" or a "moral leader," but truly a real (*maa*) king, a divine leader, and a spiritual king, concerned with the divine principles governing the world. The kings of ancient Egypt upheld the laws of the universe and of human society, which *Maat* embodied, i.e. cosmic order, truth, justice, harmony, perfection, and spiritual strength.

Maat is, thus, more than "ethics" or "moral values," because the creator-god himself lives by *Maat*. Things change (*kheper*), both in the world of nature and of human beings, but *Maat*, underlying and regulating the changes, remains (*men*) unchanging as long as the creator-god *Ra* exists. An ancient Egyptian text runs:

O *Ra*!
Master of truth (*Maat*)
Living of Truth (*Maat*)
Rejoicing in Truth (*Maat*)
Vaunted in Truth (*Maat*)
Formed of Truth (*Maat*)
Eternal through Truth (*Maat*)
Abundance by Truth (*Maat*)
Powerful by Truth (*Maat*)
Constant in Truth (*Maat*)
Rich by Truth (*Maat*)
Adorned by Truth (*Maat*)
Shining by Truth (*Maat*)
Satisfied by Truth (*Maat*)
United to Truth from his beginning.

(Litany of the god Ra)

The Immanence of Maat in African culture

The honor and awe in which the Egyptians held *Maat* was tremendous. In fact, *Maat* is still one of the principal forces in the development of African societies. The fundamental role of *Maat* is manifested nowadays in the language of various African ethnic groups:

Ancient Egyptian	:	*maat*, "truth"; *maa*, "true"
Coptic (Egypt)	:	*me, mee, mie, mei, meei*, "truth," "justice," and also "truthful," "righteous"
Caffino (Cushitic, Ethiopia)	:	*moyo*, "motive," "reason" (truth and reason are inseparable)
Kongo (Congo)	:	*moyo*, "life," "soul," "mind" (same semantic field)
Ngbaka (Central African Republic)	:	*ma*, magic medicine (in order to know the truth)
Fang (Equatorial Guinea, South Cameroon, Gabon)	:	*mye, mie*, "pure" (*tabe mye*, "to be physically and morally pure")
Mpongwe (Gabon)	:	*mya*, "to know" the truth (*mya re isome*, the "self-knowledge," which the Delphic oracle also enjoined: *gnothi seauton*)
Yoruba (Nigeria)	:	*mo*, "to know" the truth (knowledge)
Hausa (Nigeria)	:	*ma*, "in fact," "indeed" (affirmative truth: *ni ma na ji*, "I in fact heard it")
Mada (North Cameroon)	:	*mat*, "genie," "goblin" (semantic specialization)
Nuer (Nilotic, Sudan)	:	*mat*, "total," "sum up"; "forces" (*ro mat*, "to join forces with." *Maat* is indeed the total of all virtues, all forces as ideals to guide man in his personal and spiritual life).

Conclusion

The serious and careful study of African philosophy from antiquity through the present era will reveal that African philosophy has a very wide scope. All the major issues that have engaged the attention of philosophers in Asia, Europe, America, etc. can be found in African philosophy. They were discussed through many centuries in ancient Egypt, during the great kingdoms of West, Central, and Southern Africa, in modern times and in contemporary times. Any doubt about reason and rationality in Africa was chiefly due to anthropological innuendoes. Philosophy as such was not, and has never been, a mystery to the African mind. The fact is that in human history philosophy has been everywhere a mark of the triumph of the human mind.

The central concept of the Egyptian philosophy is *Maat*, meaning "levelness, evenness, straightness, correctness," in the sense of regularity and order in the world. Flowing from this is the philosophical use of *Maat* to mean "uprightness, righteousness, truth, justice." In conformity with *Maat*, individual rights were fully recognized in ancient Egypt. *Maat* gave each human being an opportunity to realize himself or herself in this life and to have hope for a future life hereafter.

Since human beings belonged also to society, not to themselves alone, the key word for the wise person was "silence," with the meaning of calm, tranquillity, humility. The god *Amon* himself was "the lord of the silent, the protector of the silent." Since "ignorant and wise are of one piece," the right to self-expression must be used in the spirit of *Maat*.

The achievements of the ancient Egyptians in art, architecture, and government and their sense of geometric order, social justice, peace, love, and happiness are reflected in the intellectual, scientific, and spiritual heights reached by Egypt, thanks to the philosophy of *Maat*.

Ancient Egypt did contribute significantly to the continuing philosophy, ethics, or world consciousness of later times by receiving and educating many Greek scholars and philosophers. For example, Plato (427–347 BC) himself records that Thales (624–546 BC), the founder of philosophy, geometry, and astronomy in the Greek world, was educated in Egypt under the priests ("*Th. epaideuthe en Aigupto hupo ton hiereon*": Plato, *The Republic* X, 600 A, scholium).

References

Breasted, James H. (1972) *Development of Religion and Thought in Ancient Egypt* (Philadelphia: University of Pennsylvania Press; 1st edn. 1912).

Brugsch, Heinrich (1968) *Thesaurus Inscriptionum Aegyptiacarum: Woerterbuch Suppl.*, 6 vols (Leipzig: Graz; orig. pub. 1883–91).

Gardiner, Alan Henderson (1957) *Egyptian Grammar: Being an Introduction to the Study of Hieroglyphs*, 3rd rev. edn. (Oxford: Griffith Institute, Ashmolean Museum).

Gillings, Richard F. (1972) *Mathematics in the Time of the Pharaohs* (Cambridge, MA: MIT Press).

Hegel, G. W. F. (1956) *The Philosophy of History* (New York: Dover).

Yu-lan, Fun (1976) *A Short History of Chinese Philosophy* (New York: The Free Press).

2

African Philosophers in the Greco-Roman Era

D. A. MASOLO

The intellectual movements and influential texts which defined what later was to be known as the Patristic period in the history of Christian thought were molded by the sociocultural and political realities of the interface between several older cultural traditions in North Africa and the new Christian faith. From antiquity, North Africa had been home to several indigenous African peoples like the Berbers, but it also was the playground of both Roman imperial politics and Greek intellectual traditions. In addition to them, North Africa was also the site of traditions of Judaism brought by Jewish immigrants from antiquity. All these traditions were richly reflected in the many intellectual movements and schools that emerged in North Africa before and well into the medieval period of the Christian era.

Christianity emerged as the culmination of the Judaic prophetic history and tradition, as the perfection and consummation of universal history. Its posture thus was one of superiority to all other traditions. Doctrinally, it emerged as a practical system, a revealed way of life rather than a system or theory of knowledge which it considered as worldly and lacking in Truth. In the North African context, the worldliness of the secular systems of thought and the ways of life derived from them were considered by Christian faithfuls as pagan belief systems whose adherents they were out to conquer and convert. Clearly, even as Christianity triumphed in this quest, the chief crafters of its doctrines assimilated the methods and many of the ideas of Greek and Roman rhetoric and philosophy. Yet this triumph came only as a result of many years of struggle and growth. Christianity started within the vast Roman empire as just one of the many religious sects of the time, both competing for recognition against and resisting persecution from believers of several astrological, divinatory, and numerous other forms of religious cults of the time. From the fourth century onwards, it was Christianity on the offensive and other belief systems and cultural practices in retreat and declining resistance.

Today's corpus of the accepted doctrines of the Christian faith is an outcome of many centuries of development and revision. In these processes, the need for definitive formulations has been driven by the desire to protect the articles of faith from confusion among believers, and from discordant secular beliefs and theories, and finally from attacks by non-believers. In so doing, part of the aim of the various councils and synods at which specific doctrines were established for the universal

Church was to present the Christian faith as a homogeneous and rational under-standing of the dependent relation of created reality to the Divine. In what fore-shadowed later missionary methods in sub-Saharan Africa in the nineteenth and twentieth centuries, the spread of Christianity in Greco-Roman Africa was closely linked to the control of knowledge through a system of education introduced as a tool for evangelization. In both the earlier and later periods, part of the outcome of this institutional set-up was that Christianity either depended on, or caused, the rise of an educated and privileged class in society.

In Alexandria and other major cities of the Greco-Roman world, there had been a solidly educated elite prior to the arrival of Christianity. This kind of personnel has been the pillar of the Church's survival through the centuries. This linkage has been true since the conversion of Constantine. Education, higher education in par-ticular, was confined to an economically privileged minority. Another striking simi-larity between the two periods is that one of the expectations underlying the Church's control of education and the school systems was to get the new and well-schooled converts to write in defense of the new faith against the local cultural traditions from which they themselves had emerged. Indeed, it was common for doctrinal schools, including religious sects, to enlist the intellectual support of re-nowned scholars as a means of legitimating their teachings. Among the Christians, such supporters, often converts, came to be known as the apologists, and their writings can be said generally to characterize the works of such African thinkers of the time as Origen (AD 185–253), Tertullian (AD c.155–c.240), and, above all, St Augustine (AD 354–430). Plotinus (AD 204–70), who was born in Egypt, also belonged to this period and school, although historians are often quick to point out his Greco-Roman ancestry.

Like Plotinus, Hypatia (AD c.370–415), one of the earliest Western female phil-osophers on record, was also an Alexandrian-born Greek philosopher. It appears from historical reports and accounts that although she was primarily grounded in mathematics and astronomy like her father, her general philosophical orientation embraced the Neoplatonism of her time. Her explications of Plato's and Aristotle's systems appear to have been popular. By being the earliest known female figure in the professional practice of philosophy, Hypatia appears to have pioneered the con-quest of what were traditional biases against women. Also, by her chastity she successfully fought off the sexual representation of women. Primarily for these reasons, the memory of Hypatia has become a source and a symbol of inspiration to the modern feminist movement. She was murdered for reasons not quite determin-able to historians. In celebration of her historical significance, the journal *Hypatia*, named for her, has become the most visible and authoritative philosophy journal dedicated to gender-related issues and social philosophy.

Another noted personality with intellectual roots in Alexandria was the Jewish philosopher Philo, usually known by some as Philo Judaeus (c.20 BC–AD 40), and by others as Philo of Alexandria. His thought developed out of an attempt to merge Jewish thought with elements of Greek philosophy in the diaspora. Some notable African personalities of this era, although of less intellectual renown than Origen, Tertullian, or Augustine, are Cyprian (born probably in Carthage between 200 and 210), a famous rhetorician and expert in eloquence who was influenced by

Tertullian and rose through Church ranks to become bishop of Carthage in 248 or 249; Arnobius, another apologist; and Lactantius, also a learned rhetorician and apologist who tutored Crispus, the eldest son of Emperor Constantine, before persecution forced him to abandon those duties. He had studied under Arnobius.

Alexandria was also the site of the translation, by Jewish scholars, of the Old Testament known as the *Septuagint*. Philo's allegorical exegesis and his doctrine of the Logos as the external revelation of the "idea" of God and as mediator between God and the world exerted a powerful influence on Christian theology of the first centuries. Generally, the Jewish presence in this intellectually rich environment facilitated the embrace, by local populations, of the monotheistic idea and also of some of the rites which later became important symbols of their conversion to Christianity.

The Alexandrian School

Alexandria, the second largest city in the Roman empire, was a well-known center of learning. It was inhabited and also frequently visited by noted scholars and thinkers of antiquity and reflected much of what the pagan world of the Greco-Roman civilization was known for: poetry, rhetoric, philosophy, astronomy, mathematics, physics, and art. It was also the seat of the Roman empire on the African continent, and thus was known for law and political organization. In the philosophical domain, Alexandria displayed much of the Neoplatonic philosophical movements which characterize the classical and medieval eras: hedonism, stoicism, and Gnosticism. By the turn of the second century Alexandria had become a noted center of theological studies, there having emerged a catechetical school which operated as the Christian Academy and whose leading affiliates included Titus Flavius Clemens (also known as Clement of Alexandria) and Origen. But because these pioneers often worked under very precarious conditions posed by both the anti-Christian persecutions from without the Church and possible charges of heresy arising from the yet uncertain doctrinal interpretations within the Church, their tenure of office was constantly threatened. Thus, for example, Clement, who was one of the earliest directors of the Alexandrian catechetical school, was forced to flee during the persecution of Septimius Severus. He was succeeded by Origen, who was himself deposed from the post after 28 years for allegedly receiving Holy Orders irregularly and teaching heresy. Origen is arguably the most influential theologian of the early Church and the most important theologian of the entire Church before Augustine.

Origen

Origen was born in Alexandria in either 184 or 185 to an indigenous Christian family, and was a victim of anti-Christian violence early in his life: his father Leonides became a victim of persecution when Origen was only 17 years old. Origen himself was captured and tortured for his beliefs later in his life during the persecution of Decius.

Several things define Origen as an African. First, eminent historians and commentators of his times refer to him as "the African," as they did Clement, Tertullian, Augustine, Cyprian, Arnobius, and other African scholars. (See, for example, Döllinger 1840: i. 40ff.) This suggests that Origen was either a Punic or a Berber like Augustine (Ferguson 1969: 184). Secondly, references, in sources on his early life, to his mastery of Greek philosophy and language as a sign of his affluent family background, which would not be such if he *was* Greek, indicate that he was an outsider to Greek culture. Also, the fact that he wrote in Latin, the preferred language of the African intellectuals of the time, rather than in Greek, as did the Romans, Jewish intellectuals, and the Greeks themselves, appears to confirm this view. Thirdly, we learn that he was expelled from Antioch, where he had gone at the invitation of Julia Mamaea, the mother of Emperor Alexander Severus, when all Egyptians were ordered out of the city. The experience of his father's killing left a deep mark on him and would be manifested in two ways in his later life: his advocacy of courageous martyrdom, and his arguments against the heretics.

At the age of 18, Origen became a teacher at the catechetical school where he himself had studied, becoming so famous there that he had disciples among both believers and non-believers. His intellectual fame became widespread in the Mediterranean region, extending as far east as Caesarea in Palestine, where he later founded a theological school. Origen is popularly remembered for his reported literal interpretation of Matthew 19: 12, and his self-mutilation thereupon, but his significance in the history of the Church lies in his theological writings. Like Clement, and in contrast to Tertullian, Origen believed, possibly under the influence of Philo, that philosophy occupied a special place in history as a means for educating pagans for Christ. This attitude toward philosophy was the foundation of Christian Neoplatonism, which would later influence Augustine as well.

Origen was an ardent learner who would go to any lengths to master what he thought to be important for understanding the problems of his time. He is reported to have studied under Ammonius Saccas, who at one time was Plotinus' teacher. At another time, probably around 212, he placed himself under a tutor to learn Hebrew so he could better counter orthodox Jews. Origen's works represent the non-heretical trajectory of the Gnostic movement. His writings have been divided into various categories which reflect his original objectives: *exegeses* (commentaries) on the Scriptures; *skalia* or *Didaskalikos* (brief notes) on especially difficult or abstruse biblical passages; and *homilies* (sermons).

Origen's principal work remains *De principiis* (*On First Principles*), which is a comprehensive presentation of Christian dogma. It consists of four books which treat of God, the Trinity, and Angels (I); of creation, man, and redemption (II); of freedom of the will, and the conflict between good and evil (III); and of Holy Scriptures and their somatic, moral, and mystical significance (IV). He drew on Plato in teaching the pre-existence of souls. The present visible world, he argued, was preceded by a world of perfect spirits (*naturae rationabiles*) who abused their free will by turning away from God and were therefore exiled in matter, which was created just for this purpose. The angels were given very refined bodies of spherical shape (the stars), while men were given animal bodies, and demons invisible and hideous ones. He taught that creation must be an external act since God's omnipotence and goodness must constantly be manifested. This, as we know, is contrary to the then current theological theory according to which the divine perfection precludes the oppositional separation between interiority and exteriority in divine nature and action. The material world, he maintained, would come to an end and the bodies of humans would rise again as pure spirits so that at the end they will be like they were at the beginning, ushering in the restoration of all things or *apokatastasis*. According to Origen's theory, this process, contrary to the orthodox belief in the existence of hell, would go on endlessly, one world following another without end.

Origen's doctrines appear to have roots culturally and historically far deeper than his engagements with them for the sake and good of Christianity. Long before Christianity, there were several rival mythical narratives, called "mysteries" by historians of that period, about the origin of the world. Some of these were entertained by various Gnostic groups, and people like Origen might have been very aware of those teachings. One such group was known as the Ophites, who, according to Döllinger (1840: i. 138), had existed before Christianity and must have been known by Origen in Egypt. One of their theories was similar to Origen's later doctrine of *apokatastasis*. The Ophites taught that there was a universal soul from which all things flowed, and to which all things would again return. It is obvious that this theory combined elements of the doctrines of creation and immortality, attaching to the latter the sub-doctrine of resurrection. Another sect of the Gnostics, the one led by Capocrates and his son, Epiphanes of Alexandria, taught something similar too, claiming that all things had sprung from the Monas, the father of all being, and would flow back again into his bosom. (Egyptian legends regarding the origin of immortality, regarded by historians as probably one of the very oldest developments of Egyptian religious thought, are gathered in the form of myths about the god Osiris.[1]) According to the followers of Capocrates, the visible world was formed by ambitious spirits that had rebelled against the Monas. To extricate oneself from the grip of the Monas, everyone has to acquire knowledge of the Monas, and that is what gives freedom. To them this was the meaning of the term or name "Jesus," that is, "The Truth shall make you free" (Döllinger 1840: i. 139). It would appear that many elements of indigenous religious beliefs and practices were not only in competition with the new Christian religion but also lent to it some of their key concepts. Historians concur that the kind of syncretism which we observed recently in the ethno-theological attempts to merge agreeable elements of African traditional beliefs with those of Christianity occurred at the turn of the first millennium as well. Döllinger writes thus:

> The ideas and dogmas of the religion of the people in the east [the Egyptian, Phoenician, Persian, and Buddhist] were again awakened, and there appeared men, who, filled with these ideas, and with the doctrines of Christianity, and in particular with the doctrine of redemption, were carried away by an enthusiasm to mingle the new with the old, to illustrate the one by the other, and to form of them a system of higher wisdom and religious knowledge. (Döllinger 1840: i. 123)

In fact much of the influence of traditions on how we think often takes place rather unconsciously and inevitably. It is therefore reasonable to think that many elements of the indigenous customs and everyday or seasonal activities and practices of the peoples of North Africa may have found their way, by way of adaptation, into the conceptions of Christianity as African thinkers endeavored to systematize Christian beliefs into an organized and coherent thought system. This had happened elsewhere too, as historians remind us.[2]

Even the concept of the divine triad, or Trinity, appears to have roots in classic Egyptian beliefs, which reflected the people's conception of the gods in families or groups. Perhaps this grouping of gods resulted from a long process of trying to merge the gods of the rural populations with those of the city dwellers, as people migrated into the cities from agricultural and nomadic, pastoralist lifestyles outside (Baikie 1926: 332–3). While it is known that Judaism was a monotheistic tradition, the Egyptians never ran short of gods and goddesses to worship. But as cities were formed and populations merged, the gods became fewer because they too merged into families. Gradually this "social evolution" of the gods led to the conception of them as a unity in plurality. For the Egyptians, this might have been a natural process (Hornung 1982).[3] Given that some of Origen's themes are known to have appeared in Egyptian texts, Egyptian influences in the matter of the Trinity cannot be ruled out.

On the question of the nature of a person too, although Origen believed in the Platonic trichotomy of personhood, his general theory has affinities with the Egyptian practice of approximating human nature to that of the divine. Thus it would not be surprising that Origen saw in human nature a reflection of the divine triad and an element of the doctrine of *Apokatastasis*. Sometimes his theory of personhood is thought to have been influenced by the Pauline letter to the Thessalonians (5: 23) rather than by the trichotomous Platonic theory of the soul. It is, however, likely that St Paul, a learned man of Greek letters himself, was also influenced by the Platonic elements of Greek thought which was widely known and influential. After all, the reason St Paul became the "Apostle to the Gentiles" was his qualifications and fame as a person well versed in Greek thought and Roman law (Bihlmeyer 1968: 52–8). His letters, called the Epistles, were, like the Gospels, all written in Greek and embodied a scheme similar to that of Philo of Alexandria, who was his contemporary. One only has to remember that St John, like Philo, found the Logos a useful concept, and identified Jesus with the Logos in a human body. Thus Origen could very well have been aware of all these sources.

At all events, Origen theorized that a person was made up of body (*soma*), soul (*psyche*), and spirit (*pneuma*), the latter being conceived during Origen's time, especially by the Gnostics, as a spiritual element which was different from the soul (*psyche*). It might, perhaps, be approximately likened to what has been called the "vital force" in more recent African metaphysical texts. As explained by Tempels (1959) and by Griaule (1965), for example, the "vital force" is conceived as an element in the composite make-up of a person that animates and individuates him or her. Many African explanations of personhood incorporate such a concept. What sometimes falls into contention is whether such explanations point to the existence of an element separate from the body, or merely to a faculty or capacity of the complex organic system of the body. Be that as it may, for Origen, the *pneuma* was not just an element of the human composite; it transcended it and participated in the divine Spirit.

In advancing this view, Origen was founding the Christian view of the person and of history. In particular, he was pioneering the conception of the supernatural vocation of humans as being "that which is oriented toward and participative in divine nature." Such a position obviously put Origen directly against some of the philosophical currents of his time, especially Epicureanism which, according to him, was the shame of philosophy and a form of true atheism. It might be noted here that in many African explanations of personhood it is believed that the life-giving element that constitutes certain systems of biologic antecedents into living persons comes directly from God and is a speck of the divine substance itself. Thus, to the many African peoples who hold this view, it is not by chance that they place great value on marriage and procreation. To them, to evade these duties is to reject the basic human responsibility for actualizing the divine order of things by which humans participate in the furtherance of creation. Origen could have been laboring with a widespread African conception of reality and of personhood, in particular.

The question of the Trinity was thus not new to the times of Origen, but reconciling the old mode of thinking about the relations between deities with the new and assertive Christian monotheism must have been problematic. Again, we can assume that the same pattern of thought used to reconcile rural and urban divinities in Egyptian thought was applied to reconcile the divine idea imported by the carriers of the Gospel with the dominant Egyptian deities, a sort of truce in which God would be one but still manage a manifestation in a triad. As Africans like Origen were absorbed into the Christian fold, they brought with them their local god or goddess, and, as was the practice of the Egyptians, says Baikie (1926: 332), "a place had to be found for this deity by the side of the great god of the larger community, and thus there grew up a kind of divine family of the city, which, for some reason, was generally arranged as a triad or trinity."[4] The powerful god of the city, which was the larger and absorbing community, was considered to be superior to the gods of the smaller communities. The notion of inequality among the members of the new divine family occurs in Origen's teachings. As a matter of fact, the theological systematization of the doctrine of the Trinity was done by African pioneer apologists. Origen taught that the two "lower Persons" of the Trinity were subordinate to the first, the Father. The *Logos* or Word was subordinate to the Father, and the Holy Spirit to the *Logos*, "and immediately below the Holy Spirit are the created spirits, who, through the power of the Holy Spirit, are lifted up to become sons of God, in union with the Son, and are finally participants in the divine life of the Father" (Copleston 1985: vol. II, 28). Some of the elements of these views were later incorporated into the Christian doctrine. For example, the doctrine of the restoration of all creation to God became part of the doctrine of the immortality of the soul and of the resurrection at the end of time. But, generally, these views did not fare well with the leaders of the time and were condemned as heresies, first by Justinian in 543 and then by the Council of Constantinople in 553.

Tertullian of Carthage

Tertullian of Carthage had a different background and approach from that of Origen. The son of a pagan who was a government official at the court in the capital city of Carthage, a suburb of today's Tunis in North Africa, Tertullian had what was considered a good and wide-ranging education at the time. He was trained as a jurist and practiced law in Rome, and is said to have been highly skilled in refuting Gnostic heresies and other anti-Christian doctrines. It is not known when he converted to Christianity, but it is thought that he was already a Christian by 197 when he wrote his first two apologist treatises, *Ad nationes* (*To the Pagans*), and *Apologeticum*. Tertullian's African descent is discerned by historians from both his literary style and his hatred for anything Greek. His *Adversus Judaeos* (*Against the Jews*), written to prove that Jesus was the Messiah, clearly indicates that he was not Jewish. He is credited with writing the first systematic Christian theological works, and with inventing such distinctive, and now received, philosophical terminology in Latin, such as *substantia*, *persona*, and others, all proof of his substantial influence on the history of Christian philosophical and theological thought.

The general corpus of his works can be divided into three categories: polemico-doctrinal, practical-disciplinary (didactic-pastoral), and Montanist. He is widely considered the first Christian writer of great theological significance. Those of his works that fall under the first category include *De testimonio animae* (*The Testimony of the Soul*), in which he defends the universality of the belief in one God as evidenced by human conscience, and *Ad Scapulam* (*To Scapula*), in which he directs his attention to the Roman Representative (Proconsul) who had reverted to persecuting Christians in the years 212–13. His *De carne Christi* (*On the Flesh of Christ*) and *De resurrectione carnis* (*On the Resurrection of the Flesh*) are especially noteworthy for their critique of two theses of the Gnostics, namely, their doctrine that Christ's body was only an "apparent" body and their rejection of the resurrection of the body. Other works of note are *De praescriptione haereticorum* (*The Prescription of Heretics*), *Scorpiace*, *De anima* (*On the Soul*), and *De baptismo* (*On Baptism*), in which, as the titles suggest, he alternates between attacking the heretics and defending his chosen doctrine,

Works in the didactic-pastoral category address primarily the kind of conduct expected of the faithful, and particularly of the Church leaders of the time. They focus on matters of morals and disciplined conduct and they include, for example, *De verginibus velandis* (*On the Veiled Virgins*), *Ad martyras* (*To the Martyrs*), *De oratione* (*On Prayer*), *De paenitentia* (*On Penitence*), *De patientia* (*On Patience*), and *De monogamia* (*On Monogamy*), among others. Finally, while it is not known with any certitude what were the causes of Tertullian's drift toward Montanism, it is suspected that envy and insults (*invidia et contumeliae*) directed at him by the Roman clergy may have driven him into association with the Montanists. These were followers of a movement that in some ways resembles the present-day Pentecostal Churches. Their faith included claims to a form of prophetism involving the ability to speak in tongues. Even more strikingly, they preached the imminent Second Coming of Christ and promised believers deliverance to a heavenly kingdom away from their current tribulations. In light of the fact that it arose during the hard times under Marcus Aurelius, this movement can further be likened to the more recent independent Church movements in Africa during colonial rule and control of all matters of faith by the missionary Church. At any rate, Tertullian's rigoristic approach found some resonance with some aspects of the Montanist movement, especially its way of life, which regarded anything mediocre with pitiless severity. In opposition to stoicism, Tertullian had defended the view that ethics evolves with rigorous self-discipline and the unrelenting observance of the moral law. Thus he adopted an approach to ethics similar to that of Kant. But this approach quickly put him out of tune with the original positions and structure of Montanism. A further complication was that the founding leaders of the Montanist movement had included two women, Priscilla and Maximilla. For Tertullian, women were not qualified to hold any priestly office, nor were they to be allowed to teach or speak at divine worship. Even if they possessed the gift of prophesy, their use of it was to be confined to private utterances. In addition, he repudiated the original Montanist eschatological idea of an imminent descent of a heavenly Jerusalem. Accordingly, he later defected and rejoined the main body of the Church.

It is frequently said that, unlike Origen, Tertullian did not believe that philosophical knowledge was of any use to faith, an observation which, if true, explains why some people have described Tertullian as anti-philosophical or anti-rationalist. Support for these observations often derives from the now classical phrase in *De carne Christi* (5, 4): "*credo quia absurdum* (I believe that which is absurd)," which foreshadows St Anselm's later "*credo ut intelligam*" and, in even more recent times, Søren Kierkegaard's definition of faith as the acceptance of that which reason rejects as absurd. Commenting on a passage from the Bible (I Cor. 1: 27–8) in relation to the Platonic system, Tertullian once observed that "it was hard to find the Maker and father of the universe, whereas the simplest Christian has already found Him" (Copleston 1985: ii. 23). One might recall in this connection also Tertullian's oft-quoted query, "What has Athens to do with Jerusalem?" He draws an adversarial opposition between Christianity, on the one hand, and philosophy and heresy, on the other. Truth and the knowledge of God could be attained only through revelation, by the recognition of the greatness of God's works. He associated philosophy with the heresies of the Gnostics who were heirs to Greek philosophy.

Yet, despite this apparent distrust of philosophy and, in particular, his sharp criticism of the Stoic influence on his adversary Marcion, Tertullian's own thought had its philosophical aspects, and that philosophy was hard to separate from Stoic materialism. He theorized that everything that exists has bodily existence. Hence God, too, was a corporeal Being. However, he argued that God's bodily nature was a *sui generis in sua effigie* (of its own kind commensurate with His likeness),[5] being simultaneously both body and spirit. His views on the corporeal nature of other substances, such as the soul, and of the fate of the soul in the afterlife, has cast some doubt on whether Tertullian was a materialist in a direct and deliberate sense. The ambiguity created by the fact that he held such views while also opposing the materialism of his opponents has led to the suggestion that the apparent materialism in his own writings was the result of the inadequate clarity of his language, by which he probably meant different things altogether. It is conceivable, however, that Tertullian's position was a middle way between materialism and standard dualism. He might be taken to have conceived of the soul as not fully but partially material. In this sense, it might not, perhaps, be out of place to speculate on the possibility of an unconscious indigenous African influence on his thinking, since such conceptions are basic to a lot of African ontologies.[6] It may be noted further that in addition to this apparent materialism, Tertullian argued that the knowledge of God could be inferred from the evidences of order in the world. This suggests that he accepted the teleological argument for the existence of God then well known to the Stoics and the Greek apologists. According to this argument, a posteriori knowledge could, by a natural way, validly lead to the knowledge of God.

Earlier in the chapter I referred to Origen's theories of the Trinity and the probable influences on the theory from the indigenous beliefs of North Africans. However, while Origen's contribution to the conception of the doctrine belonged to what later theologians referred to as the Logos christology, it was, indeed, Tertullian who, in *Adversus Praxean*, founded and systematized the doctrine of the Trinity. That work remains the most important work of Western theology on the Trinity before the time of Augustine.

Incidentally, Origen, Clement, and Tertullian helped to define the Christian catechetical method of preparing converts which was criticized by the Ugandan writer Okot p'Bitek in its twentieth-century form. According to this procedure, the catechumen, before being ready for baptism, must receive instruction on basic tenets of Christian doctrine, such as the teachings regarding the nature of God and the Trinity; the creation and order of the universe; the purpose of creation and the place of humans in it; human nature; Divine punishment for the wicked and rewards for the righteous; and God's mercy to humankind. The catechumen had to learn to proclaim these tenets and also recite "the Lord's prayer." p'Bitek argued that concepts like the absoluteness of God and *creatio ex nihilo*, which were so central to the catechism, not only were absent from the Acholi world-view, but also did not make sense within the Acholi conceptual framework.

St Augustine

Undoubtedly the most celebrated African thinker in history, and one of the greatest thinkers of all time, Aurelius Augustinus was born of Berber parents in Thagaste (probably the present-day Béjaïa in Algeria), a small North African town facing the Mediterranean at Souk Ahras (then known as Numidia). His father, Patrick, was a pagan, while his mother, Monica, was a Christian. Although brought up as a Christian from childhood by his devout mother, the catechetical regulations put in place during the time of Tertullian and other earlier Church leaders and thinkers prevented his baptism at infancy. There has never been any doubt among historians regarding Augustine's Berber ethnicity. According to Ferguson (1969: 184), not only was Thagaste a center of Berber culture, but his own name, and those of his mother and son, are all either Berber, or Berber-derived in their meanings. In Ferguson's view, while Monica is certainly Berber, Adeodatus, the name of Augustine's son, is without doubt a Latinization of Iatanbaal (given by God). Ferguson mentions additional evidence of Augustine's African heredity (ibid.), including the apparent "outsider's style" of his discussion of the Roman Empire in *The City of God* and an African nationalist attitude in the *Confessions*.

Augustine's early studies were done at local schools, where he studied mainly Latin, rhetoric, and, later, at Carthage, also eloquence and a form of what one

59

would today call the performing arts. During these years he read Cicero's works. In the *Confessions* (III, 4) he mentions, in particular, Cicero's *Hortensius* as the source of his philosophical awakening. Regarding his liking for the performing arts (theater) he confessed that this was "because the plays reflected my own unhappy plight and were tinder to my fire" (*Confessions* III, 2). Augustine's youth was filled with adventurous recklessness when he lived away from home. While in Carthage he fell in love with a young girl with whom he cohabited and had a son, Adeodatus. After the awakening Augustine would no longer accept anything on the grounds of authority, but it also left the problem of evil imprinted on his thinking. This would become the key preoccupation of the rest of his intellectual life. He reverted to reading the Scriptures, but is reported to have understood little of it. To quell his uncertainty he joined Manicheism, but before long became afflicted with disappointments with the Manicheists' inability to solve intellectual problems he considered crucial. It appears then that Augustine was affected early by the confusion arising from the many moral and religious systems peddled by the many rival schools and traditions in his time. His *Confessions* would later reflect, in part, his disavowal of Manicheism and, in the other part, his submission to Christian teaching mixed with a nationalist pride in the spirituality of his indigenous culture.

After traveling to Rome in 383, Augustine opened a school for rhetoric, but soon folded it up in order to take up an appointment as a Municipal Professor of Rhetoric in Milan the following year. By this time Augustine had lost nearly all his accommodation for Manicheism and had reverted to academic skepticism. In Milan he discovered Neoplatonic texts which helped to sweep away any residues of Manicheism, especially their materialistic view of reality. At the same time, he was drawn back to Christianity and listened to the homilies of St Ambrose, then Bishop of Milan. It is said that it was the Neoplatonic texts – probably those of Plotinus – which directed Augustine to responses to some of his earlier queries. In particular he was able to grasp the idea of immaterial being. Finally, he was able to understand that God was a spiritual rather than a material substance; that He transcends all things as opposed to being immanent in them. But if this was at the philosophical level, Augustine dramatizes his conversion in the *Confessions* (VIII, 12) by attributing it to a direct divine intervention in the form of a child's voice calling on him to open up and read the Scriptures (specifically, Romans 13: 13, 14). The drama sets forth the separation between faith and reason. Despite all his previous skepticism, Augustine was now ready to accept by faith the dictates of what appeared, from a rational standpoint, like an illusion.

Following his conversion, Augustine abandoned the mother of his son Adeodatus, abandoned any thoughts of marriage, and retreated with his mother, son, and a group of followers to Cassiciaco (present-day Cassago in Algeria) to dedicate himself to prayer, study, and dialogue. By 386 he had written *Contra Academicos* (*Against the Academicians*), *De beata vita* (*The Blessed Life*), and *De ordine* (*On Order*). The following year he wrote *Soliloquia* and also was baptized by Bishop Ambrose. His conversion had become complete. From then on, and following his return to Africa in the summer of 388, Augustine set forth a flurry of writings, most of them aimed at rejecting the intellectual positions he had been attracted to during the tumultuous period of his youth. Manicheism, in particular, is subjected to several rebuttals in these polemics. In 391 he was ordained priest in Hippo and appointed bishop there at the end of 395 or beginning of 396 following the death of Bishop Valerius. For people who wish to excuse themselves from Augustine's exegetical homilies, his two best-known works remain his amazing autobiography, the *Confessiones* (*Confessions*), whose 13 books were written in 401, and the *De civitate Dei* (*The City of God*), which is considered his *magnum opus*, written between 412 and 416, in response to the renewed attacks on Christians and their religion that followed the defeat and plundering of Rome by the Goths (also called Visigoths by some writers) in 410.

Philosophically, Augustine's work, like that of Thomas Aquinas several centuries after him, covered a great variety of topics. On all these his positions, as in the case of St Thomas, have influenced the later theories thereof. In *De civitate Dei* (XI, 26), for example, he writes of the indubitability of the conscious self in a manner that clearly foreshadows the Cartesian *Cogito*. Clearly his objectives were totally different from those under which the *Cogito* arose, yet the implications for the unity of the knowing subject and on the status of sensory experience in both cases are very similar. Augustine's "if I err, then I am" came out of the need to explain the divine Trinity by demonstrating the triple unitary nature of our own subjectivity. He writes:

> We ourselves can recognize in ourselves an image of God, in the sense of an image of the Trinity. Of course, it is only an image and, in fact, a very remote one.... For, we are, and we know that we are, and we love to be and to know that we are. And in this trinity of being, knowledge, and love there is not a shadow of illusion to disturb us... without any illusion of image, fancy, or phantasm, I am certain that I am, that I know that I am, and that I love to be and to know...if I am mistaken, I am. For, if one does not exist, he can by no means be mistaken. Therefore, I am, if I am mistaken. Because, therefore, I am, if I am mistaken, how can I be mistaken that I am, since it is certain that I am, if I am mistaken?

Similarly, he thought, the unity of the one God in three persons can be understood. The unity of the triple human subjectivity participates in the higher and perfect divine Trinity. Augustine's other theories can be derived from this basic position on self-consciousness. His metaphysical system is founded on the idea that the search for truth is the foundation and task of human nature. He taught that the grades of knowledge are the grades of our spiritual elevation. And this is accomplished by searching ever deeper into the inner self in order to transcend oneself. To philosophize is to grasp the truth inside, that is, to acquire knowledge of the soul and of God. For him, truth is not created but only discovered by reason; and it exists in itself prior to such discovery. It is obvious that Augustine identifies internal truth with God and draws a participative comparison between His Trinitarian unity with the triadic unity of self-consciousness, which imitates it. The Platonic influence comes into heavy play here, as Augustine draws the gradations of reality. We ascend from sensible knowledge at the lowest to internal, and eternal objective truth at the highest. Reason, natural *lumen*, is inferior and subordinate to truth, which is its object; but it is also inferior to the *lumen* of intelligence, which has unmediated access to truth by intuition. Above intuition is a superior *lumen*, the *lumen* of grace by which humans have access to supernatural truths. The first two aid and elevate natural reason in its operations. This theory of illumination as the instantaneous act by which reason controls and guides sensory perception toward knowledge clearly anticipates the Cartesian theory of the intuitive power and ability of the mind to discern the characteristics of the true (objective) contents of sensory experience.

Augustine's philosophy closely reflects his *curriculum vitae* which moves gradually from the lowly and reckless indulgences of worldliness and transcends them toward the realization of eternal truth. In going through this spiritual journey, Augustine realizes that humans will always remain humans even in their moments of splendor. But they undergo a spiritual transformation, which includes the rational perception of objective truth and the passionate response to the call to embrace it. In this sense, his system is fundamentally anthropological and historical, from which emanates an awareness of human weakness, limitation, concupiscence, but also of the power of reason which, when used carefully and diligently, should lead humans to the pursuit of salvation. Through reason, humans have the fundamental (that is, metaphysical) vocation to know and accept God. The correlation between these two realms can be summarized with his famous formula: *intellige ut credas* (understand [in order] to believe).

Conclusion

One can learn several things from the foregoing outline of the works and thought of Origen, Tertullian, and Augustine. First, it is not hard to realize from available historical texts, both philosophical and general, that interest in Africa in their times was focused almost exclusively on the formation of Christianity. Contrary to the popular perception of the doctrines of Christianity as divine promulgations, this history of Christianity in its nascent stages reveals the gradual and often also fragile human making of the articles of the faith. Secondly, the history reveals to us the African input in the making of Christianity as we have come to know it. These great Africans helped define some of the basic tenets of Christianity. It is therefore ironical that Christianity in its return to Africa after centuries of absence following its defeat and expulsion by Islam from some parts of Africa looks so foreign and so implicated in the colonial conquest of the continent. The reason is partly suggested by what became of the influence of the works of these African pioneers. As the Church grew and became implanted in European society following the challenge of Islam, the African roots, from which it had grown and which had shaped it into a doctrinally equipped institution, were absorbed into the Western tradition, and the Church took on a local identity.

We lack the kind of detailed and systematized documentation of indigenous knowledge systems in first-century Africa that anthropology has made available about African peoples in recent decades. One of the results of this void is the difficulty of making an adequate assessment of the degree of competition and cross-fertilization between local knowledge and belief systems and other cultural movements like Judaism and Christianity. Several attempts have been made to account for the interaction between ancient African intellectual cultures and their Greek counterparts across the Mediterranean. Both Christian and secular historians of the first five centuries tend to lump together African, Greek, and Roman cultures as pagan in opposition to the emergent Christian tradition. One thing, however, is sufficiently clear from the work of the personalities we have discussed above, especially from Tertullian and Augustine. It is that even in those early stages, Christianity, and later Islam, used its monotheistic world-view as a model for universalizing its belief system. Augustine's *Confessions* clearly and strongly condemn other ways of life as "wayward." Although the book is framed in an autobiographical format, it clearly calls for the rejection of the beliefs and practices that were in competition with Christian beliefs at the time. Through their arguments, Christianity gradually triumphed over local customs and schools of thought and propagated its own world-view as the source of universal moral and cognitive values. Nevertheless, it is difficult to resist the impression that, with the interactions between, on the one hand, local ideas and customs and, on the other hand, the Christian, Judaic, Roman, and Greek traditions, the cultural atmosphere in those days must have been characterized by a rich diversity that was both intellectually challenging and morally confusing. To get some sense of this cultural milieu, one need only think of the cultural conditions that recently have prompted the rise of African independent churches in our own time.

Notes

1   See, for example, Baikie 1926: 325–63. The curious legend of Osiris tells that following his death, his wife Isis had an immaculate conception while in mourning, leading to the birth of their son Horus who she had to protect from the wrath of Osiris' jealous brother and murderer Set. Around the legend of Osiris one finds several similarities with what would later constitute various crucial aspects of Christian beliefs, including Osiris' resurrection and ascent into heaven; and also the doctrine of judgment after death. Later, the Pharaoh was identified with Osiris, and was believed to be raised to life again in the person of the god. This doctrine of resurrection and immortality was finally extended universally to all humans, thus expressing the view that all humans were immortal if only they observed the laid down religious rites. As would be expected, these beliefs later influenced changes in the forms of interment, including mummification, especially for the kings and other people of nobility. Another instructive text on the ancient Egyptian conceptions of the afterlife is Erik Hornung 1999b.

2   See, for example, Ferguson 1970: 237–40 on the origins of what today are considered to be primarily Christian festivals, including such major ones as Christmas, Easter, and All Souls' Day. He also mentions the adaptation of the Isis-Horus representation into the Christian Madonna-child figure.

3   In yet another work, Erik Hornung calls the former theories claiming an ancient Egyptian monotheistic tradition matters of conjecture better left "definitively to the 'history' of ideas..." (1999a: 90).

4   Reference is probably made here to the social transformation, which took place both before and as a result of the Roman colonists' action of forcing African pastoralist and nomadic communities into sedentary lifestyles in cities and agricultural villages. This social process resulted in the meeting and mingling of different customary beliefs and practices, including religious beliefs and rituals.

D. A. MASOLO

5 In *Adversus Praxean* (*Against Praxeas*), 7–8.
6 See, for example, Kwasi Wiredu's defense of what he argues is the Akan non-dualist concept of mind (1987: 153–79).

References

Augustine, Saint (1958) *City of God* (New York: Doubleday Image Books).
Augustine, Saint (1961) *Confessions* (London: Penguin Books).
Baikie, James (1926) *The Story of the Pharaohs*, 3rd edn. (London: A. & C. Black, Ltd.).
Bihlmeyer, Karl (1968) *Church History*. Vol. 1: *Christian Antiquity*, revised Hermann Tüchle, trans. Victor E. Mills (Westminster: The Newman Press).
Copleston, Frederick S. J. (1985) *A History of Philosophy*. Vol. II: *Augustine to Scotus* (New York: Doubleday Image Books).
Döllinger, J. J. I. G. (1840) *History of the Church*, trans. Rev. Edward Cox (London: C. Dolman and T. Jones Publishers).
Ferguson, John (1969) "Aspects of Early Christianity in North Africa," in Lloyd A. Thompson and J. Ferguson (eds.), *Africa in Classical Antiquity, Nine Studies* (Ibadan, Nigeria: Ibadan University Press).
Ferguson, John (1970) *The Religions of the Roman Empire* (Ithaca, NY: Cornell University Press).
Griaule, Marcel (1965) *Conversations with Ogotemmeli* (Oxford: Oxford University Press).
Hornung, Erik (1982) *Conceptions of God in Ancient Egypt: The One and the Many*, trans. John Baines (Ithaca, NY: Cornell University Press).
Hornung, Erik (1999a) *Akhenaten and the Religion of Light*, trans. David Lorton (Ithaca, NY: Cornell University Press).
Hornung, Erik (1999b) *The Ancient Egyptian Books of the Afterlife*, trans. David Lorton (Ithaca, NY: Cornell University Press).
Tempels, Placide (1959) *Bantu Philosophy* (Paris: Presence Africaine).
Wiredu, Kwasi (1987) "The Concept of Mind with Particular Reference to the Language and Thought of the Akans," in Guttorm Floistad (ed.), *Contemporary Philosophy, A New Survey*. Vol. 5: *African Philosophy* (Dordrecht: Martinus Nijhoff Publishers; repr. in Safro Kwame (ed.), *Readings in African Philosophy: An Akan Collection* (New York: University Press of America, 1995).

Further reading

Budge, Wallis E. A. (1911) *Osiris and the Egyptian Resurrection*, 2 vols (London: The Medici Society).
Chadwick, H. (1980) *The Cambridge History of Later Greek and Early Medieval Philosophy* (Cambridge: Cambridge University Press).
Chadwick, H. (1988) *The Early Church* (London: Penguin Books).
Daniélou, J. (1955) *Origen*, trans. W. Mitchell (New York: Sheed and Ward).
Dodds, E. R. (1965) *Pagan and Christian in an Age of Anxiety: Some Aspects of Religious Experience from Marcus Aurelius to Constantine* (Cambridge: Cambridge University Press).
Fox, Robin L. (1987) *Pagans and Christians* (New York: Alfred Knopf, Inc.).
Gilson, Etienne (1985) *History of Christian Philosophy in the Middle Ages* (London: Sheed and Ward).

64

Hanson, R. P. C. (1954) *Origen's Doctrine of Tradition* (London: SPCK).

Hutchins, Robert M. (ed.) (1952) *Great Books of the Western World*. Vol. 18: *Saint Augustine* (Chicago: William Benton Publisher, for the Encyclopaedia Britannica, Inc.; contains complete versions of *The Confessions*, *The City of God*, and *On Christian Doctrine*).

Jaeger, Werner (1961) *Early Christianity and Greek Paideia* (London: Oxford University Press).

Jedin, Hubert (ed.) (1993) *The Early Church: An Abridgement of the History of the Church*, vols. 1–3: trans. and ed. John Dolan (New York: Crossroad).

Laistner, M. L. W. (1951) *Christianity and Pagan Culture in the Later Roman Empire* (Ithaca, NY: Cornell University Press).

Roberts, A. and Donaldson, J. (eds.) (1982) *The Ante-Nicene Fathers*, vol. 3 (Grand Rapids, MI: Wm B. Eerdmans Publishing Co.; contains Tertullian's works: *Apologeticum*, *The Soul's Testimony*, *A Treatise on the Soul*, and *The Prescription Against Heretics*).

Rudolph, K. (1983) *Gnosis: The Nature and History of Gnosticism* (San Francisco: Harper and Row).

Schaft, P. and Wace, H. (eds.) (1982) *A Select Library of Nicene and Post-Nicene Fathers of the Christian Church*, 2nd series, vol. 1 (Grand Rapids, MI: Wm B. Eerdmans Publishing Co.; contains the Origen's following works: *De Principiis* and *Against Celsus*).

Trigg, J. W. (1983) *Origen: The Bible and Philosophy in the Third Century* (London: SCM Press, Ltd.).

3

Precolonial African Philosophy in Arabic

SOULEYMANE BACHIR DIAGNE

A Tradition that has been Ignored

In his introduction to a book edited by François Constantin and devoted to the development of Islam in East Africa, Jean-Louis Triaud denounces the too narrow framework of a limited, initiation-based orientalism, open only to an erudite elite and very little concerned with the Islam of the "African margins" (1987: 9). As a matter of fact, on the one hand, Islamic Studies have often ignored the large areas in sub-Saharan Africa which became part of the Islamic world through a historic process that started more than a thousand years ago. Discourse on African cultures, spirituality, and intellectual productions, on the other hand, is quite often encapsulated in an ethnological paradigm wherein what is "authentically" African is simply assumed to be what remains once you have removed all the deposits that history has left on the continent. In this way, it seems to be thought that one reaches the very essence of African society. Islam, then, becomes just one deposit on that "authentic" Africa. The French anthropologist Jean-Loup Amselle has quite clearly demonstrated that this ethnological pursuit of the "true" African soul, supposedly expressed in ethnic religion and spirituality in contradistinction to any foreign, imported credo has been part of the colonial anti-Islamic policy he describes in a chapter entitled "White Paganism" (1990: 181–204). In another place, in connection with the example of West Africa, he concludes that Africanist anthropology has, in effect, undertaken a process of "de-politicizing, de-historicizing and de-Islamizing the Sub-Saharan West African societies" (1998: 13). As a matter of fact, in the essentialist paradigm constructed by this ethnographical logic, one ends up thinking that identity exists *in spite of* history, instead of *in* and *by* history.

The role which this logic has played in the debate in contemporary African philosophy, which has opposed the so-called "ethno-philosophers" to "professional philosophy," seems quite obvious. This is because the two camps, ultimately, do agree on the assumption that "professional philosophy," that is to say, philosophy practiced, taught, and written in formal, academic places, mainly universities, is quite a recent discipline in the African context; and that the only alternative, when it comes to the question of "what African philosophy is," is merely either to answer it "with a program," in Wiredu's words,[1] or to exhume as a philosophy what is considered to be the folk-wisdom of African traditional societies.

Apparently, no real attention had been paid by philosophers to the observation made by Cheikh Anta Diop, as early as 1960, that four centuries before Levy-Brühl wrote his famous text, *Primitive Mentality*, some African scholars in the Muslim areas were commenting on Aristotle's formal logic and were practicing dialectics. It is only recently that full notice has started to be given by philosophers to the fact that, in Kwame Anthony Appiah's words, "Muslims have a long history of philosophical writing, much of it written in Africa, so that the study of philosophy can be seen as traditional (and therefore holy) and endogenous (and therefore nationalistic)" (1992: 144).

Now two preliminary questions may be raised once we really start looking at this written philosophical legacy of ours, assuming that we seriously undertake the program of recapturing the actual history of African philosophical writing. They can be thus stated: (1) To what extent is a philosophy related to questions raised in the Islamic African context an *African* philosophy? (2) To what extent is a philosophy related to questions raised in the Islamic context (indeed in any religious context, whether Christian, Jewish etc.) still *philosophy*?[2]

The answer to the first question is just the same as the answer to the following general question: what would be *"African"* in the writings of the *African* philosophers? Was, for example, the famous Songhay scholar Ahmad Bâbâ of Timbuktu (1556–1627) more "African" when he wrote his reflections on the slavery of his own people in the Sudan[3] (where he refers to the situation of the people of Bornu, Kano, Katsina...) than when he wrote another pamphlet on Islamic mysticism[4] and the question of the need for a guide (*shaykh*) in the pursuit of knowledge by intuition (where his references are, for instance, to the writings of a philosopher like Ghazâlî – the "Algazel" of medieval Europe)?

As for the second question, answering it will mean explaining what Islamic philosophy (called *falsafa*) is, and how it is related to other Islamic sciences.

Falsafa and Other Islamic Sciences

Islamic philosophy is not to be understood as philosophy directly coming out of Islam, so to speak. As a philosophical discipline it is, rather, rooted in the classical Greek tradition (hence the loanword *"falsafa"* which derives from *"philosophia"*). The questions it is concerned with, however, are closely related to the spiritual universe of Islam, which is the reason why this tradition can be rightly said to be "Islamic."[5]

Falsafa really started as a distinct tradition among the different disciplines that developed from the Quranic Revelation around the ninth century. As a matter of fact, in the year 832, the Caliph Al Ma'mun decided to create an institution for translators to produce Arabic versions of Greek philosophical texts. That institution was called *Bayt al Hikma*, that is "The House of Wisdom" (*hikma* meaning "wisdom" being another possible Arabic word for philosophy). The story goes that the Caliph took the decision to have Greek philosophical texts systematically translated into Arabic after Aristotle appeared to him in a dream and reassured him that this foreign wisdom called philosophy would be no threat to religion, and that quite a fundamental agreement did actually exist between the two. This story expresses the nature of the dilemma the religious and political authorities were facing when confronted with what was for them, at first, just a "pagan" intellectual tradition. How then could it be welcomed among the traditional *'ulûm uid-dîn* (that is, "sciences of the religion") within which Islamic wisdom was supposed to be sought and realized?

This is why, even if philosophy did cohere with what is known as *Kalâm*, namely, the rationalist approach that had developed in Islamic theology and had in some ways prepared a place for it – in fact, the Caliph Al Ma'mun did belong to that school of rationalist theology – still the tension never ended between the traditionalist view according to which all true sciences have to be exclusively rooted in the very letter of the Revealed Text, and the questioning attitude characteristic of *falsafa*.

Partly as a consequence of this tension, and the associated disputes regarding the legitimacy or illegitimacy of various sciences, philosophy was not always part of the curriculum in the learning centers in the Islamic world generally and in Africa in particular. Very often, when the study of *falsafa* was countenanced, it was merely the study of what was regarded as the undisputed part of it, which turned out to be Logic (*mantiq*). It is an interesting fact that, in accordance with the very meaning of the Greek word *Organon*, the logical work that came from the classical tradition of philosophy, mainly the Aristotelian *Organon*, was generally considered as a metaphysically neutral *instrument* for valid reasoning. And as such, the study of the discipline was generally considered to be lawful.

But it must be noted that philosophical thought does exceed the bounds of what is technically called the *falsafa* tradition.[6] It must be noted also that philosophical questioning or reasoning is present in the discourse of *Kalâm*, that is, theology.[7] As a matter of fact, the different schools of *Kalâm* in the Islamic world were, historically, formed according to the ways in which they dealt with philosophical issues, such as human free will versus predestination, the relationship between the Essence and the Attributes of God, and the eternity and uncreatedness of God's Word, that is the Quran.

Besides theology or *Kalâm*, there is also a way in which these philosophical questions have been addressed in what is called *Tasawwuf*, that is to say, Islamic mysticism.[8] Of course, mysticism has to do with spiritual attainments and experience rather than with speculative knowledge or theoretical reasoning. But when it comes to explaining the basis of the mystically experienced knowledge (*dhawq*) in order to hand on the mystical teachings, treatises on *tasawwuf* appear to deal with philosophical questions concerning such subjects as the essential nature of God, His Attributes (or Names), the nature of the human personality and of the soul, and so on. Indeed, analysis of the doctrines and practices of the Sufis since the tenth century has disclosed a technical vocabulary (part of which may be described as Neoplatonic) in which the Sufis have endeavored to conceptualize and articulate their experience.

And finally, when we look at the question of the philosophical components of the Islamic sciences other than *falsafa*, we find that even jurisprudence (*fiqh*) was held to be cognate to logico-philosophical questions about the nature of sound reasoning.

What, we may now ask, did the Islamic sciences actually teach in the African intellectual centers?

Learning in Islamic Sciences in Africa

Historians have insisted on the fact that the intellectual centers in sub-Saharan Africa, such as Timbuktu, probably the most famous in Western Africa, were quite comparable to other scholarly centers in the rest of the Islamic world. For example, concerning the intellectual level of the 'ulamâ (learned scholars) in Timbuktu around the sixteenth century, Joseph Cuoq writes that the elite among them were "quite comparable to their colleagues in Marrakesh," the Moroccan city (1984: 222).[9] Ahmad Bâbâ was certainly the most eminent representative of that elite. And the story of his arrest by the Moroccan army and, subsequently, of his exile in Marrakesh from 1593 to 1607 needs to be recalled here as testimony to the intellectual status of some of the 'ulamâ from the Bilâd as-Sudân, "the Black people's land." The Moroccan scholars are reported to have been amazed at the knowledge of a scholar trained in Timbuktu.

The Songhay empire had been continuously declining when the Moroccan sultan, Mûlây Ahmad al-Mansûr, decided in 1591 to conquer the country in order to control the trade in salt and gold. After the conquest, the Moroccan governor in Timbuktu had to face intellectual opposition from Ahmad Bâbâ, who insisted that, from the point of view of Islamic law, the sultan of Morocco could not pretend to have any right on a Muslim land over which the Askia Muhammad, at the end of the fifteenth century, had obtained recognition as amîr (commander) from the 'Abbâsid caliph in Cairo.[10] He was then arrested and sent to the sultan who kept him for 14 years in Marrakesh. What is significant here is, first, that one of the complaints of Ahmad Bâbâ to the sultan was about the loss of the 1,600 volumes that constituted his personal library and, secondly, that during his exile in this city he became quite famous among the Moroccan 'ulamâ themselves as a prominent scholar. In his autobiography he writes: "many scholars came to me and asked me to give public lectures. My first thought was to refuse, but I finally surrendered to their insistent demands; hence I sat in the mosque of the Shurfa and inaugurated my lectures by reading Khalîl's Mukhtasar which I explained and commented on, quoting the best jurists."[11] Actually, the title of the book he is referring to is Mukhtasar fî 'ilm al-fiqh by Khalîl Ishâq, who died in 1374. It was a treatise on the Malekite school of Islamic jurisprudence, the only one to be found in West Africa, which was very well known and studied among the West African scholars.[12] A comment is in place as to the significance of Ahmad Bâbâ's life and work for African scholarship in general. Although it would be exaggerated to consider him as the champion of a Sudanese nationalism in front of the Moroccan state, he did manifest, on various occasions, the feeling that he belonged to an excellent scholarly tradition. As a matter of fact, when the issue was raised as to who might be called the reviver of Islam, he considered that "his principal teacher, whose lessons he followed for more than ten years...the Dyula scholar Muhammad Baghayogho...[was worthy of being regarded as] the regenerator (*mujaddid*) in the tenth century of the Hijra in Timbuktu" (Hunwick 1985: 19).[13]

Ahmad Bâbâ eventually returned to Timbuktu where he remained for the rest of his life. While his visit to Morocco was forced, scholars from sub-Saharan Africa often themselves decided to travel in the Islamic world seeking knowledge. As Joseph Cuoq remarks, it is surprising to notice how much people used to travel in those times either for pilgrimage or to expand their Islamic faith. He also recalls the prophetic *hadith* (dictum) enjoining it upon Muslims to seek knowledge even if they had to go to China for it (1984: 217). It was probably not rare to have students from the Bilâd as-Sudân go to the learning centers of the Maghrib, as recorded in the Sudanese Chronicles.[14] Most of the time, those scholars who could afford it would take the opportunity, while fulfilling their religious duty of pilgrimage to Mecca, to stop here and there in order to meet celebrated 'ulamâ, mainly in Egypt. This is what Askia Muhammad himself did when, on his way to Mecca on pilgrimage, he met the celebrated Egyptian scholar Jalâl al-Dîn al-Suyûtî, as we already have mentioned. In the same way, different generations of Ahmad Bâbâ's family and his own professor Muhammad Baghayogho had thus met 'ulamâ from the Islamic intellectual elite of their time.[15]

Now the information we have concerning the conditions of study in the different learning centers indicates that one burning question was the scarcity of texts. Seeking texts and copying them was one of the important activities of the 'ulamâ. Here again, as an example, we have Ahmad Bâbâ's testimony concerning his professor Muhammad Baghayogho. By his account, the master had a real passion for books, spending great amounts of money to get them or to get copies of them.[16] To underline his master's extreme generosity, he adds that Muhammad Baghayogho was always ready to give the books he had to students and scholars who needed them, never asking for them back, no matter how rare they were.

Scarcity of books also explains the incredible role played by memorization in the study of the Islamic sciences. And this is true not only of the Quranic text, but also of more "secular" disciplines like logic. In fact, in order to help the memorizing, the authors themselves will, very often, write their theoretical works in poetry. For instance, the most celebrated treatises that were used in the study of Aristotelian logic were written in verses, such as the *Rajaz* of al-Maghîlî or the *Sullam al Murwnaq* by Abd ar-Rahmân al-Akhdarî (1514–46). The latter is said to have been a celebrated textbook in Aristotelian logic taught in different mosques and other *madrasas* (schools) throughout North Africa as well as at the sub-Saharan African intellectual centers.[17]

In spite of the problems the students and the scholars encountered in acquiring books, historians have been able to establish lists of the works they used.[18] Most of them are related to jurisprudence (*fiqh*). As a matter of fact, those are the most often quoted in the Sudanese Chronicles. Among them, four had pride of place with the Timbuktu scholars ('ulamâ). They were: the *Mukhtasar fî 'ilm al-fiqh* by Khalîl Ishâq, to which reference has already been made, the *Risâla* of Abû Zayd al-Qarawânî (922–96), the *Kitâb al-Shifâ bi ta'rîf huqûq al-Mustafâ* by 'Iyâd ibn Mûsâ (1083–1149), and the *Tuhfat ul-hukkâm fî nukat al-ahkâm* by Ibn Asîm (1359–1426). All these books, except the third, are explanations and commentaries concerning the Malekite school of jurisprudence.

Some of the works dealt with *kalâm* (theology) and *tasawwuf* (mysticism). More precisely, concerning the science of *kalâm*, these works were concerned with an aspect of it called *tawhîd*. As Mervyn Hiskett explains: "the Arabic word *tawhîd* derives from a root *w.h.d*, of which the simple form of the verb, *wahada*, means 'to be one,' 'to be unique.'... Thus the Islamic science of *tawhîd* concerns the unity of God. It embraces the whole of Islamic theology and philosophical thought" (1975: 24). In other words, *tawhîd* is the part of *kalâm* particularly concerned with the relationship between God's Essence and His Attributes, which, by way of synecdoche, eventually became a synonym for theology in general. Studying the tradition of Hausa versification on the Doctrine of Divine Unity, Hiskett was able to demonstrate how much influence books by African scholars, such as *Jawharat al-tawhîd* by Ibrâhîm al-Laqânî of Egypt (d. 1668) and *Umm al-barâhîn* by Muhammad Yûsuf al-Sanûsî (d. 1490),[19] exercised in the Islamic world.

The teaching of *tasawwuf* was largely based on the commentaries and meditations of Ibn 'Atâ' Allah's *al-Hikâm al-'Atâîya*, which achieved great popularity. Ibn 'Atâ' Allah (1259–1309), a North African, was a famous member of the Sufi Order named Shâdhilîya (after its founder al-Shâdhilî, 1196–1258) who had to flee from his town in Tunisia because of persecution by the local religious jurists, who were very often hostile to Sufi thinking, to settle in Alexandria. In his *Hikâm*, Ibn 'Atâ' Allah wanted to transmit the teachings of his master in the Order, since al-Shâdhilî himself, underlining the fact that *tasawwuf* has to do essentially with transforming people into accomplished Sufis rather than lecturing them on theories, had declared: "my disciples stand for my books" (Ibn 'Atâ' Allah 1998: 21–2).

Most of what has been said concerning the conditions of learning in the Islamic sciences is about the western part of sub-Saharan Africa. To present in a few words a general picture of the situation in Eastern Africa we must first point out that the whole process of pre-independence Islamization in that region was very different. J. Spencer Trimingham, in his *Islam in East Africa*, has an oft-quoted phrase: "Islam in East Africa... bears many of the characteristics of a foreign religion" (1962: 11). And he actually drew this conclusion from the idea that Islam, since the date of its arrival on the East Coast of Africa (that is to say, as early as the eighth century), had not, until the nineteenth century, been anything other than the religion of settlers from overseas who remained in closed communities occupying off-shore islands and a narrow coastal fringe.[20] Although there may be something in this, nevertheless, as subsequent works have shown, this view of the Islamic areas of East Africa being simple extensions of civilizations grown elsewhere is quite simplistic and exemplifies again the prejudicial notion of Islam as essentially foreign to Africa. In reality, the interaction between Swahili culture and "Arab" culture reveals a more complex cultural dialectic, as the works of Randall L. Pouwels, for example, have shown.[21]

Some sense of the oversimplification just alluded to may be had from Pouwels's explanation of how Islamic learning was related to the Swahili notion of *uungwana*. This word may be rendered as "civilization." It comprised much more than the written Islamic tradition and was on very intimate terms with non-Islamic

71

mainland culture despite the townspeople's disapproval of it as, on the whole, a kind of "barbarity" (1987: 73). On the other hand, after the eighteenth century the new settlers from Oman brought with them the 'ulamâ tradition of Islamic scholarship with the more "orthodox" formal knowledge of written Islam.[22] And we are told that those 'ulamâ studied most of the time in academic centers in Arabia to which they were closely related. The "Hagiographic account," by Shaykh Abdallah Salih Farsy (d. 1982), former Chief Qadi of Zanzibar and Kenya, of the 'ulamâ of East Africa from 1830 to 1970 gives very precious information on the training of these scholars (Farsy 1989). They would often journey to the Hadhramawt in South Arabia for training "in at least one of the traditional written sciences. Among these were fiqh (law), faraydh (inheritance), hadith, nawh (Arabic grammar), sarf (morphology), bayan (rhetoric), mantiq (logic), tawhid (theology), tafsir (exegesis), and [in Islamic mysticism] tasawwuf."[23] The distinction has to be made here that, unlike West Africa, most of the East African Muslims belonged to the Shâf'i school of Islamic jurisprudence and thus were trained accordingly.

Writings in Islamic Sciences in Africa: Main Features and Themes

A great continuity runs through the teachings and the writings of those of the African scholars ('ulamâ) who actually produced some works, thus contributing to Islamic literature. In the Sudan (Bilâd as-Sudân) before the time of Ahmad Bâbâ, that is, the beginning of the seventeenth century, that production was probably quite modest. Most of the time the 'ulamâ would be authors of "Annotations" (taqâyîd) or remarks on their readings.[24] To take an example in the field of logic (mantiq), Ahmad Bâbâ's grandfather, Ahmad 'Umar Muhammad Aqît (d. 1583), wrote a commentary on al-Maghîlî's poem on logic.[25]

Also many works were pedagogically simple paraphrases of some important texts. As an example, Hiskett has given the case of Malam Usuman, "the earliest poet known to have composed in Hausa in the Kano emirate." He worked out a Hausa philosophical poem from an Arabic text that we have previously mentioned. This was a book in theology by al-Sanûsî called Umm al-barâhîn. The following illustration should give some idea of Malam Usuman's methodology. In one instance, where the Arabic text asserts the following proposition, an "onto-logical" preliminary, so to speak, to an elucidation of the notion of divine Essence and Unity, "Know that logical judgement is confined to three categories: necessity, absurdity and possibility," the Hausa poem says:

> Seek to know all those things that are necessary in respect of God,
> So also know those things that are absurd in respect of God,
> Then know what is possible in respect of God.
> (Hiskett 1975: 68–9)[26]

One philosophical theme that occupied some prominent 'ulamâ is particularly important to notice since it concerns the relation of the learned written tradition and law of Islam to the traditional customs, habits, and morals of the African people. This theme appears in the famous *Replies of al-Maghîlî to the questions of Askia al-Hajj Muhammad*. The context of the questions and replies was the political situation of the Songhay empire after Askia Muhammad had taken power from Sonni Ali's direct heirs. Sonni Ali had been depicted in the Sudanese Chronicles, that is to say, by the Islamic scholars (*'ulamâ*), as a malicious dictator, pretending to be a Muslim but being fundamentally an unbeliever. Somehow, he did represent, for the *'ulamâ*, the traditional, pagan African customs that were to be eradicated. So the questions put to Muhammad ibn 'Abd al-Karîm al-Maghîlî (d. 1504–5)[27] by Askia Muhammad, whose constant policy was to get the support of the *'ulamâ*, were concerned with that general issue of the necessity to build an alliance between the political power and true Islamic knowledge in order to reform the society. (This, in turn, posed the question of the relationship between the rulers and the devotees of the Islamic sciences and its associated dangers. Indeed, this is a theme on which the *'ulamâ* produced quite a rich literature and to which Ahmad Bâbâ devoted a book.) Al-Maghîlî's *Replies* concerned the way in which such an alliance was to be realized. He argued that it was the duty of a Muslim ruler to establish Islamic order against any kind of deviation.[28]

This question of reform is quite recurrent in African writings in connection with the question of the *jihâd* against deviations or the issue of *education*, or, quite often, both. Shaykh 'Uthmân ibn Muhammad Fodiye (d. 1817), better known as Uthman dan Fodio, is a good example of the reform attitude and the reform literature. The *jihâd* he fought is quite famous but should not overshadow his intellectual contribution to African philosophy in Arabic as well as in some African languages. He knew that his goal of a "*vilayet-i-faqîh* – a state in which the highest authority was the *faqîh*, the learned jurisprudent" (Hunwick 1997: 18) – was truly to be attained solely by way of education. And this is why, while producing a rich Islamic literature which dealt with political, social, and theological matters, "he pioneered the use of vernacular languages, writing numerous poems in Fulfulde, as did his son Muhammad Bello."[29]

To remain in West Africa, we might say that perhaps the best philosopher to be found there was a nephew and student of Muhammad Bello called 'Abd al-Qâdir b. al-Mustafâ al-Tûrûdû (d. 1864), whose works, according to the bibliography compiled by John Hunwick, are often quite plainly of the *falsafa* type. Here, for example, is a description of his *al-Futûhât al-rabbâniyya* written in 1828–9. Kani describes it as "a critical evaluation of the materialists', naturalists', and physicists' perception of life . . . matters related to the transient nature of the world, existence or non-existence of the spirit, and the nature of celestial spheres, are critically examined in the work."[30] He is also the author of *Kulliyât al-'âlam al-sitta*, about "universals" in philosophy.[31]

The issue of reform and education is also a key one in the writings of quite a few of the *'ulamâ* of East Africa. And, as a matter of fact, it is not a surprise that, in consonance with the way in which his predecessors had been dealing with this issue, the celebrated *'alim* al-Amîn bin 'Alî Al Mazrui (1891–1947) became known as a writer committed to the modernist turn in Islamic philosophy that took place during the nineteenth century in response to the colonization of most Muslim countries.[32]

73

One can conclude this general sketch of African philosophy in Arabic only by underlining again the notion of a program. Scholars in the field of Islamic African studies, such as John O. Hunwick and Rex Sean O'Fahey, have undertaken the task of providing a survey of the Arabic literature of Africa, eventually to be published in six volumes. Two volumes have already been published on the writings of Eastern Sudanic Africa to *c*.1900 and on the writings of Central Sudanic Africa (Hunwick and O'Fahey 1994). The authors, mindful of all the manuscripts kept in many private family libraries, have told me that they have just been scratching the surface of what is to be exhumed,[33] and, we could add, what is to be translated into the languages in which we are currently working. Part of this literature could then certainly be added to what Paulin Hountondji has undertaken to establish as a bibliographic survey of African philosophy (1988).[34] It would then probably not only broaden the question Hountondji and others have raised, namely, "What is African philosophy?," but also answer it.

Notes

1   I quote him from Didier N. Kaphagawani's contribution to *Sage Philosophy* (ed. H. Odera Oruka) as saying: "Thus the question 'What is African philosophy?' is at this juncture of our history at bottom, one to be answered not with a definition *per genus et differentia*, but rather with a programme" (1990: 196). The same idea of a starting tradition of genuinely philosophical thought is to be found in P. O. Bodunrin's answer to "the question of African philosophy": "Why must we lament a late start in philosophy? No one laments our late start in mathematics" (1990: 177).

2   One can think here, for example, of the very strongly worded position of Marcien Towa (1979: 19–23), who assumes that no philosophical thinking can exist in any religious atmosphere whatsoever; which appears to dismiss as non-philosophical most of what we are used to calling "philosophy."

3   *Sudân* or *Bilâd as-Sudân* (Black people's country) referred to sub-Saharan Africa in general. Ahmad Bâbâ wrote this text (the title in Arabic is *Mi'râj al Su'ûd ilâ nayl hukm majlab al sûd*) in Timbuktu in 1615 as an answer to a question raised to him by scholars from the Saharan region of Tuwât concerning the legal status of enslaved Sudanese people. In his answer, Bâbâ has, in particular, an interesting reflection concerning the notion of slavery as a curse against the race of Cham, and he argues against the idea that attributions of that kind can be made to "races." Mahmoud A. Zouber has published a useful presentation of Ahmad Bâbâ's works, including this one on slavery (1977: 129–46).

4   That pamphlet, *Risâla fî l-tasawwuf*, was written in 1616. There is a short presentation in Zouber 1977: 119.

5   Actually, the same kind of encounter took place with Christianity as well as Judaism. And, as a matter of fact, Maïmonides did belong to the *falsafa* tradition of Muslim Spain.

6   Kai Kresse, who is currently pursuing research for his dissertation "On Forms and Functions of Philosophical Discourse in Swahili Society," insists on the fact that the technical content of *falsafa* does not appear to be relevant to Swahili traditional practice of philosophical thinking for which terms such as *ufahamu* (intelligence, sense, comprehension, understanding), *elimu* (knowledge, education, wisdom), *hekima* (wisdom, knowledge, judgment), *busara* (practical wisdom, sagacity, skill), *ujuzi* (knowledge, wisdom, sagacity), are more likely to be found. I came to know about this project thanks to Rex Sean O'Fahey.

7   The exact meaning here of the science of *Kalâm* is in fact the defense of the different components of the religious creed by way of rational argumentation.

8   From the word *Sûfî* referring to the individual mystic, the word "Sufism" has been created in English as "the name given to the mysticism of Islam ... as the mystical movement of an uncompromising Monotheism," to quote A. J. Arberry (1950: 11–12).

9   Senegalese historian Penda Mbow declares that around the fifteenth century Timbuktu was "one of the greatest intellectual centers of the Islamic world" (1997: 232).

10 John Hunwick, discussing the question of Askia Muhammad's recognition during his pilgrimage to Mecca, observes that: "Whatever the case may be, when Askia Muhammad returned to his domains some two years later in 1498, he not only possessed the *baraka* of a pilgrim who had been to the 'House of God' and visited the tomb of His Messenger, he had also studied briefly with the celebrated Egyptian scholar Jalâl al-Dîn al-Suyûtî and, probably through the latter's agency, obtained from the puppet 'Abbâsid caliph a delegation of authority to rule 'the land of Takrûr' in his name" (1985: 26). ("The land of Takrûr," which refers more precisely to a region of River Senegal's valley, is here used simply as another name for the Sudan in general).

11 Ahmad Bâbâ wrote his autobiography at the end of his famous *Kifâyat al-muhtâj*, composed in Marrakesh in 1603. In that work he gives valuable indications concerning the cultural and intellectual history of the Sudan. I quote this passage from Zouber 1977: 29.

12 Ahmad Bâbâ himself had written an important commentary on that book, called *Sharh Mukhtasar Khalîl*, in his first period in Timbuktu before his exile in Morocco.

13 According to a prophetic dictum, "at the beginning of every century God sends men a scholar who regenerates their religion for them" (al-Maghîlî in Hunwick 1985: 66). Muhammad Baghayogho produced a number of important writings. But he was modest. Ahmad Bâbâ gives as an example of his modesty the fact that he not only approved some works of his student but cited them in his own and did refer to them in his teachings afterwards (see Zouber 1977: 47).

14 The most famous are the *Ta'rîkh al-Fattâsh*, by Mahmûd b. al Mutawakkil Ka'tî, ed. and trans. into French by O. Houdas (Paris, 1913); and the *Ta'rîkh al-Sudân*, by Abd ar-Rahmân al-Sa'dî, ed. and trans. into French by O. Houdas and M. Delafosse (Paris, 1913).

15 See J. Cuoq (1984: 220–2) and Zouber (1977: 38ff.).

16 Leo Africanus, on his visits to Timbuktu, reports that "Many manuscripts from Barbary were sold there and that such a sale would generate more benefits than any other goods" (quoted in Cuoq 1984: 210). It should be also mentioned that Askia Dâwûd (reg. 1549–82), being the successor of Askia Muhammad and following his policy of care and attention for the Muslim scholars of Timbuktu in pursuit of their support, is said in the *Tarîkh al-Fattâsh* to have had a workshop of copyists whose manuscripts he used to keep in cupboards.

17 Let us quote verses 15–18 of this book to underline the notion, already referred to, of the legitimacy of logic: "As to the question of knowing whether the study of logic is permitted by the dogma, there are three opinions. / Ibn es-Salâh and Nawawî forbid it while others think that it is suitable to learn this science. / The most widespread and reliable opinion is that this study is permitted to men with a sound understanding / Familiar enough with the Prophet's traditions and with the divine Book to get through its guidance towards the truth" (al-Akhdarî 1921).

18 See, for example, Mbaye (1976); Cuoq (1984); Mbow (1997).

19 See Hiskett (1975: 68). Al-Sânûsî, a theologian from Tlemcen, was the author of three works on dogmatics (*al-'Aqîdat al-kubrâ / al-wustâ / al-sughrâ*) which were, in John Hunwick's words, "popular teaching manuals in North and West Africa" (1985: 133).

20 Trimingham speaks of the "settlement mentality and Arab racial consciousness" of the Coastal Muslims and goes on to say that "neither Shi'ite settlers, nor the Arabs from South Arabia, nor the later 'Ibadis did any propoaganda among Bantu people" (1962: 11).

21 He has this quite strong warning, for example: "Indeed, probably no greater error can be made than in taking approaches to coastal history and culture principally through Arabic.... Swahili is not Arabic and coastal culture is not Arab culture, though both have borrowed some elements from the heartlands of Islam" (Pouwels 1987: 73).

22 Nevertheless "it is noteworthy that waungwana [i.e the learned ones according to uungwana standards] dismissed the Islam of the new 'ulamâ as not 'orthodox' because such beliefs and practices were not followed by their ancestors" (Pouwels 1987: 147).

23 Pouwels (1987: 149). He adds that "An 'alim [sing. for 'ulama] had to be proficient to some degree in Arabic. For example, he often was a poet in Arabic and commonly also in Swahili."

24 See, for example, Cuoq (1984: 214–15).

25 From a note by John Hunwick, we know that this work is among the 6,000 items that are kept presently in CEDRAB, the Centre de Documentation et de Recherche Ahmad Baba at Timbuktu (1992: 177).

26 We may add here the remark that African philosophical production in the Islamic areas is not to be found only in Arabic, but is quite often written in the African languages using Arabic characters, as is the case with Hausa tawhîdî versification.

27 He was a scholar from Tlemcen (whose name is linked with massacres of Jews in Tuwât – J. Cuoq calls him a new Torquemada), who visited Kano and Katsina.

28 See Hunwick (1985) for the English translation of the Replies and Mbaye (1972) for a translation into French. This attitude is in contrast with what Hunwick has called a "philosophy of tolerance" among the Dyula merchants dealing very often with non-Muslims and "arguing that God would bring folk to Islam in His good time, and that in the meantime it was the Muslim's duty to set an example to non-Muslims, but not to forestall God's plan by forceful Islamization" (1997: 17).

29 Hunwick (1997: 19). He adds that "his daughter too, Asmâ', composed numerous poems in Fulfulde and Hausa as well as some in Arabic" (ibid.).

30 Hunwick 1995: 222.

31 Ibid. 223.

32 See, for example, Ahmed I. Salim Ibid. (1987).

33 I had the great chance to be able to discuss this essay with John Hunwick and Rex Sean O'Fahey while I was invited at Northwestern University.

34 In his Combats pour le sens Hountondji calls for a transcription of the African oral heritage (1997: 227). Our written heritage is also waiting to be edited.

References

al-Akhdarî, abd ar-Rahmân (1921) Le Sullam. Traité de logique, tr. J. D. Luciani (Algiers: Jules Carbonel).

Amselle, Jean-Loup (1990) Logiques métisses. Anthropologie de l'identité en Afrique et ailleurs (Paris: Payot).

Amselle, Jean-Loup and Sibeud, Emmanuelle (eds.) (1998) Maurice Delafosse. Entre orientalisme et ethnographie: l'itinéraire d'un africaniste (1870–1926) (Paris: Maisonneuve et Larose).

Appiah, Kwame Anthony (1992) In my Father's House. Africa in the Philosophy of Culture (London: Methuen).

Arberry, A. J. (1950) *Sufism. An Account of the Mystics of Islam* (London: George Allen and Unwin).

Bodunrin, P. O. (1990) "The Question of African Philosophy," in H. Odera Oruka (ed.), *Sage Philosophy. Indigenous Thinkers and Modern Debate on African Philosophy* (The Netherlands: E. J. Brill).

Cuoq, Joseph (1984) *Histoire de l'islamisation de l'Afrique de l'Ouest. Des origines à la fin du XVIe siècle* (Paris: Geuthner).

Diop, Cheikh Anta (1960) *L'Afrique noire précoloniale* (Paris: Présence Africaine).

Farsy, Shaykh Abdallah Salih (1989) *The Shaf 'i 'Ulamâ of East Africa, ca.1830–1970. A Hagiographic Account*, tr. and ed. Randall L. Pouwels (Madison, MA: University of Wisconsin).

Hiskett, Mervyn (1975) *A History of Hausa Islamic Verse* (London: University of London).

Hountondji, Paulin J. (1988) *Philosophical Research in Africa: A Bibliographic Survey* (Cotonou: Inter-African Council for Philosophy).

Hunwick, John O. (1985) *Sharî'a in Songhay: The Replies of al-Maghîlî to the Questions of Askia al-Hâjj Muhammad* (Oxford: Oxford University Press).

Hunwick, John O. (1992) "CEDRAB: Centre de Documentation et de Recherches Ahmad Baba, Timbuktu," *Sudanic Africa*, 3: 173–81.

Hunwick, John O. (1997) "Towards a History of the Islamic Intellectual Tradition in West Africa down to the Nineteenth Century," *Journal for Islamic Studies*, 17.

Hunwick, John O. and O'Fahey, Rex Sean (eds.) (1994–) *Arabic Literature of Africa* (Leiden, New York, and Köln: E. J. Brill; vol. 1 (1994), vol. 2 (1995); 4 vols to follow).

Ibn 'Atâ' Allah (1998) *La Sagesse des maîtres soufis*, tr. Eric Geoffroy (Paris: Grasset).

Kaphagawani, Didier N. (1990) "The Philosophical Significance of Bantu Nomenclature: A Shot at Contemporary African Philosophy," in H. Odera Oruka (ed.), *Sage Philosophy: Indigenous Thinkers and Modern Debate on African Philosophy* (Leiden: E. J. Brill).

Mbaye, El Hadj Rawane (1972) "Les Réponses d'al-Maghîlî aux questions posées par Askia Muhammad," *Bulletin de l'IFAN*, No. 2 (Dakar).

Mbaye, El Hadj Rawane (1976) "L'Islam au Sénégal." Thèse de Doctorat de Troisième cycle. Université Cheikh Anta Diop de Dakar.

Mbow, Penda (1997) "Enseignement et système de pensée dans le Soudan Occidental," in *La Culture arabo-islamique en Afrique au Sud du Sahara: cas de l'Afrique de l'Ouest*, Proceedings from an International Meeting in Timbuktu (Tunisia: Fondation Temimi).

Pouwels, Randall L. (1987) *Horn and Crescent. Cultural Change and Traditional Islam on the East African Coast, 800–1900* (Cambridge: Cambridge University Press).

Towa, Marcien (1979) *L'Idée d'une philosophie négro-africaine* (Yaoundé: Cle).

Triaud, Jean-Louis (1987) "Les Chemins de l'islamologue," in François Constantin (ed.), *Les Voies de l'Islam en Afrique orientale* (Paris: Karthala).

Trimingham, J. Spencer (1962) *Islam in East Africa* (London: Edinburgh House Press).

Zouber, Mahmoud A. (1977) *Ahmad Bâbâ de Tombouctou (1556–1627). Sa vie et son oeuvre* (Paris: Maisonneuve et Larose).

4

Some Nineteenth-Century African Political Thinkers

PIETER BOELE VAN HENSBROEK

Several West African intellectuals gained great fame in the second half of the nineteenth century and are of lasting importance for African philosophy. Their work covered a range of fields, such as religion, culture, race, science, technology, and politics, and addressed pressing issues related to the rapid rise of European domination. Such issues came up first in Liberia and in the European colonial settlements along the West African coast. Subsequently, they became the central concern in most of Africa when European domination became established in the last decades of the nineteenth century. Key authors in this period, such as Edward Blyden, Africanus Horton, James Johnson, and Alexander Crummell, developed comprehensive arguments that can be considered classical positions on the issue of an African response to the West.

The nineteenth century was an exceptionally turbulent age in African history. The established political and economic structures were overturned; Islam and Christianity gained influence. A wide variety of smaller political units were clustered into a limited number of states. These political units included the Fulani empire of Sokoto, the Tokolor, the Mandinka, and Asante empires in West Africa, as well as a number of large kingdoms in East and Central Africa. Western power and ideas that remained in the margin of the physical and intellectual landscape at the beginning of the nineteenth century occupied the center at its close.

There has been elaborate philosophical thought in African societies at least since ancient Egyptian times, taking forms probably as diverse as African societies themselves. The emergence of Western domination in the nineteenth century created a new situation; it raised a new and common agenda for reflection by African intellectuals. The ideas of these intellectuals, who wrote in European languages, have often been attributed to an influx of European ideas resulting from trade, evangelism, intermarriage, and studies abroad (Shepperson 1960; Clapham 1970). Some African authors have expressed disdain for the ideas of what they called "a hybridized species" and "deserters of their fatherland" (Ayandele 1971). Others have stressed the originality of these African intellectuals and have identified the roots of their discourses within the contemporary local political situation (Langley 1973; Boele van Hensbroek 1999). Whatever the assessment and the political roots, the impact of European languages and discourses upon intellectual life had a practically irreversible influence upon African thought. Even arguments in favor of preserving African identity and traditions were framed within the parameters of these new discourses, using, for instance, concepts such as "tribe," "chief," and "civilization."

Liberia and Sierra Leone were the first context within which this new type of African discourse developed. Liberia was founded in 1817 by Africans who had returned from slavery in the United States and declared its independence in 1847. Sierra Leone had, since 1787, become the place for the resettlement of several groups of African origin, initially a relatively small group of Africans freed from slavery after its abolition in the UK and later including groups of so-called "recaptives." Recaptives were Africans who had been captured and sold as slaves, but who had been intercepted by the British navy during its mission against slavery and released in Sierra Leone.

Intellectual expression in these small coastal enclaves with a relatively large margin of freedom (as well as in the coastal cities of the Gold Coast and Nigeria a little later) became trend-setting for later discussions elsewhere in Africa (Fyfe 1962, 1972). Because intellectual developments in South Africa, French West Africa, and in East Africa came later and did not produce markedly different positions, the discussion is limited here to the main authors in West Africa writing in English.

Edward Wilmot Blyden and Alexander Crummell

The most celebrated and influential intellectual in West Africa in the second half of the nineteenth century was a flamboyant self-made and self-educated Liberian who became the most prominent West African ideologue opposing dominant European paternalism: Edward Wilmot Blyden (see Lynch 1967, 1971, 1978; July 1964, 1968). Blyden was born on St Thomas in the Caribbean in 1832. After being blocked from studying theology in the USA because of his color, he went to the free republic of Liberia to work for the Pan-Negro ideal. Arriving in 1851, only a few years after independence, Blyden taught at the Presbyterian Alexander High School, was ordained a priest, taught himself Latin, Greek, and Arabic, and quickly became a public figure.

Liberia's capital, Monrovia, was a small settlement living in near constant antagonism with the inland African population, and its internal politics was marked by a new color line between lighter- and darker-skinned Liberians, while indigenous Africans held no citizenship rights (unless "acculturated"). Blyden, being very black, sided against the "mulatto" ruling caste in what were often bitter struggles. Together with the prominent black missionary Alexander Crummell, he saw the complete integration of "natives" in educational and missionary efforts as central to the Pan-Negroist movement that was to spread from Liberia to the rest of Africa. Therefore, they both engaged actively in church work among the indigenous Africans.

Blyden had to flee to Sierra Leone in 1871 when President Roye of Liberia was overthrown and killed. In the capital of Sierra Leone, Freetown, he established the newspaper *The Negro* and undertook several official government missions into the interior, always urging the British government to expand its influence. He ran for the presidency back in Liberia in 1885, but lost. He lived mostly in Sierra Leone for the rest of his life. Blyden became a highly respected man with contacts among the most important figures in West Africa and outside, yet he was practically penniless when he died in 1912.

Blyden's thought, in all its stages, centered on the idea of race, race-pride, love of the fatherland (Africa), and belief in a brilliant African renaissance. He held the view that every race is a natural unit, having its own "home" continent, character, and mission. As a result, he is often considered the precursor of Negritude and of the idea of anti-racist racism in the twentieth century (July 1964). However, Blyden's thought can best be understood against the background of the historical process of European domination in Africa. This was a process that involved the high-spirited missionary drive of the Christian abolitionist and humanitarian movements in the mid-nineteenth century, the rapid rise of the "scientific" racist and colonial ideologies, and the full establishment of colonial rule in most parts of Africa.

When Blyden arrived in Liberia to serve the Pan-Negroist cause, his frame of mind fully reflected Christian abolitionism. He preached that, following the dictates of Providence, *Negritia* or *Ethiopia* soon shall "stretch out her hands unto God" and will be reborn. Slavery itself was considered to be part of this divine plan, because it was through the New World slavery experience that "the sons of Ham" could absorb Christianity in order to effect the regeneration of the African continent. At the same time as being a Christian abolitionist, Blyden was a Pan-Negroist striving for the reunification of black peoples all over the world. The Pan-Negroism that was taken to Africa derived from the New World slavery experience and involved the "color-line" and a racial self-definition of Africans. Both abolitionism and Pan-Negroism provide a view of Africa from a position outside of Africa, positioning Africa and Africans within grand, originally European or New World, dichotomies, such as *civilized* versus *primitive*, and *black* versus *white*. The early Christian Pan-Negroists, such as Blyden and Crummell, made a peculiar combination of abolitionism and Pan-Negroism. They applied the civilized/primitive dichotomy *within* the black race, namely, between the New World "exiled brethren," "trained for the work of rebuilding waste places under severe discipline and hard bondage" (= the civilized), and the indigenous Africans, who had to be "raised from the slumber of the ages and rescued from a stagnant barbarism" (= the primitive) (Blyden 1887: 129).

Alexander Crummell remained the purest example of this Pan-Negroist abolitionism. Born in New York in 1818, he studied at Queen's College, Cambridge, and went to Liberia in 1853 as teacher and pastor. He was a highly respected black intellectual in Liberia, the USA, and Britain. At one time he aspired to become Episcopal Bishop of Liberia, but was effectively blocked by the American mother church and the Liberian elite. Crummell's thought expresses excellently the Pan-Negroist Christian abolitionist approach in castigating slavery and its supportive ideologies, while, at the same time, expressing total confidence in Christianity and Western culture. His famous speech, "The English language in Liberia" (1862), relates the English language to nation-building and praises it as "the enshrinement of those great Charters of Liberty which are essential elements of free government, and the main guarantees of personal liberty." Crummell's estimation of African cultures was correspondingly low. In his earlier years, especially, he stressed the role of Africans from the Americas as agents of African upliftment. The diaspora experience, by infusing Christianity into the African race, could thus still benefit Africa. Crummell's theological tracts are better, particularly his "The Negro Race Not Under A Curse" (1862) which skillfully refutes arguments linking African slavery to the biblical story of the curse pronounced upon Canaan, son of Ham.

Blyden distanced himself gradually from almost every aspect of the Christian abolitionist discourse. The key to this remarkable development of his thought was that first-hand knowledge of African life and cultures corrected his negative idea of African culture. He engaged in church work among indigenous Africans in Liberia, traveled inland and to Egypt, studied African history and cultures, and learned Arabic. This exposure made him doubt the Christian abolitionist idea that "savage" African culture should be replaced by Christianity. In fact, Blyden gradually developed the opposite view – namely, that African culture should be *protected* against alien (including Christian) influence. He thus initiated a new, what could be called an "Afrocentric" or "African Regeneration," discourse that could become a vehicle for a forceful critique of the missionary (and in principle also the colonial) establishment in West Africa.

The idea of race in Blyden's writings has a number of aspects: biological, cultural, and religious. Under the last rubric, race is, for Blyden, a God-created unit of humanity:

> Each race is endowed with peculiar talents, and watchful to the last degree is the great Creator over the individuality, the freedom and independence of each. In the music of the universe, each shall give a different sound, but necessary to the grand symphony. There are several sounds not yet brought out, and the feeblest of all is that hitherto produced by the Negro; but only he can furnish it. And when he furnishes it in its fullness and perfection, it will be welcomed with delight by the world. (1903)

As a consequence of his view on race, Blyden saw nothing wrong with the term "Negro." He even insisted on writing it with a capital N and made it the title of the journal he founded in Freetown. For Blyden "pride of race" was a dictate of nature as well as a divine commandment. The great challenge for the self-conscious Negro was to bring out, discover, and develop this specifically "African" mode in all aspects of life. In his forceful speeches and writings, he would exclaim: "Be yourselves...if you surrender your personality, you have nothing left to give the world," and "the African must advance by methods of his own. He must possess a power distinct from the European."

Blyden perceived his philosophy to be part of a grand global process of peoples, nations, and races reclaiming their legitimate place in this world.

> The feeling is in the atmosphere – the plane in which races move. And there is no people in whom the desire for race integrity and race preservation is stronger than in the Negro... Within the last thirty years, the sentiment of race and of nationality has attained wonderful development.... The efforts of men like Garibaldi and Cavour in

81

Italy, of Kossnuth in Hungary, of Bismarck in Germany, of the Ashantees and Zulus in Africa, have proved the indestructible vitality and tenacity of race. (1887: 121)

The more radical implications of Blyden's identity philosophy, such as the idea of a specifically African personality, came forward only later in his life. The African personality was defined in contrast to the European, which was identified as harsh, individualistic, competitive, combative, non-religious, and materialistic. The African's contribution toward world culture would be that of peacemaker and conserver of the spirituality of the world. In a letter to Booker T. Washington, Blyden wrote:

> The spirit of service in the black man is born of his spiritual genius...the supple, yielding, conciliatory, obedient, gentle, patient, musical spirit that is not full of offensive resistance – how sadly the white man needs it!...Let him fight the battle of government on the stump, at the polls and in the legislative halls. Our kingdom in America is not this world. We cannot compete with the Anglo-Saxon. He is so dreadfully determined, so intolerant and self assertive, intent upon carrying his point at all hazards, having good in view of course; but the wheels of his mind and understanding need oiling sadly with the oil of African good nature. (in Lynch 1971: 207)

Blyden developed the idea of cultural difference with remarkable consistency, sometimes shocking his contemporaries as well as the present-day reader. For instance, he held that Christianity, as a Western religion, did not fit Africa well. He saw Islam as better suited to the needs of the African continent. Great African warriors had expelled the conquerors and adjusted Islam to accommodate the social peculiarities of the people. The idea of a divine mandate for the authenticity and the purity of African culture also involved the ideal of race purity. Blyden turned against wholesale remigration of African-Americans to Africa, against accepting mixed bloods (mulattoes) as full "Negroes," and, in his later life, even favored the prohibition of inter-racial marriages. In education, Blyden favored a curriculum specially designed for African students to be taught by Africans in indigenous institutions. In politics, however, his position was ambiguous. On the one hand, the logic of his position involved the idea of "Negro" self-assertion and unity and could lead to an outspoken anti-colonial ideology based on the idea of "Africa for the Africans," such as was advocated by Marcus Garvey in the USA after the First World War. On the other hand, a consistent elaboration of Blyden's philosophy of racial/cultural difference implied that Africans should leave politics to the race that excels in this area: namely, the Europeans.

> Thus, Ethiopia and Ethiopians, having always served, will continue to serve the world. The Negro is, at the moment, the opposite of the Anglo-Saxon. Those everywhere serve the world; these everywhere govern the world.... The one serves mankind by ruling; the other serves mankind by serving. The one wears the crown and wields the scepter; the other bears the stripes and carries the cross. (1887: 120)

According to the providential scheme of things, the British had a historical task in Africa to facilitate education, trade, and the creation of a great, unified, West

African state. However, Blyden expected that whites would be physically unfit to settle permanently on the African continent, so the colonialism that got fully established toward the end of his life would be "by nature" a temporary phenomenon. Blyden's forceful positions on such issues as an African church, an African curriculum, an African personality, history, and high culture, as well as his ideas on race pride and non-acculturation, struck forcibly at the heart of paternalistic rule in the proto-colonial enclaves on the West African coast between 1870 and 1900, and were embraced by the frustrated African "educated elite." However, when colonialism became established around 1900, when fully fledged administrative, legal, military, and economic structures were being imposed, the *political* rather than the *cultural* aspects of colonial rule became the primary issue.

Blyden's development constitutes a long journey from abolitionist *cultural paternalism* to *cultural nationalism*, from a view of Africa as still having to acquire everything to the view that Africa, in principle, has everything already, from an evolutionary discourse to an essentialist discourse, from the standard narrative of an outsider preaching to Africans to civilize and Christianize them, to a standard narrative of an African patriot addressing outsiders. Blyden's development came to its consistent conclusion in *African Life and Customs* (1908), which is a superbly elegant, idealized presentation of "the" African way of life, covering its various aspects one by one, and showing its intricate balance, wisdom, and perfect adaptation to the African environment. Blyden adapted from the dominant scientific racist ideology of his time key concepts (e.g. "race," "instinct," "natural order"), dichotomies (e.g. Negro/Anglo-Saxon), and theories (on the "serving" nature of blacks, the natural home continents of races, the degenerative effects of the mixing of races). But he overturned, as it were, the structure of racist discourse by replacing a hierarchical order of races with an order of difference.

James Africanus Beale Horton

The 1860s and '70s constituted an exceptional historical interlude in West Africa, because, despite pervasive Western influence, no one considered the possibility of colonial occupation. The political horizon appeared open, allowing for a process of rapid indigenous modernization such as was seen in Japan or in "dominions" like Australia and Canada. Several events suggested this openness. The British House of Commons decided, in 1865, on a retreat from West Africa; in the Gold Coast the Fanti Federation was established in 1870. Also, in a number of fields Africans proved able to compete successfully with Europeans: Ajayi Crowther of Nigeria was ordained bishop, Africanus Horton took a doctorate in medicine, and a class of successful African businessmen emerged. The careers of Samuel Lewis, Ajayi Crowther, James Johnson, William "Independent" Grant, G. G. M. Nicol, and Africanus Horton refuted in a most concrete way the emerging racist prejudice by showing what Africans and Africa could achieve within a lifetime.

The most comprehensive and tightly argued expression of this self-conscious African "Mid-Victorian Optimism" is found in the work of James Africanus Beale Horton. Whether it concerns race, cultural excellence, the capitalist spirit, education, or politics, he defended a thoroughly universalist position, arguing that Africans are capable of measuring up to the highest standards of achievement (July 1966; Fyfe 1972).

James Beale Horton was born in 1835 of "recaptive" parents in the village of Gloucester in Sierra Leone. His father and mother had been set free from a slave ship. The recaptives were, as Horton perceived it, "on their arrival in Sierra Leone, landed naked and in a state of abject rudeness and poverty, without the least knowledge of civilisation" (1868: 29, 59). Energetic missionary effort had Christianized and educated them. They had become part of "a nation of free black Christians," a very successful nation. In his sketch of the small settler village of Gloucester, the Nigerian historian Ayandele mentions that by 1821 missionary efforts had already been so effective that "500 out of a total population of 720 were able to read their Testaments," a literacy rate not easily matched by any other place in the world in the 1820s.

After attending Fourah Bay College in Freetown, Sierra Leone, Horton was offered the exceptional chance of studying medicine in London in order to prepare for service in the British West African forces. When he moved from King's College London to the University of Edinburgh to take a medical doctorate, he added "Africanus" to his name. He was admitted into the British army as staff surgeon in West Africa, making him the highest-ranking African in British army service. He served at many places along the West African coast, acquiring an extensive knowledge of the geological, economic, social, and political conditions in the coastal zone and participating, to the extent to which his position allowed, in political matters. The Ashantihene (King of the Ashanti) even offered him the title of Prince (see Fyfe 1972: 133). After his retirement, he resettled in Freetown, becoming active in the economic field by starting several companies and establishing the first West African bank – the Commercial Bank of West Africa. Horton died suddenly in 1883. The main body of his work is contained in the books *West African Countries and Peoples* (1868), which includes his important text "The Negro's Place in Nature," and *Letters on the Political Condition in the Gold Coast* (1870).

The basis of Horton's optimistic and universalistic position was a rather modern conception of race. Whereas his contemporaries expounded the case against scientific racism with religious arguments, Horton directly attacked the biological claims of the racists. As a medical doctor, he had no doubt that biological differences between the races are negligible. He knew, therefore, that none of the popular and "scientific" racist positions explaining Western superiority in his time could have any ground. "It is an incontrovertible logical inference that the difference arises entirely from influences of external circumstances, Truly, *Nature una et communis omnium est*" (1868: 29). Historical circumstances, he argued, had been beneficial to rapid civilizational development in the West, but Africa would soon catch up. He believed, with his contemporaries, in a world-historical civilizational progress, but indicated that different peoples contribute to that development. Nations rise and fall; the once flourishing and civilized nation can easily degenerate into a semi-barbarous state; and those who have lived in utter barbarism, after a lapse of time, become the upstanding nations. At the time of the Romans Britain was in a state of hopeless barbarism, yet now it was the cream of civilization. Horton quoted Cicero:

"the ancient Britons went about scantly clothed; they painted their bodies in fantastic fashions, 'offered up human victims to uncouth idols, and lived in hollow trees and rude habitations'." Atticus advised a friend "not to buy slaves from Britain on account of their stupidity and their inaptitude to learn music and other accomplishments."

Consistent with Horton's turn toward historical explanation and rejection of the idea of basic racial differences, he entertained a very practical idea of civilization. To be civilized is to be advanced in science, in cultural sophistication, in productive development, and thus to be powerful. Horton's universalistic conception of civilization translated into a very practical view of what is involved in development – namely, to absorb effectively all aspects of civilization achieved elsewhere and, subsequently, to improve upon these. For Horton, therefore, Africa's task was to educate, Christianize, industrialize, and acquire wealth. "Buy up the former abodes of thy European masters; carry on extensive mercantile speculations; seek after the indulgences of civilized life, and travel in foreign countries to seek after wealth...look out for a better form of government administration."

With his practical turn of mind, Horton suggested a host of initiatives in the educational, economic, and political fields. He was well ahead of his time in constantly stressing the need for a very active government policy in education, propagating compulsory education and the elevation of Fourah Bay College in Sierra Leone to a West African university. He greatly valued African entrepreneurship and, as well as establishing the Commercial Bank of West Africa, which he managed himself during the last months of his life, he also started several companies, such as the Wassaw Light Railway Company Ltd.

In politics, according to Horton, development depended on infusing "the true principles of civilized Government," including the election of rulers. Without enlightened and modern government, none of the modernizing policies which he considered essential would be possible. The "feudal lords" of the interior tribes would not promote development, neither would a hesitant and inconsistent British colonial policy. The core of Horton's vision was, therefore, the development of modern states in Africa, what he called "that great principle of self-government."

When in 1865 a Select Committee of the British House of Commons concluded that Britain should retreat from West Africa, Horton took up the challenge to give a blueprint for West African states. His major work, *West African Countries and Peoples*, provides detailed suggestions for the institutional set-up appropriate to each of the future states. The book offered a complete plan, which he expected the British to permit, supervise, and protect. The plan advocated the creation of a number of "dominions" within the British Commonwealth in West Africa entitled to an equal position with the white dominions such as Canada and Australia. In another development, in 1868, rulers and intellectuals in the coastal regions of the Gold Coast established the Fanti Confederation, indicating their political agenda in the Mankessim Constitution of October 1871. Horton published his letters to the Colonial Office in defence of the Federation in his *Letters on the Political Condition of the Gold Coast*.

However, the Fanti leaders were arrested by the British, the Confederation collapsed in 1873, and Fantiland became a protectorate, while Ashanti was defeated in 1874. Colonial influence expanded rapidly and racist ideology spread. Horton's optimistic and pragmatic approach quickly lost appeal. He was considered a so-called "Black Englishman" and became completely forgotten.

John Mensah Sarbah and Joseph Casely Hayford

The next phase in the intellectual process in West Africa developed under quite different historical conditions. After the second Ashanti War against the British (1874), initially won by Ashanti, colonial rule became established before the end of the century in most countries in Africa. In the Gold Coast, this development was somewhat more complicated than elsewhere (except Senegal), because the relationship between the African rulers in the region and the British was laid down in agreements, in particular in the Bond of 1844. The British encroachment on indigenous power was, in fact, a direct violation of these agreements. Intellectuals and traditional rulers alike resisted several key Gold Coast government laws. Western-educated intellectuals turned to the serious study of traditional institutions, legal systems, and languages, and became great defenders of these in the face of the "great disorganization of society" effected by several British laws.

John Mensah Sarbah (1864–1910), an erudite Fanti barrister trained in London, played a leading role in the opposition. He was involved in founding the first political organizations under colonial rule, the Mfantsi Amanbuhu Fékuw (Fanti National Political Society) in 1889 and the Aborigines' Rights Protection Society in 1898, as well as in establishing the newspaper *The Gold Coast People* in 1891. In the framework of protest against the colonial Land Bills, he published his *Fanti Customary Law* (1897) "to reduce into writing the Customary Laws and Usages of the Fanti, Ashanti, and other Akan inhabitants of the Gold Coast." To this sophisticated description of the Akan social and legal system, he added a number of appendices on the key historical documents and treaties, thus proving the case that the Gold Coast was never conquered by the British and dismissing the legality of their encroachment on indigenous rule. In 1906 Sarbah published another important work, *Fanti National Constitution*, to describe "the principles controlling and regulating the Akan State."

Joseph Casely Hayford was another exemplary representative of the early Gold Coast educated elite. Hayford was a journalist, a Cambridge-trained lawyer, and an important politician – the "uncrowned king of West Africa" during the first three decades of the twentieth century. As well as being a political leader, he was probably the most comprehensive and representative political theorist of these decades in British West Africa. He was eloquent, sophisticated, and witty. Where necessary, he could bolster up an argument with extensive reference to historical fact. He wrote *Gold Coast Native Institutions* (1903), *Ethiopia Unbound* (1911), *The Truth about the West African Land Question* (1913), and *United West Africa* (1919).

Gold Coast Native Institutions described the sophisticated Ashanti and Fanti political procedures, containing their own "checks and balances," and mechanisms that could promote thorough political deliberation. Typically, Hayford gave an enthusiastic description of the role of the "linguist" (or "speaker"), especially in the Ashanti system. "The Linguist is the most important personage of the Native State.

He is in some cases more influential than the Chief...He is generally the repository, or, if you like, a walking encyclopedia, of all traditional knowledge...his knowledge embraces the political history of the whole State, as well as of sister States." Furthermore, said Hayford, his speeches will sparkle with humor; he is the master in "the art of 'linguistic' oratory," and creative in guiding the discussion to a balanced conclusion (1970: 68).

Hayford's inspired representation suggests that the educated elite were not outside the traditional system, but right at its center. Thus, he welded the two major forces in indigenous politics into one model. For the "educated sons of the nation" there was an important role "to serve his country's cause" as councilor, advisor, or linguist. Hayford also urged the transcending of other divisions, such as between Fanti and Ashanti. His endeavor was at the same time a nationalist effort, a conscious attempt to establish a national Fanti-Ashanti tradition.

Hayford's most exceptional book, *Ethiopia Unbound*, appeared in 1911. It is an appeal to Africans to turn to their heritage to create the future, an appeal in the form of a magnificent fictional and partly autobiographical work. The conclusion was clear: there is no alternative for the Gold Coast except to build on the indigenous tradition; there is "no healthy growth except from within."

From the philosophical point of view, the discourse of Sarbah and Hayford is particularly interesting. The nineteenth-century ideologies, represented by Horton and Blyden, suggested a choice between *modernization* and *African tradition*, while neither provided a forceful framework for political action in a situation characterized by colonial penetration. The way out was shown by intellectuals such as Sarbah and Hayford. They suggested that there is no contradiction between tradition and modernization. African traditions, they argued, are perfectly able to adjust in their own way to modern times, if only they are given the chance. The key problem was a political one – namely, that the fair chance of "working out our own salvation as a people" was denied to them. The Gold Coast intellectuals wanted to renovate indigenous political traditions as the basis for an indigenous path to modernization, just like the Japanese, who, while facing the threat of modernized Europe, revolutionized their *own* culture under Meiji rule.

This grand ideological option of *modernization-from-indigenous-roots* involved a conception of the vitality of the indigenous traditions that is reminiscent of Blyden. But it was, in fact, different. Rather than affirming a general African identity as being different from the European, Sarbah and Hayford wanted to show the vitality of specific Fanti and Ashanti traditions as a basis for organizing social and political life on the coast. Whereas Blyden was making a cultural statement on behalf of Africa as a whole, Sarbah and Hayford were formulating a national political alternative for the Gold Coast.

However, the historical chances for this alternative had already disappeared by 1900. As J. B. Danquah analyzed the situation 30 years later:

> The age in which an independent national consciousness dawned upon the Gold Coast people came to an end in 1897.... The Gold Coast people had effectively become part of the Empire, and for weal or woe, what they could best do to foster the national cause and liberty was to work from within the British constitution itself for a liberal

recognition of our right and capacity to direct our destiny within an Empire of free nations and not as a subject Colony forming the "pocket borough" of the English Parliament. (1932: 18, 20)

Colonialism had become the dominant reality. Preservation of indigenous political systems was replaced by a struggle to attain national independence.

References

Ayandele, E. A. (1971) "James Africanus Beale Horton, 1835–1883: Prophet of Modernisation in West Africa." *African Historical Studies*, 4(3): 691–707.

Blyden, E. W. (1887) *Christianity, Islam and the Negro Race* (London: W. B. Whittingham & Co.; repr. Edinburgh: Edinburgh University Press, 1967).

Blyden, E. W. (1903) *Africa and the Africans, Proceedings on the Occasion of a Banquet* (London: n.p.; partly repr. in Albert G. Mosley, *African Philosophy: Selected Readings*. Englewood Cliffs, NJ: Prentice-Hall, 1995).

Blyden, E. W. (1908) *African Life and Customs* (London: C. M. Phillips).

Boele van Hensbroek, P. (1999) *Political Discourses in African Thought: 1860 to the Present* (Westport: Praeger).

Clapham, Ch. (1970) "The Context of African Political Thought." *Journal of Modern African Studies*, 8(1): 1–13.

Crummell, A. (1862) *The Future of Africa: Being Addresses, Sermons, etc., etc., Delivered in the Republic of Liberia* (New York: Charles Scribner; republished (n.d.), Scholarly Press).

Danquah, J. B. (1932) "Introduction," in M. I. Sampson, *Gold Coast Men of Affairs* (London: Routledge).

Fyfe, C. (1962) *A History of Sierra Leone* (Oxford: Oxford University Press).

Fyfe, C. (1972) *Africanus Horton, 1835–1883, West African Scientist and Patriot* (New York: Oxford University Press).

Hayford, J. E. Casely (1919) *United West Africa* (London: F. T. Phillips).

Hayford, J. E. Casely (1969) *Ethiopia Unbound. Studies in Race Emancipation* (London: Frank Cass; repr. from 1911).

Hayford, J. E. Casely (1970) *Gold Coast Native Institutions, With Thoughts upon a Healthy Imperial Policy for the Gold Coast and Ashanti* (London: Frank Cass; repr. from 1903).

Hayford, J. E. Casely (1971) *The Truth about the West African Land Question* (London: Frank Cass; repr. from 1913).

Horton, J. A. B. (1868) *West African Countries and Peoples, British, and Native. With the Requirements Necessary for Establishing that Self-government Recommended by the Committee of the House of Commons, 1865; and a Vindication of the Negro Race* (London: W. J. Johnsonn; repr. 1970, Nendeln, Liechtenstein: Krause Reprint).

Horton, J. A. B. (1970) *Letters on the Political Condition of the Gold Coast since the Exchange of Territory Between the English and Dutch Governments, on January 1, 1868; together with a short account of the Ashanti War, 1862, and the Awoonah War, 1866* (Africana Modern Library, London: Frank Cass; repr. from 1870).

July, Robert W. (1964) "Nineteenth-Century Negritude: Edward Wilmot Blyden." *Journal of African History*, 1: 73–86.

July, Robert W. (1966) "Africanus Horton and the Idea of Independence in West Africa." *Sierra Leone Studies*, new series no. 18 (January): 2–17.

July, Robert W. (1968) *The Origins of Modern African Thought: Its Development in West Africa during the Nineteenth and Twentieth Centuries* (London: Faber & Faber).

Langley, J. Ayo (1973) *Pan-Africanism and Nationalism in West Africa: A Case Study in Ideology and Social Classes* (Oxford: Clarendon Press).

Lynch, H. R. (1967) *Edward Wilmot Blyden: Pan-Negro Patriot 1832–1912* (London: Oxford University Press).

Lynch, H. R. (ed.) (1971) *Black Spokesman. Selected Published Writings of Edward Wilmot Blyden* (London: Frank Cass).

Lynch, H. R. (ed.) (1978) *Selected Letters of Edward Wilmot Blyden* (New York: Kto Press).

Sarbah, J. Mensah (1968a) *Fanti National Constitution* (London: Frank Cass; repr. from 1906).

Sarbah, J. Mensah (1968b) *Fanti Customary Law* (London: Frank Cass; repr. from 1897).

Shepperson, G. (1960) "Notes on American Negro Influences on the Emergence of African Nationalism." *Journal of African History*, 1(2): 299–312.

Further reading

Ayandele, E. A. (1970) *Holy Johnson, Pioneer of African Nationalism, 1836–1917* (London: Frank Cass).

Crummell, A. (1969) *Africa and America: Addresses and Discourses* (Springfield, MA: Negro University Press; orig. pub. 1891).

Curtin, P. D. (1964) *The Image of Africa: British Ideas and Action, 1790–1850* (Madison: University of Wisconsin Press).

Danquah, J. B. (1928) *Gold Coast: Akan Laws and Customs and the Akim Abuakwa Constitution* (London: Routledge).

Kimble, D. (1963) *A Political History of Ghana: The Rise of Gold Coast Nationalism, 1850–1928* (Oxford: Clarendon Press).

Langley, J. Ayo (1979) *Ideologies of Liberation in Black Africa 1856–1970: Documents on Modern African Political Thought from Colonial Times to the Present* (London: Rex Collings).

Wilson, H. S. (1969) *Origins of West African Nationalism* (London: Macmillan; St. Martin's Press).

5

Africana Philosophy: Origins and Prospects

LUCIUS T. OUTLAW, JR.

Introduction

The notion of "Africana philosophy" is of very recent origin but is being taken up by increasing numbers of professional philosophers who are African or of African descent, and by others who are not. "Africana philosophy" is very much a heuristic notion – that is, one that suggests orientations for philosophical endeavors by professional philosophers and other intellectuals devoted to matters pertinent to African and African-descended persons and peoples. "Africana Philosophy," then, is meant to facilitate the organizing of past, present, and future "philosophical" articulations and practices by and in the interests of African-descended peoples.

The production, justification, and validation of knowledge by and in the interests of peoples of African descent are hardly of recent origin. Such efforts are as old as African peoples themselves. However, recognizing articulations by peoples and persons of African descent as instances of *philosophy* is a recent matter within what is regarded as the Western portions of the world, and *very* recent – within the past two decades – for professional philosophers in the United States of America in particular. In fact, the joining of "Africana" to "philosophy" was both motivated and facilitated by institutionalized developments in several other fields of knowledge. This was particularly the case in those institutions in which there were concerted interdisciplinary efforts devoted to reclaiming, rehabilitating, and producing new knowledge by and about African and African-descended peoples. An example of this was the Africana Studies and Research Center at Cornell University (New York) during the 1960s. Nonetheless, the history of efforts of this kind include predecessor ventures, such as the African Heritage Studies Association, which, also during the 1960s, developed out of and away from the African Studies Association. There is also the much older and still functioning Association for the Study of Negro (now African-American) Life and History and other ventures such as *Phylon* magazine, founded by W. E. B. Du Bois and others. Academic philosophy, as a complex social as well as epistemological venture of ventures, is very much the latecomer to these developments and concerns, more so in the United States of America than in Africa.

Just what is the heuristic promise of "Africana philosophy"? It consists in its utility, initially, as a "gathering" notion under which to collect and organize philosophical and related articulations (writings, speeches, etc.) and practices (of research, conferencing, teaching, etc.), and traditions of Africans and peoples of African descent. (However, "Africana philosophy" is to be inclusive of the work of persons who are neither African nor of African descent but who recognize the legitimacy and importance of the philosophical concerns and discursive activities of African-descended people and contribute to such efforts.) The initial guidance implied in the notion of Africana philosophy, then, is to be sought in the philosophical discourse of a racially or ethnically identified people, specifically, people of African descent.

Still, these initial identifying efforts are only promissory. Further determinations must be made as to whether there are characteristics of the philosophical discourse of African and African-descended thinkers that distinguish them from those of other peoples *by virtue of their being products and efforts of persons African or African-descended*. This is a matter of determining what the criteria might be for classifying the philosophical efforts of particular racial and ethnic groups as a distinct species of philosophy. The question is especially important in light of the complicated historical developments involving global dispersal and the subsequent development of regional entities (e.g., the Caribbean), complex local or national identities (e.g., African Americans), and nation-state groupings (e.g. "Nigeria," "Kenya"), all involving African and African-descended peoples. Determining how it is possible to speak of "Africana philosophy" in a cogent way is work to be further pursued, in part by exploring the heuristic promises of the notion.

More of the resources needed for doing so are now available to an increasing degree. There is an impressive number of publications in the form of articles in journals in philosophy and other disciplines and in anthologies and monographs (much fewer). In evidence also are organizations of philosophers and other scholars. In Africa one can mention the Inter-African Council of Philosophy and national organizations in Kenya, Nigeria, and elsewhere. In the United States of America we have the Society for African Philosophy in North America (SAPINA); the Society for the Study of Africana Philosophy (SSAP), with a chapter in New York (which meets in the Manhattan home of Alfred Prettyman) and in Washington, DC (which meets at the Philosophy Department, Howard University). There is also the Committee on Blacks in Philosophy in the American Philosophical Association. There are somewhat regular conferences, such as the Annual Philosophy-Born-of-Struggle Conferences organized primarily by J. Everet Green, assisted by several others and hosted recently by the New School University. One might mention, besides, the Annual Alain Locke Conference, devoted to explorations of raciality and philosophy, organized and hosted by the Philosophy Department of Howard University; the Afro-Asian Philosophy Conferences held in various African nations; sessions at divisional meetings of the American Philosophical Association and at the African Studies Association. Still other conferences are hosted by persons in departments of philosophy and religion in various colleges and universities throughout the United States of America and in Africa. There are, furthermore, graduate programs in a number of universities in Africa that award PhD or equivalent degrees in philosophy. However, these graduate programs do not yet attract persons from the US. Moreover, there are no PhD programs in the US that have the critical mass of philosophers with the convictions, competencies, departmental and institutional support, and other requisite resources to become principal sites for the production, validation, and mediation of Africana philosophy. Development of a first-rate graduate program in Africana philosophy in the United States of America remains one of the pressing needs of the present and the foreseeable future.

Needed even more, and as a basis on which to develop such a graduate program, are clarified and settled conceptualizations of Africana philosophy as a disciplinary venture. Pertinent resources of this kind are available in other fields, particularly in African and African-American studies. In the latter case, the work of Maulana Karenga and Molefi Asante are particularly noteworthy and valuable, but they have yet to be taken up thoughtfully and critically by many of the philosophers working under the umbrella of Africana philosophy. The impediment here is, of course, a consequence of both sociological conditions (e.g., professional and personal networks that tend not to overlap) and ideological differences. Overall, however, much of this has to do with the deformation many professional philosophers suffer as a consequence of our culturally anemic, race-tainted yet race-denying, logocentric, and Eurocentric training. The near exclusive focus, throughout our training, on canonical "Western" figures and texts as the paragons of "philosophy," and the near total exclusion of insights from such disciplines as history, anthropology, ethnology, psychology, theology, sociology, demography, epidemiology, political science, economics, art, music, and dance leave us ill-equipped for working out appropriate conceptualizations to guide us in realizing the promises of "Africana philosophy." The relative neglect, in our philosophical training, of such other disciplines and interdisciplinary programs of studies as African, Caribbean, American, and Latin American studies and the far too little consideration of the philosophical efforts of black women have also had the same effect.

In following up the heuristic leads of the term "Africana" as intending African and African-descended peoples throughout the African continent and the African diaspora, one immediately confronts challenges to identifying the objects of investigation. One reason lies in the enormity of the geographical and historical expanses of the continent and the diaspora and of the sociocultural complexities consequent on African contacts with other peoples and cultures. It is not possible, then, to pursue studies under the heading of "Africana philosophy" without proper attention to the history of the African continent as well as of the formation and persistence of African-descended peoples in the diaspora. Further, there is the particularly important task of identifying the extent to which, and the basis upon which, it is appropriate to gather various peoples and discursive practices together under a single heading as forming a properly relational collectivity rather than an arbitrary and unrelated heap of identities and conceptions. The objects of study must form a determinate field comprising the philosophical efforts of related racial and ethnic groupings. Identifying the peoples, historically and culturally, is work best accomplished by historians, anthropologists, and ethnologists, among others. Consequently, studies in Africana philosophy *must* be historically and comparatively *ethno*philosophical. They must, that is, be attentive to the histories and cultures of the peoples, nations, nation-states, regions, etc., from which the philosophical articulations under discussion emanate. With this in mind, I shall in what follows sketch a possible orientation for conducting ethnophilosophical studies of diasporan systems of thought, encompassing their normative and aesthetic conceptions and their practical and theoretical beliefs under the heuristic rubric of "Africana philosophy." In doing this, I will draw on the reflections of Melville Herskovits (1969), one of the pioneering scholars of African and "Afroamerican" studies of a previous generation.

Giving Primacy to Sociocultural Settings

Afroamerican societies, for the most part, do not stand alone, clearly separable, as do the tribal aggregates customarily studied by anthropologists; and this holds whether we consider them on the geographical, the social or the cultural level. (Herskovits 1969: 74)

The social settings of African-descended peoples in the diaspora (the "New World" in Herskovits's words), compared to those on the African continent, have tended to involve varying degrees of intensive and influential contacts with other peoples and cultures. Consequently, determining the provenance and significance of the action-orienting belief, and value, systems of African-descended thinkers in the diaspora will require varying strategies depending, in part, on the societies and cultures to which the thinkers belong. These are, moreover, likely to contrast with studies of continental African thinkers of certain times and places. In most cases in the diaspora, particular attention must be given to the history of the dynamics "resulting from the constant and continuing contact which the descendants of Africans have had with peoples of different cultural antecedents and of different physical types." This is especially necessary in view of the *variations* in the complexity of "the character of the integration of the cultural streams in play – African, European and American Indian" in different societies. Further, for Herskovits, studies of peoples of African descent in the Americas could not proceed by using geography as "the principal organizing factor" given the ethnographic complexities of the societies as cultural continuities with continental Africa. According to Herskovits, "this obviously increases the methodological problems to be faced and the intricacy of the conceptual structure that must be employed in shaping and executing research" (ibid. 74). For example, setting out diasporan religious or artistic beliefs and value systems and identifying the African elements within them would require, Herskovits notes, knowledge of the African cultures from which the people concerned were descended. It would involve, furthermore, the determination of the extent to which the elements have undergone change in New World settings and an explanation of why and how.

Methodologically, then, studies in Africana philosophy cannot appropriately proceed by dispensing with considerations of history and culture. In other words, it would be a mistake to focus on the evaluation of thought constructs solely in terms of their logical cogency. Nor would it be any more sensible to be guided by uncritical adherence to those prevailing agendas and methods of academic philosophy that disregard the relevance of sociocultural histories. Rather, these studies should be conditioned by a heuristic mindfulness of the likelihood, in many cases, of "philosophizing born of struggle." That is, one must look at, listen to, feel, and experience what does matter most to black folks in their various life-worlds as conditioned by struggles against racial oppression.

Nonetheless, there should not be wholesale rejection of disciplinary resources *simply* because they have been determined to be "Eurocentric." Rather, here, too, careful, critical, comparative considerations must be worked out to settle issues regarding the viability of resources for assisting philosophical thinking in the interests of black peoples, and others. In particular, getting at the philosophical thought of African and African-descended thinkers in multiracial or multiethnic New World societies will require informed and critical understandings of quite complex cultural dynamics. As a rule, these cultural dynamics involve processes of retention and reinterpretation of cultural practices that originated in Africa, development of new ones, and appropriation and adaptation of elements and practices from the cultures of the non-African peoples with whom black folks have been in sustained contact. The groundwork for studies in Africana philosophy must, then, be prepared by comparative ethnohistories that, taken together, constitute connected histories of various but related African and African-descended peoples.

An important consequence of such studies will be to compel more intensive and explicit ethnohistorical, ethnophilosophical reconceptualizations of what heretofore has been categorized as "Western Philosophy." For the disciplinary impediments that Herskovits noted in anthropology more than 50 years ago continue to plague the discipline of philosophy. Herskovits commented that "the methodological and conceptual innovations of Afroamerican researches brought into play cultural resistances which, quite without being verbalized, operated so as to inhibit anthropologists from making the most effective use of the fresh approaches to the use of comparative data that the results of work in this field presents" (ibid. 72). The resistances, I submit, have to do with the failure to take responsibility for racialized investments in "Whiteness" in much of the canonical work in academic, professional philosophy. Such failure has all too often been camouflaged as insistence on rigorous adherence to epistemological norms said to be neutral with regard to "morally irrelevant," "accidental," characteristics such as raciality, ethnicity, and gender. A thorough and honest historical review of the sociology of academic philosophy will not, I contend, support such claims. Furthermore, such a review, I believe, will also make it abundantly clear that these sociological situations and their associated epistemologies are inappropriate in Africana philosophy.

Giving Primacy to the Historical and Cultural

[I]n Afroamerican research, belief systems, folklore and music are of fundamental importance in the range of data that bear on the essential comparative analysis...research into the social aspects of Afroamerican cultures is complicated...by the fact that Afroamerican groups are integral parts of larger population aggregates. This means that to analyze them requires a firm grounding in the cultures of certain key African areas if the extensive reinterpretations that characterize these social structures are adequately to be assessed. Without this background for analysis and comparison, the investigations have tended to be sociological, which is to say analytic and ahistorical, with the historical component, indispensable in Afroamerican research, foreign to direct interests and procedures. (Herskovits 1969: 79)

Studies in Africana philosophy that focus on diasporan thinkers (African-descended thinkers in the Americas) can be expected to contribute to the understanding of what Herskovits termed "the acculturative history of New World Negro societies" (ibid. 77). That is, they should advance the study of the cultural dynamics of the contacts of racial and ethnic groups in societies with substantial populations of peoples of African descent. For Herskovits, such studies necessitated the developing of a viable model of culture involving "component aspects," such as technology, economics, social organization, non-kinship institutions, religion, magic, art, folklore, music, and language. In regard to each of these "component aspects," the peoples of African descent were to be studied to determine to what degree it had been *retained* during intercultural contacts and how it had been affected by these contacts within the overall ethnohistorical "cultural stream." (This last phrase was used by Herskovits for the conception of cultures as dynamic yet bounded wholes that are subject to change through the admixture of new "currents" or by way of the recomposition of prevailing currents.) Also to be studied was the acceptance of non-African cultural elements by people of African descent, assuming, of course, in either case, that cultural elements can be distinguished either as African or non-African. Herskovits was convinced that the degree of acceptance of non-African elements "varies significantly when one compares technology or economics with religion or music" (ibid.). Elements of religion and music derived from continental African cultures and retained in the cultures of diasporan African-descended peoples tend to persist longer and are more resistant to change than beliefs and practices having to do with technology and economics.

Further, and of particular importance, Herskovits concluded from his researches that "culture-change differs in degree and intensity with the socio-economic positions of the individuals that make up a given Afroamerican society, the amount of retention of Africanism being inverse to acculturative opportunity as represented by position in the total community of a particular stratum" (ibid.). The implications for studies in Africana philosophy are momentous. Such studies must assess likely variations within and among the belief and value systems of African-descended peoples as a function of the socioeconomic positions of those who hold and propagate them. Important research questions emerge. For example, to what extent do belief and value systems vary by socioeconomic position, within and across ethnicities of African descent in various sociohistorical settings? How are the variations influenced by, say, college and graduate-level formal education or even by the type of institutions attended (public or private, historically and/or predominantly white or black) or by the historical "periods"? One might also raise the question of the relative viability of "folk" versus "professional" philosophy (a distinction invoked by a number of contemporary African philosophers).

In any case, a conclusion to be drawn from Herskovits's methodological considerations is that studies in Africana philosophy should be thoroughly situated within ethnohistorical, decidedly *cultural*, studies of African and African-descended peoples.

In this way, efforts in Africana philosophy can contribute to comparative, critical, hermeneutical studies of the various life-worlds of African and African-descended peoples.

Along the foregoing lines Herskovits took note of a matter that has frequently been of particular importance to many professional philosophers, though usually differently conceived, namely, personality formation in multicultural situations – in Herskovits's terms, "the relation between cultural setting and personality integration in acculturated societies" (ibid. 78). This continues to be a driving concern for many persons of African descent in the Americas where the education of their children, for example, is a crucial issue. This is an issue that formed the crux of the successful legal attack on *de jure* segregation of public schools in the consolidated cases decided by the US Supreme Court in Brown *v.* Board of Education of Topeka Kansas in 1954. It continues to drive campaigns for "Afrocentric" schools and curricula for black children in many urban school districts. The conclusions Herskovits draws from his research warrant serious consideration:

> In Afroamerican societies... we can see how the various cultural elements [which we brought together] have developed their own unity; a unity which, though it can be dissected by the student into its historical components, carries for the person living in the society all the subliminal sanctions of any long established social entity. When we turn to the problem of enculturation, as this has to do with personality in terms of the conflicts commonly held to assail the child in cultures of multiple derivation, we find that in Afroamerican societies the enculturative process is no necessary road to disorganization. (ibid.)

What educational and acculturative agendas will be best for the formation and development of the personalities of children and young people of African descent in our various social locations? Might there be in Herskovits's position a challenge to Du Bois' notion of "double consciousness" as definitive of the self-understandings of black folks in the New World, in the United States of America in particular? These crucial questions continue to be matters of concern for researchers, scholars, artists, and activists seeking to be of service to black folks.

Equally pertinent and no less challenging is the question, "What kinds of historical accounts should provide the bases for work in Africana philosophy?" Certainly, broad regional and continental histories would be appropriate. But so too will be particularistic histories of kingdoms, peoples, nation-states, economic units, organizations, institutions, and movements, of both continental Africa and the diaspora. Still, an important caution is to be drawn from Herskovits's contention that geography should not be used as the principal factor for organizing studies in Africana philosophy except, perhaps, for initial determination of objects of study. For geographical borders do not set impermeable boundaries to the flow of "cultural streams." On the contrary, such borders were constantly traversed as well as facilitated by the structuring practices of the political economies that became the engines of the formation of The New World. (See Gilroy 1993; Thornton 1992.)

A particular strategy employed by Herskovits that I regard as especially promising for studies in Africana philosophy is the ordering of various ethnographic data

along a continuum in terms of the degree of intensity of the persistence or transformation of a cultural element within a particular stream over time. Herskovits
took as an example

> the manner in which elements, such as the name and role of a deity or of a saint, or
> the complex of death rites, or attitudes toward twins, or the specialized use of magic as
> protective or aggressive self-help can be extracted from an original setting and be
> reworked into another. Or we can study how a whole pre-existing social complex, such
> as a tradition of polygyny, can be integrated into a different set of conventions which
> sanction monogamy, to form a new marriage pattern. (1969: 77)

Once noted, such elements and practices can be queried and critiqued with respect
to their moral or pragmatic significance for the people engaging the world through
them. Perhaps, then, such studies might help in a philosophical and historically
sophisticated way to determine what kinds of ethical, aesthetic, and practical program might be best for insuring the well-being of African and African-descended
peoples. And it will be especially important to conduct these studies in a *comparative*
manner. This can be done by taking critical account of beliefs and norms operative within particular cultural streams in various sociohistorical settings. Note will
have to be taken, in this connection, of similarities and differences, so as to determine the varying "Africanity" of the philosophical practices when compared to
relevant practices in continental Africa. In this way one might be able to determine
what Herskovits termed "the tenacity of culture." He was convinced that "Afroamerican studies have demonstrated from the first that retentions, whether in pure
or reinterpreted form, are of quite equal importance" to phenomena of cultural
change (ibid. 80):

> We have but to refer to what is known about the role of learning during the earliest
> years of life in setting behavior patterns, to recognize the fruitfulness of this approach.
> Motor behavior, concepts of time and space, ethical concepts, aesthetic tastes, and
> many other basic cultural orientations are inculcated in these years, and shape charac-
> teristic reactions manifested during the whole of the individual's life. They form the
> background against which innovations are projected; they provide the basis for his
> evaluations of what is newly presented to him; they afford the rationale for the
> conclusions today generally agreed on by students that under culture-contact, those
> innovations that are most in consonance with pre-existing custom will be accepted.
> (ibid.)

If Herskovits is right in his view that the concepts of space and time along with
ethical and aesthetic concepts are *learned*, then it might appear that Kant must be
wrong about the apriority of *the categories* (of space and time, among others) as
conditions of the possibility of experience and knowledge. Certainly, if Herskovits is
right, then a Kantian approach to Africana philosophy is ruled out. Rather, studies
in Africana philosophy must be undertaken as endeavors in comparative, historically informed ethnophilosophical investigations. One objective of such inquiries
must be to contribute to the application of "concepts derived from cross-cultural
research to the analysis of our discipline," in this case philosophy. We must, that is,

97

get round to "studying the ethnology of our own sub-culture," of professional philosophy (courtesy of Herskovits 1969: 80).

Conclusion

Is a Herskovits-inspired approach to Africana philosophy viable? This remains to be determined. Here, then, is an opportunity for work that could have a substantial impact on the future development of the heuristic promise of "Africana philosophy." The promise is that of organizing a project of cross-cultural, comparative studies of thought systems as they are found in the cultural repertoires of various African and African-descended peoples. The results could be a major contribution to the understanding of African and African-descended peoples. It will also give those of us involved in Africana philosophy new assignments for today and tomorrow more worthy of our energies and talents than arguing the case for the recognition of the humanity of African and African-descended peoples by establishing that some among them "philosophized." Let us be done with such efforts.

References

Gilroy, Paul (1993) *The Black Atlantic: Modernity and Double Consciousness* (Cambridge, MA: Harvard University Press).

Herskovits, Melville J. (1966) "On Some Modes of Ethnographic Comparison," in *The New World Negro: Selected Papers in Afroamerican Studies* (Bloomington: Indiana University Press), pp. 71–81.

Thornton, John (1992) *Africa and Africans in the Making of the Atlantic World, 1400–1680* (New York: Cambridge University Press).

6

Contemporary Anglophone African Philosophy: A Survey

BARRY HALLEN

Introduction

Contemporary academic philosophy in Anglophone Africa arose in a different and more turbulent intellectual climate than its Francophone equivalent. "Different" because philosophical paradigms in the English-language academy derived principally from the analytic tradition, which provided for a comparatively more narrow conception of the discipline than its Continental counterparts. "Turbulent" because of the competing claims about what could constitute the sources of African philosophy, as advocated by Africanists and African intellectuals from a diverse variety of disciplinary and vocational backgrounds – social anthropology, philosophy proper, missionary and religious scholarship, and, most prominently in the cases of Kwame Nkrumah and Julius Nyerere (presidents of Ghana and Tanzania, respectively), ideologically pragmatic political leadership.

Placide Tempels's *Bantu Philosophy* was originally published in French (1945/ 1949) and was intended for a Francophone readership. But these are not sufficient reasons to overlook the effects on an Anglophone African readership of its later publication (1959) in English-language translation. That Africans of a Bantu origin were said to explain and perceive the world as expressions of "vital forces" was found to be, at least initially, a satisfactorily radical alternative to Western mechanism. This "vital force" approach was shortly thereafter popularized in a fashionably lyrical, artistic, and best-selling manner with the English-language translation of *Muntu*, written by the German scholar Janheinz Jahn (1961). To develop this more specifically aesthetic dimension to the "vital force" approach, Jahn also drew heavily upon the (Francophone) theory of Negritude as expressed and propounded by Aime Cesaire and Leopold Sedar Senghor. But Tempels and Jahn share a view of the African intellect that, once better appreciated for its negative consequences, particularly where philosophy is concerned, has been enough to cause many Anglophone African intellectuals to reject it as ethnocentric and even derogatory of the African mentality generally. For Africans themselves are said to be incapable of articulating the "views"[1] reported by these studies, views on the basis of which Africans purportedly perceive and understand the world.

Africans are said to "live" in a world that is fundamentally *symbolic* and *ritualized* in character. These two terribly overworked terms are meant to convey the point that Africa's indigenous peoples express their beliefs and values most directly by means of symbolic and ritualized behavior (so-called "rites," "rituals," "masquerades") rather than discursive verbal statements. The closest such cultures come to any sort of systematic verbalization is said to be found in their myths and proverbs. More often than not, of course, this makes the participation of the alien academic fieldworker, professionally trained for the decoding (interpolating the meanings) of such behavior (symbolic and ritual), myths, and proverbs, indispensable to any scholarly, intercultural exercise. For without their active participation there could be no "studies" of the African mentality written in the systematic, reflective, critical, and discursive manner that is taken to be conventional by Western paradigms of scholarship.

Perhaps the most positive enduring heritage of these studies are their rudimentary efforts to link their theses to key concepts in the Bantu languages said to be fundamentally "expressive" of this culture's "world-view."[2] This limited, verbal articulateness of African peoples was, however, dramatically challenged in 1965 by the English-language translation of yet another widely read (and still enduringly popular) text of Francophone origin, *Conversations with Ogotemmeli*, as recorded and edited by the anthropologist Marcel Griaule. This book purports to report a series of discussions with a Dogon elder in which he comprehensively and systematically decodes, in a clear and discursive manner, much of Dogon symbolism, ritual, and myth.

With regard to the development of African philosophy generally as an independent discipline, one important and enduring consequence of Griaule's *Ogotemmeli* is that it did *not* provide a Dogon replication of Tempels's "vital force" ontology. The hierarchical, yet unified and somehow uniform, metaphysical structure to the universe outlined by Ogotemmeli – as well as its organizing principles – argues in a convincing manner for the diversity of Africa's indigenous systems of thought. That Ogotemmeli, without any formal training in the conventional Western sense (indeed he had undergone no "modern" education and spoke no Western language), is able to do this in so compelling a manner so went against the grain of previous studies in and of African "thought" that there were published insinuations that these "conversations" were, in fact, fabrications by members of a Griaule research team in search of international fame and fortune.

William Abraham

Two seminal works of Anglophone African origin are W. E. Abraham's *The Mind of Africa* (1963) and John S. Mbiti's *African Religions and Philosophy* (1969). Interestingly, both contain reasonably extensive assessments of the work of Tempels and Jahn, while the opposite is not the case.[3] Abraham is generally scathing in his assessments of Western scholarship regarding Africa. But the simple facts that he is African and was formally trained in academic philosophy had very positive consequences for the viewpoints he advocates about the *philosophical* dimensions to Africa's indigenous cultures. In doing so, he chooses an essentialist interpretation of African culture, in the sense that all of the subcontinent's cultures are said to share certain fundamental beliefs and values. He then chooses to analyze his own Akan culture (located in present-day Ghana) as an exemplar of how those beliefs and values function in a particular context.

Here for the first time one finds extensive discussion of such specifically and distinctively philosophical issues as whether there must be "African philosophers" in the conventional (Western academic) sense in order for there to be "African philosophy" (Abraham 1963: 104); and of the sources one might turn to in Africa's indigenous cultures that would be relevant to epistemology or the theory of knowledge with specific reference, for example, to the form of conceptual analysis undertaken by the British philosopher, Gilbert Ryle; and, as we shall see, of such prescient insights as the following with regard to the African context: "The resort of linguistic philosophers to what we say or do is not, therefore, shortsighted. This is where relativism might affect philosophy" (ibid. 105).

Despite his analytically orthodox philosophical training, overall Abraham might be said to advocate a methodologically pluralistic approach to the study of the philosophical in Africa's indigenous cultures. There is a place for language analysis, but also for the study and interpolation of oral literature, as well as the beliefs and values enshrined in African social institutions (religious, political, legal, etc.). At the same time he insists that African philosophy not become obsessed with the Africa that had been prior to European imperialism and colonialism. If Africa's cultural heritage is to come to terms with the latter-day problems of "modern" nation-states in a globally international community, then African social, political, and economic demands upon that community also have to be enunciated and addressed.

John S. Mbiti

Mbiti, coming, by contrast, from a theological background, sees African philosophy as subordinate to African religion (a thorny issue, as we shall discover). As had Abraham, Mbiti effectively adopts an essentialist rendering of African philosophy, in that it is said to consist of certain beliefs and values all African peoples share in common (Mbiti 1969: 2).[4] This makes his approach to African philosophy much less technical both in character and content, more in line with the popular expression that every culture must have some sort of "philosophy of life" or world-view. This means that the greater proportion of his book is devoted to discussions of conventional African views about God, creation, and the after-life, rather than of technically philosophical problems or topics.

Perhaps it is because of this more ethnographic approach to philosophy, as well as its deceptively straightforward title (*African Religions* [note the plural] *and Philosophy*) that this book became and remains so popular, virtually a best-seller, as well as *the* text in most introductory university courses taught during the 1970s in African thought, religion, or philosophy. Consequently its influence came to far outweigh its merit, at least as a work of *technical* philosophical significance. This eventually was recognized and challenged by a growing number of professional philosophers in Africa.

For example, in a chapter that is addressed to a topic of specifically philosophical importance – the notion of "time" expressed by Africa's indigenous languages[5] – Mbiti makes the remarkable claim that Africans generally have no expression for or conception of the distant (as contrasted with the immediate) future. The apparent evolutionary implications of this claim, that Africans have yet to "develop" such a notion, as well as its clear falsity with regard to any number of African languages, has led to numerous published critiques of this aspect of his work by African philosophers.[6] The salutary benefits to African philosophy that arose from this debate are threefold. First, it has led to extensive discussions of notions of "time" by philosophers in a variety of African cultural contexts. Second, it again focuses attention on the usefulness of African languages as a basis for philosophizing. And, third, it forces African philosophers to come to terms with the overriding issue of whether it truly should be taken for granted that all of Africa's cultures share certain core concepts, values, and beliefs in common.

At this point in time the two disciplines with which African philosophy inevitably had to come to terms, in order to establish itself as an independent subject of substance, were religious studies and social anthropology. In important as well as strategic respects, the interests and claims of these two fields undermine and even contradict the notion of an "African philosophy" arising from the subcontinent's indigenous cultures. Take, for example, the thesis that Africa's indigenous cultures are essentially traditional in character. By this is meant that virtually every major element of African society and culture was inherited from a distant past, is preserved relatively unchanged in the present, and will be passed on as normative to the future. This is interpreted to mean that if Africans are asked to explain *why* they hold a certain belief or practice a certain form of behavior, their response will essentially be an appeal to tradition ("because this is what we inherited from the forefathers"). All of this fits in very nicely with the idea of a people who, when persuaded or compelled, explain their culture primarily on the basis of a kind of trust or faith in the value of inherited traditions. Consequently, for years the departments in many African universities entrusted with teaching African students about African *traditional* thought were departments of religious studies.

Anglophone (essentially British) social anthropology in Africa began by concentrating primarily on appropriately social elements such as kinship and social institutions. But when such things as beliefs and values became objects of interest in their own right, the approach that predominated was once again that of *symbolism* and *ritual*. Africans do not so much articulate their beliefs as "live" them. As preliterate peoples who are relatively inarticulate when it comes to reflecting on (much less criticizing) *why* they do *what* they do, observing their behavior (the old "fly on the wall" metaphor) and then inferring its rationale are said to be the most reliable methodological keys to an anthropologically correct understanding of the "reasons" *why* they do *what* they do.

As such, social anthropology and religious studies are at one in claiming that Africa's cultures are essentially traditional (often with a capital "T") in character. And that, when it comes to characterizing the African intellect, mentality, or modes of thought, the most appropriate terms are "precritical," "prereflective," "protorational," "prescientific," "emotive," "expressive," "poetic," etc. Of course all of this did not do much for the early proponents of African philosophy. Indeed, since the discipline was defined by the Western canon as pre-eminently reflective, critical, and rational (as contrasted with "emotive," etc.), African modes of thought seemed diametrically opposed to those enunciated by philosophy as an intellectual exercise.

Robin Horton

In 1967 Robin Horton's two-part essay, "African Traditional Thought and Western Science," appeared in the interdisciplinary journal *Africa*. With formal training in philosophy, science, and social anthropology, Horton, with this controversial theoretical comparison and critique of elements of African and Western systems of thought, provided a catalyst that, for a number of philosophers in the African context, led to a more deliberate development of Anglophone African philosophy as an independent academic discipline.

Because of the vigorous critical responses it evoked from African philosophers, some may not fully appreciate the fact that Horton's position vis-à-vis African systems of thought is equally controversial within British anthropological circles. For Horton rejects the claim that the African mentality is most fundamentally symbolic and/or ritualistic in character. Regarding himself as a descendant of the "Intellectualist" anthropological tradition as epitomized by E. E. Evans-Pritchard and Daryll Forde, Horton argues that indigenous African religions, for example, are better approached as genuinely *theoretical* systems, whose purpose is to provide members of the relevant cultures with models of explanation, prediction, and control that will allow them to link events in the world of everyday life with causal forces that either transcend or underlie that world. It is this fundamental claim or insight that entitles him to compare them as explanatory vehicles with the theories formulated and proposed by (Western) science.

If Horton had stopped there, his comparative analysis probably would have received general acclaim within African academia. However, in the second part of his essay he proceeds to identify a number of logically or empirically erroneous types of reasoning, which he also claims are characteristic of African systems of thought. These seemed so to discredit the integrity of African thought as intellectual statements that many African scholars (philosophers included, of course) have responded by criticizing portions of Horton's essay as both methodologically flawed and empirically false.

To be fair to Horton, it is important to stress that the basis for his comparisons between African and Western systems of thought is meant to be at the level of what he describes as those comparatively abstract elements or forces that are said to be responsible for what happens at the level of the everyday life. One might illustrate with, on the one hand, gravity as being responsible for an object's falling and, on the other, a person's destiny as being responsible for a specific incident during their lifetime. Because Africans are said to have yet to develop a notion of objective truth, of truth as independent of any special interests or values, "truth" in their cultures is said to be fundamentally linked with whatever happens to be the local world-view (or religion).

Africans therefore are said to be only marginally capable of imagining or experimenting with alternatives to that world-view – precisely the kind of theoretical alternatives that would promote the development of a notion of objective truth. Hence they are said to be less able to reflect upon and distance themselves from their theoretical or religious beliefs as possibly true or possibly false, or to imagine what it might mean to envision, much less to embrace, alternative beliefs, and therefore to identify the nature of the logical and empirical criteria and testing that would need to be employed to facilitate serious consideration of such alternatives (Horton 1967: 155–67).

Philosophical Analysis I: Rationality as Culturally Universal

The debate about the nature of the African intellect marked a kind of watershed in the history of Anglophone African philosophy. For it incited the scholarly momentum, the motivation that led to a coalescing of philosophical discussions, debates, and endeavors in Africa that would result in an autochthonous, independently minded, analytic tradition. Many philosophers in the African context felt that religious studies and anthropology were exceeding their disciplinary limits if and when they claimed the right to define "rationality" in the African cultural context. "Rationality," as both concept and capacity, constitutes part of the core of philosophy as a discipline, and it was certainly not the case that scholars in these other two disciplines were dependably philosophically literate. In a sense, then, African philosophers were reclaiming their own territory when, by both deed and word, they reasserted the prerogative of their discipline to define the "rational" in any culture.

The most frequently footnoted critique of Horton's essay by an African philosopher is Kwasi Wiredu's "How Not to Compare African Traditional Thought with Western Thought" (1976). In it, Wiredu implies, most importantly, that Horton's basis for comparison between Africa and the West is problematic. For example, one fundamental issue on which he challenges Horton is the legitimacy of comparing (African) religion with (Western) science, particularly in terms of their respective *objectivity* – the importance attached to criticism, verification, falsification, and the revision of theories designed to explain, predict, or control human experience. Wiredu and others argue that a more realistic basis for comparison would be to contrast the role(s) and evidential and argumentative bases for *religion* between the two cultures.[7]

Wiredu continues by pointing out that science constitutes a very specialized enterprise. Its methods and theories are not things with which the ordinary man in the street is conversant. Yet the majority of African beliefs (which Horton has to reclassify as "theories" in order to justify the basis for his comparison) that Horton chooses to compare with scientific theories are things with which the ordinary African is conversant. And it is unrealistic to expect such commonplace beliefs to be the product of or subject to the rigors of scientific testing and verification. If anything, the species of African beliefs Horton discusses are of a universal ethnographic order that, Wiredu suggests, is better regarded as "folk" philosophy. These are the sorts of things that anthropologists refer to as the customs and mores of a society. Western culture certainly has its own customs and mores, and these would provide a more suitable basis for a comparison of this type. As generalized, this remains the single most important methodological legacy of Wiredu's contention that a pre-requisite for judicious comparison(s) between African and Western cultures is that the materials selected share sufficient attributes in common to constitute a legitimate basis for comparison.

In addition to this methodological critique, Wiredu (1995a) has, more recently, challenged Horton's contention that African world-views, generally, employ personal rather than impersonal models of causal explanation because of the greater senses of order and security supposedly attributed to the human community by comparison with the wilderness synonymous with nature or the "bush." He does so on the basis of a cosmological verse from Akan oral literature in which the Creator is said to have created the following in sequence: (1) Order; (2) Knowledge; (3) Death, and so forth. The point being that the Order created was not limited to the domain of the human community but to all aspects of creation – animate and inanimate – and that this Order includes a fundamental causal determinism.

Another critique of Horton's position that seems to have had lasting consequences is my own "Robin Horton on Critical Philosophy and Traditional Thought" (1977). In this essay, I argue that Horton's assessment of African systems of thought as "closed," as resistant to change or revision on the basis of critical or reflective thought, is exaggerated. I provide first-hand evidence of individuals within Yoruba society who do seem to regard fundamental beliefs with a degree of reflective objectivity.[8]

As previously remarked, there are other published articles that contributed to the debate concerning the nature of African traditional thought.[9] But what becomes of importance for the independent development of *analytic* philosophy in the African context is that African philosophers now bring the techniques of that approach to bear in a more systematic and comprehensive manner on a subject-matter that had heretofore primarily been the domain of religious studies and/or social anthropology. The late Peter Bodunrin,[10] a Nigerian philosopher, is thought of by some as having been hostile to the possibility that African philosophy could be based upon the beliefs and values of Africa's indigenous cultures. This is said to be because he contends that philosophy, as a scholarly enterprise, is quintessentially critical, argumentative, and reflective in character. The implicit and unresolved issue that demands resolution here, again, is what, in fact, is the true "nature" of the indigenous African intellect.

It is not clear from his published writings that Bodunrin ever answers this question to his own complete satisfaction.[11] What is clear is his consistent demand that philosophy of any stripe or color be distinctively reflective and critical in order to be worthy of the name. But this insistence does not necessarily exclude Africa's indigenous cultural heritage. Where that heritage contains critical and reflective elements, these could be directly incorporated into the philosophical mainstream. Where it does not, African philosophy still has an important role to play insofar as such elements can be (and should be) subject to critical analysis and reflective evaluation of the evidence and reasoning underlying their development and application. If and when these two forms of philosophical endeavor can be combined, Bodunrin would have agreed that there can be a basis for a philosophy that is at the same time reflective and critical in cross-cultural terms, and of distinctively African (cultural) orientation.

105

Kwasi Wiredu

Coming to terms with the Ghanaian philosopher Kwasi Wiredu's corpus of work is a formidable task. His publications extend over most of the philosophical spectrum – epistemology, ethics, logic, metaphysics, social and political philosophy – and are interrelated in a subtle but systematic manner. Here, I shall discuss and assess only three of the important themes to which Wiredu addresses himself: (1) the proper relationship between academic or professional philosophy and Africa's indigenous cultural heritage; (2) the problem of truth; (3) the problem of cultural universals. Reference has already been made to Wiredu's critical response to Robin Horton. But in an even earlier article, published in the Nigerian journal *Second Order*,[12] Wiredu (1972) outlines a number of themes that he has continued to develop over the years with regard to the philosophical "prepossession(s)," as he likes to put it, of indigenous African cultures. It is in this article that, to my knowledge, he first discusses the notion of "folk" philosophy.

In regard to folk philosophy Wiredu suggests that we take a closer (philosophical) look at the different kinds of belief that Africans actually do have, as well as the languages with which they are expressed. Here Wiredu is out to knock down the fences that have been erected to intellectually segregate the African mentality as somehow idiosyncratic – as "protorational," "precritical," etc. For, as we shall see, he has always been fundamentally committed to the notion that all of humanity shares certain basic rational attributes and that the exploration of the consequences of these attributes for human understanding should be assigned the highest priority for those committed (as Wiredu certainly is) to a vision of philosophy that truly crosses cultures. Hence the importance of his underlying reasons for classifying a host of relatively unsystematized beliefs in all human cultures as elements of "folk" philosophy.

Then what of Wiredu's position concerning "theoretical," "technical," or "academic" philosophy in the African cultural context? This is where his work with regard to the role of Africa's indigenous languages in African philosophy becomes of crucial importance. Africans cannot undo the past and erase the cultural consequences of European colonialism. But they certainly can come to terms with them. First, they need to remind themselves of the very limited number of Europeans who became truly fluent in an African language, and the profound consequences that this European ignorance, which also affected Western scholarship about Africa, had for communication with and hence comprehension and appreciation of the African intellect. Secondly, they need to recognize the intrinsic instrumental value of *some* of the more technical varieties of information and methods of reflection, such as scientific method, that the colonial experience has put at their disposal. Thirdly, such relatively culturally neutral and instrumentally useful elements can be adapted by Africans and used to develop their own interests.

There have always been two dimensions to Wiredu's philosophical scholarship. He addresses some purely technical philosophical problems in the treatment of which factors such as national affiliation and cultural background are, to all intents and purposes, irrelevant or, at most, happenstance.[13] In other instances he explores the philosophical "prepossessions" of select concepts or aspects of the language and culture of the Akans that happen to constitute his African heritage. In some cases, as with his ruminations about truth, the two dimensions are combined and inter-related, but always on a common basis of analytical rigor.

With reference to the first dimension, Wiredu has, for example, tried to develop a cogent, technical, philosophical theory of truth. He argues that whatever is called the "truth" is always *someone's* truth. For a piece of information to be awarded the appellation "true," it must be discovered by, known by, and defended by human beings somewhere, sometime. Furthermore, as past experience has clearly demonstrated, what human beings defend as "true" can prove to be false from an alternative point of view. Therefore, whatever is called "truth" is more starkly described as *opinion*.

Interpreting "truth" as opinion means that Wiredu rejects what, in technical, philosophical circles, is referred to as the "objectivist theory" of truth.[14] This is a theory that posits "truth" as an independent property of timeless, eternal information located in some transcendent realm that we humans must ceaselessly endeavor to reach if we are to know it (*the* truth). The truth about virtually everything is more or less "there" and always has been "there," waiting for us to discover it, or, better, decipher it. Furthermore, Wiredu suggests that such an objectivist theory of truth implies that truth is categorially distinct from opinion. But this, in effect, would make truth "as a matter of logical principle, unknowable," because every *claim* to truth would then be reduced to only an opinion advanced from a particular point of view and therefore "categorially distinct from truth" (1980: 115).

Rather than deriving from some transcendent reality, truth, in fact, arises from human endeavor and effort – from perception and rational inquiry. "We must recognise the *cognitive* element of point of view as intrinsic to the concept of truth" (ibid. 115; my italics). That truth arises from human agency does not mean knowledge will degenerate into the merely subjective or relative. "What I mean by opinion is a firm rather than an uncertain thought. I mean what is called a considered opinion" (ibid. 115–16).[15] This notion of the "considered opinion" is of fundamental importance to Wiredu's overall theory of truth. In other contexts he links it to the notion of "warrant" arising from John Dewey's pragmatism (ibid. 216–32; 1993; 1995b; 1996: chs. 2–4), although he insists it is not identical: "Something is warranted ['well-considered'] not because it is true, but true because it is warranted; better, it is true if and only if it is warranted."[16] Truth as opinion must, of course, always be entertained from some point of view. But that opinion becomes considered or warranted when it arises in a genuinely intersubjective context where it is grounded upon shared canons of rational inquiry. In his view, such intersubjectivity becomes a sine qua non to truth and is responsible for his enduring opposition to both subjectivity and relativism.

In his discussions of Akan discourse relating to the notion of truth, Wiredu is concerned to elucidate the phrase that he renders into English as something's being "so" (*Nea ete saa*; 1996: ch. 8):

> To say that something is true, the Akan simply say that it is so, and truth is rendered as what is so.[17] No undue sophistication is required to understand that although

the Akan do not have a single word for truth, they do have the concept of truth. (1985: 46)

He then goes on to suggest that the notion of something's being so is the same as something's being a fact. But if this means that in Akan truth amounts to correspondence with fact, this is nothing more than a restatement of elementary correspondence theory (of truth) and, as such, less than enlightening.

In order to be more clear about the philosophical prepossessions of Akan discourse about the truth, more information about ordinary usage would be required. And in the end the most frustrating limitation to Wiredu's (Twi, the more specific name for the language of the Asante) analyses is that he does not aim to offer a complete explanation of what is meant by saying (in Akan) that something is "so."[18] What the "it" that is "so" might correspond to or cohere with are left as speculative possibilities. This is not a criticism of his analyses, by the way. It is, rather, a consequence of the fact that there are some questions that ordinary discourse and usage do not answer – some issues they do not resolve – because there is no need for human beings to be so technically specific about such matters at the level of ordinary, everyday discourse. However, in the other dimension to Wiredu's philosophical scholarship – that devoted to purely technical philosophical problems – he has gone on to explore in further detail what might be required for something to be so. This occurs in the course of a critical evaluation of the three standard theories of truth (correspondence, coherence, and pragmatic), and the suggestion that being so may, broadly speaking, again be interpreted as being warrantably assertible (1980: ch. 10, sec. III; 1983).[19]

We have seen how Wiredu levels the intellectual, cross-cultural playing field with regard to "folk philosophy," so that it becomes a universal human attribute. An analogous process of leveling may now be seen to be taking place with regard to every culture's standing as contributor to technical, philosophical debate. Truth, as a construct of the considered opinions of human beings in *any* culture, when coupled with (as we shall soon see) a concern to demonstrate that certain rational principles are universal to *all* cultures, effectively makes reasoned debate a prerogative of every culture (Africa's included, of course) in the world.

It is perhaps because of his coining of the term "folk philosophy" to characterize unreasoned African (and Western) beliefs that Wiredu is sometimes misinterpreted as overtly hostile to Africa's "traditional" cultural heritage.[20] In fact, his position has always been that the elements of that heritage must be continuously re-evaluated with a view to gauging their negative, positive, or neutral consequences when retained as priorities of contemporary African societies. For example, several "traditional" values and practices that he recommends be carried over so as to be made of fundamental importance to the contemporary African polity are the emphases "traditionally" placed upon *consensus* and *reconciliation* (note the analogies between these terms and "considered opinion" and "warrantably assertible") as a basis for governing and government. This is an idea Wiredu first introduces in 1977,[21] but has more recently developed in detail in two essays specifically devoted to the issue of democracy in Africa (1996: chs. 13 and 14).

Wiredu is leery of the conventional (Western) multiparty system and the form of majority rule it entails. In the African context it seems to favor political parties structured and divided along ethnic lines, thereby heightening social tensions. And it can therefore lead to elected governments that fail to represent a substantial portion of the population, thereby further exacerbating social tensions. Wiredu argues that affirming and reformulating the African tradition of government on the basis of consensus, negotiation, and reconciliation (in effect, a non-party form of democracy) would better foster an impression of the entire electorate's participation in the institutions of government, and this would contain the divisiveness that has too often become a characteristic of politics in the modern African nation-state.

Wiredu has always been concerned with what he has come to describe as "the possibility of universal canons of thought and action" (ibid. 1). In a series of articles he argues that certain logical and ethical concerns are necessarily common to all human cultures simply by virtue of the fact that they are human.[22] Exemplary logical universals to which he makes specific reference are the principles of non-contradiction ("that a proposition cannot be true and false at the same time") and induction (described as "the capacity to learn from experience" (ibid. 27)). As for the ethical, the priority assigned to "the harmonization of the interests of the individual with the interests of society" (ibid. 84), when formulated as a principle, also becomes a candidate for cultural universality.

Perhaps some commentators will see these more recent steps in his philosophical development as inevitable, given his long-term, determined commitment to a universal rationalism, a commitment which consistently persuades him to reject relativism as a productive philosophical alternative. But it is also possible to see his commitment to a (universal) rationalism as motivated by an even more fundamental commitment to a form of humanism. This is a humanism that was evident in even his earliest publications. It rejects the possibility that some cultures may be of intrinsically greater merit than others because the people who founded them are, as human beings, somehow intrinsically better intellectually endowed than other human beings. It is with this in mind that Wiredu also challenges and rejects moves by some sections of Western culture to hegemonize its customs and mores (elements of its "folk" philosophy) as things that should be adopted by all the cultures of the world on pain of eternal damnation. For Wiredu, this is a superficial, false, and unphilosophical form of cultural universalization, nothing more than a manifestation of (Western) cultural ethnocentrism.[23]

To resume my characterization of Wiredu's overall strategy, in a subtle but perfectly deliberate fashion one of his aims from the beginning is to provide empirical evidence (predominantly linguistic) and a reasoned basis (universal rationalism) for Africa's liberation from pejorative cultural stereotypes. Cultures can and do differ from one another, but on a more fundamental level, as expressions of a common humanity, they manifest and share important common principles such as the above. It is on this basis that Wiredu can argue that no cultures merit second-rate status as somehow intrinsically rationally deficient or defective. It is on this basis that he can argue that, despite our apparent (and real) differences, it is this common humanity with all it may entail which, once recognized and acknowledged (ignorance is our greatest common enemy), cannot fail to unite and thereby benefit all humankind.

Standard expositions of the analytic approach to philosophy are grounded upon the thesis that philosophical questions are primarily questions of language. The main tasks of the philosopher therefore become *clarification* ("analysis" in the narrowest sense) of the meanings of the words/language with which our beliefs are expressed, and *justification* – in the sense of identifying and assessing the arguments and evidence with which those beliefs are justified. As such, orthodox analytic philosophy does not create or invent the beliefs it targets. They are received as pre-existent elements of whatever language culture happens to be its target of interest. This means that it is often relatively passive with regard to advancing alternative theses (beliefs) that might prove to be of greater truth value.

But this passive (or non-reformist) attitude toward analysis is something with which Wiredu fundamentally disagrees. He believes change is something philosophers should encourage, and that he exemplifies in his own work via the pragmatic perspective that he adapts from John Dewey. For, as we have seen from the above summary, he conceives of philosophy as a dynamic endeavor whose aim is to encourage the introduction of novel, warrantedly assertible truths about the origins of our beliefs, as well as to re-evaluate, revise, or discard "old" ones, and to introduce new ideas that might possibly achieve the status of truth. As any number of quotations from Wiredu's work indicate, the better humankind understands the world in which it finds itself (human nature included, of course), the more likely it becomes that it can procure satisfaction from it.[24] This dynamic approach to philosophizing is further demonstrated by his essays that speculate on the genetic impetus to human knowledge.[25]

Kwame Gyekye

Kwame Gyekye[26] is another Ghanaian philosopher whose publications cover a broad and important range of topics. *An Essay on African Philosophical Thought: The Akan Conceptual Scheme* (1995) uses an analytical approach that is meant to set a precedent for how material of philosophical substance can be identified in and derived from Africa's indigenous cultures. Although Gyekye's claims about the philosophical dimension to Africa's cultures may appear rhetorically more forceful and direct (he does not use the "prepossession" word, for example), the differences between his approach and that of Kwasi Wiredu to their culture seem more those of emphasis than of substance.[27]

Gyekye's presentation makes a clear distinction between the methodology he embraces and the results of that methodology when applied to elements of Akan culture. That distinction will be replicated by my interpretative synopsis. The forthright phrasing of the opening statement of *An Essay*, meant to summarize its aims, is characteristic:

> [1] to stress the fact of the universal character of the intellectual activity called philosophy – of the propensity of some individuals in all human cultures to reflect deeply and critically about fundamental questions of human experience; [2] to point out that philosophy is essentially a cultural phenomenon; [3] to argue the legitimacy or appropriateness of the idea of African philosophy and attempt a definition of (modern)

African philosophy; [4] and to demonstrate that there were sages or thinkers in Africa's cultural past who gave reflective attention to matters of human existence at the fundamental level, and, as part of the demonstration, to critically explore the philosophical ideas of the Akan traditional thinkers (of Ghana).

Gyekye's approach to Akan philosophy is significantly conceptual. He identifies terminology in Akan (Twi) discourse that is of philosophical significance. But he also emphasizes the intellectual importance of proverbs in that culture, as analogous to philosophical "nuggets" that contain highly condensed, judicious insights and wisdom, characteristic of an oral culture that could not have recourse to extensive written tracts.[28] At the same time he rejects, categorically, a purely technically philosophical, linguistic, or conceptualist approach to these materials (ibid. 64–5). This is because their function, most importantly, is not merely to express or to record wisdom – it is also to serve as *practical* guides to life and human experience.

It is to research their practical consequences[29] in Akan culture that Gyekye has undertaken what he unabashedly refers to as "fieldwork" – seeking out "sages" in traditional Ghanaian society who can explain this aspect of the concepts and proverbs he finds of interest (in effect, the relationship between theory and practice). But rather than remain with sets of random concepts and proverbs and the isolated, individuated meanings or insights they express, Gyekye sets out to weave them together (ibid. 16) so that they can then be seen to express more systematic philosophical viewpoints on such topics as God, causality, free will, and ethics or morality.

He further maintains that this philosophical substratum to Akan proverbs will turn out in many cases to replicate the proverbial wisdom of other African cultures. This is a thesis he explores in greater detail in a later book, *African Cultural Values* (1996).[30] For example, in a chapter on moral values he favorably compares specific humanistic values expressed by the Akan with similar virtues affirmed by the Yoruba ethnic group of Nigeria in West Africa and the Swahili language and culture of East Africa. Yet at the same time he wants to maintain that it would be a serious error to infer from this that there is such a thing as a *unique* – in the sense that it contains ideas not found anywhere else in the world – African (traditional) philosophy shared by all the subcontinent's peoples (1995: xvi), any more than there is a *unique* Akan cultural philosophy. What one does find in every culture in the world are certain common philosophical concerns and questions[31] to which different *answers* (destiny vs. free will) in different *formats* (proverbs vs. deductive arguments) have been proposed. The particular *combination* or *interrelation* of formats and answers to these concerns or questions found in a particular culture may somehow be distinctive, but this is of a very different order from their being literally *unique to* that culture.

As well as cultural, philosophy is also a historical enterprise. By this, Gyekye means that the issues which concerned African philosophers in precolonial or "traditional" times may not be the same as those that concern African philosophers in modern or contemporary times (ibid. xi–xii). But this does not imply that there should be no connection between the two, either. As to what exactly that connection should be, he is prepared to be flexible. From the standpoint of the *history* of philosophy in Africa, all viewpoints relevant to "traditional" philosophy would become important. But since the philosophical priorities and concerns of every society change over time, this would mean that, from the standpoint of modern or contemporary African philosophy, some "traditional" themes may prove of less interest or relevance than others.[32]

When it comes to specific examples of Akan philosophical thought as derived from that culture's concepts and proverbs, obviously there is a wide range of topics from which to choose. The one that will be selected here as exemplary of Gyekye's approach is the ultimate basis for morality in Akan "traditional" culture, and the consequences of this for the relationship between individuals and their community. A misleading stereotype of "traditional" Africa, as we have already seen in the case of Mbiti, is that every important element of such cultures, morality included, is inextricably bound up with religion. For example, the prominent role assigned by some Africanists to a notion like "taboo"[33] means that violating such injunctions leads to disastrous consequences that emanate from the level of the divine or spiritual for those concerned. For Gyekye, this is too simplistic, and he emphatically rejects so prominent a role for divine intervention by saying: "I reject the view that religion constitutes the basis of Akan morality" (ibid. 131). Gyekye's more fundamental point is that the *values* that define moral or immoral conduct or practice in Akan culture are *not*, ultimately, of supernatural or divine origin.[34] What he proposes, as an alternative philosophical and more factually correct way of interpreting morality in Akan culture, is treating it as a form of *humanism* ("what constitutes the good is determined not by spiritual beings but by human beings" (ibid. 133)). "In Akan moral thought the sole criterion of goodness is the welfare or well-being of the community" (ibid. 132). This is not to say that the Akan believe God and religion have absolutely nothing to do with the moral, either. For certain events that take place *may* be linked to supernatural approval or disapproval of an individual's or group's conduct (1996: 17–18). But the individual and communal *practical consequences* of different kinds of behavior have more to do with why certain moral values are honored and observed by members of that culture (ibid. 57).

Following upon the philosophical methodology he has embraced, Gyekye then proceeds to give a list of terms/concepts prominently associated with being moral in Akan culture whose importance, as elaborated by the sages and as systematized by himself, is illustrative of this humanism: "kindness (generosity: *ayamyie*), faithfulness (honesty, truthfulness: *ahohoye, adoe*), that which brings peace, happiness, dignity, and respect (*nea ede asomdwee, ahomeka, anuonyam ne obuo ba*)" (1995: 132). And also examples of proverbs that imply a similarly humanistic provenance: (1) "When a person descends from heaven, he [or she] descends into a human society" (1996: 36); (2) "A man must depend for his well-being on his fellow man" (ibid. 45); (3) "The person who helps you carry your load does not develop a hump" (ibid. 49); (4) " 'Given a choice between disgrace and death, one had better choose death' (*aniwu ne owu, na efanim owu*)" (1995: 139).

As for the optimal relationship between individuals and their community,[35] the Akan ideal is that both should benefit on a reciprocal, still essentially humanistic, basis. "The good is identical with the welfare of the society, which is expected to include the welfare of the individual" (ibid. 132). Gyekye acknowledges that in some circumstances individuals will be torn between favoring their own (self-) interests and those of the community (ibid. 154–62). But he also points out that the possibility of such conflicts of interest is acknowledged and to a certain degree accommodated by Akan morality, since it retains an element of flexibility on this very issue. "Akan social thought attempts to establish a delicate balance between the concepts of communality and individuality. Whether it succeeds in doing so in practice is of course another question" (ibid. 161).

In *Tradition and Modernity: Philosophical Reflections on the African Experience* (1997), Gyekye presents thoughtful and comprehensive reflections on how one might reconcile some of the more admirable qualities of "traditional" Africa with the policies, priorities, and problems of the "modern" nation-states that now con-figure the subcontinent. Much of the book is devoted to topics that are convention-ally regarded as social and political philosophy, but, as Gyekye explains in the Preface, this is because today they constitute some of the most important pro-blems with which contemporary African philosophers need to come to terms (1997: ix–xi).

Several themes from Gyekye's earlier work carry over and serve as basic struc-tural elements. He frequently refers to the "thought and practice of the Akan soci-ety of Ghana" as a basis for African cultural extrapolation (ibid. x). Furthermore, to deal with such compelling contemporary African problems as integrating the "trad-itional" with the "modern" in the nation-state, or how to overcome ethnic rivalries, or how to achieve political stability, or how to eliminate political corruption and combat increasing public immorality, he falls back upon humanism and a humanis-tic ethic as one of the most powerful remedies that the African philosopher can proffer. But with this generalization I do not mean to oversimplify his approach to these problems, for Gyekye offers important new insights into the meanings of ethnicity, of "traditional" (and of "modernity"), as well as of morality.

For example, he criticizes the notion of ethnicity ("tribalism") in Africa as a dangerous invention and tool of political ideologues and argues that it must be supplanted by notions of group identity comparable to those found in contemporary multicultural societies. As for the "traditional" and the "modern," he argues that the time has passed when these words can be used to type whole societies or cultures. Traditions, or conventions inherited from the past, also play a role in so-called "modern" societies. And the most satisfactory basis on which they can be justified, always, is that they serve a useful, positive purpose. His vision of "modern" African society, therefore, becomes one which incorporates and inter-relates the best elements of other cultures in the world[36] with those elements of Africa's cultural heritage that deserve to be similarly valued.[37] The transcendent (and universal) criterion on the basis of which the positive contribution of any of these elements can be rated is again humanistic: "bringing about the kinds of progressive changes in the entire aspects of human culture necessary for the en-hancement and fulfillment of human life" (ibid. 280).

It is tempting to speculate on possible intellectual interchanges and influences that might have taken place among these three Ghanaian philosophers (Abraham, Wiredu, and Gyekye). Certainly, there is at least one important common theme to their work – first expressed by Abraham and later not only taken up but developed in a hybrid manner by Wiredu and Gyekye. Wiredu summarizes it as follows:

> It comes out clearly, for example, in Professor Abraham's *The Mind of Africa* . . . that in theoretical sweep and practical bearing traditional African philosophies concede nothing to the world views of European philosophy. Why, then, should the African philosophy student not be steeped in his own heritage of philosophy before looking elsewhere. (1980: 28)

That this would involve demonstrating the presence and importance of the rational in traditional African thought by philosophers in Africa is a point that has already been stressed. That the forms in which it was expressed (proverbs, for example) might be different, even distinctive, also seems to have been convincingly established.

Segun Gbadegesin

I selected "Philosophical Analysis" as the subtitle for this section of my text because it seemed a more flexible heading than, for example, the more rigidly circumscribed "Analytic Philosophy." And that element of flexibility suits the topical and methodological priorities of the last philosopher whose work will be considered in some detail in the present section, Segun Gbadegesin.[38] Gbadegesin's *African Philosophy: Traditional Yoruba Philosophy and Contemporary African Realities* (1991) employs conceptual analysis and the critical evaluation of the argumentation and evidence underlying so-called "traditional" beliefs and practices as fundamental methodological techniques (1991: 4). He argues that there always has been an individualistic, reflective, and critical dimension to the formation and reformation of such beliefs and practices in African cultures (ibid. 5). And as for the "character" of African rationality, in a discussion relating to the work of Robin Horton he states, without qualification, that: "If we grant such thought systems are 'eminently logical', what else is required to demonstrate their philosophical nature?" (ibid. 18). But this is also an intensively "hands-on" text (as the expression goes), in that its author is most deeply concerned to demonstrate that philosophy can be of *practical* value for solving some of Africa's current social, cultural, economic, and political problems.[39]

But, Gbadegesin argues, Africans cannot be in a strategic position to solve current problems and plan for a better future unless they are fully informed about their cultural past, about where they're coming "from" (ibid. 216). With this in mind, the first half of his text is devoted to clarifying select beliefs and practices fundamental to his native Yoruba culture. Although he explicitly refuses to promote "traditional" Yoruba beliefs, customs, and values as if providing a paradigm or model for all of Africa's cultures, at the same time he admits to a conviction that there are common cultural priorities of "African-ness" that need to be more clearly identified, fundamental amongst which is the importance attached to the *common* good or communal welfare (ibid. 104). For Gbadegesin too will conclude that the moral values that distinguish "traditional" Yoruba and, by implication, African culture

114

determine a form of humanism: cooperation, a healthy sense of community, generosity, and respect for others.

He therefore begins by exploring a carefully chosen set of Yoruba "traditional" beliefs and values relating to: (1) the nature of personhood (the physical and spiritual components of human being, the powers it has at its disposal, and the forces to which it may be subjected while in the world); (2) the nature of the dialectic between individual and communal interests and priorities, and how they may be reconciled so as to benefit the two (here Gbadegesin defends a secularist view of Yoruba moral values or virtues, very much along the lines of Gyekye's "consequentialism"); (3) how certain beliefs fundamental to Yoruba traditional religion differ fundamentally from both Christianity and Islam, but appear to be more compatible in practice as well as theory with the humanitarian values he finds distinctive of Yoruba culture; (4) how the comparatively absolute Western dichotomy between the natural and supernatural does not fit the Yoruba world-view, and how various beliefs and practices relating to the supernatural that might appear exotic or bizarre to Westerners become eminently reasonable when sited within that world-view.

Having outlined these basic elements of Yoruba culture, Gbadegesin then proceeds to identify (in certain instances to denounce), and more importantly to propose solutions to, a cluster of contemporary social and cultural problems that are literally bedeviling Yoruba society today. It would be too simplistic to say that he sees these problems as consequences of modernity. For "modernity" itself is an ambiguous term that must combine, at least in the African context, European (economic and cultural) imperialism, colonialism, and the varieties of neocolonialism that are local manifestations of the global competition between capitalism and socialism (in all of their various forms as well, needless to say).

It is in the second half of his text, where he addresses these problems, that Gbadegesin sets out to demonstrate that the philosopher too can contribute to their solution. He provides numerous examples of how Christianity and Islam have become culturally irrelevant and socially corrupt, and recommends that Yoruba traditional religion be reaffirmed as most compatible with that culture's positive moral priorities. He denounces the negative connotations that have become associated with the idea of doing "work," especially manual labor (ibid. 215), and suggests measures and programs that need to be supported by government if Africa's notoriously low productivity is to be raised. He insists that the focus upon that ubiquitous term "development" in Africa must be upon economic development (ibid. 256), but that it can only be assured if there is political stability. Finally, if there must be a choice between capitalism and socialism, the latter in its democratic forms appears to be more compatible with the humanitarian values definitive of Africa's "communitarian" societies.

The combined impact of these philosophers, who defend the thesis of rationalism as a cultural universal, upon African philosophy has been profound. And their defense of this thesis is anything but simplistic, for they all also allow for distinctive African cultural heritages and orientations as long as they are grounded or founded upon patterns of reasoning and cognitive systems that share essential and defining characteristics in common with what it means to be "rational" in other human

115

societies, in particular with the so-called paradigm of the "rational" as propounded by the Western philosophical "establishment."

However, there is another school of thought on this subject, among philosophers in and of Africa, that queries whether African cognitive systems can be done analytic justice if they are typed as essentially universal, as somehow the "same" as their Western equivalent(s). This point of view is that perhaps African conceptual and cognitive systems may, in certain distinctive respects, deserve to be regarded as genuinely alternative pathways to the "truth." In academic philosophy the differences between these two points of view relate most directly to the old and ongoing debate between *universalism* and *relativism*.

Philosophical Analysis II: Rationality as Culturally Relative

A number of philosophers in and of Africa contend that there are elements to African cognition that are sufficiently unique or distinctive to somehow set it apart. Their major complaint against the so-called "universalists" is that, by placing undue emphasis upon the supposedly common or universal elements to African cognition, these uncommon features are underrated and fail to receive the recognition they deserve and the credibility they merit as alternative pathways to understanding.

J. Olubi Sodipo and Barry Hallen

The collaboration between myself and the late J. Olubi Sodipo when we were colleagues at the University of Ife, Nigeria is one such case in point. We set out to adapt the techniques of J. L. Austin's ordinary language philosophy to the African context in our studies of Yoruba discourse and thought. Briefly, this is an approach to philosophy that implores philosophers to avoid excessive armchair theorizing by studying the meanings of key terms in any natural language on the basis of the contexts in which those terms are actually used and thereby defined by ordinary, everyday speakers of that language. The presumption is that if the members of a particular language culture have taken the trouble to articulate, to verbalize differences between, for example, things they may claim to "know" as contrasted with things they may only claim to "believe," there is some point to or reason for their having made this distinction.

The task of the philosopher of ordinary language, therefore, becomes that of identifying the underlying criteria that govern correct application (usage) of these terms. The expectation here is that, on the basis of detailed study of everyday terminology relevant to such philosophical topics as epistemology, ethics, and aesthetics, networks of interrelated meanings (concepts) will emerge that will enable the philosopher to draw more generalized conclusions about the intellectual priorities of the language (and people) concerned and harvest some valuable philosophical insights from them.

In our conjointly published works Sodipo and I have concentrated exclusively upon the Yoruba people of southwestern Nigeria. And although some of our more important findings are discussed in detail in a separate chapter of this volume,[40] it is relevant to focus here on the arguments we formulate to defend a form of cognitive relativism. To this end we invoke the work of W. V. O. Quine (1960) with regard to that distinguished philosopher's critique of the notion of (culturally) universal propositions or meanings. For Quine challenges the apparent presupposition that underlying meanings are essentially shared, common, or universal, even if the word (or phrase) used in a particular language culture to express a certain meaning is very different from the word (or phrase) used to express the same meaning in another language culture.

Quine prefers to hypothesize that each human language may be viewed as a unique creation, with innovative meanings and conceptual networks that are compelling evidence of human genius. It may be that, for purposes of intercultural translation (between, for example, Yoruba and English), such unique elements must be downplayed, sacrificed to the need for international communication. But this practical priority is not sufficient to justify philosophers' ignoring the unique, more troublesomely untranslatable elements they may also contain.

For Sodipo and myself, as contrasted with Wiredu, one fundamental point of difference arises over the issue of whether, when the meanings of key epistemological terms in Yoruba discourse are proven to be fundamentally different from their purported English-language equivalents, it makes sense to maintain that members of different language cultures do share sufficient cognitive priorities in common so that they may be said to share the same notion of rationality. For example, on the basis of our studies of everyday Yoruba discourse and its select differences from English-language usage, we suggest that there is compelling evidence to support the contention that propositional attitudes are culturally relative (Hallen and Sodipo 1997: 84).

The term "propositional attitude" is philosophical jargon for a variety of statements in which a specific verb is used to indicate a person's thoughts and/or feelings toward a particular statement (or proposition). The following are examples: "I *know* that x" (where x is any matter-of-fact statement such as "I am late"); "I *believe* that x"; "I *doubt* that x," etc. The point now is that if the *criteria* that a statement must satisfy to *qualify* as "knowledge" in a particular culture are very different from comparable criteria in the language of another culture, does it really make sense to continue to claim that the underlying propositional attitudes (of "knowing," "believing," "doubting," etc.) still share the *same* meanings?

Godwin Sogolo and M. Akin Makinde

Godwin Sogolo, Professor of Philosophy at the University of Ibadan, Nigeria, is another African philosopher of relativistic persuasion, insofar as he argues that there are certain dimensions to African "form(s) of life" that are unique and cannot be adequately or fairly treated or understood using the techniques of a Western philosophy that originated from Western "form(s) of life." In other words, for Sogolo, philosophical methodologies, as well as theories and paradigms, are culturally relative. Africa will therefore only receive accurate and unbiased representation by this discipline when philosophers in and of Africa begin to develop methodologies for the study of their societies that are uniquely suited to the African cultural context(s). Sogolo's most comprehensive statement of this position is to be found in his book, *Foundations of African Philosophy: A Definitive Analysis of Conceptual Issues in African Thought* (1993).

M. Akin Makinde is Professor of Philosophy at the Obafemi Awolowo University (formerly University of Ife), Nigeria. His most comprehensive publication is *African Philosophy, Culture, and Traditional Medicine* (1988a). This text mounts a more forthright and radical claim that African systems of thought, including especially systems of divination, may contain and constitute alternative but legitimate approaches to and methodologies for understanding the nature of reality. Though Makinde also focuses on the Yoruba of southwestern Nigeria, he intends his claims to be more broadly based and to apply, in principle, to all African cultures. Divination, for example, may not be based upon the same methodology as science. But this need not mean that the conclusions it comes to about the nature of reality, and the prescriptions it recommends for coming to terms with that reality, are false or untrue. In a sense, the world awaits the birth of a "mastermind" who will someday be able to interrelate and thereby confirm the truths of these two apparently diverse and sometimes contradictory fields of endeavor in a syncretic manner (Makinde 1988a: ch. 1).

V. Y. Mudimbe

The appearance of V. Y. Mudimbe's *The Invention of Africa: Gnosis, Philosophy, and the Order of Knowledge* (1988) marks a kind of watershed or turning point in the overall development of African philosophy. Mudimbe, sometime Professor of Anthropology, Language(s), and Literature at Duke and Stanford Universities, and originally of Zairean (now Republic of the Congo) origin, would justifiably protest at being typed simply a "philosopher." This is because he also approaches philosophy as an historian of ideas and literature, and therefore writes about it from "outside" its confines more than he does from within.

By adapting select techniques of the French historian of ideas and sciences, Michel Foucault, and combining these with insights into the "nature of culture" (a phrase he might find amusing), Mudimbe achieves, as an African and Africanist scholar immersed first in his native culture, next in the Continental (European) academic tradition, and then in the Anglo-American (avowedly analytic and empirical) academic tradition, a breadth and depth in his writings about these subjects that many readers find remarkable. And when this is further combined with critical elements derived from the deconstructive and postmodern movement(s) – perhaps as most notably exemplified by the work of the philosopher Jacques Derrida and the sociologist Pierre Bourdieu – the power of his carefully crafted critiques of Western intellectual history and the Western intellectual "establishment" is at many points as devastating as it is, in the end, constructive.

For the central theme of *The Invention of Africa* is that whatever field of (Western) scholarship one looks to – whether anthropology, history, literature, or, in particular, philosophy – the portrait of Africa that emerges (no matter how supposedly "scientific") is as much a product of Western cultural priorities and prejudices as it is of anything African. Much of the power of Mudimbe's critically architectonic analyses derives from the fact that he shows how these accounts "of" Africa tell us as much or more about their authors' Western cultural orientations as they do about anything African.[41] Another positive point to Mudimbe's exposition is that it devotes as much attention to Francophone African sources as it does to Anglophone.

With specific reference to African philosophy, the result is that it is all reduced to an extension of various Western philosophical traditions – the analytic, the Marxist, the phenomenological, and so forth – into the African context. This does not necessarily mean it is bad philosophy, but it does allow Mudimbe to question whether it should then be regarded as authentically African. Of course, this critique extends to African scholars who have imbibed and who employ these (Western) approaches to knowledge as well. It is culture rather than birthright that determines the identity of an individual's scholarship.

The effects of this challenge upon the African studies establishment generally have been profound. It has led to much soul-searching about the supposed objectivity of the methodologies of the disciplines involved (philosophy included, of course) and of the human beings who employ them. I think this is a process that is best described here and now as "ongoing." In this particular text Mudimbe himself proposes no resolution, other than to suggest that Africa still waits to be discovered, to speak, to be understood.

Anthony Appiah

Kwame Anthony Appiah is the son of the late Ghanaian patriot, lawyer, and intellectual Joe Appiah. He was for many years Professor of Afroamerican Studies and of Philosophy at Harvard University and is now Professor of Philosophy at Princeton University. He would probably not object to being characterized as an analytic philosopher in his own right, but this has not inhibited him from introducing a postmodern dimension into his published works that includes a vigorous defense of a multicultural approach to philosophy. That the Western world has chosen to embrace analytic philosophy is all well and good, but this is no reason for it to deny other cultures in the world an equal right to develop their own ways of doing and expressing their ideas about what philosophy is and should be. Therefore in his published works he repeatedly encourages philosophers in and of Africa to claim, aggressively if need be, a legitimate place for their possibly divergent views in the international academic "marketplace" (1992: 143, 145, 149). This alone should qualify him as a form of relativist.

> Postmodernism can be seen, then, as a new way of understanding the multiplication of distinctions that flows from the need to clear oneself a space; the need that drives the underlying dynamic of cultural modernity. Modernism saw the economization of the world as the triumph of reason; postmodernism rejects that claim, allowing in the realm of theory the same multiplication of distinctions we see in the cultures it seeks to understand. (1992: 145–6)

Appiah's *In My Father's House: African in the Philosophy of Culture* (1992) is one of the few books devoted to the subject of African philosophy that has also attracted a general readership. As was the case with Mudimbe, Appiah is important because of his disciplinary breadth as much as for his disciplinary depth. As well as an astute grounding in technical philosophy, this collection of essays exemplifies a talent for interdisciplinary exegesis involving such diverse fields as literature, art, and science.

As might be expected, this text, which sets out to address a number of different issues and "hot topics" in diverse disciplines, has given rise to considerable controversy. Perhaps the most controversy has been generated by Appiah's discussion of the concept "race" (1992: chs. 1–3). His claim that this is a notion that has been proven false on both scientific (genetics) and cultural grounds, and therefore should be banished from halls of debate and the vocabularies of languages, has provoked both strong protests and wide-ranging intellectual discussion.[42] Since it is culture and not race that should define any people's identity, Appiah is also suspicious of those who claim there is some form of philosophy common to all of Africa's peoples (as he must also therefore be about claims to some common African culture) (ibid. ch. 4). But he insists that for something to qualify as philosophy in the academic sense, it must amount to something more than a mere catalogue, or mapping of beliefs, concepts, and meanings. There must, in addition, be some evidence of efforts to determine whether what is believed and what is meant also is true (ibid. 96–8). And if this is what some commentators have in mind when they refer to "critical" or to "reflective" thought, then so be it.

There is an important underlying qualification to this discussion that demands clarification. By making this assertion, is Appiah closing the philosophical "door" to those African philosophers who would insist that the beliefs, proverbs, and customs of their cultures do amount to a form of philosophy? I think not. He certainly advocates that the door be open to them as well, but once they are inside, he, as an African philosopher in his own right, would side with someone like Kwasi Wiredu in saying that what also is advisable is that these elements of a people's "folk philosophy" then be subjected to critical analysis and evaluation.

It is in another essay concerned with contemporary African philosophy per se that Appiah devotes considerable time and energy to the issue of what may or may not be distinctive about "traditional" African cognition insofar as this element of critical reflection upon beliefs and meanings may be concerned (ibid. ch. 6). Here he very clearly distances himself from those who have sought to characterize the indigenous African intellect as a-critical, non-reflective, and therefore, in Western terms at least, non-rational. On a factual basis he argues that there is substantive evidence of critical thinking on the part of some members of "traditional" societies. On a moral basis he insists that:

> unless all of us understand each other, and understand each other as reasonable, we shall not treat each other with the proper respect. Concentrating on the noncognitive features of traditional religions not only misrepresents them but also leads to an underestimation of the role of reason in the life of traditional cultures. (ibid. 134)

Finally, with an eye to the future, he discusses the seemingly inevitable problem of how Africa's cultures should come to terms with the antagonisms between the religious or spiritual and the scientific that seem to have become part and parcel of "development." This is a problem that Africans will have to work through for themselves, but he sees no reason why the results should mirror what "has occurred among educated people in the industrialized world, in general, and in the United States, in particular" (ibid. 135). For these are cultures in which the so-called "spiritual" values have been severely curtailed by the influence of science and technology, cultures which are therefore sometimes said to have "lost their soul":

> Scientific method may lead to progress in our understanding of the world, but you do not have to be a Thoreauvian to wonder if it has led only to progress in the pursuit of all our human purposes. In this area we [Africans] can learn together with other cultures – including, for example, the Japanese culture, which has apparently managed a certain segregation of moral-political and cognitive spheres. In this respect, it seems to me obvious that the Ghanaian philosopher Kwasi Wiredu is right. We will only solve our problems if we see them as human problems arising out of a special situation, and we shall not solve them if we see them as African problems, generated by our being somehow unlike others. (ibid. 135–6)

Here again one finds expressed that delicate dialectic between the "universally human" and the "culturally relative," but never, ever in a sense that should be taken as demeaning to either.

One obvious comment to make about the above synopsis of analytic philosophy in the African context is the level of technical sophistication displayed by these philosophers who have so obviously succeeded in adapting this complex methodology to a non-Western context. When I say this, I do not in the least mean to appear patronizing. If anything, this introductory comment is meant to provide the basis for a complaint against the so-called "mainstream" Western philosophical establishment. Their continuing, preponderant attitude of benign indifference to the rich harvests produced by these analyses is unacceptable. To a lesser extent the same can be said of colleagues who work in other disciplines within African studies. For African philosophy, as an autochthonous and important area of research in its own right, definitely has "arrived," as the expression goes, and it deserves far more attention from the international academy than it is presently receiving.

Another important achievement of African analytic philosophy is that it demonstrates, amply, that African scholars have regained the initiative with regard to the complex task of defining "rationality" as it relates to Africa's intellectual heritage. And there is no question that this achievement was motivated in part by the unflattering portrayals of African cognition and the African intellect that made them somehow qualitatively distinct from those of cultures that were said to be somehow better endowed with regard to these fundamentally human attributes.

One outstanding issue that merits further discussion is to reflect again on the basis for my distinction between those I have typed as "universalists" and those I have typed as "relativists." Is it really a difference in kind, or is it more one of emphasis – insofar as some African philosophers have preferred to focus primarily upon what they see as commonalities, while others have preferred to concentrate upon what they see as differences?

121

I think this may be, to some extent, true – insofar as it is a consequence of their *methodological* assumptions. For example, it is apparent that some of these philosophers prefer to begin their analyses on the basis of a presumption that there is, indeed that there must be, a shared rationality (otherwise one group would not even be able to understand the other); while others think that this kind of commitment should be avoided, or at least delayed, until sufficient piecemeal, detailed, concrete, empirical analyses of specific elements of the African intellectual heritage have been undertaken and the results assessed. This is seen as a more cautious way to proceed, and as a way that contains the ever-pervasive influence of the rationalist paradigm that is treated as a virtual sinecure of Western philosophy.

Last but not least, it is important to note that African analytic philosophers themselves are well aware of this split within their ranks. It is and will doubtless continue to be a source of vigorous debate and criticism, but that, after all, is an activity that can acceptably distinguish the discipline known as "philosophy" in any culture.

Ethnophilosophy and Philosophical Sagacity

Paulin Hountondji

Paulin Hountondji is another major figure in contemporary African philosophy whose influence spans the Francophone–Anglophone divide. He is from the République du Benin (formerly Dahomey) and for years has been a professor of philosophy at the University of Cotonou. Hountondji is best known for his critique(s) of philosophers in and of Africa who propound what he calls "ethnophilosophy."

His intention is to condemn the intellectual injustice that he believes to be enshrined in publications purporting to be African philosophy when they display the following essential characteristics. Ethnophilosophy presents itself as a philosophy of peoples rather than of individuals; in African societies one is therefore given the impression that there can be no equivalent to a Socrates or to a Zeno. Ethnophilosophy speaks only of Bantu philosophy, Dogon philosophy, Yoruba philosophy; as such its scope is collective, tribal, and of the world-view variety. Ethnophilosophy's sources are in the past, in what is described as authentic, traditional African culture of the precolonial variety, of the Africa prior to "modernity." These are to be found primarily in products of language: parables, proverbs, poetry, songs, myths – oral literature generally. From a methodological point of view, ethnophilosophy therefore tends to portray African beliefs as things that do not change, that are somehow timeless. Disputes between ethnophilosophers arise primarily over how to arrive at a correct rendering of oral traditions. African systems of thought are depicted as placing minimal emphasis upon the rigorous argumentation and criticism that are prerequisites to the sort of search for truth that involves discarding the old and creating the new. Tradition therefore becomes suspect as a justification for something's being "true" and is portrayed as antithetical to innovation.

If this material was presented as cultural anthropology or as ethnology, Hountondji would find it less objectionable. But when it is introduced as philosophy, as African philosophy, a demeaning and subversive double standard is introduced that excuses African thought and philosophy from having critical, reflective, rational, scientific, and progressive content produced by individual thinkers in any significantly cross-culturally comparative sense. African philosophy, in fact, becomes a prereflective mode of thought. Of the philosophers whose work has been discussed or mentioned in this chapter, Hountondji would certainly claim that the work of Mbiti, Tempels, Kagame, and Griaule (Ogotemelli) is of an ethnophilosophical character.[43] And he would likely characterize the approach of "analytic" philosophers who use African languages as a basis for African philosophy[44] (since languages are shared and thereby also "collective") as also guilty of the ethnophilosophical "sin."[45]

Hountondji does not hold these creators of unphilosophical African philosophies criminally responsible for their crimes. In their own intellectual circles they believe they are doing something genuinely professional and progressive in their attempts to link Africa and philosophy. Also, Hountondji appreciates the problematic sources of Africa's "modern" intellectual history that may be traced back to the colonial period. Academic philosophers – African or expatriate – were a rare species. The principal Western initiatives for serious scholarly studies of African cultures did come from ethnography and anthropology. Given the holistic parameters of the social sciences, it is understandable – if still not ideologically or professionally acceptable – that something like ethnophilosophy came about. But that is not reason enough to encourage its continued development – as African *philosophy*.

A second, prominent theme in Hountondji's published work is the importance he assigns to the development of science and technology in Africa as independent and vital research disciplines in their own right. From a practical point of view, this is the sort of enterprise, as well as knowledge, that African governments and universities must encourage if international intellectual independence is to be achieved and secured. From a philosophical point of view, the literacy, inventive critical thinking, analytic argumentation, and competitive testing of alternate hypotheses intrinsic to such disciplines, when they are brought to bear on African research priorities, are sure to encourage the kind of independent, individualized theoretical thinking that Hountondji finds essential to philosophical discourse that is truly worthy of the name.

Odera Oruka

It would be unfair to discuss the work of the late H. Odera Oruka only as a reaction or response to Hountondji's critique of ethnophilosophy. For in his methodological writings and fieldwork focused on the approach to African philosophy that Oruka christens "philosophical sagacity," he believes that he is creating a genuinely novel approach to the discipline that both suits the African context and rebuts the claims of those who insist that the philosophical enterprise in Africa must be a mirror-image of philosophy in the West.

Oruka suggests that the activity of *reflection* upon certain themes of fundamental importance to human life – the existence of a supreme being (or God), the nature of time, of freedom, of death, of education – has always been of concern to a select

123

number of people in all human societies. And this kind of thinking does not presuppose a "modern" education or even literacy, so it is false to presume that it can only take place in societies that are typed as "developed." Therefore, one task of the academically trained philosopher becomes to identify these "sages" in a culture, and then to record their potentially unique insights on these and related topics ("unique" because they may very well differ from conventional beliefs in their societies).[46] In a sense, Oruka remolds and rechristens Wiredu's "folk philosophy" as "culture philosophy," which he says does include the shared, fundamental, conventional beliefs of a society or culture on a variety of important human concerns, topics, and questions. But for this "culture philosophy" to then metamorphose into "philosophical sagacity," individual thinkers ("sages") in that society must also reflect upon and critically assess such conventional beliefs on the basis of their own experience and intellectual prowess. It is this that contributes the element of individuality that both Hountondji and Oruka insist is a sine qua non of philosophy in any culture.

Oruka first presented his position on sagacity in a seminal paper (1978) that probably should be considered the first serious attempt to write the history of contemporary Anglophone African philosophy, "Four Trends in African Philosophy." The four trends, "schools," or approaches to African philosophy he identifies are: *ethnophilosophy* (Tempels, Griaule, Mbiti, and, as this category was first introduced, Gyekye, Hallen, and Sodipo); *philosophical sagacity* (Oruka); *nationalist-ideological philosophy*, inclusive of African social-political thinkers (Fanon, Nkrumah, Nyerere); and *professional philosophy*, which he associates with the orthodox Western academic tradition (Bodunrin, Hountondji, and, as this category was first introduced, Wiredu and, most interestingly, Oruka himself again[47]). There is not space to discuss Oruka's detailed critical assessments of each of these categories, but it is important to note that he later refined their terms of reference and added on an additional two: the *hermeneutic*, to more specifically accommodate those who choose a linguistic approach[48] (Wiredu, Gyekye, Hallen, Sodipo), and the *artistic or literary*, to apply to African intellectual figures in the humanities who address themselves to themes basic to Africa's cultural identity (Okot p'Bitek, Ngugi wa Thiong'o, Wole Soyinka).

Something needs to be said about the strong reactions by both Hountondji and Oruka against a linguistic approach to African philosophy and to their view of it as a further extension of a one-sidedly ethnophilosophical approach directed only at non-Western (more specifically, African) peoples and cultures. Twentieth-century Western analytic philosophy is perhaps best known for its own "linguistic turn."[49] For what Western analytic philosophers have spent much of their time analyzing is language – either in an idealized or paradigmatic form (concerned with the "nature of" meaning, reference, and so forth in any language) or, more concretely, by identifying and evaluating the criteria governing usage of certain concepts or fields of discourse in a specific natural language that is actually used by human beings (not surprisingly, usually the English language). For example, to determine the criteria that are involved in English-language discourse for a piece of information to be classified as "true," or for a particular action to be labeled "good" or "moral." This kind of approach to English-language discourse was instrumental to the fundamental distinctions advanced in epistemology (or the theory of knowledge) between "knowledge by acquaintance," "knowledge how," and "knowledge that" (or "propositional knowledge").[50] But if both Hountondji and Oruka (at least at one point in time) would condemn the linguistic approach as misguided because it is based on a shared, collective, "tribal" enterprise like a common language, then much of the contemporary orthodox Western philosophical canon itself qualifies as perhaps *the* most gross example of ethnophilosophy ever! Therefore, it would seem there must be a place for some sort of accommodation between Hountondji and Oruka, and mainstream Western linguistic philosophy.

It appears that Hountondji and Oruka would have no objection to the individual philosopher observing and reflecting upon the world and human experience, and on that basis propounding a speculative theory derived from those sources. Indeed, in a sense this is their paradigm for the philosophical (and sagacious). So if the linguistic philosopher proposes to substitute language, either in its idealized form or as a specific natural language (English, Akan (Twi)), for "the world and human experience" as an alternative basis for his or her observations, reflections, and speculations, are the parameters involved really so different? Only, it would seem, if linguistic philosophy is made out to be so parochial and prosaic an enterprise as to amount to nothing more than the simplistic representation of a language's grammar and vocabulary that can be found in an elementary-level foreign-language textbook. On the other hand, if the networks of concepts and fields of discourse of every natural language might be looked at as potentially original and unique creations of human genius setting out to comprehend the world, theoretical incentives much more exciting than mere grammar and vocabulary become involved. Furthermore, if the philosophical backgrounds, interpretations, and critiques of the different linguistic philosophers who reflect upon and critically analyze those conceptual networks and fields of discourse differ, as indeed they do, does this not highlight or underscore that essential element of individuality, of significant creative input by the individual thinker, that Hountondji and Oruka find vital to the philosophical enterprise?

Phenomenology and Hermeneutics

As will hopefully be clear by the end of this chapter, contemporary Anglophone African philosophy is as noteworthy for the variety of *methodological* approaches it evidences as it is for the diversity of views that result from the application of those methodologies to a variety of topics and problems. Up to this point the only mainstream methodological approach to the discipline that has been explored in any detail is that conventionally referred to as *analysis* or *analytic philosophy*. Another approach that deserves consideration is that derived from the phenomenological tradition, which is conventionally, at least as far as its African manifestations are concerned, referred to as *hermeneutics*.

The modern-day founder of the philosophical approach that has come to be known as phenomenology was the German philosopher, Edmund Husserl (1859–1938). In common with the universalist aspirations of many of his analytic contemporaries, Husserl sought to formulate a methodological approach that would focus on a level of (human) experience that was universal to all peoples, in all historical periods, in all cultures. To reach this most fundamental level of experience, Husserl insists that phenomenologists will have to be trained in a rigorous manner to "see through" and to discard as well as discount all of the more superficial interpretative frameworks they have inherited from or invented in the particular historical and cultural contexts in which they happen to live, and with which they are most familiar as supposedly representing the world the way it "really" is. Such frameworks include a person's cultural identity, "common" sense, religious identity, professional identity, and, in the academy, philosophical identity. For Husserl regarded analytic philosophy itself as, relatively speaking, just another one of those comparatively superficial but fashionable "philosophical" frameworks for interpreting human experience invented by scholars who were the products of a particular phase of human history – in this case a period overwhelmingly influenced by the paradigms and propaganda of the empirical sciences.

The best known of the descendants of Husserl was Martin Heidegger (1889–1976), who is frequently, and many would say misleadingly, identified with the post-World War II literary-philosophical movement known as Existentialism. Here I shall make special mention of one of Heidegger's students and intellectual descendants, Hans-Georg Gadamer (1900–2002). I choose Gadamer because of the frequent references made to his work by African philosophers who align themselves with his distinctive form of hermeneutics. For Gadamer, it is the various frameworks that have been invented or created by human beings over the course of their history (including all the arts and sciences) that should constitute the objects of hermeneutical or interpretative exercises. There is a claim of transcendence here, apart from his encouraging us to have a self-consciously explicit appreciation of the fact that we all find ourselves in the world as products of specific historical, cultural, and intellectual contexts. Hermeneutics as "interpretation" can certainly promote understanding of the nature of those contexts, and our own self-understanding as well, of course, but always still as beings who have no choice but to continue to exist, to learn, to understand, and perhaps be critical within those contexts. In other words, human understanding is always affected by the various contexts in which it is sited; so that human *understanding* is always and inevitably *interpretation*. (Keep in mind the significance of this word for Gadamer's hermeneutics.) That interpretation is a rendering that arises from the contexts of which it is a product and which it, in turn, may thereafter transform.

Theophilus Okere

Theophilus Okere, a Nigerian philosopher, is one of the earlier advocates of a hermeneutical approach to African philosophy. In his *African Philosophy: A Historico-Hermeneutical Investigation of the Conditions of Its Possibility* (1983),[51] Okere outlines a program for how a hermeneutic approach might be implemented. The first major issue he addresses is what should be the proper relationship between such a hermeneutic philosophy and Africa's cultural heritage. He dismisses the work of the so-called "ethnophilosophers"[52] as not worthy of the label "philosophy." At the most, these collections of myths, proverbs, and world-views qualify as ethnography, as compendiums of cultural beliefs and practices. It is on such materials that hermeneutic philosophers might labor so as to render them philosophical by *interpreting* them – distilling and assessing their meaning(s), their true significance(s), and their value(s) to and for Africa's cultural present and future.

Although appreciative of the Western philosophical tradition that traces its roots to the Greeks, it is most certainly not something Okere would like to see transferred or transplanted into the African context.[53] He embraces Gadamer's notions of the relativity of cultural and social contexts ("all philosophical discourse is first and foremost an answer to problems and questions raised within a questioning horizon which means always, a culture" (1983: 64)). In other words, to be genuinely African, Africa's philosophers and philosophy must arise from and relate directly to the particular culture(s) in which they are sited. And these cultures are sufficiently distinctive, in their own right, so that it would be a reductive injustice to claim or to conclude that they are somehow the "same" as their Western counterpart(s). Clearly this again places Okere on the side of relativism when it comes to the nature of philosophical "truths" and principles.

In the final chapter of his text Okere identifies any number of "symbolic" elements and practices in his native Igbo culture that he suggests could contribute to a positive basis for a philosophy arising from that culture consequent upon a hermeneutical interpretation, such as the role of the *"Chi"* as guardian spirit and symbol of destiny, the practice of polygamy, and the nature and role of the extended family (ibid. 115).

Okonda Okolo

The Congolese philosopher Okonda Okolo applauds (1991: 201) the hermeneutical approach to African philosophy outlined by Theophilus Okere. And to further its development he proposes to provide African-oriented hermeneutical interpretations of two notions of fundamental importance to Africa's indigenous cultures – Tradition and Destiny. His decision to concentrate on them is not accidental or haphazard. Apart from their genuine importance to Africa's cultures, it also is motivated by his conviction that Western Africanists – as ethnocentric products of their own cultural backgrounds – have managed to analyze and evaluate them in ways that are both derogatory and false.

In Western anthropology, a culture based on tradition is frequently pictured as one devoid of change or development because also devoid of critical or reflective thinking. Beliefs and practices inherited from the "ancestors" are said to be preserved unchanged in the present, and then handed on to the next generation with the understanding they will be preserved and observed in a similar manner. Knowledge therefore does not progress, and those who dare to challenge established traditions put their own welfare at risk. The belief in destiny is portrayed as encouraging a rather severe manifestation of determinism, according to which it is believed that what will be, will be. This too is said to inhibit the development of independent or individual initiative.

Invoking the hermeneutic tradition arising from the work of Paul Ricoeur, Heidegger, and Gadamer, Okolo proposes to reinterpret and reappraise each of these

127

notions, and to do so as an African (rather than a Westerner) who can philosophize from within the African cultural and historical context. For example, he disagrees fundamentally with the image of tradition involving unchanging beliefs and practices that are handed on from generation to generation. Tradition does involve a sense of transmission and of reception (ibid. 202), but in a context where the meanings of any particular tradition are constantly being interpreted and reinterpreted – and therefore always changing – by different individuals and in different historical contexts over the passage of time. Tradition therefore does not inhibit invention or change, as new interpretations are made as a natural and normal part of making "tradition" meaningful to the people who "inherit" it. And because of this those societies will inevitably either eliminate or amend traditions as time passes and/or reinterpret them so that they again become newly relevant to the present generation.

Destiny, from the vantage point of African hermeneutics, is not a symbol of determinism, where everything that happens is seen as inevitable. Destiny involves a people's "vision of the world" and, as such, represents the history of a people, of a culture, in the world. It represents that people's past, present, and future, and whatever sense of identity they create and then recreate for themselves on the basis of reinterpreting and reinventing tradition(s) over the passage of time.

Reinterpreting a sense of African destiny must be linked to Africans' regaining the sense of being in control of their own societies, including the right to understand those societies in *their* own terms. These elements must constitute essential parts of the framework that will define African hermeneutics, reinterpreting the nature of the African identity as expressed by and through African culture.

Tsenay Serequeberhan

The Eritrean philosopher Tsenay Serequeberhan deserves credit for having the foresight to produce the first widely read anthology of African philosophy (1991), which includes the essay by Okolo that I have just been discussing. But here my principal interest will be in his *The Hermeneutics of African Philosophy* (1994), which presents itself as a kind of "manifesto" for what the role of hermeneutical philosophy in Africa should be. Serequeberhan identifies Gadamer as "the father of contemporary philosophical hermeneutics" (1994: 16), which, he says, unlike "orthodox" phenomenology is always explicitly and self-consciously sited in a specific historico-cultural context (ibid. 3). Indeed, as far as Serequeberhan is concerned, *all* philosophy – not just the hermeneutical – must be so situated and, no matter how meticulously neutral and universal it pretends to be, must also have a political dimension (ibid. 4). He therefore castigates the Western philosophical establishment for playing along with the intellectual and political issues involved in the portrayal of Africa as irrational and primitive, especially when viewed against the background of European colonialism. Western civilization (philosophy included) was indeed propagandized as the cultural paradigm, and most things African were viewed as negations of that ideal.

Serequeberhan is one of the first African philosophers to explicitly confront the problem posed by the fact that hermeneutics itself is a methodology of European origin (ibid. 10–11). In other words, how can it avoid being certified as just one more example of a European mentality that therefore cannot authentically apply to the African cultural context? His response to this potentially serious challenge is twofold. First, the hermeneutical approach to philosophy has already been adapted, filtered, and amended by the work within and on it by non-Western thinkers such as Frantz Fanon and Amilcar Cabral. Other non-Western intellectuals whose work is relevant to its political renovation (remember that for Serequeberhan *all* philosophizing has political ramifications) are Aime Cesaire and Cornelius Castoriadis. At the same time, Serequeberhan does not hesitate to condemn Western icons like Heidegger, Marx, Hegel, Hume, and Kant for the racist content to their writings (ibid. 60–1).

Secondly, it would be hypocrisy for contemporary African intellectuals, philosophers included, to pretend they remain unaffected by the colonial experience and the Western elements introduced thereby into Africa's own intellectual heritage. It makes more sense for Africans to come to terms with all of this in a deliberate and forthright manner. If that also involves the adaptation of an approach like hermeneutics to the African context, then that may be all well and good, provided it is done in a positive, progressive manner – a manner that will benefit Africa rather than demean it.

Serequeberhan appears to have a fairly low tolerance for other methodological approaches to African philosophy. He rebukes the so-called "ethnophilosophers" for introducing themselves to the international community (and Africa) as a kind of "new wave." They may argue that Africa's cultures have always contained a philosophical dimension, but it still took *them* to identify, codify, and somehow, in the end, take the professional credit for developing it. As for what I have been referring to as the "rationalist" approach, he criticizes Bodunrin, Hountondji, and Wiredu for too easily advocating, adopting, and imposing an essentially Western tradition of philosophy upon the African context (ibid. 5).[54]

In this regard he has some nice things to say about Gyekye's suggested program for identifying and re-examining Africa's indigenous "traditions" with a view to determining which deserve to be preserved and promoted (ibid. 6). This obviously will also be a priority of African hermeneutics. With regard to the issue of whether there was philosophy in so-called "traditional" or precolonial Africa, because Serequeberhan is so insistent upon every people's and culture's right to *define itself*, clearly he is open to the idea that Africa's cultures are entitled to claim their own philosophical heritage, even if manifested in a substantially different form from that taken as conventional by other societies:

> The foundational wondering and musing of traditional African sages have – in their continuous critical and safeguarding relation to the traditions (i.e., the ethnic world-views) they inhabit – a hermeneutic and philosophic function. To this extent, it has to be conceded in principle that their reflections and intellectual productions are products of philosophic effort. (1994: 126 n. 11)

Lewis Gordon, Lucius Outlaw, and Robert Bernasconi

There is one final dimension to African hermeneutics to which reference must be made in this discussion. In a sense, it represents its most "radical," even revolutionary, position with reference to the status and role of African philosophy. Although explicitly present in Serequeberhan's writings, it is in the publications of three other Africana philosophers – Lewis Gordon (1997), Lucius Outlaw (1996), and Robert Bernasconi (1997) – that it comes into prominence.

The theme I have in mind is introduced by Lewis Gordon as follows.

> The artificial situating of the African outside of the universal leads to a particular conception of the "scope" of reality.... African philosophy is treated by many theorists as a type of suppressed prime[55].... The white/Western philosophical reality becomes the "governing fiction." ... Now although this governing fiction suggests at first that "real philosophy" is Western, there is a logic that can show that African philosophy is broader in scope than Western philosophy because it *includes* the Western in its self-articulation. In *practice* Western philosophy may be a subset of African philosophy. (1997: 145; my italics in part)

Lucius Outlaw, for his part, employs a deconstructive critique to demonstrate how Western "philosophy" is used as an ideological weapon to denigrate the intellectual significance of non-Western, in particular African, cultures. His strategy for combating this coalesces with that of Serequeberhan and Gordon when he reviews African philosophy as a movement to displace the West from its paradigmatic role (1996: 65).

Finally, Robert Bernasconi, writing explicitly as a Westerner versed in the phenomenological-hermeneutical tradition, indicts the European-Continental philosophical tradition (the "birthplace" of modern phenomenology-hermeneutics) for being as much in need of ethnocentric cleansing as its Anglophone analytic counterpart (1997: 190). But what is most pertinent about his critique is that he too sees the real possibility and value to Western philosophy and to philosophy as a transcultural enterprise, of an African philosophical tradition, independent of the West, engaging in dialogue *with* and deconstructive critiques *of* that West.

One important concern shared in common by both analytic and hermeneutic philosophers is the determination to come to terms with the damage done to Africa by the era of colonialism and Western intellectual imperialism. Another important interest the two traditions share in common is the degree to which African languages may serve as a basis for African philosophy. The important thing, as far as Africa's overall philosophical future is concerned, is for analytic and hermeneutic philosophers to interact and communicate with one another on the professional or intellectual level. In the Western academy this is not the case and the split between them is sometimes viewed as irreparable. But as the above synopsis indicates, with reference to Africa the two do share some concerns and interests in common and these should be explored, hopefully to their mutual benefit.

Marxism

Contemporary African philosophers who identify themselves as Marxists constitute yet another and, as far as the present synopsis is concerned, final school of thought.

130

The non-Western Marxist philosophical tradition, with specific reference to Africa, has a distinguished Caribbean and South American, as well as African, ancestry and may be associated with some of the most brilliant and "radical" thinkers who address the issues of (European) colonialism, of neocolonialism, of Africa as a victim of the so-called Cold War (the ideological and political struggle between West and East), and of where Africa's best interests lie when it comes to contemporary social, political, and economic development. Here I have in mind intellectual figures such as Claude Ake (1939–96), Samir Amin (1931–), Amilcar Cabral (1921–73), Aime Cesaire (1913–), Frantz Fanon (1925–61), Paolo Freire (1921–97), Albert Memmi (1920–), and Walter Rodney (1942–80).

Many conventional (and non-Marxist) expositions of Karl Marx's and Frederick Engels' ideas and theories divide them up into two major but supposedly irreconcilable phases: (1) an earlier "humanistic" period in which Marx, in particular, was outraged by the exploitation of some groups or "classes" in certain societies, and sought to outline an alternative form of community in which such injustices might be corrected and human beings would be truly free (Marx I); (2) a later, comparatively "social scientific" period in which Marx (and Engels) sought to formulate a rigorous *economic* theory that would allow Marxist thinkers to demonstrate that the manner in which the means or modes of production in a society were controlled or administered exercised substantial influence upon its social, political, and cultural life (Marx II).[56]

It is therefore relevant to begin this introduction to the African Marxist philosophers I am about to consider by saying that the first two, each in his own distinctive way, will reject this artificially imposed bifurcation upon the development of Marx's thought. In their writings, they argue that Marx's economic theory can only be understood correctly as and if conjoined with fundamental *value* commitments to moral or legal principles and ideals.

Oladipo Fashina

For example, the Nigerian philosopher Oladipo (better known as Dipo) Fashina addresses this point in an article in which, commenting on the bifurcation between what I have labeled Marx I and Marx II, he says: "According to some philosophers, all talk about human nature or human essence [Marx I] became irrelevant in Marx's outlook as soon as he became a Marxist [Marx II]" (1988: 291). In this article Fashina argues that Marx did reject certain forms of society on moral grounds, but that because his moral theory or viewpoint itself are atypical, this aspect to his overall thought has frequently gone unrecognized or unappreciated.

Fashina argues that portraying Marx as only a defender of human *freedom* (Marx I) places undue emphasis on one precondition of human fulfillment. For what is more fundamental to Marx's thinking is his view of *human nature* and the *plurality* of conditions for its maximum fulfillment. Marx I and Marx II may therefore be better understood as reunited, in fact, as never bifurcated, in his views about the kind of society in which this can be achieved: "In Marx's view, socialism is superior to capitalism by being more conducive to the realization of *human nature*: it enhances freedom (self-mastery), community, rationality, reciprocity, the development of talents, and other essentials of human nature" (ibid. 303; my italics). That Marx links his *moral* views regarding the fulfillment of human nature to more socially scientific notions of history and economics may indeed make them atypical. But this is as much because conventional Western moral philosophy continues to treat moral values as somehow independent of *empirical* realities, and should not make Marx's more detailed views about the *empirical* preconditions for the fulfillment of that human nature any less moral in intent or content.

Finally, to return to the issue of justice and human rights in Africa, when discussing Frantz Fanon with regard to whether violent resistance by Africans to European colonization can be morally justified, Fashina argues that humanism can*not* play an important role in Fanon's justification of such violence precisely because Fanon recognizes that the contending parties do *not* share a common vision of humanity. For part of the colonizers' defining role is that as human beings they are superior to the inferior (African) human beings they colonize. This kind of double standard would negate any theoretical basis for a universal humanism. Therefore, a further, and practical, consequence of Fashina's analysis of Fanon is that anti-colonial violence is justifiable because of the prejudice and the violence (rationalized thereby) that were instrumental to Europe's colonization and enforced occupation of the African continent.

Olufemi Taiwo

The Nigerian philosopher, Olufemi Taiwo, has done interesting work in the area of African philosophy as well as on Marxism. But in this narrative I will concentrate on the latter, particularly as represented by his book *Legal Naturalism: A Marxist Theory of Law* (1996). His overall strategy is encapsulated by the title's initial phrase, "legal naturalism." For what Taiwo sets out to do is to establish a Marxist theory of natural law. He does this principally by arguing that there are *legal* priorities or principles that constitute an essential, intrinsic part of any economic system.

Perhaps the most important initial point to establish about Taiwo's text is his explicit acknowledgment that the end result will be a novel synthesis of Marxist theory with natural law theory. He distinguishes his analysis of law from that of most Marxist theoreticians because:

> [Orthodox] Marxist theories of law are dominated by a positivist orientation that sees law as the will of the ruling class in its efforts to make the subaltern classes cooperate with or accede to its dominance.... In the main they treat law within a general discussion of politics or philosophy of history. They all, in their different ways, accept the base/superstructure dichotomy of society. Thus law is usually discussed as a component of politics or economics and banished to the superstructure. (1996: 2, 45)

Yet according to Taiwo and to Marxism generally, the moral value of *any* legal system (and the economic order of which it is part and parcel) can be rated by the degree to which it facilitates freedom. "Freedom is the essence of human beings" (ibid. 23).

At this point some readers may well be wondering what exactly is meant by the "theory of natural law" or the "natural law tradition": "Natural law is identified with the ideal legal system which is striving for realization and, being ideal, is desirable and ought to be" (ibid. 37). Whether its ultimate source is said to be divine, human reason, or the material or economic basis of society (the option Taiwo favors), this is the system of legal values that humankind should strive to institute in order to fully realize the ideals that define that particular form of society (and its particular notions of what are considered to be "happiness," "freedom," "justice," etc.).

Though he also acknowledges the diversity of the natural law tradition, Taiwo suggests (ibid. 37–8) that the core of the theory may be summarized by three basic principles:

1   It is necessary to make a *distinction* between so-called "positive law" (the laws that are *in fact* enacted or legislated by a particular society at a particular point in time) and the "natural law" (the ideal law(s) that serve as guiding principles for positive law, and that *ought* to be enacted by a society to maximize its notions of "happiness," etc.).
2   In terms of both values and rationality, natural law *rates higher* than positive law, and so may be used as a *standard* on the basis of which to evaluate whatever positive law is in place at a given point in time.
3   In some instances, natural law may be invoked as a justification for *rejecting* or *disobeying* positive law because the latter is said to violate the principles of natural law and therefore, in fact, is not entitled to be regarded as "law."

Taiwo notes that any number of Marxist theoreticians have rejected natural law theory as nothing more than one more ideological invention of a burgeoning middle class out to challenge the European feudal aristocracy (ibid. 34–5). But, and this perhaps is where the originality of his approach is most evident, Taiwo wants to argue that the natural law framework may be used to make explicit the legal content inherent in any economic system. He does this, first, by arguing that it is not necessary for natural law to be immutable (ibid. 40) – that there can in fact be different "systems" of natural law that emerge as human societies undergo economic and legal change over the course of time. For if this theoretical innovation is incorporated into Marxism, it would mean that "the concept of law is not exhausted by" a society's positive law system, its legislated law(s) (ibid. 56).

Next, he argues that because it enunciates certain basic, if very generalized, values, natural law can be used as an independent but practical standard for the evaluation of the positive law(s) in place in a society at a given point in time. In other words, every variety of economic system or "social formation" has inherent in it a distinctive, defining set of natural law(s) which constitute part of its essence, whether feudal, capitalist, socialist, or communist. These natural laws also set certain limits to the positive law(s) that society may choose to enact. And if those limits are exceeded, either on the basis of ignorance or revolution, the nature and future of that society may be undermined or overturned. This allows Taiwo to offer a more comprehensive interpretation of "natural" law that he suggests is compatible with a Marxist perspective:

133

> The natural law of the mode of production provides the foundation for the positive law of each society. It is the law that positive law seeks officially to express. It is the law that legislators seek to formulate in conscious positive law.
>
> [But the so-called] "law*makers*" formulate ... [the laws they do] because they have to operate within specific or specifiable limits imposed by the natural law of the given mode of production in which they are located. For example, if a social formation is feudal, no matter how determined the legislators are they cannot make or implement laws that will guarantee capitalist commodity production and exchange, or liberty, equality, etc. (ibid. 67; my italics)

The theoretical as well as the empirical addition of this natural law framework provides a substantive basis that individuals or groups may invoke to justify demands they make upon or of their society. It also provides a more clear framework for individuals or groups whose aim is to reform or overthrow a society.

Does the fact that such individuals or groups reject the established system of positive (and natural) law mean that there are also some trans-historical criteria on the basis of which the various systems of natural law may themselves be evaluated or rated? According to Taiwo, the answer is "yes." "One can say that Marx does affirm such a normative standard of human and social evolution" (ibid. 73). Namely, "to strive to bring about better and better social orderings, where the best possible social ordering is one in which human beings are enabled to realize their human potential as fully as possible, limited only by the constraints of physical nature, human and material" (ibid. 73).

The final, major topic that Taiwo addresses in his text is Marx's controversial notion of the "withering away" of the state and, by obvious implication, the law. For in a truly communist society – in which human freedom and potential could be maximized, where the means of production were not used by some to profit off others, and where everyone's material needs could be satisfied – there would be no place for one group or "class" to administer or to govern the rest. Hence the so-called "class*less*" society.

Perhaps no other element of Marx's overall theory has been subjected to as much ridicule as these notions of the state's "withering away" and a "classless" society – both have been regularly characterized as hopelessly utopian. But Taiwo provides extended and thoughtful arguments in defense of Marx's idea that should challenge the attention of any open-minded reader. (For more discussion, see Hallen 2002.)

Another African Marxist thinker of note is the Congolese historian and philosopher, Ernest Wamba-dia-Wamba, who was for many years Professor of History at the University of Dar es Salaam, Tanzania. More recently he has attracted the attention of the international community as the leader of one of the contending forces in the post-Mobutu Republic of the Congo. Because of space constraints I cannot take up his writings here, but the reader is referred to Hallen 2002 for a discussion of his ideas.

My first thoughts, after completing this lamentably brief review of these African Marxist philosophers, were how fresh and intriguing, even exciting many of their ideas are, and how regrettable it is that this school of thought is often overlooked in more generalized discussions of African philosophy. In some measure this is no doubt a hangover from past propaganda contests between the East and West. Anything linked with the words "Marx," "Marxism," or "communism" became suspect to a substantial portion of the world's population. But it is time people learned to look beyond these labels, to the new ideas and insights being produced by Marxist philosophers in and of Africa today. For there appears to be much here that is of value and should be of common concern.

Histories of, Anthologies of, and Introductions to African Philosophy

In addition to the individual philosophers whose views we have been exploring, there are a substantial number of publications on African philosophy that are of a more diverse nature – usually because they incorporate the writings of a number of African philosophers within a single text. I want to make at least some reference to them here for several reasons: (1) they are important philosophical statements in their own right; (2) they further demonstrate the vitality and diversity of contemporary Anglophone African philosophy; (3) they may be of use to newcomers to the field who wish to pursue their interest in the subject further.

D. A. Masolo

The first truly comprehensive and detailed history of African philosophy was written by the Kenyan philosopher, D. A. Masolo. Appropriately entitled *African Philosophy in Search of Identity* (1994), this important text devotes entire chapters to all of the topics I have touched upon, and makes frequent reference to African philosophers who represent the Francophone tradition as well. Unfortunately, it is impossible for me to do justice to Masolo's much more sophisticated and detailed history in this brief historical synopsis. But it is important that I point out that this text is also a philosophical statement in its own right. Masolo does not write merely as a chronicler of ideas. He also analyzes and provides critical assessments of the various philosophers and the traditions they represent. He does this, ultimately, from the standpoint of his own philosophical position, and it is therefore appropriate that I at least say something about that here.

Masolo is skeptical about the truly *philosophical* merit of an exclusively linguistic approach to African philosophy (1994: 95–102). Ordinary language exists primarily as a practical means of communication rather than as a philosophical statement of a people's world-view or metaphysics (their most fundamental beliefs about the nature of reality). Analytic philosophers may choose to explore its meanings and grammatical structure, but for Masolo this provides an insufficient basis for drawing systematic conclusions about the most fundamental or important theoretical precepts of a given African culture:

> When through some rigorous analysis we are able to trace word formation to the word's conceptual significances, we are actually doing an exercise that is essentially out of the context of the original function of the word. In other words, at this level we would be doing our own private abstractions and ploughing into fields completely

135

unintended and possibly even unknown to the common native speaker of that language.... The philosopher's interests in meaning go beyond the limits of the linguist. His "meaning" searches for or denotes "essential" properties by which we identify things as belonging to a specific class. But this is beyond the communicative meaning that words denote in common language.... From the ordinary common language they build another language, a language of experts. The meaning of a specific word in ordinary language, on the other hand, must be sought in "what it stands for" for the majority of its speakers, who never have to qualify first as metaphysicians before they qualify as speakers of their own language, whether it is their native language or a new one. (ibid. 102)

One obvious danger to this vision of linguistic philosophy, and one apparently implied by Masolo's observations, is that the philosopher might end up creating an African world-view or philosophy, attributed to an African people via their language, that was significantly the product of his or her own imagination and speculation. This would help to explain why Masolo insists that African philosophy must be grounded upon something more than mere linguistic analysis.

What Masolo does see as one of the most important and positive developments within contemporary African philosophy is the determination on the part of African philosophers to explore the universal elements of rationality in African thought (ibid. 44). For one thing, this kind of approach – for example, as evidenced by Wiredu – does constitute one of the benchmarks of the mainstream discipline known as "philosophy." For another, it will hopefully serve to counterbalance the claims of those extreme relativists who go too far in their efforts to prove that African cognition is qualitatively different from that of other cultures and who produce essentially ethnographic treatises (Tempels, etc.) of an "African traditional thought" that is both excessively exotic and bizarre in character.

Masolo suggests that, even today, the most basic issue that continues to divide African philosophers and philosophy is precisely the degree to which cognition may be said to be distinctive in African thought:

The question of how to define the criteria of rationality has become a central theme in Anglophone philosophy.... On one side are the foundationalists [universalists], who argue that formal rational procedures are the defining features of science, which supersedes common sense and is universal. On the other side are the pluralists [relativists], who argue in favor of the diversity of human experience and systems of representation. These include the criteria for the definition of knowledge and for making judgments. (ibid. 247)

His own position is to try to strike a kind of mean midway between the two:

The position which states that our sense of the world and of personhood varies according to the varieties of experience takes a middle ground between the foundationalists and the pluralists by arguing that what are called products of the rational mind are not really conflictual with what are oppositionally referred to as the disorderly life of the body and the emotions. Rather, this third position argues, such products carry equal weight as they [both] are modes of thinking which illustrate the variant modalities of experience. This position avoids the Cartesian dichotomy which posits the cogito ["pure" reason] as separate from, opposed to, and more reliable than bodily experiences [sensory perception]. This position argues for a historical and contextual approach to the definition of knowledge and rationality. (ibid. 248)

He argues that this kind of "historical and contextual" approach will prove more beneficial because it will prevent African philosophy from being dominated by any absolute commitment to a single methodological or ideological paradigm. It will leave the future of the discipline open to the development of new insights and approaches that may prove of value or interest to philosophers working within the African context. In addition it takes more explicit account of the fact that philosophy – philosophizing – is the product of the mind of the *individual* philosopher and his or her own creative interests, insights, and genius (ibid. 251).

Anthologies

One example of a recent anthology that relates to African philosophy is that edited by John Pittman, *African-American Perspectives and Philosophical Traditions* (1997). It contains contributions by both African and African-American philosophers (the two traditions are now sometimes grouped under the common heading "Africana Philosophy"), and is of interest for the suggestions made about how the two do and should interrelate. Another example is the volume edited by Emmanuel Eze entitled *Postcolonial African Philosophy* (1997). It is particularly noteworthy for the substantial number of contributions made by philosophers who come from a Continental, phenomenological, or hermeneutical background, traditions that too often go under-represented in the Anglophone philosophical context.

There is now a fairly wide variety of "Introductions" to African philosophy, mostly in textbook format. Some are straightforward anthologies of canonical pieces. Prime examples are the collections edited by Richard Wright entitled *African Philosophy: An Introduction* (1984), and *African Philosophy: An Anthology* edited by Emmanuel Eze (1998). Some are anthologies of canonical pieces supplemented by substantive, expository, editorial commentaries. Representative examples are the collection edited by Parker English and K. M. Kalumba, *African Philosophy: A Classical Approach* (1996), Albert Mosley's *African Philosophy: Selected Readings* (1995), and *The African Philosophy Reader* (1998), edited by P. H. Coetzee and A. P. J. Roux. Some are entirely original texts that situate African philosophy in its historical context and then discuss major figures and traditions within it. Another example is *An Introduction to African Philosophy* (1998) by Samuel Oluoch Imbo.

Conclusion

I have very little to add in this "final" final conclusion – apart from the hope that those who have perused my text now appreciate how vital and dynamic a field African philosophy is. Occasionally, I hear colleagues expressing concern about its future, but, in view of the fact that most of this "history" has taken place since the

1960s, that is not a concern I share. In my opinion, its progress is not just impressive; it is staggering. My final concern, therefore, is to apologize to colleagues who feel their own work should have been included in this synopsis, or who feel their thoughts have not been adequately or correctly represented. Some of those whose work was not discussed here will find some amends made in my *Short History of African Philosophy* (2002). But even there, the shortness of exposition means, inevitably, that a lot of good work remains unmentioned. As always in a text of this nature, considerations of space, of time, and of an author's own responsibilities to his or her discipline can serve neither as sufficient justification nor as excuse.

Notes

1   The English-language technical/specialized vocabulary/terminology dating from this period used by foreign scholars to characterize things related to the African intellect has for long been a subject meriting more detailed study in its own right.
2   The African philosopher Alexis Kagame's much more detailed and thorough study (1956) of Bantu language(s) has never had the impact on Anglophone African philosophy it merits because, lamentably, it has yet to be translated from French into English.
3   As well as indicative of the one-way traffic between translations of Francophone and Anglophone African scholarship, the different times at which the original manuscripts were crafted also obviously is an important factor. Jahn does make the briefest of references to Mbiti as "the young story-teller" (1961: 212).
4   "[W]e shall use the singular, 'philosophy', to refer to the philosophical understanding of African peoples concerning different issues of life."
5   Mbiti bases his more general claims on his more specific studies of the Kikamba and Gikuyu languages (both classified as Bantu).
6   See, for example, Gyekye 1975 and Masolo 1994: 111–19.
7   See, for example, Bodunrin 1975; Emmet 1972; Pratt 1972; and Skorupski 1967.
8   Horton (1982) makes important revisions to his original position.
9   Two frequently footnoted anthologies are Horton and Finnegan (1973) and Wilson (1974).
10   Regretfully Peter Bodunrin died in December 1997.
11   Compare, for example, Bodunrin 1981 with Bodunrin 1992.
12   *Second Order: An African Journal of Philosophy*, principally under the editorship of the late J. Olubi Sodipo of the University of Ife, Nigeria, provided a vital and remarkably effective forum for the discussion of many viewpoints and issues relevant to philosophy in the African context.
13   His numerous published papers on formal logic are, I suppose, the clearest examples of this.
14   Wiredu characterizes the objectivist theory as maintaining that "once a proposition is true, it is true in itself and for ever. Truth, in other words, is timeless, eternal" (1980: 114).
15   The differences between "objective truth" and "cognitive truth" are more than rhetorical. The first claims that truth must be determined by an independent, transcendent reality to which human knowledge can be shown to correspond. The second, as expounded by Wiredu, argues that human beings have no direct access to such a "reality," and that truth can therefore only be determined by rigorous, careful reasoning and experimentation – cognition.
16   Wiredu, personal correspondence.

17 The *Concise Oxford Dictionary* records this form of usage in the English language for "so" as: "In that state or condition, actually the case," and cites as one example: "God said 'Let there be light' and it was so." The equivalence Wiredu himself favors is that "p is so" means "p is true."

18 In "it/that is so" and "what is so."

19 Wiredu, personal correspondence.

20 Also why he has sometimes been unfairly labeled an extreme "positivist." See, for example, Owomoyela 1987.

21 "Philosophy and Our Culture," *Proceedings of the Ghana Academy of Arts and Sciences*, p. 52 (rev. and repr. as chapter 1 of Wiredu 1980).

22 He goes so far as to suggest that their universality is ultimately of (human) genetic origin (1996: chs. 2 and 4).

23 See, for example, Wiredu 1996: ch. 6.

24 "I would concede, or even insist, that philosophy is ultimately political, for the understanding of reality that we seek is for the betterment of human existence" (1996: 148).

25 See, for example, "A Philosophical Perspective on the Concept of Human Communication," in his 1996: 13–20.

26 Pronounced phonetically as "Jay-chay."

27 Perhaps the most pronounced difference between the two is that Gyekye does not make as clear a distinction between *philosophy* as purely technical (universal) and *philosophy* as cultural (distinctively cultural relative). For him, all philosophy is somehow culturally related, even if human being (and all that implies) is indisputably universal.

28 "Akan proverbs are the wise sayings of individuals with acute speculative intellects. They become philosophically interesting when one sees them as attempts to raise and answer questions relating to the assumptions underlying commonly held beliefs and to make a synthetic interpretation of human experience" (1995: 21). Though Gyekye chooses to concentrate primarily on concepts and proverbs, he does not exclude aphorisms, myths, "stories," and other forms of oral literature as of potential philosophical significance.

29 Gyekye therefore characterizes Akan morality as "consequentialistic" (1995: 139).

30 "There is of course no pretense made that the moral values of various African societies are the same across the board, but there are some values that can be said to be shared in their essentials by all African societies" (1996: 55–6). Such shared beliefs and values are said to fall under the following headings: (1) metaphysics: (a) ontology; (b) causation; (c) concept of person; (d) fate/destiny; (e) the problem of evil; (2) epistemology (inclusive of the paranormal as well as the rational/empirical); (3) morality (as established and maintained on a secular rather than religious foundation); (4) communalism (that self-interest must be reconciled with communal interests) (see 1995: 195–210).

31 "I argue that philosophy is a universal intellectual activity that has been pursued by peoples of all cultures and that the propensity to raise fundamental questions about human experience can be found in peoples belonging to different cultures, even though the answers may be different, despite our common humanity, and may not all be equally compelling" (1995: xiv).

32 "By 'connection to the traditional', I was only calling for some analytic attention to be paid *also* to the traditional thought categories, values, outlooks, and so on, as a way of affirming an existing African philosophical tradition, some features or elements of which may be considered worthy of further philosophical pursuit" (1995: xi–xii).

33 Defined by the *Concise Oxford Dictionary* as a system or act "of setting apart persons or things as accursed or sacred." Gyekye rejects this as the basis for taboo in Africa and reinterprets their force as morally normative: "it is the humanistic, nonsupernaturalistic

outlook of Akan morality that in fact underpins the reasons offered by Akan thinkers for considering some things as morally taboo" (1995: 134).

34 He relates this to the fact that traditional African religion is not a *revealed* religion, the product "of a prophet claiming to have heard and received a divine message directly from God for use as a guide to the spiritual and moral life either of a specific group of people or of all humanity" (1996: 6).

35 Wiredu also suggests this as a universal ethical priority. See pp. 108–9 above.

36 He makes specific reference to a "developed economy, technological and industrial advancement, [and] the installation of democratic politics" (1997: 279).

37 He makes numerous references to the greater emphasis placed upon the importance of the community or group as opposed to individualistic self-interest (ibid. 278).

38 An adequate English-language phonetic rendering would be "Shay-gun Bah-deh (with the 'deh' pronounced like the 'de' in 'destroy')-gay-shin."

39 A theme that has already been introduced by Abraham, Wiredu, and Gyekye. Certainly, the latter's *Tradition and Modernity* has precisely this as its central aim. For Appiah's more guarded viewpoint on humanism in the African context, see 1992: 155.

40 See chapter 21 below.

41 Mudimbe's detailed, critical analyses of individual philosophers in and of Africa are of more positive value than this very broad synopsis might indicate. For example, his exegesis of the work of Placide Tempels (see above), and the cultural and historical context in which it occurred, provides important insights into the roots of Tempels's *Bantu Philosophy*.

42 See, for example, Gordon 1997: ch. 6; or Seregneberhan 1999: ch. 4.

43 "Scientific rigour should prevent us from arbitrarily projecting a philosophical discourse on to products of language which expressly offer themselves as something other than philosophy" (Hountondji 1983: 43).

44 There is anticipation of Quine's indeterminacy in the following edited quote from Hountondji, in which he derides the usually unspecified methods used by these ethnophilosophers to educe African philosophy from oral literature: "The discourse of ethnophilosophers, be they European or African, offers us the baffling spectacle of an imaginary interpretation with no textual support, of a genuinely 'free' interpretation, inebriated and entirely at the mercy of the interpreter, a dizzy and unconscious freedom which takes itself to be translating a text which does not actually exist and which is therefore unaware of its own creativity. By this action the interpreter disqualifies himself from reaching any truth whatsoever, since truth requires that freedom be limited, that it bow to an order that is not purely imaginary and that it be aware both of this order and of its own margin of creativity" (1983: 189, fn. 16).

45 For a postmodernistic defense of ethnophilosophy, see Salemohamed 1983. For a more recent, comparatively strident condemnation of virtually the whole of African philosophy as non-philosophy, as too culturally specific and descriptive (in other words, as ethnophilosophy yet again), see Pearce 1992.

46 Oruka does not regard Griaule's Ogotemelli as a sage, because basically all he does is to summarize Dogon beliefs (no matter how esoteric) on a variety of topics. He argues there is minimal evidence of critical and independent reflection upon the beliefs by Ogotemelli himself (1990a: 45–6).

47 Oruka evidently views "philosophical sagacity" as a species of the genus "professional philosophy" specially designed for accommodating "traditional" African cultures.

48 Which he understands as involving "the philosophical analysis of concepts in a given African language to help clarify meaning and logical implications arising from the use of such concepts" (1990a: xx).

49 As expressed by Rorty 1992.

50 See, for example, the "Introduction" to Moser and van der Nat 1995.

51 The book is an edited version of Okere's doctoral dissertation presented in 1971.

52 He specifically mentions Tempels, Kagame, and Mbiti by name. Although suspicious of attempts to mine African languages for philosophical insights, he does not *absolutely* rule this out as a possibility: "Our scepticism does not, of course, refuse all validity to the thesis of linguists who have drawn attention to the close relationship between language and thought. According to the best researches, language seems to affect culture and thought at some level but there is not enough material yet to help determine precisely how" (1983: 9).

53 Except insofar as it would be taught and studied as an alien philosophical tradition, like Chinese philosophy, Indian philosophy, and so forth.

54 Serequeberhan also mounts severe critiques of Kwame Nkrumah's "consciencism" (for its neo-Marxist "scientific" pretensions), and Leopold Senghor's theory of Negritude (for its racism arising from the special "traits" associated with being African).

55 "*Suppressed* prime" in the sense, perhaps, that it is portrayed as never realizing a potential.

56 See, for example, Venable (1966).

References

Abraham, W. E. (1962) *The Mind of Africa* (Chicago: University of Chicago Press).

Appiah, K. Anthony (1992) *In My Father's House: Africa in the Philosophy of Culture* (Oxford: Oxford University Press).

Bernasconi, Robert (1997) "African Philosophy's Challenge to Continental Philosophy," in E. Eze (ed.), *Postcolonial African Philosophy* (Oxford: Blackwell Publishing), pp. 183–96.

Bodunrin, Peter (1975) " 'Theoretical Entities' and Scientific Explanation," *Second Order*, 4(1): 56–65.

Bodunrin, Peter (1981) "The Question of African Philosophy," *Philosophy*, 56: 161–79.

Bodunrin, Peter (1992) "Philosophy in Africa: The Challenge of Relevance and Commitment," in H. Nagl–Docekal and F. M. Wimmer (eds.), *Postcolonial African Philosophy* (Munich and Vienna: Oldenbourg), pp. 15–35.

Coetzee, P. H. and Roux, A. P. J. (eds.) (1998) *The African Philosophy Reader* (New York and London: Routledge).

Emmet, Dorothy (1972) "Haunted Universes," *Second Order*, 1(1): 34–42.

English, P. and Kalumba, K. M. (eds.) (1996) *African Philosophy: A Classical Approach* (Englewood Cliffs, NJ: Prentice-Hall).

Eze, Emmanuel (ed.) (1997) *Postcolonial African Philosophy: A Critical Reader* (Oxford: Blackwell).

Eze, Emmanuel (ed.) (1998) *African Philosophy: An Anthology* (Cambridge, MA: Blackwell).

Fashina, Oladipo (1988) "Marx, Moral Criticism, and Political Choice," *The Philosophical Forum*, XIX(4) (summer): 291–308.

Gbadegesin, Segun (1991) *African Philosophy: Traditional Yoruba Philosophy and Contemporary African Realities* (New York: Peter Lang).

Gordon, Lewis (1997) *Her Majesty's Other Children: Sketches of Racism from a Neocolonial Age* (New York and Oxford: Rowman and Littlefield).

Griaule, Marcel (1965) *Conversations with Ogotemmeli* (Oxford: Oxford University Press).

Gyekye, Kwame (1975) "Philosophical Relevance of Akan Proverbs," *Second Order*, 4(2): 45–53.

Gyekye, Kwame (1995) *An Essay on African Philosophical Thought: The Akan Conceptual Scheme* (Philadelphia: Temple University Press; revised edn. of the 1987 text, with a new Preface by the author).

Gyekye, Kwame (1996) *African Cultural Values: An Introduction* (Philadelphia and Accra, Ghana: Sankofa Publishing Company).

Gyekye, Kwame (1997) *Tradition and Modernity: Philosophical Reflections on the African Experience* (New York: Oxford University Press).

Hallen, Barry (1977) "Robin Horton on Critical Philosophy and Traditional Thought," *Second Order*, 6(1): 81–92. Rev. and repr. as "Analytic Philosophy and Traditional Thought: A Critique of Robin Horton," in P. English and K. M. Kalumba (eds.), *African Philosophy: A Classical Approach* (Englewood Cliffs, NJ: Prentice-Hall), pp. 216–28.

Hallen, Barry (2002) *A Short History of African Philosophy* (Bloomington and Indianapolis: Indiana University Press).

Hallen, Barry and Sodipo, J. Olubi (1997) *Knowledge, Belief, and Witchcraft: Analytic Experiments in African Philosophy* (Stanford: Stanford University Press; UK edn. London: Ethnographica Publishers Ltd, 1986).

Horton, Robin (1967) "African Traditional Thought and Western Science," *Africa*, 37: 50–71, 155–87 (also in Horton 1993, pp. 197–258).

Horton, Robin (1982) "Tradition and Modernity Revisited," in M. Hollis and S. Lukes (eds.), *Rationality and Relativism* (Oxford: Blackwell Publishing), pp. 201–60 (also in Horton 1993, pp. 301–46).

Horton, Robin (1993) *Patterns of Thought in Africa and the West: Essays on Magic, Religion and Science* (Cambridge: Cambridge University Press).

Horton, Robin and Finnegan, Ruth (eds.) (1973) *Modes of Thought* (London: Faber and Faber).

Hountondji, Paulin (1983) *African Philosophy: Myth and Reality* (Bloomington: Indiana University Press).

Imbo, Samuel Oluoch (1998) *An Introduction to African Philosophy* (New York and Oxford: Rowman and Littlefield).

Jahn, Janheinz (1961) *Muntu: An Outline of the New African Culture* (New York: Grove Press).

Kagame, Alexis (1956) *La Philosophie Bantu-Rwandaise de l'être*, 8 vols (Brussels: Academie Royale des Sciences Coloniales, n.s. 12, no. 1).

Makinde, M. Akin (1988a) *African Philosophy, Culture, and Traditional Medicine* (Athens: Ohio University Center for International Studies).

Masolo, D. A. (1994) *African Philosophy in Search of Identity* (Bloomington: Indiana University Press).

Mbiti, John S. (1969) *African Religions and Philosophies* (New York: Doubleday).

Moser, P. and van der Nat, A. (ed.) (1995) *Human Knowledge: Classical and Contemporary Approaches*, 2nd edn. (Oxford: Oxford University Press).

Mosley, Albert (ed.) (1995) *African Philosophy: Selected Readings* (Englewood Cliffs: Prentice-Hall).

Mudimbe, V. Y. (1988) *The Invention of Africa: Gnosis, Philosophy, and the Order of Knowledge* (Bloomington: Indiana University Press).

Okere, Theophilus (1983) *African Philosophy: A Historico-Hermeneutical Investigation of the Conditions of Its Possibility* (Lanham, MD: University Press of America).

Okolo, Okonda (1991) "Tradition and Destiny: Horizons of an African Philosophical Hermeneutics," in T. Serequeberhan (ed.), *African Philosophy: The Essential Readings* (New York: Paragon House).

Oruka, H. Odera (1978) "Four Trends in African Philosophy." Paper presented at the William Amo Symposium in Accra, Ghana, July 24–29. Later published in Alwin Diemer (ed.), *Philosophy in the Present Situation of Africa* (Weisbaden, Germany: Franz Steiner Erlagh).

142

Oruka, H. Odera (ed.) (1990a) *Sage Philosophy: Indigenous Thinkers and the Modern Debate on African Philosophy* (Leiden: E. J. Brill).

Outlaw, Lucius (1996) "African 'Philosophy'? Deconstructive and Reconstructive Challenges," in *On Race and Philosophy* (New York and London: Routledge).

Owomoyela, Oyekan (1987) "Africa and the Imperative of Philosophy: A Skeptical Consideration," *African Studies Review*, 30(1) (March): 79–100 (repr. in Mosley 1995, pp. 236–62).

Pearce, Carol (1992) "African Philosophy and the Sociological Thesis," *Journal of the Philosophy of the Social Sciences*, 22(4) (December): 440–60.

Pittman, John (ed.) (1997) *African-American Perspectives and Philosophical Traditions* (New York and London: Routledge).

Pratt, Vernon (1972) "Science and Traditional African Religion," *Second Order*, 1(1): 7–20.

Quine, W. V. O. (1960) *Word and Object* (Cambridge, MA: MIT Press).

Rorty, Richard (ed.) (1992) *The Linguistic Turn* (Chicago: University of Chicago Press; 1st edn. 1967).

Salemohamed, G. (1983) "African Philosophy," *Philosophy*, 58: 535–8.

Serequeberhan, Tsenay (1991) *African Philosophy: The Essential Readings* (New York: Paragon House).

Serequeberhan, Tsenay (1994) *The Hermeneutics of African Philosophy* (London: Routledge).

Serequeberhan, Tsenay (1999) *Our Heritage* (New York and Oxford: Rowman and Littlefield).

Skorupski, John (1967) *Symbol and Theory* (Cambridge: Cambridge University Press).

Sogolo, G. S. (1993) *Foundations of African Philosophy: A Definitive Analysis of Conceptual Issues in African Thought* (Ibadan, Nigeria: University of Ibadan Press).

Taiwo, Olufemi (1996) *Legal Naturalism: a Marxist Theory of Law* (Ithaca, NY: Cornell University Press).

Tempels, Placide (1959) *Bantu Philosophy* (Paris: Presence Africaine).

Venable, Vernon (1966) *Human Nature: The Marxian View* (Cleveland: New World Publishing).

Wilson, Bryan (1974) *Rationality* (Oxford: Blackwell).

Wiredu, Kwasi (1972) "On an African Orientation in Philosophy," *Second Order: An African Journal of Philosophy*, 1(2).

Wiredu, Kwasi (1976) "How Not to Compare African Thought with Western Thought," *Ch = Indaba* (July–December). Repr. in R. Wright (ed.), *African Philosophy: An Introduction* (Washington, DC: University Press of America, 1977); and in A. Mosley (ed.), *African Philosophy: Selected Readings* (Englewood Cliffs: Prentice-Hall, 1995).

Wiredu, Kwasi (1980) *Philosophy and an African Culture* (Cambridge and New York: Cambridge University Press).

Wiredu, Kwasi (1983) "The Akan Concept of Mind," *The Ibadan Journal of Humanistic Studies*. Repr. in G. Floistad (ed.), *Contemporary Philosophy, A New Survey*. Vol. 5: *African Philosophy* (Dordrecht: Martinus Nijhoff Publishers and Boston: Kluwer Academic Publishing, 1987).

Wiredu, Kwasi (1985) "The Concept of Truth in the Akan Language," in P. Bodunrin (ed.), *Philosophy in Africa: Trends and Perspectives* (Ife, Nigeria: University of Ife Press), pp. 43–54.

Wiredu, Kwasi (1993) "Canons of Conceptualization," *The Monist*, 76(4) (October): 450–76.

Wiredu, Kwasi (1995a) "On Decolonizing African Religions," in *Proceedings of the Colloquium*, held at Unisa, October 1995.

Wiredu, Kwasi (1995b) "Knowledge, Truth and Fallibility," in I. Kucuradi and R. S. Cohen (eds.), *The Concept of Knowledge* (Boston: Kluwer Academic).

Wiredu, Kwasi (1996) *Cultural Universals and Particulars: An African Perspective* (Bloomington: Indiana University Press).

143

Wiredu, Kwasi and Gyekye, Kwame (eds.) (1992) *Person and Community: Ghanaian Philosophical Studies, I* (New York: Council for Research in Values and Philosophy).

Wright, Richard A. (ed.) (1984) *African Philosophy: An Introduction*, 3rd edn. (Lanham: University Press of America).

Further reading

Abimbola, Wande and Hallen, Barry (1993) "Secrecy ('Awo') and Objectivity in the Methodology and Literature of Ifa Divination," in M. Nooter (ed.), *Secrecy: African Art that Conceals and Reveals* (New York: The Museum for African Art and Munich: Prestel), pp. 212–21.

Appiah, K. Anthony and Gutman, Amy (1996) *Color Conscious* (Princeton: Princeton University Press).

Beattie, John (1966) *Other Cultures: Aims, Methods and Achievements in Social Anthropology* (London: Routledge and Kegan Paul Ltd.).

Bedu-Addo, J. T. (1985) "Wiredu on Truth as Opinion and the Akan Language," in P. Bodunrin (ed.), *Philosophy in Africa: Trends and Perspectives* (Ife, Nigeria: University of Ife Press), pp. 68–90.

Bell, Richard H. (2002) *Understanding African Philosophy: A Cross-Cultural Approach to Classical and Contemporary Issues* (New York and London: Routledge).

Bodunrin, Peter (1975) "The Alogicality of Immortality," *Second Order*, 4(2): 36–44.

Bodunrin, Peter (1975) "Values and Objectivity in the Social Sciences," *Thought and Practice*, 2(1).

Bodunrin, Peter (1978) "Witchcraft, Magic and ESP: A Defense of Scientific and Philosophical Scepticism," *Second Order*, 7(1–2): 36–50. Repr. in A. Mosley (ed.), *African Philosophy: Selected Readings* (Englewood Cliffs, NJ: Prentice-Hall), pp. 371–85.

Bodunrin, Peter (1979) "Belief, Truth and Knowledge," *Second Order*, 8(1–2): 28–46.

Bodunrin, Peter (1985) *Philosophy in Africa: Trends and Perspectives* (Ife, Nigeria: University of Ife Press).

Fashina, Oladipo (1981) "Mythical Consciousness: Neo-Kantian or Quasi-Realist?" *Second Order*, 10(1–2): 31–45.

Fashina, Oladipo (1989) "Frantz Fanon and the Ethical Justification of Anti-Colonial Violence," *Social Theory and Practice*, 15(2): 179–212.

Gadamer, Hans-Georg (1975) *Truth and Method*, trans. W. Glen-Doepel (London: Sheed & Ward).

Gbadegesin, 'Segun (1981) "Ethnicity and Citizenship," *Second Order*, 10(1–2): 3–12.

Gbadegesin, 'Segun (1991) "Negritude and Its Contribution to the Civilization of the Universal: Leopold Senghor and the Question of Ultimate Reality and Meaning," *Ultimate Reality and Meaning*, 14(1): 30–45.

Gordon, Lewis (1997) "Tragic Dimensions of Our Neocolonial 'Postcolonial' World," in Emmanuel Eze (ed.), *Postcolonial African Philosophy* (Oxford: Blackwell), pp. 241–51.

Gordon, Lewis (ed.) (1997) *Existence in Black: An Anthology of Black Existential Philosophy* (New York and London: Routledge).

Gordon, Lewis (2000) *Existentia Africana: Understanding Africana Existential Thought* (New York and London: Routledge).

Gyekye, Kwame (1974) "Substance in Aristotle's *Categories* and *Metaphysics*," *Second Order*, 3(1): 61–5.

Gyekye, Kwame (1975) "Review of John Mbiti's *African Religions and Philosophy*," *Second Order*, 4(1): 86–94.

Gyekye, Kwame (1975) "Akan Language and the Materialist Thesis: a Short Essay on the Relation Between Philosophy and Language," *Studies in Language*, 1(2): 227–34.

Gyekye, Kwame (1978) "The Akan Concept of a Person," *International Philosophical Quarterly*, 18(3): 277–87; also in Richard A. Wright (ed.), *African Philosophy: An Introduction*, 3rd edn. (Lanham: University Press of America, 1984).

Gyekye, Kwame (1981) "Philosophical Ideas of the Akans," *Second Order*, 10(1–2): 61–79.

Gyekye, Kwame (1988) *The Unexamined Life: Philosophy and the African Experience* (Accra: Ghana Universities Press).

Gyekye, Kwame (1997) "Philosophy, Culture, and Technology in the Postcolonial," in Emmanuel Eze (ed.), *Postcolonial African Philosophy: A Critical Reader* (Oxford: Blackwell, 1997), pp. 25–44.

Hallen, Barry (1975) "A Philosopher's Approach to Traditional Culture," *Theoria to Theory*, IX(4): 259–72.

Hallen, Barry (1977) "The [African] Art Historian as Conceptual Analyst," *The Journal of Aesthetics and Art Criticism*, 37(3): 303–13.

Hallen, Barry (1981) "The Open Texture of Oral Tradition," *Theoria to Theory*, IX(4): 259–72.

Hallen, Barry (1988) "Afro-Brazilian Mosques in West Africa," *Mimar*, 29: 16–23.

Hallen, Barry (1995) "Some Observations About Philosophy, Postmodernism, and Art in African Studies," *African Studies Review*, 38(1) (April): 69–80.

Hallen, Barry (1996) "What's It Mean?: 'Analytic' African Philosophy," *Quest: Philosophical Discussions*, X/2 (December): 67–77.

Hallen, Barry (1995) " 'My Mercedes Has Four Legs!' 'Traditional' as an Attribute of African Equestrian 'Culture'," in Gigi Pezzoli (ed.), *Horsemen of Africa: History, Iconography, Symbolism* (Milan: Centro Studi Archeologia Africana), pp. 49–64.

Hallen, Barry (1997) "African Meanings, Western Words," *African Studies Review*, 40(1): 1–11.

Hallen, Barry (1998) "Moral Epistemology: When Propositions Come Out of Mouths," *International Philosophical Quarterly*, 38(2) (June): 187–204.

Hallen, Barry (1998) "Academic Philosophy and African Intellectual Liberation," *African Philosophy*, 11(2) (November): 93–7.

Hallen, Barry (2000) "Variations on a Theme: Ritual, Performance, Intellect," in John Pemberton (ed.), *Insight and Artistry: A Cross-Cultural Study of Art and Divination in Central and West Africa* (Washington, DC: Smithsonian Institution Press).

Hallen, Barry (2000) *The Good, the Bad, and the Beautiful: Discourse About Values in an African Culture* (Bloomington and Indianapolis: Indiana University Press).

Hallen, Barry and Olubi, Sodipo J. (1994) "The House of the '*Inu*': Keys to the Structure of a Yoruba Theory of the 'Self'," *Quest: Philosophical Discussions*, 8(1): 3–23.

Heidegger, Martin (1962) *Being and Time*, trans. John Macquarrie and Edward Robinson (New York: Harper & Row).

Henry, Paget (2000) *Caliban's Reason: Introducing Afro-Caribbean Philosophy* (New York and London: Routledge).

Horton, Robin (1960) "A Definition of Religion and Its Uses," *Journal of the Royal Anthropological Institute*, 90: 201–26. Repr. in *Patterns of Thought in Africa and the West: Essays on Magic, Religion and Science* (Cambridge: Cambridge University Press, 1993), pp. 19–49.

Horton, Robin (1960) "Destiny and the Unconscious in West Africa," *Africa*, 31(2): 110–17.

Horton, Robin (1973) "Paradox and Explanation: A Reply to Mr. Skorupski, Parts I & II," *Philosophy of the Social Sciences*, 3: 231–56 and 289–312. Repr. in *Patterns of Thought in Africa and the West: Essays on Magic, Religion and Science* (Cambridge: Cambridge University Press, 1993), pp. 259–300.

Horton, Robin (1973) "Professor Winch on Safari," *European Journal of Sociology*, 17: 157–80. Repr. in *Patterns of Thought in Africa and the West: Essays on Magic, Religion and Science* (Cambridge: Cambridge University Press, 1993), pp. 138–60.

145

Horton, Robin (n.d.) "Traditional Thought and the Emerging African Philosophy Department: A Reply to Dr. Hallen (unpublished manuscript).

Horton, Robin (1973) "Social Psychologies: African and Western," an essay accompanying Meyer Fortes' *Oedipus and Job in West African Religion* (Cambridge: Cambridge University Press), pp. 41–82.

Hountondji, Paulin (1974) "The Myth of Spontaneous Philosophy," *Consequence*, 1 (January–June): 11–38.

Hountondji, Paulin (1985) "The Pitfalls of Being Different," *Diogenes*, 131 (Fall): 46–56.

Hountondji, Paulin (1990) "Scientific Dependence in Africa Today," *Research in African Literatures*, 21(3): 5–15.

Hountondji, Paulin (1995) "Producing Knowledge in Africa Today," *African Studies Review*, 38(3): 1–10.

Hountondji, Paulin (1996) "Intellectual Responsibility: Implications for Thought and Action Today," *Proceedings and Addresses of the American Philosophical Association*, 70/2 (November): 77–92.

Hountondji, Paulin (2002) *The Struggle for Meaning: Reflections on Philosophy, Culture, and Democracy in Africa*, trans. John Conteh-Morgan and with a Foreword by K. Anthony Appiah (Athens, Ohio: Ohio University Center for International Studies).

Husserl, Edmund (1980) *Ideas Pertaining to a Pure Phenomenology and to a Phenomenological Philosophy*, trans. F. Kersten (The Hague: Nijhoff).

Karp, Ivan and Masolo, D. (eds.) (2000) *African Philosophy as Cultural Inquiry* (Bloomington and Indianapolis: Indiana University Press).

Makinde, M. Akin (1977) "Formal Logic and the Paradox of Excluded Middle," *International Logic Review*, 15 (June): 40–52.

Makinde, M. Akin (1984) "An African Concept of Human Personality: The Yoruba Example," *Ultimate Reality and Meaning*, 7(3): 189–200.

Makinde, M. Akin (1985) "A Philosophical Analysis of the Yoruba Concepts of Ori and Human Destiny," *International Studies in Philosophy*, 17(1): 53–69.

Makinde, M. Akin (1988) "African Culture and Moral Systems: A Philosophical Study," *Second Order*, 1(2) (July): 1–27.

Masolo, D. A. (1997) "African Philosophy and the Postcolonial: Some Misleading Abstractions About 'Identity'," in Emmanuel Eze (ed.), *Postcolonial African Philosophy* (Oxford: Blackwell), pp. 283–300.

Masolo, D. A. (1999) "Rethinking Communities in a Global Context," *African Philosophy*, 12(1): 51–68.

Masolo, D. A. (1999) "Critical Rationalism and Cultural Traditions in African Philosophy," *New Political Science*, 21(1): 59–72.

Mbiti, John S. (1970) *Concepts of God in Africa* (New York: Praeger).

Mudimbe, V. Y. (1992) *The Surreptitious Speech: Presence Africaine and the Politics of Otherness 1947–1982* (Chicago: University of Chicago Press).

Mudimbe, V. Y. (1994) *The Idea of Africa* (Bloomington: Indiana University Press and London: James Currey).

Mudimbe, V. Y. and Appiah, Anthony, K. (1993) "The Impact of African Studies on Philosophy," in Robert H. Bates, V. Y. Mudimbe, and Jean O'Barr (eds.), *Africa and the Disciplines: The Contributions of Research in Africa to the Social Sciences and Humanities* (Chicago and London: University of Chicago Press).

Okere, Theophilus (ed.) (1996) *Identity and Change: Nigerian Philosophical Studies I* (Washington, DC: Council for Research and Values in Philosophy).

Oruka, H. Odera (1975) "The Fundamental Principles in the Question of 'African Philosophy', I," *Second Order*, 4: 44–55.

Oruka, H. Odera (1990) "Cultural Fundamentals in Philosophy," *Quest: Philosophical Discussions*, 4(2): 20–37.

Oruka, H. Odera (1997) *Practical Philosophy* (Nairobi and Kampala: East African Educational Publishers).

Oruka, H. O. and Masolo, D. A. (eds.) (1983) *Philosophy and Cultures* (Nairobi: Bookwise Publishers).

Outlaw, Lucius (1996) "African, African American, Africana Philosophy," in John Pittman (ed.), *African-American Perspectives and Philosophical Traditions* (New York and London: Routledge).

Oyewumi, Oyeronke (1997) *The Invention of Women: Making an African Sense of Western Gender Discourses* (Minneapolis and London: University of Minnesota Press).

Serequeberhan, Tsenay (1991) "The African Liberation Struggle: A Hermeneutic Exploration of an African Historico-Political Horizon," *Ultimate Reality and Meaning*, 14(1): 46–52.

Serequeberhan, Tsenay (1991) "African Philosophy: The Point in Question," in T. Serequeberhan (ed.), *African Philosophy; The Essential Readings* (New York: Paragon House), pp. 3–28.

Serequeberhan, Tsenay (1997) "The Critique of Eurocentrism and the Practice of African Philosophy," in Emmanuel Eze (ed.), *Postcolonial African Philosophy* (Oxford: Blackwell), pp. 141–61.

Serequeberhan, Tsenay (1998) "The Idea of Colonialism in Hegel's Philosophy of Right," *International Philosophical Quarterly*, 29(3): 301–18.

Sodipo, J. O. (1973) "Notes on the Concept of Cause and Chance in Yoruba Traditional Thought," *Second Order*, 2(2): 12–20.

Sogolo, G. S. (1981) "Universal Prescriptivism and Racial Discrimination," *Second Order*, 10(1–2): 80–90.

Sogolo, G. S. (1990) "Options in African Philosophy," *Philosophy*, 65: 39–52.

Taiwo, Olufemi (1993) "Colonialism and Its Aftermath: the Crisis of Knowledge Production," *Callaloo*, 16(4): 891–908.

Verran, Helen (2001) *Science and an African Logic* (Chicago and London: University of Chicago Press).

Wamba-dia-Wamba, Ernest (1991) "Philosophy in Africa: Challenges of the African Philosopher," in T. Serequeberhan (ed.), *African Philosophy: The Essential Readings* (New York: Paragon House).

Wamba-dia-Wamba, E. and Mamdani, Mahmood (eds.) (1995) *African Studies in Social Movements and Democracy* (Dakar, Senegal: CODESRIA).

Wiredu, Kwasi (1970) "Kant's Synthetic Apriori in Geometry and the Rise of Non-Euclidean Geometries," *Kant-Studien* (January).

Wiredu, Kwasi (1973) "Deducibility and Inferability," *Mind* (January).

Wiredu, Kwasi (1973) "Logic and Ontology, Part 1," *Second Order* 2(1): 71–82.

Wiredu, Kwasi (1974) "Carnap on Iterated Modalities," *Philosophy and Phenomenological Research* (December).

Wiredu, Kwasi (1974) "Classes and Sets," *Logique et Analyse* (January).

Wiredu, Kwasi (1983) "Morality and Religion in Akan Thought," in H. Odera Oruka and D. Masolo (eds.), *Philosophy and Cultures* (Nairobi, Kenya: Bookwise Ltd.), pp. 6–13. Repr. in Norm Allen, Jr. (ed.), *African-American Humanism: An Anthology* (New York: Prometheus Books, 1991).

Wiredu, Kwasi (1985) "Replies to Critics," in P. Bodunrin (ed.), *Philosophy in Africa: Trends and Perspectives* (Ife, Nigeria: University of Ife Press), pp. 91–102.

Wiredu, Kwasi (1991) "On Defining African Philosophy," in T. Serequeberhan (ed.), *African Philosophy: The Essential Readings* (New York: Paragon). Repr. in H. Nagl-Docekal and

F. M. Wimmer (eds.), *Postkoloniales Philosophieren: Afrika* (Vienna and Munich: R. Oldenbourg Verlag), pp. 40–62.

Wiredu, Kwasi (1992) "The Moral Foundations of African Culture," and "The African Concept of Personhood," in H. E. Flack and E. D. Pellegrino (eds.), *African-American Perspectives on Biomedical Ethics* (Washington, DC: Georgetown University Press).

Wiredu, Kwasi (1992) "Science, Technology and Humane Values," in *Paths to Human Flourishing: Philosophical Perspectives* (Seoul: Korean Philosophical Association), pp. 35–62.

Wiredu, Kwasi (1995) *Conceptual Decolonization in African Philosophy: Four Essays by Kwasi Wiredu*, intro. and ed. Olusegun Oladipo (Ibadan, Nigeria: Hope Publications).

Wiredu, Kwasi (1995) "Metaphysics in Africa," in J. Kim and E. Sosa (eds.), *A Companion to Metaphysics* (Oxford: Blackwell).

Wiredu, Kwasi (1995) "Democracy and Consensus in Traditional African Politics: A Plea for a Non-Party Polity," *The Centennial Review*, 39(1) (Winter).

Wiredu, Kwasi (1995) "Philosophy, Humankind and the Environment," in H. Odera Oruka (ed.), *Philosophy, Humanity and Ecology*. Vol. 1: *Philosophy of Nature and Environmental Ethics* (Nairobi, Kenya: African Center for Technology Studies Press).

Wiredu, Kwasi (1995) "Particularistic Studies of African Philosophies as an Aid to Decolonization," and "On Decolonizing African Religions," in J. Malherbe (ed.), *Decolonizing the Mind: Proceedings of the Colloquium Held at Unisa, October 1995* (Pretoria: Research Unit for African Philosophy).

Wiredu, Kwasi (1996) "Time and African Thought," in D. Tiemersma and A. F. Oosterling (eds.), *Time and Temporality in Intercultural Perspectives* (Amsterdam and Atlanta: Rodopi).

7

Philosophy in South Africa Under and After Apartheid

MABOGO P. MORE

Kwame Nkrumah argued that philosophy does not occur in a vacuum but that it arises from a social milieu: "The social milieu affects the content of philosophy," he contended, "and the content of philosophy seeks to affect the social milieu, either by confirming it or by opposing it" (1964: 56). Indeed, it can be asserted that Nkrumah's view finds perfect and concrete expression in philosophy in South Africa. The claim of this chapter, therefore, is that academic philosophy in South Africa has to a large extent sought to affect the social and political milieu of apartheid by confirming or opposing it.

In 1996, just before the adoption of the new South African Constitution, Nelson Mandela's successor to the presidency, Thabo Mbeki, opened his address to the country's Constitutional Assembly with the firm declaration: "I am an African." In response, white opposition leaders such as the former president of the apartheid regime, F. W. De Klerk, also declared, "I am an African." This response subsequently led to a question that has been at the center of popular discourse in the country and has a bearing on the conception of African philosophy: who is an African? Is South African philosophy African philosophy simply because South Africans consider themselves African? When considering African philosophy in South Africa, it may be argued that philosophy as professed and practiced by most white South African philosophers is not conceived as African philosophy, their claim to being African notwithstanding.

The history of philosophy in South Africa cannot, for reasons of sheer quantity, be adequately covered within the confines of a short chapter such as this one. Research has been conducted on individual philosophers and traditions, but no single historian of philosophy has thus far covered the entire field. What follows therefore is merely a quick mapping out of the terrain with the hope that such an account will provide enough information for readers to undertake a more thorough investigation.

Institutionalized Philosophy

South Africa has been, and still is, to a large degree, a racially, culturally, linguistically, and ideologically divided society. The same applies to institutions of higher

149

learning and the philosophy studied in those institutions. Therefore a brief background of university education in the country might help us understand the role of philosophy within that society.

Prior to 1960, universities in South Africa were divided broadly in terms of the two official languages, English and Afrikaans (South African or Cape Dutch), and also according to ideological positions. While the English-language universities (Cape Town, Witwatersrand, Rhodes, and Natal), in accordance with their liberal universalism, admitted some "non-white" students, the Afrikaans-speaking (volk) universities (Potchefstroom, Orange Free State, Pretoria, Stellenbosch, Port Elizabeth, and, later, Rand Afrikaans University), on the other hand, excluded black students. As the only correspondence institution, the University of South Africa occupied the unique position of being both an English and Afrikaans university despite the fact that, ideologically, it was aligned with the Afrikaans universities.

A peculiar South African phenomenon in relation to universities, therefore, is that no university is simply and purely a university without qualification. They were all predicated on racial and cultural identities. They are either Afrikaans, English, or black. In the last category were Fort Hare University (originally for Xhosas), University of Zululand (for Zulus), University of the North (for North and South Sothos, Tswanas, Tsongas, and Vendas), University of Durban-Westville (for Indians), and University of the Western Cape (for Coloreds). These, however, were products of one of the apartheid laws called the Extension of University Education Act (No. 45 of 1959), which empowered the Minister of Bantu Education and Administration to "provide for the establishment, maintenance, management and control of university colleges for non-white persons." Even though these – with the exception of the University of the Western Cape – were English-medium institutions, the staff and managers were predominantly Afrikaans speakers, whose function was more that of policing black people than teaching them.

Despite the fact that South Africa has a variety of philosophical orientations and traditions within the small community of professional philosophers, philosophy is still broadly divided into two traditions, namely, the Anglo-Saxon tradition, which is mainly the preserve of English-medium universities, and the Continental, which is generally associated with the Afrikaans-speaking universities. Ideologically, English-medium universities and most English-speaking philosophers generally link their philosophical practice specifically with the political ideals of liberalism, while some of the Afrikaans-medium universities and philosophers have embraced Afrikaner (volks) nationalism or have developed a Calvinistic philosophy which is supposed to have its roots in the specific historical experience and consciousness of the Afrikaner.

Western philosophy is taught at all black universities, with the exception of the University of Durban-Westville which, because originally established for the Indian population, has, in addition to Western philosophy, a department of Indian philosophy. At these universities, one or the other and sometimes a mixture of the Anglo-Saxon and the Continental traditions is offered, depending, of course, on who chairs the department at a particular point in time. Academic philosophy in South Africa has always been the terrain of whites, particularly white males.

150

Philosophy Before Apartheid

There is a general misconception about the origins of apartheid. The name "apartheid" emerged – in its legal sense – in 1948 as a means of strengthening and perfecting an already existing system of racial discrimination and domination rooted in the attitudes and values of the whites ever since they came into contact with the African. So the Afrikaner Nationalist Party, which first came to power in 1948 and introduced the name "apartheid," established its fortification on grounds already prepared by the first Dutch settlers in the Cape of Good Hope under Jan van Riebeeck in 1652, and later by the British settlers in 1820. Therefore philosophy before apartheid was fundamentally and ideologically no different from philosophy during apartheid.

According to Andrew Nash (1997: 63), philosophy as an academic discipline can be traced back prior to 1873 with the publication of the first philosophical text designed specifically for the use of students at the South African College. After the establishment of a theological school at Stellenbosch in 1859, in order to "compensate for the inadequate preparatory studies of their students" (van der Watt, quoted in Nash 1997: 63), a number of professors offered tuition in the history of philosophy, thus heralding the earliest institutionalization of philosophy in South Africa. After Stellenbosch, several Afrikaans-medium universities emerged in the Orange Free State and around Johannesburg and Pretoria. From the cultural and religious traditions of the Afrikaner people a certain distinct Calvinist and neo-Fichtean philosophy developed, especially at Potchefstroom University. Most of its advocates came from or studied in Europe under philosophers such as Schelling, Herder, or Fichte and were also under the influence of Kant, Kierkegaard, Husserl, Abraham Kuyper, etc. – mostly German and Dutch philosophers.

From the outset, the dominant tradition in most Afrikaans universities has been Kuyperian neo-Calvinism combined with neo-Fichtean nationalism, both of which provided the bases for the apartheid system. One of the characteristic tenets of Calvinism is "the election by predestination of the few through grace to glorify God... and the damnation of the rest of mankind, also to the glory of God" (Loubser, quoted in Du Toit 1985: 212). This idea of divine election and predestination to a large extent provided the justification for the social ideology of a chosen people and legitimized racial conquest and domination. In his famous Address to the German Nation, "in which are plainly visible the violent racism and nationalism that have caused some of his critics to regard him as a direct ancestor of Nazism" (Aiken 1956: 54), Fichte invoked the concept of "nature" to justify the maintenance of the separation between groups of different "origins" or "languages." Coupled with his view that the individual is subordinate and only an aspect of the self-development of the Absolute Spirit as that which reveals itself historically in the life of a community, Fichte's philosophy found favor with apartheid ideologists.

Nico Diederichs (later Minister of Finance in the late 1960s and early '70s) who, on returning from his studies in Germany and Holland, took over the chair of political philosophy at the University of the Orange Free State, constructed a social metaphysics opposed to human equality. In his 1935 book *Nasionalisme as Lewensbeskouing en*

151

sy Verhouding tot Internasionalisme (*Nationalism as a Weltanschauung and its Relation to Internationalism*), he argued that man is a spiritual being and as such an instrument of God. The individual exists only as a member of the national whole within which self-realization can be achieved:

> Without the uplifting, ennobling and enriching influence of this highest unity, which we call a nation, mankind cannot reach the fullest heights of their human nature.... Only in the nation as the most total, most inclusive human community can man realise himself to the full. The nation is the fulfilment of the individual life. (in Moodie 1975: 156)

The real unity of the nation, for Diederichs, rests upon a single spiritual characteristic, namely, a common culture. Thus a nation is constituted by a unique cultural principle and its unity is a result of a community of commitment to the active realization of this cultural principle in the everyday life-world. In terms of this neo-Fichtean metaphysics, culture as the defining characteristic of a people of a common racial descent (nation) "must continually struggle to remain itself" because God "ruled that there should exist a multiplicity and diversity of nations, languages and cultures" (in ibid. 158, 159). Each nation has something of a unique, Heideggerian, "calling" in accordance with God's plan. It is this explicit articulation of separatism and nationalism that provided the foundation for the pillars of apartheid, especially the later establishment of Bantustans (arid and small remote pieces of land called Homelands for Africans). The neo-Fichtean and neo-Calvinist separatist ideology was officially reiterated by M. C. de Wet Nel, Minister of Bantu Affairs, during the heyday of apartheid in 1959 in a House of Assembly speech, which I shall quote at length:

> The philosophy of life of the settled white population in South Africa, both English-speaking and Afrikaans-speaking in regard to the colour or racial problem...rests on three basic principles.... The first is that God has given a divine task and calling for every People in the world, which dare not be destroyed or denied by anyone. The second is that every People in the world, of whatever race or colour, has an inherent right to live. In the third place, it is our deep conviction that the personal and national ideals of every individual and every ethnic group can best be developed within its own national community. Only then will the other groups feel that they are not being endangered. *This is the philosophic basis of the policy of apartheid....* To our People this is not a mere abstraction, which hangs in the air. It is a divine task, which has to be implemented and fulfilled. (quoted in Sizwe 1979: 82; italics added)

Academic philosophy at English-speaking universities started at the University of the Cape of Good Hope established in 1873. Undoubtedly, the general trend in English-speaking universities was a preoccupation with British philosophical traditions, such as empiricism, and with philosophers such as Locke, Hume, Mill, Russell, and so on. This does not, however, mean that other traditions, such as Greek philosophy, were not taught. One of the early philosophers to occupy the chair of philosophy in 1908 at the South African College in Cape Town (later to become the University of Cape Town) was R. F. A. Hoernle. He became one of the major figures in the intellectual formulation of South African liberalism. Influenced by T. H. Green, Bernard Bosanquet, R. B. Perry, and W. F. Hocking, Hoernle attempted to apply liberal idealist concepts to the South African situation. In his inaugural lecture as Professor of Philosophy at the English-speaking University of the Witwatersrand (1923) he stressed the significance of pluralism in a multiracial society such as South Africa. Later, in his famous *South African Native Policy and the Liberal Spirit* (1939), he argued for a policy of racial separation as opposed to parallelism or assimilation. This resembled in a significant manner apartheid's later legislation, such as the *Group Areas Act, Separate Amenities Act, Mixed Marriage Acts*, and so on, and therefore could be said to have provided arguments for the apartheid policy of the Nationalist Party.

Both philosophical traditions – the Anglo-Saxon and the Continental – therefore, in varying degrees, may have been used to provide justification for racial and cultural discrimination before official apartheid in 1948 and during apartheid in the years that followed.

Philosophy During Apartheid

When the Afrikaner Nationalist Party came into power in 1948, it introduced a number of apartheid laws in accordance with the basic tenets of neo-Calvinism and neo-Fichtean nationalism in order to extend and entrench its hegemony. There was, according to Hilda Kuper, "a terrifying, almost lunatic 'rationality' as laws moved from the prohibition of body contact to prohibition of the exchange of ideas" (Berghe 1979: 31). Laws were promulgated – for example, the Prohibition of Mixed Marriage Act of 1949, the Group Areas Act of 1950, the Immorality Amendment Act of 1950, the Bantu Education Act of 1953, and, of course, the Extension of University Education Act of 1959, which literally brought ethnic universities into existence. Thus Diederichs' Calvinist nationalism was realized in all domains: social, cultural, educational, religious, and political.

Three types of philosopher emerged after 1948: defenders, neutralists, and dissidents.[1] Most Afrikaans university philosophers explicitly defended apartheid. The defense was so vigorous and extensive, encompassing a variety of philosophical traditions, that even Rawls's theory of justice was construed to be compatible with the basic tenets of apartheid.[2] But it was phenomenology that most rendered itself vulnerable to this kind of misuse. Husserlian and Heideggerian phenomenology were put especially into the services of the apartheid state philosophy of education referred to as *Fundamentiele Pedagogie* (Fundamental Pedagogy), spearheaded by the Afrikaans-speaking University of Potchefstroom for Christian Higher Education. Phenomenological categories such as "life-world," "essences," "world-view," "epoch," "givenness," etc. easily lent themselves to manipulation as ideological instruments. For example, Article 1 of the Christian National Education Report combines phenomenological categories with neo-Fichtean notions:

> We believe that the teaching and education of the children of white parents should occur on the basis of the *life* and *world-view* of the parents. For Afrikaans-speaking

> children this means that they must be educated on the basis of the Christian-National
> life and world-view of our nation. In this life and world-view, the Christian and Na-
> tional principles are of basic significance and they aim at the propagation, protestation,
> and development of the Christian and National being and nature of our nation.... By
> the national principle we understand love for everything that is our own, with special
> mention of our country, our language, our history and our culture.

From the phenomenological categories of "life-world" and "world-view" is derived the fundamental tenet of apartheid, namely separation on the basis of culture, language, and history.

Philosophy at most English-speaking universities, while still embracing the liberal spirit, increasingly became associated with analytical philosophy. It is in this group that we find most neutralists, those who believe that "philosophy ought to be pursued for its own sake" without intervention in social and political issues of the day. Since philosophy, according to the neutralists, is a second-order activity concerned mainly with the logical analysis of concepts, the task of the philosopher is therefore the clarification of the logic of concepts and their meanings. Social and political issues are not, accordingly, the responsibility of the philosopher *qua* philosopher but *qua* active citizen. These are philosophers who Ronald Aronson characterized as "professionally indifferent to what goes on in South Africa today. Whatever their personal commitments, professionally they have no difficulty staying out of politics" (1990: ix). As I have argued elsewhere,[3] and as the quotation from Nkrumah at the start of this chapter suggests, the adoption of a particular conception or tradition of philosophy is simultaneously an expression of one's ideological position. Moreover, philosophical traditions function not only as ideologies but also as particular political agendas.

The dissidents generally come from the Marxist and, sometimes, liberal traditions. The Marxist tradition has not been strong within philosophy departments; rather, it tended to have considerable following in other departments and outside the university establishment. This group of philosophers came from both the Afrikaans and English-medium universities. A prominent figure among the English philosophers representing the dissidents was Richard Turner, who was assassinated by apartheid agents in 1977. Some few Afrikaans-speaking philosophers, not necessarily Marxist, located at Afrikaans universities such as Stellenbosch, also risked ostracism from the Afrikaner community by publicly denouncing apartheid. For example, Willie Esterhuyse (1981) took a strong stand against social and political discrimination, and both Johan Degenaar (e.g. 1978, 1982a, 1982b) and Andre Du Toit (e.g. 1982) have made contributions to anti-apartheid social and political philosophy.

African Philosophy in South Africa

In response to Mbeki's Africanist declaration, most whites, especially Afrikaners, declared themselves African. Is philosophy in South Africa therefore African philosophy simply because whites have assumed an African identity? More precisely, the whites of Dutch and French descent who landed at the Cape of Good Hope in 1652 called

154

themselves Afrikaner. Loosely translated, the name "Afrikaner" means African. Can we then refer to "Afrikaner" philosophy as African philosophy? If African philosophy is philosophy by people who regard themselves as African, then, by their own admission in the Constitutional Assembly, white South African philosophers have produced African philosophy ever since 1652. If by African philosophy we mean a philosophy that is a product of the geographical space called Africa, then, since South Africa is part of the continent of Africa, white South African philosophy must be African philosophy. If African philosophy *à la* Hountondji is that discursive field articulated by Africans concerning problems that are not necessarily related to African experience, then, if white South Africans are Africans, philosophical works produced by them concerning problems that are related to Europe qualify as African philosophy.

Yet most white South Africans would not agree to the above conclusions. By their own admission, whether Afrikaner or English, they certainly do not regard either themselves or their philosophy as African. Apartheid has created two distinct South Africas, one that sees itself as white, Western, civilized, and developed, the other as black, African, presumably uncivilized, and underdeveloped. Consequently, a widely shared prejudice among whites and some blacks is that while white South Africa is a part of Africa geographically, it is not culturally, politically, or certainly economically, African. Evidence of this attitude, which Mahmood Mamdani aptly calls "South African exceptionalism" (1996: 27), is abundant not only in the political, social, religious, and cultural domains but also in philosophical discourse.[4]

Given this exceptionalist attitude, the question of African philosophy, not only as an academic discursive field but also as reality, was never on the agenda of the dominant white philosophical voices in South Africa. If raised at all, the response was decidedly dismissive. The two journals of philosophy in the country – obviously under white control and editorship – until very recently, hardly published a single piece on African philosophy during their long history, even though located within the geographical space of Africa. The obvious reasons are, first, the European construction of the African as the absolute Other, and, second, the constructed self-image and self-conception of philosophy itself. Africa and the Africans supposedly lack what both the European and philosophy share: rationality.[5]

If not rejected *tout court*, African philosophy was used as an instrument by apartheid apologists and defenders to legitimize and justify their ideologies of separate ethnic and racial development. One of the oft-quoted and most abused texts by defenders of apartheid was John S. Mbiti's *African Religions and Philosophy*. F. J. Engelbrecht, a philosophy professor at one of the Historically Black Universities, relying heavily on Mbiti's account of the African conception of time, produced a text entitled *Tyd en Neurose by die Bantoe* (The Bantu, Time and Neuroses 1972), according to which "The life-world of the Bantu is totally different from that of the white. *Integration* and *equation* would not only create confusion but also psychological and social disturbances" (p. 2). The difference between the "Bantu" and white life-worlds is, according to Engelbrecht *à la* Mbiti, a consequence of the African conception of time, a two-dimensional conception that places a heavy emphasis on the past and the present, with virtually no reference to the future.

Out of approximately 21 universities, only 2 introduced African philosophy in their syllabi in the 1980s and very little research was done in this area. However, events following the release of Nelson Mandela from jail necessitated a repositioning in the intellectual terrain in terms of the (re)articulation of issues pertaining to the African continent.

A great deal has happened in the field of African philosophy outside mainstream university departments. Literary and political figures such as Es'kia Mphahlele, Mazisi Kunene, Bessie Head, Miriam Tladi, Mongane Serote, Dennis Brutus, Sipho Sepamla, Chief Albert Luthuli, Nelson Mandela, Robert Sobukwe, Steve Biko, Archbishop Desmond Tutu, and so on, have been articulating metaphysical, ethical, epistemological, social, and political philosophies defined by the peculiarities and actualities of South African social, political, and economic circumstances. In his classic, *The African Image* (1962), Mphahlele strongly rejects Senghor's Negritude from a literary point of view. However, he agrees with his philosophical interpretation of African humanism, a theme that constitutes the basis of his literary and educational works. In 1977 Kunene gave a lengthy interview on African philosophy which was followed by an article entitled "The Relevance of African Cosmological Systems to African Literature Today" (1980). Politically, the efforts of Mandela's nationalism, Sobukwe's "Pan-Africanism," and Biko's Black Consciousness have definitely contributed to the development of African philosophy. It is, in fact, in this political sphere that African philosophy has been vibrant in South Africa.

Three important developments in African philosophy have received very little attention in South Africa. First, Chabani Manganyi, an African existentialist, has, since the mid-1970s, articulated the philosophy of Black Consciousness (see, for example, 1973, 1977a, 1977b, and 1981). Second, Mathole Motshekga, who is now the premier of the Gauteng Province in the new South Africa, established the Kara School of African Art, Culture, and Philosophy and co-published *An Introduction to Kara Philosophy* (1983). Third, there has been a re-emergence of the concept of "*ubuntu*," popularized by Archbishop Desmond Tutu, and the concept of "African Renaissance," popularized by President Thabo Mbeki.

When political violence intensified during the late 1980s and after Mandela's release from prison, Archbishop Desmond Tutu, together with other political leaders, made an impassioned plea for an African moral philosophy of *ubuntu/botho*. Like most fundamental concepts, *ubuntu* defies a single definition or characterization. Consequently, it has been variously equated with African communalism or African humanism, and has been associated with values such as caring, sharing, hospitality, forgiveness, compassion, empathy, honesty, humility, or "brotherhood."[6] The humanistic nature of *ubuntu* is expressed in the words of M. Buthelezi as follows:

> Long before Europeans settled in South Africa a little more than three centuries ago, indigenous African peoples had well-developed philosophical views about the worth of human beings and about desirable community relationships. A spirit of humanism – called *ubuntu* (humanness) in the Zulu language and *botho* in the Sotho language – shaped the thoughts and daily lives of our peoples. Humanism and communal traditions together encouraged harmonious social relations. (1984: 2)

In one sense, *ubuntu* is a philosophical concept forming the basis of relationships, especially ethical behavior. In another sense, it is a traditional politico-ideological concept referring to socio-political action. As a moral or ethical concept, it is a point of view according to which moral practices are founded exclusively on consideration and enhancement of human well-being; a preoccupation with human welfare. It enjoins that what is morally good is what brings dignity, respect, contentment, and prosperity to others, self, and the community at large (Wiredu 1980: 6).[7] *Ubuntu* is a demand for respect for persons no matter what their circumstances may be.

In its politico-ideological sense it is a principle for all forms of social or political relationships. It enjoins and makes for peace and social harmony by encouraging the practice of sharing in all forms of communal existence. *Ubuntu* in this sense expresses an understanding – a societal bond – and forms the basis for consensus. Fundamental to African political philosophy and ontology is the view that an individual is not a human being except as he or she constitutes part of a social order. This is a conception of the self as intrinsically linked to, and forming a part of, the community. In this communal orientation the self is dependent on other selves and is defined through its relationships to other selves. This dependency on the other is epitomized by the expression: "*Motho ke motho ka batho ba bang*" (Sotho) or "*umuntu ngumuntu ngabantu*" (Xhosa, Zulu) meaning, respectively, "a person is a person through other persons," "I am, because we are." While the term *ubuntu* is of South African origin, the phenomenon contains a wider African reality enshrined in African humanism, communalism, and what Nkrumah calls "consciencism." As Wiredu confirms:

> The sense of solidarity and fellowship which, as it were, spills over from the extended family to the larger community and the well-known spontaneity of our people . . . combine to infuse our social life with a pervasive humanity and fullness of life which visitors to our land have always been quick to remark. (1980: 21)

Philosophy in Post-Apartheid South Africa

Since the release of Nelson Mandela in 1990, certain things have changed dramatically, but others simply have refused to change. Philosophy in South Africa after apartheid has both changed and not changed. Departments of philosophy in most universities have not changed at all structurally, ideologically, or academically. "Believe It or Not," to use Leonard Harris's phrase, there is only one black person teaching philosophy at a Traditionally White University. All philosophy departments, even at the Historically Black Universities – except two – are dominated by white males. Out of a population of more than 80 academic philosophers, 8 are black (Africans, Indians, and Coloreds) with only 3 as professors.

Since the appearance of Du Toit's "Philosophy in a Changing Plural Society" (1982), Wolff's "Philosophy in South Africa Today" (1986), and Aronson's *Stay Out of Politics* (1990), all of which question the manner in which philosophy has been practiced in South Africa, nothing much has come out of English-speaking philosophers, except politically correct utterances to the effect that philosophy must deal with socio-political issues of the day. Responding to Wolff, Miller and Macdonald concede that in South Africa "philosophy, and in particular philosophy

157

applied to certain social, political and moral issues, ought to receive much greater emphasis" (1990: 446). Among some Afrikaans-speaking philosophers the trend is now an immersion in postmodernist articulation of cultural diversity, difference, or multiculturalism that sometimes smacks of old apartheid attitudes dressed in post-modern clothes.

Is African philosophy possible after apartheid? Much progress has been made in legitimizing African philosophy in South Africa. At the University of Cape Town, Augustine Shutte offered a course called "Philosophy in the African Context," which he was apparently forced to abandon. This was followed by his groundbreaking and controversial text *Philosophy For Africa* (1993). Despite its shortcomings, the text was definitely a contribution to the general consciousness of Africa. Probably anticipating possible pressure for transformation and relevancy and a concomitant move away from Eurocentric discourse and curricula, the University of South Africa established a Research Unit for African Philosophy (RUFAP) in 1994. The announcement for the founding had the following as some of the general aims of the research project:

- to lay a foundation for an emerging indigenous African philosophy;
- to support the development of a non-Eurocentric identity in South Africa;
- to implement a philosophy course in African philosophy;
- to undertake a critical investigation into the establishment of a curriculum of African philosophy and related study fields;
- to establish a database with a full bibliography of primary and secondary sources on African thinking, and to make this material available to the research community;
- to publish competitive scientific publications with contributions from authorities and acknowledged researchers in the field of African thinking.

Indeed, tremendous progress has been made in relation to some of the aims of the unit. Published under the title *Decolonizing the Mind*, an interdisciplinary collection of papers in the field of African philosophy has appeared from the unit (see Melherbe 1996; see also Coetzee and Roux 1998). This collection boasts papers from prominent African philosophers such as Wiredu, Godwin Sogolo, etc. Several conferences on African philosophy have been hosted by the unit. Several schools have also since emerged, amongst which are the Ubuntu School of African Philosophy and the Kara School of African Art, Culture, and Philosophy, Inc.

Conclusion

The above barely constitutes a fraction of the history of philosophy in South Africa. The aim, however, was merely to highlight the historical complicity of philosophy – like almost everything else – in the evil system of apartheid. I have said very little indeed about this system, precisely because of its worldwide notoriety. The demise of statutory apartheid – even though racism is not dead – has created some space and opened up various possibilities for the development and growth of a South African philosophy that is truly an African philosophy. That will be a philosophy that transcends racial and ethnic boundaries, a philosophy born of experience and struggle.

Notes

1   A quick glance at the *South African Journal of Philosophy* and the predominantly analytical philosophy journal of the English-speaking universities, *The Philosophical Papers*, and the predominantly Afrikaans journal *Koers* will reveal the ideological content of philosophy in South Africa.

2   See Wolff 1986 for a discussion of G. J. C. Van Wyk's "Rawls, Justice and Apartheid."

3   See More 1996b and Wolff 1986 for a sustained argument against the neutralist position.

4   This exceptionalism is expressed in Shutte 1993; Georgiades and Delvare 1975; Rauch 1996; Walt 1997; Merwe 1994, 1997. This list is not exhaustive.

5   See More 1996 for a detailed treatment of the questions of rationality and African philosophy in South Africa.

6   See Khoza 1994; Sindane 1995; Mphahlele 1982; Boon 1996; Bhengu 1996; Teffo 1996; Prinsloo 1998; Makhudu 1993; and Motshekga and Motshekga 1983 (for a full linguistic account of roots and stems of African concepts such as "*Ubuntu*," see especially pp. 59–66).

7   This is not to suggest that Wiredu has articulated the theory of *Ubuntu*, but that there are similarities and common philosophies that are shared by Africans.

References

Aiken, H. D. (1956) *The Age of Ideology* (New York: New American Library).

Aronson, R. (1990) *Stay Out of Politics: A Philosopher Views South Africa* (Chicago: University of Chicago Press).

Berghe, P. L. van den (ed.) (1979) *The Liberal Dilemma in South Africa* (London: Croom Helm).

Bhengu, J. M. (1996) *Ubuntu: The Essence of Democracy* (Cape Town: Novalis).

Boon, M. (1996) *The African Way: The Power of Interactive Leadership* (Sandton: Zebra Press).

Buthelezi, G. M. (1984) "The Legacy of African Humanism," *Natural History*, 12.

Coetzee, P. H. and Roux, A. P. J. (eds.) (1998) *Philosophy for Africa: A Text with Readings* (Johannesburg: Thomson).

Degenaar, Johan (1978) *Afrikaner Nationalism* (Cape Town: Centre for Intergroup Studies).

Degenaar, Johan (1982a) *The Roots of Nationalism* (Cape Town: Academia).

Degenaar, Johan (1982b) *Ideologies: Ways of Looking at South Africa* (Cape Town: UCT).

Du Toit, Andre (1982) "Philosophy in a Changing Plural Society," *South African Journal of Philosophy*, 1(4).

Du Toit, Andre (1985) "Puritans in Africa? Afrikaner 'Calvinism' and Kuyperian Neo-Calvinism in the late Nineteenth-Century South Africa," *Comparative Studies in Society and History*, 27(2).

Engelbrecht, F. J. (1972) *Bantu, Time and Neuroses* (Pietersburg: University of the North).

Esterhuyse, W. P. (1981) *Apartheid Must Die* (Cape Town: Tafelberg).

Georgiades, D. S. and Delvare, I. G. (eds.) (1975) *Philosophy in the African Context* (Braamfontein: Wits University Press).

Hoernlé, R. A. F. (1939) *African Native Policy and the Liberal Spirit*, Phelps-Stokes Lectures (Cape Town).

159

Khoza, R. (1994) *Ubuntu – African Humanism*, discussion paper (Johannesburg: HSRC).

Kunene, M. (1980) "The Relevance of African Cosmological Systems to African Literature Today," in Eldred Durosimi Jones (ed.), *African Literature Today: Myth and History* (London: Heinemann).

Makhudu, N. (1993) "Cultivating a Climate of Co-operation Through Ubuntu," *Enterprise*, 68 (August).

Mamdani, M. (1996) *Citizen and Subject: Contemporary Africa and the Legacy of Late Colonialism* (Princeton, NJ: Princeton University Press).

Manganyi, N. C. (1973) *Being-Black-in-the-World* (Johannesburg: Sprocas).

Manganyi, N. C. (1977a) *Mashangu's Reverie and Other Essays* (Johannesburg: Ravan).

Manganyi, N. C. (1977b) *Alienation and the Body in Racist Society: A Study of the Society that Invented Soweto* (New York: NOK).

Manganyi, N. C. (1981) *Looking Through the Keyhole* (Johannesburg: Ravan).

Mbiti, John S. (1969) *African Religions and Philosophy* (New York: Doubleday).

Melherbe, J. G. (ed.) (1996) *Decolonizing the Mind: Proceedings of the Second Colloquium On African Philosophy* (Pretoria: Department of Philosophy, Unisa).

Merwe, W. L. van der (1994) "Facing the Challenges of Diversity," *South African Journal of Philosophy*, 13(4).

Merwe, W. L. van der (1997) "African Philosophy and Multiculturalism," *South African Journal of Philosophy*, 16(3).

Miller, S. and Macdonald, I. (1990) "Philosophy in South Africa: A Reply to Robert Paul Wolff," *The Philosophical Forum*, 21(4): 442–50.

Moodie, D. T. (1975) *The Rise of Afrikanerdom* (Berkeley: University of California Press).

More, Magobo P. (1996a) "African Philosophy Revisited," *Alternation*, 3(1): 109–29.

More, Magobo P. (1996b) "Complicity, Neutrality or Advocacy Philosophy in South Africa," *Theoria*, 87.

Motshekga, N. and Motshekga, M. (1983) *An Introduction to Kara Philosophy* (Freiburg: Bundschun).

Mphahlele, Es'kia (1982) "Towards a Humanistic Philosophy of Education," *The Capricon Papers* 1(1) (Johannesburg: The Council for Black Education and Research).

Nash, A. (1997) "Wine-Farming, Heresy Trials and the Whole Personality: The Emergence of the Stellenbosch Philosophical Tradition, 1916–40," *South African Journal of Philosophy*, 16(2): 55–65.

Nkrumah, K. (1964) *Consciencism* (London: Panaf).

Prinsloo, E. D. (1998) "Ubuntu Culture and Participatory Management," in P. H. Coetzee and A. P. J. Roux (eds.), *Philosophy for Africa: A Text with Readings* (Johannesburg: Thomson).

Rauch, G. A. (1996) "In What Sense can there be Talk of African Philosophy? A Methodological Hermeneutics," *South African Journal of Philosophy*, 15(1).

Shutte, A. (1993) *Philosophy for Africa* (Rondebosch: UCT).

Sindane, J. (1995) *Democracy in African Societies and Ubuntu*, discussion paper (Pretoria: HSRC).

Sizwe, N. (1979) *One Azania, One Nation* (London: Zed Press).

Teffo, L. J. (1996) "The Other in African Experience," *South African Journal of Philosophy*, 15(3).

Walt, B. J. van der (1997) *Afrocentric or Eurocentric* (Potchefstroom: Potchefstroom University).

Wiredu. K. (1980) *Philosophy and an African Culture* (Cambridge: Cambridge University Press).

Wolff, Robert Paul (1986) "Philosophy in South Africa Today," *The Philosophical Forum*, 18(2–3): 94–104.

8

Philosophy in North Africa

MOURAD WAHBA

In *The Rise and Fall of the Roman Empire* Gibbon describes the tragic end of Hypatia, the female Egyptian philosopher of antiquity. She taught Greek philosophy and found that there is no contradiction between Neoplatonism and Christianity. From this standpoint she adopted Nestorius' theory of Christ as having two natures, the divine and the human, loosely united. At that time Nestorius, as a result of this theory, was condemned at the council of Ephesus in 431 and was declared a heretic. Hypatia was, accordingly, execrated as a follower of a heretic, and in 415 she was killed in an unspeakably gruesome manner by some monks in an assassination endorsed by Cyril, patriarch of Alexandria.

In a nutshell, one can say that the second half of the fifth century was the end of philosophy in Egypt. But in Europe, in the eighteenth century, the age of Enlightenment, Hypatia appeared for the first time as a cause célèbre in religious and philosophical polemic. In 1720 John Toland published a long historical essay titled *Hypatia* in which he focused on the Alexandrian clergy headed by the patriarch Cyril, who was the contriver of so horrid a deed as the murder of Hypatia, and his clergy, who were the executors of his implacable fury. Voltaire used the figure of Hypatia to express his repugnance for the church and revealed religion. In his view, Hypatia was murdered because she believed in rational thinking and trusted the capacities of the human mind freed of imposed dogma (see Dzielska 1995: 109–10). That comment was made in the eighteenth century. In the twentieth century Bertrand Russell, quoting Gibbon's description of the murder of Hypatia, comments wryly that after it Alexandria "was no longer troubled by philosophers" (1946: 368).

In 1198 an even more dramatic incident took place in Cordoba, Spain, in which the Islamic philosopher Ibn Rushd (Averroes, in Latin) was accused of being an atheist. His books were burnt and he was banished to Lucena. The reason for this persecution was his concept of interpretation. He writes:

If the apparent meaning of Scripture conflicts with demonstrative conclusions it must be interpreted allegorically, i.e., metaphorically. This being so, whenever demonstrative study leads to any manner of knowledge about any being, that being is inevitably either unmentioned or mentioned in Scripture. If it is unmentioned there is no contradiction and it is in this case an act whose category is unmentioned, so that the lawyer has to infer it by reasoning from Scripture. If Scripture speaks about it, the apparent meaning of the words inevitably either accords or conflicts with the conclusions of demonstrations about it. If this apparent meaning accords there is no argument. If it conflicts there is a call for allegorical interpretation of it. The meaning of allegorical interpretation is: extension of significance of expression from real to metaphorical significance.

The reason why I think that this definition of the term "interpretation" is the explanation for the persecution of Averroes is that it legalizes diversity of interpretation and, consequently, eliminates the illusion of absolute truth. Obviously, if this illusion is negated, no one has the right to charge another of unbelief and, hence, *ijma* (conformity) and its concomitant dogmatism will be negated. Consequently, Averroes has been marginalized in Islamic culture, or, strictly speaking, neglected. On the other hand, in Europe his books were translated into Latin and Hebrew in the thirteenth century on the political decision of Emperor Frederick II. Frederick made this decision having grown up in a society where a new culture – that is, a secular culture – was in the making. Hence, Averroes' philosophy played a decisive role in the emergence of two complementary movements.

The first movement was the Reformation led by Luther, with his motto "Free inquiry into the Scripture." This motto is analogous to Averroes' statement (1976: 53) that unanimity cannot be established in the interpretation of the Quran. Both Luther and Averroes were accused of being heretics for holding basically the same position. Jean de Jandun of France (1275–1328), who politically opposed the papacy, claimed that there is no principle of belief except reason and experience. He supported a doctrine of the distinctness of the philosophical and religious levels of discourse that was adopted by the Latin Averroists in the fourteenth century. His political collaborator, Marsile de Padou, drew a distinction between reason and faith, the temporal and the spiritual, the church and the state, in the domain of politics. In terms of this distinction, he maintained that the basis of politics should be secular and not religious.

The second movement was the Enlightenment, which is considered the age of reason, or of the sovereignty of reason. The writers of the mid-eighteenth century challenged views of the history and nature of man and of the universe that were endorsed by the Church of Rome. Kant is considered the philosopher who summed up the achievements of the Enlightenment. In his *Critique of Practical Reason* moral duty was withdrawn from possible determination by the material world of perceived phenomena. This implied a refusal to subordinate moral duty to the authorities of the world. The concept of social contract was adopted as a doctrinal counterbalance to the theory of the divine right of kings. It was adopted to show the sovereignty of reason as the ultimate source of moral authority. Averroes was the forerunner of this point of view.

But the propagation of the ideas of these two movements was not an easy task for the Averroists. They faced a severe struggle, especially in the European universities. Albert the Great published a book entitled *Unity of Intellect Against Averroists* and Thomas Aquinas wrote *Contra Averroistas*. Thus Averroism was condemned in 1265 as a heresy. In December 1270 the Bishop of Paris, Etienne Tempier, condemned 15 doctrines; 13 of them were of Averroist inspiration. Here I mention only the doctrines concerning the mortality of the soul, the unity of the active intellect, and the negation of divine providence.

Now, what happened in the Arab world with respect to Averroes? As previously mentioned, he was totally rejected, even by Muslim reformists such as Muhammad Abdou. The Islamic thinkers objected to the secularization that was one of the important features of Averroes' rationalism. This opposition was, in fact, an echo of the collective reaction in the Arab world that may be classified into three types: traditionalism, abortive modernism, and moderate modernity.

Traditionalism is to be viewed as a negative attitude toward Western civilization, and toward any futuristic outlook, on the grounds that the locus of the Golden Age was the past and not the future. Abortive modernism is to be understood as a positive attitude toward the West, but it is at the same time tradition-bound. It is not much more than what one might call an enlightened traditionalism. And that is why abortive modernism, in its fundamental premises and ultimate conclusions, opposes the secular elements of social modernization even more effectively than traditionalism. Moderate modernity may be regarded as a proposed remedy for the previous two conditions of the mind. It sought to interpret tradition within a secular framework free from cultural taboos.

The two most influential figures in the traditionalist movement were Jamal al-Din Afghani of Afghanistan or Iran (1939–97) and Muhammad Abdou (1949–95). It must be stressed from the start that this movement, spearheaded by these two Muslim thinkers, did not question Islamic dogma. Its primary motivation was to meet the challenge the West posed to the Arab world by strengthening Islamic dogma rather than exposing it to rational criticism.

Afghani put the issue of the decadence of Islam in clear and terse words, "Every Muslim is sick, and his only remedy is in the Quran" (1995). Thus, the problem of the Muslim world was not how to be strong, but how to understand religion and live in accordance with its teachings. Pursuing this theme, Afghani published a book entitled *The Refutation of the Materialists*, which became the model for traditionalist thought. Those he attacked under the name of materialists included virtually all, from Democritus to Darwin, together with all those in Islam who gave an explanation of the world without invoking the existence of a transcendent God. Afghani's preoccupation with Western materialism reflected a general Muslim bias against science, which was regarded as responsible for the disintegration of traditional Christianity, and which was now threatening Islam. It is, therefore, not surprising that this stand blocked logically oriented discourse and contributed to deflecting interest in rational criticism.

Thus, Afghani formulated the general direction of traditionalism, but it was Abdou who, using Afghani's teachings as a springboard, gave it its precise formulation. The task he set himself involved two things: first, a restatement of what Islam really was; second, a consideration of its implications for modern society. Regarding the first point, Abdou was of the opinion that reason must accept everything that is in the Quran without hesitation. Once reason acknowledges that Muhammad was a prophet, it must accept the entire content of his prophetic message. The second point proceeds from the first. If reason is controlled by the Quran, then the ideal society will have to be granted to be that which submits to God's commandments, since these commandments are also the principles for the well-ordering of human society. The behavior that the Quran teaches to be pleasing to God is also that which modern social thought must teach as the key to progress. Islam is the true sociology, the science of happiness in this world as well as in the next. So when Islamic law is fully obeyed, society flourishes; when it is rejected, society decays.

For Abdou, this is not just the ideal society, but one that once actually existed. His imagination is fixated on the golden age of Islam and that is why he was against secular society. One proof of this fact is the dispute between Abdou and Farah Antun on the occasion of a book published by the latter in 1903 on the life and philosophy of Ibn Rushd. In his dedication, Antun declares that the book is meant for "the new shoots of the East," by which he meant "those men of sense in every community and every religion of the east" who have seen the danger of mingling the ordinary affairs of the world with religion in an age like ours, and have realized the necessity of moving "with the tide of the European civilization, in order to be able to compete with those who belong to it, for otherwise it will sweep them all away and make them the subjects of others" (1903: 3).

A little further on, Antun explains why he writes about Ibn Rushd: it is to separate temporal from religious authority. There are five reasons why this is necessary. The most important is the third one in which he states that, since the religious authorities legislate with a view to the next world, their control would interfere with the purpose of government, which is to legislate for this world. Implicit in this reason lies the presupposition that the state must be neutral toward all religions, and hence tolerant. This was in direct opposition to Abdou's belief for two reasons. First, for Abdou, the separation of religion and the state was not only undesirable, but also impossible, for the ruler must belong to a specific religion. Second, he maintained that if religion is purified, it could be the basis of political life. Antun's reply was that states are no longer based on religion, but on national unity and modern science and technology. But Abdou's philosophy prevailed with the rise of the Muslim Brotherhood, headed by Hassan al-Banna (1906–49), the initiator of Islamic fundamentalism in Egypt in the 1940s.

We come now to the second movement, that is, abortive modernism. The most influential figures are: Youssef Karam (1886–1959), Osman Amin (1905–73), Zaki Naguib Mahmoud (1905–93), Abdel-Rahman Badawi (1917–, Egypt), Malek Ben Nabi (1905–78, Algiers), Lahbabi (1923–93, Morocco). We begin with Youssef Karam, the advocate of moderate rationalism. He wrote the history of Greek, medieval and modern philosophy, commenting on every philosophic system, either supporting or rejecting it, on the basis of his own system of "moderate rationalism," which is propagated in his two books *Reason and Existence* and *Physics and Metaphysics*.

Karam's "moderate rationalism" reflects the influence of the neo-Thomism that was advocated by Jacques Maritain, under whom Karam studied philosophy at the Catholic Institute in France at the beginning of the First World War. According to Karam's system, the mind can strive toward truth and, thus, can attain certainty. Through its capacity for abstraction, which is the mediator between mind and object, the mind attains to the essence of things. It is this mediation that guarantees scientific objectivity. Karam, therefore, is against the sensualists, because they exclude reason and believe only in the senses. But he is also against those rationalists who deny abstraction, since they fail to locate the real cause that relates the mind to objects.

Abstraction also provides a justification for metaphysics. Due to abstraction, the mind is able to transcend sensible nature to her non-sensible origins and conditions and is thus able to grasp existence per se, which is the subject of metaphysics. Justifying this science in this manner leads Karam to investigations that result in proofs of the immortality of the soul and the existence of God.

The immortality of the soul rests on three proofs. The first is a metaphysical proof, which holds that the human soul is independent of the body in its existence and in its exercise of the mind and the will. The soul, therefore, is immortal and is not annihilated with the extinction of the body. The second is a psychological proof, derived from the basic natural inclination toward eternal survival. And the third is a moral proof resulting from the necessity of final and total sanctions for our free actions. Such sanctions necessitate another life, since they cannot be realized in nature because it is non-mortal. Neither can they be realized in society because society deals only with our outward actions, nor by the conscience because it cannot judge itself. For the existence of God there were plenty of proofs. The most important of these, according to Karam, are the following three: the proof from motion to an unmoved mover, from the fact of order to the existence of its designer, and from the contingent to the necessary. The third argument, like the first, depends upon the principle of causality and is formulated in the statement: "There is a cause for everything that exists." The second relies upon the principle of teleology and is formulated in the statement: "Every action must have a purpose." Karam argues that the principles of causality and teleology are a priori principles of the mind. Such principles are universal because they are presupposed by the existence of mind and perception.

For Karam, the function of mind is judgment, not action, which pertains to the will. As to the question of the relation between the mind and the will, Karam's answer is that each is a cause that is in some way related to judgment. However, they differ in that the will is the *cause efficace* of the mind's activity in judgment because it directs the mind in a direction. The judgment of the mind is the *cause finale* of the will because it offers to the will a specific cause. The direction of the mind by the will forestalls the clash between the mind and religion, since it is the will rather than the mind that fosters faith. Karam writes: "If a person's behavior is straight and firm, his will is ready for faith, and it will direct the mind towards finding support for this belief." The significance of this statement is that the mind per se neither accepts nor refuses belief. That is, it does not gravitate toward a specific belief. The mind is directed toward a specific belief by accepting external reasons under the influence of the will. The inevitable consequence of this "moderate rationalism" is that faith is beyond reason.

Osman Amin is the advocate of the "Philosophy of Inwardness" (*al-Gouwania*) (1964). It is a philosophy that tries to see people and things from a spiritual angle. In other words, it tries to see the invisible world by not limiting itself to the visible. It seeks the inward being, not stopping at the outward. Many traditions traced to the Prophet Muhammad emphasize this opposition between the invisible and the visible. For example: "God does not look at your face and wealth, but at your heart and your actions" (Amin 1964). In this religious sense, *al-Gouwania* is a synonym for freedom. Freedom must not be sought in the possession of objects, like wealth and honors, but in the soul, that is, in something of absolute autonomy, namely, faith in God and attachment to the dignity of man. In this connection Amin thinks that he combines Western philosophy with the framework of the Islamic tradition. He says: "I now go back to the philosophical explanation of *al-Gouwania*. In this respect Maine de Biran is of great help. He says that there is much difference between knowing a truth through our intelligence and having it always present in our soul" (ibid.). Later on he states that the philosophy of *al-Gouwania* adopts the distinction made by Bergson between two very different ways of knowing: "the one being the way of inward vision, penetration by the spirit, by intellectual sympathy; the other the way of exterior vision, effected by using the testimony of the senses or by applying logical analysis alone."

Concerning his concept of freedom, Amin assumes that it is found in Cartesian ethics, which aims at establishing the mastery of the soul over the passions, and in Kant's idea of the moral law, which is wholly inward and a priori, that is to say, preceding and conditioning all experience and not being derived from the exterior world.

Because of his idealist tendencies, Amin is against logical positivism and historical materialism. He is against logical positivism because, in his view, it stops at the limits of the senses and experiment and denies the capabilities of reason, and he is against historical materialism on the grounds that it uses science to abolish man and, consequently, religion, since man, according to Amin's definition, is a religious animal.

The consequence of this is that Amin approaches social issues not only in an idealist manner, but also in a religious manner. He uses the question of socialism as an example of this double approach. According to him, the idealist approach regards the notion of socialism, above all, as an absolute truth that exists in the mind as an impersonal existence, unlimited either by time or by space. In the religious approach, neither the non-temporal nor the non-spatial can serve as a theory or ideology, nor can they be subject to any law, but can only serve as a subject of religious faith. Therefore, socialism has to be Islamic socialism, and its pioneers are Jamal al-Din al-Afghani, Muhammad Abdou, al-Kwakbi (1848–1902, Egypt), and Muhammad Iqbal (1873–1938, India), because they awakened the socialist consciousness of the society.

The purpose of such a philosophic system, according to its advocate, is to restore to our atomic age, the age of historical materialism and logical positivism, faith in God, and allegiance to man. However, in all the lectures he delivered at Cairo University in the late 1950s Amin harshly criticized logical positivism rather than historical materialism. This can be explained by the fact that Zaki Naguib Mahmoud, who was professor of philosophy at the same department, adhered to logical positivism.

Zaki Naguib Mahmoud adopts the attitude of logical positivism toward science. Science, for him, is natural, experimental science, and the basis of scientific knowledge is constituted by the senses, which are the only source of knowledge. The scientific outlook obliges us not to deviate from ascertainable fact. Since basing our investigations on data arising from reality as ascertained through sense experience is the only legitimate methodology of scientific research, the scientific outlook leads to positivism. If the data that preoccupy the researcher are of a linguistic character, dealing with the structure and relationships of statements, positivism in that case becomes "logical." Hence, the label "logical positivists" denotes a group of thinkers who do not accept that there can be any reality transcending sense experience and who concern themselves with the structure and significance of the language of science. Hence, philosophy should be limited to the linguistic analysis of scientific statements.

Zaki Naguib Mahmoud (1955) reaches two important conclusions through his linguistic analysis. The first is that the logical analysis of mathematical sentences indicates that they are tautologies, and that their certainty is due to the fact that they say nothing. He writes: "This strange discovery about the nature of the mathematical sentence justifies the contention that there is only one source of knowledge for man, namely, the senses and that nothing can justify an element of belief beyond the senses, and deriving from an independent faculty, such as the mind." The second conclusion is that value "is purely a subjective expression which has nothing to do with the external world." The significance of this is that, if two people disagree about a value judgment, "the only alternative would be to resort to an external criterion to decide who is wrong and who is right."

The question now is: what is Zaki Naguib Mahmoud's motive for adopting this interpretation of science? The motive is a social one. In one of his later books, he says (1971) that his aim is to reconcile the Arab tradition with modernism. But what is meant by the Arab tradition? According to him, it is the configuration of techniques by which our ancestors lived. Our task then is to choose the techniques that can help us in our contemporary living. Hence, the Arab tradition is not a matter of ideology but of technology.

What now is meant by modernism? According to Zaki Naguib Mahmoud, "Logical positivism represents the spirit of modernism." That is why it is an essential part of Mahmoud's philosophy to affirm a distinction between factual judgment and value judgment. One is scientific, the other is not. As a consequence, one cannot speak of a scientific approach to the study of social change, since this is essentially a matter of values. Hence, ideology also is non-scientific, and it is nonsense to talk of an ideological struggle. That is why, according to Mahmoud, the terms "capitalist society" or "socialist society" are to be replaced with "technological society" or "post-industrial society."

This conception has defined the main tendency in modern bourgeois ideology, and it has received the name of "de-ideologization," which is an attempt to propagate an apolitical state of mind that does not care either for social change or for society. That is why Mahmoud is consistent in his philosophy when he writes "Owing to my philosophical position, I approve of anything that can strengthen the individuality of the individual and that can destroy society in case solidarity were to grow at my own expense. There is no real fact except my own being, and everything else is but an instrument for strengthening this being" (1955: 10). This statement confirms our point of view that de-ideologization is an ideological weapon used against social change.

167

Abdel-Rahman Badawi comes to the same conclusion but through atheistic exist-entialism. According to him, existence and time are synonymous. In his book, *Existential Time*, he declares that any existence that is not temporalized is an abso-lute impossibility. Since time, for Badawi, is divided into physical and subjective time, there is, likewise, physical and subjective existence. Physical existence is the existence of objects in the world in which man exists, while subjective existence is the existence of the self as an independent and quite isolated being. Consequently, communication between selves is initially totally absent. However, this chasm may be overcome by means of a certain kind of leap. But this leap cannot be explained rationally, according to Badawi. The reason is that nothingness is an essential factor in the structure of existence, and the irrational is the intellectual expression of existential nothingness. Modern physics, he argued, corroborates the notion of the irrational. The indeterminism of quantum theory and wave mechanics is quite irrational in the sense that it cannot be reduced to a purely rational system. In this matter, Badawi relies on Louis de Broglie's assumption that physics should reject the idea of causal continuity and limit itself to deducing laws which are necessarily of a statistical nature.

Badawi held also that self-knowledge cannot be attained by reason but by an-other faculty, namely, intuition. The logic of intuition is tension. This tension means the inability to resolve a contradiction. And this is the meaning of the dialectic, which functions only within the self and not outside of it.

Badawi considers his system an appropriate ideology for Arab society. In an article published in 1967 he argues in justification of this claim of appropriateness by appealing to the Islamic heritage as represented in Sufism. He finds a close connection between Sufism and existentialism. Both start from subjectivism and place subjective existence above physical existence. The purpose of discipline in Sufism is to release the self from external encumbrances so that the self can be left alone to develop. The notion of the perfect man for the Sufis means a self-realization that is possible only in man. In this way, humanity becomes a substitute for God. But such humanity is a subjective, rather than an objective, humanity.

The main theme of the Algerian philosopher Malek Ben Nabi is the reconstruc-tion of Islamic society so that it can be free from exploitation and imperialism and capable of coping with modern civilization. This is impossible, Ben Nabi maintains, unless the Islamic idea becomes efficient. By efficient, he means being able to change the world radically to create history. He says that this kind of efficiency was realized during the Prophet's time in the creation of the Islamic empire and the establishment of Islamic truth. One might object that truth is to be identified with not one point of view but many. Although this objection might be well taken from Ben Nabi's standpoint, he insisted that no one can deny the efficiency that was achieved during the period in question.

What does this mean, according to Ben Nabi? It means that truth is subjective, while efficiency is objective. Hence, objective factors are required for the realization of efficiency. Unfortunately, these conditions are absent nowadays for two reasons: the presence of imperialism and the absence of ideas. The first reason is obvious, but the second one is obscure and has to be explained in detail. According to Ben Nabi's theory, there are three worlds that are necessary for any civilization: the world of ideas, the world of persons, and the world of things. The leading world is the world of ideas because man is distinguished from animal by reason, and this means that our idea of a thing precedes its realization in reality. Therefore, ideas have the ability to change the world of persons and the world of things.

Here, the question may be raised: what is the matter with the world of ideas in the Islamic world at the present time? Ben Nabi's answer is that the world of ideas is absent, and its absence is due to two factors: the first is objective, the second subjective. According to Ben Nabi, imperialism is the objective factor. It negates the creative powers of man by involving him in the world of things instead of ideas. In this way, man regresses to the infantile stage, which is characterized by handling things without knowing what they are. That is why imperialism is always keen to sell us things rather than ideas. Even when it does sell us ideas, it sells them only after distorting and falsifying them. But, as an objective factor, imperialism would be ineffective without the subjective factor, which is the susceptibility to imperialism on the part of the victim. This susceptibility is seen in the inability to utilize one's potentialities for raising one's standard of living. Ben Nabi says further (1970) that liberation from imperialism implies liberation from the susceptibility toward capitalism. Hence any revolution neglecting this subjective factor condemns itself to failure.

But how could a revolution avoid such failure? Through a cultural revolution, replies Ben Nabi. It turns out, however, that such a revolution is put forward as a necessary but not sufficient condition. To achieve efficiency through the Islamic idea there is also the need for an "explosive economic policy" to liberate the productive forces. But what is the definition of this technical term "explosive economic policy?" Ben Nabi's definition is that it is neither the capitalist pattern nor the Marxist pattern. But what is it specifically? We get no answer from Ben Nabi, and this is his dilemma, for one cannot control and orientate social change if one lacks a clear idea of what is required for such a change.

I come now to Lahbabi. He gives a radical analysis of the decadence of the Muslim world in the light of the original fountains of Islam, that is, the Quran and the Sunna (the biography of the Prophet). On that basis, he calls for a sweeping transformation of the status quo and the attitudes allied to it, which are extremely backward. He advocates going back to original Islam and shedding off all blind faith in holy texts (*taqlid*) and insists on an *ijtihad*, that is, a rethinking for oneself of the meaning of the original message. In the light of this conception of Islamic revivalism (*Salafiya*), Lahbabi outlines what he takes to be the radical difference between the *Salafiya* and the Western Renaissance.

The Renaissance in the West was, according to Lahbabi, a rupture in the continuity of the given civilization. One was freed from the medieval style of thinking to enslave oneself in the ways of antiquity, thus instantiating the tactic of taking one step forward and two steps backward. On the other hand, the *Salafiya* goes back to the sources of Islam without rejecting any fresh cultural acquisitions, whether Islamic or not. There is a going back to the Quran and the Sunna to liberate the dogma and the laws from superstition. The *Salafiya* is a search for the original force of Islam. It is a creative going back, whereas the Renaissance was a reaction against the Middle Ages. By a paradoxical process, progress is realized through reaction, through the imitation of the thought of the Greeks and Romans. For the

Muslims, by contrast, the Middle Ages was a time of creativity, of free interpretation in all fields. In this sense, one might say that a marriage was struck between the sacred and the secular. The classics of Greek antiquity, especially in philosophy and the sciences, were taken not as perfect models, as they were during the Renaissance, but as something that could be adapted.

But in my opinion, Lahbabi's theory suffers from two weaknesses. The first is that he does not fully elaborate a specific method; the second is that he does not tackle the social implications of his thesis. Thus, it is noticeable that Lahbabi has not been able to subdue the ever-haunting ghost of the West. It is certain that the medieval religious output of Muslims cannot give any intelligible guidance either for today or for the future, even though there is much that is highly valuable in this medieval body of thought.

This is why Lahbabi is right when he assumes that the weakness of the Arab intellectuals is their confinement to two approaches, the traditionalist (*Salafi*) and the eclectic. Together, these tendencies have the effect of abolishing the historical dimension. But ahistorical thinking has but one consequence: failure to see the real. The only way to transcend these two modes of thought consists in strict submission to the discipline of historical thought and the acceptance of its presuppositions. These are the existence of laws of historical development, the unity of the meaning of history, and the effectiveness of the political role of the philosopher. But these are not accepted. The *Salafi* believe in Providence and the eclectics are at the mercy of every passing fashion. But, in my opinion, it is not easy to adopt historical thinking, which requires a certain stage of civilizational development such as is exemplified in the Enlightenment – that is, the liberation of human reason from any authority save reason itself.

As for the third type of orientation in modern Islamic philosophy, namely moderate modernity, its representative figures are M. Arkoun (Algiers) and M. El-Gabri (Morocco). Arkoun claims that there are two kinds of text, the oral and the written, which is the Quran. But this written text has nothing to do with revelation. The sacred language is liable to be secularized. If this is done quietly, there is no trouble. On the other hand, this same sacred text might be transformed into an orthodoxy. When that happens, any thinker who tries to secularize it is liable to be accused of being an apostate and a destroyer of the political system. In the latter situation, it might seem as if religion rules. But if we dig deeper, we find that religion does not really rule and that the ruler does not really yield to God either. What happens, one might ask, if we are late in digging deeper? In that case we may be deceived into thinking that our beliefs are not open to argument. Accordingly, we may wallow in the imaginary beliefs embedded in religious language and rituals.

Thus, according to Arkoun (1993), we have, on the face of it, two types of reason, the dogmatic and the secular. But our task is to fuse the one with the other so as to eliminate the false dichotomy. In this way, we could establish what Arkoun calls Islamic humanism with a secular flavor. This kind of Islam was aborted in the eleventh century on the pretense that Islam is against secularization due to cultural taboos. However, in defense of his thesis, Arkoun argues that secularization, in fact, emerged in the year 661, that is, within 30 years of the death of Prophet Muhammad. Thus, true secularization is not opposed to religion per se.

As for El-Gabri (1991), he is engaged in the analysis of the Arab mind within the tradition (*taqlid*). Hence, he tackles the problem of modernity and authenticity for the sake of a Renaissance project that will confront backwardness. The problem, he finds, is that Islamic culture is unable to produce new things and hence displays little creativity. This means that the contemporary Arab milieu is synonymous with tradition. The paradox here, according to El-Gabri, is that the Arabs are the only people on earth whose tradition is contemporaneous with their contemporary thought.

Note

This chapter is based, in part, on the author's "Contemporary Moslem Philosophers in North Africa," in P. O. Bodunrin (ed.), *Philosophy in Africa: Trends and Perspectives* (Ile-Ife, Nigeria: University of Ife Press, 1985).

References

Afghani, Jamal el-Din (1995) *The Refutation of the Materialists*, trans. M. Abdou, 2nd edn. (Cairo: Al-Halabi).

Al-Makhzumi, Muhammad (= M. Abdou) (1931) *Kharitat Jamal al-Din Afghani al-Husayni* (Thoughts of Jamal al-Din Afghani al Husayni) (Beirut: Dar Al Kindi).

Amin, Osman (1964) *Al-Gouwania or the Philosophy of Inwardness* (Cairo: Dar al Kalam).

Antun, Farah (1903) *Ibn Rushd and His Philosophy* (Cairo).

Arkoun, M. (1993) *Secularization and Religion* (Dar el-Saki).

Averroes (1976) *The Decisive Treatment*, trans. G. Hourani (London).

Ben Nabi, Malek (1970) *Vocation of Islam* (Beirut: Dar El Fikr).

Dzielska, M. (1995) *Hypatia of Alexandria* (New York: Harvard University Press).

El-Gabri, M. (1991) *Tradition and Modernity* (Morocco).

Lahbabi, A. (1967) *Le Persalisme Musulman* (Paris: PUF).

Mahmoud, Zaki Naguib (1955) *Days in America* (Cairo).

Mahmoud, Zaki Naguib (1971) *Revival of Arab Thought* (Beirut: Dar Al Sherouk).

Russell, B. (1946) *History of Western Philosophy* (London: Allen and Unwin).

9

The Light and the Shadow: Zera Yacob and Walda Heywat: Two Ethiopian Philosophers of the Seventeenth Century

CLAUDE SUMNER

Introduction

The shadow is a witness to the light! Since the allegory of the cave in Plato's *Republic*, philosophers have been concentrating on the light – seeking the light, analyzing it, attempting to penetrate into its radiance, and neglecting the shadows, leaving them to themselves to their obscure fate, to the ashes of an all-embracing fire. In this chapter, I would like to focus on the shadow. Because the shadow is luminous in its own way. Because the shadow, with its fleeting, all too brief silhouettes on the wall, is closer to the human condition. And yet the whole soul of the shadow is the Light. This is exactly what has happened in Ethiopia. When at long last, after three centuries of quasi-oblivion, it became aware of the great light that was Zera Yacob the Philosopher, it left in the dark his disciple Walda Heywat. And when the continent of Africa, nay the world at large, discovered in Zera Yacob a rationalist, a free thinker, the glow of an enlightenment in the shadows of the African past, it opened its arms to the original master, and left the disciple amidst the embers of the night.

This, in a way, is the fate of any disciple. Like the Prophet, his mission is to let the light increase, while he himself decreases. But is this not the grandeur of his very mission? And so it is that Walda Heywat, the disciple and promoter of Zera Yacob's thought, has hardly left any trace in history up to our own days. This chapter purposes to focus on him – not in any way denying the centrality of the fulgurant figure of Zera Yacob, but converging upon the reflection of such glare on the more practical and down-to-earth educator that was Walda Heywat.

The Master and the Disciple

My chapter is necessarily comparative: there is no shadow without a source of light, no disciple without a master. But the only rationale for delineating the life and thought of Zera Yacob is to bring into full light the life and thought of Walda Heywat.

172

Zera Yacob: a great philosopher of seventeenth-century Ethiopia

In 1667 (Gregorian calendar) an Ethiopian philosopher by the name of Zera Yacob (which means "The Seed of Jacob") wrote a *Treatise* (*Hatata*) in which he recorded both his life and his thought. To the person with some acquaintance with Ethiopian history, the name of Zera Yacob brings to mind the fifteenth-century emperor of that name. He reigned from 1434 to 1468, was the consolidator of the First Shoan Kingdom, a religious zealot, a literary figure of considerable repute, and an efficient administrator. Zera Yacob, the philosopher, lived about a century and a half later.

In terms of originality of thought, the philosopher was much more important than the king. He begins his treatise with the story of his life. It is the only known autobiography in Ethiopic literature. He was born on August 28, 1599, near Aksum, into a family of poor farmers. Aksum was the capital of a kingdom and the cradle of a civilization, which from the most ancient times up to the ninth century AD extended from the Red Sea coasts to the Nile plain and covered a great part of northern Ethiopia. Zera Yacob attended the traditional schools of Ethiopia, studying in particular the Psalms of David, the *zema* (sacred music taught in Church schools), the *qene* ("poetry" or "hymns"), and the *sewasewa* ("vocabulary"). *Sewasewa* designates the interpretation of the Holy Scriptures and is somewhat equivalent to "belles lettres." This is a point of special importance. The prose of Zera Yacob reflects the language that is taught in the *qene* school; it is the jewel, the masterpiece of Ethiopian literature. Moreover, his thought is imbued with the spirit of discussion and criticism, which is inculcated in such schools, although the criticism took a very personal and original direction in the case of Zera Yacob.

In 1626, King Susenyos made his solemn profession of the Catholic faith. Shortly afterwards, Zera Yacob was denounced before the king and was compelled to flee for his life. He took with him three measures of gold and the most precious of his possessions – the second great influence in his life together with *qene* language and culture – the Book of Psalms, the *Dawit*. On his way to Shoa in the south (where the modern capital Addis Ababa is located), he found a beautiful uninhabited location: a cave at the foot of a valley south of the Takkaze River. Here he lived for two years. (The modern bridge over the Takkaze River is 120 kilometers from Addis Ababa.) There, in the peace and solitude of the cave, far from the conflicts among his people, he elaborated his philosophy. Just as his contemporary René Descartes, during a winter in Neubourg, was forced to stay in a locality where, as he found no society to interest him, he remained in seclusion, undisturbed by any cause or passion, and there occupied his attention with his own thoughts, thoughts that were later embodied in his *Discourse on Method* (1637), likewise, Zera Yacob, in the quietness of a cave where he meditated on the Psalms and reflected on the roots of the antagonisms in the hearts of people, developed a new approach to life and thought, which later on would constitute the subject of his treatise (1667).

The exact location of Zera Yacob's cave is unknown, but, no doubt, the refuge was roughly in the area described by Henry Salt some 108 years later. Henry Salt came to the Takkaze River from the north (1809–10), exactly as Zera Yacob did, and he recorded his impressions upon his arrival at Takkaze:

After another slight descent, a broad expanse of country opened before us, and we found ourselves at a short distance only from the banks of the Takkaze. I immediately ran forward, prompted by a sort of natural impulse, till we came to the edge of the stream, where, seated on the bank, I remained for some time contemplating with delight the smooth course of the water gliding beneath. (1814: 247)

Zera Yacob's philosophy is an absolutely original work, the fruit of his own personal reflection and not a translation or an adaptation from foreign sources, as most Ethiopic literature is. The philosophy that later on will be developed in his treatise is clearly rationalistic. Rationalism (religious) is here considered as the view which recognizes only that content of faith that can be made to appeal to reason. In Ethiopia, traditional philosophy in its written form is intimately linked with Christianity, in general, and monasticism, in particular. It is precisely in this sense of the absolute and exclusive sufficiency of human reason, which denies all dogmatic assertions that reason cannot adequately comprehend and establish by its own means, that Zera Yacob is said to be rationalist (see Jolivet 1951: 162).

After the death of Susenyos, Yacob left his cave to live again amongst his fellow men and women, and at last settled down in Enfraz (590 kilometers from Asmara), with a certain rich merchant Habtu, who became his patron. For him, Yacob wrote the Psalms in a beautiful hand, which all admired, taught his two sons, and married a maidservant of his family. It was at the request of one of Habtu's sons, Walda Heywat, on whom this chapter would like to focus, that Zera Yacob wrote his famous treatise. The work was completed when the author was 68 years old. He was to live in Enfraz for 25 more years. The brief account he gives of his harmonious and happy family life, of his property, and the birth of his children and grandchildren is very striking in its patriarchal simplicity. He died in 1692 at the age of 93.

Perhaps the best judgment on the value of Zera Yacob's treatise has been given by Enno Littmann: "a real contribution to the history of human thought."[1]

Walda Heywat: a great educator of seventeenth-century Ethiopia

Cervantes has placed side by side Don Quixote, a country gentleman with his addled idealism, Sancho Panza, a peasant bent on earthly acquisitiveness. And likewise it happened during the second half of the seventeenth century and at the beginning of the eighteenth that the great philosopher Zera Yacob had at his side a man who, although he did not share the originality of his master, turned out to be a magisterial exponent of his thought. His name, as mentioned above, was Walda Heywat, "The Son of Life." This is what the master wrote of him in his treatise:

[Walda Heywat] was closely associated with me in science and in my great affection; he knew all my secrets; there was nothing I kept hidden from him. After his constant entreaties, I wrote this small book just for the sake of his love. (HZY 26: 12–16)[2]

We may easily visualize a scene which must often have taken place in the house of the rich merchant in Enfraz: two young men are seated at the feet of Zera Yacob, but the face of one of the two is lit with the glow of understanding and admiration. Walda Heywat is aware that his master is not just one more teacher in Ethiopia, but a profound and original thinker. He will treasure the memory of Zera Yacob until his death. Not only will he encourage his master to write the story of his life and to expound his own thought, but after his master's death in 1692, Walda Heywat, while well advanced in age, will write a book on the things taught him by Zera Yacob for 59 years.

This second treatise, however, is no mere repetition of the first. Although Walda Heywat's ideas are basically those of his master, his presentation is quite different. Walda Heywat is remarkable for his pedagogical qualities. For instance, he is a skillful storyteller. Each of his stories is an illustration in practical life of the principles he wishes to inculcate. Each of these, also, shows the deep influence of the folk literature of Ethiopia upon Walda Heywat, although these short stories are far more dramatic and picturesque in Walda Heywat than in the traditional wisdom literature. Here is an example.

> There was a man whose wife was lazy and unkind. So the husband disliked her and began going to another woman. Then the wife became jealous; she went to a doctor and said: "My husband hates me; give me a medicine that will make him love me." He said: "I shall prepare it for you, but first go and get me three pieces of hair from the mane of a lion. I need them for the potion." While she was going away, she asked herself: "How can I approach a lion and yet avoid that he devour me?" Then she took a sheep with her and went to a field. The lion came out seeking to devour her. She threw the sheep to it and ran away. The lion, having found food to eat, did not chase her. On the next day, she did the same thing, and for many days she repeated the same action, because jealousy for her husband had taken hold of her. As the lion saw that the woman was bringing her food, it no more turned against her. When she came with the sheep it received her with delight, swishing its tail; and, like a dog, it licked her hand and played with her. Then the woman plucked three pieces of hair from its mane and brought them to the doctor. She said to him: "Here, I have brought to you what is needed for the medicine." He said: "How did you manage to pluck them?" When she had narrated to him all she had done, he said to her: "Go, do to your husband what you did to the lion, and your husband will like you. Do you think that your husband is wilder than the lion? As you won the love of the lion by giving it food, so you can win the love of your husband." Then she went and began to follow the doctor's advice. She pleased her husband in all things and was patient. After a few days the husband thought in his heart and said: "Why should I love other women more than my wife; she is good and helps me more than they do?" Then he turned to her and loved her very much. (HWH 57: 17–58: 6)[3]

But the pedagogical value of Walda Heywat goes much beyond the literary qualities of his presentation. He seems to have selected from amongst the ideas of his master those whose significance for human life is the greatest. These he expresses in a forceful way, often addressing himself directly to his readers as if they were his disciples. This is essentially an oral style – that of the parents teaching their sons, of the sage talking to his pupils. Walda Heywat is first and foremost an educator, using pedagogical techniques. He is in constant communication with his "students," asks questions, foresees objections, answers them, sets queries within his replies, and keeps his audience in a living rapport through imperatives. The combination of practical significance and educational concern is such in Walda Heywat that present-day Ethiopia has set in the limelight many aspects of his thought.

175

These include his social philosophy with all its practical applications as manifested in the vigorous affirmation of the value of work, the equality of all human beings irrespective of their different creeds, and the assertion of the beauty of marriage and of family life against their detractors (see Sumner 1981b).

The Light and the Shadow

The brief remarks that precede this section have hardly touched upon "the heart of the matter." We are here in the presence of a rare phenomenon in the history of philosophy: two great philosophers, one basic thought, shared by the master and the disciple. I would like to take this opportunity to investigate, in some depth, a living, personal case of real "analogy," where there is similarity and dissimilarity, not in an even proportion, but with the preponderance of the difference over the sameness, usually – but not always – in favor of Zera Yacob. Although this analogy could be shown on the linguistic and literary levels, I would like to concentrate on the philosophical level in terms of methodology, theodicy, principles of ethics, individual ethics, social ethics, and psychology.

Methodology

In a sense Zera Yacob is the only one of the two philosophers who presents in a complete, systematic, and original manner the methodology of his philosophy. Criticism is the initial condition of his method, division the occasion for his inquiry, and the *hatata* its principle. The driving presupposition of his method consists in the belief in the necessity of inquiry, in the light of reason, and in the goodness of the created thing. It is true that each of these six items is also found in Walda Heywat, but it appears each time in a different *optique*: it is but an echo of, a reference to, a borrowing from Zera Yacob. The starting point and the dialectical development of these ideas are not to be found in Walda Heywat. There are exceptions, however, and each exception manifests the predominantly moral, parenetic, sapiential, and practical approach of Walda Heywat.

Even in minor aspects of each of the items, for instance regarding criticism as the initial condition of method, one notices a difference of approach. Zera Yacob's skepticism is never left in suspense, in mid-air as it were; whereas Walda Heywat freely admits his ignorance, at least as far as such things as the immortality of the souls of animals or the theory of the transformation of fallen angels into human beings are concerned.

When we pass from methodology to its applications in such areas as theodicy, ethics, and psychology, the following pattern emerges. Theodicy and ethics with respect to individual conduct belong mostly to Zera Yacob, while social ethics and psychology belong mostly to Walda Heywat.

Theodicy

Theodicy[4] is the privileged domain of Zera Yacob. The very important problem of the existence of God is tackled only by Zera Yacob. He and only he propounds a philosophical demonstration of his existence. The divine attributes are basically the same in the two treatises. But although there is unanimity in doctrine, there is a significant difference in approach. Let us take only one example: the notion of providence and governance in the two *hatatas*. In very general terms, we can say that Zera Yacob's treatment of the subject is personal, while Walda Heywat's is impersonal.

Zera Yacob is writing an autobiography, and the manifestations of divine providence tend to find their place within the framework of his life. God is provident because, for instance, he (Yacob) was once playing with his friends at the *qene* and *sawasewa* school and fell into a ravine and "God as it were snatched [him] from the claws of death." Rescued "by a miracle of God [he does not cease] thanking God for saving [him.]" God, writes Zera Yacob, "protects *me*, helps *me*, draws *my* soul, is *my* guardian" (HZY 3: 21, 3: 29; ZY + WH, p. 4; CEP, p. 230). It is true that Zera Yacob does occasionally speak of divine providence and governance in more general terms. Such texts are, however, exceptional and, moreover, have a psalmic background. It remains true despite these texts that, by and large, Zera Yacob speaks of divine providence in personal terms, in its relation to himself and to people who are significant to him, such as his children and his compatriots.

There is no such personal aspect in Walda Heywat. The "historical Creator" is known to him as the one who deals with human events in general. He willingly speaks of God's decree, decision, order, and precept for the whole of mankind. He mentions the "precept of the creator, who created man and woman," "the will of God who ordered all men," "who directs all." Even after introducing the first person singular, Walda Heywat passes immediately to the first person plural as soon as he touches upon divine governance, as if he were placing himself together with others as the object of God's benevolence.

Characteristic of the different approach of each author to the subject of providence and divine governance is his way of speaking of God's justice in his dealings with human beings. "Justice" in Zera Yacob has very personal connotations. At the beginning of his treatise, as he is about to describe his own life, and search for wisdom, he invokes "God who alone is just" (HZY 3: 1; ZY + WH, p. 3; CEP, p. 230). While he is pondering on the divisions among Christians and, more broadly, among all believers, he remarks on how people lack wisdom and truthfulness and, hence, he asks for intelligence for himself – intelligence, which is deplorably lacking in others. The approach and language of Walda Heywat is impersonal. He situates divine justice on an objective and universal level.

Principles of ethics

The establishment of the principles of ethics is the domain of both Zera Yacob and Walda Heywat; but, once more, the difference in approach is considerable. Take, for instance, their philosophy of sanctions. Zera Yacob shows how sanctions are not only not opposed to freedom but presuppose it and flow from its very nature. The original thought of Zera Yacob, however, fell on soil that did not give rise to any kind of mechanical response. The soil was rich with the traditional elements of Ethiopian wisdom, featuring the prevalence of moral concern, Platonic and

Neoplatonic dualism and sense of measure, the Christian and Oriental sentiment of mystery, and the deep consciousness of the inadequacy of the human understanding in the face of problems that transcend it and the Semitic biblical notion of time. Even if none of these elements, taken in isolation, is original with Walda Heywat, their harmonious blending is his own type of originality.

Individual ethics

Individual ethics belongs mostly to Zera Yacob. And yet, on the points that are common to both authors, like prayer, the difference of approach is very great. Zera Yacob's prayers are deeply influenced by the Psalms.[5] They spontaneously throb with words, expressions, quotations, thoughts, and sentiments which explicitly or implicitly are psalmic. On the other hand, Walda Heywat's prayers are hardly influenced by the psalter at all.

In the choice of the Psalms that he quotes explicitly, Zera Yacob is guided by the extent to which they express a personal lament, invocation, or supplication. Is this personal or individual approach a reflection of his secluded life and of the deep personal seal of his philosophy? The only dialogue that was available to him during his period of forced seclusion was with his Lord and Creator. Hence the spontaneous and constant invocation. His direct appeal takes the form of the lament. How could he not find a parallel with himself in the life and prayer of the psalmist who was unjustly accused, banned, and outlawed, and who cried out his suffering, sometimes with an indignant sense of innocence? By contrast, there is but one explicit quotation from the Psalms in Walda Heywat, but this single excerpt is very typical. No lament of an individual here, but a wisdom psalm. And even this sapiential motif is not original; it is an old proverb that has become a song and which exhibits a strong collectivism – all of it formulated in the third person.

Social ethics

Social ethics is very developed in Walda Heywat. Zera Yacob, in spite of his authentic humility, may boast that he surpassed all his fellow people in love. The Golden Rule is not for him a mere statement of principle: his whole life is a witness that he himself practiced it and even became, so to speak, one with it. Mutual love in Christian teaching is the one tenet that he accepts and welcomes, while he considers so many elements as adventitious. It is out of a warm personal love for his disciple that he wrote his treatise. Walda Heywat is less personal in his approach, but no less vigorous. The ethics of love is based on the doctrine of our reason. This, in turn, expresses the will of our Creator, since it is the principal precept God gave us and is engraved on the Tablets of the hearts of all.

It must therefore come as a surprise that after the beauty and the wide-ranging scope of the statement on "love" in the treatises one should find any hint of a need to mistrust one's friends. Such a narrowing of the scope of love, however, is nowhere to be found in Zera Yacob. But it occurs in Walda Heywat. We are here in the presence of a preconception of the traditional type of sapiential literature, more akin to *The Book of the Philosophers* than to *The Treatise of Zera Yacob*. Thus when Heywat warns: "Do not trust your friends" (HWH 61: 21; *ZY + WH*, p. 55; *CEP*, p. 284), he is echoing *The Book of the Philosophers*, which says "Beware of your friend!" (N59b 8).[6] Again, Heywat says: "Your secret is bound in your heart as long as it is in your heart; once it is spoken out from your mouth, you are bound to the love of your listener" (HWH 61: 10; *ZY + WH*, p. 55; *CEP*, p. 284) and *The Book of the Philosophers* says, "You shall tie your word and your secret with a rope. But if you speak, you will be tied by them" (N16a 5; *CEP*, p. 66).

The personality of Walda Heywat comes out clearly from the analysis of his social ethics. He is a disciple of Zera Yacob, no doubt. He has been influenced by his master's thought. But he did not break away from traditional patterns of thought and expression as his master did. His was a process of assimilation, growth, and development, and not of cleavage or splitting away from tradition, not even on the purely intellectual level. From an intellectual viewpoint, Zera Yacob was a dove, free and independent, as he soared over the jagged divisions of the earth with its mountains and chasms huddled one against the other. Walda Heywat, on the other hand, is a tree. The branches spread all around him and reach out towards light, warmth, and free space. But the roots are firmly anchored in the rich soil of ancient Ethiopia. The status of woman affords a unique case, in the treatises, of a clear, explicit, and blunt opposition between Zera Yacob and Walda Heywat. Man and woman are equal for Zera Yacob – "Husband and wife are equal in marriage" (HZY 22: 29; *ZY + WH*, p. 21; *CEP*, p. 248); whereas Walda Heywat professes that women are inferior by nature – "O man, remember that a woman is weak by nature and less intelligent than man" (HWH 57: 9; *ZY + WH*, p. 51; *CEP*, p. 279).

Up to now we have seen that the differences between Zera Yacob and Walda Heywat bore on approach and method of development rather than intellectual content. Why the stark opposition in this case? This can only be explained by reference to the influence that traditional sapiential ideas, as illustrated by the story of the woman and the lion (cited in full above), had on Heywat in spite of the overwhelming influence of the original thinking of his master.

Psychology

Psychology[7] as a whole is the area in which Walda Heywat's thought easily expands. He devotes five chapters (4, 8, 10, 12, and 34) entirely (or nearly entirely) to the general principles of psychology. Moreover, three of his chapters (19, 20, 21) are concerned with the more practical aspects of psychology and the care of one's health. One may also find here and there throughout his treatise some 22 units where particular aspects of general psychology are briefly mentioned.

No such elaborate discussion of general and practical psychology is to be found in Zera Yacob. And yet, although he does not devote one single chapter to the subject, we find that it is treated in some 17 units dispersed from beginning to end of his treatise. Not only do these units correspond, in relative terms, to the number of such units in Heywat's treatise, but also the topical headings are exactly the same. We may therefore conclude that the longer treatment of psychology in Walda Heywat is but a development of the master's intuitions on the subject.

The difference between the human being and the animal is the explicit object of Walda Heywat's study in two chapters: 8 and 12. The soul and its relation to the body is again studied by him in chapters 4, 10, and 34.

As to the immortality of the human soul, it is presented in both treatises, but in a very different way. Zera Yacob alone presents arguments in its favor. The first is metaphysical and is based on the desire for happiness, which is inherent in the human soul and is not fulfilled in the present life. The second is psychological, and is based on the spiritual power of the soul. Our soul is able to have a mental concept of God, and hence of immortality. He who gave the power also gives the reality. The third is moral and is based on the existence of injustices in this world. The light of reason requires that an all-perfect God will re-establish perfect retribution after death. Walda Heywat, on his part, simply points to a contrast between the question of the immortality of the souls of animals and that of humans. While, in regard to the souls of animals, he held that we do not know the answer one way or the other, he maintained that with regard to the souls of humans, there was no doubt as to their immortality. And he exhorts his reader not to fear the things that frighten the wicked at the hour of their death.

The philosophy of nature that is found in the two treatises is enlightened from above by an all-encompassing doctrine of creation. The closer one is to the Creator the more developed is the *hatata*; the further away, the less developed. There is thus a scale of beings, a gradation of perfection. This gradation, however, is presented by Zera Yacob in a personal manner, and by Walda Heywat in an impersonal way.[8]

Conclusion

To sum up, the main difference between the thought of Yacob and that of Heywat lies in the sources of their work. The autobiography gives us the key to Zera Yacob's philosophy. It is the direct fruit of his own personal reflection upon events that have affected his life. Each one of his introspective moments not only follows upon an event, but also springs from it, or, more exactly, is a penetrating intuition into the sense of history as it conditions his life. It is a kind of philosophical *midrash* based on a personal story. The themes that he develops in his autobiography, like gratitude to the saving power of God, discretion in the expression of his opinions, tolerance in his teaching and his attitude to life, the importance of prayers based on his meditations on the Psalms, and his sadness over the divisions among believers – all are the epiphany in his heart of the meaningfulness of events in his life. This does not mean that there are no sources extrinsic to himself. There are, indeed, such as the Book of Psalms, the spirit of the *qene* school so favorable to a certain form of criticism, his encounter with the Portuguese Jesuits, and his philosophico-theological discussions with them. But these external sources have been so integrated into his own inner fabric that they are expressed as the overflowing of an internal source. The "creative incorporation" which is a characteristic of "The Ethiopian Response"[9] to "outside" influences has come to a summit in Zera Yacob. The incorporation has become an identification, so that the "outside" has been transformed into the "inside." All the philosophical items mentioned above are strongly colored by personal, and even autobiographical, hues.

In Walda Heywat, there is also a degree of "creative incorporation," but the "outside" is explicitly characterized as the "outside" vis-à-vis Zera Yacob. However, the "inside" is never explicitly formulated. Only a deeper investigation reveals its characteristic elements, namely, the traditional folk literature of Ethiopia and the sixteenth-century collection of sayings known as *The Book of the Philosophers*. It is in the junction of the radical and the traditional that lies the individuality of Walda Heywat as a parenetic educator of the nation as a whole. His students are explicitly the men and women of Ethiopia. The personal and autobiographical have flowered, through the medium of one disciple, into the practical concerns of generations of followers. Through Walda Heywat, Zera Yacob's cave has opened its narrow rocky entrance into a world so wide that it may very well have no limit.

Notes

1 See Littmann 1909: 202. For the section, "Zera Yacob: a great philosopher of seventeenth-century Ethiopia," see Sumner 1981a.
2 HZY = *Hatäta Zera Yacob* ("The Treatise of Zera Yacob"). See also Sumner 1976: 24 (abbr. *ZY + WH*); 1985: 251 (abbr. *CEP*).
3 HWH = *Hatäta Walda Heywat* ("The Treatise of Walda Heywat"). See *ZY + WH*, pp. 51–2; *CEP*, pp. 279–80.
4 The term "theodicy" was coined by the philosopher and mathematician Gottfried Wilhelm Leibniz (1646–1716) who used it in his *Essays on Theodicy* to express the justice or the righteous manner of God's dealings with humankind, which he defended against those who felt that the evils of life are an argument for atheism. The term "theodicy" thus literally means "God's justice" or "God's righteous way." But this original meaning was quickly expanded to include not only God's Providence, but the whole of the philosophy of God: his nature, attributes, and operations. In a word, *theodicy* became a synonym for *natural theology*. Theology had long been distinguished as (a) *natural theology* which is a part of philosophy, and which is the science of God as knowable by human reason without the help of any revelation; and (b) *supernatural theology* or *divine theology* which is the science of God as manifested by Divine Revelation. The term "theodicy" came in handily to replace the more cumbrous "natural theology" and to allow the simple name "theology" to be used for the supernatural science. Convenience and long usage have established the term "theodicy" in its present meaning.
5 It might seem strange that in a paper concerned with philosophical issues, one speaks of "prayer" and of the Psalms. But prayer is never understood in a theological sense. Several scholars have singled out what may be termed the "reasonableness" of Zera Yacob's prayer (Carl Bezold, Wilhelm Wey, Benno Erdmann, J. M. Hardon: *ZY + WH*, pp. 198–200). St Augustine intersperses his philosophical investigations with prayers to the Source of all Light – St Thomas Aquinas never does. Zera Yacob is close to the African scholar's approach, not to that of the European doctor.

As to the Psalms, let us remember that Zera Yacob considered all religious revelation as invention and lies made by humans. But the Psalms are an exception to his criticism, since they express a theological anthropology. For indeed, the Psalms are not strictly a revelation but the human prayerful response to it, how the human person has understood

181

itself in front of God, how and what the person has really integrated into his spiritual life from the mass of events and words which makes up revelation. (See von Rad 1958: 352–405.)

6 N is the name I have given to the twentieth-century manuscript of *The Book of the Philosophers* found in the National Library of Addis Ababa. See *CEP*, p. 105.

7 The object of this section is the study of the human being from a philosophical viewpoint. It refers to psychology of a philosophical type, and not to contemporary schools of experimental psychology, like the gestalt, the eidetic, and the behavioristic schools, or of non-experimental psychology, like the psychoanalytical and the criteriological schools. It is the equivalent of anthropology in the Kantian sense, not in the ethnological sense. See Sumner 1973: 22–4.

8 For the section, "The Light and the Shadow," see *ZY + WH*, in the "Conclusions," sect. 8, "The dual authorship of the *Hatätas*," pp. 260–75.

9 See Sumner 1988.

References

Jolivet, Régis (1951) *Vocabulaire de la philosophie* (Lyon-Paris: Emmanuel Vitte).

Littmann, Enno (1909) "Geschichte der äthiopischen Literatur," in Carl Brockelmann, *Geschichte der christlichen Literaturen des Orients*, vol. II (Leipzig: C. F. Zmelangs Verlag).

Salt, Henry (1814) *A Voyage to Abyssinia* (London: F. C. and J. Rivington).

Sumner, Claude (1973) *The Philosophy of Man*. Vol. I: *From the Upanisads to the British Empiricists* (Addis Ababa: Central Printing Press; repr. New Delhi: Rekha Printers, 1989).

Sumner, Claude (1976) *Ethiopian Philosophy*. Vol. II: *The Treatise of Zera Yacob and of Walda Heywat. Text and Authorship* (*ZY + WH*) (Addis Ababa: Commercial Printing Press).

Sumner, Claude (1978) *Ethiopian Philosophy*. Vol. III: *The Treatise of Zera Yacob and of Walda Heywat. An Analysis* (Addis Ababa: Commercial Printing Press).

Sumner, Claude (1981a) "An Ethiopian Summit," *Interline. The Magazine of Ethiopian Airlines*, 3: 5–11.

Sumner, Claude (1981b) "Ethiopian Philosophy (Part II)," *Interline. The Magazine of Ethiopian Airlines*, 4: 5–11.

Sumner, Claude (1985) *Classical Ethiopian Philosophy* (*CEP*), sponsored by Alliance Ethio-Française d'Addis-Abéba (Addis Ababa: Commercial Printing Press; US edn. Los Angeles: Adey Publishing Company, 1994).

Sumner, Claude (1988) "The Ethiopian Philosophy of Greek Origin," in Uhlig von Siegbert and Tafla Bairu (eds.), *Aethiopistischen Forschungen*. Vol. 26: *Collectanea Aethiopica* (Stuttgart: Franz Steiner Verlag Wiesbaden GMBH).

von Rad, Gerhard (1958) *Theologie des Alten Testaments* (München: Chr. Kaiser; *Old Testament Theology*, 2 vols. trans. D. M. G. Stalker (Edinburgh and London: Oliver and Boyd, 1962)).

10

Zera Yacob and Traditional Ethiopian Philosophy

TEODROS KIROS

Introduction

Ethiopian philosophy is unique in Africa because it is both written and oral. In the written tradition, Zera Yacob is undoubtedly the dominant figure. The oral tradition is present in songs, poems, proverbial sayings, etc. These have been systematically translated and analyzed by Claude Sumner, the foremost scholar of Ethiopian philosophy, in his editions of *The Book of the Wise Philosophers* and *The Life and Maxims of Skendes*.

Zera Yacob was born in 1599 in Aksum, the ancient capital and religious center of learning in northern Ethiopia, and died in 1692. The little information we have about his life is derived from the rare autobiographical introduction to his philosophical treatise on meditation written during the reign of the Ethiopian Emperor Susenyos (1605–32). Zera Yacob followed a traditional religious training within the Coptic church, while acquainting himself with the teachings of the Catholic Church introduced by the Portuguese Jesuit missions that had been in Ethiopia since the middle of the sixteenth century. Through this rare autobiographical act, Zera Yacob becomes the first self-conscious founder of a philosophical tradition in Ethiopia. Indeed, it is a mild exaggeration to assert that it is Zera Yacob who gave the continent of Africa an original autobiography, something that was at that time confined to literate traditions outside of Africa. His treatise is a masterful example of self-presentation. The times during which he lived were very troubled times. King Susenyos had converted to Catholicism, and the Jesuit missionaries were propagating their own interpretations of the scriptures. It was to these powerful forces that Zera Yacob was responding with his independent reading of the Bible, in which he was seeking support for the philosophically inspired mission of saving Ethiopia from foreign intellectual invasion. I will present Zera Yacob's thoughts on three topics of philosophy, namely, the method of knowing God and the disclosure of truth, human nature, and the obligations of human beings.

Method of Knowing God

Zera Yacob's method may be roughly called a discursive subjection of faith, any faith, to a critical examination by intelligence or natural reason. This takes the form of honest searching or uncovering, called *hasasa* or *hatata*. Central to this project is the idea that reason itself is incomplete without God's guidance. Yet reasonable human beings must subject their faith to critical self-examination before they believe, since God's guidance can only be apprehended through reason. Faith in God, then, must come only after profound reasoning. All human perceptions, imaginations, judgments, and apprehensions should be carefully subjected to this discursive method. Nothing should be accepted without being tested by intelligence or natural reason.

For Zera Yacob, truth is clearly revealed to whoever seeks it "with the pure intelligence sat by the creator in the heart of each man." Faith then is not the irrational procedure of giving oneself to an unknown external power called God.

According to Zera Yacob, God does not order absurdities such as "Eat this, do not eat this; today eat, tomorrow do not eat, do not eat meat today, eat it tomorrow ... neither did God say to the Mohammedians: 'eat during the night, but do not eat during the day.'" For Zera Yacob, these are unreasonable laws made by human beings. God could not possibly stand behind them. These absurdities could not have emanated from the careful exercise of human intelligence. God does not subject the human body to such traumatic deprivations. God loves his children too much to create cruel laws that disfigure the body, not to say the soul. God knows the power of necessity, and the difference between necessity and luxury.

To begin with, Zera Yacob instructs, humans are all equal in the eyes of God. This equality is shown in the fact that God created all humans with intelligence. Again, because humans are fated to die, they are equal. Death does not discriminate. It is the ultimate equalizer. The human body is not entitled to immortality. Also, all persons, given their intelligence, can understand God's wishes, through revelation, which for Yacob comes in the form of the deliverances of reason. These revelations were the moments of truth. False faith is manifestly non-truth, and cannot be revealed to persons who are fated to experience truth. Truth occurs only when all persons agree on a given matter or value. Whereas it is possible for all to agree on truth, it is not possible for all to agree on falsity. Truth compels singular agreement, whereas falsity or false faith does not. For example, the fact of the existence of created things leads one to agree on a true proposition such as "Humans are created beings with a body and soul." The believer experiences the proposition as a true object of faith; whereas its opposite, "Created things are because they created themselves," would not be true. More to the point, Zera Yacob argues that the love of others is a singularly true and compelling value that all humans can agree on, whereas hate, any form of hate, cannot be elevated to a value without serious resistance from human reason. The second is effectively an example of a false faith that cannot pass the test of reason guided by God's doctrine. It is a failure of human intelligence, an abortion of reason. Such a situation is brought on not by God's refusal to reveal a majestic truth that commands love, but rather by the notorious weakness of human beings that prevents them from loving deeply and unconditionally. In an attempt to address the question why humans sometimes believe in falsities, of which false faith is a particular example, he develops the thought that God has given reason to everyone, hoping that it will be used for the search for truth and the avoidance of falsehood. But human nature is too sluggish and weak to withstand the challenge. This leads to a discussion of Zera Yacob's views of human nature.

Human Nature

Human beings are exceptional beings, in that, if they exercise their willpower to its fullest capacity, they can decipher truth from falsehood and unfailingly choose truth over falsehood. However, the nature of humans, when they resort to themselves only, is not strong enough to be enabling. Under their own direction, they cannot know the difference between truth and falsehood. God's direction, in the secular form of intelligence, is that power that enables individuals to judge and choose correctly. Note that the stress is not on blind faith, but on a faith that is guided by God's gift of reason. Humans, when unaided by their God-given reason, are so weak that they cannot choose truth over falsehood. They get easily lured by the trappings of falsehood, wealth, status, and power.

There are two kinds of law, Zera Yacob contends: the law of God and the law of humans. In order for humans to be self-governing in the realm of the moral life, they must at all times consult the law of God. It is the law of God that completes the incomplete and deficient law of humans. An exclusive reliance on the latter leads to falsehood. The use of God's law, by contrast, enables humans to recognize truth as truth, not as a semblance of falsity. It is only God who knows "the right way to act," and when persons want to act rightly, they ought to consult the law of God, which is in the heart of each person. It is crucial, Zera Yacob adds, that one knows the humbling fact that everything that is of and by humans is of limited use and duration, whereas that which comes from the original source, God's dispensation, is illuminated by a total intelligence. Ultimate truth cannot be reached by the efforts of humans alone. Humans are liars, and that which comes from them is falsehood and false glory. True, the lies of humans cannot affect the solid structure of the world in which they live. Lies are effective only in the defilement of human character. Thus, when we lie, it is our souls that we destroy. The world created by the original source remains the same.

On Obligation

The fundamental obligation of humans is toward God. That is the first wisdom, the beginning of all knowledge. God created humans and endowed them with intelligence in the hope that they would use the endowment for knowing Him. As the philosopher put it, "God created us intelligent so that we may meditate on his greatness, praise him and pray to him in order to obtain the needs of our body and soul." It is after we are imbued with the knowledge of God, the source of reason, that we become willing to be obligated toward all *others*. Thus, the first foundational obligation of human beings is to love others as you would yourself, and not to do to others what you would not do to yourself. It is reason, God's gift to us, that commands us absolutely to love others as we love ourselves. Our obligations to ourselves may be expressed, in the secular form, as meditations or, in the religious form, as prayers. Prayers are, perhaps, the deepest modalities of thinking. The Ethiopian philosopher's prayers are deeply steeped in the Psalms of David. It is via these intimate prayers that the moral principles governing the relations among human beings are illuminated. It is out of these prayers that an original mode of African philosophy was born.

The Oral Tradition

Traditional Ethiopian philosophy also has a powerful tradition of orality. *The Book of the Wise Philosophers* is a collection of sayings that seeks to locate meanings in the tradition. Most of the sayings are Ethiopianized Greek counsels. The book is a collection of sayings by great philosophers of the past. These are mostly Greeks (Plato, Pythagoras, Aristotle), but the contents are still Ethiopian, by virtue of the originality of their style of formulation. Ethiopians never translate literally: they adapt, modify, add, and subtract. For the sake of brevity, and in order to be systematic, I will choose three perennial moral categories – wisdom, moderation, and faith – to highlight some of the concerns and preoccupations of the author of *The Book of the Wise Philosophers*. Whenever appropriate, I will interject limited analytic interpretations. I use below a style of exposition reminiscent of *The Book*, which frequently introduces a maxim with "A wise man said" or some variation thereto.

Wisdom

A wise man said, "Nothing is nobler than the mind. Kings condemn people and the learned condemn the kings." This particular saying, like many that follow, is very Greek in spirit. It is distinctively Platonic. In the saying, the mind is privileged over everything else, including the power of Kings. Wise is the one, then, who can go beyond the glitter of kings and their worldly power and is only attracted to the wealth of the Mind. Knowing the difference is what distinguishes the wise from the fool.

The wise man said, "There are four kinds of men. The person who knows and teaches, he himself being educated: he is a scholar; ask him questions and learn from him. The person who knows and does not teach, although he is a scholar: he is intelligent; remember him. The person who does not know but teaches: he is in need of guidance; teach him and guide him. The person who does not know and does not want to learn: he is a fool; keep away from him." The wise person specifies various kinds of knowledge and the types of person who embody them. He knows that different occasions require dissimilar modes of knowledge. Accordingly, the following cases are discriminated: the discourses of a scholar to whom we should listen; the silent reflections of a mediator from whom we can learn by example, through critical remembrance; the self-righteousness of a teacher who needs guidance and therefore should not be imitated. Finally, there is the mental situation of the most dangerous teacher who does not know that he is ignorant. He is the most dangerous of all and must be avoided at all costs. This type is the perfectly extreme example of ignorance, the farthest opposite of wisdom. Such a type should be banned from the pupil's gaze. Those who imitate such an impostor will destroy their souls and infest their minds with false idols, very much like persons who

186

choose the wealth of ignorant kings over the wealth of the mind, as noted in the saying of the wise man recalled above.

One of the wise men said, "Wisdom is not good if the action is not good." *The Book of the Wise Philosophers* is guided by a central concern with action. It holds that "Wisdom springs from man's good nature or good character." Ethiopian philosophy does not separate wisdom and moral goodness from their manifestation in action. A person is wise only when his or her practices reveal it. A practice that is evil is one that is not grounded in wisdom.

It has been said: "Sorrow is of two kinds. One type is that of conscience: the rational soul becomes sad out of lack of knowledge. The animal soul feels sorry out of lack of food and drink and the like." The thought is that any action that is not watered by the fountain of wisdom starves for food, very much as a dry plant thirsts for water. It is only the ignorant who do not care for their soul by furnishing it with wisdom. Good persons at least know what the soul hungers for. When they act on it, their sorrow is lessened. The origin of sorrow is thus revealed to the soul, and the soul learns by effective examples of living practice or lived action.

The wise Solomon was asked: "Where is the dwelling place of wisdom?" He said, "In the tongue." The tongue, which is capable of becoming a dangerous instrument of speech, occupies a prominent place in classical Ethiopian philosophy. Sumner puts the matter thus, "The wise man is he who knows the time, the time to speak and the time to keep quiet, the time to listen and the time to reply. We are destined to be in language; and that is why we should speak sparingly and carefully. The word can humanize us when we use it carefully; the word can also victimize us when we are lax with it." I think here that classical Ethiopian philosophy shares remarkable similarities with the concerns of Heidegger, for example, for whom Being is language. For Heidegger, human beings are linguistic beings, and our thought reflects the contingent structure of language itself. There is a similar understanding of language in the Ethiopian analysis of language, as *parole*.

It has been said that man becomes lord by four things. They are: counseling, purity, knowledge, and faith. For me, this says that wisdom is not a natural given. It is developed with time. Conscience is the essential human power which aids humans to attain wisdom. The repeated use of conscience matures in the womb of historical time. Through counseling by those radiant models, that is, the wise as such, those who are seekers after wisdom can become wise. In the end the wise person is distinguished by his or her willingness to be counseled by those who know as well as by oneself in moments of self-counseling, and most importantly by faith in the creator.

The wise Pythagoras said, "If the soul does not conquer the flesh, then the flesh becomes the grave of the soul. When you warn a wicked person, do it tactfully with soft words, so that he does not run away from you and develop a sinful inclination into a habit like eating and drinking." Central to classical Ethiopian thought is the battle between the flesh and the soul. The confrontation between the appetites and reason was also a crucial concern for Plato, following the Pythagorean problematic. Plato comes down on the side of Reason, as does the author of *The Book of the Wise Philosophers*. The overcoming of the desires of the flesh is the only remedy for the struggling self. This theme is repeated throughout *The Book of the Wise Philosophers*. Consider the following passage, for example:

> Solomon, the son of David, said: Drinking wine with excess is the destruction of many. Wine causes the storm of evil. Again he said: Drinking wine with moderation will be like fresh water that quenches one's thirst. It will please the heart. Drinking wine with excess harms and sickens.... My son when you drink wine you must not talk too much, but praise God and give thanks to him. Saying good things while drinking wine is like a precious stone of high value, a pearl alloyed with gold. A wise and honorable man avoids evil words and reveals what is in his heart.

The second passage is considerably milder than the first. It enjoins the self to moderately enjoy the objects of desire. It does not say, "Deny the needs of the flesh." Rather, it says, "Regulate the amount. Pay attention to the dangers of quantity." The flesh does not understand restraint; whereas the vigilant self should and must, lest it be consumed by the flames of desire.

It is theses such as the foregoing that ought to make classical Ethiopian philosophy an ideal candidate for critical interrogation in the manner of, say, Foucault's postmodernistic criticisms of the genealogy of morals. The flesh may be a burden only to those who do not know how to use their bodies in accordance with a self-constructed yardstick of moderation guided by reason. Existence can be intimate and private, and philosopher kings and priests cannot tell others how to live their lives, how to use their bodies economically. These styles of existence and ethics of living can be determined only by autonomous individuals. Indeed, no two individuals are the same; consequently, one cannot develop a model of the appropriate use of the flesh that can satisfy everybody.

Faith

Faith is one of the most dominant categories in *The Book of the Wise Philosophers*. It appears as frequently as does wisdom. Recall that *it was* said that "man becomes lord by four things...counseling, purity, knowledge, and faith." Faith, then, is one of the four cardinal categories in the evaluation of persons. A few sayings illustrate the importance of faith in the sculpting of character.

It has been said: "Religion and the King are equal. One is not greater than the other. Religion is for the faithful and the King is its keeper. He who has no faith is vain, and he who has no keeper disappears." Again, *it has been said*: "He is respected whose faith is just, whose living is good to the very end and who honors his fellow man. His conscience and patience are the resources of his respect; his purity is his protector, his speech and his equanimity are his rank." According to Sumner, faith and wisdom are inseparable. As he puts it, "Wisdom has come out of the mouth of God, whose name covers all the earth like a cloud. Human temporal wisdom not only springs from an eternal origin, it also leads to an eternal glory at the end of man's presence in the world." Furthermore, "Wisdom is the foundation of Faith, which renders to the creator the glory He deserves. Its head and crown are the fear of God."

On The Life and Maxims of Skendes

I come now to *The Life and Maxims of Skendes*. In introducing it I will follow the same method of exposition I used in the case of *The Book of the Wise Philosophers*. I will first select unique statements about human nature, and then provide my own interpretations.

It is significant to note that the story of Skendes (Secundis in Greek) is a celebrated story that has occupied the imagination of Greek, Syriac, Arabic, and Ethiopian scholars over the centuries. The Ethiopic text is based on the Arabic, although some scholars maintain that it is based on the Greek. The Ethiopic text recalls the story of Skendes, who was the son of sagacious parents who decided to send him to the ancient cities of Berytus (modern Beirut) and Athens for further studies. Skendes was only 13 at the time. While abroad, he heard and read a statement made by some of the wise philosophers about women to the effect that all women are prostitutes. He was highly angered by such a speculative proposition and eventually decided empirically to test it.

So he returned home after 24 years, and resolved to test it against his own mother. Through the services of a maid servant whom he met at a public well where the people drew water, he managed to trick the servant of his mother to convince her to let him into his mother's house to spend the night with her in exchange for 100 dinars. So he spent the night with his mother. However, in the morning he revealed to his mother that he was her own son. Thereupon, exactly as in the Oedipus story, where the mother after discovering the identity of her new lover, hanged herself, Skendes' mother hanged herself. Skendes was so saddened by the action of his tongue, which spoke the truth at the cost of the life of his own mother, that he resolved never to speak again. He became permanently silent. During those days, Andryanos was the emperor. He heard the extraordinary story and was intrigued about the philosophy of silence, as a law established for philosophers. He sent orders for Skendes to be brought to the palace. Skendes was ordered to speak, which he refused to do. Instead, he wrote his thoughts in the form of answers to questions organized in two sections. The first section has 55 questions, and the second section has 108. The questions center on the human condition. The philosopher develops questions concerning the mysteries of humans and the world. In the first section, he answers questions that deal with the essence of God, the world, the sun, the moon, the earth, the stars, the angels, the sky, the clouds, the winds, thunder, air, water, the ocean, the soul, the mind, the spirit, man, and woman. Many others deal with the emotions (peace, anger, hatred, cursing, weeping, sadness, laughter), death, sleep, and pleasure. After Skendes gave outstanding philosophical discourses on the above themes, the Emperor was deeply impressed by what he read and did not try to force the philosopher to speak. In the second section, the philosopher reflects on 108 questions, some of which deal with wisdom, the nature of evil, and crime. The philosophy of Skendes is treated as a national treasure and is preserved in the archives of the priests.

The obstinate silence of Skendes, the wise philosopher, is responsible for the immanent motif of wisdom through silence in classical Ethiopian philosophy. The theme of wisdom is pervasive in *The Life and Maxims of Skendes*, and Skendes is constantly called "the wise" throughout its biographical sections. The human condition is the general theme of Skendes' wisdom. Human life is afflicted by "miseries, death, folly, stupidity, anger, wrath, labor, fetidity, war, killing, slaying, abstention, and fear." The difficult questions which he answered are about these perennial ethical and sapiential themes.

Further reading

Kiros, Teodros (1994) "The Meditations of Zera Yaquob," in *Working Papers in African Studies* (African Studies Center, Boston University).

Kiros, Teodros (1997) "Claude Sumner's Classical Ethiopian Philosophy," *Northeast African Studies*, 3(2), Spring.

Kiros, Teodros (1998) "The Meditations of Zera Yacob," *Proceedings of the Twentieth World Congress of Philosophy*, Boston, August 10–16.

Kiros, Teodros (Forthcoming) "Claude Sumner's Classical African Philosophy," in Samuel Yohannes (ed.), *From Dusk to Dawn*.

Sumner, Claude (1974) *Ethiopian Philosophy*. Vol. I: *The Book of the Wise Philosophers* (Addis Ababa: Central Printing Press).

Sumner, Claude (1976) *Ethiopian Philosophy*. Vol. II: *The Treatise of Zera Yacob and of Walda Heywat. Text and Authorship* (Addis Ababa: Commercial Printing Press).

Sumner, Claude (1994) *Classical Ethiopian Philosophy* (Los Angeles: Adey Publishing Company; this includes *The Life and Maxims of Skendes*).

11

Anton Wilhelm Amo

WILLIAM E. ABRAHAM

Anton Wilhelm Amo (*c*.1703–58), physician and philosopher, was born at Axim in western Ghana. Transported to the Netherlands at the age of 3, he was quickly offered to the Duke of Wolfenbüttel. He mastered German, Dutch, French, Latin, Greek, and Hebrew, and became adept at law, philosophy, and medicine. Best known as a professor of philosophy at the universities of Halle, Jena, and Wittenberg, he also taught courses in medicine, psychology, cryptology, etc. He was in the thick of struggles to rescue university education from political and clerical suffocation, and debates advancing the supremacy of mechanistic explanations of natural phenomena. Personal vicissitudes and a theatrical satire eventually induced him to return to Ghana to some members of his family in the Axim area. Eventually brought to the Dutch Fort San Sebastian at Chama, he probably died there. Two of his works are extant.

Though their African mission was to acquire slaves for the Americas, the Dutch West Indies Company also fitfully relied on Dutch ministers to bring Christianity to the local inhabitants. In 1706, the local preacher resolved to send a child of local Christian parents, Amo, to the Netherlands for baptism, education, and training as a predicant. However, experiencing difficulty in placing him, the Company transferred Amo in 1707 to Duke Anton Ulrich of Brunswick-Wolfenbüttel. Upon his death, responsibility for Amo passed to the Duke's son, Wilhelm August.

With Amo's placement now resolved, the Company's governing Assembly reacted sharply to the local preacher's initiative. They promptly replaced the local director, who had permitted this emphasis on Christian education, and enjoined his substitute to focus on the slave trade and restore it to its proper state. Finally, they urged the preacher in Ghana to send no more children to the Netherlands for baptism. Amo's baptism (1708) and confirmation (1721) duly occurred in the Saltzthal Chapel of Wolfenbüttel Castle. Now he was Anton Wilhelm Rudolph, having adopted the names of his benefactors.

Duke Anton Ulrich was an ardent promoter of the arts and sciences, a prolific composer of hymns, a theologian, and a novelist. After publishing his *Fifty Reasons why one must be a Catholic*, he recanted the Augsburg Confession in 1710, and, with 50 impelling reasons, successfully petitioned to be received into the Roman Catholic Church, an act of apostasy that incurred public condemnation from his son and heir.

Between 1717 and 1720, Amo acquired the necessary pansophic preparation for a university education at the Ritter Academy of Wolfenbüttel. His later attendance at Helmstedt University qualified him to take postgraduate courses in law upon enrolling at Halle in 1727. His probable dates at Helmstedt would have been 1721–4, leaving 1725 and 1726 unexplained. Helmstedt University was then a principal center of Protestant orthodoxy and learning. Most of its professors and students embraced the recognized social hierarchies and espoused Lutheran doctrines and usages, successfully rendering the climate inclement for would-be nonconformists. It is probable that Amo was not able to defend any thesis there which interested him, and so he needed to seek out another institution.

Halle was different, having grown rapidly in intellectual tolerance and emancipation under the inspiration of Hermann Francke, Christian Wolff, and Christian Thomasius. Francke founded the Pietistic School and preached internal disciplines and mutual tolerance. Wolff had joined the faculty in 1706 on Leibniz's recommendation. Renowned philosopher, mathematician, scientist, indefatigable instigator of the German *Aufklarung*, and disseminator of Leibniz's theories, he ardently sought to secularize education. Thomasius embraced the maxim "unlimited freedom accords the best life to all spirits" for his personal motto, and demanded unrestricted freedom of research and immunity from persecution for opinions honestly formed and sincerely held. His endeavors swelled the number of Halle's nonconformist faculty and students, including Amo.

Soon, Halle became notorious for its freethinking professors and students, and attracted those disaffected with the establishment. Their agitation provoked the Pietists, and caused Joachim Lange to persuade Frederic Wilhelm I that Wolff's ideas were inimical to the state. Francke was dismissed for his biblical revivalism and social activism. Wolff was dismissed and banished in 1726. After this, Thomasius continued his influence, but he died in 1728.

The influence of these three pioneers had made Halle irresistible to Amo. The thesis which he intended to establish, the legal, social, and philosophical interpretations which engrossed him, and his own origins and dependency all combined to make his continuation at Helmstedt virtually unsustainable. Those theories could at least get an airing at Halle, even if only an embattled one.

A notice of his dissertation in the university journal at Halle in 1729 read:

> There resided here for some time an African called Antonius Wilhelmus Amo who belonged in the household of His Royal Highness. As he had before then thoroughly mastered the Latin language, he very diligently and with great success studied here in the School of private law. As a result, he became most accomplished in that field. With the knowledge and consent of his patrons, who had maintained him up till that time, he registered with Dean von Ludewig to give a public defense of a dissertation under him. To make the argument of the dissertation appropriate to his status and circumstance, they approved for him the theme "De Jure Maurorum in Europa": in other words, on the rights of Black Africans in Europe. In it, not only has he shown, basing himself upon Law and History, that African kings were once vassal to the Roman Emperor, and that every one of them had an Imperial Patent, which Justinian, too, had granted, but he especially also examined the question to what extent the freedom or servitude of Africans in Europe, who had been purchased by Christians, accorded with laws commonly accepted at that time.

192

This dissertation earned him candidature in both private and public law. The eminent diplomat and legal scholar, Johann von Ludewig, chaired its defense. His coolness towards Wolff and Thomasius and his sedulous diplomatic service to the Prussian King should have endeared him to the clerical faction, but did not: he opposed clericalism also. Ludewig's involvement with a successful obviously anti-establishment dissertation was a courageous act, and he remained Amo's political shield until his own death in 1743, an occurrence early believed to have featured in Amo's eventual decision to return home.

From sacred history, Amo expounded the crucial contribution of Africa to the development of Christianity, its doctrines, practices, and roll of martyrs. From secular history, he directly applied provisions of the Constantinian settlement and the Justinian Code, particularly the Pandects, to Africa, since African Kings had been vassals of the Roman Emperor under renewed imperial patents granted up till Justinian. Arguing from law and history, he concluded that the servitude of Africans in Europe, who had been bought by Christians, was in conflict with commonly accepted laws. "Africa" in that dissertation referred to its Roman provinces, from Constantine to Justinian, as well as to the continent at large.

Its anti-clerical and anti-establishment contentions would have created a stir at a university such as Halle. This is almost certainly what led to the notice and abstract in the Halle journal, and also to Amo's hurried departure from Halle in 1729 soon after the successful defense. He was probably directed by Ludewig to seek refuge at the nearby Wittenberg University, where Ludewig's friend, Gotthelf Loescher, resided. There, Amo was, on October 10, 1730, granted the degree of Master of Philosophy and the Liberal Arts, renamed Doctor of Philosophy a few years later, enabling him to lecture in Wittenberg from 1730 till 1734.

The Hamburg journal of June 2, 1733 noted Amo's role in events surrounding the visit of the Prussian King at Wittenberg. A commander led each of the university's parading corporations, and "right in front of the student corporations stood Magister Amo, an African, in the middle of the road, as commander of the entire corps."

In April 1734, Loescher chaired Amo's successful defense of his second known dissertation, *Of the Apatheia of the Human Mind, namely, the absence of sensation and the faculty of sense in the Human Mind and their Presence in our Organic and Living Body*. The Rector's address ran thus:

> Great once was the dignity of Africa, whether one considers natural talents of mind or the study of letters, or even institutions for safeguarding religion. She has given birth to several men of the greatest pre-eminence, whose talents and efforts have advanced the totality of human knowledge...
>
> In Christian teaching, too, how great are the men who have come out of Africa. Of the more distinguished, it is enough to mention Tertullian, Cyprian, Arnobius... and Augustine, the refinement of all whose minds rivals the learned of every race.... Those who say that the African Church has always been a mere receiver of instruction do her immeasurable wrong.... When the Moors crossed into Spain, their ancient writers brought along with them considerable assistance to Spain in the cultivation of letters during the darkness which had overwhelmed that country...
>
> Although in our own times, that part of the world is reported to be more prolific in other things than in learning, nevertheless, that it is by no means bereft of genius,

193

Anthony William Amo here, that most distinguished master of Science and the Liberal Arts, would, by his example, teach.

Born in a very distant region of Africa, where it faces the rising sun, he came to Europe as a very little child. He was initiated into sacred rites in the Julian Halls, and so enjoyed the kindness of Guelph, of Augustus Wilhelm, and of Ludwig Rudolph, which was so great that in the matter of his education no bounty of paternal love was lacking. Because of his proven teachability of spirit, he attended Saxon institutions, and came to us, already well grounded in various disciplines.

By continuing the curriculum with diligence, he so won the affection of the School of Philosophy that, with the unanimous vote of the superiors, he was decorated with the laurels of Philosophy. The honor was won by merit of his ability, his outstanding integrity, industry, erudition, which he has shown in both public and private assignments, and his praise expanded. By his comportment with the best and most learned, he acquired great influence: among his equals, he easily shone out. In consequence, trained and stimulated by his study of these matters, he became a private teacher of philosophy. But now, having examined the opinions of the ancients as well as of the moderns, he garnered all that was best, and what he selected he interpreted with precision and with lucidity. This work proved that his intellectual ability was as great as his powers of teaching; nor have these powers proved unequal to the office of teaching which by some natural instinct he is at length exercising in the University.

Therefore, since he has completely justified our expectation, there is no reason whatever why we should deny him our public acclamation and attestation to which he has a right. Indeed, we hope for all the best things from him, and we adjudge him worthy of that Princely favor which he dutifully respected, and which he publicizes in every address.

And now, for good fortune in order that he may be able to enjoy this destiny for a long time to come and attain to the most renowned fruition of his hope, for the well-being of the good and great Prince, Ludwig Rudolph, for the preservation of the whole House of Brunswick ... celebrated for so many great services to all Germany.

John Godfrey Kraus, Doctor,
Rector of the University

Loescher's address ran as follows:

We proclaim Africa and its region of Guinea, separated by a very great distance from us, and formerly the Gold Coast, so called by Europeans on account of its abundant and copious yield of gold, but known by us as your fatherland, in which you first saw the light of day, the mother not only of many good things and treasures of nature but also of the most auspicious minds: we proclaim her quite deservedly! Among these auspicious minds, your genius stands out particularly, most noble and most distinguished Sir, seeing that you have excellently demonstrated felicity and superiority of genius, solidity and refinement of learning and teaching, in countless examples before now, and even in this our University, with great honor in all worthy things, and now also in your present dissertation.

I return to you still intact, and absolutely unchanged in any respect, that which you have conscientiously and with elegance worked out, supported by your erudition, in order that the power of your intellect may shine forth henceforth all the more strongly.

It now only remains for me to congratulate you wholeheartedly on this singular example of your refined scholarship, and with a more abundant feeling of heart than words can convey. I solicit for you all good fortune; and to the Divine Grace and also to the Highest and Most Noble Prince Ludwig Rudolph, for whose health and safety I shall never tire of worshiping the Divine Majesty, I commend you.

.... Wittenberg in Saxony . . . April, 1734.

Though, in his boyhood, Amo had met Leibniz, who was researching ducal history at Wolfenbüttel, his actual encounter with Leibnizian theories was chiefly through Wolff. Amo also made a special study of Descartes' writings. The problem of this dissertation concerned the character of the dualism to which appeal could be made in the attempt to clarify the relation between mind and body. He claimed inconsistency and confusion in Descartes' position.

Descartes' ontological dualism made mind and body subject to incomparable principles and concepts of explanation: mind was a non-extended substance, whose essence was to think, while body was a non-thinking substance whose essence was to be extended. As not every action of an external body on us results in cognition, sensation was conceived as the basic link between the human mind and an external world of which it is able to gain cognizance through its own association with a living and organic body. Such actions were thought to be accomplished through transference, penetration, or immediate contact. Descartes had, however, admitted that the human mind was purely active, never passive. It was therefore inconsistent of him, Amo contended, to have ascribed to it a feature like sensation, which would require it to be both passive and extended.

Amo claimed confusion in Descartes' presentation of the thesis that it was the function of an organ to receive sensible forms (e.g. by feeling) while to judge forms when received (e.g. by taking cognizance of what is felt) was the function of the mind. Yet, taking cognizance of bodily pain or contact should not require the mind itself to *feel* pain or contact, or *sense* anything at all. A faculty of sense is not an apposite feature of minds. Hence, Amo denied that the mind could *feel*, urging that sense organs were only a medium, but not an instrument, in a theoretical conception of the occurrence of sensing. In this theory, without sense organs, there would be no sensing; and the entity with the faculty of sense should be the entity comprising living organs, namely the body.

Barely a month after his own defense, Amo chaired the defense of Johannes Theodosius Meiner's dissertation, which he had supervised. While finishing his own dissertation, Amo concurrently attended Loescher's lectures in medicine, physiology, and psychology, earning him the Master's Degree in Medicine, which now enabled him to lecture in medicine also.

Between 1734 and 1736, resurgence in Wolffian activism caused the indefatigable Lange to complain bitterly. Although Wolff was still in royal disfavor, this revival induced Amo to return to Halle. He promptly received an appointment to deliver university lectures, and advertised several series, including one on Christian Wolff's political philosophy. Such recrudescence inflamed Lange, who induced the king to issue a reprimand against university faculties. But the Wolffian philosophy, in which Amo had now become a propagator, had already established a definite stronghold.

So respected was Amo's learning and disputative ability that he acted as devil's advocate at the defense of numerous dissertations. One of his final records at Halle involves the dissertation of Moses Abraham Wolff. Wolff registered in September 1733 at the University of Duisburg medical school, but did not earn his degree there. Since 1350, when Jews were blamed and killed for the great plague, Jews had hardly lived in Duisburg. It took government decrees in 1726 to accord Jewish medical students the same treatment as others. Even at Halle, local students had once gone on a rampage, razing the local synagogue, the rabbi's residence, and several Jewish homes.

Moses Abraham Wolff completed his studies at the University of Halle. His two known professors were Frederick Hoffman and Amo. A genuine friendship between Amo and Wolff is reflected in Amo's German congratulatory poem:

> Your nimble mind, so swift in contemplation;
> In profound study, so unceasing in toil,
> Has, noble soul, made you in the scholar's world
> A star, intense star of the first magnitude.
> Shining ever brighter, your fame is enlarged
> As honors multiply. Great is wisdom's gift
> To those who are her sons. Enough. From heaven,
> Let uncommon joy fall upon you and yours,
> And blessings pure.
> ...appended for his most highly honored friend by Anton Wilhelm Amo, from Guinea in Africa, Magister and University Lecturer in Philosophy and the Liberal Arts.

Wolff's dissertation discussed the treatment of diseases sent into apparent remission by another disease. Encouraged by Amo and Hoffman, Wolff favored physiological explanations for medical conditions, over metaphysical ones. This advocacy constituted provocation in the mind of Lange, who had, in 1735, attacked mechanistic tendencies in his *Clear Proof that the 130 Questions of the New Mechanic Philosophy, especially the Metaphysic* (SIC). Hoffman joined the Wolffians in regarding living organisms as machines, which could be explained by the principles of mechanics. The clericalists and Lange co-opted Hoffman's rival, proponent of the phlogiston theory of combustion, Georg Ernst Stahl, who insisted on the necessity of a force called *anima*, for understanding and explaining life.

Wolfram Suchier, post-war Librarian at Halle, remembered another dissertation wherein Amo had signed his congratulatory poem simply "Amo," but misplaced the details.

The final notice of Amo's second period at Halle was the report of his major work *Tractatus de Arte sobrie et accurate philosophandi* (*The Art of clear-headed and correct philosophizing*). This was his final salvo at the followers of Lange and Stahl. A work of criticism and analysis, it discussed the nature and boundaries of mind, the classification and grounding principles of species of knowledge, the relation of philosophy to other intellectual pursuits, and presented philosophy as logic, ontology, rational psychology, ethics, and politics. It exuded mechanistic bias wherever possible. The *Transactions of the Faculty of Philosophy of Halle* (1737) selected it for a brief account, and the published work came out in 1738.

The worsening unrest at Halle and Amo's penchant for Wolffianism contributed to his departure for the University of Jena, then a thriving Wolffian center, where he applied for a teaching position:

> Following a habit of excellent public service, but pierced by the sharp dart of poverty (for I have a poor home), I have, to the best of my ability, been giving private lessons in philosophy, and have taught both in the universities of Wittenberg and Halle, where also I very frequently engaged in public disputation. These tasks I have performed with diligence. I therefore hope that you, gentlemen of outstanding reputation in the world of letters, will grant me similar acceptance in this your famous seat of the Muses. Once you have kindly shown me this indulgence, I shall give you thanks for your action, and shall never weary of praying to heaven that you, my excellent patrons, may enjoy forever a most desirable happiness.

Dean Friedrick Andreas Hallbauer immediately canvassed the faculty members, successfully urging deferment of Amo's nostrification fees, until he had earned enough from lecturing. Amo commenced teaching immediately. A notice advertised his lectures on "the valuable portions of philosophy" and on "the refutation of superstitious beliefs" in his continuing assault on Stahlians and followers of Lange.

The last confirmed document bearing Amo's hand is an album of another friend, Gottfried Achenwall of Elbing, originator of statistics in Germany. It contained personal memorials of eminent men of science and learning. Amo, who had been elected a member of the Dutch Academy of Flushing and other learned societies, inscribed the book on May 5, 1740 in Jena, selecting a quotation from Epictetus for his personal motto: "He who can accommodate himself to necessity is wise and has an inkling of things divine." He ruefully added: "These words Antony William Amo, an African, Master and University Lecturer in Philosophy and the Liberal Arts, has set down in everlasting memory of himself."

An article by Johann Friedrich Blumenbach, often referred to as father of physical anthropology, states:

> Our honored Professor Hollman, while he was still in Wittenberg, conferred the degree of Doctor of Philosophy on a Negro who proved his great talent both in his writings and in his lectures, and who later came to Berlin as counselor to the King. I have two of his treatises before me, of which one especially contains much unexpected and well-digested reading in the best physiological works of that time.

The call to Berlin must have come after 1740 from Friedrich II, who, for a few years, had liberalized the Prussian regime, encouraged humanitarian projects, and showed tolerance and sympathy for enlightened intellectual movements. Amo's sojourn in Berlin would explain the absence of further information about him on university campuses.

The last known record of Amo in Germany comes in a 1747 Halle report on a satirical play, *A Comic Student, the false Academic Virgin, and Magister Amo's proposal*. It depicted the rejection of Amo's ardor and suit by a courtesan masquerading as a virgin student. The billing at Halle suggests that Amo may have returned there, especially since the new dispensation of Friedrich II had been reversed. Jacob Eliza

197

Capitein, another Ghanaian who had studied in Holland, had returned to Ghana as a religious educator in 1742. He spent the next five years chiefly in the areas surrounding the Dutch-held Elmina Castle, but made occasional treks to the Dutch Fort San Sebastian at Chama, a few miles down the coast. The absence of any mention of Amo in Capitein's records all but conclusively establishes that Amo arrived in Ghana after Capitein's death in 1747. The 1747 lampoon at Halle was probably the final impulse.

The main source on Amo's life back in Ghana is Winkelman's obituary insertion in *Proceedings of the Zeeland Academy of Science* (Middleburg, 1782) on David Henri Gallandet, a Swiss-Dutch physician and ship's surgeon on a vessel that called at Axim in 1753:

> While Gallandet was on this trip to Axim on the Gold Coast...he went to visit the famous Mr. Antony William Amo, a Guinea-born African, Doctor of Philosophy and Master of Arts. He was a Negro who lived about thirty years in Europe. He had been in Amsterdam in the year 1707, and was presented to the Duke Anton Ulrich who gave him later to his son August Wilhelm. The latter made it possible for him to study in Halle and in Wittenberg. In the year 1727, he was promoted Doctor in Philosophy and Master in the Liberal Arts. Some time after this, his master died. This made him so depressed that it influenced him into returning to his fatherland. Here, he lived like a hermit, and acquired the reputation of a soothsayer. He spoke different languages including Hebrew, Greek, Latin, French, and High and Low German. He was skilled in astrology and astronomy, and was generally a great sage. He was then about fifty years old. His father and one sister were still alive, and resided at a place four days' journey inland. He had a brother who was a slave in the colony of Suriname. Later he left Axim and went to live in the fort of the West Indies Company at Chama, Fort San Sebastian.

The eminent philosopher and historian, Ivor Wilkes, has observed that the Dutch West Indies Company recruited volunteers in Ghana for military corps deployed in Suriname and Indonesia. However, brigands occasionally snatched and transported individuals across the ocean to be sold. One such incident prompted instructions (in 1749) to the Director at Elmina about the enormous trouble and expense of finally repatriating the victims from Suriname to Ghana. Six men had been thus abducted by Christian Hogeroop, commander of the privateer *Africa*, and sold as slaves. The Assembly represented to the brother and relations of Atta that his carrying off was done without their consent or blame, and he would have been brought back, had he lived. Skipper Christian Hogeroop had, at their request, been arrested and clamped in irons. If, however, they were not satisfied by this, and persisted in their claim, the local director was to avert bad consequences by offering a sum not exceeding 6,800 guilders.

At the date of this letter, Amo had been back in Axim for at least a year. The brother and relations who had to be appeased were himself, his sister, and his father. The person who raised the objection and demanded redress was undoubtedly Amo himself: Atta had been Amo's twin brother.

When Amo left Ghana, he had already internalized the basic structure of the Nzima language. Polyglot that he had become, Amo would easily have regained competence in it. His reputation as a soothsayer, which probably derived from his medical prognostications, would have required the use of Nzima.

Sometime after 1753, the Dutch authorities took Amo to Fort San Sebastian. The Wolffian professor who lectured against superstition would inevitably have offended the local healers with their superstitious etiologies, while the composer of the dissertation on the rights of Africans would have constantly menaced the Dutch slave trade. The chances are that Amo's sojourn at Fort San Sebastian was involuntary.

No further record of Amo has been found. Professor Donatie's subsequent expedition toured the West African coast sometime after April 1759 making nature observations. His records did not mention Amo. The diaries of the two governors at Fort San Sebastian in the 1750s, Mr. Sandra and Mr. Soyer, have not been found. The fort was in any case in ruins by 1769, and Amo was by then presumably dead.

Further reading

Abraham, W. E. (1964) "The Life and Times of Anton Wilhelm Amo," *Transactions of the Historical Society of Ghana*, 7: 60–81.

Ahuma, S. R. B. Attoh (1905) *Memoirs of West African Celebrities, 1700–1850* (Liverpool: D. Marples).

Amo, A. W. (1968) *Antonius Gulielmus Amo, Afer of Axim in Ghana*, ed. D. Siegmund-Schultze, trans. L. A. Jones and W. E. Abraham (Halle: Martin Luther University Halle-Wittenberg).

Brentjes, B. (1977) "Anton Wilhelm Amo in Halle, Wittenberg and Jena," *Universitas* 6(1): 39–55.

Hountondji, P .J. (1983) "An African Philosopher in Germany in the Eighteenth Century: Anton Wilhelm Amo," in *African Philosophy: Myth and Reality* (London: Hutchinson University Library for Africa), pp. 111–30.

Gregoire, Henri Abbe (1800) *De la littérature des Nègres* (Paris; translated into German in 1809, and into English in 1826).

Lochner, Norbert (1958) "Anton Wilhelm Amo," in *Ubersee Rundschau* (Hamburg).

Suchier, W. (1916) "A. W. Amo, Ein Mohr als Student und Privatdozent der Philosophie im Halle, Wittenberg, und Jena, 1727/40," *Akademische Rundschau*, 4 Jahrg. H 9/10 (Leipzig).

Suchier, W. (1918) "Weiteres uber den Mohren Amo," in *Altsachen Zeitschrift des Altsachsenbundes und Heimatkiunde* (Holzminden), pp. 7–9.

12

Amo's Critique of Descartes' Philosophy of Mind

KWASI WIREDU

Anton Wilhelm Amo was carried, in missionary-related circumstances, to Holland from his birth place in Axim, Ghana, then the Gold Coast, sometime in the first decade of the eighteenth century at the age of about three. He was soon afterwards donated to a German prince (Duke Anton Ulrich of Brunswick-Wolfenbüttel), who brought him up with the kindness and solicitude of a step-grandfather. At college he studied such subjects as philosophy, physiology, medicine, jurisprudence, history, and some other less orthodox ones, in all of which he shone brightly. He became a respected professor of philosophy and wrote a number of works, among which was *The Rights of Negroes in Europe*. In 1959 William E. Abraham, on the suggestion of Kwame Nkrumah, then President of Ghana, and I, as a fellow traveler of the former, searched in libraries in Europe and could not find this work. Unfortunately, it may be lost. Some of his other works are, however, extant, including his inaugural dissertation, *The Apatheia of the Human Mind* (1734), translated from the Latin by Abraham, which is the subject of this discussion. Amo returned home around 1748 in somewhat unhappy circumstances (see chapter 11 in this volume). Incredibly, he was able, with but sparse local documentation, to trace his family.

In 1978, at a UNESCO-sponsored conference in Accra, Ghana, in commemoration of the matriculation of Amo (in the organizing of which I had a considerable part) an appreciative delegation of members of his family (or, more strictly, lineage) headed by the chief of his town was received amidst color and pomp.

It is impossible not to perceive in Amo a relentless quest for knowledge and excellence. There is an anecdote that as a child he overheard his patron arguing with a visitor who questioned the mental capacity of black people. Perhaps he consciously offered his own life and work as one answer.

The *Apatheia* is a vigorous critique of Descartes' conception of the mind, which is interesting in itself. But to me, it has a special, or I might say, a tantalizing interest, which I will explain before long. The main contention of the dissertation is that, contrary to Descartes, there is neither the faculty nor the phenomenon of sensation in the human mind, these only being appropriate to the body. But let us start with Amo's characterization of the mind, which he develops first from its general and then from its "species" nature. In its general nature, mind, according to Amo, is *spirit*, by which he means: "whatever substance is purely active, immaterial and always gains understanding through itself (i.e. directly), and acts from self-motion and with intention in regard to an end and goal of which it is conscious to itself" (Amo 1968: 66). "As regards its species," the human mind is an immaterial substance, which "inheres" in the body as a subject and uses it as an instrument and as a medium (ibid. 69). In respect of immateriality, all spirits are the same. But the human mind is an incarnate spirit and different in this regard from unincarnate spirits. The latter species of spirits do not have knowledge through ideas, for an idea is defined as "the instantaneous action of our mind, by which it represents to itself things perceived before through the senses and the sensory organs" (ibid. 68). But "God and other spirits placed outside matter are entirely destitute of sensation, sensory organs and an organic living body." In God, in particular, "representation is impossible for otherwise there would occur in God a representation of the future, past, and in general of absent things, whereas... all things are directly present in his knowledge, and hence there cannot be any representation in him, since representation presupposes the absence of what must be represented" (ibid.). In our case, however, "our own mind knows and operates through ideas on account of the closest link with the body and its intercourse with it" (ibid.).

It would be quite a subtle inquiry to explore the further implications of Amo's remarks about God's mode of knowing. For example, in what sense, if any, is the concept of knowledge applicable to the state of a mind to which "all things are directly present"? We must, however, let the divine conundrum hang on high, for our present project revolves around only human cognition. And with respect to that, Amo seems to hold positions that are Cartesian enough. There is the supposition, first, that our cognition involves the activity of an immaterial substance; second, that (at least in some cases) the process involves the mediation of "ideas," and, third, that there is an "intercourse" between mind and body. What, then, one might ask, is the great difference between Amo and Descartes?

The difference arises from Amo's conception of the mind as *purely active* and of sensation as *purely passive*. Sensation is necessarily bound up with materiality, whilst mind is, in its very essence, immaterial. Knowledge by ideation is knowledge through sensation. The problem is to determine what the role of mind is, or can be, in such a process. Does the mind itself *feel* the sensations in cognition by ideation? If so, then the faculty of sensation will be a faculty of the mind itself. To Amo's dismay, Descartes seems to hold exactly such a view. Quoting from Descartes' *Correspondence* (part 1, letter XXIX – Amo's reference), he notes that Descartes speaks of there being "two factors in the human soul on which depends the whole cognition which we can have concerning its nature, of which one is the part that thinks and the other that which, united to the body, moves it and feels with it." It is against this view of Descartes that Amo's thesis that "Man has sensation of material objects not as regards his mind but as regards his organic and living body" is "asserted" and "defended" in the dissertation. The Cartesian position under fire is expressed even more clearly in the Sixth Meditation, where Descartes says:

> I am not merely present in my body as a sailor is present in a ship, but...I am very closely joined and, as it were, intermingled with it, so that I and the body form a unit. If this were not so, I, who am nothing but a thinking thing, would not feel pain when

the body was hurt, but would perceive the damage purely by the intellect, just as a sailor perceives by sight if anything in his ship is broken. (1984: 56)

It is not the idea, per se, of the union of mind and body that Amo finds insufferable philosophically. For him, the error lies beyond that, in the notion that something that is supposed to be nothing but a thinking thing could *feel* pain, as opposed to merely apprehending the fact of the pain intellectually. In opposition to this, Amo's view is that in sensible perception "the act of understanding" should not be confused with "the business of feeling" (1968: 74; note that, as a matter of his usage, "sensation, feeling, sensing are for me [Amo] synonyms," p. 71). This is not to say that, on Amo's view, it is inappropriate to suppose that persons, on occasion, feel pain. They do indeed, on his view; but, on that view, a person cannot be said to be, *à la* Descartes, "nothing but a thinking thing." "There are two *essential* parts of man, mind and body" (Amo 1968: 69; my italics).

This difference between Amo and Descartes on the nature of the ego is profound. In the Cartesian view the ego does not need a body in order to exist, even upon this earth. It does, by Cartesian inference, have a body; but that is, metaphysically speaking, accidental. Anyone even vaguely mindful of the dependence of some, at least, of our conscious states on physiological conditions must have premonitions of paradox in the face of the Cartesian view. Descartes had enough common sense to acknowledge the two-way interrelationships between mental and physiological functions, and enough intellectual honesty to recognize that he had a problem on his hands. But the most charitable evaluation still cannot credit him with a clue. It is generally supposed that the problem here is that of explaining how an immaterial substance can enter into a two-way or even one-way interaction with a material one. But if the material parts of our being are an accident, there is the logically prior problem of how the existence of the *essential* can come to depend in any way on the *inessential*. Amo's more even-handed dualism, although not escaping the problem of how the immaterial mind can be in union with the material body, is quite evidently exempt from this last.

Amo's view, then, is that a living person is *necessarily* both a thinking and a sensing being. The thinking belongs to the mind, but the sensing to the body. Descartes, on the other hand, seems to want to have it both ways. The I, the self, the ego, is an immaterial substance and "consists solely in the faculty of thinking," but, nevertheless, he supposes it to have the faculty of sensory experience. Indeed, in the Sixth Meditation Descartes insists not only on this but also on the idea that sensible experiencing is not something that is done by a part of the mind, but rather by the mind as an indivisible whole: "As for the faculties of willing, of understanding, of sensible perception and so on, these cannot be termed parts of the mind, since it is one and the same mind that wills, and understands and has sensory perceptions" (1984: 59). When Descartes talks like this, says Amo, "he openly contradicts himself" (Amo 1968: 73). The argument is that, since the mind, being spirit, is immaterial, it cannot admit of a sensible faculty or the feeling of sensations, which result from contact of our bodily organs with material objects. This he takes to be plain from the definitions of sensation and the faculty of sensation. "Sensation," he says, "is in general the result of the sensory organs obstructing the

202

sensible properties of material objects immediately present" and the faculty of sensation is "such a disposition of our organic and living body as by whose mediation all animal being is affected by material and sensible objects" (ibid. 71).

Does this mean that in sensible perception, such, for example, as in the seeing of a triangular ashtray on a polished brown table, there is not an essential involvement of the mind? Amo's answer is, in effect, that the mind is involved, but at the level of recognition not of "feeling." This emerges – with, admittedly, a certain unaccustomed diminution of clarity – in his further explanations of the notions of "sensation" and "idea": "Sensation is considered to be either logical or physical. When logical all sensation is either mediate or immediate. People call that an idea ... when physical, all sensation is either pleasant or unpleasant" (ibid.). The notion of a logical sensation seems to be intended to capture the conceptual aspect of what goes on when there is a perception of the kind represented by our ashtray example. Given the virtually unlimited broadness of the usage of words like "sensation" and "idea" in much of the Western philosophical tradition under which Amo is laboring, the apparent incongruity of the idea of a *logical* sensation might be passed over. What Amo would seem to be trying to get at is the element of conceptualization in sensible perception of the sort under consideration. This impression is strengthened by the following remark about ideas: "Idea is a composite entity, for there is an idea when the mind makes present to itself a sensation pre-existing in the body, and thereby brings the feeling before the mind" (ibid. 74). Now, Amo insists that to bring the "feeling" or sensation before the mind is not to feel it. Accordingly, there can be nothing else for the mind to be conversant with, when it "makes present to itself a sensation," than its conceptual identity. On this showing, the "feeling" dimension of a sensation is its physical, and the conceptual dimension its "logical," aspect. We might, perhaps, call the "feeling" component of sensation its physiological aspect, though this is not intended to denude it of what might be called brute consciousness. It is exactly this aspect of sensible experience that Amo is excluding from the province of mind.

Some of the reasoning behind this exclusion has already become apparent. But there is a further angle to his argumentation, which has to do with the purely active character of mind and the purely passive character of "feeling." As is clear from our earliest quotations from Amo, mind (spirit), for him, is, by definition, purely active and admits of no passivity. But to "feel" (given the explanation of the concept of feeling at work here) is to be *affected* by a material object. To be affected in this way is to be passive. Therefore, the mind cannot be said to feel. But what if a thinking spirit is affected by another thinking spirit? In such a case, however, Amo maintains that "spontaneity or freedom of action remains preserved, as does also the faculty of response" (ibid. 68). There is a certain amount of elaboration of this basic argument (ibid. 67, 68, 69), but it is doubtful if this particular phase of his argumentation adds much to his case against Descartes.

How strong is that case? Recall that both Amo and Descartes share the persuasion that mind is a kind of substance and, further, that it is an immaterial one. Upon this common premiss it seems clear that logic is on the side of Amo. The idea that an immaterial substance can have a sensible faculty and through it feel sensations is an inconsistency that runs through not only Cartesian dualism but also through all kinds of idealisms in the history of Western philosophy. The proof of the inconsistency is, I think, essentially as Amo has laid it out above.

However, both Amo and Descartes face the threat of shipwreck in their common dualism. They are exposed to objections on at least three points. There is, first, the fundamental assumption, which, by the way, dualism shares with materialism, that the mind is a substance or an entity of some kind. This, in my opinion, is the deepest incoherence in the philosophy of mind. There is, second, the idea that the substance in question is a spiritual one. Unhappily, no clarification of the notion of a spiritual substance ever seems forthcoming, barring the purely negative and max-imally unenlightening one to the effect that a spiritual substance is one that is not material. And, third, there is the suggestion that this immaterial substance some-how resides within the material body. Indeed, regarding the last point, the minutest twist in some of Amo's own arguments would have sufficed to derail it. If, as Amo validly argues, a spiritual entity cannot be in *contact* with a material body, then neither, on exactly the same ground, can a spiritual entity be incarnated in the human flesh. It hardly needs to be pointed out that we are dealing here with a conceptual inconsistency dear to much Western metaphysics, secular as well as theological. (This is not the place to pursue these issues, but I might mention that I have ventured some thoughts on them with respect to the philosophy of mind in "The Concept of Mind with Particular Reference to the Language and Thought of the Akans" in Floistad 1983, esp. sections III–V.)

Our finding, then, is that Amo's strength lies in his disagreements, and his weak-ness in his agreements, with Descartes. But for me, this is not the end of the matter. A question that has always forced itself upon me is: why was Amo so keenly opposed to ascribing the feeling of sensations to the mind in spite of his acceptance of the basic tenets of the dualistic philosophy of mind? I have not been able to erase the following hypothesis, though speculative in the extreme, from all the recesses of my consciousness. May it not be that some recess of Amo's consciousness was impregnated by the concept of mind implicit in the language and thought of the Akans, the ethnic group among whom he was born and initially raised before being taken away in tenderest infancy? As I have argued in the paper cited in the last paragraph, in the Akan conceptual framework, insofar as this can be determined from the Akan language and corpus of communal beliefs, the feeling of a sensation does not fall within the domain of the mental, if by "mental" we mean something like "having to do with the mind." Mind is intellectual not sensate. This is obvious even at the pre-analytical level of Akan discourse. The Akan word for mind is *adwene*, and I would be most surprised to meet an Akan who thinks that one feels a sensation – a pain, for instance – with his or her *adwene*. No! You feel a pain with your *honam* (flesh), not with your *adwene*. The latter is just for thinking. And this is exactly what Amo seems to have been arguing as far as his thesis of *apatheia* is concerned.

The principal issue here, of course, is not whether the Akan conception is or is not valid, but whether there may have been traces of it in Amo's theory of *apatheia*. Admittedly, he was heavily influenced by the dualistic ideas current in his time and place of sojourn. The puzzle is why he was so insistent on the absence of the faculty of "feeling" in the mind, an idea that was out of tune with that intellectual milieu and in tune with that of his homeland. A philosopher supplies the ratiocinative basis of his views in his own pages, and that is what is germane to their cognitive evaluation. But when puzzles such as the one just mentioned arise, it is legitimate to be curious about their psychological provenance. Inevitably, one must inquire into circumstances transcending his pages. Granted that we are on shaky ground here, it may still not be altogether irrelevant to note in this connection that, even though Amo was removed from his motherland in his infancy, he retained an uncompromising sense of pride in his origins, usually adding to his name the title "Afer" (the African). Did he, perhaps, retain more than pride from his place of origin? Certainly, somebody without a deep mental and emotional identification with his origins might well have been at a loss as to the whereabouts of his family when he returned home after more than 40 years of unbroken oceanic separation dating back to his infancy. Perhaps, then, the non-sensate conception of mind was a kind of "cultural survival" in Amo's psyche, kept in place by the sheer depth of his attachment to his motherland.

That, to be sure, is just speculation. But an issue that must evoke more than mere speculation is the following. Amo was an African and a philosopher. Therefore, he was an African philosopher. But does his work fall within African philosophy? The question sounds simple, but it may not have a simple answer. If his philosophical thinking had conscious or even unconscious African cultural traces, in part or in whole, its African identity might be proportionately capable of being validated. The speculation we have indulged in above, however, does not give us anything much to go by. It does not follow, though, on pain of the sin of denying the antecedent, that if his philosophy showed no such traces, then it could not have an African belonging. Other grounds of such belonging are possible. For example, was his philosophy – again, in part or in whole – motivated by African concerns? If it was, then to that degree and in respect of the appropriate parts, it might have a just claim to an African standing. We know that Amo did have explicit African concerns: witness the very title of his lost work *The Rights of Negroes in Europe*. But a lost work is a lost potential of proof.

Even so, there is a criterion of African identity, more basic than any of the foregoing that still remains open. To be part of an intellectual tradition, a given thought content need only be taken up and used therein. If Amo's work engages the sustained interest of contemporary workers in African philosophy, it will become part of that tradition of philosophy by dint of use or assimilation. The fact alone of his origins may help the process, but is not decisive. In fact, the work of an alien can become part of modern African philosophy by the same criterion of use or assimilation. The prospects, in the case of Amo, are by no means negligible. The Department of Philosophy at the University of Ghana has a dedication to Amo, and Nigeria can boast of a William Amo Centre for African Philosophy at the University of Nigeria, Nsukka.

These considerations prompt another reflection of the greatest contemporary significance. In principle, the question raised about the African standing of Amo's work can be raised about the work of any present-day African philosopher. Her work does not automatically acquire a place in the African tradition because of her racial identity. There are, as must be apparent from the last two paragraphs, a number of sufficient conditions for determining this issue of status. The one most relevant to the present paragraph is a matter of linkage. If the work links up with elements of the African tradition, its claims for a place in it are legitimate, irrespective of the nature of its content. Let it be about the philosophical intricacies of quantum cosmology. No matter, the criterion still holds; which is important, for this is one of the ways in which a tradition may expand and develop. The multiplicity of criteria of belonging underlies the possibility and also, indeed, the desirability, of a wide-ranging division of labor among the individual workers in a tradition. The optimal flourishing of the tradition itself, however, requires the confluence of all the various ways of forging its identity.

References

Amo, William (1968) *The Apatheia of the Human Mind*, trans. William Abraham in *Antonius Gviliemus Amo, Afer of Axim, Translation of his Works* (Halle: Martin Luther University, Halle-Wittenberg).

Descartes, René (1984) *The Philosophical Writings of Descartes*, vol. II, trans. and ed. John Cottingham, Robert Stoothoff, and Dugald Murdoch (New York: Cambridge University Press).

Wiredu, Kwasi (1987) "The Concept of Mind with Particular Reference to the Language and Thought of the Akans," in G. Floistad (ed.), *Contemporary Philosophy, A New Survey*. Vol. 5: *African Philosophy* (Boston: Kluwer Academic Publishers).

Further reading

Abraham, William (1964) "The Life and Times of Anton-Wilhelm Amo," *Transactions of the Historical Society of Ghana*, vol. VII.

Brentjes, B. (1977) "William Amo, An Eighteenth-Century Ghanaian Philosopher in Germany," *Universitas: An Inter-faculty Journal of the University of Ghana*.

Hountondji, Paulin (1976) "An African Philosopher in Germany in the Eighteenth Century," in *African Philosophy: Myth and Reality* (Bloomington: Indiana University Press).

Nwodo, Christopher S. (1985) "The Explicit and the Implicit in Amo's Philosophy," in P. O. Bodunrin (ed.), *Philosophy in Africa: Trends and Perspectives* (Ile-Ife, Nigeria: University of Ife Press).

13

Albert Luthuli, Steve Biko, and Nelson Mandela: The Philosophical Basis of their Thought and Practice

MABOGO P. MORE

Most of the contributors to the trend of African philosophical literature described by Odera Oruka as nationalist-ideological have been freedom fighters, politicians, or statesmen. For obvious historical reasons, South Africa is blessed with world-acclaimed political figures who can easily be categorized under that label. Among them are Nelson Rolihlahla Mandela, Steve Bantu Biko, Chief Albert Luthuli, Robert Mangaliso Sobukwe, and Archbishop Desmond Tutu. Like other nationalist-ideological philosophers of the African continent, their philosophical orientation and focus were directed toward political, social, legal, and religious change in pursuit of justice, equality, human dignity, and democracy. Characteristic of this group is the fact that they did not assume that Western philosophy is radically different from or irrelevant to the African. Secondly, they recognized the peculiarity of their situation and therefore did not make generalized claims about the entire African continent. Lastly, they combined theory and praxis in their fight against colonialism, racism, imperialism, and apartheid.

What is common to all of them is not so much the geographical space in which they were located as the moral, political, social, religious, and historical conditions that produced them, conditions characterized by colonialist violence of an unprecedented nature in the history of colonialism. As a consequence, they consistently focused not just on what *is* the case but also on what *ought* to be the case. Three of them (Biko, Luthuli, and Sobukwe) died under violent circumstances. And three of them (Luthuli, Mandela, and Tutu) have, ironically, been honored with the most internationally prestigious prize in the world, the Nobel Peace Prize.

If the colonial encounter between Europe and Africa, as Frantz Fanon states, was predicated on violence, then apartheid, being colonialism of a "special kind," was doubly violent. Hence, the question of political violence in the liberation struggle in South Africa became doubly compelling and urgent. Tsenay Serequeberhan (1994) laments the paucity of discourse on violence in African philosophy in spite of the fact that colonialism in Africa was predicated on violent confrontation between Europe and Africa. This chapter is an attempt to respond to Serequeberhan's incisive observations and to engage this question in the historical context of South Africa.

There has lately been a somewhat disturbing tendency to misrepresent most South African liberation leaders as pacifist. Consequently, the revolutionary impulse of some leaders has been under erasure. Understandably, part of the reason is that the great pacifist, Mahatma Gandhi, started practicing his philosophy of non-violence while in South Africa. Further, three of these leaders are Nobel Peace Laureates. But given the primacy of violence in the history of South Africa, my purpose here is to explore the philosophical bases of the thought and practice of Luthuli, Mandela, and Biko in relation to the question of violence in the liberation struggle. My claim is that not all of them chose the non-violent route on grounds of moral principle, as they are widely thought to have done.

The Question of Violence in South Africa

The question of violence as a means of social and political transformation has been a source of moral anguish to African nationalist leaders. It is common practice when dealing with the question of revolutionary violence in Africa to situate it within the context of the contrast between Mahatma Gandhi and Frantz Fanon. Gandhi's philosophy of non-violence, in particular, and Fanon's much misunderstood view that violence is necessary in anti-colonial liberation struggles are the two most influential positions regarding the question of violence in the national liberation struggles of Africa. In South Africa, a society in which structural, psychological, and physical violence were visible in the extreme, these two seemingly opposing influences were both operative. Gandhi in fact developed his non-violent ethics of *Satyagraha*, *Ahimsa* and *Tapasya* while resident in South Africa. For this reason (in addition to any other) the philosophy has had a tremendous influence on the African National Congress (ANC) and its leadership, especially Luthuli. On the other hand, Fanon's revolutionary philosophy of anti-colonial violence and his existential-phenomenological humanism have had varying degrees of influence on some important South African liberation leaders, such as, in particular, Biko and the Black Consciousness Movement.

From the landing of Jan Van Riebeeck in 1652 at the Cape of Good Hope, resistance to white colonization and domination has been violent. The Kaffir wars in the Cape, the Zulu wars, the Basotho wars, and the Bapedi wars are evidence of this violent struggle against colonization. In 1906, after the Bambata Rebellion, Africans came to accept the futility of violent struggle without weapons to match those of the oppressor. Gandhian non-violent resistance became a reasonable moral choice.

Albert Luthuli

Chief Albert Luthuli (1898–1967), the bearer of the torch of Gandhian non-violence, was first and foremost a Christian in belief and practice and can be regarded as one of those rare men of nobility whose very existence proclaimed the dignity of human beings. He was a Christian liberal "realist"[1] whose belief in the Gandhian philosophy of non-violent passive resistance was unquestionable. For him, violence was not only destructive in essence but also inhumane, primitive, and uncivilized. A former president of the ANC, Luthuli was awarded the Nobel Peace Prize in 1961.

As a devout Christian, a Zulu chief, teacher, and politician, Luthuli did not only give himself completely to his people, he also had to face the ultimate issue of the choice between revolutionary violence and reconciliation, which no one who is both a Christian and leader of an oppressed people can escape. In terms of Christian teachings, people can be reconciled with one another only insofar as they are reconciled with God. When reconciliation with God occurs, they give themselves in thought, word, and deed to the liberation of the oppressed and to the struggle against violence and dehumanization. Just as Jesus renounced violent methods as a means to liberation, Luthuli believed in "the spirit that revolts openly and boldly against injustice and expresses itself in a determined and non-violent manner" (1963: 209). Such a revolt, he held, remains the permanent duty of Christians. "The Road to Freedom," he declared, "is via the cross" (ibid. 211). The cross symbolizes Christian heroism depicted by Christ's suffering and humiliation on the cross. Victory, on this view, is best brought about by suffering and adherence to the principles of non-violent resistance.

The philosophy of non-violent resistance, borrowed largely from Gandhi, was therefore chosen precisely because it dealt with injustice in such a way as to reconcile the oppressed with the oppressor and to avoid sowing the seeds of hatred and bitterness. Non-violence, then, was a positive policy of reconciliation and love, a moral and ethical struggle for the good. Thus Luthuli declared:

> I have embraced the non-violent Passive Resistance technique in fighting for freedom because I am convinced it is the only non-revolutionary, legitimate and humane way that could be used by people denied, as we are, effective constitutional means to further our aspirations. (ibid.)

Luthuli advocated the consistent employment of non-violent methods to achieve desired political and social objectives on the grounds, first, that such methods were morally superior to violence and, second, that, at least in the long run, they will be practically more effective. The moral duty to reconcile the oppressor and the oppressed finds expression in both the 1952 Defiance Campaign against unjust apartheid laws and the Freedom Charter of 1955 which Luthuli, as the chairman of the ANC's National Action Campaign, played a major role in drafting.

If by pacifism we do not only mean the belief that violence is evil, but also that it is morally wrong to use violence to resist or prevent violence, then Luthuli was without doubt a pacifist. His position was reminiscent of the early Kenneth Kaunda's absolutist declaration: "I reject absolutely violence in any of its forms as a solution to our problem" (quoted in Mazrui 1978: 107).

Although pacifism is often thought to be a noble moral ideal, it can be shown not only to be a false moral view, but sometimes to have pernicious consequences as well. It is false because it denies us the right of self-defense, an objection that both Mandela and Biko articulated against the Christian "Turn the other cheek" philosophy, as we shall see later. It is flawed because it operates from the undiscriminating premise that all violence is equally wrong. The limitations inherent in the Gandhian

209

non-violence philosophy for Africa have been well articulated by Ali Mazrui and will not be dealt with in detail here.[2]

Nelson Mandela

What, in more detail, is Mandela's position regarding the principle of non-violence? If Luthuli is described as a Christian pacifist, Mandela has been regarded as a humanist pacifist. He has been classed with famous Nobel Peace Prize-winning pacifists, such as Gandhi and Martin Luther King Jr. Mandela personifies suffering under the most severe conditions and moral courage against an evil of a unique kind – apartheid. For this, he has earned widespread admiration.[3] After spending 27 years in the notorious Robben Island prison, he was in 1993, like Luthuli, awarded the Nobel Peace Prize and subsequently became the first African President of the newly established free and democratic South Africa in 1994. One effect of this sequence of events is that there is a tendency to perceive him only in terms of the post-Robben Island Mandela, a man of peace and reconciliation who preferred non-violence and negotiation as instruments of political liberation to revolutionary violence. The post-Robben Island Mandela, however, I would argue, is distinct from the pre-Robben Island Mandela. The latter was a radical.

Dominated by his intense commitment to justice and respect for the rule of law – witness his training as a lawyer – Mandela believed that although peace is desirable, it may be overridden by certain humanistic principles such as justice, equality, and human dignity. These have been the dominant principles that have guided his political actions and are reflected in the Freedom Charter. The South African liberal Constitution of 1996, which in many ways is largely an offshoot of the Freedom Charter, is an expression of his belief in justice, equality, and dignity as natural rights derivable simply from the fact of being human. This locates him, apart from his avowed African nationalism, squarely within what Kibujjo Kalumba calls "the natural rights tradition of ethics and political philosophy" (1995: 161).

Though he always considered himself a "loyal and disciplined member" of the ANC, as a young man he differed with some prominent members of the organization in the interpretation of Gandhi's philosophy. Unlike Luthuli, Manilal Gandhi (Mahatma Gandhi's son) and others in the ANC, the young Mandela believed non-violence to be not a purely moral or inviolable principle, but "a tactic to be used as the situation demanded . . . a practical necessity rather than an option" (Mandela 1994: 147). Confronted, therefore, by ever-increasing and unabating repressive state violence, such as the 1960 Sharpeville and Langa police massacres of the African anti-Pass campaigners, Mandela became increasingly disillusioned with the non-violent tactic. He considered it "wrong and immoral to subject our people to armed attacks by the state without offering them some kind of alternative" (ibid. 322). This was evidently a critique of Gandhi's ethical principle of *Tapasya*, that is, the willingness to suffer so that one can win the sympathy and respect of one's adversary. Mandela's point was that asking that those who suffer violence should not use violence, in fact, means sanctioning the violence of the oppressor and encouraging the oppressed to turn the other cheek.

Probably independently of Fanon, Mandela was, by 1952, already thinking along Fanonian lines in relation to violence. Fanon's theory moves from the premiss that the violence of the colonized manifests itself as counter-violence. Through the violence of the colonizer, the colonized begins to understand that violence understands only the language of violence. Hence, in 1961, amid serious objections from Luthuli and others who were morally committed to non-violence, Mandela argued for a counter-violent military struggle for liberation, insisting that "violence is the only language the government understands. *Sebatana ha se bokwe ka diatla* (The attacks of the wild beast cannot be averted with only bare hands)" (ibid. 321).

For the existentialist Sartre, too, counter-violence of this nature is justified under the following conditions: (1) It must be only provisional and should not produce systems that keep human beings perpetually in a condition of sub-humanity. (2) It should never be the first resort or the easy way out. It must be the "sole possible means to make man." (3) It should be born of the masses. (4) One should struggle against it even in using it so that it is rigorously limited to what is absolutely necessary. (5) It must be presented as subhuman to those subject to it, so that it does not hide their true goal from them (Anderson 1993: 127). These conditions are echoed in Mandela's argument for counter-violence, which requires quoting:

> At the beginning of June, 1961, after a long and anxious assessment of the South African situation, I, and some colleagues, came to the conclusion that as violence in this country was inevitable, it would be unrealistic and wrong for African leaders to continue preaching peace and non-violence at a time when the Government met our peaceful demands with force. This conclusion was not easily arrived at. It was only when all else had failed, when all channels of peaceful protest had been barred to us, that the decision was made to embark on violent forms of political struggle, and to form *Umkhonto We Sizwe* [the Spear of the Nation]. We did so not because we desired such a course, but solely because the Government had left us no other choice. (1994: 433)

Indeed, the apartheid government left him no choice in life. Denied the choice of leading a "normal, family, social life which exists in every civilized community" (ibid. 393), Mandela had no choice but to struggle. Even the choice to struggle non-violently was denied. The denial of free choice forced a choice upon him – specifically, the choice of armed struggle. Little, if any, of this revolutionary Mandela surfaces in the popular image of him today. Not so much, even, as the image of the Mandela who refused to renounce violence as a condition for his release from Robben Island prison seems to be vivid in the popular imagination. In fact, if one bears in mind the image of Mandela as a boxer and the commander in chief of *Umkhonto We Sizwe*, it might seem plausible to argue that he cannot be a disciple of Gandhi.

Indeed, Mandela's considered endorsement of violence might be viewed by some absolute pacifists as a rejection of Gandhi and an orientation toward Fanon. However, neither Gandhi nor, certainly, some of his disciples was an absolute pacifist. Gandhi, in his loyalty to the British constitution, was often ready to legitimize the violence exercised by the British state. For example, during the 1906 Bambata Revolt by the Zulus against the British, Gandhi offered the British the services of the Indian community to crush the rebellion. In a declaration on the question of the use of

211

violence in defense of rights, Gandhi said: "Where the choice is set between coward-ice and violence. . . . I would a thousand times prefer violence to the emasculation of a whole race. I prefer to use arms in defence of honour rather than remain the vile witness of dishonour" (quoted in *Sechaba* 1969: 10).

Given this declaration, Mandela's option for the armed struggle was not a contra-diction of Gandhi. Neither was it a movement toward the glorification of violence. It was, rather, a challenge to all those who preferred freedom to cowardice to join in the fight against oppression, a position of which both Gandhi and Fanon would have approved. There is therefore a paradoxical convergence between Gandhi and Fanon that renders the binary opposition associated with them tenuous.

Luthuli, Tutu, and Martin Luther King Jr. received the Nobel Peace Prize for their unbending moral commitment to non-violence. If Mandela advocated the use of revolutionary violence and was not as committed to non-violence as the rest, why was he awarded the Nobel Peace Prize jointly with F. W. de Klerk in 1993? And what of de Klerk? If a leader is judged by the policies of his/her movement or party, then de Klerk's racist National Party cannot, by any measure of the imagination, come near being described as non-violent and peaceful. Its history as the party of apartheid and de Klerk's role in it were undoubtedly predicated on unjustified vio-lence and inhumanity against African people.

The Prize, I suggest, was a recognition of the reconciliatory spirit Mandela dis-played and pursued subsequent to his release from prison. The post-prison Mandela underwent a tremendous transformation and can thus legitimately be contrasted with the revolutionary pre-prison Mandela, commander-in-chief of the revolution-ary guerrilla wing of the ANC, *Umkhonto We Sizwe*. Any person arbitrarily incarcer-ated for so long ought to be gripped by intense anger. Moral anger is a human reactive attitude which is felt toward those one believes to have wrongfully harmed one (Hughes 1995). Accruing from moral anger are resentment, indignation, wrath, rage, hatred, and fury – reactive attitudes that might lead to non-forgiveness and the desire for revenge. Mandela certainly had the legitimate right to believe that he was wrongfully harmed by the history of violence, dispossession, expropri-ation, and exploitation, which produced the apartheid regime.

Yet Mandela was resolutely determined and made a great personal effort to tran-scend and overcome personal moral anger, hatred, feelings of revenge, strife, and racial divisions by forgiving those who had wrongfully harmed him even before they could acknowledge their guilt and responsibility by apologizing to him. "Re-nouncing personal moral anger," as Hughes asserts, "is surely part of what is involved in forgiving" (ibid. 107). It is this moral act of forgiveness that turned Mandela into a modern-day moral saint, an epitome of goodness, and an inspirer of admiration. His resolute decision to negotiate the terms of the new non-racial democratic South Africa with the apartheid regime (headed by F. W. de Klerk) rather than choose a winner-takes-all, violent revolutionary route, made him, to-gether with de Klerk, a strong candidate for the Nobel Peace Prize. Thus, it is the post-prison, older Mandela and not the early commander-in-chief of *Umkhonto We Sizwe* who espoused non-violence as a moral principle. If Luthuli was a realist, Mandela is an early rebel become realist through the mellowing of his world-view by time.

212

Steve Biko

The thing about Biko that appealed to me is that he doesn't conform to the standard Freedom Fighter image. Mandela might have been more typical but...he is very much in the tradition of Kenyatta or Nyerere.... Steve Biko was much more of a philosopher. (Richard Fawkes, cited in *The Sunday Star*, May 31, 1992)

Unlike the two ANC leaders discussed above, Steve Biko cannot be said to have been a disciple of Gandhi. On the contrary, Fanon contributed much to Biko's philosophical and political thought and praxis. So much, indeed, that he may easily be categorized as a Fanonian. Philosophically, his concern was not with the speculative abstractions characteristic of much philosophy, but with the concrete and existential struggles which shape human, especially African, existence. His belief in the primacy of consciousness is based on the philosophical assumption that consciousness is the ultimate unifying principle, the agent of the synthesis and unification of different perspectives. His aim, therefore, was the restoration of the lost African consciousness and the establishment of unity among all those who had similar existential experiences in racist societies. As Lou Turner and John Alan observed, "What is powerful and new about Biko's ideas is that he always centres the possibility for change *within the subject of the oppressed*, and not simply within the South African economy or in the hierarchy of the system" (1986: 22). His philosophy, they continue, ushered in the "re-discovery of self-consciousness as an objective force within the process of liberation" (ibid. 23).

Biko, too, has been portrayed as opposing violence to a point where he is almost seen as a pacifist of the same sort as Martin Luther King.[4] This is based primarily on the following statements by Biko: "We believe that there is a way of getting across...through peaceful means" and, further, "We are not interested in armed struggle" (1996: 134, 136). First, these statements must be understood within their historical context. Biko was testifying as a willing witness for the defense in a trial involving nine of his friends and comrades accused of high treason. Biko's testimony was probably not for posterity, but simply to defend his comrades. Hence, the non-violent posture.

It may be objected that Biko espoused non-violence in several interviews which are "clearly not as threatening...as a courtroom" (Lotter 1993: 16). But it should be recalled that, as Biko put it, "we decided to actually form an *above-board* Movement" with a two-phased strategy. Phase 1 was "Psychological liberation (Conscientization)" and phase 2 "Physical liberation" (1996: 134). To publicly advocate violence as a means of political liberation would have been suicidal, for it would inevitably have invited the wrath of the apartheid regime and therefore defeated their purpose. Therefore, the public denunciations of violence by Biko may suggest a tactical move rather than a moral commitment to non-violence. As Nolutshungu argues, it was recognized by Biko and the Black Consciousness Movement that:

No organisation engaged in violent subversion could long survive to carry on propaganda inside the country.... But it was equally widely understood that the desired overthrow of apartheid could not be brought about by . . . non-subversive politics and the wizardry of consciousness, without the intervention of the liberation movements. (1983: 180)

Second, at the personal or individual level, Biko certainly did not subscribe to the pacifist principle. He seems to have long understood Fanon's view that, at an individual level, violence is a cleansing force which frees the colonized individual from inferiority complex, despair, inaction, and fear (Fanon 1968). "We had a boxing match the first day I was arrested," Biko once reported. "Some guy tried to clout me with a club. *I went into him like a bull*" (1996: 152). On another occasion Biko recounts how he reacted on being slapped hard across the face by a security policeman: "I hit him right against the wall," he said; "bust his false teeth" (cited in Woods 1987: 89). A person with such a reactive attitude toward violence can certainly not be a pacifist at all.

Third, Biko was against two of the fundamental pillars of Christian pacifism: the "turn the other cheek" philosophy and the "love your enemies" precept. He did not think it made any sense to address such a philosophy to an oppressed and destitute people (1996: 58). This is an implicit rejection of Luthuli, Gandhi, and Martin Luther King's Christian pacifistic principle, which, deriving from the Sermon on the Mount, enjoins the oppressed not to judge or resist evil or return evil with evil, but to endure wrong and suffering. As is known, implicit in this principle is the belief that the conscience of the oppressor will eventually be repulsed by the sight of undeserved suffering. Biko understood too well that within the context of a Nazi-like racist situation, such as South Africa, where the oppressors imagined themselves under an African siege, Christian pacifism with its insistence on suffering would be disastrous.

Conclusion

I have attempted to show that Luthuli and the post-Robben Island Mandela can reasonably be called pacifists and therefore deserved the Nobel Peace Prize. But, as I have tried to indicate, the same cannot be said either of the early pre-Robben Island revolutionary Mandela or of Biko. Their place among the world's respectable freedom fighters – such figures as Fanon, Mao Tse Tung, Malcolm X, Huey Newton, Che Guevara, Fidel Castro, Regis Debray, Jomo Kenyatta, Patrice Lumumba, and Amilcar Cabral – should not be overlooked. If part of the definition of African philosophy as understood by Tseney Serequeberhan, Marcien Towa, Okanda Okolo, and Ernest Wamba-dia-Wamba consists in "a historically engaged and politically committed explorative reflection on the African situation aimed at the political empowerment of the African people" (Serequeberhan 1991: xxi), then Luthuli, Mandela, and Biko may without effort be classified under the nationalist-ideological rubric in African philosophy together with Nyerere, Nkrumah, Senghor, and Cabral.

Notes

1   For a distinction between realists and rebels among South African black leaders in the liberation movements, see Gerhart 1978: 39–44.

2 For a detailed critique of Gandhian non-violence in Africa, its limitations and failures, see Mazrui 1978: 103–19.

3 See Derrida and Tlili 1987 (see esp. pp. 11–42).

4 See Woods 1987. Jack Briley, who had made a movie on Gandhi and was the screen-writer of *Cry Freedom*, a film on Biko directed by Richard Attenborough, sought to portray Biko as a pacifist like Gandhi and Martin Luther King Jr (see also Toussaint 1979). For example, Briley accused Biko not only of being a "liberal" and an "idealist," but also a pacifist who lacks an understanding of the mass struggle (1979), while Lotter approvingly portrays him as rejecting violence and seeking liberation through peaceful means. For a lively debate on whether Biko espoused non-violence or not, see Lotter 1992 and 1993; Teffo and Ramose 1993.

References

Anderson, T. C. (1993) *Sartre's Two Ethics* (Chicago: Open Court).

Biko, S. (1996) *I Write What I Like* (Randburg: Ravan Press).

Cabral, A. (1973) *Return to the Source: Selected Speeches* (New York: Monthly Review).

Derrida, J. and Tlili, M. (eds.) (1987) *For Nelson Mandela* (New York: Henry Holt).

Fanon, F. (1968) *The Wretched of the Earth* (New York: Grove Press).

Gerhart, G. M. (1978) *Black Power in South Africa* (Berkeley, LA: University of California).

Hughes, P. M. (1995) "Moral Anger, Forgiving, and Condoning," *Journal of Social Philosophy*, 25(1): 103–11.

Kalumba, K. M. (1995) "The Political Philosophy of Nelson Mandela: A Primer," *Journal of Social Philosophy*, 26(3): 161–71.

Lotter, H. (1992) "The Intellectual Legacy of Stephen Bantu Biko (1946–1977)," *Acta Academica*, 24(3).

Lotter, H. (1993) "On Interpreting Biko and the 'New' South Africa: A Reply to Teffo and Ramose," *Acta Academica*, 25(2–3): 14–26.

Luthuli, A. (1963) *Let My People Go* (Glasgow: Collins).

Mandela, N. (1994) *Long Walk to Freedom* (London: Abacus).

Mazrui, A. A. (1978) *Political Values and the Educated Class in Africa* (London: Heinemann).

Nolutshungu, S. C. (1983) *Changing South Africa* (Cape Town: David Philip).

Oruka, H. O. (1990) *Trends in Contemporary African Philosophy* (Nairobi, Kenya: Shiroki).

Sechaba, 3 (March 1969).

Serequeberhan, Tsenay (ed.) (1991) *African Philosophy: The Essential Readings* (New York: Paragon House).

Serequeberhan, Tsenay (1994) *The Hermeneutics of African Philosophy* (New York: Routledge).

Teffo, L. J. and Ramose, M. B. (1993) "Steve Biko and the Interpreters of Black Consciousness: A Response to Lotter," *Acta Academica*, 25(2–3).

Toussaint, J.-P. (1979) "'Fallen Among Liberals': An Ideology of Black Consciousness," *African Communist*, 78.

Turner, L. and Alan, J. (1986) *Frantz Fanon, Soweto and American Thought* (Chicago: News and Letters).

Woods, D. (1987) *Biko* (New York: Henry Holt).

14

Frantz Fanon (1925–1961)

TEODROS KIROS

Introduction

Frantz Fanon was born in Martinique in 1925. After his upbringing in Martinique, he studied psychiatry from 1947 to 1951 in France, where he then began clinical work. Following his marriage to Marie-Joseph Duble, he decided to work in Africa, and in 1953 accepted the position of *Chef de service* at the Blida-Joinville psychiatric clinic. He remained there for three years, acquiring significant clinical experience through work on 165 European women and 220 Algerian men. These were formative years, during which he sharpened his ideas on the social and political causes and effects of many mental illnesses. He resigned from the clinic in 1956 and joined the Front de Libération Nationale (the FNL), the movement that successfully waged the armed struggle for the independence of Algeria from France. He immediately threw himself into the anti-colonial revolution.

In December 1958 Fanon spoke before a Pan-African Congress in Accra as a member of the Algerian delegation. There he encountered Nkrumah, the President of independent Ghana, Lumumba, who represented the Mouvement National Congolais (MNC), Tom M'boya, the Secretary of the Kenyan Trade Union, and Roberto Holden, who later became the leader of the Uniao das Populacoes de Angola (UPA). It was at this crucial meeting that the black Martinican identified the Algerian movement as part and parcel of the pan-African movement. He frequently served as the official diplomatic representative of Algeria at international conferences, for example, at the Conference for Peace and Security, Accra, April 7–10, 1960; the Afro-Asian Conference, Conakry, April 12–15; and the Third Conference of Independent African States, Addis Ababa, June 1960. He was a pan-Africanist who did not divide Africa into north and south, and he made it his mission always to remind the Algerians of their Africanity, and other Africans of the Africanity of the north of the continent. His activities and writings were always guided by a pan-African lodestar.

Fanon's major books – *Black Skin and White Masks* (1952), *A Dying Colonialism* (1959), *The Wretched of the Earth* (1961), and *Toward the African Revolution* (1964), all published after his death – profoundly influenced twentieth-century thinking about the image of the black race, decolonization and violence in the third world, the problematic post-independence African state, and nationalism and national consciousness. His essays and political articles, which were always rich and astute, dealt with a wide array of subjects, ranging from strategic theories of revolution, philosophical reflections about continental Africa, visions of the postcolonial state to the psychological problems of the colonized, and advice to the youth, among other things. To this corpus should be added journalistic contributions to the Algerian underground newspaper, *El Moudjahid*, which, though originally unsigned, have been authenticated by his wife. In addition to all this, Fanon made extensive lecture tours all over the world and also gave two important speeches at the pan-African congresses of writers in 1952 and 1959.

Fanon's life was cut short in 1961 at the tender age of 36 by leukemia. He died in Washington DC, where he had gone for treatment. An accomplished writer, Frantz Fanon is regarded by many as one of the greatest revolutionary thinkers of the twentieth century. Four weeks before his death, he wrote to a friend, Roger Tayeb,

> Roger, what I wanted to tell you is that death is always with us and what matters is not to know whether we can escape it but whether we have achieved the maximum for the ideas we have made our own. What shocked me here in my bed when I felt my strength ebbing away along with my blood was not the fact of dying as such, but to die of leukemia in Washington, when three months ago I could have died facing the enemy since I was already aware that I had this disease. We are nothing on Earth if we are not in the first place the slaves of a cause, the cause of the peoples, the cause of justice and liberty. I want you to know that even when the doctors had given me up, in the gathering dusk I was still thinking of the Algerian people, of the peoples of the third world, and when I have persevered, it was for their sake. (cited in Zahar 1974)

All his books are articulations of a singular vision, and address three main themes: the racial gaze, violence, and the nature of the state. Fanon's great significance for Africa derives not only from his total dedication to the liberation and the postcolonial well-being of Algeria and Africa at large, but also from the continuing relevance of his thought to Africa and its increasing influence among intellectuals in Africa (and elsewhere).

The Racial Gaze

The nature of the gaze or the subtle racial look is the subject of *Black Skin and White Masks*. The human self is given a personality through the act of recognition. Ways of seeing, of thinking, of doing things, in the form of customs and traditions, are all dependent on the way others direct their subtle gazes upon our very being, upon those things that mean everything to us, upon our different and culturally and psychologically nuanced ways. However different or eccentric they might be, they are intimately ours, they constitute our private and cultural selves. We are the children of geography and history, born to a given race, a given region, at a particular time, in a particular place.

For Fanon, the black person is not only burdened by geography, history, time, and place, he or she is most particularly saddled with the heavy weight of difference, the

217

difference exacted by the idea of race. It is Fanon, the brilliant psychiatrist, who subjected the construction of the black self to searching analyses in terms of the gaze. He unraveled the architectonics of racism, via the machinations of the gaze, the racist look. The racist gaze, Fanon argued, indicts, judges, humiliates, and deliberately and cruelly denies human recognition to the black body. Paradoxically, however, the white racist, who subjugated, enslaved, and colonized the peoples of African descent, also secretly desires their black bodies and their ways of doing things.

The gaze is haunted simultaneously by hate, fear, anxiety, and by sexual desire for the black body. The racist gaze suffers from a double consciousness, the consciousness of superiority and the consciousness of inadequacy, incompleteness, an incompleteness that is manifest in the visual desire of the other, the black other. The black person, for his part, needs to free himself or herself, Fanon explains, from the inferiority complex, which the gaze and the brutality of colonial subjugation have inflicted on his or her soul. This dis-alienation of blacks from themselves is the central task of emancipatory psychology. As Fanon put it in *Black Skin and White Masks*, "This book, it is hoped, will be a mirror with a progressive infrastructure, in which it will be possible to discern the Negro on the road to dis-alienation. The black must realize that his alienation is not an individual problem. Its cause can be found in the interiorization of an historically and economically determined inferiority complex" (1967a: 184).

A subjugated race of people is kept dangling in the air, suspended between a yearning for recognition and an internalized self-hatred for belonging to a species of humanity condemned to suffer, chosen for annihilation, with the blessing of religious leaders and the Gospels themselves. Fanon unsparingly and unsentimentally exposes the Bible, the church, the religious leaders, and the modern academy for participating in the humiliation of blacks by way of slavery and colonization.

According to Fanon, the "Negro" has to free himself from the insulting gaze cast on him in the streets of the metropolis. He has to protect himself from all those who think that the Negro is immoral, unethical, and a liar. Most particularly, he has to learn to love his looks, his physique, his very physical being, otherwise the internalized inferiority complex will eventually destroy him.

An issue that haunted Fanon was the various ways in which love relations among and between human beings had been destroyed. This destruction is most visible in the relations between the black man and the white woman, and the black man and the black woman, and the white man and the black woman. There are haunting and tragic pages in *Black Skin and White Masks*, unmasking alienated and poisoned sexual relations devoid of love and of human understanding. No one since Fanon has analyzed these distorted relations with such psychological and moral acuity. Fanon's sustained scrutiny of this disturbing phenomenon constitutes a seminal contribution to the genealogy of the black self.

Indeed, the problems of the colonized are deep and intricately connected with the racist gaze and the oppressive colonial state which is fully equipped with language, books, teachers, experts, and even the Bible, which it uses to oppress the colonized subjects. The state systematically teaches them to hate their looks, their ways, their traditions, their language – even their clothes. Colonialism did not leave any stone unturned in its strategy of destroying the natives' cultural heritage.

218

The Martinican doctor was fully cognizant of the depth of the syndrome of self-hate that he observed in his clinical study of his Algerian patients. *A Dying Colonialism* is, at once, a long meditation and psychological probing of Algeria, a careful sociological study of the Algerian family, a shrewd study of medicine and colonialism, and, finally, a study of Algeria's European minority. Fanon shows, with remarkable skill, how the veil, as part of tradition, and the radio, as part of modernity, had become instruments of change during the struggle for revolutionary change. The veiled woman hides a revolutionary bomb and the radio becomes surreptitiously the voice of a New Algeria. The conservation of tradition is replaced by the progress of revolution. As Fanon put it: "The Algerian woman's body, which in an initial phase was pared down, now swelled. Whereas in the previous period the body had to be made slim and disciplined to make it attractive and seductive, it now had to be squashed, made shapeless and even ridiculous. This, as we have seen, is the phase during which she undertook to carry bombs, grenades, machine-gun clips" (1967b: 62).

Violence

Fanon is best known to his admirers as well as detractors for his views on violence. This theme, a central one in Fanon, has been the subject of a veritable cottage industry. Perhaps his most celebrated passage on the notion of violence is the dramatic introduction to *The Wretched of The Earth*: "National liberation, national consciousness, the restoration of nationhood to the people, commonwealth: whatever may be the headings, decolonization is always a violent phenomenon" (1991: 35). Several pages later, he dramatizes even more boldly, shocking the reader with an almost surrealistic effect, when he writes, "At the level of individuals, violence is a cleansing force. It frees the native from his inferiority complex and from his despair and inaction; it makes him fearless and restores his self-respect ... illuminated by violence, the consciousness of the people rebels against any pacification" (ibid. 94).

The inferiority complex that Fanon speaks about was first introduced in *Black Skin and White Masks*, ten years earlier. In that book Fanon introduced us to a profound psychological problem, without providing solutions. Here, he returns to the issue, advancing a solution. One way, however unpleasant to many readers of Fanon, of solving the problem is through violence. Only through violence can the tortured and anguished colonial subject expunge from the depth of his or her soul the fear of the colonizer, who is just another human being. The interiorized invincibility of the colonizer can be washed away only by violence. In violence, then, Fanon thought he had found a solution to the apparently insurmountable presence of the oppressor's gaze, the oppressor's wealth and power, the oppressor's self-perpetuating colonial machine.

The colonial machine must be broken, Fanon declares. Violence is precisely what the natives must fearlessly master in order to cleanse themselves of their wretched condition. Fanon is not celebrating violence for its own sake. He is arguing that, unless this violence is vented out, unless the pent-up energy is discharged onto the

219

body of the oppressor, the "natives" are going to turn it upon themselves, and they will never cure themselves of fear, resentment, bitterness, and sorrow. Renate Zahar, a noted Fanon scholar, explains:

> The unceasing violent confrontation of the colonized person with its norms and institutions of the colonial system leaves its imprint on his personality structure and produces mechanisms of defense and processes of compensation in the psychic makeup. If the defense mechanisms collapse under extreme pressure, psychosomatic disorders ranging from general indispositions to manifest physical changes are the result: "There is thus during this calm period of successful colonization a regular and important mental pathology which is the direct product of oppression." (1974)

What is more, we can hear Fanon questioning why we should be shocked by the counter-violence of the colonized in the first place, when the colonial enterprise itself is so violent? Those responsible for that enterprise created monsters that were destined to devour the oppressors themselves. The violence inherent in the colonial project can only be erased from its deep roots by the counter-violence that is the essence of the struggle for freedom. It is unfortunate – and Fanon, the psychologist, knew the depth of the tragedy – that decolonization can only be a violent phenomenon, but that is only because colonialism itself is violent.

Oppressed colonial subjects everywhere will have to resort to violence to free themselves and become self-determining subjects. Only after this, Fanon maintained, can the process of healing begin, and the moral project of founding a new nation and turning a new leaf of radical humanity become a reality.

Race and Class

Fanon attached considerable importance to the factor of race in his analysis of the colonial situation. In this respect he differed from the Marxists. He felt strongly that the Marxists forgot the autonomous factor of race, by relegating it to a secondary, superstructural status. For Fanon, race is the determining factor in the compartmentalization of the colonial world. The Marxists needed to extend the boundaries of their class analysis to embrace race, and, in appropriate contexts, to put it on a par with class. However, to argue that race is central in the phenomenon of colonial oppression is not by any means to suggest that race should displace class. Nowhere in his extensive writings does Fanon ever adumbrate such a useless argument. He knew rather well how brilliant Marx's notion of class is. No category can *replace* class as an explanatory concept. How can we ever understand the foundations of imperialism without the role of the class-generating effects of the profit motive, that powerful motivator of human behavior?

It is clear from the foregoing that Fanon's defense of race is a limited one. Nevertheless, it is profoundly useful in the understanding of the subordination and subjugation of peoples of African descent. Race and class interact on an equal footing to determine the plight of the colonized and oppressed subjects. Racial stratification is used as a tool for insidiously justifying the supposition of the inferiority of the "natives." Their racial identity is used to dehumanize them so as to denude them of rights, since rights pertain only to full human beings. Although political independence has brought changes, these have turned out to be, by and large, inconsequential. Accordingly, the overall pattern of racially grounded subordination of Africans and peoples of African descent, noted by Fanon, still remains in place.

The Postcolonial State

Years of subjugation have produced dangerously envious "natives," who would not mind displacing, in order to replace, their masters. In effect, their permanent dream is to become themselves the masters, the persecutors. The police, the prisons, the security systems – all of them signify their presence as masters. It is this uninvited and oppressive presence that induced in the psyche of the "natives" the notion of their inferiority, in the earlier language of *Black Skin and White Masks*.

The language of *The Wretched of the Earth* is radically different. It is bold, determined, confident, lyrical, visionary, and programmatic. Fanon writes as a thinker and dreamer, but as one disciplined by the realism of a hardened revolutionary. For Fanon, the true nation of the future, the nation that is to replace the colonial state, must be a *functional* state. This is a new argument and a development in Fanon's intellectual growth. For the first time he begins to use the category of class and draws his sword against the "native" intellectuals who profiteered from formal independence by taking their colonial masters' place. They became the new masters of the masses of the third world. These are the masses who live in tin shacks and shanty towns, walk on unpaved roads to fetch water from dried-up wells, who die before they turn 30, and whose children die of malnutrition. They suffer so that the new masters might live in gated communities, deposit their money in foreign banks, and send their children to the best universities in the West.

When the masses insist that the revolution should continue, it is the comfortable new masters who insist that it should end, because its mission has been accomplished. When some of the more fearless masses continue to light the fire of morality and insist that the revolution has not yet begun for them, that they expected far more, that they made sacrifices for change only to discover that nothing has changed, then the torture machine of the new dysfunctional state of the third world is mobilized against them. Exactly like the colonial regime, the regime of the new masters is cruel, exacting, and calculating. It devours everyone. It eats its own children. It is a shameless regime manned by shameless individuals. Note that this portrait of the postcolonial state, painted at the close of the 1950s, fits the realities on the ground today with photographic accuracy.

The ineffectual functionaries alluded to above are the ones responsible, in the eyes of Fanon, for aborting the revolution. They are not even a real bourgeoisie in the classical capitalist sense, for they are unproductive; they are merely conspicuous consumers. They are "musketeers," as Fanon calls them. In any case, the harbingers of radical change are neither the "native" intellectuals nor the "native" bourgeoisie. They are the peasantry and the enlightened but disadvantaged sections of the city dwellers. These are the people whose energies and potentials have never been tapped. They should fill the ranks of the new state. It is to them that the future

221

belongs. But they too have to be taught to eschew the blind nationalism that does not distinguish friends from foes and does not know how to craft alliances of common interests based, not on dead customs and traditions, but on new ways of seeing and doing things, stimulated by a true national culture. It is national culture that serves as a vehicle for the transformation of national consciousness. The transformation of national consciousness is one of the fundamental activities of national culture. The two processes are inextricably intertwined for Fanon. They interpenetrate as the conditions of the birth of an African consciousness. The construction of a national culture will announce the birth of a new national consciousness. Alternatively, a national consciousness is born only because a national culture has been born.

National consciousness is radically different from nationalism, Fanon points out in *The Wretched of the Earth*. He notes, "To fight for a national culture means in the first place to fight for the liberation of the nation, that material keystone which makes the building of a culture possible.... The condition for its existence is therefore national liberation and the renaissance of the state" (1991: 233, 245).

The masses need a new political party, a party that is truly of their making. Fanon remarks, "The political party may well speak in moving terms of the nation, but what it is concerned with is that the people who are listening understand the need to take part in the fight if, quite simply, they wish to continue to exist" (ibid. 207). Nigel Gibson, a leading scholar of Fanon, has put it brilliantly:

> The new person is not created from a blank slate but fashioned in the revolutionary process. Fanon's liberatory ideology is made more difficult because rather than being a party line, the process of establishing meaning demands a constant back-and-forth between the people and the militants. The militant intellectual becomes a practitioner aiding the growing awareness of the people's ability for self-government. Liberatory ideology, then, just like the colonial ideology described in the *Wretched*, is in one sense transparent; it mirrors reality. In another it seeks to uncover all the mystifications that block the people's self-activity. Fanon's example of building a bridge is a metaphor for the political matter of building bridges between the organization and the "people", "a lived experience": if the process of building does not "enrich" the awareness of those who work on it, then the bridge ought not to be built. (1999)

Gibson is right. The party for Fanon is a learning experience. It is in the process of constructing a party that the masses learn the important virtues of responsibility and accountability. These political virtues were systematically hidden from the people both by the colonial state and its leaders and the new dysfunctional state and its inept leaders. Fanon sought to liberate the new state from the old and ineffective ways. The virtues are learned by practicing them. The people proudly create the history of developing a state and its institutions. They discover that it is they who are creating the state. The state is no longer alien to them. It is their state. When the state fails to work, it is the people, who created its institutions, who fail. When the state works, it is their self-activity that has succeeded. The relationship between the state and the people is intimate, direct, and is lived every single day.

These vital relationships can be built only by the activity of national consciousness. This is a rational effort by which the people willingly undertake to make themselves a conscious and enlightened part of a new state of their own making. Fanon puts the matter eloquently thus:

> The consciousness of self is not the closing of a door to communication ... National consciousness which is not nationalism, is the only thing that will give us an international dimension. This problem of national consciousness and of national culture takes on in Africa a special dimension. The birth of national consciousness in Africa has a strictly contemporaneous connection with the African consciousness. (1991: 247)

Fanon takes us back to *Black Skin and White Masks*, where we began. The African, who was shattered by the *gaze* and the colonial brutality that accompanied it, can be freed through both the instrumentality of violence and the emergence of a critical and confident new African consciousness, which is part and parcel of the dawning of a universal humanistic consciousness. The humanist consciousness that was so important to him cannot, however, be built until after the last remnants of self-hate and the deeply sedimented effect of colonial brutality is rooted out from the black soul. Fanon the psychologist never fails to remind us of the "native's" shattered past. But what he seeks to facilitate is the birth of a new person equipped with the language of hope and political action.

Central to that possibility is the conquest of disease, hunger, and poverty on the African soil. Once the material necessities are overcome, then the newly acquired African freedom can be galvanized to heal the interiorized African shame and self-hatred. This was the ultimate vision of the Martinican visionary, who gave his life for the sake of the "Wretched of the Earth."

Fanon's *The Wretched of the Earth*, his last and greatest book, the galleys of which he read in the last moments of his life, a book full of philosophical and psychological insights, ends with a call to action, for a radical humanism: "This new humanity cannot do otherwise than define a new humanism both for itself and for others" (ibid. 246). Fanon continues: "the building of a nation is of necessity accompanied by the discovery and encouragement of universalizing values" (ibid. 247).

References

Fanon, Frantz (1967a[1952]) *Black Skin and White Masks*, trans. Charles Lam Markmann (New York: Grove Weidenfeld).

Fanon, Frantz (1967b[1959]) *A Dying Colonialism*, trans. Haakon Chevalier (New York: Grove Press, Inc.).

Fanon, Frantz (1967c[1964]) *Toward the African Revolution*, trans. Haakon Chevalier (New York: Grove Press, Inc.).

Fanon, Frantz (1991[1961]) *The Wretched of the Earth*, trans. Constance Farrington (New York: Grove Weidenfeld).

Gibson, Nigel (ed.) (1999) *Rethinking Fanon: The Continuing Dialogue* (Amherst, NY: Humanity Books).

Zahar, Renate (1974) *Frantz Fanon: Colonialism and Alienation. Concerning Frantz Fanon's Political Theory*, trans. Willfried F. Feuser (New York: Monthly Review Press).

Further reading

Arendt, Hannah (1968) "Reflections on Violence," *New York Review of Books*, 12(4), February 27: 19–31.

Coles, Robert (1965) "What colonialism does," *The New Republic*, August 9.

Gibson, Nigel (1999) "Beyond Manicheanism: Dialectics in the Thought of Frantz Fanon," *Journal of Political Ideologies*, 4(3): 337–64.

Wallerstein, Immanuel (1968) "Frantz Fanon," in David L. Sille (ed.), *International Encyclopaedia of the Social Sciences*, vol. 5 (New York: Macmillan and the Free Press), pp. 326–7.

15

Theory and the Actuality of Existence:
Fanon and Cabral

TSENAY SEREQUEBERHAN

Frantz Fanon and Amilcar Cabral are two of the most important political-philosophical thinkers produced by the African struggle against colonialism. Fanon was born in 1925 in Martinique and died in 1961 of leukemia in a hospital in Washington, DC. He was buried in the then liberated zone of Algeria. In 1953 he was appointed Head of the Psychiatric Department in Blida-Joinville Hospital, Algeria. In 1954–6 he assisted the Algerian revolution and in 1956 he resigned his position at Blida-Joinville Hospital and joined the Algerian resistance.

Amilcar Cabral was born in 1924 in Bafata, in what was then "Portuguese" Guinea, and he died, assassinated by the Portuguese, in 1973 in the Republic of Guinea. Cabral was educated as an agronomist in Portugal and in 1956 was a founding member (with five others) of the PAIGC (Partido Africano da Independencia da Guine e Cabo Verde), the liberation front that finally defeated the Portuguese a year after Cabral's assassination.

At the dawn of the twenty-first century, it is important for us to properly explore, grasp, and appreciate the character of our theoretic inheritance. In view of the above, I focus here on understanding how Fanon and Cabral understood the character and content of theoretic work as it relates to the actualities and exigencies of lived experience. The chapter will explore the dialectical relation of reflection to the lived actuality out of which it is generated, and on which it is grounded, in the thinking of Fanon and Cabral.

Frantz Fanon

In the summer of 1960, in a logbook entry entitled "This Africa to Come," Frantz Fanon wrote:

Colonialism and its derivatives do not constitute, truly speaking, the actual enemies of Africa. In a short time this continent will be liberated. For my part, the more I penetrate the cultures and the political circles [of Africa], the more the certitude imposes itself on me that the great danger that threatens Africa is the absence of ideology. (1964: 211)

These lines, hurriedly jotted down in a logbook while the author was on a recon-
naissance mission aimed at opening up a Southern Front for the Algerian Revolution, conceal, in their simplicity, the depth of the thought they express. This Front
was to be the direct and physical link of the Algerian Revolution with Black Africa
– the concrete entry point for continental solidarity. But how was this solidarity to
be established in the absence of a grounding ideological-theoretic perspective? This,
then, is the danger – the gap or lacuna – that Fanon identifies. How then is it to be
remedied?

These words, written by a partisan "on the move" in the actual process of
eluding the French colonial secret service on the front lines of the African liberation
struggle, point to a problem that to this day plagues the political culture of the
African continent. Indeed, Fanon was right; what concerns us today is not "colonialism and its derivatives" per se, but the painfully incongruent actuality of a postcolonial Africa.

What is this actuality? It is a depraved actuality controlled by a tyrannical,
dependent, and Westernized elite who beg for foreign aid by exposing their own
citizens, whom they have subjected to inhuman conditions, to the glare of Western
TV cameras. For these leaders, famine is a convenient and sure way of "earning"
foreign exchange.[1] Indeed, the national budgets drafted by this elite always keep in
view the NGO monies and disaster assistance rendered to them by the West.

This understudy elite, to be sure, is a "derivative" of colonialism. But its mimicry of
the lifestyles of its Euro-American patrons (see Fanon 1974: 98–9) and its callous
disregard for human life cannot be wholly attributed to the colonial past. Lacking in
any proper self-knowledge, this elite persists in perpetuating the hegemony of a dom-
ineering and cruel past.[2] The continental predicament resulting from this thought-
lessness, in all its tragic and comic poignancy, confirms Fanon's prophetic insight.

Indeed, Africa is threatened by the "absence of ideology." But what does Fanon
mean by the term "ideology"? A year later, the last of his life, he writes: "The
concrete problem in front of which we find ourselves is not that of a choice, cost
what it may, between socialism and capitalism such as they have been defined by
people of different continents and epochs." If it is not a choice between the established hegemonic ideologies, what then is it? In the lines that precede the sentence
just quoted, Fanon asserts: "The Third World ought not to be content to define itself
in relation to values that precede [précédé] it. The underdeveloped countries, on the
contrary, have to exert themselves to bring to the light of day their own proper
values, methods, and a style specific to themselves" (1974: 56). The non-European
peoples have to "exert [s'efforcer] themselves" in order to originate "values,
methods, and a style" grounded in their own lived historicity. For Fanon "ideology"
is a programmatic self-understanding. It should be the end result of the efforts of
formerly colonized peoples to forge out a system of "values, methods, and a style"
in their struggles. Just as socialism and liberalism were worked out within the
struggles of the differing classes of European history, the non-European world has
to "exert" itself to bring forth its own originary conceptions of the social-political
forms through which its existence can be lived. It should be noted, in this regard,
that this exertion is not to take the form of a facile and empty essentialism. Nor, of
course, should it be an attempt to force borrowed ideologies on the African people.[3]

226

For Fanon, the effort of non-European peoples to "bring to the light of day," through concrete struggles, "values, methods, and a style specific to themselves" is a question of being open to the emancipatory possibilities that their historic struggle, by its very nature, brings forth. It is an effort aimed at utilizing reflection in the service of social transformation, and, as such, the articulation of a practical rationality. Understood in this manner, "ideology" is aimed at opening anew, out of the exigencies of the present, the originative ground of historic existence that was closed off by colonial conquest and subjugation.

Even when one is open to the emancipatory value of an established ideology, one has to rethink its theoretic and practical cogency. Thus: "[M]arxist analysis should always be lightly distended [*légèrement distendues*] every time we have to do with the colonial problem" (Fanon 1974: 9). As Fanon saw, such distending, in calling for a creative rethinking, entails the critical scrutiny of various aspects of the Marxist metaphysic (see Serequeberhan 1990). This is what Fanon calls his readers to in *Les Damnés de la terre* and in *L'An cinq de la Révolution Algérienne*. In the very act of confrontation, the anticolonial struggle unleashes a process of concrete self-transformation in which, as the Algerian revolution had shown in the 1960s, what was needed was to think anew the practical possibilities disclosed by the struggle. Fanon had a prophetic awareness of impending failures in this connection.[4] It is for this reason that he concludes *Les Damnés de la terre* with a call to invention and discovery: "*il faut inventer, il faut découvrir.*" In the process of invention and discovery, one cannot but give full force to one's own "proper values, methods, and a style specific," that is, to one's own historicity. For, as Fanon knew so well: "We today can do everything on condition that we do not ape or mimic [*singer*] Europe" (1974: 230). But what exactly does this mean? At this point, let us look at the work of Cabral, who, in my view, appropriates Fanon's prescription within the context of Guinea-Bissau.

Amilcar Cabral

In 1971, a decade after the death of Fanon and two years prior to his assassination by Portuguese agents, Cabral was asked, by a European journalist, to elaborate on the character of his ideological-theoretic orientation:

> *Question*: Besides nationalism, is your struggle founded on any ideological basis? To what extent has the ideology of Marxism and Leninism been relevant to the prosecution of the war in Guinea-Bissau? What particular peculiarities, if any, have necessitated the modification of Marxism-Leninism? (Cabral 1971: 21)

Cabral's answer is as complicated and nuanced as the question is blunt. He begins by noting that "a struggle like ours is impossible without ideology" (ibid.). Indeed, there is no equivocation on this basic and central point. The problem is seeing what the term "ideology" means in the context of a multiethnic African society in a protracted process of struggle against colonialism.

At this point it is necessary to note that Cabral was asked the question about "ideology" from within the specific context of the Europe of the early 1970s. More

227

specifically, it was asked from the standpoint of the culture of the European Left of the time, entangled in the ideological strife of the Cold War and its own confessional squabbles, splits, and disputes.

Thus, after noting that "ideology" is a sine qua non of the kind of struggle that the people of Guinea-Bissau and Cabo Verde are involved in, Cabral states sarcastically: "I will perhaps disappoint many people here when I say that we do not think ideology is a religion" (ibid.). Cabral castigates the dogmatic and sectarian-confessional nature of the political culture of the European Left. A religion tells a story, prescribes a belief, a way of life, "one believes it or one doesn't believe it ... one practices the religion or one doesn't" (ibid.). This religious perversion of politics, the reduction of politics to a kind of religiosity, for Cabral, was a fundamental shortcoming of the European Left. This was a Left nurtured not on its own political needs but on the Sino-Soviet split and the consequent polemical feud between "revisionism" and "dogmatism," a feud obsessed with ideological purity.

In opposition to this construal of ideology as if it were a religious belief-system Cabral expressed his own understanding of the term "ideology" as follows:

> Moving from the realities of one's own country towards the creation of an ideology for one's struggle doesn't imply that one has pretensions to be a Marx or a Lenin or any other great ideologist, but is simply a necessary part of the struggle. I confess that we didn't know these great theorists terribly well when we began. We didn't know them half as well as we do now! We needed to know them, as I've said, in order to judge in what measure we could borrow from their experience to help our situation – but not necessarily to apply the ideology blindly just because it's very good. This is where we stand on this. (ibid.)

The point, then, as Cabral makes it, is that one has to theorize starting from a grasp of the "realities of one's own country." This does not preclude studying and borrowing from the theoretic reflections of others, produced under radically different cultural, historical, and political conditions. It does, however, preclude mimicry and the acceptance in toto of ideological or theoretic conceptions developed elsewhere.

What matters, then, for Cabral is that the work of theory be a practice originating from a situated openness to the needs of a concrete situation. We are to be open to that which arises out of "the realities of" our own "country" and critically gauge it in terms of theoretic constructs, such as social justice, the emancipation of women, economic growth, participatory democracy, etc., which are themselves the theoretic sediments of an antecedent engagement with practice. One should note here that there is a circular dialectical interplay between theory and practice. Thus, for Cabral:

> Our desire to develop our country with social justice and power in the hands of the people is our ideological basis ... If you want to call it Marxism, you may call it Marxism. That's your responsibility. A journalist once asked me: "Mr. Cabral, are you a Marxist?" Is Marxism a religion? I am a freedom fighter in my country. [W]e do not like those kinds of labels ... People here [i.e., in Europe] are very preoccupied with the questions: are you Marxist or not Marxist? ... Just ask me, please, whether we are ... really liberating our people, the human beings in our country, from all forms of

oppression? Ask me simply this, and draw your own conclusions...This doesn't mean that we have no respect for...Marxism and Leninism...But [it does mean that] we are absolutely sure that we have to create and develop in our particular situation the solution for our country. (ibid. 21–2)

It is obvious, from the above quotation, that Cabral is formulating his answer regarding the question of "ideology" in a milieu dominated by Marxism-Leninism. Nevertheless, he makes his central point unequivocally, namely, that to theorize properly is "to create and develop" the "solutions" called for by a "particular" situation. For Cabral, we must "create and develop" the "solutions" to the "particular" problems and exigencies that we encounter precisely because theoretical work is a "necessary part of the struggle." In this regard the work of theory is not something done once and for all. *Theôria* as a beholding of that which shows itself has to be, of necessity, an ongoing interpretation and reinterpretation of the concrete situation. Short of this, for Cabral, "ideology" or theory is reduced to dead dogma, and theorizing becomes a self-falsifying process of forcing the signification of events in view of an ossified and brittle orthodoxy. Indeed, for Cabral, "every practice produces a theory" (1969: 93), and the African situation is no exception.

Conclusion

By way of a conclusion, then, we can say that for both Fanon and Cabral, theorizing (or ideology) is the formulation, as a program for action, of what is called for by the concrete process of struggle. Each situation, each struggle, calls for its own indigenous self-understanding. The work of theory is a never-ending labor of situated seeing and self-understanding, a constant interpretation and reinterpretation, within the context of each new historical occasion. For each historical occasion, of necessity, presents differing vistas for theory. Fanon, like all of us, tied to the exigencies of his time, lamented the absence of such an understanding of ideology in "This Africa to Come," for which he fought and died. Cabral, on the other hand, within the circumstances of his struggle, combated the sterile and brittle notion of ideology. As he noted in 1972, a decade after Fanon, to have "ideology" does not "necessarily mean that you have to define whether you are [a] communist, socialist, or something like this. To have ideology is to know what you want [and what is possible] in your own condition" (1973: 88). It is this ignorance of what one wants that struck Fanon as the central problem of "This Africa to Come," a problem that challenged and stimulated Cabral's work and still challenges the politics of contemporary Africa.

Notes

1 Just in case one thinks that this is a hyperbole: Mobutu's Zaire and Mengistu Haile-Mariam's Ethiopia are concrete examples of this situation.
2 For a general depiction of the character of this elite, see Ousmane (film and novel) 1976 and 1972. In this regard, see also Ake 1996.

3 On this point see my critique of Senghor and Nkrumah (Serequeberhan 1994: ch. 2).
4 That the gains of the Algerian revolution, or what was known as the African revolution, were never consolidated does not detract an iota from the concrete achievements, which Fanon documents, that occurred in the process of the struggle. It just points to the fact that Fanon's theorizing had a rather limited effect on the Algerian situation.

References

Ake, Claude (1996) *Democracy and Development in Africa* (Washington, DC: The Brookings Institution).
Cabral, Amilcar (1969) "The Weapon of Theory," in *Revolution in Guinea: Selected Texts* (New York: Monthly Review Press).
Cabral, Amilcar (1971) "A Question and Answer Session Held in the University of London, 27 October 1971," in *Our People are Our Mountains*, speeches of Amilcar Cabral, collected by the British Committee for Freedom in Mozambique, Angola and Guinea-Bissau (Nottingham, UK: Russell Press Ltd).
Cabral, Amilcar (1973) "Connecting the Struggle: An Informal Talk with Black Americans," in *Return to the Source: Selected Speeches* (New York: Monthly Review Press).
Fanon, Frantz (1964) *Pour la révolution africaine* (Paris: François Maspero).
Fanon, Frantz (1974) *Les Damnés de la terre* (Paris: François Maspero).
Ousmane, Sembene (1972) *The Money Order*, trans. Clive Wake (Portsmouth, NH: Heinemann Books).
Ousmane, Sembene (1976) *Xala*, trans. Clive Wake (Chicago, IL: Lawrence Hill Books).
Serequeberhan, Tsenay (1990) "Karl Marx and African Emancipatory Thought: A Critique of Marx's Euro-Centric Metaphysics," *Praxis International*, 10(1/2) (April and July): 161–81.
Serequeberhan, Tsenay (1994) *The Hermeneutics of African Philosophy* (New York: Routledge).

16

Alexis Kagame (1912–1981): Life and Thought

LIBOIRE KAGABO

Alexis Kagame is without doubt a giant of contemporary African thought. He may only be compared to Amadou Hampate Ba, from Mali, with whom he has many similarities. Both of them were born early in the twentieth century and grew up when colonization was triumphant, but also when African traditions were still vibrant. They were lucky enough to experience African traditions at the right moment and gifted enough to conceptualize those traditions and make them known to both contemporary Africans and Europeans. For that, they both deployed an intense literary activity which has no other equivalent in Africa.

Unfortunately, until now, Alexis Kagame has not received due recognition. One reason is that a big part of his work was published in Kinyarwanda, his mother tongue, and has never been translated. The other reason is that Kagame has been best known exclusively as a philosopher. All his other writings have been forgotten. Moreover, his philosophy has been trapped under a kind of ideology, the ideology of *ethnophilosophy*, which has impeded the appreciation of other aspects of his work.

Life and Works

According to his biography, Alexis Kagame was born at Kiyanza, Mugambazi Commune, Kigali District, in Rwanda, on May 15, 1912 (see Smet 1975: 92). He entered the minor seminary at Kabgayi in 1928 and the major seminary at Nyakibanda in 1933. During his studies in the major seminary, he had the opportunity to collect and analyze tales, poems, and other oral traditions from ancient Rwanda. He became a Catholic priest on July 25, 1941. From that time on he was proud to sign his writings as "Member of the Indigenous Clergy of Rwanda (Butare)." Referring to this, Mudimbe says of him: "without any doubt, this scholar was ... a priest in the most classical but also most ordinary meaning of this word: a man dedicated to the requirements of the sacred and to the privileges of self-donation and sacrifice. Simply, a priest" (1982: 74–8).[1] This is certainly the best compliment one could pay to Kagame, the scholar, the philosopher, but also and above all "a Catholic priest."

Two years after his ordination, Kagame began to publish the results of his researches, especially on Rwandese traditional poetry, literature, history, and cultural traditions. When he was sent to Rome for further studies in philosophy in 1952, he had already published more than 40 writings, mostly articles, but also books such as *Isoko y'amajambere* (*The Sources of Progress*), a book of poetry of about 300 pages in three parts and 6,100 verses, published between 1949 and 1951. He had also published the first part of *Umulirimbyi wa Nyili-ibiremwa* (*The Singer of the Master of Creation*) in 1950,[2] *La Poésie dynastique du Rwanda* (*Dynastic Poetry of Rwanda*) in 1951, and *Le Code des institutions politiques du Rwanda précolonial* (*The Code of the Political Institutions of Precolonial Rwanda*) in 1952. At that time Kagame was already a well-known scholar. He had been appointed correspondent member of the famous Académie Royale Belge des Sciences Coloniales in 1950. During the preparation of his doctoral thesis in philosophy, that is, between 1952 and 1955, he produced at least ten publications, including a 355-page book, *The Socio-Familial Organisations of Ancient Rwanda*. His doctoral dissertation was presented in June 1955. In the same year a part of it was published, and the book as a whole (*La Philosophie bantu rwandaise de l'être*) came out in the following year. Twenty years later, he published what he himself considered a continuation of his dissertation under the title *La Philosophie bantu comparée* (*Comparative Bantu Philosophy*) (1976). Kagame had used all this time collecting information in the entire Bantu language zone, which, according to him, covers a third of Africa. In this work he gathered data on 180 languages from that zone, read more than 300 books on all the various languages, and interviewed more than 60 informants (ibid. 12–45). That certainly makes his research the most comprehensive that anybody has done on those languages.

All this time, Kagame was teaching philosophy, history, and literature at the major seminary of Nyakibanda, the Institut Pédagogique National de Butare, and the Université Nationale du Rwanda. At the same time, he continued to write and publish, especially on the history of traditional and modern Rwanda, on Rwandan literature, and on many other subjects. At his death in 1981, the bibliography of his work included more than 100 publications (see d'Hertefelt and Lane 1987). Alexis Kagame was also a member of many scientific societies.[3]

Where is Kagame's Philosophy to be Found?

Of all his writings, only six deal directly with philosophy. These are the two books mentioned above, which, in fact, are one (*La Philosophie bantu rwandaise de l'être* and *La Philosophie bantu comparée*), and four articles (1969, 1971, 1975, 1976b). It might even seem that Kagame did not spend as much time, either in his research or his teaching, on philosophy as he did on, say, the literature or history of Rwanda. In fact, however, his philosophical work was intimately linked to his literary work on at least two levels. The first level is explicit. The conviction of Kagame is that "in a culture without writing, such as that of the Bantu, the philosophical conceptions are either incarnate in the structure of words, or condensed in some proverbs, or developed in one or another literary genre (tales, stories, narratives, poems), or finally mixed with religious doctrines or social institutions" (Smet 1975: 96).[4] The author himself assures us (1956: 22) that this relationship is exemplified in his doctoral thesis.[5] Thus though P. J. Hountondji is right (1977: 30) in not regarding Kagame's literary materials as *primarily* philosophical – something that Kagame himself knew – they were shown to be susceptible to philosophical uses. The second level is that of the unity of Kagame's thought. His scientific work is very diverse, encompassing poetry, literature, linguistics, history, anthropology, religion, and spirituality. But despite this diversity, it is noticeable that they all have a common goal, namely, to rediscover all the richness of African cultures, so that they can match other cultures, especially the Western one, which seriously challenged them because of colonization. For Kagame, philosophy underlies this entire project. Thus, philosophy is the inspiration of all his literary, poetic, and historical works.

Bantu Philosophy: Placide Tempels and Alexis Kagame

Still, however, it is through his strictly philosophical writings that Kagame is known as a philosopher. In this regard, the immediate catalyst for his philosophical exertions was the well-known *Philosophie bantoue* published in 1945 by the Belgian missionary in Congo (Kinshasa), Placide Tempels. Kagame himself recognized that if Tempels had not written his book, he would not himself have chosen to write his own doctoral dissertation on Bantu philosophy (1976a: 7, 217–18). It might be said, indeed, that both authors had the same aim: to show that the Bantu have a philosophical system of their own. Kagame accords to Tempels the role of a pioneer in Bantu philosophy: "he has the honor to have been the first one to raise the problem of Bantu Philosophy." He adds, "This shall surely immortalize his name among the thinkers of our civilization" (ibid. 7; 1971: 95). However, having said this, Kagame rejected Tempels's whole enterprise on both methodological and philosophical grounds.

What method for Bantu philosophy?

According to Kagame, Tempels's method in his account of Bantu philosophy was "gravely deficient" (ibid.). The first reproach was that it was based on only one Bantu tribe, namely, the Baluba of Kasai. The second is more important. For Kagame, Tempels's approach to the culture of the Baluba of Kasai was more ethnological than philosophical. For this reason, even if he recognized a "certain philosophy" in what Tempels did, still he considered the whole enterprise as the "personal reflections" of the author rather than as Baluba philosophy (ibid. 7, 218). Against all this, Kagame proposed his own method, which he regarded as more appropriate to Bantu philosophy. This method consisted of two steps: first, "To take a determinate cultural zone and identify the philosophical elements embedded in the language and institutions, in tales, narratives and proverbs, avoiding those aspects which depend solely on ethnology." And, second, "Afterwards, [to] extend those researches to the whole Bantu area in order to verify whether the same elements can be found or not. The outcome should then enable one to establish either the real

233

existence or nonexistence of a Bantu Philosophy" (ibid.; 1971: 96). He regarded his two main books on philosophy as representing the two steps, *La Philosophie bantu rwandaise de l'être* representing the first step and *La Philosophie bantu comparée* the second.

Ethnology and philosophy

How does Kagame conceive the distinction between Bantu ethnology and Bantu philosophy? To clarify this question, he devotes to it a number of pages of *La Philosophie bantu rwandaise de l'être*. For him, philosophy is "the science which deals with beings from the special angle of their most profound causes, which, that is, tries to reach the ultimate principles of their being" (1976a: 17). Ethnology, on the other hand, deals with "historical factors that are subject to the laws of social evolution" (ibid.). In other words, philosophical principles are "invariable" because, says Kagame, "since the nature of the beings remains what it is, their ultimate explanation is inevitably immutable" (ibid.). However, since Kagame himself recognized that "ethnological data, such as social, juridical, religious and even sometimes purely cultural institutions rest upon philosophical principles" (ibid. 16) it is not clear where precisely ethnology ends and philosophy begins.

Which concept of philosophy for Bantu reality?

The concern of Kagame to begin the analysis of Bantu philosophy with a clear concept of philosophy from which ethnological considerations have been excluded is, of course, methodologically important, even if the distinction is difficult to make. That concern gives more rigor to his analysis. It must also be said to his credit that he tried to follow this methodological imperative throughout his philosophical investigations.

However, when the concept Kagame uses in his account of Bantu philosophy is seriously examined, it turns out to be the classical Aristotelian conception of first philosophy, that is, metaphysics as it was understood and elaborated by the scholastics.[6] The question now is whether the whole of philosophy and, in particular, Bantu philosophy are to be restricted to metaphysics and to one specific concept of metaphysics, namely, the Aristotelian. Coming back to Tempels, Kagame is certainly right in finding that Tempels lacked a precise concept of philosophy in contradistinction to ethnology. But if Tempels's problem is vagueness, Kagame's would seem to be narrowness.

Bantu Philosophy: Its Divisions

In his work (1945) Tempels develops the idea that Bantu philosophy is different from the European one in that it is founded on the notion of *force vitale* (vital force). According to him, for the Bantu, "force is being and being is force," that is, force is the essence of being. Kagame disputed the accuracy of this interpretation of Bantu philosophy, arguing that the central notion of Bantu philosophy is being in the general sense rather than just as force. It is, according to him, in this general sense that Bantu philosophy is a philosophy of being. Following the scholastic division of philosophy into ontology, criteriology (or epistemology), rational psychology, and ethics (to which he adds cosmology and philosophical theology), Kagame traces out the Bantu philosophy of being as it plays itself out in all those branches of philosophy. Let us see how he does this.

Logic and criteriology

Logic and criteriology (or epistemology) are considered by Kagame as introductory to philosophy, Bantu or otherwise. He begins his exposition of Bantu philosophy with formal logic (1956: ch. 2). In *Comparative Bantu Philosophy*, he also begins with formal logic (1976a: ch. 3), but he continues with criteriology (ibid. ch. 4). For Kagame, "formal logic is the same in all cultures" (1956: 37). And this turns out, in fact, to be the classical Aristotelian scholastic logic, beginning with terms and ending with the syllogistic. He claims that any culture has all those procedures of reasoning, even if it doesn't formulate them explicitly.

What is Bantu theory of knowledge? What criteria of truth do the Bantu use? What, in other words, is their criteriology? Like other people, says Kagame, the Bantu use, first of all, the first principles of reason, which are the principles of identity, non-contradiction, and excluded middle. To these, he adds the principles of teleology and causality. The second level of criteriology is more interesting. It deals with specific Bantu criteria of truth. An important criterion, according to Kagame, is testimony (see 1971: 597; 1976a: 109–16). This may be either from ancestral traditions, or from the authority of the ancients, or that of people who are supposed to know better than others, such as specialists of various kinds.

Of course, reliance on testimony is not peculiar to the Bantu. But the question arises whether testimony is a sufficient criterion of truth. Kagame does not address this issue directly, though he notes that some testimonies are believed "blindly" and followed "sheepishly." This, he argues, is as true for people living in technologically advanced countries in Europe or America as it is for the Bantu (1976a: 116). This, however, does not solve the problem of adequacy. Still, it is extremely interesting to note how Kagame uses (copious) examples from Rwandese traditions, literature, and history to illustrate the importance of testimony in Bantu epistemology.

Bantu ontology: the categories of being

Without any doubt, Kagame's theory of the Bantu categories of being is the most fundamental and original part of his account of Bantu philosophy. As his starting point, he takes language, which he considered to be the most important of "institutionalized documents." Analyzing the grammatical structure of Kinyarwanda in his doctoral thesis, Kagame recognizes four categories of being, which he compares to those discovered by Aristotle from the Greek language. Taking the Bantu term *Ntu* to mean Being, he states that *Mu-ntu* means Being with Intelligence, *Ki-ntu* Being without Intelligence or Thing, *Ha-ntu* the Being of Space and Time, and *Ku-ntu* the Modality of Being. Kagame insists on the correspondence between these four

235

categories of being: *Mu, Ki, Ha, Ku*, and those of Aristotle (1956: 120). In *La Philosophie bantu comparée* he extends the same analysis to the entire zone of Bantu languages (1976a: 120–4).

It is possible to question Kagame's claim of correspondence between the Bantu and the Aristotelian categories. It might be noted, for example, that while Aristotle's categories were classes of *predicates*, Kagame's are classes of *beings*. Nevertheless, as far as the Bantu languages are concerned, he is right to stress that "any conceivable entity comes down to one of those four, and there is no entity that remains outside those four categories" (1971: 102). And his account certainly constitutes an insightful philosophical analysis of the structure of the Bantu languages.

Bantu cosmology

According to Kagame, the *Ki-ntu* category is divided into three kinds of beings: the insensitive or inanimate,[7] the assimilative or vegetative, and the sensitive (1956: 152). Bantu cosmology deals with the metaphysics of the first two groups of beings, which, by and large, encompass the physical universe. Kagame discusses this subject in considerable detail, and we cannot pursue it in this brief forum. Let us, instead, take a brief, indeed an all too brief, look at his account of the Bantu philosophy of sensitive existence.

Bantu rational psychology

According to Kagame, Bantu rational psychology deals with all "sensitive" beings. This comprehends all beings "endowed with senses and spontaneous movement" (1971: 606–7), in other words, those that "spring up, grow up and die."[8] This is the class of animals and human beings. Their common characteristic is that they all have life. What distinguishes them is that the first are merely sensitive, while the second are both sensitive and intelligent. The "vital principle" that they all have in common, Kagame notes, is what is called *Igicucu* (literally, shadow) in the Kinyarwanda language. This "vital principle," which is identified as the "soul," is supposed to disappear when an animal or a human being dies. Death is conceived precisely as the separation of the *igicucu* from the body (1956: 171–2, 205–7).

But here is an important difference between the two classes of living beings. When the separation between the body and the *igicucu* occurs, for both an animal and a human being, the *igicucu* completely "vanishes" (ibid. 172). However, in the case of an animal, absolutely nothing is left besides the dead body, whereas in the case of a human being something survives which is called the *muzimu*. This entity, which is unperceivable while a human being is still alive, becomes a reality after death; it is the bearer of human immortality.

Bantu philosophical theology or philosophy of the first cause

In his writings, Kagame develops Bantu philosophical theology in two steps. First, he argues that God is conceived as first principle or first cause, both in Rwandese thought and in Bantu thought in general.

236

The first thing to notice in this connection, however, is that Kagame changes his way of analyzing Bantu-Rwandese conceptions. Previously, Rwandese philosophy had been analyzed first through the Kinyarwanda language and its structure. Now, on the contrary, he chooses as a starting point the European concept of God, not the Kinyarwanda word *Imana* by which he translates it. The question is, does the Kinyarwanda concept coincide with the European one? Kagame doesn't seem to see this as a problem.

However, after this European starting point, Kagame settles down to the exposition of Bantu philosophical theology with meticulous attention to the indigenous languages concerned. He first expounds Bantu theology, showing that traditional Rwandese people recognized the category of "efficient cause" and were interested in tracing the series of efficient causes to the "first cause," that is, the "uncaused cause." According to him, the traditional Rwandese identified this first (efficient) cause as "*Immana*" (1956: 315–20).[9]

To demonstrate this, Kagame undertakes a large inquiry into Kinyarwanda thinking about the concept of *Imana*. He begins with an analysis of nine "divine names" related to *Imana* (ibid. 321–31),[10] and goes on to discuss further attributes given to *Imana* in Kinyarwanda sayings, proverbs, and people's names (ibid. 338–55). This inquiry is interesting. It shows convincingly that *Imana* was conceived in Rwandan traditional culture as "first cause." If Kagame had started with this analysis, it would have given him a more legitimate way of showing how the concept of *Imana* does correspond to the concept of God in Judeo-Christian culture.

As usual, in *La Philosophie bantu comparée*, Kagame extends the same inquiry to the whole Bantu region. He compares successively what he calls "primary attributes," "secondary attributes," and the "official names" given to the "Pre-existent" (the designation he gives here to the supreme being) (1976a: 130–52). The result of this comparison is also interesting. It shows a widespread common conception of the "Pre-existent" in that region. Despite the great territorial extension of the Bantu zone and the great number of languages, Kagame succeeds in showing that the names of the "Pre-existent" are few and the attributes he is given the same. The most important ones are "the Creator," "the Great One," "the Almighty," and "the Immortal" (ibid. 153–5).

After this inquiry, Kagame thinks it even possible to conclude to the total uniformity of the conception of the Pre-existent in the entire Bantu region (ibid.). Certainly, this needs more investigation. Still, this inquiry appears to be the best way to discover Bantu philosophical theology.

Bantu ethics or Bantu philosophy of final cause

In all his writings, ethics is treated by Kagame as the last part of Bantu philosophy. The reason is that ethics is the part of philosophy that deals with final causes from his perspective, which is that of Aristotelian-Thomistic philosophy. This, in fact, is the explanation Kagame himself gives. But his exposition begins with, and rests upon, a fundamental difference between European and Bantu ethics. This difference revolved round the conception of human teleology.

Human teleology according to Bantu philosophy Following Aristotelian-Thomistic philosophy, Kagame says that the fundamental rule of action for any being depends on the purpose for which this being is specifically created. As an intelligent being, a human being is specifically created for knowledge and love. Using an expression of Thomas Aquinas, Kagame says that "a human being is created to know and love God." He concludes from this that, for European philosophy, the ultimate purpose is God. For Bantu philosophy, on the other hand, says Kagame, the ultimate purpose of human existence does not lie in God, but in the continuity of life through procreation. Correspondingly, for Bantu ethics, neither reward nor punishment is to be awaited in the next world. Everything is finished in this world, whether it be reward or punishment. In Bantu ethics, again, the gravest misfortune that may happen to any human being is to die without a descendant. This means missing the whole purpose of his bodily existence; it is to die in the most total sense, that is, to disappear completely, as far as his body is concerned. "All the Bantu zones are unanimous about this," says Kagame (1971: 110).[11] The meaning of individual immortality in Bantu thought derives from this belief. Anyone is immortal insofar as she survives in her descendants. Here, Kagame develops an original and interesting theory, which he claims to be Bantu. The idea is that, even though the body dies, in reality it survives, because it is transmitted to the descendants through procreation. So there are two kinds of immortality: that of the soul, which survives in the next world, and that of the body, which survives in this world through the living descendants of each individual (see Kagame 1969: 233).[12] This conception of the meaning of human existence is considered by Kagame to be the foundation of Bantu ethics.

Bantu rules of action Thus the most important rule is that of "blood." All individuals descending from the same ancestor are brothers and sisters; they possess a common ancestral heritage of consanguinity. This situation gives them rights and duties. They have the right to be protected by the whole "family" or, better, lineage. But they have to avoid anything that could cause evil to any one of the group or, most of all, to the group as a whole. It is the duty of each one to reinforce life for the whole group. Also, according to this rule, the family group has to extend relationships to other groups in order to strengthen its own group, and this may be done either by intermarriage or by a blood pact.

The other principal rule of action relates to ancestor worship. This is also based on the community of blood. It is a kind of worship that exclusively involves people of the same blood. And the main objective of the worship is to implore the help of the ancestors to send away all misfortunes that threaten their descendants.

Good and evil The last issue of Bantu ethics that Kagame considers is the moral significance of good and evil. He does this in terms of the Bantu conception of the ultimate meaning of human existence. In *La Philosophie bantu rwandaise de l'être*, Kagame undertakes a long and serious discussion of the notions of good and evil in Rwanda culture. In the Kinyarwanda and Kirundi languages these notions are expressed, respectively, as *-iza* and *-ibi*. From an analysis of these expressions, he

238

concludes that, as moral concepts, the substantives "the good" and "the bad" have no equivalents in Kinyarwanda (or Kirundi). Nevertheless, concrete human acts can be, and are often, morally evaluated as "good" (-iza) or "bad/evil" (-ibi).[13] But even with concrete human acts, things are not so simple, according to Kagame. It is not always clear when what is good or bad is so in the moral sense. Here Kagame introduces a distinction between *juridical laws* and *religious laws*. Juridical laws are those that are established by juridical authorities and are punishable by them. They do not necessarily have any moral significance. Frequently, if you are not caught while transgressing a law, there is no consequence. You can even be considered clever or intelligent or fortunate.

On the other hand, the religious laws are related to religious taboos. Those laws have the characteristic that they are formulated in the negative. They require from people not that they should do something, but rather that they should abstain from doing something. In a word, they are interdictions (*imiziro*). Only those laws can be said to have moral significance and to generate moral obligation. The transgression of interdictions is something that is absolutely bad, even if done unwittingly. To avoid this kind of transgression is supposed to be good. What is important in that conception of ethics is that the sanctions pertaining to those laws are immanent in terms of both reward and punishment. And the sanctions derive from the conception of the meaning of human existence. Thus the most important reward is the strengthening of personal and group life, while the most important punishment is the weakening of this life or, worse, its extinction. The realization of meaning in human life, then, is the first principle of Bantu ethics.

Bantu Philosophy and Aristotelian-Thomistic Philosophy

Kagame's intention is to develop Bantu philosophy. He does it using a specific conception of philosophy, namely, the Aristotelian-Thomistic one. It is evident that he regards this philosophy as a model and its principles as universal and invariable. This is the reason why any structure of thought claiming to be philosophy has to prove that it does correspond, in all its parts, to this philosophy. That is what Kagame did for Bantu philosophy. It is, however, not clear why one brand of European philosophy should be privileged in this way.

More importantly, the following question naturally arises: What happens if some Bantu conception resists an Aristotelian-Thomistic analysis? Kagame himself sometimes faces this resistance, notably when Bantu conceptions and Aristotelian-Thomistic ones are mutually incompatible. It is interesting to observe Kagame's attitude in such cases. Sometimes he seems to indicate the differences without taking a position. In some other cases he seems to accept and reject the Bantu conception at the same time. In still other cases of incompatibility, he appears to content himself with saying that the Aristotelian-Thomistic conception is "technicalized" (*technicisée*) or "theologicized" (*théologicisée*) while the Bantu one is not. Apart from other problems, this approach raises the question of the relevance of Bantu traditional philosophy at the present time. The question is, how can it face scientific and technological thought today?

239

Matters become even more complicated when Kagame, as a Catholic priest, is faced with conflicts between Bantu and Catholic ideas. Here he seems to adopt a double position. On the one hand, he accepts the Catholic position. But, on the other, he seems to suggest that the Bantu conception may still be suitable for those still unconverted to the Catholic faith. Another important question about Kagame's treatment of Bantu philosophy relates to the issue of "collective thought." Kagame presents Bantu traditional philosophy as "a philosophy without philosophers" (1976a: 286). And it is true that his enterprise consists of eliciting the philosophy underlying institutional "documents," literary texts, proverbs, poems, maxims, etc. It might seem then that Bantu philosophy is the collective philosophy of a whole ethnic group, a philosophy without individual philosophers and without philosophical texts (1971: 94).

Kagame has been strongly criticized on this precise point, especially by Hountondji (1977: 22). Because of this "collective" character, this author and many others have characterized Kagame and Tempels's philosophy as "ethnophilosophy" rather than philosophy as such (ibid. 14).[14] For those critics, philosophy has to be individual; it has to have an author so that evaluation and criticism can be made. Kagame himself recognized the advantage of this way of doing philosophy (1971: 94) but he thought it was only a technical issue not a civilizational one (1976a: 47–51).

We would add that we can imagine a situation in which a collective traditional discourse builds itself up as a philosophy. Generations of real but anonymous thinkers could produce new ideas and improve common ones, thus creating an organized and coherent system of thinking with its own internal mechanisms of criticism and interpretation. It is in this way, for example, that some formulations, such as proverbs, emerge. This is precisely what Kagame experimented on in his researches in the historical and literary tradition of Rwanda.[15]

On any reckoning, Alexis Kagame has his place in the history of African philosophy. Already philosophical encyclopedias and dictionaries give him a place.[16] Nevertheless, very few serious studies have been devoted to his thought in general and his philosophy in particular. Apart from some articles and undergraduate term papers, the only such book we know is *La Philosophie du langage d'Alexis Kagame* (1987) by Bwanga wa Mbenga from the Democratic Republic of Congo. Let us hope that a comprehensive study of the whole literary work of Alexis Kagame will be done as soon as possible. That would certainly help the understanding of his contributions to African philosophy and African scholarship in general.

Notes

1 The translation is mine.
2 This book is a religious epic poem written by Kagame between 1941 and 1969. It is composed of 150 songs and 35,752 verses. It tells the Christian history of salvation using the traditional Rwandese way of composing poetry. Its ambition is to inculturate Christianity into Rwandese society.
3 The longest list I know speaks of nine academic societies. See Ntagara 1987.

4   The translation is mine.

5   The author presents what he calls the "institutionalised documents" as the only ones he will use in his thesis, and he really does it abundantly.

6   Aristotle, *Metaphysics*, notably Book A, 982a1–33; 982b1–11.

7   The French term Kagame prefers is difficult to translate into English; it is *être figé*.

8   These are expressions Kagame uses very often. See, for instance, 1971: 607; 1956: 204; and many other places.

9   Kagame writes the word *Imana* with a double "m." He doesn't give any explanation, but it is not necessary to write it that way.

10 The names analyzed by the author are: *Iya-mbere* – the Eternal One (or the First One); *Iya-kare* – the Initial One (or the Earlier One); *Rurema* – the Creator; *Rugira*: the Efficient One (or the Maker); *Rugabo* – the Powerful One (or the Strong One); *Rugaba* – the Giver (that means the One who possesses and distributes goods); *Rwagisha* – the Giver of Wealth; *Nyamurunga* – the One who gives birth; *Immana* – the Great Spirit. See 1956: 338.

11 Kagame had begun his inquiry about this question in *La Philosophie bantu rwandaise de l'être* (1956: 366–79). He continued it in *La Philosophie Bantu Comparée* for the whole Bantu zone (1976a: 281–9). He concluded that the samples he got proved that the situation was the same in that zone (ibid. 286).

12 Kagame recognizes that he had not realized this in his previous writings, notably in *La Philosophie bantu rwandaise de l'être* (1956: 233).

13 See, for the whole discussion, 1956: 379–400. In fact, Kagame's claim, according to which there is no concept of good and evil as substantives, because those words are formulated in an adjectival form, is not valid. Even in European languages they were first used in adjectival forms. Note that το αγαθον and το κακον in Greek or *bonum* and *malum* in Latin were first used in the adjectival form.

14 According to Hountondji, ethnophilosophy is "ethnology" claiming to be "philosophy."

15 See the testimony of a German friend of Kagame, Mr Eike Haberland, in Kagame 1983: 364.

16 To mention a few in English and French: Huisman 1984; Brown et al. 1996; Riviere 1992.

References

Brown, Stuart, Collinson, Diané, and Wilkinson, Robert (eds.) (1996) *Biographical Dictionary of Twentieth-Century Philosophers* (London and New York: Routledge).

d'Hertefelt, Marcel and de Lame, Danielle (1987) *Société, culture et histoire du Rwanda. Encyclopédie bibliographique 1663–1980/1987*, vol. I: A–L (Musée Royal de l'Afrique Centrale, Tervuren).

Hountondji, P. J. (1977) *Sur la "philosophie africaine": Critique de l'ethnophilosophie* (Paris: Maspéro).

Huisman, D. (ed.) (1984) *Dictionnaire des philosophes* (Paris: PUF).

Kagame, A. (1954) *Les Organisations socio-familiales de l'ancien Rwanda* (Bruxelles: Académie Royale des Sciences Coloniales).

Kagame, A. (1956) *La Philosophie bantu rwandaise de l'être* (Bruxelles: Académie Royale des Sciences Coloniales).

Kagame, A. (1969) "Le Fondement ultime de la morale bantu," *Au Cœur de l'Afrique*, 5: 231–6.

Kagame, A. (1971) "L'Ethnophilosophie des bantu," in *La Philosophie Contemporaine*, Institut International de Philosophie, vol. 4 (Florence: La Nuova Italia Editrice), pp. 589–612.

Kagame, A. (1975) "Aperception empirique du temps et conception de l'histoire dans la pensée bantu," in *Les Cultures et le Temps* (Paris: UNESCO, Payot).

Kagame, A. (1976a) *La Philosophie bantu comparée* (Paris: Présence Africaine).

Kagame, A. (1976b) "Le problème de 'l'homme' en philosophie bantu," Séminaire d'Addis-Abeba. Pub. in Claude Sumner (ed.), *African Philosophy* (Addis Abeba: Central Printing Press, 1980), pp. 105–12.

Kagame, A. (1983) "Journée Alexis Kagame: vie et œuvres," in *Sagesse et vie quotidienne en Afrique* (Actes du symposium de philosophie, Kigali, July 31–August 7 1983). Repr. in *Education, Science et culture*, 15 (Jan–March 1987): 345–469.

Mbenga, Bwanga wa (1987) *La Philosophie du langage d'Alexis Kagame* (Ottignies-Louvain-La-Neuve: Editions Noraf).

Mudimbe, V. Y. (1982) "In memoriam. Alexis Kagame (1912–1981)," *Recherche, Pédagogie et Culture*, 56: 74–8.

Ntagara, Abbé Augustin (1987) "Alexis Kagame Philosophe: Témoignages et Documents," *Education, Science et Culture* (January–March): 419–20.

Riviere, C. (ed.) (1992) *Encyclopédie philosophique universelle*, vol. III: *Les Œuvres philosophiques* (Paris: PUF), p. 4180.

Smet, A. J. (1975) *Philosophie africaine. Textes choisis I* (Kinshasa: Presses Universitaires du Zaïre).

Tempels, Placide (1945) *Philosophie bantoue* (Kinshasa, Congo: Belgian Missionary).

17

Post-Independence African Political Philosophy

OLÚFÉMI TÁÍWÒ

Introduction

There is a dearth of serious academic studies of the political philosophies of Africa's post-independence leaders. This is partly due to the fact that many of them produced their ideas under the pressure of direct problems of governance. To the extent that this is true, their ideas may sometimes have an ad hoc quality to them, a situation that often is anathema to purist academic philosophers. Immediate problems, however, can have perennial implications, and a close study of the African thinkers suggests that this was not lost upon them.

Doubtless the failures of political experimentation in many African countries in the post-independence era as well as the tendency toward "maximum leadership," or, if the truth be explicitly told, toward authoritarianism, make it easy for scholars to downgrade the ideas that were fashioned to inform their practice. It is as if scholars are saying that if, for example, Kwame Nkrumah's ideas informed his statecraft at Ghana's helm, then given the failure of his practice, it follows that the ideas could not have been that good to start with. The same has seemed to be the attitude toward Nyerere's Ujamaa philosophy of socialism or Kaunda's Zambian humanism.

It should be pointed out that African leaders are not alone in having their ideas discounted in this way. It is a staple objection among anti-Marxists to insist that since the defunct Soviet Union and erstwhile Eastern European socialist regimes collapsed, then, given that they were ruled by Marxists, it must be the case that Marxism is not worth any attention as a philosophical system. But it should be obvious that this is a non sequitur. No matter how strongly philosophers from Plato through Kant to Marx and Nkrumah have affirmed a connection between theory and practice, it remains true to say that theory and practice are logically distinct and conceptually separate or separable. The question whether or not a theory yields a successful practice only arises when those who subscribe to it do try to embody it in their actual practice. Most ideas that we deal with in philosophy never have any embodiments in practice and that has never stopped us from spending entire lifetimes trying to see how good they are as theories when we test their plausibility, cogency, coherence, adequacy, and, on rare occasions, correctness.

In what follows, I shall examine the philosophical ideas of a small number of the post-independence African leaders cum thinkers. The number is small only because of space constraints. First, I present the philosophical anthropologies that under-pinned the ideas advanced by these African thinkers. Then I discuss the defense of one-party rule as made by some of them. Finally, I examine the discourse of African socialism. I do not mean to suggest that my three themes exhaust the ideas that occupied the thinkers under reference. I only focus on these three because the first almost always lurks beneath any discourse about political systems in any human community and the second and third have riveted a lot of attention in discussions of Africa's (mis)fortunes in the post-independence era. At all events, I would like to suggest that in all cases, wittingly or unwittingly, the theories put forward by the thinkers in question are best understood as attempts to answer fundamental ques-tions of political philosophy. Such questions include, but are by no means limited to, those raised below.

The Central Questions of Political Philosophy

Outside of the crudest excesses of structuralism, few would deny that the ultimate end of any political order is the well-being of its members. One can hardly speak of the well-being of an entity unless one is apprised of what type of being it is and what will best conduce to its being the best of its type that it can be. This is the sense in which some conception, however rough, of human nature is germane to the design and operation of any political order. For, in a sense, no political order can escape some assumptions about what type of humans will occupy or benefit from its arrangements and how the interests of those humans might best be served. It is against this background that we must consider the metaphysical principles concerning human nature espoused by various African political philosophers in the post-independence period. Although, as far as I know, it was Kenneth Kaunda of Zambia who deliberately dubbed his philosophy "humanism," the issue of human nature agitated quite a few others, including Sekou Toure of Guinea, Obafemi Awo-lowo of Nigeria, Kwame Nkrumah of Ghana, and Nnamdi Azikiwe of Nigeria.

The importance of the issue of human nature attracted more urgency from Afri-can thinkers because, in their experience, one of the pylons of colonial rule was the denial by colonizers of the humanity of Africans. It was a principal justification of colonialism advanced by colonial apologists that the African occupied the lowest rungs of the human ladder, if at all, and that it would take centuries before the African could be sufficiently suited to self-rule, an attribute that is considered essen-tial to human dignity. Thus, in some sense, the repeated affirmations of the human-ity of the African were nearly directly proportional to the severity of the denial, on the part of the colonialists, of the same in the African.

The second question central to political philosophy to which African thinkers responded is the following: who may rule, given that not all can rule? Generally speaking, in political philosophy, answers to this question attempt to provide justifi-cation and legitimacy for political arrangements under which some exercise power and others are required to obey. For those who subscribe to divine ordainment,

244

those who rule are rulers by the grace of God. Under contractarianism, the only basis for legitimacy is the consent of the governed. When African leaders of the immediate post-independence period embraced one-party rule as the best or, in some cases, the only legitimate form of rule, they were trying to come to grips with this issue of who is entitled to rule. However, in focusing on the arguments for one-party rule, it needs to be remembered that there were serious philosophical divergences among Africa's political leaders on the question of who may rule. Not only those who favored the one-party system addressed the question. On the contrary, there was a considerable body of theoretical opinion that confessed a clear bias for liberal parliamentary democracy. Examples of the latter category of thinkers included Obafemi Awolowo of Nigeria and Kofi Busia of Ghana.[1]

The third and final question central to political philosophy that is of moment in this discussion is the following: how ought we to organize society for purposes of governance and social living? Put differently, what political and other social arrangements are likely to conduce to the efflorescence of that which is best in us? No doubt, the question of what the best arrangements are for African, nay, any human, society imports a pragmatic component into the discussion. But the issue is also theoretical for, given the variety of possible arrangements available, we must try to give cogent reasons for privileging some arrangements over others. It was in their attempt to answer this question that many African thinkers adopted socialism. In their estimation, socialism was the arrangement that held the most promise of delivering the fruits of independence to Africans. Additionally, they were persuaded that the arrangements enjoined by socialism were most in tune with their understanding of Africa's history and culture. Some of them defended what they called "African socialism." Others defended other variants of socialism. To the former group belonged the pre-1966 Kwame Nkrumah, Julius Nyerere of Tanzania, and Tom Mboya of Kenya (see Nkrumah 1970; Nyerere 1966, 1968, 1969; Mboya 1963). The latter group included Obafemi Awolowo and the post-1966 Nkrumah, who embraced Marxism-Leninism after his overthrow from the presidency of Ghana in that year by the Ghanaian military (see Awolowo 1968; Nkrumah 1969).[2]

Making Sense of Human Nature

As hinted above, many African thinkers were agitated by the question of human nature. From Senghor to Nkrumah, from Azikiwe to Nyerere, at different times and in as many contexts, they advanced various versions of the philosophy of humanism. It is no accident that Senghor declared apropos of this commitment: "*Man remains our first consideration: He constitutes our measure*" (1964: 65). Senghor defines humanism by way of critically engaging Marxist humanism. He argues:

> The anxiety for human dignity and the need for freedom – man's freedoms and freedoms of collectivities – that animate Marx's thought and provide its revolutionary ferment, this anxiety and this need are unknown to Communism whose major deviation is Stalinism.... "The Soviet Union," said a Senegalese on his return from

Moscow, "has succeeded in building socialism, but at the sacrifice of religion, of the soul." (ibid. 46)

By this, Senghor means that a key shortcoming of Marxism was its abandonment of a commitment to the spiritual side of human nature. He writes:

> [Marxian humanism's] weakness lies above all in the fact that, as Marx proceeded in his writing of *Capital*, he increasingly stressed materialism and determinism, *praxis* and means, to the detriment of dialectics and ethics – in a word, to the detriment of man and his freedom. I shall no longer say, as I did in my *Report*, to the detriment of philosophical thought; for, rejecting the spirit of his *Philosophical Works*, Marx surreptitiously and paradoxically reintroduced *metaphysics* in the conclusion. But it is a terribly inhuman metaphysics, an atheistic metaphysics in which mind is sacrificed to matter, freedom to the determined, man to things. (ibid. 76)

In place of this "terribly inhuman metaphysics," Senghor substitutes a historicized, *nation*-bound, humanism that he dubs "Negro-African – I mean Negro-Berber – humanism" (ibid. 78). He continues:

> Hence, for us, Man is not without a country, nor is he without a colour or a history, a fatherland or a civilization. It is West African man, our neighbour, exactly defined in time and space. He is Malian, Mauritanian, Eburnian, Wolof, Targui, Songhai, Hausa, Fon, or Mossi. He is a man of flesh and blood, nourished on milk, millet, rice, and yams. He is a man humiliated for centuries, less perhaps in his nudity and hunger than in his skin and civilization, in his dignity. (ibid. 78–9)

I have quoted Senghor at length because his insistence on historicizing human nature, contextualizing it in definite cultural, geographical, and other boundaries, sets the stage for his program of retrieving Africa's past civilizations as a precondition for restoring the colonized and dehumanized Africans to their dignity. The elements of this dignity are only partly contained in material artifacts; they are more to be found in the culture of the people, a product solely of their spiritual genius. This emphasis on culture emanates from Senghor's primary metaphysical standpoint which accepts the "*Priority* of matter," but affirms at the same time the "*Primacy* of Spirit" (ibid. 84). Thus, in order to move forward and come to the world's table with its own unique offering, Africa must first attain self-consciousness. But, at the same time, it cannot be an inwardly directed, autarkic consciousness:

> Thus, though our humanism must have West African man as its major objective, it cannot, without peril, end with West Africa, not even with all of Africa. An effective humanism must be *open*; it obviously includes not only *Malianism* – since we are not only Malians here assembled – but also nationalism and pan-Negroism (I do not say Négritude), pan-Africanism and, with greater reason, pan-Arabism. The one "Pan-ism" that meets twentieth-century requirements is, I dare say, pan-humanism – a humanism that includes all men on the dual basis of their contribution and their comprehension. (ibid. 80)

The preceding forms the basis of Senghor's insistence on the creation of a Civilization of the Universal as the end of history. But, for our limited purposes, it provides the foundation for his later arguments for an African way to socialism that makes use of the conflicting legacies of indigenous African civilizations, on the one hand, and, on the other, the European and Arab conquests. The goal always is the enhancement of human dignity.

Obafemi Awolowo (1909–87), one of the most famous politicians in the modern political history of Nigeria, offers us a philosophical anthropology that is Christian inflected but shares a lot in common with theories of human nature to be found in many philosophical traditions. Very much mindful of the role of a theory of human nature in philosophical systems, Awolowo writes: "A study of some of the writings of political philosophers from Plato to Aristotle, through Hegel, Hobbes and Locke, to Marx, Engels and Lenin, would appear to suggest that all philosophies or theories have certain basic underlying principles on the nature of man, and the concept of the structure and origin of the State" (1981: 40). He proceeds to offer us his view of human nature:

> Man is an animal; but an animal with considerable difference. He has something in him which puts him apart in a class by himself. The Christian Bible says, correctly in my view, that God forms man from the dust of the ground. He then breathes into his nostrils the breath of life, and man becomes a living soul. He is not a body with a Soul, but a Soul covered with body. He is ordained to have dominion over all other created things, and to be monarch of the earth. On these grounds, his body must be made as sound as suitable and adequate food, shelter, and clothing, as well as health care, can make it; and his mind must be nurtured and polished by his being educated to the full extent of his capacity. His body is like an electric bulb; his mind like the filament in the electric bulb; and the breath of God in him is like the electric current which flows through the filament, and is reflected to the outside world by the bulb. (ibid. 174)

We need not go into the specifics of Awolowo's theory of human nature. But I hope that the reader can see that he comes to place as strong an emphasis on the soul as the characteristic component of human nature as Senghor does using a different argument. Precisely because of this emphasis, it is no surprise that education becomes a key element for Awolowo in the improvability of human beings. This yields two consequences for Awolowo's analysis of human equality and the goal of the *polis*. Although he believes in the basic equality of all human beings as children of God, he believes that inequalities abound, some of which may be traced to the differential manner in which different human beings exercise their capacity for self-improvement through education and other forms of self-discipline. Those who attain the highest levels of self-discipline and self-improvement through the unceasing development of their minds and bodies enter into what Awolowo calls:

> the regime of mental magnitude, properly and eminently equipped with a considerable measure of intellectual comprehension and cognition, insight, and spiritual illumination. In this regime, we are free from: (1) the negative emotions of anger, hate, fear, envy or jealousy, selfishness or greed; (2) indulgence in the wrong types of food and drink, and in ostentatious consumption; and (3) excessive or immoral craving for sex.

247

> In short in this regime we conquer what Kant calls "the tyranny of the flesh", and become free. (1968: 230; see also 1966: 158–9)

One implication of Awolowo's position is that it is only those who have satisfied the requirements for entry into the regime of mental magnitude who *may* aspire to the rulership of the state. But Awolowo preserves his egalitarian credentials by insisting that everyone should have the equality of opportunity, within the limits imposed by nature's lottery in the distribution of abilities, to be the best that they can be, including being suited for entry into the regime of mental magnitude. The job of ensuring this equality of opportunity is the principal task of the state in Awolowo's political philosophy. Thus, for Awolowo, the state exists to subserve the purpose of creating the maximal conditions for the realization by individuals of all that is best in and about their nature as *Imago Dei*. It is for this reason that Awolowo repudiated capitalism, preferring instead socialism. But his preference for socialism did not deter him from insisting that liberal parliamentary democracy was the best structure of government with which to usher in the socialist paradise.

We turn now to the final philosophical anthropology that we look at in this chapter: that of Ahmed Sekou Toure (1922–84), first post-independence President of the Republic of Guinea from 1958 until his death in 1984. One commentator has remarked that, "Of all African presidents, Sekou Toure of Guinea has given most attention to theoretical matters" (Andrain 1967–8: 103). One does not have to concur fully with this judgment to acknowledge Sekou Toure's sterling philosophical contributions. What is Sekou Toure's view of human nature? Unlike the two views discussed above, Toure held an *organicist* view of human nature, a development traceable to his "monistic view of reality" (ibid. 103). He argues that it is impossible for an individual to be human outside of her consort with other human beings in society.

> The lower animals, vegetables, and minerals can exist cut off from their kind without a change in *their nature, but man would lose his human nature and his essential qualities if he were to isolate himself from other men, who constitute his natural sphere*. This way of looking at the question makes it easier to understand the close link between man and his fellows, the uninterrupted bond with society. (Toure 1987: 485)

Given this view of an organic connection among human beings, it is no wonder that Toure believed that a preoccupation with individuals considered *as if* they could be apart from their fellows is a wrongheaded philosophy. By the same token, given that all human beings are vulnerable to the threat of dehumanization when left bereft of human fellowship, there is a fundamental equality that all humans have which is traceable to this fundamental need for fellowship.

> No man can be considered inferior to another. His equality is a measure of his liberty, and the solidarity which governs the quality of his relationship with the various group organizations to which he belongs, ranging from his family to the whole of society, is a measure of his unity with humanity. This is why racialism, regionalism, and religious sectarianism are objectively reactionary and inhuman. (ibid. 484)

248

It is on the basis of these reflections that Toure argues that the interest of the individual should be subordinated to that of society. At the same time, however, he insisted that society must be organized in such a way that it is able to develop a "collective personality" made up not of "the sum of the consciousness and faculties of the individuals involved, but the synthesis of [these] wills and transcendental aspirations" (ibid. 485). Needless to say, this synthesis is without prejudice to the presence of conflicts and contradictions among the individuals within the society concerned. But part of the measure of the progress of a society on the road to developing the requisite collective personality is the extent to which its organization of its members' social existence "progressively and finally [removes] the bases for all contradictions, the reasons for all oppositions, by substituting a collective conception, collective determination, and collective action, tending towards a social harmony which will reflect greater social justice, greater solidarity, and a richer humanism" (ibid. 486).

I am aware of some of the problems usually associated with the kind of organicist philosophy of human nature represented above. Since my primary aim in this chapter is expository rather than critical, I shall not go into any discussion of those problems. Nevertheless, I believe that my exposition does show that the political choices made by African leaders respecting specific political principles and arrangements were not made without serious, even if not unimpeachable, philosophical thought.[3]

Why One-Party Rule?

It cannot be denied that some of the African leaders who chose one-party rule in post-independence Africa did so out of a penchant for personal rule and sometimes a proclivity for megalomania. Yet, we should not conclude that all partisans of one-party rule were cut from the same cloth. For instance, given what we have just reported of his view of human nature and, by extension, of society, it is easy to see why Sekou Toure's sentiments would incline in the direction of one-party rule, or "national democracy," as he preferred to call it. We cannot always be sure, though, that anyone who subscribes to a monistic view of reality and an organicist conception of human nature would, for those reasons alone, embrace one-party rule. Thus, we may not affirm a one-to-one correspondence between people's metaphysical conceptions and their political choices.

Be that as it may, some of the African thinkers who embraced one-party rule did so on articulate philosophical grounds. Take, for instance, Sekou Toure's defense of his ideology of "national democracy." He identified two opposing possibilities that Guinea, and Africa at large, might consider. The first is that of "class struggles" under which a society is riven by class divisions and contradictions. In such a society, social and political life is much dominated by struggles between and among these classes over the allocation of the society's resources and its direction of development. The second is that of "rival factions" in a plural society motivated by divergent sectional interests in the struggle for power and for the wealth of the society. By his own estimation, neither option was appropriate for Guinea in light of her history and her specific needs. First, Guinea had not reached the level of economic development in which class boundaries had crystalized enough to warrant talk of class struggles. Secondly, the country had had to discourage political factionalism in the struggle for independence from a hostile colonial power, France, that would have been all too happy to pit one faction against another as a way to perpetuate its iniquitous rule. Thus, he concluded, the preference for one-party rule derived from the peculiar history of Guinea and the goals that the Guinean people had chosen. He wrote:

> What are the principles on which "national democracy" is founded? First of all the principle of the *people's unity, founded on common aspirations and fundamental interests belonging to the social group. Then from this springboard, one has to proceed to organize this unity into an active force, which can become an effective means of reinforcing the elements of unity in the people, so that their interests are really served.* This is not a unity which sacrifices men to its ends, a unity which is an end in itself, but unity which is a means at the service of the people and of man. (1987: 494)

The party, as the embodiment of the will of the people united in the pursuit of the goal of enhancing human dignity, is the organizational mode of this unity and the sole instrument of collective action. Needless to say, the danger of this type of party becoming the instrument of one-man rule and a threat to heterodoxy and individual freedom cannot be overemphasized. Indeed, the Parti Démocratique du Guiné did become such a party and it wreaked murderous havoc on ordinary Guineans and intellectuals alike. Beyond its practical excesses, one can ask serious questions concerning the plausibility of the contention that there is a unity of interests among the people and that it is necessary to eradicate all social contradictions from society or that individual interests are subordinate to the collective will. Although I cannot do so here, I believe that the arguments advanced for one-party rule by Sekou Toure can be shown to be flawed.

Kenneth Kaunda (b. 1924, first President of Zambia, ruling from 1964 to 1991 when he lost power in multiparty elections after being repeatedly re-elected in one-party elections) provided a different justification for one-party rule. According to him, the nations that Africans inherited at independence were so in name alone. The nationalism that had served as the rallying cry of the anti-colonial struggle might have appeared more solid than it really was as long as it had for its focus the colonial powers. This is how he poses the problem:

> Whatever combination of factors has influenced the development of African nationalism, the important question is this: what happens to nationalism as a movement of protest when the basic target of its protest – the colonial power – has been removed? The withdrawal of the colonial power, whilst solving one great problem, raises another equally acute for the nationalist leader. The discipline and solidarity of the national movement and the impetus built up during the freedom struggle are vital to the success and survival of the new nation. Yet, unless new, exciting and worthwhile goals can be proposed for nationalism, there is danger of the movement of protest turning inwards upon itself and becoming destructive of the national good. (1987: 468)

250

The fragility of the sentiments of nationality developed in the African nations cobbled together by the colonialists necessitated, in Kaunda's view, an instrumentality for transforming this nationalism into "patriotism," "a zealous love for one's country" in the aftermath of independence (ibid.).

> The vehicle of these sentiments of loyalty is the party, which marshals, channels, and controls it. And the person of the leader provides an especially intense focus of loyalty. He is the people's mouthpiece. He suffers with them and on their behalf. They speak through his voice and he leads them where they have trusted him to take them. (ibid. 469)

We see here that the party is called forth to ensure that the fragile solidarity among the many particularist traditions within African countries was not shattered on the morrow of independence. The leader at the helm of the party provides, according to this way of thinking, a symbolic embodiment of this aspiration to unity. Kaunda was aware of criticisms of one-party rule. One criticism, for example, dealt with the many ways in which the party could be subverted to subserve sectional interests and in which the leader could become a scourge to his people. In reply to this, he argued that the risk is unavoidable in the particular terrain of post-independence Africa and that, ultimately, the people would provide the requisite brakes on the excesses of both party and leader.[4]

There were additional arguments advanced by Kaunda for the movement by independent African states "away from the Westminster Model [of parliamentary democracy] imposed upon them in the closing stages of colonial rule to the one-party system" (1987: 475). In the first place, he contended that the liberation movements that rid the colonies of British rule "enjoyed the overwhelming support of the people – in former British territories this was often the most important criterion by which the British government decided when the time had come to withdraw" (ibid.). Given the fact of this overwhelming support of the people, Kaunda argued, "many one-party states are the natural consequence of this process" (ibid.). For this reason, Kaunda could not see the rationale for, as he puts it, the artificial creation of "an Opposition solely to accommodate those theorists who regard a government-in-waiting as essential to the democratic process" (ibid.).

Secondly, Kaunda suggested that "in Africa the things which divide contending groups tend to be of such fundamental significance that continuity of government could hardly be achieved through a change in the party in power" (ibid. 476). The issue here turns on the alleged absence in Africa of what he terms "political values" to which all groups subscribe, as in, say, Britain, and which provide the glue that binds together opposition and government parties alike. In light of the absence of similar values in Africa and the presence of divisive factors of a "fundamental significance," to allow an official opposition or governments-in-waiting "too much latitude to inflame opinion" would be to risk having the "very foundations" of the state being "torn out." This second argument rests on the instrumental value of one-party rule as a guarantor of the survival of the African state. Kaunda did not mince words in this regard: "Hard though it may sound," he avers, "in my view survival [of the state] is more important than freedom of expression.... The great enemy of freedom is not totalitarianism but chaos" (ibid.).

Finally, Kaunda maintained that "the idea of an institutional Opposition is foreign to the African tradition." This is so because, according to Kaunda and others who canvass this view, "in our original societies we operated by consensus" (ibid.). Julius Nyerere (1922–98), first President of Tanzania from 1962 to 1985 when he voluntarily retired from the presidency after operating a one-party system for many years, offers a variant of the same argument in his essay on "Democracy and the Party System." According to Nyerere, "in African society, the traditional method of conducting affairs is by free discussion. Mr. Guy Clutton-Brock, writing about a typical African village community puts it neatly...'The Elders sit under the big trees, and talk until they agree...' In larger communities, however, government by the people is possible only in a modified form" (1987b: 478).

Kwame Nkrumah canvassed a variant of the preceding argument. According to Nkrumah, pre-Islamic and pre-Christian Africa had a specific "face" which "includes an attitude towards man which can only be described, in its social manifestation, as being socialist. This arises from the fact that man is regarded in Africa as primarily a spiritual being, a being endowed with a certain inward dignity, integrity and value. It stands refreshingly opposed to the Christian idea of the original sin and degradation of man" (1970: 68). This background belief in the inherent dignity and integrity of every human being provides, in Nkrumah's view, "the theoretical basis of African communalism" (ibid. 69). It had its institutional embodiments in such forms of social living as "the clan" in which all members were equal and where obtained "the responsibility of many for one." He concluded: "In traditional African society, no sectional interest could be regarded as supreme; nor did legislative and executive power aid the interests of any particular group. The welfare of the people was supreme" (ibid.). Absent the requisite cleavages in the society, African society did not need any institutionalized opposition parties.

The arguments by Kaunda, Nyerere, and Nkrumah appeal to the putative alienness of the idea of two-party or multiparty democracy to the collective psyche of Africans. This fundamental preference for consensus necessitates a model in which *all* are represented and membership is not denied to anyone. Such a system will be closer to the spirit and historical experience of Africans than one in which division is taken as a datum and persons are generally expected to line up behind one party or another. Nkrumah puts it succinctly:

> A people's parliamentary democracy with a one-party system is better able to express and satisfy the common aspirations of a nation as a whole, than a multiple-party parliamentary system, which is in fact only a ruse for perpetuating, and covers up, the inherent struggle between the "haves" and the "have-nots." (ibid. 100–1)

Furthermore, if no one is excluded from membership and the essence of democracy is the free participation of all in governance, then it must be that one-party democracy of this sort is more democratic than one in which people are forced to divide. Nyerere too, for his part, concludes: "I am now going to suggest: that, where there is one party, and that party is identified with the nation as a whole, the foundations of democracy are firmer than they can ever be where you have two or more parties, each representing only a section of the community" (1987b: 478).

252

Nyerere has an additional argument for one-party rule. But it is an argument that features premises that run counter to some of those advanced by Kaunda and Nkrumah, discussed above. On this argument, the only time that a multiparty system can be justified is "when the parties are divided over some fundamental issue; otherwise, it merely encourages the growth of factionalism" (ibid.). If their division is not over some fundamental issue, then their pretense to real division can only induce cynicism and apathy on the part of the electorate who come to see politics as no more than a game. But if the division is fundamental, then what we have in such a country, Nyerere submits, will be "a civil war" situation. He concludes that there is a lack of the appropriate division in Africa because of the particular historical experience of Africans:

> Our critics should understand that, in Africa, we have to take our politics a little more seriously. And they should also remember the historical differences between parties in Africa and those in Europe or America. The European and American parties came into being as the result of existing social and economic divisions – the second party being formed to challenge the monopoly of the political power by some aristocratic or capitalistic group. Our own parties had a very different origin. They were not formed to challenge any ruling group of our own people; they were formed to challenge the foreigners who ruled over us. They were not, therefore, political "parties" – i.e., factions – but nationalist movements. And from the outset they represented the interests and aspirations of the whole nation. (ibid. 479)

The argument has come full circle. Running like a single thread through all the arguments advanced by Sekou Toure, Kenneth Kaunda, Kwame Nkrumah, and Julius Nyerere for one-party rule are claims of (1) the unity of the historical experience of African peoples; (2) the foreignness of two-party or multiparty models of governance in the context of African tradition; and (3) the danger that the delicate fabric of the recently cobbled together and fragile African nations might be rent by the embrace of two-party or multiparty rule.

Although I cannot develop the criticisms at any length in this chapter, one still can show in capsule form some of the problems with the foregoing defenses of one-party rule. In the first place, it is interesting that Kaunda suggests that the divisive factors in African countries possess a "fundamental significance," while Nyerere suggests that there are no such fundamental dividing factors in African society. Both of them use these apparently divergent descriptions of African society to support their arguments for one-party rule. What this shows is that the defenders of one-party rule could not even agree on the character of the society on which they based their advocacy.

Furthermore, all the arguments are vulnerable to the charge of hasty generalization. After all, Africa is quite a diverse continent and it would be a surprise if all African countries – not to mention all African societies – exhibited the same or similar characteristics. Add to this the fact that the model of Africa that our thinkers deploy was more a propaganda trope than a product of scientific research into the nature of African societies, past and present, and the upshot is that much of the empirical support for one-party rule based on the nature of African societies is, at worst, false and, at best, tenuous. For example, contrary to Nyerere's assertion, parties were formed in Nigeria to oppose aristocratic monopoly of political power in some parts of the country. The Northern Elements Progressive Union (NEPU) and the Action Group (AG) both claimed to want to liberate the *Talakawa* (the poor masses) from the thrall of feudalism in northern Nigeria supposedly represented in the leadership of the Northern People's Congress (NPC) in the post-independence era. Anyway, even if one grants the plausibility of the empirical support adduced for the arguments for one-party rule, it does not follow that one must embrace one-party rule. Motivated by the same considerations of delivering on the promise of independence for their populations, Obafemi Awolowo contended that Western parliamentary democracy anchored on a multiparty model held the most promise for African countries. He wrote in his *Autobiography* in 1961: "There are two distinct ideological camps in the world today: the Western democracies and the communist bloc. For reasons which I will presently give, my preference is unhesitatingly and unequivocally for the Western democracies" (p. 309).[5] This was an abiding commitment for Awolowo that continued after he embraced socialism and through to his death in 1987.[6] Unfortunately, because scholars have not bothered to subject the philosophical ideas of Africa's statesmen philosophers of the immediate post-independence era to scrutiny, it has been difficult for the world to know of the subtle philosophical debates that transpired among some of Africa's political leaders.

There are other queries that one can raise concerning the arguments for one-party rule. The assumption of the uniformity, perhaps unanimity, of views in African societies is dubious in light of the well-known divergences and conflicts in even the smallest African communities. One must also remark our philosophers' simplistic treatment of the danger of the single party becoming the vehicle of personal rule and terror; which, as a matter of history, is what actually happened.

Why Socialism?

The choice of socialism was supported by the thinkers with many of the same arguments that we have discussed above. But the choice was built on additional argumentative foundations. Recall what was said earlier about the third basic question of political philosophy, namely, "How ought we to organize society for purposes of governance and social living?" One aspect of this question pertains to the best, most efficient, most rational way of organizing social production, distribution, exchange, and consumption. This aspect was extremely urgent on the morrow of independence because, given the predatory nature of colonialism in Africa, few countries had the social and economic foundations for improving the living conditions of their citizens, not to mention facilitating the efflorescence of that which is best in them. It was as an answer to this latter question that African political philosophers opted for socialism. Again, as in the case of one-party rule, each of the leaders had a different take on what socialism meant and what opting for it entailed. Here I can only present in summary form the case for socialism as the thinkers we have selected for attention in this chapter made it.

Senghor, born in 1906 and first President of Senegal from 1960 to 1980, when he retired from the presidency, deliberately takes Marxism as his starting point. He finds a lot that is agreeable in Marxism, not least the dialectical method. He departs from Marxism on two key points. First, he believes that Marxism ultimately betrays humanism. It is to correct this betrayal that he affirms a peculiar conception that he calls "Negro-African" or "Negro-Berber" humanism (1964: 77–8). Negro-Berber humanism is not so merely because people who are "Negro-Berber" embrace it. It is so precisely because to be "Negro-Berber" is to have a specific history, a given outlook on life that has emerged from this history, and a model of a specific way of being human. In so far as Marxism with its metaphysical corollary, Marxian humanism, is a product of a particular history and is, by implication, a model of a specific way of being human, any attempt to apply it, without thought of possible modifications, to other societies would be a betrayal of Marx and his philosophy. Senghor calls upon his African compatriots to take a cue from other peoples who have taken hold of Marxism and have run with it in different directions: "The Israelis, like the Chinese, have been able to find their ... road to socialism and have adapted it to the spirit and realities of their native soil. Theirs are exemplary efforts to inspire us" (ibid. 77). He then proceeds to describe the West African realities that ought to shape the model of socialism to be adopted for that specific region.

> West African realities are those of underdeveloped countries – peasant countries here, cattle countries there – once feudalistic, but traditionally classless and with no wage-earning sector. They are community [the French word is *communautaires*] countries where the group holds priority over the individual; they are, especially, religious countries, unselfish countries, where money is not King. (ibid.)

If Senghor is right, then it stands to reason that Marxian humanism, which had its inspiration from, and is a reaction to, capitalist individualism, competition, and the triumph of Money as King, cannot be an appropriate model for constructing the best society possible in West Africa of which Senegal is a part. Senghor sets as his objective "an ideal society that will integrate the contributions of European socialism with our traditional values" (ibid. 93). His preference for socialism is unyielding because he believes that this is the best way to achieve the "community society" specific to Africa's historical experience.

In similar vein, Nkrumah insists that Africa's future could not unfold without due attention to her historical experience made up of her heritage of Islamic and Christian influences. He advances "Consciencism" as that philosophy which can do justice to Africa's multiplex heritage. *"Philosophical consciencism* ... will give the theoretical basis for an ideology whose aim shall be to contain the African experience of Islamic and Euro-Christian presence as well as the experience of the traditional African society, and, by gestation, employ them for the harmonious growth and development of that society" (1970: 70).

Julius Nyerere, also, predicates his preference for socialism on two grounds. In the first place, socialism "is an attitude of mind. In a socialist society it is the socialist attitude of mind, and not the rigid adherence to a standard political pattern, which is needed to ensure that the people care for each other's welfare" (1987c: 512). According to Nyerere, this attitude of mind is indigenous to Africa and the task of theorists like him is to wend their way past the exploitative capitalist

255

system introduced by colonialism, which was at the root of the problem of back-wardness in Tanzania and other African countries. The foundation of African socialism is to be found in the idea of "Ujamaa" or "familyhood." This itself is traceable to the African institution of the *extended family* under which there were no distinctions of class and to which the notion of "class struggle" was completely foreign, even anathema. The extended family in this sense was defined neither by blood nor by lineage or other restrictive conditions. On the contrary, for Nyerere, the African "regards all men as his brethren – as members of his ever extending family" (ibid. 515). If this is the case, it is easy to see why socialism, an essentially distributive system which is concerned "to see that those who sow reap a fair share of what they sow" (ibid. 512), will be closer to the sentiments of those in whose indigenous societies there was no class of exploiters or of the exploited, of those who worked and those who lived off the toil of others. Insofar as *all* were workers, their entitlement to a share of the social production could not be questioned. By the same token, they could not be denied access to the means of production, mainly land. However, under the new mode of production midwifed by colonialism, land became "a marketable commodity" and the pursuit of individual wealth even at the expense of the collective well-being became an acceptable fact. The call to socialism was, for Nyerere, a clarion call back to what made precolonial Africa a much more humane social context. In embracing socialism, the African was merely returning to her roots. Nyerere declares: "We, in Africa, have no more need of being 'converted' to socialism than we have of being 'taught' democracy. Both are rooted in our own past – in the traditional society which produced us. Modern African socialism can draw from its traditional heritage the recognition of 'society' as an extension of the basic family unit" (ibid. 515).

There is a second ground that Nyerere provides for his preference for socialism. Simply put, it is that socialism holds the promise of a better society in which what is best about our nature can be realized. This is laid out more fully in what has come to be known as "The Arusha Declaration: Socialism and Self-Reliance."[7] I quote from Part One, entitled "The TANU Creed":

> The policy of TANU is to build a socialist state. The principles of socialism are laid down in the TANU Constitution and they are as follows:
> [Whereas] TANU believes:
> (a) That all human beings are equal;
> (b) That every human individual has a right to dignity and respect;
> (c) That every citizen is an integral part of the nation and has the right to take an equal part in Government at local, regional, and national level;
> (d) That every citizen has the right to freedom of expression, of movement, of religious belief, and of association within the context of the law;
> (e) That every individual has the right to receive from society protection of his life and property held according to law;
> (f) That every individual has the right to receive a just return for his labour;
> (g) That all citizens together possess all the natural resources of the country in trust for their descendants;
> (h) That in order to ensure economic justice the state must have the effective control over the principal means of production; and

(i) That it is the responsibility of the state to intervene actively in the economic life of the nation so as to ensure the well-being of all citizens, and so as to prevent the exploitation of one person by another or one group by another, and so as to prevent the accumulation of wealth to an extent which is inconsistent with the existence of a classless society. (Nyerere 1987a: 516)

Many of the provisions of the TANU Creed are designed specifically to exclude the fundamental tenets and practices of a capitalist mode of production. For example, (g) and (h) effectively outlaw private property in the principal means of production; (f) trumps the right of capitalist employers or the market mechanism to fix the wages of workers. In this connection, socialism is at one and the same time a means and an outcome. The implicit assumption is that the way of being human articulated by the TANU Creed is superior to that enjoined by capitalism or any other form of social living. Although it helps that the antecedents of this way of being human can be found in African history and cultural experience, it seems to me as if it would not have mattered to Nyerere if this had not been the case. The point is that he considered a socialist society per se as superior to a non-socialist one. That is why I believe that this provides a different justification for socialism from that founded on its African genesis.

The last argument for socialism to be considered here is that advanced by Obafemi Awolowo in his book *The People's Republic*. Awolowo's defense of socialism merits attention because, unlike the previous two discussed above, he rejects any appeal to cultural rootedness as a reason for embracing socialism. He dismisses the notion of "African socialism" out of hand. According to him, socialism is a normative social science and it must be appraised and embraced or rejected as such. If it is good science, regardless of its genealogy, it ought to be accepted; if it is bad science, then even if it is homegrown, it ought to be rejected. "If any principle is purely and strictly peculiar to a given institution, region, or state, it may be a custom, practice, or even a theory, but it certainly cannot lay claim to the status of science. Just as there can be no African ethics *qua* Ethics as a science, or African logic, so there can be no African socialism" (1968: 208). His defense of socialism represents a significant departure from the dominant defenses of socialism. These are usually developed from the perspective of its alleged African pedigree or from the standpoint of unvarnished adoption of Marxian scientific socialism.

According to Awolowo, socialism is "a politico-economic ideal whose sole aim is social justice":

By social justice, in this context, is meant the just and equitable distribution of the nation's wealth amongst those factors which have made positive, necessary, and effective contributions to its production. And such factors are labour and entrepreneurship, which are two species, degrees or gradations of the same phenomenon – the application to the land of the efforts of man, assisted by capital which is wealth accumulated from an antecedent union of labour and entrepreneurship with land. (ibid. 36)

Awolowo's preference for socialism arises from his repudiation of capitalism. Capitalism is to be rejected because, according to Awolowo, it contradicts the principles of the dialectic, the ultimate ideal of which is "LOVE." He does not deny that capitalism does cater to and builds upon some aspect of human nature. He argues only that capitalism is founded upon what is most base in our nature. If this is the case, the best capitalist society will still remain a less than good society and will ultimately self-destruct because the traits of human nature that it fosters will eventually lead it to perdition:

> Since greed, selfishness or naked self-interest is the essence and predominant motivation of capitalism, the system is bound to generate secular social disequilibrium in the society in which it is operative, and to diminish and degenerate through time until it suffers extinction, yielding place to another and better system which either approaches or approximates to the ideal of LOVE. (ibid. 188–9)

Socialism is to be preferred, therefore, because it alone can ensure the form of social living that best conduces to the realization of what is best in our nature as humans. That, ultimately, rather than its genealogy, is what recommends socialism over competing models for organizing social living and governance within it.

Conclusion

I hope that this mostly expository discussion will encourage more students and scholars, especially professional philosophers, to take more seriously the philosophical thought of the African political leaders of the immediate post-independence period.

Notes

1 See Awolowo 1968; Busia 1967. I am ignoring others like Sir Seretse Khama of Botswana, who held similar views but never offered any philosophical defense of his preference.
2 I have left out latter-day Marxists like Amilcar Cabral, Eduardo Mondlane, Agostino Neto, and Samora Machel. I have also left out earlier Marxists such as Mohammed ben Barka of Morocco, for he was not really a politician in the mode of those upon whom our focus is directed in this chapter.
3 I have also refrained from the dubious practice of passing off African thinkers as unoriginal parodies of various European thinkers. The ones that I have examined here may have been influenced by any number of European thinkers, but they were by no means mere imitators of the latters' ideas. What I find in them are serious attempts to beat their own paths through the dominant ideas inculcated in them through their education in European and European-inspired academies.
4 This seems to be the view of Bechir Ben Yahmed (1987: 504).
5 For similar sentiments against one-party rule, see Senghor 1964: 145.
6 Nor was Awolowo alone in this commitment. See also Busia 1967; Azikiwe 1961.
7 This is strictly speaking a Party Document. But it is based on a draft submitted by Nyerere to the National Executive Committee of the TANU Party.

258

References

Andrain, Charles (1967–8) "The Political Thought of Sekou Toure," in W. A. E. Skurnik (ed.), *African Political Thought: Lumumba, Nkrumah, and Toure* (Denver: The Social Science Foundation and Graduate School of International Studies Monograph Series in World Affairs).

Awolowo, Obafemi (1961) *Awo: An Autobiography* (Cambridge: Cambridge University Press).

Awolowo, Obafemi (1966) *Thoughts on the Nigerian Constitution* (Ibadan: Oxford University Press).

Awolowo, Obafemi (1968) *The People's Republic* (Ibadan: Oxford University Press).

Awolowo, Obafemi (1981) *Voice of Wisdom: Selected Speeches*, vol. 3 (Akure: Fagbamigbe Publishers).

Azikiwe, Nnamdi (1961) *ZIK: Selected Speeches of Dr. Nnamdi Azikiwe* (Cambridge: Cambridge University Press).

Busia, Kofi Abrefa (1967) *Africa in Search of Democracy* (New York: Praeger).

Kaunda, Kenneth (1987[1966]) "The Future of Nationalism," excerpted in Mutiso and Rohio (eds.), *Readings in African Political Thought*. Orig. in *A Humanist in Africa* (London: Longman, 1966).

Mboya, Tom (1963) *Freedom and After* (London: Andre Deutsch).

Mutiso, Gideon-Cyrus M. and Rohio, S. W. (eds.) (1987) *Readings in African Political Thought* (London: Heinemann).

Nkrumah, Kwame (1969) *Class Struggle in Africa* (London: Panaf).

Nkrumah, Kwame (1970) *Consciencism: Philosophy and Ideology for Decolonization* (London: Panaf).

Nyerere, Julius (1966) *Freedom and Unity/Uhuru na Umoja* (Dar es Salaam: Oxford University Press).

Nyerere, Julius (1968) *Ujamaa: Essays on Socialism* (Dar es Salaam: Oxford University Press).

Nyerere, Julius (1969) *Freedom and Socialism/Uhuru na Ujamaa* (Dar es Salaam: Oxford University Press).

Nyerere, Julius (1987a[1966]) "The Arusha Declaration: Socialism and Self-Reliance," excerpted in Mutiso and Rohio (eds.), *Readings in African Political Thought*. Orig. in *Freedom and Unity/Uhuru na Umoja* (Dar es Salaam: Oxford University Press).

Nyerere, Julius (1987b[1966]) "Democracy and the Party System," excerpted in Mutiso and Rohio (eds.), *Readings in African Political Thought*. Orig. in *Freedom and Unity/Uhuru na Umoja* (Dar es Salaam: Oxford University Press).

Nyerere, Julius (1987c[1966]) "Ujamaa – The Basis of African Socialism," excerpted in Mutiso and Rohio (eds.), *Readings in African Political Thought*. Orig. in *Freedom and Unity/ Uhuru na Umoja* (Dar es Salaam: Oxford University Press).

Senghor, Leopold Sedar (1964) *On African Socialism*, trans. and intro. Mercer Cook (London: Pall Mall Press).

Toure, Sekou (1987[1975]) "National Democracy," in *The Doctrine and Methods of the Democratic Party of Guinea* (new edn.), vol. X, excerpted in Mutiso and Rohio (eds.), *Readings in African Political Thought*.

Yahmed, Bechir Ben (1987) "For or Against the Single Party," in Mutiso and Rohio (eds.), *Readings in African Political Thought*.

Part II

METHODOLOGICAL ISSUES

18

Some Methodological Controversies in African Philosophy

A. G. A. BELLO

Introduction

Philosophers are wont to talk about the nature and methodology of their discipline. African philosophers, especially the "professional" variety, have been engaged in some discussion, sometimes acrimonious, about the nature and methodology of African philosophy. Methodological controversies, sometimes engendering very lively discussions, have revolved around issues including the tensions between "universalism" and "particularism," and between the "modern" and the "traditional." Also germane here are the problem of the relation between philosophy and language in African philosophizing and the question of "ethnophilosophy." At the root of these controversies lie the basic problems of the nature, methodology, and relevance of African philosophy, its relation to philosophy in general and to Western philosophy in particular, and its relevance to the search for the good life for the peoples of Africa.

Particularism vs. Universalism

In his "Four Trends in Current African Philosophy," Odera Oruka classifies the work of African philosophers into "ethnophilosophy," "philosophic sagacity," "nationalist-ideological philosophy," and "professional philosophy." The professional philosophers can be broadly divided into two groups, namely, particularists and universalists. The universalists include Peter Bodunrin, Odera Oruka (both of blessed memory), Paulin Hountondji, and Kwasi Wiredu, while the particularists include Godwin Sogolo and Olusegun Oladipo. It must be pointed out that this is only a broad classification, since there is no absolute uniformity in the views of members of each group. On the contrary, there are significant differences between them.

According to Wiredu, particularists see African philosophy as "coterminous with philosophical investigations having a special relevance to Africa" (1996: 149). The particularist conception is that no philosophy is African philosophy unless it deals with a specifically African theme, topic, or problem, for example, the Yoruba conception of the human person, the Akan conception of truth, Bantu philosophy, the Luo concept of God, Igbo philosophy, or African sage philosophy.

There is some merit in the particularistic position for, first, if we accept, if only for the sake of the argument, the definition of philosophy as the "criticism of the ideas that we live by" (see Staniland 1979), it goes without saying that African philosophy should be concerned with the criticism of the ideas that Africans live by. Secondly, to admit all manner of discussions, for example, of logic and ontology, Greek science and religion, the bundle theory of substance, the a-logicality of immortality, modal metalogic, or theoretical identities (as suggested by, for instance, Bodunrin 1981), into African philosophy will be to miss the point about the "ideological" and existential necessity of cultivating African philosophy. This is especially because these latter theories, topics, or problems belong to another philosophical tradition, to wit, the philosophical tradition of our erstwhile colonizers.

However, what the particularists lose sight of is that the universalist agenda is more inclusive than their own. All universalists will agree with Wiredu that it is important to engage in a "serious study of African culture and its philosophical heritage" (1996: 149). But, in addition, they insist, first, that such a study ought to be "critical and reconstructive" (ibid.) in order for the result to qualify as philosophy, properly so called, and, second, that contemporary African philosophers should attempt to appropriate any modern "resources of philosophical insight not already exploited in our culture" (ibid.). This can only be done by cross-cultural and interdisciplinary comparisons.

The universalist case, in my view, has greater merit, in that, first, the insistence on criticism and reconstruction is to make the efforts of contemporary African philosophers truly philosophical. All philosophizing involves assertion, explanation, and justification (cf. ibid. 114), and anything less than that will be less than philosophy. Secondly, it is unrealistic for Africans to pretend to uniqueness or purity in the matter of culture, since Africans, apart from being part of the human race with which it shares universal biological features, have been influenced, for better or for ill, by, among other factors, Islam, Christianity, colonialism, urbanization, industrialization, and globalization. Lastly, cultural products are best seen as the common wealth of mankind to be appropriated as the need arises. This is the only way Africans can cope with the challenges and needs of the modern world.

Modern vs. Traditional

Does the distinction between the modern and the traditional apply to African philosophy? If it does, are there criteria for distinguishing one from the other? If there are, what are they? In attempting to answer these questions, it is useful to note that various classifications, sometimes overlapping, have been made in African philosophy. These include "oral" philosophy, ethnophilosophy, "folk" philosophy, "communal" philosophy, traditional philosophy, written philosophy, contemporary philosophy, modern philosophy, sage philosophy, and nationalistic-ideological philosophy. The very fact of these classifications indicates that, however we look at it, there is African philosophy in some shape or form, thus finally laying to rest the vexatious and sometimes vituperative debate about its existence. As a corollary, we may also claim that there are African philosophers.

The sources of African philosophy are also of a great variety. They include proverbs, maxims, tales, myths, lyrics, poetry, art motifs, and cultural practices like worship and sacrifice, and institutions like chieftaincy. Many of these sources are transmitted orally, though some of them have been committed to writing for some time, or are more or less textual. Apart from the "communal" transmissions discernible in linguistic and cultural usages, there may be identifiable living individuals in the culture (for example, Oruka's philosophic sages – see his 1991: 34), some of whom are able to transmit the folk wisdom, and explain or criticize it. There are still others, who are not necessarily lettered, but who hold what we may call original philosophical positions.

Problems, however, arise as to whether these sources can be called philosophy *simpliciter*, or can only be said to be source materials for philosophizing. My own ideal of philosophy is the written work of a live flesh and blood person or groups of persons (or schools) which contains assertions, explanations, and justifications. It is only in such cases that there is little doubt as to what is said and who says it. It is also in such cases that we can evaluate what is said with respect to philosophic content, methodology, influence(s), or originality.

As a proposed approximation to this, let us take the case of an African traditional sage who is interviewed or, if you like, is engaged in dialogue by a professional philosopher. How are we to ensure that what we have is solely the respondent's ideas and not his ideas mixed with the interpolations of his interlocutor? Is there indeed a "proper dialogue" between the sage and the philosopher (see Oladipo 2000: 90)? For the avoidance of doubt, this is not to impute any moral lapse to the interlocutor. It is just that by the nature of the situation, it is difficult to fully ascertain the respondent's real thoughts. [See, further, chapter 19 in this volume.] Socrates provides a historical example of reporting. What were Socrates' real teachings? This question continues to agitate the minds of historians of ancient philosophy in the West.

At any rate, this is not what we mean by philosophy in other cultures. In the history of philosophy, we discuss the ideas of identifiable persons or schools, whether the philosophy is Western, Indian, Islamic, Chinese, or Japanese. For sure, all these cultures also have the types of linguistic and cultural material that we investigate in African philosophy. Surely, they also have their own "literary" men and sages.

Thus, when we want to investigate British philosophy, we do not start looking at English proverbs, myths, tales, and their system of governance. We look, rather, at the writings of Locke, Berkeley, Hume, and others of British origin. Similarly, in investigating Islamic philosophy, we do not look at the Arabic language and literature, or tenets of Islam, or the Quran; we look, rather, at the writings of Farabi, Ibn Sina, Ibn Rushd, and so on. If we are doing something different for African philosophy, we must do so knowing full well that it is only because of the absence of a better alternative.

This is why, in my view, materials obtained from all these sources, apart from the written ones, are only raw materials for philosophizing. Even concerning the written sources, it is quite clear that some of them do not have the characteristics of assertion, explanation, and justification. Such written sources do not qualify as philosophy *simpliciter*. This is because philosophy is different from the study of religions and from mythology, literature, and folklore. It is useful to keep the distinctions between these disciplines clear.

Contra Sogolo (1993: 6), this does not mean that there were no philosophers in African traditional culture. There must have been, even if, for want of written records, we do not know their identities or thoughts. Their fate is like that which might have befallen Socrates if Plato, Aristotle, Aristophanes, and Xenophon had not recorded some of his thoughts or biography. They can be called philosophers only in a generous sense. Even in cases like *Odu Ifa*, which is believed to have been transmitted orally for centuries and is now partially committed to writing, the fact that it cannot be ascribed to any identifiable individuals or schools detracts from its being called philosophy *simpliciter*.

Philosophy and Language

What can African philosophy claim from an African language? There are some general points about language that can be made before attempting to answer this question. First, while it may be true that no language is intrinsically superior or inferior to another one, it is safe to say that some languages may be better in some respects than others. Thus, for example, it can be conceded that some African languages are inferior to some European languages in respect of scientific vocabulary or the language for expressing "modern" knowledge. The inferiority arises from the fact that these African languages are underdeveloped in that respect. This, indeed, does not mean that they cannot be developed in that respect or that they do not have the requisite potential.

Secondly, Quine's "principle of indeterminacy of translation" cannot be invoked to discredit the attempts by African philosophers writing in English to elucidate philosophical theses using the vernacular. Sogolo (ibid. 30–1) tries to do this in connection with the attempt of J. O. Sodipo and B. Hallen to elucidate the *mo/gbagbo* (knowledge/belief) distinction in Yoruba and the dispute between J. T. Bedu-Addo and Kwasi Wiredu on the concept of truth in the Akan language (ibid. 26–8). It seems to me that Sogolo misunderstands the whole point of the latter dispute; which is not surprising, since he knows no word of Akan. Moreover, in the dispute between Bedu-Addo and Wiredu, we are not in a radical translation situation, since the two disputants are superbly competent to think in terms of both Western philosophy and the relevant African philosophy.

Now, to return to our question, we may start answering it by noting that the sources of African philosophizing enumerated some paragraphs above – proverbs, maxims, tales, myths, lyrics, poetry, etc. – presuppose, in their use, an intimate knowledge of a given vernacular. Thus, in attempting to discuss the Yoruba concept of mind, I must have an intimate knowledge of the Yoruba language and the culture of which it is a part. The general assumption here is that useful philosophical insights can be drawn from linguistic facts (cf. Bello 1987: 7).

In particular, African languages can be employed in the task of supporting or refuting "popular" (or "unpopular," if you like) conceptions about African thought and culture. They can also be employed in elucidating the concepts that Africans live by. Such elucidations can be enhanced by comparing the concepts in question with corresponding concepts in other philosophical traditions. Such concerns with language do not necessarily amount to linguistic philosophy, ordinary language philosophy, philosophy of language, or analytic philosophy, as Sogolo suggests (1993: 25–32).

Wiredu's work in this area is highly commendable. He has doggedly pursued the twin program of "domesticating" some Western philosophical ideas and "decolonizing" certain African philosophical ideas. His program covers a wide area of philosophy – metaphysics, epistemology (e.g. theory of truth, skepticism, relativism), morality, social and political philosophy, and philosophy of culture. His arguments are very constructive, rigorous, and sophisticated. In pursuing his program of domestication and conceptual decolonization, Wiredu appears to be observing the following three conditions enunciated by him: (1) the necessity and importance of the enterprise must be clear; (2) the ideas and techniques to be thus rendered in our language must have universal intelligibility and applicability; (3) there must, in any particular case, be an adequate mastery of the given African or foreign language and the body of knowledge concerned (1996: 85).

Of the three conditions, the first and the third are unexceptionable. However, the same cannot be said of the second one, which I find objectionable, and it is the one I wish to address presently. Let me make a start with Wiredu's observation, with which I fully concur, that "language can only incline, not necessitate" (1980: 35). If we need any evidence in support of this observation, it is simply that philosophers speaking the same language often come to different, even antagonistic, positions using the same linguistic data. The moral I draw from this evidence is that linguistic facts cannot be used as a decisive argument for or against a philosophical position.

For example, Wiredu draws our attention to some conceptual contrasts, namely, the Material and the Spiritual, the Secular and the Religious, the Natural and the Supernatural, the Mystical and the non-Mystical. If we take the contrast of the material and the spiritual and apply it to the concept of mind in the Akan language, according to Wiredu, "one can straightaway rule out any prospect of a Cartesian dualism of body and mind" (1996: 125). My reaction to this claim is that this finding, using the Akan language, is not a new philosophical insight, for Cartesian dualism has been contested since the days of Descartes himself. This, however, has not stopped philosophers from proposing other forms of body–mind dualism.

Again, take the example of the conception of God as creator *ex-nihilo*, which, according to Wiredu, is incoherent within the framework of the Akan language. That conception of God has been attractive to religious or ultra-religious thinkers from antiquity, but it has also been disputed since those times. It was disputed, for instance, by Muslim philosophers like Ibn Sina and Ibn Rushd, and it formed the basis of one of their disputes with a fellow Muslim thinker, Al-Ghazzali. Part of the philosophers' arguments was that *creatio ex-nihilo* was impossible or unintelligible. The Akan denial of *creatio ex-nihilo* or of a creator *ex-nihilo* is therefore not necessarily new. In spite of this opposition, however, there are still modern adherents to the doctrine of creation (as opposed to evolution, for example) or to the notion of creator *ex-nihilo* (as opposed to cosmic architect).

The lesson to be drawn from these examples, in my view, is that it is neither necessary nor important to classify problems, ideas, concepts, or techniques as either universal or particular, especially since Wiredu himself concedes that the universality of a mode of conceptualization does not guarantee its objective validity (1996: 55). Rather, we should attempt to domesticate as much non-traditional material as possible. It is just possible that some of our kinsmen, now or in the future, may find some of the ideas we have labeled "particular" more acceptable, for whatever reason(s). As the saying goes, "let a thousand flowers blossom!" Let us not limit our thought to ideas we reckon universal, for whatever reason(s), whether linguistic or independent of language.

Thus, we may, like the early Muslims, attempt a mass translation of available classics into our indigenous languages. The translation of Greek philosophical literature into Arabic is particularly instructive here. The translators strove, as faithfully as the state of knowledge at the time permitted, to render Greek philosophical ideas and conceptions into Arabic, borrowing non-Arabic words, where necessary, or adapting old words to new uses. That did not stop subsequent Muslim thinkers from making original contributions to philosophical literature, or from criticizing Greek ideas or conceptions. In other words, to embark on a wholesale translation will not prevent thinkers from holding independent positions or criticizing received ideas or opinions.

In the matter of domesticating and decolonizing ideas, what Wiredu appears to be doing can be described roughly as follows. He has mastered Western philosophical ideas, conceptions, and arguments, and has found good reasons to accept, modify, or reject some. He has then taken a close look at his traditional culture to see how he can make sense, in his vernacular, of the positions he has taken on independent grounds. Though such considerations serve as additional grounds to confirm him in his opinions, it is just possible that his prejudices predispose him to ignore or overlook countervailing evidence.

Conceptual Decolonization and the Question of Democracy and Consensus

One turn that Wiredu's program of conceptual decolonization has taken is the critique of majoritarian democracy together with the plea for a non-party polity based on consensus. His unhappiness with majoritarian democracy stems partly from the frustrations or ideological marginalization that is apt to befall an ethnic or ideological minority in the face of domination by an ethnic or ideological majority (1996: 189). However, Wiredu seems to play down the fact that the kinship ties that made consensus – which, in my view, he over-idealizes (ibid. 200–1) – possible are no longer practicable. On the contrary, majoritarian multiparty democracy, if properly engineered, and if based on a well-conceived system of education in democracy, can produce greater dividends than Wiredu's "new" consensus politics.

After all, the new arrangement, like multiparty democracy, will rely on elections (ibid. 189). The cause of the failure of multiparty democracy in Africa lies not in the idea, but in the practice. One malaise that afflicts the practice is our inability, in Africa, to hold, and abide by the results of, transparently free and fair multiparty elections. The reasons for this failure must be located elsewhere than in the idea of the multiparty system itself.

I must confess that I am enamored of the Western conception and practice of democracy, involving, among other things, periodic elections, peaceful change of government, the rule of law, the plurality of parties, the equality of citizens, the freedom of the press, transparency, and consensus, when necessary, as in times of national emergency. This is not to say that all is well with either the democratic idea or its practice, since aspects of both continue to be criticized and modified or improved.

As to consensus, it is doubtful that it is always a virtue, or that it always leads to the best results. It is arguable that even in traditional culture consensus was not always attained, otherwise there would have been perpetual peace; but quite clearly there was not (cf. ibid. 182). It is also arguable that decisions reached by consensus are not always the best. If they were, traditional society would have been able to meet the challenges of European infiltration and colonization. Quite obviously they were not able to do so. In my view, the politicians who idealize consensus are those who want a one-party state or do not want opposition to their rule. I doubt if the non-party consensual democracy proposed by Wiredu will produce any better result.

By contrast, the multiparty democracy starts with the assumption that groups of people having the same vision of the good society may come together to promote their vision. This has worked in Western multiparty democracies and has given people a real choice of alternatives. For instance, the economic boom of the late 1990s in the United States or the impetus to peace in the Middle East in that period might not have been possible in a consensual arrangement. How, for example, would Mr Ehud Barak have got the hawkish Likud to reach any consensus that could satisfy Israel's Arab neighbors and the international community? Similarly, how could Mr. Bill Clinton, President of the United States (1992–2000), have got his Republican opponents to reach a consensus on his economic and social policies that have obviously worked?

The Problem of Linguistic Inadequacy

To return to the question of language, Wiredu also seems to me to underrate the enormity of the task involved in formulating modern thought in African languages. As an illustration, let us consider Yoruba-language news writers attempting to translate into Yoruba language a news bulletin read in English. Frequently occurring English words or phrases like "genocide," "war crimes," "bombardment," "democracy," "state government," "rule of law," "sovereignty," "territorial integrity," "violation of human rights," "constitution," "proclamation of the national assembly," "international election monitors," "vice-chancellor" are translated with varying degrees of circumlocution, distortion, or inexactitude. Oftentimes, the modern educated person may find it difficult to understand what is being talked about if she has not already heard the news bulletin in English. The various ranks in the army, to take another example, are indistinguishable in Yoruba language, since all of them – General, Lieutenant-General, Major-General, Brigadier-General, Colonel, Lieutenant-Colonel, etc. – are translated as *oga'gun* or *olori-omo-ogun*, which translates into English as a head or leader of warriors, which is a glaringly non-symmetrical translation (cf. Wiredu 1996: 91). The situation regarding more "abstract" words or concepts, such as "philosophy," "number," "absolute," "supernatural," "natural," "transcendental," "substance," is bound to be more precarious. I venture to think that this is true of other African vernaculars.

These observations, in my view, contra Wiredu, argue grave deficiencies in our languages that need to be made up for by a vigorous program of borrowing, adapting, or whatever. Thus, if we have no Akan or Yoruba equivalent of the English word "cousin," to take Wiredu's "simple" example, then we do not have it. For sure, the strength of kinship bonds cannot be cited to justify or explain away this deficiency, as Wiredu tries to do (ibid. 93–4). At any rate, the strength of kinship bonds will not be diminished because we have a different word to translate the word "cousin." It is similarly not acceptable to explain or justify the absence of certain abstract concepts in Akan by observing that the intellectual orientation of the Akan is empirical (ibid. 99). To be sure, the intellectual orientation of most human beings and human groups starts by being empirical. It is only later in their development that they become "metaphysical." That is why many "abstract" words, for example, words that describe mental phenomena, have affinities with the physical (cf. Gyekye 1977: 237). I venture to say that we have not felt the need to invent, adopt, or adapt words for some of these "abstract" concepts because we have not thought for long enough in or about them.

There is one last point about the use of African vernaculars in philosophizing, namely, that no third person can participate in a dialogue between speakers of the same language unless the third person also has some competence in the language in question. This sounds to me reasonable enough, for without some knowledge of a language, it is difficult, if not impossible, to determine if an interpretation is correct or not. Take the case of the correct word for the English "God" in the Luo language. Is it "Rubanga" as some suggest or "Nyasaye" as others claim? The honest answer is that I do not know, since I know no word of the Luo language.

However, I am willing to concede that after a period of sustained discussion in or about the philosophical concepts and conceptions in a vernacular, some common agreements may emerge. Such common agreement may form the basis of further discussions among native as well as non-native philosophers. Thus, for example, it is now generally agreed among Yoruba-speaking philosophers who have discussed the concept of a person in Yoruba, that *ori* (lit. head), *ayanmo* (lit. that which is chosen for one), *akunleyan* (lit. that which is chosen kneeling down), *akunlegba* (lit. that which is received kneeling down), and *adamo* (lit. that which is created along with an individual) are all synonyms and refer to part of the non-physical constituents of a human person.

270

I am, further, willing to concede that a period of sustained discussion can yield parallels in conceptions in our vernaculars. Thus, for example, it has been shown that the word *iro* in Yoruba, like the word *nkontompo* in Akan, has primarily a moral meaning, since it means "lie." *Iro* (*nkontompo*) is the opposite of *otito* (*nokware*), which means "truth." But the opposite of "truth" in English is "falsehood," not "lie." This means that both the Yoruba and Akan languages have affinities in the matter of the concept of truth and its cognates. Wiredu appears, from what he does with examples across vernaculars, to consider such cautions unnecessary.

Whither African Philosophy?

In concluding this chapter, I would like to consider the question, "Whither African Philosophy?" This is necessary in view of the damning criticism of what Olusegun Oladipo (2000) calls "the traditionalist program" and "the analytic challenge." He attempts to "shift the focus of the debate [in African philosophy] from metaphilosophical preoccupations to the normative issue of what should be the commitment of the African philosopher in the contemporary world" (ibid. 93).

The commitment of the African philosopher, according to Oladipo, should be directed to the solution of three basic problems confronting Africa today. They are, in his words:

1. The problem of cultural identity, which is the problem of how we can achieve significant human development on the continent without compromising our identity;
2. The problem of knowledge, defined as the problem of how we can acquire and apply scientific knowledge and utilize mankind's accumulated wisdom to promote human well-being; and
3. The problem of social control, which concerns the issue of the development and maintenance of social orders within which individuals can exercise their rights, perform their obligations and realize their genuine human potentials. (ibid. 114)

Though Oladipo denies it, it is clear that his prescription leads to an exclusively "practical" orientation in African philosophy. The "practical" here has to do with proposing or formulating and implementing policies in such spheres of life as the social, educational, cultural, political, and the economic. Oladipo's emphasis seems to be on *techne* (art) as opposed to *episteme* (knowledge). Maybe what Oladipo is suggesting, like Plato, is either that philosophers should take over the rulership or leadership of African countries, or that African rulers or leaders should turn philosophers. Or, perhaps, what he is suggesting is that the solution of these problems can be achieved only after the theoretical framework or foundation has been laid by philosophers, the task of raising the superstructure being then left in the hands of practical men of affairs, for example, politicians, civil servants, and economists. However this is interpreted, it is clear that it is too idealistic and unattainable.

I truly sympathize with Oladipo's concerns about Africa, its problems, and how African philosophers can show their relevance by contributing to the solution of these problems. My worry, however, is that he would seem to place African philosophers in a philosophic straitjacket, thus stifling their freedom, initiative, and genius. It is, in principle, wrong for anyone to prescribe to another how to think or what to think about. A research program should not be set by one person and imposed on another in the name of relevance.

For one thing, the idea of relevance is not always clear. There can be grave doubts about what is relevant or not relevant in any situation. There is always some ambiguity about immediate or long-term relevance. For example, is logic relevant to our developmental needs? Or, is genetics relevant to medicine? Or, is nuclear physics relevant to medical practice? Relevance cannot be defined too narrowly. As Wiredu has shown (1980: 58), the notion of truth, which is investigated in epistemology, has relevance for ideology. Similarly, as I. M. Copi has shown (1986: vii), the study of logic has relevance for democratic living. For another, Oladipo exaggerates the "metaphilosophical preoccupations" of contemporary African philosophers. Philosophers in all cultures continually discuss the nature and methodology of their discipline. So there is nothing amiss if African philosophers do the same. Furthermore, as a matter of fact, some of the discussions that have been going on in African philosophy have been concerned with the basic problems enumerated by Oladipo. Lastly, contra Oladipo, it must be said that some philosophical problems are perennial and universal. Such, for example, is the problem of social control, which Oladipo himself considers the most fundamental of Africa's problems (2000: 114).

From the foregoing, it is clear that I favor a universalist or, better still, "pluralist" orientation in African philosophy. Such an orientation will allow research programs in various areas of philosophy, including logic, metaphysics, epistemology, ethics, social and political philosophy, and the history of philosophy. Such programs will draw on our culture and other philosophic traditions, Eastern or Western. Contra Sogolo, we can, and do, understand the philosophies of other cultures. There is also a need for us to let philosophers of other cultures understand our own tradition. This is the only way we can participate in, and contribute to, the "conversation of mankind."

References

Bello, A. G. A. (1987) "Philosophy and an African Language," *Quest: Philosophical Discussions*, 1(1) (June).
Bodunrin, P. O. (1981) "The Question of African Philosophy," *Philosophy*, 56(216).
Copi, I. M. (1986) *Introduction to Logic*, 7th edn. (New York: Macmillan Publishing Company).
Ghazzali, Abu Hamid (1958) *Tahafut al-Falasifah*, trans. into English by S. A. Kamali (3rd imp., 1974).
Gyekye, Kwame (1977) "Akan Language and the Materialist Thesis: A Short Essay on the Relation Between Philosophy and Language," *Studies in Language*, 1(2).
Oladipo, Olusegun (2000) *The Idea of African Philosophy*, 3rd edn. (Ibadan: Hope Publications).
Oruka, H. Odera (1981) "Four Trends in Current African Philosophy," in A. A. Diemer (ed.), *Philosophy in the Present Situation of Africa* (Wiesbaden: Steiner).

Oruka, H. Odera (1991) *Sage Philosophy: Indigenous Thinkers and Modern Debate on African Philosophy* (Nairobi, Kenya: Acts Press).

Rushd, Ibn (1969) *Tahafut al-Tahafut* (London: Luzac & Co.; trans. into English by Simon Van den Bergh as *Averroes' Tahafut al-Tahafut*).

Sogolo, Godwin (1993) *Foundations of African Philosophy* (Ibadan: Ibadan University Press).

Staniland, H. S. (1979) "What is Philosophy?" *Second Order – An African Journal of Philosophy*, 8(1).

Wiredu, Kwasi (1980) *Philosophy and an African Culture* (Cambridge: Cambridge University Press).

Wiredu, Kwasi (1996) *Cultural Universals and Particulars: An African Perspective* (Bloomington and Indianapolis: Indiana University Press).

273

19

Sage Philosophy: Its Methodology, Results, Significance, and Future

KIBUJJO M. KALUMBA

Introduction

For historical reasons, African sage philosophy focuses on the views of traditional indigenous sages. I will not attempt to expound these reasons immediately, as my first concern is to shed some light on the nature of sagaciousness.[1]

Most people will agree that a sage is a person who is exceptionally wise. In addition to exceptional wisdom, Henry Odera Oruka suggests a second criterion for sagaciousness. A true sage, he urges, must habitually use the gift of wisdom for the ethical betterment of his or her community. Consequently, he or she has to be consistently concerned with the ethical and empirical problems arising in his or her community with the intention of finding insightful solutions to them. In Oruka's view, the second criterion is what distinguishes a sage from a sophist (1990: xvii–xviii).[2] I agree.

Three works stand out as sage philosophy's most widely accepted specimens: Marcel Griaule's *Conversations with Ogotemmeli* (1965), Odera Oruka's *Sage Philosophy* (1990), and B. Hallen's and J. O. Sodipo's *Knowledge Belief & Witchcraft* (1997).[3] This chapter revolves around these classics. I have chosen this classical approach for its double advantage. Besides familiarizing the reader with the general character of sage philosophy, it exposes him or her to some of the major substantive issues that have arisen within this trend of African philosophy.

Methodology

Every work of sage philosophy involves a professional philosopher interviewing some person whom he or she regards as a sage. The conjunction of this chapter's opening statement and the two criteria of sagaciousness provides a threefold methodological checklist for any philosopher desirous of contributing to this trend of African philosophy. Such a philosopher must ensure that all his or her interlocutors are traditional, exceptionally wise, and satisfy the ethical criterion. Let us now examine the extent to which the authors of our classics have utilized this checklist.

274

Griaule makes no direct attempt to argue the traditionality of his interlocutor. Presumably, he saw no reason to question Ogotemmeli's traditionality, hailing as he did from Dogon country, a region of present-day Mali, whose inhabitants "were thought to present one of the best examples of primitive savagery" (1965: 1) at the time of the interview (1947). Hallen and Sodipo argue for the traditionality of the Yoruba *onisegun* (medicine men) on whose analysis of epistemic terms their work is based. To those who would insist that the *onisegun* are not traditional on the grounds that they have been touched or influenced by a "scientific" outlook that is not indigenous, their reply is that none of the *onisegun* they relied on "have undergone formal education or speak the English Language. Consequently there is no significant avenue by which such influence could have been conveyed" (1997: 74). Likewise, to ensure reliance on "genuine representatives of traditional Africa in a modern setting," Oruka limits his interviews to those who are "free from the effect of Western scholarship." Ideally, such people are rural and illiterate (1990: xviii, 6).

When it comes to deciding the exceptional wisdom of his interlocutors, Oruka's practice is to follow the lead of the community from which they hail (ibid. xviii). Hallen and Sodipo follow the same practice and base their work on the analysis of some twelve *onisegun* regarded as wisest within their community by both their clients and the members of their professional society, the *egbe* (1997: 13). Griaule describes Ogotemmeli as a person "endowed with exceptional intelligence and a wisdom the fame of which has spread throughout his country" (1965: 2). So, his own estimation of Ogotemmeli came to coincide with that of the Dogon community in granting him an eminent epistemic status. What Griaule does not specify is what role, if any, communal consensus played in shaping his conviction that Ogotemmeli was exceptionally wise. A brief discussion of the role of communal consensus in the exploration of sage philosophy is appropriate at this juncture.

A philosopher interested in sage philosophy typically plunges him or herself into a rural African village and solicits from a cross-section of the villagers names of community members they believe to excel in wisdom. He or she then proceeds to interview and to record those individuals who receive a preponderance of nominations. This is what following the lead of the community means. But, as Oruka points out, communal consensus alone does not guarantee an individual's exceptional wisdom. Hence, the philosopher must habitually assess the wisdom of his or her interlocutors. Additionally, to eliminate sophists from his pool, he or she must regularly scrutinize the behavior of those interlocutors he or she deems to be wise to ensure that they use their wisdom for the ethical betterment of their communities (Oruka 1990: xviii). Furthermore, the philosopher must remain vigilant for any information that could detract from the interlocutors' traditionality. It is imperative for the philosopher to constantly assess the traditionality, the exceptional wisdom, and the ethical character of his interlocutors throughout the course of his or her research. For what is at stake is a threefold checklist for constant referral rather than a series of chronologically ordered steps. We will now examine the extent of our authors' utilization of the third item of the checklist (the ethical criterion).

Since Oruka personally suggested the second criterion of sagaciousness, it is safe to assume that he regularly assessed the behavior of his interlocutors to ensure that they used their wisdom for the ethical betterment of their communities. The other authors don't make explicit reference to the ethical criterion. However, since they portray their interlocutors as popular counselors, the latters' compatriots must have perceived them as altruistically motivated. This is how Griaule describes Ogotemmeli's communal involvement: "Indeed his name and his character were famous throughout the plateau and the hills, known (as the saying was) to the youngest boy. People came to his door for advice every day and even by night" (1965: 15). Similarly, after describing the *oniseguns'* unparalleled epistemic status within their community, Hallen and Sodipo conclude as follows: "One therefore finds the onisegun being asked to give advice and counsel about business dealings, family problems, unhappy personal situations, religious problems, and the future, as well as about physical and mental illness" (1997: 13).

Beyond the threefold checklist, our authors don't share much else in common besides transcribing and translating the original dialogues. Oruka exhibits the least degree of "tampering" with the original data, as his final product comprises no more than English translations of the original dialogues. In contrast, Griaule rarely quotes Ogotemmeli directly. His book is so dominated by his own summary statements of Ogotemmeli's expositions of the Dogon world-view that it is difficult to distinguish the interlocutor's message from Griaule's speculations.

Hallen and Sodipo's involvement with the original data goes beyond mere translation as well. Their main project consists in comparing the meanings of the Yoruba terms *mo* and *gbagbo* with those of their supposed English equivalents.[4] According to certain Yoruba-English dictionaries which Hallen and Sodipo regard as the "established translation manual" (etm), the respective English equivalents are the terms "know" and "believe." Their first step consists of a four-tier analysis of the two English terms to determine their respective references, objects, criteria, and varieties. They base this analysis on several "standard Western philosophical works and a bit of common sense" (1997: 40). Next, they proceed with a similar analysis of the terms *mo* and *gbagbo*, relying on data gathered from the Yoruba *onisegun* mentioned above. They do this by collating these diverse data and then comparing them to select the meanings for the terms they deem most representative of the Yoruba conceptual system. Finally, they compare these meanings with the meanings of "know" and "believe." Hallen and Sodipo characterize their overall method as "conceptual analysis," and regard the *onisegun* as "colleagues" in a "collaborative analysis" of the Yoruba terms (ibid. 8, 10, 124).

Because Griaule and Hallen and Sodipo communalize their results by attributing them to entire societies, Oruka describes their works as anthropology rather than philosophy (1990: xxvi). As we shall see in the next section, he reserves the label "philosophy" for portions of his final product.

Results

Griaule believes the *Conversations* to be a synopsis of Dogon metaphysics as "laid bare" by Ogotemmeli in the course of 33 days of "conversations." At least this is the picture emerging from the book's first 15 pages, in which an impression is created that Griaule is about to do for the Dogon what Tempels did for the Bantu in

Bantu Philosophy (1959). Tempels, to whose work Griaule likens his (1965: 2), reconstructed what he regarded as the basic explanatory ontological principles underlying Bantu culture. Unfortunately, one searches the *Conversations* in vain for any explanatory ontological principles comparable to those of Tempels except for occasional references to the notion of the life force.[5] Griaule's explanations of Dogon beliefs and practices are in terms of mythology rather than ontology.

The main conclusion of Oruka's sagacity research in western Kenya is that there are two kinds of sage in traditional Africa: folk sages and philosophic sages. Whereas both kinds of sage excel in their knowledge of traditional cultural thought, they are distinguishable by their attitude toward it. Folk sages take a first-order attitude toward cultural thought in that their thought never manages to transcend the traditional confines. In contrast, a philosophic sage adopts a second-order attitude toward cultural thought: he or she rises above cultural thought and makes an independent, critical assessment of it, accepting only those aspects of it that satisfy his or her rational scrutiny. Oruka believes that unlike the utterances of folk sages, which are all best characterized as cultural thought, the critical utterances of his philosophic sages deserve the label "philosophy."[6]

The "meanings" Hallen and Sodipo obtain from their four-tier analysis of "know" and "believe" turn out to be significantly different from those they obtain from the analysis of their Yoruba counterparts of *mo* and *gbagbo*. From this they conclude, contrary to the etm, that neither of the English terms has the same meaning as its supposed Yoruba equivalent.

The sharpest contrast in meaning revealed by Hallen and Sodipo is between "know" and *mo*. This is due to one of the criteria they assign to the term *mo*. According to their analysis, the two criteria for *mo* are *ri* (visual perception) and the recognition of the perceiver's *eri okon* (etm: heart and mind, apprehension) that what is perceived is *ooto* (etm: truth). In other words, where P is a proposition, a person S has *imo* (the noun form of *mo*) that P only if S has seen that P and S's *eri okon* has witnessed that it is *ooto* that P. When it comes to *knowledge that*, Hallen and Sodipo contend that its two uncontroversial criteria are truth and belief. That is, a person S knows that P only if it is true that P, and S believes that P. The criterion of *ri* so sharply distinguishes the meaning of *imo* from that of *knowledge* that it is possible for a person who possesses knowledge that P to fail to possess *imo* that P. For example, the average American knows that Christopher Columbus was the first European to visit the Americas. But he or she cannot *mo* anything about Columbus whom he or she cannot see first-hand. Like all information based on second-hand sources or testimony, any information the average American possesses about Columbus is relegated by the Yoruba to the second-best epistemic level of *igbagbo* (the noun form of *gbagbo*).

> The point of difference between the two systems that we find to be of greatest significance is the relative role of testimony or second-hand information. In the Yoruba system any information conveyed on the basis of testimony is, until verified, *igbagbo*. In the English system a vast amount of information conveyed on the basis of testimony is, without verification, classified as "knowledge" that. Much of the latter is information that the individual concerned would not even know how to verify. Yet it is still "knowledge" that. (Hallen and Sodipo 1997: 81)

Is it possible to have instances of belief that fail to be *igbagbo*, or vice versa? This question cannot be answered from Hallen and Sodipo's analysis alone. Despite their effort to dissociate *gbagbo* from "believe" by rendering it as "agreeing to accept what one hears from someone" (ibid. 64), Hallen and Sodipo do not provide a clear-cut criterion comparable to what was given in the case of *ri* that sharply distinguishes the meaning of "believe" from that of *gbagbo*.

Significance and Future

Sage philosophy was conceived as part of a general reaction to the position of classical anthropology regarding traditional Africa that dominated the first three decades of the twentieth century. Epitomized by the works of Levy-Bruhl, classical anthropology denied all abstract thought to the traditional African, whom it described as a savage with a primitive mentality (see Irele 1983). Griaule responded to this description by undertaking a study of the cultural thought of a traditional African people, the Dogon, using one of their leading traditional sages, Ogotemmeli, as his informant. This study convinced Griaule that, contrary to the claim of classical anthropology, Dogon culture had produced an abstract metaphysic whose principles grounded and animated all Dogon institutions, customs, laws, rituals, and so on. Griaule attached such great significance to his "discovery" that he believed it would put to rest the claim of classical anthropology as well as "revolutionize all accepted ideas about the mentality of Africans and of primitive peoples in general" (1965: 2).[7]

The "discovery" of abstract thought among traditional Africans was not enough to convince all Africanists that the best of traditional Africa's thinkers operated at the same level of intellectual sophistication as their Western counterparts (the scientists). Robin Horton (1967) typifies these skeptics. He claims that there is a remarkable similarity between traditional thinkers and scientists in that both groups seek to explain the visible world in terms of the invisible world. Traditional thinkers try to do this in terms of the actions of gods and spirits, and scientists in terms of theoretical entities such as atoms and waves. So, the thought systems of both groups contain a theoretical component. But Horton sees a big difference between traditional thinkers and scientists when it comes to the attitude toward their respective theoretical beliefs. For traditional thinkers, the theoretical postulates constitute a revered, closed system that must be accepted uncritically: a system of indubitable beliefs that renders empirical testing superfluous. In contrast, scientists regard their theoretical postulates as open to criticism, further empirical testing, and subsequent revision.

Hallen and Sodipo believe their research puts a critical check on Horton's generalizations. They argue that the *imo/igbagbo* distinction among the Yoruba shows that these traditional people (and, a fortiori, their leading thinkers) do not revere their theoretical beliefs to the extent claimed by Horton. This is true, they urge, because the Yoruba do not use the highest epistemic term *imo* to describe these beliefs. Since they are not acquired visually, all theoretical beliefs are relegated by the Yoruba to the second-best epistemic level of *igbagbo*, the level of things one

278

agrees to accept from others. Most importantly, Hallen and Sodipo argue that the *imo/igbagbo* distinction suggests, contrary to Horton, that the traditional Yoruba possess a critical attitude as well as an appreciation of empirical testing. This is true, they contend, because the distinction calls for treating all information critically as merely hypothetical (as *igbagbo*) until and unless it can pass the empirical test (1997: 72–81, 119–25).

But the authors of the abstract metaphysic "unearthed" by Ogotemmeli are anonymous, and their thoughts are portrayed as the unanimous possession of an entire people. The same is true of the exponents of the Yoruba conceptual system explicated by Hallen and Sodipo. Does traditional Africa provide instances of individualized, critical, second-order thinking? Yes, according to Oruka. He believes the existence of traditional philosophic sages in Kenya proves that this sort of thinking is a permanent feature of Africa (1990: 5–6).

The reader should now be in a position to understand why sage philosophy focuses on the views of traditional sages. It is because, from the moment of its conception and throughout the course of its development, its overarching goal has been to prove that rational thought in its various forms is native to Africa. Sagacity researchers have pursued this goal in one of two ways. Some, such as Griaule and Hallen and Sodipo, have chosen to study traditional African thought systems utilizing those indigenous experts least likely to smuggle foreign elements into them, namely, the traditional sages. Others, such as Oruka, have preferred to look for evidence of second-order rational thought among those Africans most likely to possess it who are also least influenced by Western culture: the traditional sages again.

In addition to its historical role of demonstrating traditional Africa's rationality, Oruka has identified three other roles for sagacity. First, named individual sages sometimes make valuable philosophical contributions worth the attention of professional philosophers (ibid. xvii, 36). This is true of Mbuya Akoko's argument for monotheism. Classified as a philosophic sage by Oruka, Akoko disagrees with the traditional polytheism of his ethnic group, the Luo, and offers a *reductio ad absurdum* argument for monotheism:

> God is One Supreme Being for all people. This I can show by reference to the fact of the Uniformity of nature. If there were many gods with similar powers, nature would be in chaos, since there would be conflicts and wars between the gods. But nature is uniform not chaotic: a dog, for example, brings forth a dog not a cat. And a cat produces a cat not a dog or a hen. All this is a proof of One Supreme Mind ruling nature. (ibid. 32–3)

Sagacity's second role consists in providing "raw data" for further philosophical reflection (ibid. xvii). A good example is the "psychology" Griaule attributes to the Dogon according to which the self is a compound entity comprising the soul (will and consciousness) and the life force. The life force itself is depicted as a composite entity "made up of portions of the forces of its genitors... and various ancestors..." According to Griaule, the Dogon view death as the separation of the soul from the life force and the disintegration of the latter into its components (1965: 172–3, 180–2). But this psychology is remarkably different from the one reported by

Tempels. From the conviction that the Bantu regard every being as a force, Tempels infers that they equate an individual's self with his or her life force. Tempels characterizes this life force as a simple (non-compound) entity "endowed with intelligence and will." According to Tempels (1959: 49–55), it is this undivided life force that the Bantu regard as surviving physical death. Do these disparate accounts reflect actual differences in the way the Dogon and the Bantu view the self? Do they result from misrepresentation of traditional psychology by either Tempels or Griaule? These questions call for serious reflection by African ethnophilosophers, especially those, such as Innocent Onyewuenyi (1991), who seem to see in *Bantu Philosophy* the definitive statement of traditional African philosophy.

Sagacity's third role is in the area of socio-economic development. Convinced that genuine development must be pursued in light of the concrete circumstances of the people whose lives it is meant to improve, Oruka urges African leaders to enlist the input of traditional sages in the process of designing and implementing development policies and programs. This is because he believes the sages understand their people's culture and the nature of their problems better than most people (1990: 61–2). Indeed, Oruka himself has done a study on family planning involving the inputs of several traditional sages (see Presbey 1998: 10).

A fourth role for sagacity is entailed by Hallen and Sodipo's work. It consists in supplementing Western philosophy. Because it has developed in relative independence of the rest of the world, Western philosophy has tended to absolutize many untested presuppositions. Sagacity research has the potential to validate, invalidate, or modify some of these presuppositions. One of these is the claim that propositional attitudes are universal. In English, these are expressed by verbs such as "believe," "know," "doubt," "wish," and "want," which indicate a person's attitude toward a subordinate proposition introduced by the word "that," as in the sentence "John believes that philosophy is hard." The claim is that these verbs have equivalents in all natural languages. Hallen and Sodipo take their research to invalidate this claim. As we have seen, the two conclude from their analyses that there are no exact Yoruba equivalents for "know" and "believe." From this they infer that propositional attitudes are not universal (1997: 84). Unfortunately, this inference comes too early. It needs to await further analyses encompassing a more representative sample of propositional attitudes.

Is there a future for sage philosophy, given the growing Westernization of Africa and the resultant gradual disappearance of traditional sages? The answer depends on what the driving force behind future sagacity research will turn out to be. If future research continues the current trend of being driven by the desire to showcase individualized, unwesternized second-order thinking or to utilize uncontaminated expertise in traditional African systems, then sage philosophy has a bleak future. For then, it will have restricted itself to traditional sages, and their demise will mean its demise. But while sagacity research has to focus on the thought of sages, these sages need not be traditional. The traditionality of its sages is just an accidental feature of African sage philosophy. As we have seen, it was the purely historical concern of demonstrating traditional Africa's rationality that led our classical authors to focus on traditional sages. It is reasonable to think, then, that sage philosophy's future lies in the hands of those researchers who will be willing to transcend this concern. Freed from this constraint, such researchers will be able to dialogue with all Africa's sages: traditional, modern, literate, and illiterate. A wealth of results is bound to emerge from such interactions, which could serve various purposes. They could be valuable as raw data for philosophical reflection or as, in themselves, independent philosophical counsel. Besides, they could yield insights useful for thinking about socio-economic development. In all these connections, moreover, sage philosophy might possibly offer fresh options to Western philosophical issues. Sage philosophy has to adapt to survive.

Notes

1 For the rest of this chapter, the expression "sage philosophy" will be used to designate African sage philosophy.
2 Even though it appears to be an independent criterion of sagaciousness (1990: xviii), consistent concern with society's problems is, in my view, best treated as a necessary condition for what I am presenting as the second criterion.
3 Hallen and Sodipo's book was first published by Ethnographica in 1986. All the references in this chapter are to the 1997 Stanford edition.
4 I say "main project" because in chapter 3, Hallen and Sodipo also compare the meaning of the Yoruba term *aje* with that of its supposed English equivalent "witch." My focus is on their main project.
5 Griaule 1965: interviews for days 20, 21, 26, and 27.
6 The distinction between folk sages and philosophic sages is articulated on several occasions in Oruka's *Sage Philosophy*: see, for example, pp. 28–9, 44–5. Chapter 6 of *Sage Philosophy* reproduces the interviews of seven traditional thinkers Oruka classifies as folk sages; chapter 7 is devoted to extended interviews of five philosophic sages.
7 But recall what I have said about the lack of explanatory metaphysical principles in the *Conversations*.

References

Griaule, Marcel (1965) *Conversations with Ogotemmeli* (London: Oxford University Press).
Hallen, Barry and Sodipo, J. O. (1997) *Knowledge, Belief, and Witchcraft* (Stanford: Stanford University Press; orig. pub. Ethnographica, 1986).
Horton, Robin (1967) "African Traditional Thought and Western Science," *Africa*, 37(1 & 2): 50–7, 155–87.
Irele, Abiola (1983) "Introduction," in Paulin Hountondji, *African Philosophy: Myth and Reality* (Bloomington: Indiana University Press).
Onyewuenyi, Innocent (1991) "Is There an African Philosophy?" in Tsenay Serequeberhan (ed.), *African Philosophy: The Essential Readings* (New York: Paragon House).
Oruka, Henry Odera (1990) *Sage Philosophy: Indigenous Thinkers and Modern Debate on African Philosophy* (Leiden: E. J. Brill).
Presbey, Gail M. (1998) "H. Odera Oruka on Moral Reasoning: Rooted in the East African Prophetic Tradition," Paper read at the American Philosophical Association Symposium on "Sage Philosophy: Celebrating the Life and Works of Odera Oruka," Los Angeles, California.
Tempels, Placide (1959) *Bantu Philosophy* (Paris: Presence Africaine).

Part III

LOGIC, EPISTEMOLOGY, AND METAPHYSICS

20

Logic in the Acholi Language

VICTOR OCAYA

Introduction

The language of the Acholi, more or less understood also by the other Luo peoples of Uganda, the Sudan, Kenya, and Tanzania, is spoken by the Ugandans of the Gulu and Kitgum districts. When the Acholi settled in present Acholiland, they, as a whole, preserved their language. Later contacts with the Arabs (Uma 1971: 34) and Europeans had their impact on the language. But the Acholi language appears to have developed always toward simplicity (Crazzolara 1938: xiv).

Every language, including Acholi, suffers from variations in spelling, pronunciation, and accent, as it gets spoken in a wider geographical area. The language used as illustrations in this chapter is heard mainly in the central areas of Acholiland.

Because of space limitation, we will take a brief excursion through the Acholi language, identifying only those ideas deemed of importance in logic. Thereafter we will consider some logical concepts and rules to show that the Acholi language has all the elements sufficient for the business of logic. Finally, I will call upon logicians to rethink certain logical laws.

The language and its characteristics

The Acholi language has all the letters of the alphabet of the English language except the letters h, q, s, x, and z. Its vowels have, as a rule, the Italian value: they are pronounced the way they are written. However, linguists say that the language has many more vowels and consonants and follows standard orthography (Tucker 1971: 633; Crazzolara 1938: 4–7).

It is, however, important to note that Acholi is a tonal language. The function of a word in a given context is determined by tone or pitch. Linguists use tone-marks to indicate different tones (Tucker and Bryan 1966: 405–8). In this work I will avoid all that and follow Savage (1955), Malandra (1952), and Kitching (1932).

Parts of speech

The Acholi language has all the eight parts of speech (noun, pronoun, verb, adverb, preposition, adjective, logical connective, interjection). The language does not have articles ("a," "an," "the," as in English); nor does it have every grammatical gender. There is, however, a neuter gender.

Nouns Nouns in Acholi describe the nature of the thing named. The names of persons, in particular, often express relation. Though largely ignored today, Acholi names describe the circumstances prevailing at the birth of the child.

There is also in the language a great preponderance of concrete nouns over abstract ones. This indicates that reality, relationship, and similar concepts are nearly always looked at from a concrete point of view. This observation is of some importance, as logic is also concerned with description, relation, and class. Thus, a logician handling arguments involving certain aspects of Acholi life will have to be cognizant of these facts.

Pronouns Personal pronouns in Acholi take two forms, namely, as independent forms and as prefixes or suffixes. They are essential in the formation of tenses and in determining possession. Besides, by the manipulation of nouns and pronouns, it is possible to see other unusual features of the language. All this goes to indicate that, in Acholi, words are, generally speaking, heavily loaded with meaning. When translating into another language or formal system, care has to be taken if justice is to be done to those meanings.

It is in place to emphasize that there is perfect gender equality in Acholi. He, him, his, and she, her, hers are alien in Acholi. In Acholi the gender problem arises elsewhere.

Verbs There is no copula in Acholi language. Attributes of any kind are obtained by the juxtaposition of adjectives to nouns, or of nouns to nouns. And very significant is the absence of the passive voice in the language. There is only the active voice. Thus, *Ocaya ocoyo buk-ki* (Ocaya wrote this book) is the active voice. To say "This book is written by Ocaya," one might say something that translates back to English literally as "This book Ocaya is the one who wrote it": *Ocaya aye ocoyo buk-ki*. Consequently, any relation in Acholi, to be worthwhile, has to be active (Ocaya 1988). And this is of no small bearing on logic.

Adverbs These are numerous in number and diverse in form. Of interest to logic are adverbs of a descriptive nature and those that express manner, degree, precision, and quantity. A logician will have to take pains to ascertain the precise meanings of the adverbs, as he is unlikely to encounter similar patterns in other languages.

Prepositions These are few in number. But many of them are taken from parts of the body and are further evidence of the practicality of the Acholi language, which is more adept at handling down-to-earth facts than abstract truths.

Adjectives Acholi adjectives behave in a way that is suggestive of a many-valued logic and this, I think, calls for a rethinking of the law of excluded middle (Quine 1970: 83–7). We shall return to this question later.

286

Logical connectives   We know that logical connectives are important in logic and in Acholi there is a variety of logical connectives, which allow for different kinds of proposition. The following may be mentioned. *Ki* (and), *bene* (also), *onyo* (either or), *ka* (if), *ci* (then; but); *ka...ci...* (if...then...). Every natural language must, of necessity, possess negation-words in order to function. In Acholi they are *pe*, *ku*, *bong(o)* (not). Few logical connectives in Acholi have exact equivalents in English. Indeed this linguistic problem has to be borne constantly in mind while reading this chapter.

The Logic of Proposition

The Acholi language, as noted earlier, has all the elements of logic even if, unlike English and other European languages, it has had no connection with Greek or Latin (Ocaya 1979, 1989). Words like "argument," "proposition," "premise," "truth," "falsehood," and "soundness," so frequently used in logic, have no exact equivalents in Acholi. But they can still be translated into Acholi using the word *lok*, which, like the Greek *logos*, translates a multitude of concepts. It means, "word," "speech," "question," "problem," and many other things. Accompanied by an adjective, pronoun, or even another noun, *lok* will translate the key English words mentioned above and will, more or less, convey these ideas and reveal the distinctions between them.

Argument is *lok-mukubbe* (related assertions); proposition = *lok-awaca* (the matter which is said); premise = *tyen-lok* (*tyen* = foot: grounds for a statement); conclusion = *latwe-lok* (that which ties up speech); soundness = *lok-atir* (straight talk); truth = *lok-ada* (real talk); falsehood = *lok-nguna* (halved talk).

Assuming familiarity with the above logical terms, I will take leave of their definitions and proceed instead to examine select logical concepts and principles in the Acholi language.

Negation

Negation, usually symbolized "$-$," in logical texts is the denial of a proposition as contrasted with its affirmation. In a bivalent logic a proposition is either true or false; its negation either false or true. In Acholi the particles that express negation, as we have seen, are *pe*, *ku*, and *bong(o)*. Thus *Odong laco* (Odong is a man), when negated, may become *Odong pe laco*, *Odong laco ku*, *Odong bong laco*, *Odong laco bongo* (Odong is not a man). But generally anyone disagreeing with *Odong pe laco* (Odong is not a man) simply says *Odong laco* (Odong is a man). In Acholi one does not normally affirm or deny a statement by employing two negation words as in the English sentence "It is not the case that Odong is not a man." There is either one or no negation word at all.

Double negation

According to this law, denying a proposition twice is equivalent to affirming it. In English to say that Acholi is in Uganda and it is not the case that Acholi is not in

287

Uganda is to make two equivalent statements. The two propositions are interderivable. The lack of natural facilities for handling two negation words in ordinary speech suggests that the Acholi language does not explicitly use the law of double negation. But the principle exists implicitly in the language. An incident involving a father and his son makes this clear: *In pe iwaco ni maa-ni pe iot?* (Did you not say that your mother is not in the hut?). The principle of negation is essential to any form of communication, in that it must have instruments for including and excluding. And a system contains the essential elements of logic, if it is capable of performing that function.

Conjunction

Conjunction denotes the conjoint truth of the propositions combined by the conjunctive connective (and), and the proposition is true only when all the conjuncts are true. The Acholi language uses *ki* (and) to construct a conjunction as in *Opio ki Ocen beco* (Opio and Ocen are good). And, given a conjunction as a premise, an Acholi easily draws any of its conjuncts as a conclusion or a conjunction as a conclusion if he is given two or more propositions as premises.

Logical contradiction

From the standpoint of a predicative logic, there is a logical contradiction when a quality is attributed to, and denied of, a thing at one and the same time and under the same circumstances. In propositional logic a contradiction is a logical conjunction in which one of the conjuncts is the negation of the other. Such a proposition is always false. It is self-contradictory, and its negation is a tautology known in logic as the law of non-contradiction. The Acholi language prefers atomic propositions to molecular ones. So a compound proposition which clearly expresses a logical contradiction is hard to come by. But, implicitly, there is a constant use of the principle of non-contradiction in the language.

Children frequently (unwittingly) get people confused. On being sent by their mother to fetch *opoko* (gourd) from their elder sister, two children (as always) run to win the race. One says: *Maa mito agulu* (Mother wants a pot); the other immediately retorts: *Maa gire pe mito agulu* (Mother does not want a pot). The confused sister discovers later that the mother actually wants a gourd. The point is that she was never tempted to suppose that both siblings might be right.

A man once returned from Kitgum and reacted: *Kitgum ber, ci pe ber* (Kitgum is good and not good). The contradiction here is only apparent. What the traveler meant was that under certain circumstances Kitgum is good; but from other points of view the town is not good.

The Acholi will often express notions of the interplay of opposites: *Kongo ni mit marac* (This beer is very good. Literally: This beer good bad). The Acholi, like the Greeks of old, insist that any given thing contains opposites. The seeming contradiction is, in fact, an endeavor to explain the interplay of conflicting forces in nature. It is a "contradiction" that can easily be explained away, unlike the real contradictions of Hegel and Marx.

Disjunction

The inclusive disjunction, usually symbolized "v," is a compound proposition which is true if and only if at least one disjunct is true. And an exclusive disjunction "/" is true if and only if one principal disjunct is true and the other is false. Disjunctive connectives in Acholi are *nyo, onyo* (or). The Acholi language recognizes only the exclusive disjunction. For example, *Okello ka pe paco, ci tye i poto* (Okello is either at home or in the fields). It is always "either...or...and not both." When both propositions hold, then it is a logical conjunction. So, from an exclusive disjunction and any of its disjuncts as premises, the Acholi validly conclude the negation of the other disjunct. According to the Acholi language, therefore, a situation such as that envisaged by the inclusive disjunction does not make sense.

Law of excluded middle

This principle says that between a statement and its negation there is no other alternative. The Acholi language, however, has a peculiar way of repeating an adjective in a manner that seems to suggest a third possible alternative between a statement and its negation. For example:

1   *Piny lyet*: It is hot. (P)
·2   *Piny pe lyet*: It is not hot. ($-$P)
3   *Piny lyet-lyet*: It is rather hot. (?)

In (3) the English "rather" does not capture the Acholi idea of *lyet-lyet*, which is somewhere between (1) and (2). *Piny lyet-lyet* quite unambiguously asserts that it is neither "hot" nor "not hot" and the law of excluded middle rules out just this possibility. This is evidence against the law of excluded middle, from an Acholi standpoint.

Natural language may be open to the influence of psychological and social factors that are too complex to be reduced to the all-inclusive dichotomy of true or false. So, perhaps, a polyvalent logic may be needed to provide for more than two values. This Acholi inspired questioning of the law of excluded middle has a practical rationale when one thinks about a certain very common range of facts. There is clearly a problem of continuous variation in the context of certain attributes and their negation (Thouless 1930: ch. 9). For example, some countries used to be referred to as developed and others as underdeveloped. Today we hear of developed and developing countries. The inadequacy of the law of excluded middle is at work here. Exactly when is a country developed and no longer developing? This problem may perhaps be settled by re-examining the law of excluded middle.

Zadeh (1972), Gaines (1976), Haack (1978), and Sainsbury (1986), who argue that the existence of vagueness in ordinary discourse is a fact and should be taken seriously, would have no hesitation in supporting the Acholi contention. Unlike Russell (1923) and Black (1937), who maintain that natural language is totally vague and ought to be eliminated from formal language altogether, Zadeh and others believe that fuzzy thinking may be a blessing in disguise. They maintain that fuzzy thinking may solve puzzles that defy precise analysis, and that a multivalued logic might yield better answers to the problem of vagueness. The Acholi language would lead one to single out the law of excluded middle as simply failing to perform the job it is supposed to do.

Implication

In natural language implication is expressed in the form of a conditional proposition, and it is false only when the antecedent is true and the consequent false. The connective "→" used to translate it into symbolic language raises great difficulties. Some of the problems can be seen below:

1 *Ka mani obino, ci mi-ne lagony* (If your mother comes, then give her the key).
2 *Ka icamo kic i dwar ma nongo ceng lyet, ci oryo neki matek* (If you eat honey during a hunt when the sun is hot, then you get very thirsty).
3 *Ka in lacan, ci pe inyomo* (If you are poor, then you cannot marry).
4 *Ka Gulu pe tye i Acholi, ci maa pe onywala* (If Gulu is not in Acholiland, then my mother did not beget me).

In sentence (2) the relation between the antecedent clause and the consequent is a causal link. In sentence (3) the consequent clause is derived from its antecedent, but there is no causal nexus. In the three sentences (1), (2), and (3) there exists a relationship of relevance between the antecedent clauses and their consequents. In example (4), on the other hand, there is no nexus of this kind whatsoever between the antecedent and consequent. The link between them is entirely logical.

As can be seen, the notion of implication, common also in Acholi, is a complex one. Like other languages, the Acholi language has additional connectives for rendering implication. However, such variations bring with them certain changes in meaning or syntax. In sentence (1), *teke* (as soon as) may be substituted for the connective *ka...ci...* (if...then...). One might say, *Teke mani obino, mi-ne lagony* (As soon as your mother comes, give her the key). Here the idea of urgency is suggested. Hence there is a shade of difference between this form of statement and the conditional form noted above.

Conditional sentences of the form of (4) are frequently heard in Acholi:

Latin-na pe lakwo (My son is not a thief) (−P).
Ka latin-na lakwo (If my son is a thief) (P), *ci maa pe onywala* (then my mother did not beget me) (−Q).

The form of the utterance is, "−P because P → −Q." The mother, convinced of her child's integrity, is prepared to accept the impossible should the child turn out to be a thief. This is an enthymeme. The complete argument would run:

If my son is a thief, then my mother did not beget me.
My mother did beget me. (Suppressed premise.)
Hence, my son is not a thief.

290

Symbolically, we have, P → −Q, Q ∴ −P. This is a *modus tollens*, a valid form of argument in which one can validly conclude the negation of the antecedent, given a conditional statement and the negation of its consequent as premises. But the next example, another enthymeme, although acceptable in logic, sounds strange in the ears of the Acholi people:

Awich rwot Payira (Awich is the chief of Payira) (P).
Ka jobi ger (If buffaloes are fierce) (Q), *ci Awich rwot Payira* (then Awich is the chief of Payira) (P).

This is of the immediate form "P because Q → P." Fully stated, it becomes "Q → P, Q ∴ P" which is a *modus ponens* with *Jobi ger* (Buffaloes are fierce) (Q) as the suppressed premise. It is a valid argument because the consequent of a conditional follows validly from the conditional statement and its antecedent as premises. But the Acholi regard with suspicion anyone who reasons in this way.

We have already observed that a conditional statement is false only when the antecedent is true and the consequent false. The assumption is that truth does not lead to falsehood, whereas falsehood may lead to truth. The Acholi easily see this point in the context of fables. Indeed, among the Acholi fables, as false stories with true implications, are a suitable vehicle for explaining the nature of logical implication, provided analogies are not pressed too hard.

Anderson and Belnap (1973) argue that logical concepts such as that of validity, deducibility, or entailment must always take relevance into account. According to them, there is, for instance, deducibility only if a person's unspoiled sense intuitively tells him that an inference is valid. The Acholi concur with this view.

Logical equivalence

Two propositions are equivalent if they entail each other, and to be the case both must either hold or not hold. The notion of logical equivalence is easily seen by the Acholi in the context of certain kinds of riddle. They may be helpful in understanding the idea of equivalence. But, as with fables in the case of implication, care must be taken not to capitalize too much on them. A riddle of the kind in question is made up of an indirect description of an object (the problem). The object, when named, is the solution of the problem. In Acholi traditions it is generally acknowledged that the problem as set is equivalent to the correct answer given. For example, *Akuri aryo ongolo nm* (Two doves crossed the river) is equivalent to *wang* (the eyes). Here again riddles may help to see that the concepts of logical equivalence (and of identity) exist in the Acholi language. With adequate qualifications, riddles may be helpful in the interpretations of these concepts.

Further, certain apparently simple conditionals express relationships that are equivalencies. For example: *Opia ka pe paco, ci tye i te kongo* (If Opia is not at home, then he is at the beer party). Such statements, as commonly understood in Acholi, are best symbolized as biconditionals: (−P←→Q). This is equivalent to an exclusive disjunction.

291

Identity

The law of identity states that any given thing is itself. In traditional logic, this law is given as A is A. This formulation is ambiguous in the English language because the copula has various possible meanings like formal implication, identity, and formal equivalence. This problem does not arise in the Acholi language. Identity is expressed by juxtaposition of nouns: *dano dano* (man is man). This law is perhaps best identified with the mathematical theorem $a = a$. In this respect, too, the Acholi expression of the law of identity is precise.

Predicate Logic

In this section it is shown that the logic of syllogisms and quantificational logic are easily formulated in Acholi.

Syllogism

The central assumption of syllogistic logic is that every statement has a subject of which something is predicated. According to that logic, there can be only four kinds of statement: (1) universal affirmative (A), e.g. *Dano ducu to* (All men are mortal); (2) universal negative (E), e.g. *Dano ducu pe to* (No man is mortal); (3) particular affirmative (I), e.g. *Dano mukene to* (Some men are mortal); (4) particular negative (O), e.g. *Dano mukene pe to* (Some men are not mortal).

A syllogism is made up of any three of these categorical propositions, two of which are premises (major and minor) and the other the conclusion. Traditional logic developed definitions and rules sufficient for checking the validity or invalidity of syllogistic arguments.

That the traditional logic of the syllogism can be done easily in the Acholi language is seen by noting the following. In the above examples, the three terms in each statement are clearly distinguishable (*dano, to, Awich*). The symbols of quality (*pe* (not)) and quantity (*ducu* (all); *mukene* (some)) are readily discernible. Absent, of course, is the copula. The job of the copula is to indicate the presence of subject-predicate relationships. This service does not, however, require the existence of another word.

Quantifiers

One of the functions of predicate logic is to lay bare the inner structure of propositions to enable logicians to discover whether arguments in which subject-predicate distinctions are necessary are valid or invalid. This is also true of traditional logic, which also is a predicate logic. In modern logic quantifiers ((x) and (Ex)), individual variables (x, y, z), and predicate letters (F, G, H) are used for that purpose. The quantificational sentence *Dano ducu to* (All men are mortal) contains a universal quantification. This may be written as follows: "For every x it holds that: If x is *dano* (man), then x *to* (is mortal)." The general form of such a statement is (x)(Fx → Gx), where F and G represent any properties. The existential quantifier (Ex) appears in *Lee mukene ger* (Some animals are fierce) and is paraphrased as: "There exists at least one x such that it has the property of being *lee* (animal) F and also being *ger* (fierce) G." This yields: (Ex)(Fx & Gx). Quantificational formulations are quite natural in Acholi.

Logical equivalents

The quantifiers (x) and (Ex) can be expressed in terms of each other as in the following, where G stands for the characteristic of being *ber* (good):

1   *Jami ducu beco* (Everything is good), (x)Gx, is equivalent to *Pe tye gin mo ma pe ber* (There is nothing that is not good), i.e. −(Ex)−Gx. In short, we have: (x)Gx ←→−(Ex)−Gx.
2   *Gin moni ber* (Something is good), (Ex)(Gx), can be put in another way: *Pe gin ducu beco* (Not everything is not good), −(x)−Gx. Briefly, (Ex)(Gx) ←→ −(x)−Gx.
3   *Pe gin ducu beco* (Not everything is good), −(x)(Gx), is another way of saying *Gin moni pe ber* (Something is not good), (Ex)−Gx. We then have: −(x)(Gx) ←→ (Ex)−Gx.
4   *Pe tye gin mo ma ber* (There is nothing good), −(Ex)(Gx). This is equivalent to *Gin ducu pe beco* (Everything is not good), (x)−Gx. In symbols: −(Ex)(Gx) ←→ (x)−Gx.

All these hold in virtue of the equivalence noted in (1). But they are spread out here to illustrate the ease with which the Acholi language accommodates quantifiers. Similarly, the logic of classes and relations presents no difficulties to Acholi, and we will here skip the details. In traditional Acholi discourse statements involving classes are often concerned with the world of living things, but that exercises no undue constraints on more generalized class reasoning. Again, in relational discourse, kinship relations are of special interest and deserve special study in their own right. But the symbolism and principles of the logic of relations fall into place without any unusual problems.

Conclusion

In surveying those principles of logic considered basic, it is clear that logic is not strange to the Acholi language. Where certain laws are not explicit in the language, they exist in it implicitly. In some cases, however, as illustrated by the problem of the excluded middle, Acholi would seem to suggest some departures from classical logic.

Any language, because of its unique position in the universe, deserves to be explored and investigated, as it is likely to contribute to knowledge and human development. Besides, no human activity is a finished product. There will always be room in it for further improvement. Any aspect of human life can be enhanced by re-examination and re-evaluation. This examination of logic in the Acholi language should, it is hoped, spur scholars on to do the same for other languages.

References

Anderson, A. R. and Belnap, N. D. (1973) *Entailment*, vol. 1 (Princeton: Princeton University Press).
Black, M. (1937) "Vagueness," *Philosophy of Science*, 4.
Crazzolara, J. P. (1938) A *Study of the Acholi Language* (London: Oxford University Press).
Gaines, B. (1976) "Foundations of Fuzzy Reasoning," *International Journal of Man-Machine Studies*, 8.
Haack, S. (1978) *Philosophy of Logics* (London: Cambridge University Press).
Kitching, A. L. (1932) An *Outline of the Acholi Language* (London: Sheldon Press).
Malandra, Alfred (1952) A *New Acholi Grammar* (Nairobi: Eagle Press).
Ocaya, Victor (1979) "Logic within the Acholi Language: Elementary Notions." MA dissertation, Makerere University, Uganda.
Ocaya, Victor (1988) "Ultimate Reality and Meaning According to the Acholi of Uganda," *Ultimate Reality and Meaning*, II(1), March: 11–22.
Ocaya, Victor (1989) "Logic and Culture with Particular Reference to the Acholi of Uganda: A Survey," *The South African Journal of Philosophy*, 8(2) (May): 88–93.
Quine, W. V. (1970) *Philosophy of Logic* (Englewood Cliffs, NJ: Prentice-Hall).
Russell, B. (1923) "Vagueness," *Australian Journal of Philosophy and Psychology*, 1.
Sainsbury, R. M. (1986) "Degrees of Belief and Degrees of Truth," *Philosophical Papers*, XV.
Savage, G. A. R. (1955) A *Short Acholi-English and English-Acholi Vocabulary* (Nairobi: Eagle Press).
Thouless, R. H. (1930) *Straight and Crooked Thinking* (London: Hodder and Stoughton; rev. edn. London: Pan Books, 1974).
Tucker, A. N. and Bryan, A. N. (1966) *Linguistic Analysis: The Non-Bantu Languages of North-Eastern Africa* (London: Oxford University Press).
Tucker, A. N. (1971) "Orthographic Systems and Conventions," in Thomas Sebeck (ed.), *Current Trends in Linguistics: Linguistics in Sub-Sahara Africa*, vol. 7 (The Hague/Paris: Mouton).
Uma, K. F. (1971) "Acholi-Arab-Nubian Relations in the Nineteenth Century." BA dissertation, MUK, Kampala.
Zadeh, L. A. (1972) "Fuzzy Languages and Their Relation to Human Intelligence," *Proceedings of the International Conference: Man and Computer* (S. Karger).

Further reading

Crazzolara, J. P. (1950–3) *The Lwo*, 3 vols. (Verona: Editrice).
Girling, F. K. (1960) *The Acholi of Uganda* (London: HMSO).
Ocitti, J. P. (1973) *African Indigenous Education as Practiced by the Acholi of Uganda* (Nairobi: EALB).
Okot p'Bitek (1971) *Religion of the Central Luo* (Nairobi: EALB).
Onyango-ku-Odongo and Webster, J. B. (1976) *The Central Luo During the Aconya* (Nairobi: EALB).
Wild, John Vernon (1954) *Early Travelers in Acholi* (Nairobi: EALB; London: Nelson).

294

Further reading (in the Acholi language)

Anywar, Reuben S. (1954) *Acoli ki Ker Megi* (Nairobi: Eagle Press).

Cave-Brown-Cave, P. (1949) "Carolok Acholi (Acholi Proverbs)," *Acholi Magazine*, II.

Latigo, Nekodemo (1949) "Mony Macon Ikom Rok Ma Gurumu Acholi," *Acholi Magazine*, III.

Ocitti, J. P. (1959) *Lacan Makwo Pe Kinyero* (Nairobi: EALB).

Ocitti, J. P. (1974) *Acam To-na* (Nairobi: EALB).

Okot, p'Bitek (1966) *Wer pa Lawino* (Nairobi: EALB).

Okot, p'Bitek (1953) *Lak Tar* (Nairobi: EALB).

Pellegrini, V. (1949) *Acoli Macon (Acholi History)* (Kitgum).

Wild, John Vernon (1946) *Wot Pa Ladit Baker in Lobo Acholi* (Nairobi: EALB).

21

Yoruba Moral Epistemology

BARRY HALLEN

The original impetus for the modest body of literature that is coming to be associated with the term "moral epistemology" arose from a research project in which I participated during the period 1973–85, when I was teaching philosophy in the Nigerian federal university system. In the mid-1970s there was really very little material to teach that had been published under the heading "African philosophy." What there was usually painted a portrait of the African intellect that made it out to be qualitatively distinct from its Western counterpart, at least where theoretical or abstract thought was concerned.

In the West such thought was said to be associated primarily with critical reasoning and empirical evidence, while in Africa's indigenous cultures such thought was said to be expressed primarily in and by myths, stories, proverbs, and rituals. Comparative studies of abstract thought in the two cultures appeared to suggest that there was little point in asking whether its African forms were "true" because, even if believed so by members of the relevant cultures, they were too obviously "fictions" and "exercises" invented to permit Africans at least to *feel* that they did understand and thereby could exercise some control over the forces underlying life's sometimes paradoxical events. As such, they were said to fulfill people's emotional needs as much as or more than pre-eminently intellectual ones (Beattie 1966).

The more troubling consequence of this assessment, of the dominance or predominance of emotional needs and feelings over abstract thinking in Africa, was how to relate or to reconcile it with an academic philosophy that was overwhelmingly rationalistic in orientation. Senghor's Negritude (Senghor 1970) proved to be, in the end, a less than successful attempt to do this because it more or less confirmed and reinforced the reason/emotion dichotomy between the West and Africa. Many African intellectuals protested that critical reasoning also had to play an essential role in African systems of thought and that, in any case, dividing the person up (purportedly on a "scientific" basis) between a rational self and an emotional self was an hypothesis of Western cultural orientation (Fanon 1967, 1978; Hallen 2000). Other African scholars suggested that lumping all of African "abstract" thought into a single category and then comparing it with the theories of so deliberately and painstakingly refined a subject as academic philosophy was not fair. Africa has its own folklore, folk thought, or folk philosophy (relatively popular beliefs, superstitions, etc.), as also is the case with the West. This distinction in the two cultures' respective modes of thought or beliefs had first to be made clear before a neutral basis for intercultural comparisons would be established. Otherwise elements of African folklore might end up being contrasted and compared (unfavorably, of course) with technical philosophical theories (Wiredu 1980).

In the latter half of the twentieth century the two most influential Western schools of philosophical thought proved to be analytic philosophy (Rorty 1967) and phenomenology-hermeneutics (Gadamer 1975). Since the latter derives from and is primarily associated with Continental European philosophers, it was not well represented in the Nigerian academic context. There, British analytic philosophy reigned supreme even if, as I have already mentioned, there was scant evidence within it of anything to do with Africa. Indeed, the disinterest in things African on the part of Western analytic philosophy was almost certainly a consequence of the fact that its practitioners passively (or perhaps impassively) had tacitly acquiesced in the portrait of Africa as a place where people did not assign a high priority to reason, to critical thinking, in formulating their views of the world.

Much of (Western) analytic philosophy is rightly identified with the analysis of language. This may involve the *clarification* of the *meaning(s)* of individual concepts that are of particular philosophical interest, such as "knowledge," "belief," "truth," and so forth. It may involve as well studying the kinds of *justification* given to prove, for example, that a certain piece of information is worthy of being described or classified *as* "knowledge," etc. One very remarkable oddity about the analytic tradition as practiced within the academy is that virtually the only language that it has been used to analyze is the English language. The most obvious explanation for this is that analytic philosophy is a product of English-language culture. But was this really sufficient to explain why its method and techniques had never been applied in even an experimental manner to any *non*-Western language? Was there not here also evidence, albeit implicit, of a tacit judgment on the part of the Western academy that such endeavors were likely not to be philosophically rewarding?

The point of the Hallen/Sodipo research project on African thought/philosophy became to apply the techniques of analytic philosophy, as adapted for use in a culture that was substantially oral in nature (Hallen 1998), to the language of the Yoruba of southwestern Nigeria. The Yoruba vocabulary or fields of discourse preselected as of particular interest were those relevant to three primary foci of academic philosophy: epistemology or the theory of knowledge, ethics and aesthetics, and the philosophy of the natural world. It is the exploration of the *interrelations* between elements of the Yoruba conceptual system relating to the first two of these special interests (epistemology and ethics) that has resulted in the publications associated with the term "moral epistemology" (Hallen and Sodipo 1997; Hallen 1998, 2000).[1]

In Western epistemological theory the most problematic and controversial subcategory of information is what has come to be known as propositional knowledge.[2] Generally, this is associated with information in written or oral propositional (sentential) form that is supposed to be knowledge and therefore true, but which the individual recipient is in no position to test or to verify. When one reflects upon what a member of Western society may "learn" in the course of a lifetime, it

297

becomes clear that most people's "knowledge" consists of information they will never ever be in a position to confirm in a firsthand or direct manner. What they "find out" from a history book, "see" via the evening news on television, or "confirm" about a natural law on the basis of one elementary experiment in a high school physics laboratory – all could be (and sometimes are!) subject to error, distortion, or outright fabrication.

Propositional knowledge is therefore generally characterized as *secondhand*, as information that cannot be tested or proven in a decisive manner by most people and therefore has to be *accepted as true* because it "agrees" with common sense or because it "corresponds" to or "coheres" with the very limited amount of information that people are able to test and confirm in a firsthand or direct manner. Exactly how this coherence or correspondence is to be defined and ascertained is still a subject of endless debate in (Western) epistemological theory. What is relevant to the present discussion is that this debate is evidence of the intellectual concern and discomfort – in academic parlance it becomes one of the "problems" of philosophy – on the part of (Western) philosophers about the weak evidential basis of so much of the information that people in that culture are conditioned to regard as knowledge, as true.

The distinction made in Yoruba-language culture between *imo* (putative "knowledge") and *igbagbo* (putative "belief") reflects a similar concern about the evidential status of firsthand versus secondhand information. Persons are said to *mo* (to "know") or to have *imo* ("knowledge") only of something they have witnessed in a firsthand or personal manner. The example most frequently cited by discussants, virtually as a paradigm, is visual perception of a scene or an event as it is taking place. *Imo* is said to apply to sensory perception generally, even if what may be experienced directly by touch is more limited than is the case with perception. *Imo* implies a good deal more than mere sensation, of course. Perception implies cognition as well, meaning that the persons concerned must comprehend *that* and *what* they are experiencing. The terms *"ooto"/"otito"* are associated with *"imo"* in certain respects that parallel the manner in which "true" and "truth" are paired with "know"/"knowledge" in the English language. In the English language "truth" is principally a property of propositional knowledge, of statements human beings make about things, while in Yoruba *ooto* may be a property of both *propositions* and *certain forms of experience*.

The noun *igbagbo* (and its verb form *gbagbo*) does in fact arise from the conflation of *gba* and *gbo*.[3] The two components are themselves verbs, the former conventionally translated into English as "received" or "agreed to," and the latter as "heard" or "understood." Yoruba linguistic conventions suggest that treating this complex term as a synthesis of the English language "understood" (in the sense of cognitive comprehension) and of "agreed to" (in the sense of affirming or accepting new information one comprehends as part of one's own store of secondhand information) is perhaps the best way to render its core meaning. *Igbagbo* encompasses what one is not able "to see" for oneself or to experience in a direct, firsthand manner. For the most part this involves things we are told about or informed of – this is the most conventional sense of "information" – by others.

What makes it different from the English language "believe"/"belief" is that *igbagbo* applies to *everything* that may be construed as *secondhand* information. This would apply to most of what in English-language culture is regarded as propositional knowledge: the things one is taught in the course of a formal education, what one learns from books, from other people, and, of particular interest in the special case of the Yoruba, from oral traditions. While English-language culture decrees that some propositional or secondhand information, since classified as "knowledge," should be accepted as *true*, Yoruba usage is equally insistent that, since classified as *igbagbo* (putative "belief"), it can only be accepted as a possible (*o seese*) truth.

The cross-cultural ramifications of these differing viewpoints on the truth status of propositional or secondhand knowledge are worth considering. Yoruba-language speakers would likely regard members of English-language culture, who are willing to assign so much certainty to and put so much trust in information that they can never test or verify, as dangerously naive and perhaps even ignorant; while members of English-language culture might criticize their Yoruba counterparts' identification of optimal knowledge with "you can only know what you can see" as indicative of a people who have yet to discover the benefits of institutionalized knowledge and formal education.

The criteria that define the respective extents of and the interrelations between *imo* and *igbagbo* stipulate that any experience or information, which is not firsthand, personal, and direct, must by definition fall under the heading of *igbagbo*. The sense of *igbagbo* may therefore be paraphrased as "comprehending, and deciding to accept as possible (as 'possibly true' rather than as 'true'), information that one receives in a secondhand manner." *Imo* (firsthand experience) and *igbagbo* (information gained on the basis of secondhand experience) together exhaust all of the information that human beings have at their disposal. If and when my *imo* is challenged by other persons who have not undergone a similar firsthand experience and who therefore doubt what I say I actually saw happen, the best way to convince them would be to arrange for some kind of test whereby they will be able to see the thing happen for themselves.[4] If I cannot arrange for this kind of direct testing, the next best I can do is to ask any others who may have personally witnessed my own or a similar experience to come forward and testify. In this case my firsthand experience cannot become the challengers' own (*imo*), but if they are influenced by the combined testimony they may decide to "believe" me and accept the information on a secondhand basis, as *igbagbo*.

A simple example may serve to clarify things. If I claim I have seen for myself (*imo*) that a certain friend drives a specific make and model of car and another friend challenges my claim, the best way to resolve the dispute is to visit the friend and see (*imo*) what kind of car she actually has. If the friend lives a thousand miles away, a more practical solution would be to ask other mutual friends who have seen (*imo*) the car themselves to tell us (*igbagbo*) what kind it is. Or perhaps to telephone my friend direct and ask her to tell us (*igbagbo*) what kind of car she is driving.[5]

If and when my *igbagbo* is challenged by another person, again the best solution would be to arrange some form of empirical test. In this case, since this is information I myself only know secondhand, the most reliable solution for all concerned would be to test it directly, so that the information would progress from being *igbagbo* to being *imo* for all concerned, myself included. Next best would again be to call upon all relevant witnesses who may have heard the same or similar secondhand information (*igbagbo*) or, even more definitively, have firsthand (*imo*) experience of what I can only claim to know on a secondhand (*igbagbo*) basis.

When agreement or a consensus among disputants is reached on the level of *igbagbo*, the applicable term (comparable to the role of "truth" with reference to knowledge, or of "*ooto*" with regards to *imo*) is *papo*, which may be rendered colloquially as "the words have come together."[6] The antecedent process of testimony, discussion, and reflection on the basis of which the consensus is reached is described as *nwadi* – an expression whose meaning may be compared to the English-language "let's get to the bottom of this matter."[7]

A suitably modified version of our simple example may also be helpful here. Although I myself have not seen it, I have heard (*igbagbo*) that a friend drives a specific make and model of car. If another friend disputes my *igbagbo*, the best way to resolve the dispute would be for both of us to go there and see for ourselves (*imo*) what kind of a car the friend actually drives. If the friend lives a thousand miles away, a more practical solution would be for us to ask other mutual friends to tell us (*igbagbo* + *nwadi*) what kind of car they have seen (*imo*) or heard (*igbagbo*) that she drives. Or perhaps to telephone the friend direct and ask her to tell us (*igbagbo*) what kind of car she is driving.

The system that emerges from these criteria appears to be three-tiered. *Imo* is the sole category of experience or of propositions entitled to be regarded as certain and as true (*ooto*). *Igbagbo* that is in principle open to empirical testing, verification, and thereby transformation into *imo* (*ooto*) is the next best. *Igbagbo* that can never be verified and can only be evaluated on the basis of testimony, explanation, discussion, and reflection (*nwadi*) is the least certain.

The significance of all this for cross-cultural understanding and comparisons is complex. The most obvious and perhaps important point is that Yoruba discourse does employ terminology and systematic criteria for the evaluation of any type of information. This is a priority to which African systems of thought were once said not to attach special importance. Their most important knowledge was said to be preserved in the form of oral tradition, which could encompass anything from medicinal recipes to children's stories. The bias against tradition has always been epistemological – its questionable reliability as a source of and justification for knowledge. What was said to be distinctive about African oral traditions was the relatively uncritical manner in which they were inherited from the past, preserved in the present, and passed on to future generations. So regarded, traditions resembled "rules" governing the "game of life" that determined in a relatively absolute manner what Africans believed and how they behaved, and which they therefore had no intellectual incentive to articulate, explain, or challenge.

One problem for this (admittedly simplified) portrait of the African intellectual attitude toward tradition is that it is contradicted by the manner in which the Yoruba employ *mo* and *gbagbo* in discourse. If my grandfather tells me that he knows the recipe for a potent headache medicine (that he in turn learned from his grandfather), and teaches it to me – this exchange of information would still be on the level of *igbagbo*, of secondhand information. I could not be said to have *imo* of this medicine as medicine until I myself had prepared it, administered it to someone, and witnessed its curative powers.

The same would hold for other traditions inherited from the past. Whether a military strategy or an agricultural technique, a tradition only deserves to remain as a tradition if it proves effective, if it does what it is supposed to do. Until this has been proven in a direct and personal manner, its empirical status can be no more than hypothetical, something that may *possibly* be true (or false) and therefore must be classed as *igbagbo*.[8]

The moral underpinnings to this discussion of Yoruba epistemology become evident once one recognizes that the primary source of propositional or *secondhand* information in an oral culture is other persons. For, if that is the case, knowledge of those other persons' moral characters (*iwa*) – their honesty, their reliability as sources of information – becomes a fundamental criterion to evaluating the reliability of secondhand information obtained from them.

Knowledge of another person's moral character is said to be obtained, most reliably, from observing (firsthand) their behavior (*isesi*). And in Yoruba discourse behavior conventionally extends to "what they say" and "what they do," which also pretty much corresponds to the standard Western notions of verbal and non-verbal behavior. But what is again in evidence here is the priority the Yoruba place upon hard evidence, upon only being able to "know" what you witness in a first-hand manner. For the point is that a person's verbal and non-verbal behavior are construed as firsthand evidence (*imo*) of their moral character (*iwa*).

Needless to say, a person's moral character (*iwa*) is not as readily observable as everyday material objects, such as a tree or a table. Obviously a process of inference is involved in order to move from observing a multiplicity of individual actions to a generalization about character. But with specific reference to epistemological concerns – the person as a source of reliable secondhand information – the interplay between knowledge (*imo*) and belief (*igbagbo*) appears to be as follows. On the basis of a number of specific previous occasions when you have had the opportunity, firsthand (*imo*), to verify the truth (*ooto*) of a person's statements, you are justified in using these firsthand experiences as the basis for a generalization about their moral character. This generalization may then serve as a kind of character reference for evaluating the reliability of future statements made by this same person but, strictly speaking, such evaluations must remain hypothetical or tentative until also confirmed in a firsthand manner.

What the overall process appears to involve is a kind of sliding scale for gauging varying degrees of epistemic certainty about the moral characters of and/or information provided by other persons. Those you have associated with directly and therefore have had ample opportunity to observe in a firsthand manner are those whose character you are in a position to know best. You are thereby in a position to judge whether information of which they are the source is likely to be reliable or unreliable. Those you have not associated with at all and therefore have had no opportunity to observe in a firsthand or even a secondhand manner are those whose character you do not know. Consequently, you have no substantive basis on which to judge whether information of which they are the source is likely to be reliable or unreliable.

A person who makes an informative statement may be obliged to recount the precise circumstances in which he or she came by it. A person is expected to say whether there is any cause for uncertainty or imprecision about the information. Determining whether the information is derived from the speaker's firsthand (*imo*) or secondhand (*igbagbo*) experience is part of this process. A person's diligence in doing all of this also is considered important evidence of their moral character (*iwa*). With specific reference to moral epistemology, at least four positive behavioral values are emphasized: (1) being scrupulous about the epistemological basis for whatever one claims to know, to believe, or to have no information about; (2) being a good listener, with the emphasis upon cognitive understanding rather than a polite and respectful demeanor; (3) being a good speaker, with the emphasis upon speaking in a positive, thoughtful, and perceptive manner rather than merely having beautiful elocution; (4) having patience, with the emphasis upon being calm and self-controlled in judgment and intellect rather than merely in manner and demeanor.

The public in Western societies have become concerned about exercising control over the quality of information put out by the media. In an oral culture the media are people's mouths. These four values, in effect, set broadcasting standards for those mouths. "Speaking well" and "hearing well," as values, further reinforce the importance of providing accurate information or reliable advice and being forthright about the epistemological origins of that information and advice. A consciousness that cultivates "patience," especially in difficult or problematic situations, is more likely to maintain self-control and thereby optimal communication with its environment. "Speaking well," "hearing well," and "patience" are not, then, *moral* values in any conventional sense. They are rather *epistemological virtues* because of their *instrumental* value for promoting the accuracy of information.

Notes

I wish to dedicate this essay to my colleague, co-author, and friend, the late J. Olubi Sodipo. Olubi Sodipo passed away in December 1999 in Nigeria. Friends of African philosophy will remember him for his multiple, major accomplishments: first Nigerian Professor of Philosophy; founder and Chair of one of Africa's most academically and intellectually influential Departments of Philosophy at the University of Ife (now Obafemi Awolowo University); founding editor of *Second Order*, for some time Africa's most noteworthy journal of philosophy; founding Vice-Chancellor of the Ogun State University; multiple-term President of the Nigerian Philosophical Association; life patron of the Nigerian National Association of Philosophy Students; co-author of *Knowledge, Belief, and Witchcraft: Analytic Experiments in African Philosophy* (Stanford University Press, 1997).

1   I most explicitly acknowledge my gratitude to Kwasi Wiredu for coming up with this apropos phrasing.
2   For example most of the "Introduction" to Moser and Nat 1995 is devoted to the issue of propositional knowledge.
3   The *Dictionary of Modern Yoruba* compiled by Abraham (1958) usually serves as the standard reference for Yoruba-English translations of this variety. Abraham treats *ooto* as a straightforward equivalent of the English-language "truth," and the same is the case with *igbagbo/gbagbo* (p. 233) and the English-language "belief"/"believe." Both are

302

examples of the understandably "loose" translation equivalences that are a necessary evil for the conventional, cross-cultural translation of everyday affairs, and which cannot afford to take account of all semantic differences, even if they happen to be more than nuances.

4   One expression used regularly for testing was *danwo* ("try to do").

5   Speaking to her directly by telephone still would not be *imo* about the car because one is not actually seeing it. One is only hearing a voice, another form of testimony, albeit a particularly relevant one given the circumstances.

6   Since it may now be said that the various disputants are reconciled.

7   According to Abraham, *nwadi* is a participial conflation of the verb for "looking" or "seeking" with the noun *idi* (1958: 272) for "bottom," "base," "reason," or "cause." See also Hallen and Sodipo 1997: 70.

8   This is also indicated by the various rhetorical idioms used in Yoruba discourse when reference is being made to traditions. See Hallen and Sodipo 1997: 67–8, and 67 nn. 14–16. The active rather than passive relationship that holds between the Yoruba and their traditions has been similarly documented with reference to the oral literature. See Barber 1991 and Yai 1991.

References

Abraham, R. C. (ed.) (1958) *Dictionary of Modern Yoruba* (London: University of London).

Barber, Karin (1991) *I Could Speak Until Tomorrow* (Washington, DC: Smithsonian Institution Press).

Beattie, John (1966) *Other Cultures: Aims, Methods and Achievements in Social Anthropology* (London: Routledge and Kegan Paul Ltd.).

Fanon, Frantz (1967) *Black Skin, White Masks* (New York: Grove Press).

Fanon, Frantz (1978) *The Wretched of the Earth* (London: Penguin Books).

Gadamer, Hans-Georg (1975) *Truth and Method*, trans. W. Glen-Doepel (London: Sheed and Ward).

Hallen, Barry (1998) "Moral Epistemology – When Propositions Come Out of Mouths," *International Philosophical Quarterly*, XXXVIII/2 (Issue No. 150; June): 187–204.

Hallen, Barry (2000) *The Good, the Bad, and the Beautiful: Discourse About Values in an African Culture* (Bloomington and Indianapolis: Indiana University Press).

Hallen, Barry and Sodipo, J. Olubi (1997) *Knowledge, Belief, and Witchcraft: Analytic Experiments in African Philosophy* (Stanford: Stanford University Press).

Moser, P. and Nat, A. van der (1995) *Human Knowledge: Classical and Contemporary Approaches*, 2nd edn. (Oxford: Oxford University Press).

Rorty, Richard (1967) *The Linguistic Turn* (Chicago and London: University of Chicago Press; reissued in 1992 with two retrospective essays).

Senghor, Leopold (1970) "Negritude: A Humanism of the Twentieth Century," in W. Cartey and M. Kilson (eds.), *The African Reader: Independent Africa* (New York: Random House).

Wiredu, Kwasi (1980) *Philosophy and an African Culture* (Cambridge: Cambridge University Press).

Yai, Olabiyi (1991) "In Praise of Metonymy: The Concepts of 'Tradition' and 'Creativity' in the Transmission of Yoruba Artistry over Time and Space," in R. Abiodun, H. Drewal, and J. Pemberton (eds.), *The Yoruba Artist: New Theoretical Perspectives on African Arts* (Washington, DC: Smithsonian Institution Press), pp. 107–15.

22

Ifá: An Account of a Divination System and Some Concluding Epistemological Questions

OLÚFÉMI TÁÍWÒ

Ifá Defined

What is *Ifá*? It is usual to think of *Ifá* simply as a Yoruba system of divination. In fact, however, it is also a form of worship undertaken by *Ifá* devotees as well as a compendium of performances including praise singing, engaged in by *babaláwo*. Although all these are integrated, in this discussion I propose to focus on its divinatory dimensions. I do this without wishing to minimize the complexity of *Ifá*.

I propose therefore to proceed according to the following plan. First, I describe what divination in *Ifá* entails, how it is done, what types there are, and what goals it sets out to achieve. Second, I shall point out the many ways in which *Ifá* intersects everyday life, the circumstances under which divination is performed or sought, and the expectations of all parties in the process. I shall then proceed to identify various philosophical issues arising from the many ideas, practices, orientations, injunctions, and so on, germane to *Ifá* divination. The ultimate aim is to provide some way of grasping the philosophy of *Ifá* and the philosophical puzzles that it elicits.

Ifá Divination

According to Wande Abimbola,

> *Ifá* is a special divinity among the Yoruba. The Yoruba believe that it was Olódùmarè who sent *Ifá* forth from the heavens and who charged him to use his wisdom to repair the world. The wisdom, knowledge, and luminosity with which Olódùmarè endowed *Ifá* account for *Ifá*'s preeminence among divinities in Yoruba land. "The-young-but-immensely-wise one" is *Ifá*'s cognomen. (1983: 6; my translation)

William Bascom described it thus:

> *Ifá* is a system of divination based on 16 basic and 256 derivative figures (*odù*) obtained either by the manipulation of 16 palm nuts (*ikin*) or by the toss of a chain (*òpèlè*) of 8 half seed shells. The worship of *Ifá* as the God of divination entails ceremonies, sacri-

fices, tabus, paraphernalia, drums, songs, praises, initiation, and other ritual elements comparable to those of other Yoruba cults; these are not treated fully here, since the primary subject of this study is *Ifá* as a system of divination. (1991: 3)

I have cited the above passages because they come from two of the pre-eminent scholars of *Ifá*. Each one of them proceeds to describe the mechanics of divination. Only Bascom offers a serious analysis of the deeper theoretical issues raised by *Ifá* including those of its professional ethics, its predictions, the system of belief that underpins it, and its multifarious epistemic checks on the truth that it avails (ibid. chs. 5–9, 11). But, as definitions go, the citations from Abimbola and Bascom do not help us much. Let us see why.

In Abimbola's account, he identifies *Ifá* as, among other things, one of the most important of Yoruba gods, one sent by Olódùmarè, the supreme God, from on High, charged with the responsibility of using his God-given incomparable wisdom and capacity for omniscience to order the world aright, and to ensure that both it and its inhabitants do not spin out of their proper orbit. Hence, *Ifá*'s nickname, "*A-kéré-finú-sogbón*," which is an allusion to the fact that *Ifá* is reputed to be among the youngest gods, yet *Ifá* is endowed with unsurpassable knowledge. It would appear that Bascom takes a different, apparently non-religious turn in his characterization of *Ifá* when he describes it as a system of divination. But he goes on to identify *Ifá* as "the God of divination" and talks about the worship of *Ifá*. He does insist, however, that his focus is on *Ifá* as a system of divination. So does Abimbola in other areas of his work. We propose to do the same here. Nevertheless, the identification of *Ifá* as a god does hold some implications for *Ifá* as a system of divination. Let us go back for a moment to Abimbola's description.

Ifá is omniscient; it is a repository of unsurpassable knowledge and wisdom. This means that *Ifá* transcends the limits of human cognitive capacities, has the capacity to know from several perspectives at the same time, and is not bound by the time–space constraints of human knowing. Now, if one proceeds from the religious stand-point and identifies *Ifá* as a god, the capacity that we have just mentioned follows as a matter of course. While this may offer an easy way out of the perennial problems of epistemology, it limits the appeal of *Ifá* to only those who are religiously inclined. Even a slight familiarity with *Ifá* in its many aspects will show that its religious dimension is only one among several other characteristics. More importantly, the *babaláwo*, the *Ifá* diviner or priest, does not ask the client to affirm a faith in *Ifá* before, during, or after consultation, and the capacity of *Ifá* to know a client's fate is not affected by the non-membership of a supplicant in the *Ifá* tradition.[1] Additionally, the religious dimension of *Ifá* is separate and separable from its various forms of divination. The problem is that, all too often, ritual is assimilated to religion and the rituals involved in different forms of divination are mistaken for religious observances. That need not be so.[2] I suggest therefore that, regardless of one's stand on the matter of whether or not *Ifá* is a religion, one can analyze it purely as a system of divination and seek to lay bare its presuppositions, its criteria of correctness and adequacy, and its philosophical assumptions. We shall now proceed to this task.

When people consult *Ifá*, they do so because they are convinced that *Ifá* has answers and that knowing those answers will enable them to solve, or at least make sense of, the problem or the circumstances that have led them to the *babalá-wo's* door. We need not go into the grounds of this belief or how good they are. It is sufficient for our purposes to affirm that such is the minimum requirement for anyone to go to *Ifá*.

So far we have talked of two parties in divination: *Ifá* and the supplicant. *Ifá* does not "speak" directly to the supplicant; hence the *babaláwo* must be interposed between the two. This is the classic or standard structure of *Ifá dídá* (casting *Ifá*). We shall call this *Ifá eni*, literally, divining for a specific individual. On occasion, we have *Ifá egbé* (society or club), *ògbà* (age grade), or *ilú* (town, nation, country), where the client is not an individual person but some group or another. On still other occasions the supplicant may be an individual who comes before *Ifá* not in his or her personal capacity but as the holder of an office. We call this last instance *Ifá ipò* (divining for an office or its holder). In this discussion we shall concentrate on the first type of *Ifá* supplication.

What circumstances usually warrant consultation with *babaláwo?* It used to be the case that when children were born Yoruba parents would go to the *babaláwo* to have *Ifá* tell them the newborn's *àkosèjayé*, that is, what the child's path through life might be. Individual adults consult *Ifá* on diverse occasions. When an individual is about to embark on a new venture, he or she would want to know whether or not the proposed venture will be profitable.[3] The new venture may be starting a business, going on a journey, changing occupations, constructing a house, getting married, and so on. Furthermore, an individual might consult *Ifá* in times of illness, especially when other diagnoses and reputable treatments have failed. These are all instances of *Ifá eni*.

Ifá is also consulted when things are not going the way they are supposed to for individuals, groups, or the society as a whole. The same is true of when the normal order of life is upset. For example, if there is a rash of deaths of young people,[4] or when the harvest is not bounteous or the community is afflicted with a run of natural disasters such as flood or drought. It should be noted, however, that it is only when events are inexplicable by the normal explanatory stratagems available that *Ifá* is summoned to avail people of the abstruse wisdom that they ascribe to it. This caution is inspired by veneration for *Ifá*. These are instances of *Ifá egbé*, or *ilú*.

Ifá is, in light of the preceding discussion, regarded as a compendium of knowledge and wisdom. It bespeaks a sophisticated society in which people, ordinary folk and experts alike, are agitated by questions of causality, proof, consistency, clarity, efficacy, correctness, and the like. Add to this the human need to know, to anticipate the imponderables of human existence in an often hostile and inscrutable world, and we can better appreciate the premium that is placed on *Ifá* as an "omniscient intelligence" (Makinde 1988: 5–10).

The Process of Divination

One of the crucial elements of the process of *Ifá eni* (individualized supplication) is that the *Ifá* in that case must be made specific to that particular individual who seeks *Ifá's* wisdom. One cannot overemphasize the importance of this factor in the cogency and accuracy of the outcome of any particular consultation. To make this point more clear, we need a description of the process of divination. This is how Wande Abimbola describes the process:

> When the client enters the house of the *Ifá* priest, he salutes him and expresses a wish to "talk with the divinity." The *Ifá* priest then takes out his divining chain and lays it on a mat or a raffia tray in front of the client. The client whispers his problem to a coin or a cowry shell and drops it on the *Ifá* instruments. Alternatively, the client could pick up the divining chain or the *ibò* and whisper his problem to it directly. In either case, it is believed that the wishes of the client's *orí* (God of predestination who knows what is good for every person) have been communicated to *Ifá* who will then produce the appropriate answer through the first *Odù* which the *Ifá* priest will cast when he manipulates his divining chain. (1977: 9)

Let us now discuss the various elements in the consultation situation. In the first place, the client does not talk with the *babaláwo*; she expresses a wish to "talk with the divinity." This is a critical element in *Ifá*'s epistemology. In not talking directly with the *babaláwo*, the client underscores the intermediary role of the *babaláwo* and the process simultaneously denies the *babaláwo* any ambition to play god or play seer. The insight that is sought is *Ifá*'s, not the *babaláwo*'s. The client whispers her problem to a coin or a cowry shell that is then dropped on the instruments of *Ifá*. In so doing, two ends are served. First, a physical connection is established between the client and *Ifá* as symbolized by the instruments. Secondly, given that the client's "scent" is on the coin or cowry shell that she whispered her problem on, *Ifá* is *by that token* personalized for her. That is, *Ifá* does not have to decide *whose* destiny is to be figured out. It is as if some aura of the client's is imparted to the shell or coin such that *Ifá* will know that the *orí* whose preferences are to be divined is *this*, the client's *orí* and not just any *orí*. This is significant because it is part of the received wisdom about Yoruba and, nay, all African societies that they are so collectivistic or communalistic that some might think that they hardly, if ever, have room for individuals. But here, in what is supposed to be the ultimate symbol of Yoruba genius, we are in a process that must be made specific, tailored to a named individual whose *orí*'s wish is to be deciphered by *Ifá*, the "omniscient intelligence."

Secondly, the process is interactive in ways that are significant for the kinds of knowledge produced in *Ifá*. After the initial steps we have described, the *babaláwo* "throws the divining chain in front of himself and quickly reads and pronounces the name of the *Odù* whose signature he has seen. The answer to the client's problem will be found only in this *Odù*" (ibid. 9–10). *Ifá* has 256 *Odù* which derive from 16 basic or original *Odù*. Each of the *Odù*, loosely identified variously as "verses of *Ifá* divination poetry" or "categories of *Ifá* divination," has a signature which is determined by the pattern that emerges from the throwing of the divining medium – chain, palm nuts, kola nuts, etc. The 16 original *Odù* and their patterns are as shown in table 1.

We need not go into the details of how the *babaláwo* identifies the *Odù* that emerges from the different sequences of throwing or manipulating the divination instrument. But once an *Odù* appears:

307

Table 1 The original *Odù* and their patterns[5]

I	II	II	I	I	II
I	II	I	II	I	II
I	II	I	II	II	I
I	II	II	I	II	I
(1) *Ogbè*	(2) *Òyèkú*	(3) *Ìwòrì*	(4) *Òdí*	(5) *Ìrosùn*	(6) *Òwónrín*

I	II	I	II	II	II
II	II	I	I	I	II
II	II	I	I	II	I
II	I	II	I	II	II
(7) *Òbàrà*	(8) *Òkànràn*	(9) *Ògúndá*	(10) *Òsá*	(11) *Ìká*	(12) *Òtúúrúpòn*

I	I	I	II
II	I	II	I
I	II	I	II
I	I	II	I
(13) *Òtúá*	(14) *Ìretè*	(15) *Òsé*	(16) *Òfún*

Source: Abimbola 1977: 16

[the *babaláwo*] then begins to chant verses from the *Odù* which he has seen while the client watches and listens. The priest chants as many poems as he knows from that *Odù* until he chants a poem which tells a story containing a problem similar to the client's own problem. At that stage, the client stops him and asks for further explanation of that particular poem. The *Ifá* priest will interpret that particular poem and mention the sacrifice which the client must perform. (ibid. 9–10)

This is another interactive element in *Ifá dídá*. Because each *Odù* has 600 *ese* (roughly: verses), the process of chanting the *ese* of a single *Odù* can take several days. However, in spite of this time-consuming dimension, the *babaláwo* may not stop, save for fatigue, to tell the client that he, the *babaláwo*, has decided that a particular *Odù* is the appropriate one for the client's problem. On the contrary, the client is the *only* person in this instance of *Ifá eni* who may stop the *babaláwo*, ask him to explain some *ese* or another, seek clarification, and then *decide* that the problem spoken of in the text is the same as or akin to her problem. This is a very important requirement that bears significantly on the veracity of *Ifá*'s prediction and prevents the *babaláwo* from insinuating himself in an inappropriate way into the talk between the client and the divinity. In this way, it takes *Ifá* out of the orbit of fortune-telling. It requires the client to be an active participant in the process of finding an efficacious remedy for whatever problem has led her to *Ifá*'s door. It is a corollary that only an individual who is capable of exercising agency can participate in this instance of *Ifá dídá*.[6]

But it is not the case that the client merely chooses the verses most directly related to his own problem. After all, as we have pointed out, the stories told in the *Odù* originally concerned other persons who lived in times and places vastly different, and very distant, from that of the client who has come to *Ifá* on this particular occasion. Additionally, given the multiplicity and variety of clients who might at different times recognize themselves in the same *Odù*, it must be that the client is not a mere recipient of *Ifá*'s message coming through the *Odù*. He or she must also assume the role of a decoder, an interpreter, who is capable of mapping *Ifá*'s often cryptic message onto his or her own life's grid.

The interactive aspect of *Ifá dídá* raises many questions of profound significance for epistemological analyses. One question pertains to the hermeneutics of *Ifá*, given that, as we have seen, *Ifá* does not speak directly to the client. In fact, *Ifá*'s message is doubly indirect: first, the *babaláwo* must correctly identify the *Odù* whose signature results from his casting his divining instruments and proceed to chant the *ese* in which the *Odù* is represented. Many things could go wrong at this stage. The *babaláwo* must be a master of the language of the original. He must possess a superb memory from which the *ese* are chanted.

Ifá's message is indirect in a second manner. The client, too, must be able correctly to identify a particular *Odù* and the pertinent *ese* as containing *her* story. As in the *babaláwo*'s case, language and its mastery are of the essence here too. In exactly the same way that the *babaláwo* should refrain from rushing the client to make a choice prematurely, the client must know better than to find her story in every *ese*. That is, she must be careful in her interpretation, meticulous in her mapping of the stories of *Ifá*'s mythological characters onto her own life's grid. Furthermore, we must not discount the possibility of mischief on the part of the client deliberately to "mislead" *Ifá* or frustrate the *babaláwo* by choosing a story that is clearly at variance with the problem that has led her to *Ifá*.

Given the possibility of mischief, fraud, and sheer incompetence on the part of *babaláwo* and client alike, it is right to ask whether there are corrective mechanisms within *Ifá* with which *Ifá* handles these contingencies and preserves its integrity as a cognitive system. There are at least two such mechanisms. The first is integral to *Ifá dídá*; the second is the phenomenon that is supposed to complete the dialectic of *Ifá dídá* and, therefore, plays an *ex post facto* role as an epistemic check on the entire process. We examine them *seriatim*.

One of the instruments for *Ifá dídá* is the *ibò*, which consists of "a pair of cowry shells tied together and a piece of bone. The cowry shells stand for an affirmative reply while the bone stands for a negative reply [from *Ifá*] in respect of every question posed" (ibid. 7). The *ibò* represents an epistemic check on the initial identification of an *Odù* made by the *babaláwo* and on the initial identification of the same *Odù* by the client as reflective of his story or his problems. When an affirmative answer is obtained after several other possible subjects of the *Odù*'s narrative have been eliminated, that is taken to be a sign that there indeed is a match between the *Odù* and the client, a convergence between the *babaláwo*'s identification and the client's appropriation of *Ifá*'s story as her own.

At this stage, the second corrective or corroborative mechanism becomes operative. After the necessary determinations have been made, the client is called upon to offer a sacrifice, *ebo*, to the god *Òrúnmìlà* or whatever other deity is found to be in need of propitiation if the client's problems are to be solved. The belief is that if the client offers *ebo* as the mythological characters in the *Odù* did in the past, his efforts will be attended with success and the problems that have brought him to *Ifá* will be solved. If, after the sacrifice is offered, the client's fortunes change for the better, that is taken to be the ultimate confirmation of the prediction that emerged from the specific instance of *Ifá dídá*. Although it is possible for alternative explanations to be offered for this turn of events, given the processes we described above, a successful outcome is taken as evidence of the "omniscient intelligence" ascribed to *Ifá*. It would be used counterfactually to explain the change in the client's fortunes. It would be said that had the client not consulted *Ifá* and done what *Ifá* enjoined in the process of *Ifá dídá*, his circumstances would not have altered.

If, on the other hand, after he had followed *Ifá*'s direction and done the sacrifice prescribed therein, there was no improvement in his situation, that would not ordinarily be taken as evidence of *Ifá*'s misdirection. On the contrary, that will be an occasion to review the process of *Ifá dídá*. Did the *babaláwo* read the signature correctly – i.e. did he correctly identify the *Odù* that appeared? Did he chant the appropriate *ese* so that any mistake might be attributed to the client's inability, due to a character flaw or inattention, to identify the appropriate story as hers? Did the client lie to *Ifá* in disclosing the contents of her hand when the *ibò* was administered? Did the client misconstrue a metaphor in the narrative? Did she misunderstand a phrase? However the miscarriage may have occurred, the failure of sacrifice unhinges the dialectic of *Ifá dídá* and sends *babaláwo* and client alike back to *Ifá*'s drawing board as long as the client remains desirous of solving the problem that triggered off the initial consultation with *Ifá*.

Now, epistemologically, some might object that protecting *Ifá* itself from doubt approaches the dimensions of unreasoned faith. That is, *Ifá* is protected from questioning, much less of falsification. This objection has less force than at first appears. As Thomas Kuhn (1962) has shown, even in Euro-American science, where Karl Popper mistakenly suggested that scientists abandon "falsified theories," the truth is that it takes a considerable time before scientists give up on theories that have been found to be productive of adequate explanations in at least some situations. In the interim, they go to great lengths to explain away counter-instances or to construct subsidiary explanations for such anomalies as may arise. But they never doubt that science has within itself the resources with which to correct anomalies. So it is with *Ifá*. William Bascom points out that, "as in the case of a doctor whose patient dies, a number of explanations are possible, and while the doctor's skill or knowledge may be questioned, the system of medicine itself is not" (1991: 70).

At least three other epistemological issues arise. There is no doubt that analogical reasoning plays a large part in the "divination" system. The principle is obviously that what has worked for past clients will work for current ones in similar situations. The question is: did the original diagnoses and prescriptions depend similarly on empirical reasoning? The idea, implicit in the above account, that *Ifá* divination rests on the cognitive resources of an omniscient entity, namely, *Ifá*, suggests that the knowledge generated by the system itself does not depend on empirical inference alone. The second epistemological issue, then, concerns the clarification and justification of this attribution of omniscience or at any rate of unsurpassed knowledge to *Ifá*. Interestingly, since, in any supplication, the solution is partly, at least, elicited by an act of inference and interpretation on the part of the fallible supplicant, the role of empirical thought remains, to all practical intents and purposes, highly significant.

We need to account for the many ways in which divergences might emerge in the divination process from the fallibility not just of the supplicant but also of the *babaláwo*. Most difficult, perhaps, is the epistemological problem of how chance and probability, on the one hand, and any supposed extra-empirical cognitive mechanisms, on the other, play out in the manipulation of the divination instruments (as shown in table 1). These philosophical issues obviously should challenge the most sustained examination. One hopes that time and scholars will oblige.[7]

Notes

1 This characteristic may help explain *Ifá*'s portability and its capacity for syncretism, especially in the Americas.
2 For a similar distinction between the religious worship of *Òrúnmìlà* and *Ifá* divination, see Idowu 1994: 77.
3 I cannot go into the metaphysics of the self on which this quest is founded in Yoruba philosophy in this chapter. For discussions, see Makinde 1985; Gbadegesin 1991; Hallen 1989; Abimbola 1973.
4 Instances of bad death in Yoruba metaphysics.
5 The binary logic exhibited by the signature of the different *Odù* has elicited an attempt by Olu Longe (1983) to explore the parallels between *Ifá* divination and computer science. I would like to thank Dapo Olorunyomi for bringing this reference to my notice and making it available to me.
6 Other conditions seem to be necessary in this respect. It is difficult to imagine one who is not proficient in the original language in which the *Odù* are articulated being able to exercise the requisite agency. Nor can this be done from a distance.
7 I would like to express my gratitude to Kolapo Abimbola who pointed out some crucial errors to me and whose spirited divergences from my positions require more than I can accommodate in this short piece. My thanks also go to the editor of this volume, Professor Kwasi Wiredu, for some significant editorial suggestions.

References

Abimbola, Wande (1973) "The Yoruba Concept of Human Personality," *Bulletin du Centre National de la Recherche Scientifique*, 544.

Abimbola, Wande (1977) *Ifá Divination Poetry* (New York: Nok Publishers).

Abimbola, Wande (1983) *Ìjìnlè Ohùn Enu Ifá, Apá Kíìní*, 2nd edn. (Oyo: AIM Press).

Bascom, William (1991) *Ifá Divination: Communication Between Gods and Men in West Africa* (Bloomington: Indiana University Press).

Gbadegesin, Segun (1991) *African Philosophy: Traditional Yorùbá Philosophy and Contemporary African Realities* (New York: Peter Lang).

Hallen, Barry (1989) "'Èniyàn': A Critical Analysis of the Yoruba Concepts of Person," in C. S. Momoh (ed.), *The Substance of African Philosophy* (Auchi: African Philosophy Projects).

Idowu, E. Bolaji (1994) *Olódùmarè: God in Yorùbá Belief* (New York: Wazobia; reprint of original 1962 edn.).

Kuhn, Thomas S. (1962) *The Structure of Scientific Revolutions* (Chicago: University of Chicago Press).

Longe, Olu (1983) "Ifa Divination and Computer Science." Inaugural Lecture (Ibadan: University of Ibadan).

Makinde, Moses (1985) "*Orí*: A Philosophical Analysis of the Yoruba Concepts of *Orí* and Human Destiny," *International Studies in Philosophy*, 12(1).

Makinde, Moses (1988) *African Philosophy, Culture, and Traditional Medicine* (Athens: Ohio University Center for International Studies).

23

Toward a Theory of Destiny

SEGUN GBADEGESIN

Introduction

In earlier works (1984, 1987, and 1991), I grappled with the concept of destiny as it features in Yoruba philosophical discourse. In this chapter, I will pursue the discussion a little further.

The Odu Corpus and Two Stories

In the Odu Corpus, the collection of verses constituting the basis of the Yoruba divination system, there are at least two references to the concept of destiny as it features in traditional Yoruba philosophy. In *Ogbegunda*, is told the story of how *ori* (the bearer of a person's destiny) is prenatally chosen in *orun* (heaven), and how, once chosen, it is irrevocable. It is the story of three friends – Oriseeku (the son of Ogun), Orileemere (the son of Ija), and Afuwape (the son of Orunmila). Obatala had finished molding their physical bodies, and they were ready to go to the house of Ajala, the heavenly potter of *ori*, to choose their *ori*. The three friends were warned by their friends to go directly to the house of Ajala, and not to break their journey for any reason. While the other two friends took this advice seriously, and went straight to the house of Ajala, the third, Afuwape, decided to first see his father before going to choose his *ori*. Oriseeku and Orileemere got to the house of Ajala first and picked the *ori* of their choice, and proceeded straight to the earth. Afuwape got to his father and met with a group of divination priests, divining for his father. These diviners advised Afuwape to perform a sacrifice so that he may choose a good *ori*. He did, and proceeded to the house of Ajala. Though he met some obstacles on the way, he overcame them all, apparently due to the sacrifice he had performed. He chose a good *ori*, with the help of Ajala, and he was able to succeed in life. His two friends, Oriseeku and Orileemere, did not make a good choice and were never successful in life. Each got stuck with his choice until the end of his life.

The second reference is in *Ogunda Meji*, an *Odu*, that is a unit of verses in the Ifa Corpus, which emphasizes the importance of *ori* to a person. In the story, each of the gods (major and minor) is asked if he or she is willing to follow his or her devotee to the grave, that is, to literally die with his or her devotee. None of them is willing, not even Orunmila, the most important of them, who then concludes that it is only a person's *ori* that will go with him or her to the grave. Literally, *ori* means head, and the conclusion is therefore literally true: the heads of dead persons are never cut off before they are buried. But it is also meant to be a metaphorical truth: *ori* is a god, just like *Ogun* or *Oya*. But more than these two, the Yoruba believe that a person's *ori* is his or her paramount god. Therefore the story concludes that no *Orisa* blesses a person without the consent of his or her *ori*; and we should therefore leave other *Orisa* alone and worship our own *ori*.

In these two stories, we have the conundrum of the concept of destiny. I can identify at least seven fundamental questions, which have to be addressed to make sense of the concept. First, is the choice of *ori* the same as the choice of destiny? Second, is there really a choice involved? Third, does the concept of responsibility have a role in the explication of the concept? Fourth, does the concept allow for a connection between destinies, for instance, between those of a mother and a daughter? If so, does this happen by accident or by design? Fifth, how does the belief in reincarnation affect the concept of destiny? Sixth, is there only personal destiny or is there also communal destiny? Seventh, what is the significance of destiny, and is the belief in destiny rational? I will address each of these questions as a basis for a coherent theory of destiny.

Ori and Destiny

Ori, in the Yoruba language, as noted above, means head. What has it got then to do with destiny? *Ori* is an important part of the make-up of the human person. *Emi* and *okan* are the others. *Ori*, like *okan*, has a dual meaning. It refers to the physical head, which is considered vital to the physical status of a person. It is, for instance, the seat of the brain. But when a typical Yoruba talks about *ori*, she is, more often than not, referring to a non-physical component of her person. For there is a widely received conception of an *ori* as the bearer of a person's destiny as well as the determinant of one's personality. How does this element come into the picture?

There is a common agreement in the tradition and in its literature about the make-up of the human being. According to this tradition, the human being is made (created?) by the combined effort of the god Obatala, the maker of the physical body, and Olodumare, the Supreme being, who gives *emi*, the life-force or soul. *Emi* is a non-material force responsible for life. Its presence ensures life and its absence means death. But the *emi* is itself immortal, and it may reincarnate in another body. The problem this belief raises for the concept of destiny will be discussed later. *Okan*, the other component of the human person, also has a dual nature, being material and non-material. In its former nature, it is the heart; in its latter nature, it is the mind, as a center of consciousness responsible for thinking, desiring, wishing, deliberating, etc. As such, its contents include *ero* (thought), *ife-okan* (desire), *eru* (fear), etc.[1]

After Olodumare has put the *emi* in place, the newly created body-plus-*emi* proceeds to the house of the god Ajala, the potter of *ori*, to get an *ori*. *Ori* is the bearer of each person's destiny. This, as previously noted, is not the same as the

314

physical head; though, for a reason that has to do with the important role of the latter in the life of a person, it is taken as a symbolic representation of an inner head, which is then taken to be the bearer of destiny. This inner head is *ori-inu*, or simply *ori*. Therefore, though *ori* is not identical with destiny, it is its bearer and, as such, the controller of a person's life.

Destiny is the preordained outcomes of life, wound and sealed up in the *ori*. Every human being is believed to have an allotment, and it determines what they will be in life.

Ori, Destiny, and the Problem of Choice

How does a person get his or her destiny? Is it by choice? Or is it by imposition? There are various conflicting accounts in the interpretive literature, due largely to the existence of numerous accounts in the traditional literature, including the literature of *Ifa* itself. One has to pay attention to all in the interest of full understanding, even if it leaves the puzzle largely unsolved. Three accounts stand out: *ayanmo*, *akunlegba*, and *akunleyan*.

Ayanmo

Literally, *ayanmo* means "that which is chosen and affixed to one." Here we have the idea that destiny is chosen and affixed. We do not, however, have an idea of who does the choosing. It is either the deity or the human. If it is the deity, then the problem of choice does not arise. But the problem of responsibility does. For, if I do not myself choose my destiny, and it is chosen for me, what right does anyone have to blame me for being what I have been predestined to be without any input from me? If I do the choosing, the problem arises about what kind of choice it is which an unconscious entity makes. I will go into this in a moment.

Akunlegba

Akunlegba literally means "that which is received while kneeling." Here, destiny is conceived as the portion which is imposed on one, most likely by the deity. One just receives it, and one has no choice in what it turns out to be. In this conception of destiny, the problem of choice does not arise, but the problem of responsibility does.

Akunleyan

Akunleyan means "that which one kneels down to choose." Here it is the human entity that makes the choice of a particular destiny. In the first story above, this is the model of destiny that is used. Afuwape and the others make their own choices. One might picture the procedure this way. The body-plus-*emi* entity goes to the house of Ajala. There are numerous *ori inu* (inner heads) with various destinies sealed up in them. The body-plus-*emi* entity looks round the room and makes a choice of one. In the Afuwape story, we are told that Afuwape was looking for one that is beautiful on the outside. But Ajala helped him to pick a really good one. This is because he

315

performed the sacrifice recommended by the divination priests. In any case, the emphasis here is on choice, and this is what creates the problem of choice. How so?

Choice presupposes freedom, information, and genuine alternatives. None of these conditions is present in the case of the "choice" of destiny. The body-plus-*emi* entity is unfree since he or she has to have a destiny. So he or she cannot avoid making a "choice" and cannot walk away. Second, this entity is unfree to choose in the sense that he or she has no personality, without which it is impossible to have preferences of life-patterns. Destiny is what confers personality; for it is what confers tastes and preferences, important elements of personality. But without a specific personality, one has no basis for choice. Third, this being has no full information to make a choice. There is no recitation of what is in each of the *ori*. So this being has no basis for comparison between them, without which it is impossible to make a real choice. Finally, there are no genuine alternatives, since there is no way of differentiating in any intelligent way between the available *ori*, at least as far as their real essence is concerned. On the outside, each *ori* looks exactly like the other. With all these observations, it appears clear that the concept of choice is problematic when applied to the choice of destiny (Gbadegesin 1991).

Ori, Destiny, and Responsibility

If destiny is really not a product of a genuine choice, as must be the case when we look at *akunlegba* (what is received while kneeling) as the source of destiny, the question arises as to the appropriateness of praise or blame. Is a person responsible for what he or she has not really chosen? Yet, the traditional Yoruba do not shy away from praising and/or blaming people for their actions. How then does one reconcile the apparent inconsistency? It should be easy if individuals are truly responsible for the choice of destiny. Then it would make sense to praise or blame them. Thus it may be argued that the car-jacker who got jailed chose his punishment along with his choice of the car-jacking profession. But if the choice was not his, and it was imposed on him (through *akunlegba*), then there is a problem that cannot be brushed aside. There are two approaches to the issue.

From one perspective, destiny is not a cut-and-dried phenomenon, and it is alterable. Indeed the average Yoruba acts as if destiny is alterable. Therefore, even if a bad destiny has been imposed on one, one has a responsibility to try to change it for the better. Divination for a newly born baby about its future prospects is the direct means of doing this. The rationale is that the diviner has the power to discern the destiny of everyone, and to do something about an unfavorable destiny. Since the procedure is available to everyone, the argument is that whoever does not take advantage of it is to blame for any problem he or she may have in life, not the initial destiny. Yet this conclusion does not take into consideration the fact that even after all is said and done, an unfavorable destiny may not go away, or at least so does the belief go. For is it not true, in the language of the tradition, that *ayanmo ko gboogun*? That is, destiny does not succumb to medicine. The question then must be faced: "Why do the typical Yoruba refuse to accept an unfavorable destiny only to end up accepting that a bad destiny cannot be altered?" Second, why do the typical

Yoruba proceed on the assumption that a good destiny may be negatively altered by the machinations of others, and therefore continually arm themselves against evil-doers?

The answers to these questions are at the heart of Yoruba philosophical thought. As a prelude to an answer to the first question, we have to note the following. A typical Yoruba has an optimistic attitude toward life. He or she is born into a family that is loving and caring. He or she also knows that the gods are there for the protection and prosperity of the individual. Therefore the first attitude to life is one of optimism. Secondly, the divination process never comes up with a purely negative prediction for a client. The logic of divination is to predict in such a way that the goodness of life's prospects is not permanently blocked out. Thus even if a diviner "sees" a problem, he puts it in a positive light, and may recommend sacrifice. For instance, the diviner is not expected to say: "You are destined to die." Rather, he would say, "You are advised to perform 'xyz' sacrifice to avert an untimely death." Or "You are advised to avoid going on a long journey for xyz number of days to avoid an accident." These examples show that even the diviner brings forth the optimistic aspect of the belief in destiny. It is therefore this attitude that informs the behavior of the people, and why they proceed on the assumption that all is well. However, suppose that even after the sacrifice against untimely death, the client still dies in mysterious circumstances. Here the recourse is made to the notion that it always was her destiny, and could not possibly be avoided. It may be said, then, that the doctrine of destiny does not induce resignation at first blush. But if one puts together the two phases of the thinking process, the first of which is the initial optimism and the second the appeal to fate, it would appear that an uncharitable critic may sense an inconsistency, where a sympathizer might sense pragmatism.

A second approach is even more problematic since it proceeds on the assumption that a bad destiny may be the result of the individual's own character subsequent to the attribution of an otherwise good destiny. Thus, a person destined to be a success-ful surgeon may turn out to be a failure because of his or her laziness and fraudulent activities, and a case like that is considered to deserve blame. In other words, destiny only guarantees the potentials, not the actualization of a life prospect. The latter depends on the efforts of the individuals. Hence the emphasis on *ese* (leg) and *owo* (hand) in the elaboration of the concept. The leg and the hand are the symbols of hard work without which a good destiny cannot come to fruition. Yet the problem is only partially resolved by this approach. For if one can make sense of destiny as it pertains to success or failure, it does not appear that the same answer will do for misfortunes which have no noticeable source in a person's character. This is the case with an innocent victim of earthquake or flood, and one cannot blame such a bad destiny on the character of the victim without assumptions about an earlier life.

The Interconnectedness of Destinies

The very idea of destiny suggests that there must be some connection between the destinies of various peoples: mother and child; spouses; friends and relations. For the child whose destiny is to die in infancy is born to a family whose destiny it is to

317

mourn its child. Therefore, one can assume that each of the parents must also have chosen (or received) a related destiny. And by extension, could it also mean that all the members of a particular community chose related destinies, at least to the extent that significant events in the lives of each would have an impact on the others? For one thing, a queen's destiny is to rule her people, whose destinies include being ruled by this particular queen. Could it also not mean that the car-jacker's destiny includes the choice of his victim whose destiny then is to be robbed and perhaps killed by this particular person? This insight about the interconnected-ness of destinies probably reflects the traditional communal mode of living among the Yoruba, and may provide an intellectual rationale for the appeal to the notion of a common destiny that political leaders are apt to make when it suits them.

Individual and Communal Destinies

Individual destinies determine the outcome of individual lives. Destiny is the mean-ing of a person's existence, the purpose of existence. However, this personal life-purpose cannot be separated from the communal reality of which the individual is only a part. This is due, in part, to the interconnectedness of destiny discussed above. However, it is also due to the fact that the purpose of individual existence is intricately linked with the purpose of social existence, and cannot be adequately grasped outside it. While confirming the personality of an individual, destiny also joins each one to the community, and personality becomes meaningful only by appeal to destiny and community. In any case, destiny is itself a community con-cept, a means for the community to provide its members with meaning. In the final analysis, a person is what she is in virtue of her destiny, her character, and the communal influences on her.

But what does it mean to say that destiny is the purpose of existence? Simply put, an individual's destiny is what he or she is supposed to live for. I have argued elsewhere that destiny is like a message to be delivered. The deity sends the message through each person, and it is the person's own contribution to the totality of the good in the community in particular, but also in the universe. Conceived in this way, there is bound to be raised the problem of an apparently bad or even wicked destiny, for example, the car-jacker's destiny. How is that supposed to promote the totality of the good in the universe? It appears that one cannot consistently main-tain the view that destiny is to promote the good, and acknowledge the fact that some destinies are clearly evil.

The Akan view, as interpreted by Kwame Gyekye, avoids this dilemma. For, according to that view, God disposes destiny, and it is always good. The occurrence of evil in the world is then attributed to the existence of wicked people. However, as I have argued elsewhere (1991), the problem here is that the three theses by Gyekye cannot be consistently maintained. The three theses are: God imposes des-tiny; destiny is always good; destiny is unalterable. If we add to these theses the obvious fact that there is evil in the Akan community – people die prematurely; natural disasters are real forces that the people contend with – then it becomes clear that one of the three theses must be false. Gyekye admits that the path of a person may be "strewn with failures, either because of his or her own actions, desires, decisions, and intentions or because of the activities of some supposed evil forces" (1987: 116). If these evil forces are human, then their own apportioned destiny must be bad, which means there is bad destiny. Or if they originally have good destiny, which was changed, then, it means that destiny is alterable. If they are natural forces, then again, there is bad destiny.

Destiny and Reincarnation

Two other important related beliefs of the Yoruba are the beliefs in the immortality of the soul and reincarnation, and it is necessary to clarify how the belief in destiny fits in with these two. The Yoruba seek three goods in the world: *ire owo*, *ire omo*, and *ire aiku pari iwa* (the good of wealth, the good of children, and the good of immortality). The latter is, for them, the most important, because it is the crown of existence (*iwa*). *Aiku* is immortality. The belief is that bodily death is not the end of one's life, for the soul lives on in a different plane of existence. This soul (*emi*) may then reincarnate in a different form of existence at a later time. Thus a dead parent may reincarnate in the form of a child to her own daughter or granddaughter. With respect to the belief in destiny, this belief in immortality and reincarnation raises a number of questions. First, how does one conceptualize the connection between the original destiny allotted to the original person in her first life and the new destiny in her second life? Is it the same destiny that is only temporarily suspended at death, or indeed is this death one phase of the entire long destiny that has to be "lived" out? Or does the first destiny lapse at the first death, and a new destiny begin at each reincarnation? It does not appear that much thought is given to this puzzle in the traditional philosophical speculation about destiny.

We could try and see how the various options fare. First, suppose it is the same first destiny that extends over all the "lives" of the person. It would follow that one is not really dead until all the details of one's destiny are worked out in the various lives. Indeed, some of the mythical stories, which illustrate the belief, suggest something to this effect. There is, for instance, the story of a certain young man. As he was about to go into the world for the first time, he recited his destiny for the approval of Olodumare, the Supreme Being. His destiny was to go into the world, live to a youthful age, have a girl friend, fix a date for the wedding, and, on the wedding day, go into the bush to relieve himself, and be bitten by a poisonous snake. Then, as he put it, "I would come back." In other words, he would end his life in this way. In this account of the matter, reincarnation is just the continuation of the same life. But if so, there would be no need for the choice of a new destiny. "I would come back" would then have to be followed by a further narrative about what will happen next. Perhaps "then, I would stay for a little while and go back to be born into my original father's family again." This would account for the phenomenon of *abiku*, born-to-die children.

But suppose the person has a different allotment of destiny at each reincarnation. Then can it be said that the same person is reincarnating after each death? This would raise a serious problem regarding the meaning of being the same person. For if it is true that one's personality is really determined by the kind of destiny one has, then each new round of destiny chosen by the *emi* would appear to turn up a different person, provided the destiny chosen is not identical. So even if, this time around, this new being were brought into the world through the same mother as before, it would not mean that it is the same person. It all boils down to what a person is, and in the tradition, a person is a combination of *ara* (body), *emi* (soul or life force), and destiny (*kadara* or *ipin*).

The Significance of Destiny: Addressing the Question of Rationality

The belief in destiny has a special place in the world-view of the Yoruba. Like the way chance and causality are conceptualized, which is in terms of personal idioms connoting the activities of gods and other spiritual entities, the belief in destiny fits perfectly well into the Yoruba traditional system of thought. Furthermore, if one explores it carefully, one discovers its rationale. There is no doubt that the belief serves a purpose. It is to assure human beings that they have a role to play in the world, even if it is an assigned role. There is implied, further, the assurance that they are not alone, all by themselves, because that role has been endorsed by the deity. There is, finally, the assurance that their lives have a meaning, which is encoded in the message of destiny. Two lessons are, accordingly, drawn. First, people should not worry unduly about failure, since that may be their destiny. But, second, since destiny may be just an indication of potentiality, they should not be complacent either. The belief also suggests to us that the Yoruba have some anxiety about situations that are beyond the control of anyone, and are keen on providing some psychological cushion against the rough and tumble of life.

From the last paragraph, one may concede that the belief in destiny has its rationale. But a further question is in order: Is the belief rational? This is the question posed by the late Peter Bodunrin. As he puts his argument:

> [S]howing why a people hold a particular belief is not sufficient to show that the belief is rational. Given any social practice one can always find a reason for it . . . an explanation of an event in terms of the motives of a person or a god is rational only if evidence is given for the existence of the person or god, or sufficient reasons given why their existence must be assumed and arguments adduced as to why the person or god should be supposed to be implicated in the particular event. Surely, to show that a belief arises from emotional needs, if this is in fact true, can hardly be construed as having shown it to be rational. (1984: 15)

Bodunrin's point is that a traditional belief, like any other belief, must be evaluated from a philosophical point of view. No one can fault this demand. All that we have said about destiny providing meaning for people's life may be true, but the question must still be posed: how rational is the belief? This may be addressed from various perspectives. I will identify three. First, is the belief coherent? That is, are its internal components consistent with one another? Second, is the belief consistent with other beliefs the people hold about the world? Third, is the belief or theory compatible with reality (practice), as we experience it?

320

To the first issue, from our discussions above, it seems obvious that there is a tension between the various components of the belief in destiny. On the one hand, there is a tension between the idea of a predestined life and the idea of individual responsibility. It is similar to the relation between the belief in determinism and free will. If we assume a changeable destiny, then we may draw an analogy between destiny and soft determinism, which is consistent with free will. One may then suggest that destiny is also compatible with responsibility. But this only moves the problem of incoherence to another arena. Here it is instructive to quote from Barry Hallen:

> A Yoruba will say that once destiny is "fixed" by Olorun it cannot be changed. It must take place. Nevertheless on other occasions the same person will say that it is possible to "miss" the destiny one has been apportioned, in the sense of becoming confused and lost during one's lifetime and doing things for which one is not at all suited. Or an external force can interfere with one's destiny. Neither of these is entirely consistent with the belief that once destiny is fixed, it is unalterable and must take place. (cited in Bodunrin 1984: 16)

This surely appears to be an example of inconsistently held beliefs within a single structure of beliefs, and as far as Bodunrin is concerned, it must be seen and evaluated as such. But Hallen does not; hence Bodunrin objects to Hallen's account. For Hallen, the inconsistency is only there if we look at the Yoruba belief from the perspective of a Westerner. He sees the various beliefs that may be called upon when an explanation is required as comparable to

> the various partitions that are ranged along the wings of a stage and may be swung into position depending upon the demands of the next scene. Each partition corresponds to a certain belief. There are other belief-panels in the wings that would be inconsistent with it if they were brought into play simultaneously. But this does not happen (except in very exceptional circumstances) because when a certain kind of problem occupies stage centre the same partition is always moved out to serve as its explanatory background. (cited in ibid. 17)

Bodunrin is not pleased with this approach, which he sees as "a good account of why the Yorubas do not find it odd to live with inconsistent beliefs." But, as he puts it, "Hallen's account can hardly be construed as showing that the Yorubas hold consistent views on destiny as expressed in their concept of *ori*; rather his account explains why the Yorubas do not see any inconsistencies in their belief system. But this does not remove the inconsistency" (ibid.). On this issue, I think Bodunrin is right. This is the position I have argued elsewhere (1987). I am, however, not implying that one cannot find arguments to remove the inconsistency.

The question is what kind of argument is there to remove the apparent inconsistency? The question of the belief in the alterability of destiny is fundamental to the theory. The issue we have raised in this connection is whether this belief is compatible with the idea of a fixed and unalterable destiny. Now, one way out of the apparent dilemma is to see the belief in an unalterable destiny as fatalism, and to argue that this is not the Yoruba position. Many scholars have argued this way. Thus Moses Makinde (1985) has drawn a distinction between strong destiny, which he identifies as fatalism, and weak destiny, which he identifies as the Yoruba concept of *ori*. If fatalism entails inalterability, weak destiny, as in *ori*, does not. Therefore, the argument goes, there is no inconsistency in the belief. Another argument is that even the strong notion of destiny is open to alteration, as far as the Yoruba are concerned. According to this interpretation, the concept of *ase* (special divine edicts) is superior to that of *ori* or *ayanmo* (destiny) because it issues from Olodumare. The point here, then, is that Olodumare can effect a change through *ase* once a supplication is made and accepted. The fact that the Yoruba act as if they believe that destiny is alterable would seem to support this interpretation.

The second issue has to do with whether the belief is consistent with other beliefs the Yoruba hold about the world. A list of major Yoruba beliefs about the world will include at least the following. There is God; there are *Orisas* (minor gods); death is inevitable; work is the cure for poverty; good character is beauty; it is the king of all talismans; moderation is the source of honor and respect, etc. From this list of beliefs, can it be said that there is one that is inconsistent with the belief in destiny? Again, it would appear at first that the belief that *ori* is the determinant of success or failure is inconsistent with the belief that work is the cure for poverty. However, as observed above, the Yoruba acknowledge the importance of hard work in the realization of a good destiny. This is why *ese* (leg) and *owo* (hand) are brought into the picture. The meaning of this is that both the hand and the leg are important instruments in the realization of one's destiny. Therefore, it might appear that there is no conflict between the two beliefs. With respect to character, it has also been observed above that one of the ways in which one's destiny may be altered is through one's own character. Of course, one may question how one's character could contribute to the altering of one's destiny, since it is supposed to be a component of the destiny in the first place. I do not myself see an adequate answer to this problem within the structure of the belief.

The third issue is whether the belief or theory is compatible with reality or practice, as we experience it. For instance, since the theory of destiny suggests that one has a preordained allotment before coming into this world, one possible practical implication is resignation. Yet in practice, no one adopts a philosophy of resignation. Does this suggest, then, that the theory is incompatible with our practice? Again, one way of addressing this issue may be to call attention to the complexity of the theory of destiny with its in-built correctives. Destiny does not, even in theory, imply resignation, one might argue, because the notion is one of potentiality. A potentiality is something that still has to be fulfilled. Second, one may argue that, since destiny is only a potential, one cannot, even in theory, consistently adopt a philosophy of resignation until one has made persistent efforts without success. But, of course, there are other beliefs in the system, which reject measuring success in terms of wealth or position. Furthermore, as discussed above, it may also be pointed out that the theory of destiny allows for the concept of *ase* (divine edicts) with the consequence that even a strong notion of destiny is liable to alteration with the involvement of Olodumare (God). Therefore, the theory is apparently not inconsistent with practical efforts to avert failure. It seems, then, that what is needed is a thorough analysis of the full logic of the theory. Then, one can expect a better fit between the theory and practice of destiny.

Conclusion

From the foregoing, it seems clear that the concept of destiny, as it features in Yoruba philosophical discourse, has good potentials for a rewarding philosophical investigation. I have only attempted to raise some of the issues that call for further analysis and investigation. I am sure that there is a lot more to be done, and that, even with regard to those that I have tried to address here, there is a lot more to be said and not a few objections to be considered. But I think it is clear that one cannot dismiss the concept as irrational without further argument. It also seems clear that one cannot drive a wedge between the theory and the practice of destiny without plenty of argument. Finally, since the belief in destiny continues to feature prominently in the social lives of the people, serious philosophical efforts will continue to be required to deal with the various issues that need to be resolved to move us toward the formulation of an adequate theory.

Note

1   For an extensive discussion and defense of my account of *okan*, see Gbadegesin 1991: ch. 2.

References

Bodunrin, Peter (1984) "The Question of African Philosophy," in Richard Wright, *African Philosophy: An Introduction*, 3rd edn. (Lanham, MD: University Press of America), pp. 1–23. (Orig. in *Philosophy*, 56 (1981): 161–81.)

Gbadegesin, Segun (1984) "Destiny, Personality and the Ultimate Reality of Human Existence: A Yoruba Perspective," *Ultimate Reality and Meaning*, 7(3): 173–88.

Gbadegesin, Segun (1987) "God, Destiny and Social Injustice: A Critique of a Yoruba Ifa Belief," in Gene James (ed.), *The Search For Faith and Justice in the Twentieth Century* (New York: Paragon Press).

Gbadegesin, Segun (1991) *African Philosophy: Traditional Yoruba Philosophy and Contemporary African Realities* (New York: Lang Publishing).

Gyekye, Kwame (1987) *An Essay on African Philosophical Thought: The Akan Conceptual Scheme* (New York: Cambridge University Press).

Makinde, Moses (1985) "A Philosophical Analysis of the Yoruba Concept of Ori and Human Destiny," *International Studies in Philosophy*, 17(1): 53–69.

24

On the Normative Conception of a Person

IFEANYI A. MENKITI

Group solidarity is most often cited as a key, perhaps the defining, feature of African traditional societies. There are many formulations of this general view, but the one that seems most appropriate for our purposes in this chapter is from John Mbiti. He notes that an individual's relation to the group is best described as one of "I am because we are" (1970: 141). His formulation provides a useful starting point for our discussion.

It will be noted, I should point out, that Mbiti's claimed connection between the individual and the community takes on a particular form, moves in a trajectory not to be confused with others. Although Mbiti himself does not spell this out in his own work, it bears mentioning, rightaway, that the force of the statement "I am because we are" is not such as to directly translate into another set of related statements, for example, "He is because we are" or "You are because we are." Its sense is not that of a person speaking on behalf of, or in reference to, another, but rather of an individual, who recognizes the sources of his or her own humanity, and so realizes, with internal assurance, that in the absence of others, no grounds exist for a claim regarding the individual's own standing as a person. The notion at work here is the notion of an extended self.

In looking at the African conceptualization of the person, one acknowledges, of course, that it is a given fact that every individual has a body apart from the body of every other individual within his or her own community. That sort of given fact is a brute biological fact. But it need not be read as conveying a message that each stands alone. Normative standing is one thing, and superficial biological considerations quite another. I use the word "superficial" advisedly because, on a deeper level, both norm and biology do tend to converge.

I have in mind here the lucid example of the human navel and the way it points us to umbilical linkage to biological generations going before. And I have in mind, also, the fact that human language, which is a biologically anchored fact, points us, one and all, everywhere in the world, to a mental commonwealth with others – others whose life histories encompass past, present, and future. In both of these examples, biology intimates a message, not of beingness alone, but of beingness together. And to the extent that morality demands a point of view best described as one of beingness-with-others, to that extent does deep biology link up nicely with the direction of movement of the moral order.

Up to this point I have used the terms "individual" and "individual person" as if they were fully interchangeable. But in the context of an investigation of African understandings of the person, a clarification might be in order, so as to avoid confusion later on. The clarification is this: if we began first with a context in which the talk is already about persons, so that we are plainly counting out individuals judged from the point of view of a personhood already established, then there is no question that we are counting individual persons. But a confusion might arise if we began with an unspecified context of counting out individuals. For we can count, having in mind different aspects of human agency in the world, though not necessarily agency as person. For considered as an individuated source of consumption, a bundle, as it were, of primary appetites, the individual could still count as an agent in the world. But to go beyond the raw appetitive level to the special level marked by the dignity of the person, something more would seem to be needed. In this regard, "individual" and "individual person" may carry somewhat different weight and it is the context of discussion that spells out whether they converge or diverge.

I think that it would be best, regarding the African story, to conceive of the movement of the individual human child into personhood, and beyond, as essentially a journey from an *it* to an *it*. I shall explain shortly what I mean by this formulation. But before doing so, let me note that since the child's journey, or ontological progression, takes place in time, a word might also be in order regarding the nature of time in African thought. Time's movement was generally from the present to the past, so that the more of a past one has, the more standing as a person one also has. In this regard, a remark to the effect "I am looking forward to my own past" would be a remark well placed within the thought system.

Ontological progression, then, in taking place in time, demands that time be considered relevant to the in-gathering of the excellences of the person as one ages. Hence the Igbo African proverb: "What an old man sees sitting down, a young man cannot see standing up." A statement of this nature signifies that passage through time helps create not only a qualitative difference between young and old, but also an ontologically significant one. The issue here is not gradation pure and simple, but gradation based on the emergence of special new qualities seen as constitutive of a level of being not only qualitatively superior to, but also ontologically different from, the entity with which one first began.

Fundamentally, it is the emergence of moral, or quasi-moral, qualities considered useful to the enrichment of the human community, or at least useful to the internalized rejection of attitudes directly inimical to community, that accounts for the shift in classification. The thinking here is that in the normal process of growth and maturation, the heart does grow increasingly wiser, morally speaking. But it all takes time, and there are no short cuts.

Consider now, for a moment, that although we would not have a great deal of difficulty talking about an 18-year-old mathematical giant, we would have a great deal of difficulty talking about an 18-year-old moral giant. The reason for this is that morality and the maturation of the human person are so intimately bound up that a still evolving specimen of the person, lacking a full record in the area of lived experience, would be hard-pressed to present the sort of personal history needed for

325

an elevation into the status of a moral exemplar. Mathematics is another thing altogether: as long as the young man or woman can maneuver the equations better and faster than his or her aging professor, the road to mathematical sainthood is clear for him or for her. In fact, it is often said that mathematicians tend to do their best work while in their early years. It is a field in which lived experience is not necessary to achieve greatness.

In the stated journey of the individual toward personhood, let it therefore be noted that the community plays a vital role both as catalyst and as prescriber of norms. The idea is that in order to transform what was initially biologically given into full personhood, the community, of necessity, has to step in, since the individual, himself or herself, cannot carry through the transformation unassisted. But then what are the implications of this idea of a biologically given organism having first to go through a process of social and ritual transformation, so as to attain the full complement of excellences seen as definitive of the person?

One conclusion appears inevitable, and it is to the effect that personhood is the sort of thing which has to be achieved, the sort of thing at which individuals could fail. I suppose that another way of putting the matter is to say that the approach to persons in traditional thought is generally speaking a maximal, or more exacting, approach, insofar as it reaches for something beyond such minimalist requirements as the presence of consciousness, memory, will, soul, rationality, or mental function. The project of being or becoming persons, it is believed, is a truly serious project that stretches beyond the raw capacities of the isolated individual, and it is a project which is laden with the possibility of triumph, but also of failure.

Since triumph and failure have their consequences, and the consequences cut beyond the life cycle of the assignable individual, affecting others in the community as well, it follows that societies, both large and small, are in need of recognizing that they are caught up in an inextricable dance with their component individuals. And one of the ways to act on that recognition is to join the task of transforming the individual into a true person, in other words, a moral being or bearer of norms.

For married to the notion of person is the notion of moral arrival, a notion involving yardsticks and gradations, or, more simply, involving an expectation that certain ways of being or behaving in the world may be so off the mark as to raise important questions regarding the person-status of their doers. This, it seems to me, is the import of the insistence on the part of Placide Tempels's native informants that the word "muntu," which stands for the human person, implies the idea of an excellence attaching to what it designates (1959: 10); in other words, that it does not simply refer to individuals considered as crude existents.

I had earlier suggested that it were best to regard the movement of the individual human child into full personhood, and beyond, as essentially a journey from an *it* to an *it*. The so-called "ontological progression" begins at birth with the child basically considered an "it" – essentially an individual without individuality, without personality, and without a name. Then the born child is brought through the various naming ceremonies, and, in the process, begins the first phase of that special journey toward incorporated personhood via the community. Later, there will be puberty and the ceremonies, which mark it as an entry into young adulthood. And through the years of adulthood, there will be other acknowledgements,

326

through ceremony, of other important transitions such as marriage, the producing of children, the taking of titles, etc. Finally, there will arrive old age and elderhood, and, after elderhood, ancestorhood.

Now, a most important point has to be made regarding ancestorhood. That point is that ancestors are themselves still continuing persons, still very much a part of the living community. Here, the person that the child became, at some stage in the described journey, does not abruptly go out of existence at the stage of physical death. The sense appears to be that the person, once arrived, can only depart slowly, yielding incrementally his or her achieved status. Only when the stage of the nameless dead is joined does the person once again become an "it," going out of the world the same way the journey first began. Thus the movement is a movement from an *it* to an *it*. The moral magic of personhood happens in between, and, after the magic, it is silence at the end-point that we call the stage of the nameless dead. There is no heaven or hell, no final judgment warranting an ascension into the ranks, above, of the saved; nor descent into the ranks, below, of the damned.

This point is important to bring up because, as Kwasi Wiredu has so rightly pointed out, to think of the ancestors as continuing into pure spirithood, for example, into some sort of personalized deities deserving of worship, is to suggest that Africans are caught up in the grip of a kind of collective megalomania (1977: 40). Wiredu's point is that since it is well known that traditional folks aspired to become ancestors upon physical death, then surely, to think of ancestors in terms of person- alized deities is to imply that traditional folks aspired to become transformed into god-like entities deserving of worship after the point of physical death. Which is a very loud desire, indeed. Because of this sort of consideration, Wiredu contends that the term "ancestor worship" must be considered misleading – ancestor reverence, perhaps, but not ancestor worship. The conclusion that I myself wish to draw from all of this is that since our settled understanding is that worship, properly con- ceived, belongs to deities, not persons, what we are dealing with in speaking of ancestors are not other-worldly non-persons, but persons in other worlds – persons whose person-standing will eventually be over once the nameless dead stage is reached.

At different points in this chapter, I have maintained that the movement that anchors the metaphysical situation of the person is a movement from an *it* to an *it*, with the depersonalized reference which marks the beginning of existence also marking the very end. I wish now to make a final point in support of this observa- tion. Regarding the beginning, consider now, for example, our natural ease in using an *it* type designation to refer to a young child, as in the expression: "We rushed the child to the hospital, but before we got there *it* died." This is an expression we would never use in regard to a teenager or an adult man or woman. Of course, the young child could still be referred to by name, or by a personal pronoun; but that is not the point. The point, rather, is that there is a flexibility in the way we refer to the child, but which we do not have in regard to an older person. Given these considerations, the reader who is tempted to retort that an entity either is or is not a person, that there can be no gradation about the matter, no ontological progres- sion, should perhaps think again. This is not to say that all of language always carries ontological weight, but I think that, in this case, language does.

Now regarding the *it* status of the nameless dead at the very end of the described journey, I believe that the *it* designation also carries the ease of natural use, and is the way it should be. The one contrast worth noting is that in the case of the nameless dead, there is not even the flexibility for the use of a named or pronominal reference, as with the case of the young child. The nameless dead remain *its*, and cannot be designated as something else. For this reason, Mbiti's description of the nameless dead stage as a time of "collective immortality" (in contrast to what he calls the "personal immortality" of the living dead stage of ancestor existence) is, I believe, problematic and misleading. For at the stage of total dis-incorporation marked by the *it* expression, the mere fragments that the dead have now become cannot form a collectivity in any true sense of the word. And since, by definition, no one remembers them now, it also does not make much sense to say of them that they are immortal either. They no longer have any meaningful sense of self, and, having lost their names, lose also the means by which they could be immortalized. Hence it is better, I believe, to refer to them by the name of *the nameless dead* rather than designate their stage of existence by such a term as "collective immortality," thereby suggesting that they could somehow be described as "collective immortals," which is not only odd, but also inaccurate. But this emendation apart, Mbiti is quite right when he observes that for African men and women no ontological progression is possible beyond the spirit world: "Beyond the state of the spirits men cannot go or develop. This is the destiny of man as far as African philosophy is concerned" (1970: 34).

The observation can therefore be correctly made that a metaphysically significant symmetry exists between the opening phase of an individual's quest for personhood and the terminal phase of that quest. Both are marked by an absence of incorporation – an absence underscored by the related absence of collectively re-enacted names. Just as the child has no name when it comes into the world to begin the journey toward selfhood, so likewise, at the very end, it will have no name again. At both points, we use an *it* type designation, because there exists a telling lack of incorporation. And since it is incorporation that guarantees not only the achieving, but also the retention, of personhood, it cannot but be the case that a lack of embeddedness in an ongoing community of reciprocal obligations will have negative consequences insofar as personhood attributions are concerned.

Up to this point, I have been exploring certain hierarchies, certain gradations, in the ontological perception of the individual, as he or she moves toward ancestor-hood and beyond. Perhaps a diagram will be of some help – see figure 1. In the diagram, the ranked movement which we have been describing has involved the categories of "Human" and "Spirit," and very little has been said about the category "Divinity." What the representation makes clear is that not only is there a ranking within each category, but also a ranking between the different categories. Where it gets complicated is in trying to capture in diagrammatic form the categorial ranking relationship between the ancestor (living dead) level of existence and the nameless dead level, both within the general category of Spirit.

For it appears that insofar as raw seniority is concerned, the fragments of former persons comprising the class of the nameless dead have to be ranked higher than the class of living dead ancestors. However, in regard to moral function, the ancestors occupy first position. Thus, if the left vertical numerical ordering represents

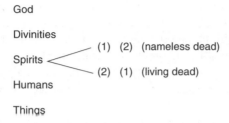

God

Divinities

Spirits   (1)   (2)   (nameless dead)

              (2)   (1)   (living dead)

Humans

Things

ranking according to raw seniority, it will be found that the nameless dead come first, but in regard to moral function (right vertical numerical ordering) they come second. On the other hand, though ranked second, age-wise, to the nameless dead, the ancestors occupy first ranking in regard to moral function. This is not an insignificant asymmetry and I hope I have been able to say enough here to show why the asymmetry is there, and furthermore what conclusions we ought to be able to draw from its being there.

Explicitly stated, the conclusions bear on the following. First, when a split exists between age and moral function, as it does in the case of the nameless dead, it is clear that, given the African context, something truly interesting is happening. For one thing, it argues that the reason age has tended to count so heavily in African thought is because of its link to the acquisition of moral function, so that where moral function is no longer an issue, by the very nature of a situation, age itself becomes something not particularly significant. In other words, it is being around for a very long time as a particular kind of human agent that counts, not being around for a very long time, simpliciter.

Second, given the absence of any beliefs in survival ad infinitum for the human individual, after the end of lived time, it means that the moral drama of existence can only be played out this side of the grave. This being so, the job of shoring up the nexus of consensual community takes on an existential urgency. Ethical salvation for the group, for the individual, is in the here and now, not later in an unrealized, and perhaps unrealizable, future. Because the metaphysical grounds do not obtain for the sort of elongated future against the background of which survival in perpetuity of the person can occur, immortalization can only go so far into ancestorship. This state of affairs, I believe, results from the empirical temperament in the thought system of traditional society. One goes by known things, by the flow of time that has occurred, not the flow of time to occur. It would, of course, be nice for immortality to come to everyone beyond the ancestor stage, but the actual experience of the direction of time's flow does not cooperate in that judgment.

Third, the aforementioned empirical temperament, or attitudinal posture having to do with staying put with known things – with things attested to, or attestable to, by experience – also lies behind the generic response to the young child. Since the child for the most part is preoccupied with its physical needs, and younger persons

329

often lack in moral perception, tending toward self-centeredness in action, traditional society often found itself with an evidentiary knowledge that the young are not ready to join the elders in the play of reciprocal moral obligations. This being so, it tended to be guarded in its attitude toward the young, though still continuing to be open-minded, until they, the young, show themselves capable of becoming full participants in communal life through the discharge of the various obligations defined by their stations. For it is the carrying out of these obligations that transforms them from the *it*-status of early childhood, marked by an absence of moral function, into the person-status of later years, marked by a widened maturity of ethical sense.

Fourth, and finally, in examining the importance of moral sense in the definition of the person within the African context, let me add that the traditional understanding in this area is something which makes a great deal of sense given the special worth attached to persons, not only within Africa, but also elsewhere in the world. John Rawls makes explicit part of what is meant by the general ethical requirement of respect for persons, noting that those who are capable of a sense of justice are owed the duties of justice, with this capability construed in its sense of a potentiality which may or may not have been realized. He writes:

> Equal justice is owed to those who have the capacity to take part in and to act in accordance with the public understanding of the initial situation. One should observe that moral personality is here defined as a potentiality that is ordinarily realized in due course. It is this potentiality which brings the claims of justice into play.... The sufficient condition for equal justice [is] the capacity for moral personality. (1971: 505–8)

Here it seems to me that an important implication of Rawls's claim is that if an individual comes to deserve the duties of justice (and the confirmation therein implied of the individual's worth as a person) only through possession of a capacity for moral personality, then morality ought to be construed as essential to humans' sense of themselves as persons. But, then, it is the depth of a culture's understanding of this fact and the practices flowing therefrom that determine whether and to what extent the perception holds for a general public. Philosophy can contribute its clarifications, but ultimately it is culture and its practices that modulate with what force an idea holds for a general population. Africa's understanding of the relationship of norms to the conception of a person is deep seated as a matter of cultural fact.

References

Mbiti, John (1970) *African Religions and Philosophy* (New York: Doubleday).
Rawls, John (1971) *A Theory of Justice* (Cambridge, MA: Harvard University Press).
Tempels, Placide (1959) *Bantu Philosophy* (Paris: Presence Africaine).
Wiredu, Kwasi (1977) "African Religions from a Philosophical Point of View," in Philip L. Quinn and Charles Taliaferro (eds.), *A Companion to the Philosophy of Religion* (Oxford: Blackwell Publishers).

Further reading

Menkiti, A. (1984) "Person and Community in African Traditional Thought," in Richard A. Wright (ed.), *African Philosophy: An Introduction*, 3rd edn. (New York: University of America Press).

Wiredu, Kwasi and Gyekye, Kwame (1992) *Person and Community: Ghanaian Philosophical Studies, I* (Washington DC: Council for Research in Values and Philosophy).

25

African Conceptions of a Person: A Critical Survey

DIDIER NJIRAYAMANDA KAPHAGAWANI

Introduction

The concept of person or personhood has drawn the attention of a great many scholars in African philosophy, generating inevitably a diverse volume of literature. What immediately come to mind are discussions by, for instance, Abraham (1962), Busia (1954), Danquah (1944), Rattray (1916), Parrinder (1951), Tempels (1959), Kagame (1989), Mbiti (1969), Wiredu (1987), Gyekye (1995), and Gbadegesin (1998).

It would be too presumptuous, here, to attempt to discuss and evaluate in detail such a volume of literature on African conceptions of person. Rather, I merely aim to survey such literature, while pointing out some similarities, differences, and problems. For no reason other than geographical, I present West African, followed by East and Southern African concepts of person, giving expositions of both Akan and Yoruba conceptions, and Bantu ones respectively.

West African Conceptions of Person

Quite a lot of research has been conducted on how a person is conceived in West Africa, particularly from the perspective of the Akan and Yoruba cultures. This section is an exposition of the Akan and Yoruba conceptions as rendered by Wiredu, Gyekye, and Gbadegesin.

Akan Conception of Person: Wiredu vs. Gyekye

Many scholars who have researched and written on the Akan concept of person seem to be in agreement that, from the Akan perspective, a person is composed of three fundamental elements: "*nipadua* [body], *okra* [life-giving entity], and *sunsum* [that which gives a person's personality]" (Wiredu 1987: 160–1). The *okra* is "the innermost self, the essence, of the individual person," "the individual's life, for which reason it is referred to as *okrateasefo*, that is, the living soul," "the embodiment and transmitter of the individual's destiny [fate: *nkrabea*]," the "spark of the Supreme Being [*Onyame*] in man." The *okra* is, according to Gyekye's exposition, "described as divine and as having an ante-mundane existence with the Supreme Being" (1995: 85).

There is, however, a controversy between Wiredu and Gyekye on how the Akan term *okra* should be translated into English. Wiredu claims that *okra* should not and cannot be translated as "soul" on the grounds that in Western philosophy this term refers to "a purely immaterial entity that somehow inhabits the body. The *okra*, by contrast, is quasi-physical. It is not, of course, supposed to be straightforwardly physical, as it is believed not to be fully subject to spatial constraints. Nor is it perceivable by the naked eye. Nevertheless, in some ways it seems to be credited with para-physical properties" (1987: 161).

Gyekye disagrees with Wiredu and insists that "the *okra* can be considered as the equivalent of the concept of the soul in other metaphysical systems. Hence, it is correct to translate *okra* into English as soul" (1995: 85). The reason, in Gyekye's view, for translating *okra* as soul and as immaterial, not quasi-material, is that describing it as quasi-physical as Wiredu does "runs counter to the belief of most Akan people in dis-embodied survival or life after death. For a crucial aspect of Akan metaphysics is the world of spirits [*asamando*], a world inhabited by the departed souls of ancestors" (ibid. 86). Wiredu, for his part, maintains that the Akans, as indeed many African peoples, famously conceive the afterlife itself in a quasi-material manner (1992: 139–40).

Clearly, for a non-Akan like me, the disagreement between Wiredu and Gyekye on this front is not so much on the existence of the *okra* as a constituent of a person, as on its nature. Though philosophically interesting, this dispute is beyond the scope of this chapter.

The second component of a person in Akan thought is *sunsum*. This is described by various scholars as "that which is responsible for the total effect communicated by an 'individual's personality'" (Wiredu 1987: 162); "the basis of a man's person-ality" and, as such, according to Gyekye, "it cannot be a physical thing, for qual-ities like courage, jealousy, gentleness, forcefulness, and dignity are psychological, not sensible or physical" (1995: 90). One interesting feature of the *sunsum* is that it is believed "to perish at death" (Wiredu 1987: 163), and that during sleep the *sunsum* is capable of leaving and later returning to the body at will, as it were (Gyekye 1995: 91). But typical of a philosophical debate, Gyekye (ibid. 90–1) claims that the *sunsum* is immaterial, divine, and immortal, whereas Wiredu (1987: 163) doubts. But again, that is not our concern here.

The third, and apparently less controversial, component of a person in Akan thought is *honam* or *nipadua* (body), which is the flesh, bones, and blood of which humans are made at the material level.

All these three constitute a person in Akan thought. But whether or not they interact – and, if so, how – are questions hotly debated among scholars steeped and well equipped in Akan culture.

Yoruba conception of person

According to Gbadegesin, the word for a person in Yoruba is *eniyan*, but he observes that this term has both a normative and a literal meaning. The former indicates "the moral standing of the human being who is thus determined as [either] falling short [or living up to the expectations] of what it takes to be recognized as such" (1998: 149). In this regard, the Yoruba seem to be at one with the Bantus of Eastern and Southern Africa, as will be observed below. However, Gbadegesin makes a further debatable claim: "In Yoruba language greater emphasis is placed on this normative dimension of *eniyan* than is perhaps placed on the concept of person in the English language" (ibid. 149). This issue requires a lengthier and more in-depth discussion and evaluation than this chapter allows. I therefore leave it for the moment for further consideration in other endeavors.

What seems incontestable about the *eniyan* is that it consists of four elements: the *ara*, *okan*, *emi*, and *ori*. The *ara* is a "physical-material part of the human being. It includes the external and internal components: flesh, bone, heart, intestines, etc." (ibid. 149). Interestingly, the Yoruba regard it as fruitless and pointless to articulate the nature or essence of the body. Nor do they consider significant the question whether or not a person is all body "because it appears too obvious to them that there is more to a person than the body" (ibid. 150).

The second element of *eniyan* is *okan*. "In Yoruba language it appears to have a dual character." "On the one hand," claims Gbadegesin (ibid. 150), "it is acknowledged as the physical organ responsible for the circulation of blood, and it can be thus identified. On the other hand, however, it is also conceived as the source of emotional and psychic reactions." It is interesting to note that although the *okan* is amenable in essence to materialistic interpretations in its first character, it seems to have some resemblance to the *sunsum* of the Akans in its second character, according to Gyekye's exposition.

The third component of *eniyan* is *emi*. To Gbadegesin (ibid. 153), it is "nonphysical," "the active principle of life, the life-giving element, put in place by the deity." It is also construed as part of the divine "breath." It should be noted at this point that the nature of *emi* has been open to dispute and debate. Some scholars claim that it has an immaterial and independent existence; and others, that it is merely a principle or force which brings about various activities and actions in human beings without itself being an entity. Whether or not the *emi* is an entity is subject to further philosophical discussion.

Lastly, the fourth element of the *eniyan* is the *ori*. And like the *okan*, the *ori* has a dual nature. "On the one hand, it refers to the physical head and, given the acknowledged significance of the head vis-à-vis the rest of the body, *ori* is considered vital even in its physical character" (ibid. 154). However, the dual nature of the *ori* lies in the fact that it is "recognized as the bearer of the person's destiny as well as the determinant of personality" (ibid. 155). How this is done is a point of controversy among Yoruba thinkers and scholars. But again, the *ori* has striking similarities with the *sunsum* of the Akans.

East and Southern African Conceptions of Person

Some literature has also accumulated through researches on conceptions of person in Eastern and Southern Africa. Of particular interest are works by Tempels,

Kagame, and Mbiti. This section, therefore, is merely an exposition of their views with a sprinkling of personal comments, since I belong to one of the so-called Bantu languages, which are spoken in this region of Africa.

The Force Thesis

What I have termed the "Force Thesis" was propounded by Placide Tempels (1959), who strongly believed in a radical conceptual difference between Africans and non-Africans on the essential nature of beings and entities in general, and human beings in particular. Africans, or the Bantu in particular, conceive of entities or beings, claims Tempels, as nothing more than essential energies or vital forces. Using Bantu or, to be precise, Luba expressions of greeting, sympathy, and hunger, Tempels (ibid. 45) concludes that every Bantu language contains words or phrases denoting a *force*, which constitutes "the integrity of our whole being." And he goes on to claim that those words or phrases, *kufwa* and *kufwididila* in Luba, and *kufa* and *kufadi* in Chichewa, for instance, indicating different degrees of loss of vital force "the superlative of which signifies total paralysis of the power to live," should not be translated in English as "to die" and "to die entirely" precisely because, for Tempels (ibid. 47), Westerners "hold a *static* conception of 'being', [and Africans] a dynamic [one]" (ibid. 51). For Tempels, specifically what is wrong with such translations is that they fail to capture what he regards as the processual connotation of the Luba words which refer to points in a processual continuum. Indeed, according to Tempels, for a Bantu, " 'Force' in his thought is a necessary element in 'being', and the concept 'force' is inseparable from the definition of 'being' ... without the element of 'force', 'being' cannot be conceived" (ibid. 50–1).

What needs to be pointed out immediately is that by claiming, as Tempels does in the passage above, that force is an essential property of being, he might seem to be implying that, although "force" is a necessary attribute of "being," it is nevertheless not its sufficient condition, so that "being" might be thought to possess some properties or attributes other than that of force. However, the picture becomes clearer a few lines later when Tempels (ibid. 51) insists that force is not only a necessary attribute of being, but *is* (the essence of) being in Bantu thought: "Force is not for [the Bantu] an adventitious, accidental reality. Force is even more than a necessary attribute of beings: *Force is the nature of being, force is being, being is force.*"

A number of questions immediately arise in the Tempelsian force thesis. Importantly, the thesis seems to beg the question; for, given that being has been defined in terms of force, the question arises what force is in Bantu languages and thought. And this is not at all clear. Chichewa, for example, one of the Bantu languages, provides us with no clue as to how the word "force" is to be comprehended in Chewa thought and language. Even Tempels himself does not indicate how the concept of "force" might be translated in the Luba language. However, it should be pointed out here that this idea of force among the Luba seems to have similarities with that of *sunsum* and *okan* among the Akan and Yoruba respectively.

Secondly, I find it quite baffling that Tempels regards it as a mistake to translate *kufa* as "to die" and *kufadi* as "to die indeed," for if there are words and phrases in Chichewa that admit of easy translation, *kufa* and *kufadi* must be among the easiest.

335

To say "X *akufa*" in Chichewa is no more to regard death or dying as a process than when it is uttered in English that "X is dying." Similarly, to say "X *akufadi*" in Chichewa is not so much to specify the ultimate degree of loss of life as to demonstrate the degree of one's certainty about X's actual death. And to regard these dictions as expressions of degrees and intensities of force is to take too literally a mode of expression or manner of speech that is figurative.

Thirdly, proceeding in the same vein noted above, Tempels (ibid. 55) insists on the distinction between "a human" and "a person," and claims, rather surprisingly, that *munthu*, in Chichewa, for example, should not be translated as "a human," but rather as "a person," because "*Muntu* signifies vital force endowed with intelligence and will." But one cannot help but ask what the term "human" means if it does not denote entities in possession of intelligence and will. On this Tempels leaves us in the dark as if there are humans (*wanthu* in Chichewa) who do not possess intelligence and will. On this point, Chichewa has counter-evidence: *munthu* denotes as much a "human being" as it does a "person."

However, this point has to be made with a qualification. In Chichewa, it is said: *Azungu siwanthu*. On a literal translation this statement means "Whites are not human," which would seem to indicate that the Chewa deny humanness to whites. Yet with a little analysis, this statement is seen not to be uttered to assert the non-humanity of whites; rather, it denies that whites are Chewa persons insofar as their looks and behavior are at variance with that of the Chewa. Thus, this statement should not be translated as "Whites are not human," but rather as "Whites are not Chewa persons." And to this extent, Tempels (ibid. 57) is quite right in advising against translating *munthu* as "human," but, rather, as "person."

But some situations warrant translating *munthu* as "human." For example, to say that *Achewa ndi wanthu* is more to assert the humanness of the Chewa than their personhood. Similarly *Azungu ndi wanthu* means that whites are just as human as the Chewa except for pigmentational differences. Here, *munthu* refers to the species of human beings and has universal applicability, whereas when this word is translated as "person," it involves a sociocentric view of personhood, which varies from one culture to another and from one time to another due to the dynamic nature of culture and society.

Fourthly, although Tempels tries to steer clear of the Western conception of being in his account of the concept of a person in Bantu thought, he surreptitiously reverts to the very distinctions employed in Western philosophy to distinguish humans from other entities. He claims that in Bantu thought humans are beings distinct from other beings by their properties of reason and volition. Thus, on the Tempelsian thesis of being as force, it should apparently be possible to distinguish between rational and non-rational forces, and voluntary and non-voluntary forces. For, according to the Force Thesis of beings as forces, there must be a radical difference between vital forces that have intelligence and those that do not. But it does seem that what it means for a vital force to have intelligence and will or, for that matter, what an intelligent vital force or a voluntary vital force is, cannot be accounted for in the Tempelsian framework. In any case, the properties of intelligence and will are precisely what, in Western philosophy, are taken to be properties distinguishing the genus "humans" from the species "animals." To assume that this way of making the distinction is adequate in Bantu thought is open to question. These are some of the problems bedeviling the Force Thesis. So much for the Force Thesis.

The Communalism Thesis

This thesis has Tempelsian origins, although Mbiti is now closely associated with it. In *Bantu Philosophy*, Tempels is quite explicit in claiming that in Bantu thought, persons or humans are defined and individuated communally:

> This concept of separate beings, of substance...which find themselves side by side, entirely independent one of another, is foreign to Bantu thought. Bantu hold that created beings preserve a bond one with another, an intimate ontological relationship, comparable with the causal tie which binds creature with Creator. For the Bantu there is interaction of being with being, that is to say, of force with force. (1959: 58)

And a few pages later it is remarked that the "child, even the adult, remains always for the Bantu a man, a force, *in causal dependence and ontological subordination* to the forces which are his father and mother. The older force ever dominates the younger" (ibid. 60).

Reflecting in the same vein, Mbiti writes:

> In traditional life, the individual does not and cannot exist alone except corporately. He owes his existence to other people, including those of past generations and his contemporaries. He is simply part of the whole. The community must therefore make, create, or produce the individual; for the individual depends on the corporate group.... Whatever happens to the individual happens to the whole group, and whatever happens to the whole group happens to the individual. The individual can only say: "I am, because we are; and since we are therefore I am." This is a cardinal point in the understanding of the African view of man. (1969: 108–9)

That Mbiti is propagating a sociocentric view of personhood, in which the status of an individual is determined through cultural criteria, is quite evident from the assertion that a society "makes, creates or produces the individual." And although Mbiti does not spell out some of the criteria societies use, Shaw (2000) has provided us with an example of a conception of personhood as dependent on the quantity of secrets an individual holds.

As with the Force Thesis, the Communalism Thesis is also confronted with a number of problems. First, it should be conceded that in putting this thesis in a form reminiscent of the Cartesian *cogito* argument, namely, that in Africa *we are* therefore *I am*, Mbiti aims at underscoring the extent to which communal life is esteemed in Africa. For example, in the Chewa language it is crisply and proverbially said: *Kalikokha nikanyama; tuli tuwili nituwanthu* (What is alone is a brute animal; whatever or whoever has a partner/neighbor is a human being), suggesting that it is in the nature of a human being to lead a communal life of one form or another.

However, and this is the second point, the validity of Mbiti's argument is questionable. Although the *cogito* argument could have pretensions of validity when

337

provided with "Whatever thinks exists" as a suppressed premiss, I find it difficult to imagine quite what suppressed premiss would render Mbiti's argument valid.

Thirdly, to assert African communalism is not in any way to imply the denial of the recognition of individual human beings qua individuals. African communalism, in fact, takes cognizance of ontological pluralism; and to start, as Mbiti does, with the assertion that *we are* presumes prior recognition of the individuality of those making up the "*we.*" For although it is mathematically possible to imagine a set which happens to be empty, it seems impossible to imagine the existence of an empty human society. And to claim that "whatever happens to the individual happens to the whole group" and vice versa is no doubt to forget the difference between individuals, on the one hand, and *sets* of individuals on the other. Africans, certainly the Chewa, are aware of this important difference as exemplified by the following expressions: *Chaona mnzako chapita mawa chili paiwe* (What your neighbor has experienced is gone, tomorrow it will be your turn); *Mvula ikakuona litsiro siikata* (When the rain has seen that you are dirty it does not stop pouring); and *Wanthu ndi mchenga saundika* (Human beings are like sand out of which one cannot make a mountain). All these proverbs and maxims are reflective of the Chewa's recognition of the individuality of human beings, their fates, predicaments, and experiences.

Fourthly, it is indeed the case that the elders tended to have an epistemological monopoly over the young. But to concede this point is not to assert an ontological distinction between the elders and the young; rather, it is merely to point out an epistemological difference; the young are not ontologically less human than the elders. Furthermore, although African cultures in general, and the Chewa culture in particular, contain expressions extolling the elders as the seat of wisdom, for instance *Mau wa akuluakulu akoma atagonela* (The elders' words are still sweet after a year), there is also evidence demonstrating the rebellious tendencies of the young. To such a proverb, they would retort: *Tsobola wakale sawawa* (Old pepper is never hot), meaning that what held sway before need not necessarily hold sway now or in the future and that the advice of the elders is likely to be obsolete and irrelevant on that count. Thus, the most serious problem of the Communalism Thesis is that it conflates the epistemological with the ontological status of a human being.

However, one advantage of this doctrine is that it underscores the processual nature of personhood, the constant and gradual remaking of persons through, inter alia, the acquisition and mastery of both cultural and esoteric knowledge. And to acquire such knowledge, "the ontological priority of the collectivity" is indeed *presupposed*. Moreover, "the ontological uniqueness" of each individual is recognized even if not underscored. Though different, these two perspectives are complementary; for "the integrity and perpetuation of every *collective* order depends in the last analysis on the initiatives and actions of *individual* persons" (Jackson and Karp 1990: 27–8).

The Shadow Thesis

The shadow doctrine has been proffered by Alexis Kagame, who claims, in certain respects quite rightly as will be shown below, that for the Bantu a human being is both a *complete* animal and a being endowed with *intelligence*; complete, because he or she possesses "the vital principle of animality known as shadow," and intelligent insofar as he or she "is animated by a second vital principle which is immortal and in which are anchored the intelligent operations proper to man" (1989: 35).

However, Kagame points out (ibid. 36) other considerations which clearly demarcate humanity from animality in general. The Bantu, he claims, do not only possess intelligence, but also "the heart." With the intelligence, the human being is not only capable of reflecting and meditating "upon the data of his senses," he is also able to "compare the facts of the knowledge he has acquired," and "*to invent* something new by combining previously acquired knowledge." All these operations are open to a human being by virtue of being in possession of the faculty of reason or intelligence.

But as regards the "heart," Kagame claims that it "integrates all that the interior man is; it harmonizes the operations and acquisitions of intelligence, by adding to them the acts which other cultures attribute to the will" (ibid.). Kagame's remark is, as it stands, quite misleading, because physiologically humans cannot be said to be more in possession of a heart than, say, pigs. However, precisely because he claims that the Bantu regard this human "heart" as the being in charge of the operations of the intelligence, then pigs definitely are to be denied possession of such a "heart."

Now, what exactly is this "heart"? In almost all Bantu cultures, and certainly in Chewa culture, by the "heart" is meant the *personality* of an individual human being: "in the heart lies the *personality* of man"; "it is that by which this man is himself and not another" (Nothomb, quoted in ibid.). Thus, the "heart" understood as personality is what characterizes human beings, and is one of the criteria for distinguishing one person from another. And on this, Kagame is quite right; and his observations are quite in unison with the sayings and practices extant in Central and Southern African cultures in general, and in the Chewa culture in particular. Indeed, in the Chewa language it is generally said: *Ujeni ndi wokoma mtima* (So-and-so has a *sweet* heart), meaning that "So-and-so" has a good or kind personality.

One advantage of Kagame's thesis, having regard particularly to the significance of the personality of a human being, is that it is a move toward the resolution of the problem of personal identity; for an individual person would, in Bantu languages and thought, be distinguished from another *at least* because of his or her personality and behavior.

But problems arise with regard to Kagame's claim that human beings are *complete* animals; for a cow could be said to be as complete in itself as a goat. Thus, the question arises what could possibly be meant by a *complete animal*. On this issue, Kagame leaves us in the dark. Instead of tackling this question, he addressed to his interlocutors in his interactive research among the Bantu the question at what point a man becomes a complete animal, in response to which he got such varied answers as: "from the moment he exists in his mother's womb" (East Africa); "when a name has been given him" (Zaire, now Democratic Republic of Congo) (ibid. 30); and "from the moment he puts reason to good use" (Malawi/Southern Africa) (ibid. 37).

339

It should be noted that the important question is not at what point in time an individual becomes a person, but rather what constitutes the completeness of humanhood. And this can only be extracted and analyzed from specific intimations from the various cultures of the world (see, for example, Wright 1984: 183ff; Floistad 1987: 153ff).

True, the significance of naming an individual has been emphasized by a number of scholars in Africa. But what should be borne in mind is that the acquisition of a name is of a cultural significance, not of an ontological significance. And to say that a child is "fully a man only when a name is given him" (Kagame 1989: 36) is no doubt to underscore the cultural significance at the expense of the ontological status. For, before an individual is given a name he or she is an existent human being who happens to be nameless. The significance of the name is more to do with, inter alia, what the society expects or wishes him or her to be. Before the act of naming, he or she is not any the less human; he or she is endowed with feelings and senses, and an intellect which is yet to be put to some use.

It might very well be argued that among the Chewa a child that dies before coming out of "maternity," that is, before the time when baby and mother are seen in public after customary seclusion just before delivery, is always buried by women without any ceremony or mourning whatsoever. Such a child is referred to as *kansenye* (a tiny gazelle), allegedly indicating that a being becomes human only after coming out of a maternity (*chikuta* in Chichewa). But such an inference, in my opinion, is not warranted. Lack of a funeral ceremony is not indicative of the denial of humanhood. Rather, it is due to cultural reasons, two of which are, surely, that although such babies are indeed human, they never had a chance to utilize their faculty of reasoning, and were not socialized into the society.

Kagame, it should be conceded, fails to define what he means by the *completeness* and the *shadow* of human beings. And the picture is further complicated by his remarks on what the Bantu believe happens to a person at death. He claims that, to the Bantu, death marks the dissolution of the union between the *shadow* and the *intelligence* of a person; and that after death the shadow completely disappears. Indeed, it is still believed among the Chewa that a dead person is devoid of a shadow even when exposed to the light of the sun. But how to comprehend what *shadow* exactly means seems quite difficult.

However, it seems uncontestable that the Chewa do not mean literally that a dead person has no physical shadow; rather, what seems to be meant is a symbolic or metaphorical shadow. This symbolic shadow presumably refers to the departure or absence, at death, of an individual's personality and individuality. Since personhood is not static, but a dynamic, gradual, and persistent process in which personality is continually reinvented, death marks the end of this creative process, thus signaling the end of the quality of personality which is as elusive as a shadow. And among the Chewa, as also among the Bantu of the Lower Congo, the "shadow of a person is a perfect symbol of individual identity" (Jackson and Karp 1990: 18). Individual identity is felt to be as problematic to pinpoint as personhood. Thus, ascribing a metaphorical meaning to "shadow" seems to lead to the conclusion that the Chewa in particular, and possibly the Bantu in general, regard personhood more as a process than as an essence, whereas using a literal meaning of "shadow" does not seem to lead us anywhere. It seems, then, on the whole, that the Shadow Thesis, its problems notwithstanding, holds some promise in the analysis of the Chewa conception of personhood.

Interestingly, this concept of the shadow among the Bantu is quite similar in some respects to that of *sunsum* among the Akans. For, as Kwasi Wiredu pointed out to me in personal communication, the word *sunsum* literally means "shadow." However, that is something awaiting further research and discussion.

Concluding Remarks

I have attempted to survey and expound various conceptions of a person in Africa. The survey does not claim to be exhaustive; rather, it is simply a summary of what, to my knowledge, has been produced so far. However, I might be criticized for not explicitly mentioning work done in Southern Africa on *ubuntuism* as a concept of person. My brief response is that *ubuntuism* falls within the communalistic conception of person discussed in this chapter.

References

Abraham, W. E. (1962) *The Mind of Africa* (Chicago: Chicago University Press).

Busia, A. K. (1954) "The Ashanti of the Gold Coast," in Daryll Forde (ed.), *African Worlds: Studies in the Cosmological Ideas and the Social Values of African Peoples* (Oxford: Oxford University Press).

Danquah, J. B. (1944) *The Akan Doctrine of God: A Fragment of Gold Coast Ethics and Religion* (London: Lutterworth Press).

Floistad, G. (ed.) (1987) *Contemporary Philosophy: A New Survey*. Vol. 5: *African Philosophy* (Dordrecht: Nijhoff).

Gbadegesin, S. (1998) "'*Eniyan*': The Yoruba Conception of a Person," in P. H. Coetzee and A. P. J. Roux (eds.), *Philosophy from Africa: A Text with Readings* (Johannesburg: Thomson Publishing).

Gyekye, K. (1995) *An Essay on African Philosophical Thought: The Akan Conceptual Scheme* (Philadelphia: Temple University Press).

Jackson, M. and Karp, I. (eds.) (1990) *Personhood and Agency* (Washington, DC: Smithsonian Institution).

Kagame, A. (1989) "The Problem of 'Man' in Bantu Philosophy," *Journal of African Religion and Philosophy*, 1.

Karp, I. and Masolo, D. (eds.) (2000) *African Philosophy as Critical Inquiry* (Bloomington: Indiana University Press).

Mbiti, J. (1969) *African Religions and Philosophy* (London: Heinemann).

Parrinder, E. G. (1951) *West African Psychology* (London: Lutterworth Press).

Rattray, R. S. (1916) *Ashanti Proverbs* (Oxford: Oxford University Press).

Shaw, R. (2000) "'Tok Af Lef Af': A Political Economy of Temne Techniques of Secrecy and Self," in I. Karp and D. Masolo (eds.), *African Philosophy as Critical Inquiry* (Bloomington: Indiana University Press).

Tempels, Placide (1959) *Bantu Philosophy* (Paris: Presence Africaine).

Wiredu, K. (1987) "The Concept of Mind with Particular Reference to the Language and Thought of the Akans," in G. Floistad (ed.), *Contemporary Philosophy: A New Survey*. Vol. 5: *African Philosophy* (Dordrecht: Nijhoff).

Wiredu, K. (1992) "Death and the Afterlife in African Culture," in Kwasi Wiredu and Kwame Gyekye (eds.), *Person and Community: Ghanaian Philosophical Studies, I* (Washington DC: The Council for Research in Values and Philosophy).

Wright, R. (ed.) (1984) *African Philosophy: An Introduction* (Lanham, MD: University Press of America).

Further reading

Gwengwe, J. W. (1970) *Kukula ndi Mwambo* (Limbe, Malawi: Malawi Publications of Literature Bureau).

Kumakanga, S. (1970) *Nzeru Zakale* (Nairobi: Longman).

Menkiti, J. (1984) "Person and Community in African Traditional Thought," in R. Wright (ed.), *African Philosophy: An Introduction* (Lanham, MD: University Press of America).

Onwanibe, R. (1984) "The Human Person and Immorality in Igbo Metaphysics," in R. Wright (ed.), *African Philosophy: An Introduction* (Lanham, MD: University Press of America).

26

Quasi-Materialism: A Contemporary African Philosophy of Mind

SAFRO KWAME

Introduction

Let me assert, categorically and unambiguously, that I am neither a materialist nor a physicalist. My reason is that I am a quasi-physicalist, and a quasi-physicalist, strictly speaking, is not a materialist nor even a physicalist. Physicalism as a contemporary philosophy of mind, it seems to me, will be reductive or else not at all. Yet, if contemporary Western philosophers of mind such as Willard Quine and Richard Rorty are right, reductive physicalism is dead, and it is apparent, or it ought to be, that a "non-reductive physicalism" is really not a kind of physicalism even though, possibly, it is a quasi-physicalism of some sort.

It is my opinion that when the distinctions between physicalism and what, for want of a better term, may be called quasi-physicalism are drawn and noted, the latter may be perceived as being more representative of traditional African philosophies of mind, such as that of the Akans, than the former. In the light of recent developments in neurophysiology, cognitive psychology, and computer science, and the resulting critique of some influential Western traditional philosophies of mind, it seems to me that a contemporary African philosophy of mind will have to take quasi-physicalism into consideration in characterizing traditional African conceptions of mind. Otherwise it might seem to be grappling with a false dilemma. If I am right, the suggestion that traditional African conceptions of mind are either dualistic in a Cartesian sense or else monistic in a spiritual sense presents the contemporary African philosopher of mind with one such false dilemma.

Physicalism

Physicalism may be characterized in various ways and each characterization may have several synonyms. While most characterizations are not inconsistent with each other, they are not exactly interchangeable. Consequently, in telling you why I am not a physicalist, it is advisable to tell you what kind of physicalist I am not. For it may turn out that my anti-physicalism passes for physicalism on some definition of the term. Simply stated, physicalism is the thesis that only physical objects exist or everything that can be said to exist can be described in the language of physics or in a physical language. As Antony Flew puts it in his *Dictionary of Philosophy*, it is the doctrine that all propositions asserting matters of fact and real existence can be formulated as statements about publicly observable physical objects and processes (1984: 267).

Physicalism espouses a materialism of sorts and a reductionism of some kind. As David Rosenthal explains, "the reduction in question would be accomplished if the terms needed for physics, and only those terms would be sufficient to express all the claims and explanations of psychology" (1987: 2). He adds that "this view, often called 'the thesis of the unity of science,' has the force of a prediction about the future development of science" (ibid.). Rosenthal explains that according to one defense of the unity thesis, commonly known as materialism, "in spite of the difference in meaning between any psychological and physical descriptions, still whatever is described in psychological terms can also be described equally well (though differently) in solely physical terms" (ibid.).

According to Quine, the physicalist "is content to declare bodies to be fundamental in this sense: there is no difference in the world without a difference in the positions of states of bodies" (1977: 196). In Quine's opinion, it is a way of saying that the fundamental objects are the physical objects and according physics its rightful place as the basic natural science (ibid. 187) without advocating reductionism in a strong sense (ibid. 192). With regard to the mind, it is saying, indifferently, that we are dispensing with mental states and events in favor of bodily ones or explaining mental states and events as bodily ones (1987: 133). "Each individual episode of someone's thinking about Vienna, for example," Quine explains, "is a neural event, which we could describe in strict neurological terms if we know enough about the specific case and its mechanism" (ibid. 133).

A physicalist, according to Rorty, is "someone who is prepared to say that every event can be described in micro-structural terms, a description which mentions only elementary particles, and can be explained by reference to other events so described" (1991: 144). He adds, however, that a physicalist need not deny that these same events can be described in mentalistic or non-microstructural (macrostructural) terms:

> So to be a physicalist is, on this non-reductionist account, perfectly compatible with saying that we shall probably continue to talk about mental entities – beliefs, desires and the like forever.... Further, it would be wrong to suggest that talk about minds is necessary for convenience but is not to be taken as "the truth about the way the world is." (ibid. 113)

The Argument for Physicalism

Quine lists three main reasons against dualism and in favor of physicalism. The first is that dualism cannot provide us with any conceivable mechanism with which to account for the interaction of two radically different substances such as the mind and the body (1987: 32). The second is that while physicalism is compatible with the highly regarded law of conservation of energy, dualism is not (ibid.). Lastly, it is claimed that our current knowledge, together with Ockham's razor, suggest that every mental event is associated with some bodily event:

> Today's conventional wisdom is that no thought or feeling occurs without an impulse or twitch of some nerve or fiber or its bodily implementation...Granted this much, it becomes a flagrant breach of William of Ockham's maxim of parsimony to admit mind as a second substance at all. (ibid.)

"If there is no mental difference without a physical difference," Quine argues, "then there is pointless ontological extravagance in admitting minds as entities over and above bodies" (1977: 187). He adds that we cannot similarly argue for dispensing with bodies in favor of minds unless we are idealists and wish to suggest that there is no physical difference without a mental difference (ibid. 188).

I do not see that any reason has been given for avoiding idealism, for the argument for physicalism, as stated above, is compatible with idealism. In the first place, we are aware of the *limits of our scientific knowledge and evidence* concerning the existence of corresponding mental events for every physical event. I believe that the attempt by some physicalists to avoid reductionism is based simply on our ignorance of the facts that would warrant saying that all psychological events are reducible to physical events. As both Quine (ibid. 187) and Rorty (1991: 115) admit, there is very little hope of our being able to specify all mental events in physiological terms. Quine calls such optimism an utopian dream (1977: 187).

However, it seems to me that any kind of physicalism which rejects dualism must in some minimal sense, at least, be reductive. It must seek to reduce all mental, spiritual, or non-physical entities and events to physical ones. Yet, it provides no decisive evidence in support of that. After all, idealism is also a monistic theory and, hence, it does not need to explain how two substances interact. It does not multiply entities beyond necessity; neither does it violate the law of conservation of energy. My second point, then, is that *there is no crucial philosophical evidence* in favor of physicalism. The main reason for Quine's preference for physicalism over idealism seems to be his concern to begin with what is clear or apparently commonsensical: "If clarity can be ascribed to things as well as words," he remarks, "then bodies are things at their clearest." "If inquiry is to begin with what is clear," he continues, "then let us begin as physicalists" (ibid. 181). But even if we assumed that it is clear in the sense of obvious that there are (physical) bodies and we wanted to start our argument and inquiry by assuming that physical objects exist, there is no good reason for ending as physicalists rather than, say, quasi-physicalists.

Quasi-Physicalism

Quasi-physicalism does for physicalism what physicalism did for materialism expressed exclusively in terms of atoms and other elementary particles. It stretches the limits of matter or materialism as far as is compatible with what we know or do not know, without embracing dualism. It admits the possibility of quasi-physical objects as belonging to a category between the realm of the obviously physical, i.e. those objects that obey the known laws of physics, and the realm of the so-called spiritual or completely immaterial objects that do not obey any of the known laws of physics. These are the "fuzziest" objects that quasi-physicalism recognizes as being compatible with a limited version of physicalism. They, unlike outright spiritual or immaterial objects, are recognized as existing together with atoms, fields, energies, sets, and numbers. While rejecting spiritual entities as conceptually confused or unclear and in violation of Ockham's razor, it wishes to acknowledge science's state of ignorance and leave open the possibility of there being entities which are not completely physical and may not as yet be discovered.

Quasi-physicalism is a term that Kwasi Wiredu coined to capture a view of the traditional Akans of West Africa. These traditional Akans consider the mind (*adwene*), in a non-substance way, as a capacity of an individual or entity while acknowledging the existence of God, "souls," and ghosts as non-human objects that may eat, drink, clothe themselves, and be spatially located without obeying all the known laws of physics (1987: 161).[1] The traditional Akan, as a quasi-physicalist, categorically asserts the existence of God, "souls," and ghosts as quasi-physical entities. The modern or contemporary quasi-physicalist merely refuses to rule out the possibility of quasi-physical entities in the light of epistemic modesty and fallibilism. They, unlike their traditional counterparts, assert that if such beings or objects exist at all, it is instructive to consider them as quasi-physical objects on the following conditions: (1) we do not wish to multiply entities beyond necessity, and (2) we are already inclined toward physicalism. In other words, they admit that, for all we know, there may be God, "souls," and ghosts who, for simplicity and other reasons, are best categorized as quasi-physical objects.

There is, at best, a difference in degree between these and human beings, but not a difference in kind. It is noteworthy that the modern or contemporary quasi-physicalist does not deny that as our discovery of physical laws proceeds and our scientific knowledge increases, we may come to accept some or all the quasi-physical objects as bona fide physical objects. The quasi-physicalism of today may then turn out to be the materialism or physicalism of tomorrow. After all, all forms of materialism are relative to the physics of the day, however unmaterialistic their theories may sound to their predecessors (see Gregory 1987: 491).

The quasi-physicalist has no objection to characterizing his or her ontology and philosophy of mind as functionalist so long as they are not confused with Hilary Putnam's functionalism, which, according to him, is a variant of the identity theory and monism while being compatible with dualism. "On the functionalist view," Putnam writes, "there is indeed an identity here, but Smart was looking at the wrong sort of brain property to figure as the other term in the identity" (1981: 78).

> According to the functionalist, the brain has properties which are in a sense not physical.... The suggestion of the functionalist is that the most plausible "monistic" theory in the twentieth century, the most plausible theory that avoids treating mind and matter as two separate sorts of substances or two separate realms of properties is that psychological properties are identical with functional properties. (ibid. 79)

He also notes that the advantage of functionalism over traditional forms of the identity theory is functionalism's compatibility with dualism (1987b: 157).

While being opposed to treating the mind as a separate substance or a separate set of properties exclusively of physical beings, quasi-physicalism, unlike Putnam's functionalism, is neither compatible with dualism nor with the identity theory, nor with any traditional form of monism. The reason, as Kwasi Wiredu points out, is simple. On the Akan conception, the mind, rendered in Akan by the word *adwene*, which is merely the noun form of the verb *dwen* ("think"), is not a substance at all. And that is why mind (*adwene*) is never listed by the Akans as one of the constituents of a person (1987: 159, 160–1). Mind excludes sensations and is, as Wiredu puts it, a logical construction out of actual and potential thoughts (ibid. 158). "Neither a thought nor the mere possibility of thought," Wiredu notes, "could, as a matter of logical impossibility, be any kind of object" (ibid.). "The truth is that thought, not being an entity, is neither material nor immaterial, physical nor non-physical" (ibid. 169). Further, to the extent that dualism or monism rests on the assumption that the mind is either an entity or a property of a completely physical or nonphysical entity, it is unacceptable from an Akan point of view (ibid. 175). As we pointed out earlier, quasi-physicalism recognizes the *possibility* of quasi-physical objects that have minds of their own.

Why then do some Africans, such as Kwame Gyekye, characterize the Akans as dualists? The reason, I believe, is that they ignore the category of the quasi-physical and, hence, have no other choice once they acknowledge that traditional Akans believe in entities that are not completely materialistic in the classic sense. "Such [a quasi-physical] description of the *okra* (soul) in Akan thought," Gyekye argues, "runs counter to the belief of most Akan people in disembodied survival or life after death" (1995: 86). Gyekye concludes as follows:

> The Akan conception of the person, on my analysis, is both dualistic and interactionist. It seems to me that an interactionist psychophysical dualism is a realistic doctrine. Even apart from the prospects for disembodied survival that this doctrine holds out it has had significant pragmatic consequences in Akan communities, as evidenced in the application of psychophysical therapies. There are countless testimonies of people who have been subjected to physical treatment for months or years in modern hospitals without being cured, but who have been healed by traditional healers applying both physical and psychical (spiritual) methods. (ibid. 102–3)

In the first place, since traditional African healers use both obviously physical as well as the not-so-obviously physical or "psychical" methods, their success does not automatically establish the efficacy of the so-called psychical methods. It may be that they use other physical methods that are more effective in the treatment of some diseases. After all, some people who are unsuccessfully subjected to so-called physical treatments in one modern Western hospital (in, say, Pennsylvania) may be successfully treated by so-called physical treatment in another Western hospital (in, say, Ohio) in the same country. Similarly, sometimes people who cannot be cured by traditional African healers are cured by Western physicians. Neither proves that there are spiritual entities or that traditional African healers do not use physical or quasi-physical methods; because success in and of itself is not a spiritual entity, and the examples in question have no controls and are not designed to test the existence of completely non-physical entities. To test the existence or non-existence of completely non-physical entities and methods, the traditional African healers would have to be barred from employing any physical entities or methods in their therapies and procedures. They never are.

As for life after death, it ought to be noted that, if it exists, it is compatible with a quasi-physical existence or even a completely physical existence, as in some forms of reincarnation. If I believed that when people die they shed their human legs and develop amphibious ones or frog legs and proceed to live under the sea, I would believe in a life hereafter that could not, in any significant sense, be said to be spiritual even if it is acknowledged to be different from the preceding human life after birth. As Wiredu has on occasion pointed out, there is nothing distinctly spiritual about the Akan belief in a life hereafter in which the *akra* or Akan "souls" clothe themselves, occupy space, drink water, and eat human food. There is a danger, to which we all sometimes succumb, in translating African categories into the most obvious Western ones. My guess is that this is why Gyekye, understandably, I think, chooses to categorize the Akans as dualists. Not much, however, is said in Gyekye's account about the Akan conception of mind that offers any solid grounds for a dualistic conception of mind.

I understand Gyekye's concerns about using the term "quasi-physicalism" (ibid. 86). It seems that quasi-physicalism has the same kind of legitimacy or illegitimacy that the preference for "physicalism" has for materialists. As D. M. Armstrong notes, some writers prefer the term "physicalism" to "materialism" because materialism misleadingly seems to conjure up a Newtonian account of matter (in Gregory 1987: 491). Similarly, the preference for "quasi-physicalism" over "physicalism" would seem to free us from confinement to the physics of the day or to the narrow boundaries of current physicalism.

It should be apparent from the foregoing that any meaningful physicalism will have to be either reductive or nothing at all. For physicalism is a monistic theory that is opposed to not only idealism but also dualism as an ontological thesis. And a monistic theory that is opposed to ontological dualism, standardly, asserts that there is only one irreducible reality. Hence, the belief that we could maintain a non-reductive physicalism or a monistic theory of a completely physicalist or functionalist nature while discovering something profound about Cartesian dualism seems to me to be misguided. After all, almost every definition of physicalism admits, as does the *Paragon House Glossary of Cognitive Science*, that physicalism embraces the view that, ultimately, nothing exists over and above or other than physical reality (Dunlop and Fetzer 1993: 98).

In my view, this is part of why Putnam's functionalism did not work. The attempt to go beyond what Putnam now characterizes as minimal functionalism (1988: xii) toward a defense of physicalism fails. It fails not just because, as he now acknowledges, the same mental state can be a property of systems which are not of the same computational structure even if they are of the same species (ibid. xiv, 74, 84, 104). As he puts it, "the different *computational* states one might be in while believing that a cat is on the mat need not have anything 'in common' that can be

348

specified in *computational* terms" (ibid. 74). But more importantly, neither can it be specified in physical or chemical terms (ibid.). "The 'intentional level,'" he recapitulates, "is not reducible to the 'computational level' any more than it is to the 'physical level'" (1987a: 15).

For our purpose here, it is important to note that it is not just that the mind is not reducible to one program or a number of programs; but, more importantly, it is neither reducible to nor identifiable with the program or programs of any physical or monistic entity. The belief that the mind is both compositionally and computationally plastic is so ontologically barren that I do not see how it can provide Putnam or anyone else with evidence of a completely physical or strictly monistic ontology. Quasi-physicalism, unlike Putnam's earlier functionalism, consistently maintains that it is wrong to think that the essence of our mind is in our "hardware" (1988: xii); and also wrong to think that this insight generates physicalism as opposed to, say, quasi-physicalism or even idealism.

Conclusion

In conclusion, I can find no (sufficient) reason from either the functionalists or non-reductive physicalists for being a physicalist. Further, if the non-reductive physicalists are right in claiming that reductive physicalism is not promising, then the only other theory I can think of, which is consistent with both scientific and philosophical considerations, is quasi-physicalism. This is not to say that quasi-physicalism is true beyond the possibility of doubt. For all I know, it may be just as confused as any of its more popular rivals. The history of metaphysics and the spirit of fallibilism in which quasi-physicalism was proposed forbid us from asserting otherwise. They do not, of course, forbid us from trying to come up with better theories.

It is obvious that the mind–body problem does not arise in the philosophy of mind that is inspired by an African tradition such as that of the Akans. Since the mind is not conceived as an entity, there cannot possibly be a problem of how mind as a "spiritual" entity is related to the material body. For some Western philosophers not to raise such a question would be a defect.

This may be a natural way of thinking of Western theories of mind, since the history of Western philosophy of mind has been largely a history of the mind–body problem. The history of the philosophy of mind in the West is not coextensive with the history of the philosophy of mind *simpliciter*. Needless to say, there have been historical philosophies of mind in Africa and the East in which the mind–body problem is not a member of the class of legitimate problems. After all, from a purely logical, as opposed to a merely historical point of view, a theory of mind need not be a theory of the mind–body problem.

Further, if a theory is to be illuminating, its objective or one of its objectives should be to eliminate eliminable problems, not to create them. It would seem, then, that there is much to say in favor of, rather than against, a theory of mind which eliminates the mind–body problem rather than raises it, provided, of course, that the elimination is achieved by sound methods. A contemporary African philosopher of mind, then, who inherits a tradition such as that of the Akans and is

349

aware of the history of the Western philosophy of mind with its mind–body problem, should be willing to explore quasi-physicalism in the light of models presented by today's computers. A reflection on the possibility of using computers as models of the mind should reinforce one's belief in quasi-physicalism so long as we do not repeat the mistake of those functionalists who took the idea that a physical entity like a computer could think to imply that physicalism is right.

If it is true that computers can think, which is still debatable, depending on what one understands by *thought*, all that it proves is that René Descartes was wrong in believing that a completely physical being was incapable of thinking and that thinking requires something that is, by essence, non-physical and capable of disembodied survival. A computer, after all, is a completely physical machine that, as far as we know, is incapable of disembodied survival. The fact that a physical machine can think, if indeed it turns out to be a fact, would not mean that thinking is a physical thing or a machine or even that only machines or physical things can think. To argue to the contrary is to confuse essence with capacity. If a dog can walk, it does not make walking a dog or a thing that only dogs can do. It would not follow that only dogs can walk or that you must have a dog in you to be able to walk. This point is implicit in the Akan conception of a person. Quasi-physicalism is one philosophy of mind that seems to me to be consistent with that African perspective.

Note

This is a revised version of "Why I am not a Physicalist," which originally appeared in *The Personalist Forum*, 7(1), Spring 1992 Supplement: 191–6.

1   In describing the Akan conception of the soul as quasi-physical, Wiredu notes that it is credited with para-physical properties, it is not straightforwardly physical, and not fully subject to spatial constraints.

References

Dunlop, Charles and Fetzer, James (1993) *Paragon House Glossary of Cognitive Science* (New York: Paragon House).

Flew, Anthony (1984) *A Dictionary of Philosophy* (New York: St. Martin's Press).

Gregory, Richard (ed.) (1987) *The Oxford Companion to The Mind* (New York: Oxford University Press).

Gyekye, Kwame (1995) *An Essay on African Philosophical Thought* (Philadelphia: Temple University Press).

Putnam, Hilary (1981) *Reason, Truth and History* (Cambridge: Cambridge University Press).

Putnam, Hilary (1987a) *The Many Faces of Realism* (La Salle, IL: Open Court Publishing Company).

Putnam, Hilary (1987b) "The Nature of Mental States," in David Rosenthal, *Objectivity, Relativism, and Truth: Philosophical Papers*, vol. I (Cambridge: Cambridge University Press).

Putnam, Hilary (1988) *Representation and Reality* (Cambridge, MA: MIT Press).

Quine, W. V. O. (1977) "Facts of the Matter," in R. W. Shawan and K. R. Merrill (eds.), *American Philosophy* (Oklahoma: University of Oklahoma Press).

Quine, W. V. O. (1987) *Quiddities: Intermittently Philosophical Dictionary* (Cambridge, MA: The Belknap Press of Harvard University Press).

Rorty, Richard (1991) *Objectivity, Relativism, and Truth: Philosophical Papers*, vol. I (Cambridge: Cambridge University Press).

Rosenthal, David (ed.) (1987) *Materialism and the Mind-Body Problem* (Indianapolis: Hackett Publishing Company, Inc.).

Wiredu, Kwasi (1987) "The Concept of Mind with Particular Reference to the Language and Thought of the Akans," in Guttorm Floistad (ed.), *Contemporary Philosophy: A New Survey*, vol. 5 (Dordrecht: Martinus Nijhoff Publishers).

Part IV

THE PHILOSOPHY OF RELIGION

27

Religion in African Culture: Some Conceptual Issues

OLUSEGUN OLADIPO

The role of religion in African culture is one of the central issues in contemporary African philosophy. The story of its importance goes somewhat like this. There was a European discourse that denied that religion had any significant role to play in African culture. According to this discourse, exemplified by the reports of early European travelers and missionaries in Africa, Africans lacked those religious and moral beliefs and attitudes that define a genuine human civilization. This is how Samuel Baker characterized this lack of religious and moral refinement among Africans:

> Without exception, they are without a belief in a Supreme Being, neither have they any form of worship or idolatry; nor is the darkness of their minds enlightened even by a ray of superstition. The mind is as stagnant as the morass which forms its puny world.[1]

In other words, for Baker, Africans were pagans, a people without a religion.

Although not all the early accounts of African beliefs are as negative as Baker's, they all, in various ways, portray Africans as spiritually inferior to Europeans – a view that was also propagated by evolutionary anthropologists, such as de Brosses, Edward Tylor, and James Frazer. For these anthropologists, the African religious heritage was at the lowest of "man's religious history." Hence, the description of African religions as "fetishism" or "animism."

The ethnocentric accounts of African religion highlighted above invariably generated a "counter discourse." The aim of this discourse, key participants in which were Bolaji Idowu and John Mbiti, was to reject the "claims of Western scholarship which presented their peoples as primitive pagans." For these scholars, Africans not only had religious categories, which were similar in some essential respects to Western ones; more than this, their view of the world was "profoundly religious." According to John Mbiti, whose view on this subject has often been quoted:

> Because traditional religions permeate all departments of life, there is no formal distinction between the sacred and the secular, between the religious and the non-religious, between the spiritual and the material areas of life. Wherever the African is, there is

his religion: he carries it to the fields where he is sowing seeds or harvesting a new crop; he takes it with him to the beer party or to attend a funeral ceremony; and if he is educated, he takes religion with him to the examination room at school or in the university; if he is a politician he takes it to the house of parliament. (1969: 2)

Thus, for Mbiti, Africans are religious in all things.

It was this rather exaggerated picture of the role of religion in African culture, which became an anthropological commonplace in African scholarship,[2] which provided the basis for the centrality of the issue of the place of religion in African philosophy. Three main questions define the focus of this issue. First, there is the question of what the substance of indigenous African religions is. The second is that of the extent to which the central categories of these religions and those of Western religions, in particular Christianity, are intertranslatable. The third question concerns the nature of the relationship between indigenous African religions and other aspects of life, for instance, morality. This chapter is primarily an attempt to address these questions.

Let us begin with the first question. A convenient point of departure in discussing this question would be Bolaji Idowu's definition (1973) of the nature of African traditional religion when he identifies the structure of African traditional religion to include the following:

- belief in God;
- belief in divinities;
- belief in spirits;
- belief in ancestors;
- the practice of magic and medicine.[3]

It is the pervasiveness of these beliefs in African culture that has provided the basis for the assertion that Africans are in all things religious.

This claim has generated two questions. These are: the question of the extent to which the non-human powers and agencies identified above can be regarded as religious entities; and that of whether the attitude of the Africans to them can be regarded as a religious attitude.

Before we begin to address these questions, it is important to note that religion is an expression of a relationship between individuals and God. It is both a belief and an attitude. It is the belief that God (or whatever is regarded as the ultimate reality in each culture) created (or made) the world and everything in it, and that it is on Him that we are dependent for our being and sustenance. As an attitude, it is devotional; it expresses our sense of dependence on God.

The two aspects of religion identified above, namely, that of belief and that of attitude, arise from the recognition by human beings that they are not alone in the world-process. It is recognized that we are in our daily activities dependent on other elements in this process. This dependence invariably places some limitations on our powers, our knowledge, our values, our identity, etc. We can therefore say with Feuerbach (1969: 16) that religion is identical with the distinctive characteristic of human beings, which is self-consciousness. But although the recognition of the limitations already mentioned is not unique to the religious interpretation of experience, it is at least its starting point. In other words, it is what provides the basis for the belief in, and devotional attitude to, that which is perceived to have the ontological significance of being the ground and source of human existence and sustenance. Thus, central to the understanding of religion is an awareness of a certain ontological ultimacy. Hence, a typically religious object is one which has the ontological significance of being the ground of human existence and its source of sustenance, while a religious attitude is a devotional attitude to this object.

With this definition as background, we can now tackle the question of what should be regarded as the substance of African traditional religion. In tackling this question, our focus will be on the non-human powers and agencies that have been identified as defining the structure of African traditional religion. To what extent are these religious entities? Even if they are religious, can the attitude of Africans to them be regarded as a typically religious attitude?

A careful examination of the various conceptualizations of these agencies and powers would suggest that the Supreme Being in African cultures can be regarded as a typical religious object. He is, in most cases, regarded as the maker of the world and its sustainer and ruler; the origin and giver of life who is above all divinities and man; a supreme judge and a controller of human destiny. These attributes show that the Supreme Being in African culture is regarded as the ultimate reality. And He is a religious object. After all, they constantly mention Him in prayers and in times of difficulties, even though no direct worship of Him is entertained in most cases. Generally, then, the Supreme Being, called *Onyame* by the Akans, *Chukwu* by the Igbos, and *Olodumare* by the Yoruba, to cite a few examples, can be regarded as the ultimate point of reference in whatever may be called African traditional religion.

It should be noted, however, that although the belief in a Supreme Being is widespread in African culture, the people do not worship Him, as the Christians, for example, do their God. Rather, they relate more directly to the divinities or deities. These divinities are believed to be more accessible, and it is to them that the people take their immediate problems.[4] Here is a contrast between the idea of the Supreme Being in African culture and the Christian notion of God, which makes the identification of the one with the other problematic. More on this later.

Now, it has earlier been observed that Africans believe in the existence of many divinities, together with "a whole host of other extra-human beings and forces" (Wiredu 1996a: 56) and that this has also been taken as an expression of their profound religiosity. However, it is doubtful that these divinities can appropriately be regarded as religious objects to which the people have a religious attitude. This judgment is based on the following considerations.[5]

First, most of these divinities are man-made in the sense that they are originated and maintained by human beings. (This is clearly revealed in the Yoruba proverb: *Ibití ènìà kò sí, kò sí imalè* – "Where there is no man there is no divinity": see Idowu 1962: 63.) They are made either in response to a perceived threat to human existence – the threat of a pestilence, for example – or in acknowledgment of a specific human need, for example, the need for security, social harmony, knowledge, and guidance. Hence the nature of these divinities is, as T. U. Nwala has

357

observed with regard to Igbo divinities (1985: 136), influenced by the people's physical environment and the ideals they cherish. Another manifestation of the dependence of these divinities on human beings is the fact that it is their devotees that maintain their secrets. Any betrayal of a divinity by its devotees reduces it "to an empty word, an object of ridicule" (Barber 1981: 738). Indeed, the divinities do "die" when they are abandoned by their devotees.

This brings us to an important feature of the attitude of the people to these divinities, which compromises their supposed religious essence. This is the pragmatic nature of the belief in and devotion to these divinities. They are feared or venerated on the basis of the people's perception of their utilitarian value, that is, their ability to aid or hinder human activities. This feature of the attitude to divinities in African culture is aptly captured in the Igbo proverb rendered in English by Chinua Achebe thus: "A deity who does as he says never lacks in worshippers" (1988: 103). It is also reflected in Ezeulu's rationalization of his decision, cited in Achebe (1974) to send one of his sons, Oduche, to the church, even though he was the Chief Priest of Ulu, the local deity. Ezeulu wanted Oduche to go to church because:

> I want one of my sons to join this people and be my eye there. If there is nothing in it you will come back. But if there is something there you will bring home my share. The world is like a mask dancing. If you want to see it well you do not stand in one place. My spirit tells me that those who do not befriend the white man today will be saying *had we known* tomorrow.

Here, indeed, is a clear expression of the pragmatic nature of the relationship between the people and their divinities!

It should be clear from the analysis above that Senghor's observation that "neither fear nor material cares dominate African religion...it is dominated by love and charity which is love in action" is mistaken (1976: 38–9). For, as this analysis has shown, the people fear or respect the divinities, they acknowledge their powers, but only to the extent that the divinities are able "to prove themselves" by delivering the desired goods. This kind of attitude can hardly be regarded as a religious attitude.

It would seem, therefore, that most of what is regarded as African religion by many writers on African culture is nothing but what Basil Davidson calls "Systems of advice and explanation" (1978: 49) misleadingly described as religions. And we have cultural nationalism to blame for this distortion of an important aspect of African culture. As already indicated at the beginning of this chapter, the claim that Africans are religious in all things is a dominant aspect of a counter-discourse which tried to show that Africans were not irreligious and immoral as some Europeans were wont to suppose. It is interesting to note, however, that this protest discourse was articulated through the medium of the languages of those whose views of Africa were being rejected. This brings us to the issue of the extent to which the religious categories borrowed from these languages fit or fail to fit the African reality they are used to describe.

Our answer to this question is already foreshadowed in the discussion of the substance of African religion attempted above. A major point of this discussion is that the characterization of the African belief in extra-human beings and forces as religions is a kind of conceptual superimposition. We have a specific case of this superimposition, which misrepresents the African cultural experience, in the attempt to draw a one-to-one correspondence between the Christian notion of the Supreme Being and African notions.

A brief listing of the defining characteristics of God in the Christian religion would go somewhat like this. He is a Supreme Being, who is the creator, sustainer, and ruler of the universe and the controller of human destiny. He is a supernatural being who is both transcendent and immanent. This transcendence means not only that He is beyond sense perception, but also that other things in the universe are absolutely dependent on Him for their existence. He is also believed to be immanent in the sense that He exists everywhere in a purely spiritual form. Above all, He is conceived to be omnipotent, omniscient, and supremely good.

Some aspects of the idea of the Supreme Being as conceived in African culture are similar to the Christian notion whose essential elements are highlighted above. In Yoruba culture, for instance, Olódùmaré (the Supreme Being), who stands at the apex of the theoretical entities in terms of which the Yoruba explain human experience, is regarded as the creator (Elédàá) and maker (Asèdá) and the origin and giver of life (Elémì í). He is also conceived as the undying king (Oba Aikú), whose habitation is in the heavens above (Oba Òrun) and who is above all divinities and humans; a being whose work is done in perfection (Asè-kan-má-kù); a supreme judge who judges in silence (Adákédájó); and the controller of humankind's destiny (see Idowu 1962: 39–42).

The similarities between the Christian notion and this African conception of the Supreme Being, which is shared by many African cultures, are too obvious to require any elaboration. However, there are significant "divergences of cultural perception" which make the identification of one with the other problematic. One area of divergence can be found in the creative works attributed to these Supreme Beings. God in Christian thought is believed to have "brought all things out of nothing." However, in the Yoruba conception of the Supreme Being the idea of *creatio ex nihilo* is absent. Indeed, the Yoruba believe not only that our earth was made out of what "was once a watery, marshy waste" (ibid. 19), but also that its making involved some divinities, particularly Òrìsà-nlá (the arch-divinity), animals like the chameleon, hen, and pigeon, and even vegetation like the palm tree, silk rubber tree, and white wood, etc. (ibid. 19–20). Thus, for the Yoruba, the Supreme Being is like Plato's demiurge, who did what he could do with pre-existing materials in making the world.

A consequence of the above observation on the creative work of Olódùmarè is that He cannot be said to be transcendent like the Christian God. For, if he made the world out of pre-existing materials, then it follows that he had always been part of the world-order. And, if this is the case, He cannot be said to exist beyond the world. Indeed, for the Yoruba, Olódùmarè exists somewhere in the sky, which, in the beginning, was so near the earth that people could travel to and back from it, as they wished.

Thus, Olódùmarè is unlike the Christian God with respect to the attributes of transcendence and immanence. He is neither "wholly other," nor is He a purely

359

spiritual being. What is more, He does not even possess the quality of omnipotence, which is another important characteristic of God. If omnipotence implies "infinite power," then to say that Olódùmarè is omnipotent is to say that He is almighty in the sense that He is not subject to any constraints in the exercise of his powers. However, it is doubtful that Olódùmarè can be said to be all-powerful in this sense. A crucial consideration in this regard is the acknowledgment, by the people, of other powers and principalities – divinities, spirits, magic, witchcraft, and so on. Some of these powers and forces are treated as ends in themselves. Hence, the people endeavor, through sacrifice, to be on good terms with them in recognition of their powers to aid or hinder human activities. It may be said, therefore, that what we see in the Yoruba world-view, like other African world-views, is a plurality of divinities and forces, which are "linked to various material forces" and are expected to fulfill specific needs. This is a kind of metaphysical pragmatism, which exposes the incorrectness of the claim that the divinities and forces stand to the Supreme Being as angels and saints stand to the Christian God.

We see, then, that the identification of the Supreme Being in African culture with the Christian God is a specific example of conceptual superimposition, which has for long prevented a proper appreciation of the nature of indigenous African religions. It is this superimposition which has obscured the humanistic characteristic of these religions.[6]

The point of the foregoing analysis is to show that the place of religion in African culture has been exaggerated, through the "uncritical assimilation" of Western conceptual categories in African religio-anthropological, and in some cases philosophical, scholarship. We have another example of this exaggeration in certain characterizations of the relationship between religion and morality in African culture. Before we discuss the nature of the distortion involved in these characterizations, it is important to note that morality in African culture is given expression in the concept of character. Idowu makes this point with specific reference to the Yoruba when he invites that: "Ìwà [character], according to the Yoruba, is the very stuff, which makes life a joy.... It is therefore stressed that good character must be the dominant feature of a person's life. In fact, it is one thing, which distinguishes a person from a brute" (1962: 154). Gyekye makes a similar point with respect to the Akans. According to him: "The concept of character, *Suban*, is so crucial and is given such central place in Akan moral language that it may be considered as summing up the whole of morality" (1987: 147).

Good character has the following components, among others: hospitality, selflessness, kindness, humility, abhorrence of wickedness, respect for truth, and rectitude, regard for covenants, high regard for honor, and respect for old age. The question which now arises is this: what is the basis of our judgment of good character?

For some scholars of African culture, the elements of good character identified above are inextricably linked to religion. For these scholars, there is a necessary connection between religion and morality in African culture. Kofi Asare Opoku, for instance, writes about Akan morality thus: "Generally, morality originates from religious considerations, and so pervasive is religion in African culture that ethics and religion cannot be separated from each other.... Thus, morality flows out of religion" (1978: 2). And writing about the Yoruba, Idowu asserts that:

With the Yoruba, morality is certainly a fruit of religion. They do not make any attempt to separate the two, and it is impossible for them to do so without disastrous consequences. What have been named taboo took their origin from the fact that people discerned that there were things which were usually approved or disapproved by the Deity. (1962: 146)

Thus, for Opoku and Idowu morality and religion are inseparable in African culture.

To support this position, it is argued, first, that in traditional society, religion is so pervasive that "it is not easy to isolate what is purely religious from other aspects of life" (Opoku 1974: 286). Second, it is observed that a sense of right and wrong is necessary for morality and, for Africans, this sense is an endowment of the Deity. Consequently, African moral values cannot be separated from the various conceptions of the Deity in Africa.

These arguments are far from being persuasive. First, as we argued earlier, the view that religion is all-pervasive in African culture is mistaken. Second, it has been observed that most indigenous African religions are non-revealed religions. In these religions, there are no founders through whom divine truths or commands are revealed. Thus, the idea that there is a set of rules decreed by a Deity is untenable. Furthermore, the pragmatic attitude of the devotees to the various divinities, which we noted earlier, suggests that even the divinities are open to moral assessment. It follows that the people's conception of what is right and wrong is a product of "their own moral perception or understanding or knowledge" (Gyekye 1987: 6). Finally, a careful examination of some African proverbs will reveal a this-worldly, essentially pragmatic, moral orientation (see, e.g., Owomoyela 1981; Oluwole 1984; Oladeji 1988).

The point of the foregoing arguments is not to deny that there are aspects of morality in African culture that are associated with the various conceptions of the Deity. The point, rather, is that there are other foundations of morality in African culture, not the least of which are "the happiness of man and the welfare of all" (Liyong 1997: 79).[7]

In all, the role of religion in African culture has been, to a very large extent, misrepresented. The correction of some of these distortions should be one of the tasks of an African philosophy of religion.

Notes

1 Samuel Baker, in an address to the Anthropological Society of London in 1866, quoted in Evans-Pritchard 1965: 16–17.
2 Kwame Gyekye re-echoes this view: "It would be correct to say that religion enters all aspects of African life so fully – determining practically every aspect of life, including moral behavior – that it can hardly be isolated. African heritage is intensely religious. The African lives in a religious universe: all actions and thoughts have a religious meaning and are inspired or influenced by a religious point of view" (1996: 3).
3 See Idowu (1973: 13–202) for a detailed discussion of each of these items.
4 For instance, it has been reported of the Arogbo-Ijaw people in the Niger Delta area of Southern Nigeria that: "There are 21 denominations of Churches in Arogbo-Ijaw

kingdom.... Yet, they (the people) seem to relate more with Egbesu than with the almighty God." And the reason for this, given by a Chief at Arogbo, is that Egbesu (the local deity) "responds more quickly to their needs than the Almighty God." Thus, although they believe in God, "they take their immediate problem to Egbesu." See Williams 1998: 29.

5   For more detailed arguments for this claim, with particular reference to the Akans of Ghana and the Yoruba of Nigeria, see, for example, Wiredu 1996a: ch. 5; Wiredu 1996b; and Oladipo 1990.

6   It is this humanistic orientation of indigenous African religions that Taban Lo Liyong explores in his "exciting collection of poems and a short article" entitled *Homage to Onyame* (1997).

7   Kwasi Wiredu has argued (1983 and 1992) convincingly for a humanistic conception of African moral values.

References

Achebe, Chinua (1974) *Arrow of God*, 2nd edn. (London, Ibadan, Nairobi: Heinemann Educational Books Ltd.).

Achebe, Chinua (1988) *Anthills of the Savannah* (Ibadan: Heinemann Educational Books Nigeria Ltd.).

Barber, Karin (1981) "How Man Makes God in West Africa: Yoruba Attitudes Towards Orisa," *Africa: Journal of the International African Institute*, 51(3).

p'Bitek, Okot (1970) *African Religions in Western Scholarship* (Kampala, Nairobi and Dar es Salaam: East African Literature Bureau).

Davidson, Basil (1978) *Africa in Modern History: The Search for a New Society* (England: Penguin Books Ltd.).

Evans-Pritchard, E. E. (1965) *Theories of Primitive Religion* (London: Oxford University Press).

Feuerbach, Ludwig (1969) "The Essence of Christianity," in Joseph D. Bettis (ed.), *Phenomenology of Religion* (London: SCM Press Ltd.).

Gyekye, Kwame (1987) *An Essay on African Philosophical Thought: The Akan Conceptual Scheme* (Cambridge: Cambridge University Press).

Gyekye, Kwame (1996) *African Cultural Values* (Philadelphia, Pa/Accra, Ghana: Sankofa Publishing Company).

Idowu, E. Bolaji (1962) *Olodumare: God in Yoruba Belief* (London: Longman Group Ltd.).

Idowu, E. Bolaji (1973) *African Traditional Religion: A Definition* (London: SCM Press Ltd.).

Liyong, Taban Lo (1997) *Homage to Onyame* (Lagos: Malthouse Press Ltd.).

Mbiti, John S. (1969) *African Religions and Philosophy* (London, Ibadan, Nairobi: Heinemann Educational Books Ltd.).

Nwala, T. Uzodinma (1985) *Igbo Philosophy* (Ikeja, Lagos: Lantern Books).

Oladeji, Niyi (1988) "Proverbs as Language Signposts in Yoruba Pragmatic Ethics," *Second Order: An African Journal of Philosophy*, new series, 1(2): 45–55.

Oladipo, Olusegun (1988) "Metaphysics, Religion and Yoruba Traditional Thought: An Essay on the Status of the Belief in Non-Human Agencies and Powers in an African Belief System," *Journal of the Indian Council of Philosophical Research*, 7(2) (January–April): 72–83.

Oluwole, S. B. (1984) "The Rational Basis of Yoruba Ethical Thinking," *The Nigerian Journal of Philosophy*, 4(1/2): 14–25.

Opoku, Kofi Asare (1974) "Aspects of Akan Worship," in C. Eric Lincoln (ed.), *The Black Experience in Religion* (New York: Doubleday).

Opoku, Kofi Asare (1978) *West African Traditional Religion* (Accra: FEP International Private Limited).

Owomoyela, Oyekan (1981) "The Pragmatic Humanism of Yoruba Culture," *Journal of African Studies*, 8(3): 26–32.

Senghor, Leopold Sedar (1976) *Prose and Poetry*, ed. and trans. John Reed and Clive Wake (London, Nairobi, Ibadan and Lusaka: Heinemann African Writers Series).

Williams, Alabi (1998) "Taste of Ijaw Lifestyle," *The Guardian on Sunday* (Lagos, Nigeria), October 2.

Wiredu, Kwasi (1982) "Morality and Religion in Akan Thought," in H. Odera Oruka and D. A. Masolo (eds.), *Philosophy and Cultures* (Nairobi: Bookwise Ltd.).

Wiredu, Kwasi (1992) "Moral Foundations of an African Culture," in Kwasi Wiredu and Kwame Gyekye (eds.), *Person and Community: Ghanaian Philosophical Studies, I* (Washington DC: The Council for Research in Values and Philosophy).

Wiredu, Kwasi (1996a) *Cultural Universals and Particulars: An African Perspective* (Bloomington and Indianapolis: Indiana University Press).

Wiredu, Kwasi (1996b) "On Decolonizing African Religions," in J. G. Malherbe (ed.), *Decolonizing the Mind* (Pretoria: University of South Africa).

28

Okot p'Bitek's Critique of Western Scholarship on African Religion

SAMUEL O. IMBO

> The religion of a people is perhaps the most important aspect of their culture. What they believe governs their lives. It provides their "world-view" – the general direction along which they live their lives, and relate to each other and the universe. It guides them in their conduct of war and peace. It is the basis of their behavior towards one another. The knowledge of the religions of our people is the key to the knowledge of our culture.
>
> Okot p'Bitek, *Africa's Cultural Revolution*

Okot p'Bitek was born on June 9, 1931 in Gulu, Uganda to parents who were ardent exponents of Acoli culture. His mother was a famous dancer and composer, while his father was a storyteller and also a dancer, cultural pursuits that they both continued even after becoming Christians. Okot was educated in Uganda and the UK, where he studied education (Bristol University), law (Aberystwyth University), and social anthropology (Oxford University). At Oxford he studied with such famous scholars as E. E. Evans-Pritchard, Godfrey Lienhardt, and John Beattie. His close encounter with Acoli rituals, dances, and storytelling, together with his experience of Western culture, would, in one way or another, be the theme of all his writings. He established himself as a poet and a cultural critic with the publication of two "songs": *Song of Lawino* (1966) and *Song of Ocol* (1970), both poetic satires on the negative influence of Western culture on African culture. He took up this theme again, in prose, in his *Africa's Cultural Revolution* (1973). In 1966 he was appointed the first African Director of the National Cultural Center in Kampala, Uganda. Two years later, during the brutal dictatorship of Field Marshal Amin, he left Uganda. In the ensuing 11 years of exile he taught at universities in the United States, Nigeria, and Kenya. Okot p'Bitek died of a liver infection in Kenya on July 20, 1982.

Okot's writings take the oral traditions of his people, as expressed through their songs, dances, funeral dirges, and material culture, as the primary texts of what he calls the people's "philosophy of life." Though deeply philosophical in content, his vast body of work has thus far not been discussed as contributions to African philosophy. His fiction, poetry, translations between Acoli and English, interviews, and critical studies have generated a respectable volume of commentaries, biographies, dissertations, interviews, and conference papers (see Ofuani 1985; Lindfors 1977). These responses to his work have focused mainly on his views on oral literatures and Western interactions with African religions. Any serious engagement with

Okot's work must begin with an appreciation of his interdisciplinary approach and the deep connections he made between diverse issues. None of his poems, songs, or critical essays can be easily catalogued. Each work at one and the same time reflects ongoing tensions between tradition and modernity and points to the difficulties inherent in translations between European and African languages. They also alert us to the dangers of assumptions about Africans smuggled into cross-cultural discussions, raise questions about what constitute appropriate texts for critical study, and take an unequivocal stand on authentic African identity and selfhood and on the question of who the real experts are in matters of interpreting and evaluating evidence on things African. This subtlety of thought makes it difficult to isolate works that primarily deal with religion.

Okot p'Bitek directly addresses Western scholarship on African religions in *African Religions in Western Scholarship* (1971a), *Religion of the Central Luo* (1971c), and in a number of essays finished just two weeks before he died and collected in *Artist, the Ruler: Essays on Art, Culture, and Values* (1986). He also directly addresses African religion in his essay "African Religion in An African University" (in 1973), in his review (1964b) of Placide Tempels's *Bantu Philosophy*, as well as in his own responses (1972) to reviews of *African Religions in Western Scholarship*. But indeed, the theme of religion permeates all of Okot's "Songs," particularly *Song of Lawino* (1966) and *Song of Ocol* (1971d). For Okot, the absence of a word for "religion" in all African languages means that there is no special compartment that the African calls "religious" that is separate from the day-to-day participation in the life-process. It is from this all-encompassing view of religion in African traditional life that Okot criticizes Western scholarship. He construes Western scholarship broadly to include the work of Western social anthropologists, missionaries, historians, ethnographers, philosophers, and their African apologists. His criticisms of Western scholarship on African religions move on at least the following seven interconnected issues.

1. The definition of the religious and the spiritual.
2. The sources of information about African religion.
3. Who the real experts on African traditional religion and philosophy are.
4. The possibility of translating Western religious ideas into African languages.
5. The intellectual smuggling of Western concepts into African religions.
6. The relevance of Western religions in Africa.
7. The hasty generalization that what is casually observed among one African people applies to all Africans.

Looking in all the Wrong Places

To understand African religions, one only needs to look at life as it is actually lived by the ordinary person in the village. Observe the person busy at work and play, at the joyous occasions of birth and marriage, and at the sad moments of war and death. Observe also the interactions of the living with the dead, for that is where the meaningfulness of life is. For Okot, religion is integral to the structures around which Acoli life is organized:

> The first step is to open your eyes. Listen to the bird's song and the talk of the monkeys. Go to the clan shrine; the diviner-priest is dressed in his frightening regalia, rattle gourd in one hand, and in the other his spear of office; listen to him addressing the dead, and the chorus of the assembled clansmen and clanswomen. And at the chiefdom shrine, listen to the priest invoking the gods. Go to the funeral dance and study the dirges – the outbursts of the grief and wailing in sorrow, the passionate cry of a soul in pain. Attend the "oiling" ceremony of a new chief; and as the men and women of the entire chiefdom dance the chiefly *bwola* dance, listen to the proud songs in which are embodied the history of the chiefdom. (1973: 24)

Okot's chief criticism of Western scholarship is its seemingly congenital blindness. There are major obstacles that prevent the Westerner from opening her eyes and truly "seeing" the oral literature and traditional religion that weave together the values of an African community. Reading Okot make this case reminds one very much of Ralph Ellison's *Invisible Man* (1990). African religion is like the invisible man Western scholars keep bumping into without seeing because of the peculiar "construction of their *inner* eyes, those eyes with which they look through their physical eyes upon reality" (ibid. 3). This chosen blindness, a recurrent theme in Okot's criticism of Western scholarship, exhibits itself in different ways.

Okot p'Bitek criticizes Western scholars from classical times onwards for searching in all the wrong places for the real expert practitioners of African religions. The countryside is populated by "religious leaders, diviners, priests; I see men and women involved in religious ceremonies and rituals, which are the practical aspects of their belief" (1972: 30). In their blind groping, anthropologists and missionaries searched for African metaphysicians and theologians when the ordinary man in the countryside had the answers the whole time.

> In Africa what you have is a wealth of traditional ideas, and it is this that forms the subject matter of study for the student of African philosophy. The most useful preparation for this kind of study is for the student to soak himself thoroughly in the everyday preoccupations of the people whose thought system he attempts to describe. (1964a: 6)

If the real experts on authentic African ideas about philosophy, culture, and religion are everywhere in the villages, why does the foreign scholar have so much difficulty finding them? Tempels could not find a single Luba elder to give a complete account of Bantu philosophy. Okot relates how the missionary Samuel Baker came to absurd conclusions about the people of the Nile Valley. Baker concluded, by talking to a Lutoko chief called Commoro, that the people lacked any concept of the spiritual, or even of the *superstitious*, because the elder showed no comprehension of a future existence after death or even of the separation of the body and soul (in 1973: 91–2). The Western scholar, such as Baker, must conclude that the people represented by Commoro either do not know what they believe or cannot articulate it. Okot p'Bitek's analysis of the situation is unequivocal. It is as if Western scholars come heavily laden with *prêt-à-porter* robes from Europe *with the sole mission of finding* Africans on whom to fit them. Just as high fashion makes explicit distinctions between the chic and the uninitiated, Western scholarship from classical times classified human societies into nobles and savages. Civilized Europeans were contrasted with the African, American-Indian, or Australian aborigines, who were seen as wild men or noble savages (1971a: ch. 5). Also, high fashion is rarely practical or relevant. In the voice of Lawino, Okot laments the imposition of meaningless "civilized" Christian names (such as Clementine, Erina, Benedeta, Jackson, Francis, William) at the expense of, for instance, meaningful bull names given for leading one's age-mates. And what about the meaningless incantations of the Catholic priest about "Maria the clean woman, mother of the hunchback?" (The hunchback spirit is the real translation of the Acoli word *Rubanga* that is used by the missionaries to render the Christian concept of the creator.) How relevant is that incantation when everyone else is out in the moonlit night with their lovers singing songs everyone understands and dancing meaningful dances (1966: 8)? Lawino is pained that much of the catechism classes are taken up with teachings about Yesu (Jesus) encouraging his followers ritually to eat human flesh and drink human blood in the ceremony of *communion* when she would rather be in the arms of her lover, or leading her age-mates in dancing, or learning the history of her people.

Okot's point here is that it is doubtful that Christianity could provide a blueprint for organizing African societies. How could a religion that has little practical value to Lawino and also seems in some ways to encourage asceticism provide a philosophy of life for living in the African world? How could the African be expected to organize her life on the basis of a religion whose major ideas are, as Okot argued, untranslatable into her language? Okot has an unassailable point here. Western scholars are unprepared or unable to read the "texts" that may inform them on African religion. In the same way, African Christian apologists like Mbiti look in the wrong place if their aim is to address African culture meaningfully.

For Okot, there was an oppressive irrelevance about Christianity and its mission to Africa that may be explained by reference to the discordance between Christian teachings and African philosophies of life. Those teachings are irrelevant because they do not speak meaningfully to the religious, social, political, and philosophical foundations on which the social institutions are constructed. Why then, one wonders, did large numbers of Africans go to Christian churches? For the practical advantages they thought they could gain, Okot says.

> The African of tradition who went to church did not reject his culture. He had no alternative offered to him. He saw the church as a necessary ladder to power and material gain.... Power, status and wealth were the main attractions of the Christian missionary at the height of the colonial regime. It was not salvation from sin that attracted the African to the altar. (1986: 66–7)

A Dialogue Across World-views?

A dialogue presupposes the ability and willingness of all involved to listen to each other. Further, there are presuppositions of mutual interest and relevance. The missionary was certain that Christianity had universal truths of which the Africans were ignorant, and that there was a way to communicate these truths across

languages. But, in truth the colonial situation offered no setting for dialogue between Western scholars and indigenous Africans. There was merely a pretense at
dialogue. Each party to the "dialogue" had their reasons for this charade. In order
for the Africans to get access to useful things like scientific medicine, they mouthed
empty slogans and meaningless alien doctrines of faith. To accomplish this charade,
the African had to live a lie: "A big lie, first to the fellows with the goods – the
missionaries: that he had left all 'black things' and had become 'saved.' Then to his
parents and the clan that he was their link man between their tradition and the
new one" (1986: 67). Dialogue at this price was costly indeed. This dissimulation
weighed heavily on the African Christian not least because it had to be hidden from
the missionary.

Western scholars for their part were not, as a rule, really interested in African
religions. They came with their minds made up and did not want to be confused by
African reality. The missionary, like his anthropologist colleague, had fixed ideas
about the proper classification of human societies (i.e. civilized or primitive), and
the proper religious doctrines worth propagating, such as the doctrine of a Supreme
Being who created the world out of nothing. The missionary therefore "built
churches and attached to them places of instruction in a number of skills. The
curriculum was based on the aim of producing loyal, grateful, but inferior gradu-
ates, rootless, nay, self-hating Africans who would always look to Europe for each
and everything" (ibid. 74). Those who could not be lured into the mission education centers were to be engaged in Christian "dialogue" in their degenerate condition
– as people steeped in "animist" traditional beliefs. While all this may seem mag-
nanimous on the part of the missionary, the Western classificatory blueprint did not
allow the missionary to encounter the African as anything other than an "animist." As a representative of a higher civilization whose mission was to civilize the
heathen, how else was the African to be seen except as an immature and primitive
being? Okot explains the so-called missionary "dialogue with animism" as wholly
imaginary. It is impossible to carry out a dialogue with animists if, as Okot declares,
there are no animists in Africa. Okot reports a perfect example of such a "dialogue"
at cross-purposes in *Religion of the Central Luo* (1971c: ch. 3) in the encounter
between Samuel Baker and the Lutoko elder Commoro. While Baker's questions are
abstract and metaphysical ("Have you no belief in a future existence after death?"
"Have you no idea of the existence of spirits superior to man and beast?" "Do you
see no difference between good and bad actions?"), Commoro's answers are characteristic in their focus on the practical ("How can a man get out of his grave unless
we dig him out?" "I am only afraid of elephants, and other animals at night."
"Good and bad [men] all die.") The "dialogue" leaves Commoro wondering why
the white man cares about such things with no practical usefulness, while Baker
concludes that the savage has no religious feeling whatsoever.

The false humility that lulls the missionary into thinking that such "dialogue"
takes another culture seriously is, in fact, further evidence of an arrogant mindset.
The only way to engage meaningfully in a dialogue would be for the missionary to
thoroughly immerse herself in the day-to-day beliefs of the people. These beliefs can
only be properly understood in the respective indigenous languages after an appropriate period of experience and study. The missionary must therefore learn the

language, sing its songs, and experience its dances – in other words, participate fully, even if experimentally, in the culture. This crucial knowledge does not come by asking abstract questions or by merely being a spectator. Okot's golden rule for anyone who would desire dialogue is this: "Shut your mouth and ask no questions. Open your ears wide, and sharpen your eyes" (1973: 91). There was something that consistently kept Western scholars from heeding this sound advice. Samuel Baker could not stop himself from asking Commoro, "Have you no belief in a future existence after death?" The Catholic priests could not help asking the Acoli elders, "Who created you?" With such loaded questions, it is no wonder there was no dialogue between Western scholars and Africans. Since the Europeans could only define religion as belief in a deity who rewards and punishes, the African, who was found to have no such belief – was declared to be of no religion. The diviner priest was seen as a sorcerer. The funeral drum was interpreted as entertainment. At best, this could only be a dialogue characterized by leading questions, blinding assumptions, and an unwillingness and inability to truly *see* the African.

Intellectual Smugglers

Okot p'Bitek offers the questions by Samuel Baker and the Catholic priests as evidence of what he famously called intellectual smuggling. He distinguished smugglers of different kinds – social anthropologists, colonial officers, missionaries, and even African nationalists. The common bond between them is that they surreptitiously import alien (Western) themes and concepts into the African context and then claim that these themes and concepts are indigenous to Africa. The most frequently smuggled concepts are those of a "creator," a High God who is omnipotent, omnipresent, and omniscient; the mana principle; an African theology; fetishism; and animism. The following story told by Okot captures the essence of such smuggling:

> In 1911, Italian Catholic priests put before a group of Acoli elders the question "Who created you?" and because the Luo language does not have an independent concept of *create* or *creation*, the question was rendered to mean, "who molded you?" But this was still meaningless.... The elders told the visitors that they did not know.... One of the elders remembered that, although a person may be born normally, when he is afflicted with tuberculosis of the spine, then he loses his normal figure, he gets "molded." So he said, "*Rubanga* is the one who molds people." This is the name of the hostile spirit which the Acoli believe causes the hunch or hump on the back. And, instead of exorcising these hostile spirits and sending them among pigs, the representatives of Jesus Christ began to preach that Rubanga was the Holy Father who created the Acoli. (1971a: 62)

In this story Okot makes clear the mechanics of smuggling. One must begin with the belief that there are some universal religious beliefs (such as belief in a supreme all-powerful god). If such a God has a name, then the task of the missionary is that of finding out what the equivalent name is in the African languages. *Mungu* in Kiswahili, *Jok* in Acoli, *Allah* in Arabic, *Rubanga* also in Acoli must therefore be the

369

local names of the Christian God. Okot notes that the missionaries did not carry out lengthy and systematic studies in the African languages concerned to find out what the true beliefs of the Africans were. They were simply looking for local confirmation of their cherished preconceptions.

This is Okot's criticism of Tempels. Not once in *Bantu Philosophy* does the Belgian missionary admit that he is serving up his own interpretations. Without carrying out the kind of study Okot recommends and therefore knowing little about the religion of the people, Tempels went on to write about "what the Bantu think." He completely forgot that "Bantu ontology" and "vital force" were merely tools constructed by him and not really what the people believe.

Okot considers some African writers equally guilty of this kind of smuggling. K. A. Busia, L. S. Senghor, J. B. Danquah, J. S. Mbiti, B. Idowu, and Kenyatta are all led into sin by their methods of research and interpretation of African culture. John Mbiti earns the title "Africa's chiefest intellectual smuggler. He earned this title because he smuggled enough Greek metaphysical material to Hellenize three hundred African deities" (1972: 29). Mbiti and the others, by merely aping Western scholars, fail in the crucial task facing African scholars. Which African elder, he asked, talked to Willie Abraham about "Akan theology"? What diviner informed Danquah of "architectural origin and form"? In systematizing the thought of his people, Mbiti sounds more like a Christian theologian and priest than an African. The Greek metaphysical terms and concepts they introduce are foreign to African thinking and incomprehensible to the practitioner of African culture. Christian apologists, African nationalists, and missionaries are all addressing the wrong audience when they focus on the European or the African elite. Okot accuses them all of singing empty songs. A song is empty if it does not meaningfully address the structures within which the person of tradition lives. In this criticism, Okot disarms anyone who might want to classify him as an ethnophilosopher. He does not merely advocate tradition and an uncritical return to the good old days. Authentic tradition, for him, is self-critical, relevant, and useful.

Lost in Translation

A recurring charge that Okot makes against the missionary project in Africa is that attempts at converting the African were, despite appearances, unsuccessful because the bulk of the message was lost in translation. The philosophical issues here are twofold. First, Okot disagrees with the missionaries on whether European and African languages share universal meanings. Okot's disagreement is at two levels. At the level of vocabulary, he argues that some English words have no equivalents in Acoli. At the level of concepts, he argues that there may be words that are translatable in different languages although they do not point to the same (or equivalent) concept. He does not always neatly make the distinction and therefore sometimes leaves the erroneous impression that if an African language lacks the word for an alien concept, then the African language must lack the concept too. Secondly, Okot raises the problem of how the Western scholar should communicate his findings about an alien culture to an audience back home in the West. This second problem is of course one of reporting about an alien and unique system of meanings with the use of one's native concepts. Okot reports that when Western scholars wanted to tell the African story, "This they could only do in terms of Western concepts. The anthropologists to whom the soul and gods had no reality interpreted African religions in terms of psychological, biological or sociological theories. Christian anthropologists, on the other hand, described African religious beliefs in Christian concepts, and called African deities God" (1971a: 66). The two stories, recounted above, of the Catholic priests interviewing Acoli elders in 1911 and of Samuel Baker with the Lutoko elder Commoro, illustrate Okot's point about how meanings can be lost in translation. He makes the point even more forcefully using a familiar biblical passage:

> The first verse of St. John's Gospel in Luo reads as follows: *Nia con ki con Lok onongo tye, Lok tye bot Lubanga, Lok aye ceng Lubanga.* Retranslated into English, it goes, "From long long ago there was News, News was with the Hunchback Spirit, News was the Hunchback Spirit. (ibid. 85)

Note that the aim was supposed to be to render into Acoli St John's "In the beginning was the Word, and the Word was with God and the Word was God."

Okot's disdain for Christianity was well known, and it is entirely possible that in the retranslation above he is taking liberties with the Acoli language at the expense of Christianity. In another essay, after all, he characterized Christianity as a religion that wooed Africans to worship in "Huge, ugly Gothic houses, called churches" and lured them "to think that wifelessness, husbandlessness, childlessness, homelessness, were a virtue" (1986: 14, 15). Nevertheless, he raises some serious problems about cross-cultural communication. Kwasi Wiredu has, in his essay about formulating modern thought in African languages (1966: ch. 7), analyzed the issues raised by Okot's retranslation more comprehensively than can be done here. Okot and Wiredu make the point that violence is done to the Acoli language by the mindset that makes the hasty assumption that concepts that exist in a European language will, *ipso facto*, appear in the vernacular. The meaninglessness of the translation is due to two factors. First, according to Okot, the Luo do not think metaphysically. This is a controversial statement that itself needs explanation. He does not, of course, mean to impute a mental disability to the Luo. He means only that one does not find among the Acoli a barren preoccupation with certain kinds of abstract question. Religious beliefs always have practical aspects. Because of the European penchant for metaphysics for its own sake, there are many European concepts that cannot find expression in an African language. Okot argues that the concept of logos that is intended in that opening passage of St John's Gospel is absent from the Luo framework of concepts. Also, the concept of a creator spirit is alien to the Luo. This is why the end result is the comical "The news was with Rubanga [the Hunchback Spirit]." But secondly, the conceptual concerns that are meaningful to the Luo do not include questions about the beginning of the world, or its end. So, having no way in the local languages to render "In the beginning," the translation becomes simply "Long long ago." To compound matters, the concept of creation *ex nihilo* is meaningless to the Acoli. Lawino, who is familiar with how pots are made but unfamiliar with her Christianized husband Ocol's new and foreign concepts, such as that of *creation*, is therefore understandably reduced to wondering:

> The Hunchback
> Where did he dig the clay
> For molding things?
> Where is the pot
> He dug the clay
> For molding Skyland,
> And the clay for molding Earth?
> From the mouth of which River? (1966: 138)

Okot p'Bitek and his Critics

Okot p'Bitek was many things to many people – cultural critic, poet, nationalist, defender of traditions. His critics therefore had many targets. In the introduction to *Africa's Cultural Revolution*, Ngugi wa Thiong'o raises a polite criticism about Okot's preoccupation with the cultural at the expense of the political and economic bases of African societies. Okot's answer is short. It is not easy to make divisions between politics, economics, and culture. Culture is all-encompassing. A people's culture is their practical philosophy, their world-view. In his review of *African Religions in Western Scholarship*, Rigby (1971) criticized Okot for unfairly attacking Western scholars, especially social anthropologists, by citing only the worst works as typical of Western scholarship while ignoring many excellent studies. A similar criticism was raised by Ali Mazrui in the "Epilogue" of *African Religions in Western Scholarship*: Okot's response is dismissive. Even those "excellent studies" cited by Rigby propagate the same myths that were used by colonialists to dominate Africans. They harbor the same oppressive prejudices about classifications of human societies and what counts as knowledge. Few of those studies have the interests of the African at heart. B. A. Ogot (1971) pleaded on his own behalf and that of J. S. Mbiti to be declassified from the category of intellectual smugglers. Okot's retort is a familiar one in his writings. He could not find among the Luo any part of the African metaphysics Ogot writes about. And African deities continue to suffocate under the *prêt-à-porter* robes directly delivered by Mbiti, Danquah, and other African theologians. Regarding Western ideas on African religions, Okot remained consistent. In all his writings he urges his critics and all other African scholars to "reflect, reject, recreate."

References

p'Bitek, Okot (1964a) "Cool, Sober, Methodical: A Reply to R. G. Harris," *Transition*, 16.

p'Bitek, Okot (1964b) "Fr. Tempels' Bantu Philosophy," *Transition*, 13.

p'Bitek, Okot (1966) *Song of Lawino* (Nairobi: East African Publishing House).

p'Bitek, Okot (1971a) *African Religions in Western Scholarship* (Nairobi: Kenya Literature Bureau).

p'Bitek, Okot (1971b) "Intellectual Smugglers in Africa," *East Africa Journal*, 8(12).

p'Bitek, Okot (1971c) *Religion of the Central Luo* (Nairobi: Kenya Literature Bureau).

p'Bitek, Okot (1971d) *Song of Ocol* (Nairobi: East African Publishing House).

p'Bitek, Okot (1972) "Reflect, Reject, Recreate: A Reply to Professors B. A. Ogot, Ali Mazrui, and Peter Rigby," *East Africa Journal*, 9(4).

p'Bitek, Okot (1973) *Africa's Cultural Revolution* (Nairobi: Macmillan Books for Africa).

p'Bitek, Okot (1986) *Artist, The Ruler: Essays on Art, Culture and Values* (Nairobi: Heinemann Kenya).

Ellison, Ralph (1990) *Invisible Man* (New York: Vintage International).

Lindfors, Bernth (1977) "A Checklist of Works by and About Okot p'Bitek," *World Literature Written in English*, 16: 300–3

Ogot, B. A. (1971) "Intellectual Smugglers in Africa," *East Africa Journal*, 8(12).

Ofuani, Ogo A. (1985) "Okot p'Bitek: A Checklist of Works and Criticisms," *Research in African Literatures*, 16(3).

Rigby, Peter (1971) "Review of *African Religions in Western Scholarship*," *Mawazo*, 3(1), June.

Wiredu, Kwasi (1966) *Cultural Universals and Particulars: An African Perspective* (Bloomington: Indiana University Press).

29

Islam in Africa: Examining the Notion of an African Identity within the Islamic World

SOULEYMANE BACHIR DIAGNE

Is "African Islam" something other than just Islam *in* Africa? In other words does the adjective "African" convey the idea that there is something radically different and specific about the way in which part of the Black continent has been Islamicized and is *living* Islam? It has been said that "Africanness" was some sort of incomplete essence, longing for a consummation that could only come under one or the other of the two *revealed* monotheistic religions present on the continent today, namely, Islam and Christianity. Take the example of Christianity. One strongly held view, which became a major philosophical thesis in Placide Tempels's *Bantu Philosophy*, is that the ontology of the Bantu people and, more generally, of African peoples, when truly understood, appears to be a call for its own perfect realization within the Christian faith.[1] One can also find in the literature, as an explanation for the rapid spread of Islam in Africa, the idea that, in contrast to Christianity, Muslim customs, in particular the Islamic toleration of polygamy (to quote the example most commonly given), are very close to the traditional African world-view and way of life. There is, however, in the literature a third view opposed to these two. According to it, there is something permanent about the traditional African view of the world, some cosmological outlook embedded in African religion, so fundamental and so deeply entrenched that it remains essentially untouched in any apparent external influence, be it by way of a conversion to Christianity or to Islam. This cosmological outlook is such that "philosophy, theology, politics, social theory, land law, medicine, psychology, birth and burial, all find themselves logically concatenated in a system so tight that to subtract one item from the whole is to paralyze the structure of the whole."[2]

All these statements, conflicting as they are, are a clear indication that there is undoubtedly a need to examine the notion of an *African difference* in trying to clarify the idea of the indigenization of "alien" religions in the context of philosophical discourses about Africa, its cultures and identities. The basic question appears to be that of *the test of difference*,[3] which raises two related issues. First, in what way, if any, has the Islamic religion passed the test of difference in Africa? This is particularly important, since we can define the universality of a message by its capacity to keep speaking, that is, communicating significance to a community of believers (as envisaged in the Islamic notion of an *Umma*) which transcends its original geographical and historical frontiers. Second, have Muslims in the Black continent (re)created themselves, as Africans, in their Islamic identity?

I would like to discuss these issues through an examination of the contrast between two concepts which look, at first sight, quite similar, namely, that of a "Black Islam," and that of the "Africanization of Islam." The present chapter will focus on these two notions. But, before that, a short historical sketch of Islam's penetration of Africa seems appropriate.

Muslim Africa: A Historical Sketch

The history of Islam in Africa is first and foremost the history of the penetration of the continent by a religion born in Arabia in the beginning of the seventh century. Just ten years after the death of the Prophet Muhammad (in 632) the Muslims had conquered Egypt and, from there, expanded into North Africa. And as early as around the eleventh century Islam had started to take root in the sub-Saharan areas of the continent, in West Africa and in East Africa. In West Africa the Islamic presence in the valley of the Senegal and Niger rivers was already a deeply rooted reality by the first decades of the eleventh century. Al Bakrî, whose work is one of the important sources for African history in Arabic, wrote around 1068 that Wâr-jâbî was the first king of Tekrûr, previously a province of the kingdom of Ghana situated on the basin of Senegal, to become a Muslim and to bring Islamic law into his newly independent kingdom. Thus Tekrûr was a Muslim territory by the time the king died, in 1040. More generally, the medieval empires that developed in the Sahelian areas of West Africa soon came to have Muslim leaders like, for example, Mansa of the Mali kingdom. In a parallel process around the twelfth century, the Islamic religion had become an important part of the history of the East African littoral and islands.

Islam did not penetrate the southern areas of West Africa until the nineteenth century. In eastern Africa too, Islam remained restricted to the coast until the colonial period. But then came the historic phase of expansion in West Africa by way of holy wars (jihâd), and, in particular, the war led by the fulânî Shaykh Umar al Fûtî from 1852 to 1864 in present-day Mali. This followed the one led by another fulânî, Uthman dan Fodio, at the beginning of the nineteenth century and which created the Sokoto caliphate in northern Nigeria. As a result of these developments, the Islamic religion was widely spread in western and eastern Africa by the time of the colonial administration.

Through an ironic dialectic, the socio-political destruction caused by colonization brought about, among other things, a massive Islamization of the interior regions of the continent. By pursuing its own ends, colonialism created a physical and social space favoring Islamization:

> The colonialists opened paths for peddlers and hawkers. The roads and railways they constructed helped Muslim traders to travel everywhere, preaching by example to populations which had witnessed the collapse of traditional micro-cultures which, outside the homelands they were rooted in, no longer made any sense. And the process

375

was facilitated by the sentiment that in some way to embrace Islam was to avenge the
fact of colonial domination. (Diagne 1993: 276)

The result of this historical process was not uniform but rather varied according
to the character of the various African cultures that encountered the Islamic
cosmology.

The penetration of Islam in sub-Saharan Africa is extensive, and it is a force in different
degrees in west, east and South Africa, along with Christianity. The nature of its
presence and the effect, which it has, through its presence, on traditional cultures, is,
however, diverse. In some cultures, it is hardly a factor. Among others, it is overwhelming. (Abraham 1992: 27)

The Construction of the Concept of "Black Islam"

Does the notion of a "Black Islam" help us to understand this reality of a Muslim
Africa? And, first of all, what is "Black Islam"? The notion of a Black Islam was
coined for the "black" societies of Muslim West Africa. And, as David Robinson
says, "at its 'worst', or in its least 'Muslim' variants, it faded into the 'paganism' of
the societies of the south" (1999: 122). "Black Islam" was an expression made
famous by the French scholar in African studies Vincent Monteil, who in 1964
wrote a book entitled *L'Islam noir, une religion à la conquête de l'Afrique* (1980), in
which he discussed that expression from various standpoints. It is significant, by the
way, that the second chapter was devoted to a discussion of "la pensée sauvage,"
the savage mind, an expression taken from the ethnologist Claude Lévi-Strauss.

One of the things discussed was the fact that the term "Black Islam" was used in
the colonial context to, so to speak, separate from the rest of the Muslim world a
supposedly "purely African [meaning: sub-Saharan] Islam" that Robert Arnaud, in
1912, proposed to call "Muslim Ethiopianism." It is interesting to note that Arnaud
was appointed by Governor-General Roume as an Islamic specialist to the Political
Bureau in 1905. His *Handbook for Muslim Policy* (*Précis de la politique musulmane*)
was commissioned to provide guidelines for administering an Islamicized sub-
Saharan African territory. These facts provide clear indications that this category of
a "Black" specificity within the *Umma*, the Islamic community of believers, was
politically and ethnologically constructed in derogation of the notion of the Islamic
Umma. It endured as a designation of a body of "ethnological knowledge" as well as
a means of control throughout the colonial period (Robinson 1999: 107). In 1962,
in *Les Musulmans d'Afrique noire*, J. C. Froelich insisted that there exists quite "a
specific black Islam, very different from the Mediterranean or Middle-eastern one,
different also from the Moor one; an Islam rethought, re-kneeled, negrified, adapted
to the psychic characteristics of the black races" (1962). This does nothing to
eliminate the fact that the notion of a Black Islam was needed by the colonial
system for political purposes, mainly to shield the sub-Saharan areas from the so-
called pan-Arabic or pan-Islamic threat to Western colonial domination.

This political agenda was also supported, from a theoretical standpoint, by the
colonial ethnology that held the essentialist view that an *ethnos* was to be defined as

something in the soul that remains permanent under any change that may occur. Hence, history – and, in particular, the history of Islamization in sub-Saharan Africa – becomes just a geological story of the outer layer of what will always remain, in cosmological terms, authentically "black" African in its deeper strata. In fact, this involves the mistake of considering identity as something that lasts *in spite of* encounters and *in spite of* history. Lost here is the fact that identity is continually recreated *through* and *by* history, through the encounters that function as a matrix for reconstructing identities. What was consequently missed is the very movement of self-invention that is an important aspect of the history of the peoples under study. And this could go as far as rewriting, in an Islamicized way, one's own history; which did happen in many African ethnic groups. To give but a single example, the way in which the ruling dynasty of the Keita, who founded the Mali empire, reconstructed their own origins as descendants of the first muezzin of Islam, the Prophet Muhammad's companion from Abyssinia Bilal ben Rabah, is quite emblematic of this rewriting of history.

Having insisted on the political and ethnological significance of the term "Black Islam" in the colonial context, we must still not forget that this ethnologism, as I would like to call it, does exist within the Muslim world too. In this new context it exists as a form of tribal thinking – something that Islam is meant to fight – that considers the Arab peoples to be at the center of the *Umma*. From such a chauvinist viewpoint Muslim Africa is sometimes looked upon as belonging to the periphery of the "truly" Islamic world. From this perspective, Africa is regarded as not yet fully integrated, impregnated, as it is, with "magical" thinking. The French colonial administration, incidentally, did play on this type of chauvinistic feeling by distinguishing, in Africa, between the categories of "Black Islam" and "Moor Islam." This differentiation was based on the fact that the Moors, generally Berbers but usually claiming an Arab descent (often from the Prophet himself) and calling themselves *beydân* (white) to establish the difference with the *sûdân* (Blacks), thought of themselves as "natural" Muslims in contrast to their neighbors to the south (see Robinson 1999). By and large, ethnologism, on the one hand, and, on the other, this centering of Islam around the Arab world contributed to the separation of the study of Africa from that of the Islamic world at large.

What now about the internal understanding of "Black Islam"? What meaning does it convey to the Africans themselves, which, ultimately, is what really matters? Vincent Monteil recalls the interesting reaction of the reformist leader Cheikh Touré, who was totally hostile to the very expression "Black Islam": "What makes the difference between black Islam and yellow Islam?" he is quoted to have asked in a quite infuriated manner (1980: 63). And he made it plain that, as far as he was concerned, the concept of "Black Islam" had done nothing but harm to Africa through the collaboration of some religious leaders with the colonial institution of The Bureau for Muslim Affairs (Bureau des affaires musulmanes). In other words, Cheikh Touré considered that notion to express the relation that objectively existed between the socio-religious order and the political order in the governance of the society.

Eventually, Monteil found that he needed to reconsider this concept, which did contribute to the great success of his book. In the Introduction to the third edition of *L'Islam noir* (1980) he explained that he had, since the first edition in 1964, been

377

gathering more information about the concept and that he himself had undergone a personal change as well. He then added that the only reason he was keeping the concept of "Black Islam" in the title was that this was the title by which his book had been so widely known.

Let us now see what it would mean to replace the notion of "Black Islam" with that of the "Africanization" of Islam. This is a notion that was metaphorically expressed by a famous Muslim master from Mali, Ceerno Bokar Tall (d. 1940), through his disciple Amadou Hampâté Bâ. The latter wrote that in Africa, as anywhere else, Islam has no more color than water. As far as he was concerned, Islam adopts the color of the homeland in which it happens to be.

Africanity of Islam

Of course, just to show the way in which colonial ethnography used the concept of "Black Islam" does not suffice to illumine the notion of an *African* way of living Islam within the global Muslim community. Certainly, to speak, instead, of the "Africanization" of Islam is much more than a nuance. It is meant to mark the difference between an ethnological *essentialist* approach and an *historico-anthropological* one. Operative here is a distinction between an approach that postulates a radical difference of essences or an inherent conflict of cosmologies, on the one hand, and, on the other, one that proceeds by a precise analysis of the tensions between the local and the global as they are manifested in the African regions of the Islamic community. The development of a true "anthropology of Islam," what Launay (1992) has characterized as "a burgeoning field," should promote such an analysis. Thus, far from indulging in any essentialist approach, Launay's study of the Muslims of the region of Koko stresses the importance of the key notion of *re-evaluation*: "Beliefs and practices are constantly shifting – subject to re-evaluation, if not rejection – though not necessarily in uniform and entirely predictable ways" (ibid. 223). As a matter of fact, the idea of the Africanity of Islam is just as different from that of "Black Islam" as the phenomenon of belief re-evaluation is from the supposed confrontation between an indigenous "pervasive cosmology that straddles space and time"[4] and an "alien" world-view implied by the Islamic faith.

One illustration of such a re-evaluation concerns the worship of the ancestors, which has been considered a permanent trait of the African identity, perduring under any change introduced by foreign influences. Thus it has been said that the belief that the departed ancestors remain living forces that do influence the living is one of the prominent aspects of the pervasive ontology of the African peoples. Referring to Kagame's philosophical account of the Kinyarwandan language, Janheinz Jahn, for example, characterizes the *"magara* principle" (*magara* meaning "spiritual life") as the essence of "Africanness." He writes: "The *magara* principle, which makes the living and the dead...close kin, who can mutually 'strengthen' one another, seems to us characteristic of African culture" (1961: 112).[5] Interestingly, poetry is the most often quoted type of evidence to support the notion of an African belief in the continuous presence of the ancestors. This is regarded as so fundamental as to constitute a definition of Africanness, since it is seen as a continuing common denominator to all the forms of the traditional religions of the continent in spite of the new cosmologies introduced by Islam or Christianity. Accordingly, the fact that the presence of the dead is a poetical theme for various African writers, such as Senghor, Amos Tutuola, and Birago Diop, is invoked not only by Jahn (ibid. 113–14), but also by Césaire, Roumain, and Langston Hughes as testimony to the unique importance of that belief. Not surprisingly, that belief is supposed to be perfectly epitomized in Birago Diop's poem *Souffles* (*Sighs*):

Hear more often things than beings,
The voice of the fire listening,
Hear the voice of the water.
Hear in the wind
The bushes sobbing,
It is the sigh of our forebears.

Those who are dead are never gone:
They are there in the thickening shadow.
The dead are not under the earth:
They are in the tree that rustles,
They are in the wood that groans,
They are in the water that runs,
They are in the water that sleeps,
They are in the hut, they are in the crowd,
The dead are not dead.

Those who are dead are never gone,
They are in the breast of the woman,
They are in the child who is wailing
And in the firebrand that flames.
The dead are not under the earth:
They are in the fire that is dying,
They are in the grasses that weep,
They are in the whimpering rocks,
They are in the forest, they are in the house,
The dead are not dead.

Can we really consider that the poetic inspiration of a writer like Birago Diop, born and raised a Muslim, is traceable to an everlasting indigenous cosmology? Only the habit of taking it for granted that modern African literature is essentially a documentary of the African "mind" could overshadow the fact that this notion of the living dead is a universal poetic theme in any period of history and in any part of the world.

Now, from an ethnographical point of view, it has been said that the worship of departed individuals perceived in popular piety as "saints" (the *awliyâ* in Islamic terms) is a sign that the old cosmology based on the *magara* principle is still alive in the new conceptual and spiritual frame. Also this has been linked to one important feature of African Islam, namely, the pervasive influence of Sufism among African Muslims, particularly in the form of Sufi brotherhoods. Sufism can be defined as the interior, mystical aspect of the Islamic faith. It may be described "as the urge to reach out to the Infinite...in some mode of intellectual communion or 'conjunction', as in Neoplatonism; or through some kind of visionary illumination, as in [its] moderate forms...or finally in a total dissolution of personal identity, as in...the 'extravagant' forms of Sufism" (Fakhry 1997: 73). Historically, the first phase of Sufism was characterized by the appearance, in the Muslim world, of individual Sufis devoted to asceticism and to worshipping God in solitude or in small circles under the guidance of a master (a *Shaykh* or, to use a popular word, a *marabout*). Subsequently, the movement took the form of large institutionalized brotherhoods or Orders or Fraternities (the *turuq*, meaning literally the "paths") centered on the teachings of a *Shaykh* considered as a path to the ultimate truth of the religion. In other words, Sufism sought to penetrate beyond the merely legal aspects of religion (*shari'a*) to its deepest and truest meaning (*haqiqah*) attainable through devotion to the *Shaykh* and obedience to his commands.

What I. M. Lewis has said specifically about Islamic brotherhoods in Somaliland is, admittedly, true of Africa in general: "So well-developed indeed had these religious organizations become in the nineteenth century, that the Somali profession of the faith was now synonymous with membership of, or more frequently, nominal attachment to a Sufi brotherhood" (1965: 63).[6] But then can it be said that the reason for this situation is that, because the Islam of the brotherhoods exalts the charismatic powers of saints, it is particularly adapted to a "system in which clan ancestors readily become transposed into Muslim saints"?[7]

First of all, what we have said about the history of Sufism and the brotherhoods in the global Islamic *Umma* shows that the pervasiveness of this mystical form of piety in Africa does not indicate any African specificity within the Muslim world. Most of the Sufi orders to be found on the continent are widespread outside Africa. An example is the *Qâdiriyya* fraternity, founded in Baghdad by 'Abd al-Qâdir al-Jîlânî (d. 1166), and present everywhere from Senegal and Mauritania to Zanzibar. There is, indeed, a trend in the Muslim world that may be characterized as "fundamentalist," which is quite radical in its opposition to the Sufi brotherhoods. The explanation for this is that it sees Sufism as expressing an unorthodox form of the religion that favors, through devotion to dead "saints" in particular, popular beliefs and practices which are contrary to the very spirit of Islamic monotheism. As a matter of fact, because mystics in different religions are generally more open to the different forms of piety, since they see all of them as implying ultimately the same Infinite Reality,[8] it is true that Sufi brotherhoods appear to be receptive to local traditions and customs; which is taken by the "fundamentalists" to be simple complacency in the face of "paganism." But once again, comparison with the rest of the Muslim world shows that this opposition is not between Islam and its African adaptation or "transplantation," but a manifestation of the tensions between "different *global* standards" (Launay 1992: 225) within the Islamic community at large. In particular, the so-called worship of saints cannot be considered as an adaptation of a traditional African cosmology. On the contrary, it is to be understood within the context of the Sufi view of the metaphysical meaning of "sanctity" (*wilâyah*).[9] Kwasi Wiredu rightly insists on the fact that the belief in ancestors is founded on a concept of immortality that is radically different from that to be found in Christianity, for example (and, one can add, Islam as well): "The African land of the dead...is not heaven" (1992: 144). If this is true in regard to Christianity, it is even truer in the case of Islam where "conversion appears to be a relatively total condition of mind" (ibid.). Hardly any admixture of Islamic and indigenous elements is to be found in the ways of mourning the dead in Islamic Africa. As a matter of fact, a complete break with beliefs *about* the ancestors and therefore with the belief *in* the ancestors is central to the Quranic message.[10]

Let us conclude with a reflection on an account, by the Moroccan traveler Ibn Battuta, of his experience of the African difference within the Islamic world. Writing about his visit to the kingdom of Mali (in 1375) Ibn Battuta is particularly intrigued by the social status of the women in the city of Wâlata. A remark concerning their "extraordinary beauty" is followed by the observation – a surprise to him – that they have more force of personality than the men do. He is particularly struck by the importance of the maternal uncle for children and by the fact that the women are not "ashamed" of appearing in the presence of men. He notes that, although the inhabitants of Wâlata are Muslims who practice religious observances, such as praying five times a day, and who have learned the Islamic law and know the text of the Quran, their wives are not cloistered. He also relates that he once expressed to one of his acquaintances in Wâlata, a man who was a *Qâdi*, that is to say, a judge, his surprise at seeing this man's wife having a conversation with another man. He had remarked to the man, "you have lived in our Arab countries and you know the legal aspects concerning the subject." Here is the answer he got from the judge: "In our societies we do not consider the company of women and men, which has its regulations, with suspicion and mental reservation. Our women are not like the women in your (Arab) countries."[11]

This report and the judge's answer (which infuriated his interlocutor) convey an important aspect of the question of diversity within the Islamic world. One can suppose here that what the judge had in mind is the difference between prescriptions in matters of religious practice (called *'ibâdât*) and matters of interpersonal relations (called *mu'âmalât*). His answer may then be interpreted as follows. When it comes to religious practices embodying the Islamic faith, there is no room for any major divergence. But when it comes to cultural customs, as distinct from prescriptions actually in the Quranic text, difference is not only unavoidable but also necessary. This is because difference carries the seeds of evolution and openness. The ultimate meaning of the judge's answer, on an issue as crucial as the cloistering of women, then, is this: cultural diversity is richness, and blind imitation of models found in another society a failure at the test of difference.

Notes

1 "We arrive...at the unheard of conclusion that Bantu paganism, the ancient wisdom of the Bantu, reaches out from the depths of its Bantu soul towards the very soul of Christian spirituality. It is in Christianity alone that the Bantu will find relief for their secular yearning and a complete satisfaction of their deepest aspirations...Christianity...is the only possible consummation of the Bantu ideal" (Tempels 1959: 186).

2   Adesanya Adebayo, the author of these lines (Adebayo 1958), is cited here by Janheinz Jahn (1961: 97).
3   In the Quran, the Islamic Holy Book, difference is presented as a test for human intelligence and faith: "If Allah had so willed, He would have made you a single people, but (His Plan is) to test you in what he hath given you; so strive as in a race in all virtues. The goal of you all is to Allah; it is He that will show you the truth of the matters in which ye dispute" (Sûrah – corresponding to ch. 5, v. 48).
4   I am here quoting with a change, using "cosmology" instead of "ontology," Archie Mafeje, who spoke of a "pervasive ontology that straddles space and time" (2000: 67).
5   There is an ontological scale of "life force" characteristic of African cosmology which Jahn describes in the following words: "The individual dead are therefore of different 'strengths', according as they have many or few living descendants who honor them and sacrifice to them. Thus an ancestor, who is an aggregate of magara, can transfer to many newborn individuals the small share of magara that they need to begin their lives. This 'quantity' is not great, and it must be constantly 'strengthened' in the course of the individual's development, and even as an adult he will always beg the ancestors to 'strengthen' him further" (1961: 112).
6   Joseph M. Cuoq's vast inquiry concerning the Muslims in Africa, Les musulmans en Afrique (1975), gives the details of the different brotherhoods to be found in the different African countries where Islam is a significant reality. It shows the pervasive presence of the Sufi brotherhoods, though their weight is to be differentiated. In a country like Senegal this presence is overwhelming and the fact that the secular political power, whether colonial or postcolonial, has come to terms with the considerably influential brotherhoods is a significant aspect of what Leonardo Villalón has called "the Senegalese model of religion and politics" (1999: 129). On the other hand, Cuoq makes the remark that in Eastern Africa in general the brotherhoods can be said to have lost some importance (1975: 466).
7   This suggestion is made by Cuoq (1975: 63) specifically concerning Somali culture.
8   This notion of a unique transcendence that goes beyond any form of piety is well expressed in these verses of the Sufi master Muhyiddîn Ibn 'Arabî (d. 1240), cited in Corbin 1981: 135:

> O marvel! A garden among the flames...
> My heart has become capable of all forms.
> It is a meadow for gazelles and a monastery for Christian monks,
> A temple for idols and the pilgrim's Ka'aba,
> The Tables of the Law and the book of the Koran.
> I profess the religion of Love, and whatever direction
> Its steed may take, Love is my religion and my faith.

9   We find this conception in, for example, the following: "To become initiated into a Sufi order and to accept the discipleship of a master is to enter into a bond that is permanent, surviving even death. For the disciple, the shaykh is always mysteriously present.... His effect upon his disciples is permanent and the seed he has sown in their hearts continues to be nurtured and cared for, even after the temple of his body has fallen into dust" (Nasr 1991: 59).
10 Many passages from the Quran put much emphasis on the total break with the religion of the forebears: "When it is said to them: 'Follow what Allah has revealed,' they say: 'Nay! We shall follow the ways of our fathers:' What! Even though their fathers were void of wisdom and guidance?" (Surah 2, v. 170).

11   This report from *The Travels of Ibn Battuta* is at the center of a discussion, by Saaliu Kanji, on the rights of the African woman, in the past and for the future (1997: 18).

References

Abraham, W. Emmanuel (1992) "Crisis in African Cultures," in Kwasi Wiredu and Kwame Gyekye (eds.), *Person and Community: Ghanaian Philosophical Studies I* (Washington DC: The Council for Research in Values and Philosophy).

Adebayo, Adesanya (1958) "Yoruba Metaphysical Thinking," *Odù*, 5 (Ibadan).

Corbin, Henry (1981) *Creative Imagination in the Sufism of Ibn 'Arabî*, trans. Ralph Manheim (Princeton: Princeton University Press; orig. French edn. 1958).

Cuoq, Joseph M. (1975) *Les Musulmans en Afrique* (Paris: Maisonneuve et Larose).

Diagne, Souleymane Bachir (1993) "The Future of Tradition," in Momar C. Diop (ed.), *Senegal: Essays in Statecraft* (Dakar: Codesria).

Fakhry, Majid (1997) *A Short Introduction to Islamic Philosophy, Theology and Mysticism* (Oxford: Oneworld).

Froelich, J. C. (1962) *Les Musulmans d'Afrique noire* (Paris: Orante).

Jahn, Janheinz (1961) *Muntu: An Outline of the New African Culture*, trans. Marjorie Greene (New York: Grove Press).

Kanji, Saaliu, S. M. (1997) *Des Droits de la femme africaine, d'hier à demain* (Saint-Louis, Senegal: Xamal Editions).

Launay, Robert (1992) *Beyond the Stream: Islam and Society in a West African Town* (Berkeley, Los Angeles, Oxford: University of California Press).

Lewis, I. M. (1965) *The Modern History of Somaliland. From Nation to State* (London: Weidenfeld and Nicolson).

Mafeje, Archie (2000) "Africanity: A Combative Ontology," *Codesria Bulletin*, 1 (Dakar).

Monteil, Vincent (1980) *L'Islam noir: une religion à la conquête de l'Afrique*, 3rd edn. (Paris: Seuil).

Nasr, Seyyed Hossein (1991) *Sufi Essays*, 2nd edn. (New York: Suny Press).

Robinson, David (1999) "France as a Muslim Power in West Africa," *Africa Today*, 46 (summer/autumn).

Tempels, Placide (1959) *Bantu Philosophy*, trans. A. Rubbens (Paris: Présence Africaine; orig. French edn. 1945).

Villalon, Leonardo (1999) "Generational Changes, Political Stagnation, and the Evolving Dynamics of Religion and Politics in Senegal," *Africa Today*, 46 (summer/autumn).

Wiredu, Kwasi (1992) "Death and the Afterlife in African Culture," in Kwasi Wiredu and Kwame Gyekye (eds.), *Person and Community: Ghanaian Philosophical Studies I* (Washington DC: The Council for Research in Values and Philosophy).

Part V

ETHICS AND AESTHETICS

30

Some African Reflections on Biomedical and Environmental Ethics

GODFREY B. TANGWA

In the domain of morality correct practice without theory is preferable to correct theory without practice.

Introduction

The last quarter of the outgoing century/millennium witnessed two very important developments – one at the theoretical level and the other at the practical. At the theoretical level, there was a significant shift of emphasis in the theoretical concerns of the Western world (the home of the dominant culture of the last two centuries of the millennium) from overly speculative and abstract issues to more practical matters. This shift of emphasis was, perhaps, dictated by an increasing realization of the very grave dangers posed to our entire planet by what might be described as the most successful aspect of Western culture, namely, its science and technology. Practical or applied philosophy, eco-philosophy, environmentalism, developmentalism, medical ethics, feminist ethics, bioethics – these are some of the fruits, among many others, of this intellectual shift of focus.

At the practical level, there has been the phenomenon of *globalization*. The concept of globalization can be considered as referring to both a descriptive and a prescriptive process. As a descriptive process, globalization has been made possible and inevitable by advances in Western science and technology, especially in locomotion and communication technologies. This has led to increased contact between the various peoples and cultures of the Earth. As a prescription, globalization arises from increasing awareness of both the diversity (ecological, biological, cultural, linguistic) and the interdependence of the various parts of the world. It arises also from the simple deduction from this last consideration that the dangers facing the world as a whole, even if emanating largely from only a small part of it, can best be tackled only from a global perspective.

Human technology in general, and biotechnology (agricultural and human) in particular, have narrowed the gap between the natural and the artificial, between nature and humanity, between "God's work" and "work of human hands," to the extent that some have proclaimed God and/or nature dead. Human tinkering with nature, which can be said to have begun with the discovery of agriculture about ten millennia ago, and which seems both inescapable and unobjectionable, has evolved, thanks to modern technology, into wholesale interventions in the processes of nature, exemplified by the engineering of novel artificial life-forms. Such developments have gradually turned the perennial moral concern with the physical environment and with medical practice into moral disquiet and even moral alarm (Beck 1992; Kassiola 1990; McKibben 1989; McLaughlin 1993).

As Frederick Ferré pointedly remarked at the Nairobi World Conference of Philosophy, on "Philosophy, Humanity and the Environment" (July 21–25, 1991):

> By the time organisms are sufficiently artificial to be patentable, it is clear that the relative weights of nature and culture have reversed themselves. Culture is in the driver's seat and nature is hanging on for dear life (literally!) as we hurtle down unexplored roads, with poor visibility, and with uninspected and untried brakes. (1994: 237–8)

The cogency of this remark, made before mammalian cloning became a scientific fact in 1997, is today even more evident than before. Nevertheless, biotechnology also holds a certain justified fascination for human beings, because of its positive potential in such domains as preventive and therapeutic medicine and in agriculture.

In the face of these developments, human ethical sensibilities and responsibilities are urgently called for. As human beings, we carry the whole weight of moral responsibility and obligations for the world on our shoulders. The claim that humankind is the apex of biological existence, as we know it, has sometimes been dismissed as an arrogant speciecist claim and contested by some human militants for the rights of animals and/or plants. Less disputable, however, is the fact that, while human beings have putative moral responsibilities toward inanimate objects, plants, and the "lower" animals, these latter cannot be considered, without absurdity, as having any reciprocal moral obligations toward humans. Human interventions in nature could plausibly be justified by appeal to this asymmetrical responsibility, although this does not imply that every intervention is justifiable.

For these reasons, the recent focal attention on eco-ethics, environmental ethics, developmental ethics, medical ethics, bioethics – all of which can be gathered into one basket labeled *"eco-bio-ethics"* – is not only appropriate, but also quite timely.

The African perspective that I hope to draw attention to can be no more than a broad and rather untidy general framework of beliefs, attitudes, dispositions, outlooks, and practices. If in the course of this discussion I sometimes say things that sound overly critical of Western culture and the Western world, it is not because I am unaware of the positive values and advantages of Western culture or of its technology in particular. I could write a whole book in praise of the Western world, its culture and technology, but this is not the occasion for it. I may, on the other hand, also appear to be exaggerating and "romanticizing" African culture and its traditional past, particularly. But I am also not unaware of some of the shortcomings and weaknesses of African culture, traditional and modern. I could equally catalogue these in a whole book, but this is not the appropriate occasion.

I use the word "African" throughout in the same way that I use "Western," without any necessary implication that some differences or exceptions may not be found within what is thus bracketed. I insist on this point because, quite often,

people who themselves use such terms as "the Western world," "Western civilization," "Western liberalism," "Western democracy," "Western technology," "West-
ern philosophy," "Western ethical values," etc. have objected to my description of
something as "African" on the ground that they happen to know some part of
Africa where the description does not apply.

African Outlook

Variety is the most remarkable attribute of the African continent. Africa is one of
the richest and most variegated continents on earth, ecologically, geographically,
climatically, biologically, historically, culturally, linguistically, natural-resources-
wise, etc. Almost any ecological niche, taken at random, anywhere in Africa, presents remarkable and fascinating diversities. In Cameroon, my own country, for
instance, with a land surface of only circa 475,000 square kilometers, and a population of fewer than 13 million inhabitants, there are more than 240 distinct lin-
guistic/cultural groups which have all experienced German and English or French
colonization and influences. Moreover, the ecology, the flora, and fauna are truly
representative of what is available elsewhere in Africa. Africa also happens to be the
continent that has been, and continues to be, exploited by the powerful predatory
nations of the world.

African ethical, religious, and metaphysical ideas have, over the ages, been influenced, shaped, and colored by this background of diversity. The precolonial traditional African metaphysical outlook can be described as eco-bio-communitarian
(Tangwa 1996: 192), implying recognition and acceptance of interdependence and
peaceful coexistence between earth, plants, animals, and humans. This contrasts
with the Western outlook, which might be described as anthropocentric and individualistic. Within the African traditional outlook, human beings tend to be more
cosmically humble and therefore not only more respectful of other people but also
more cautious in their attitude to plants, animals, and inanimate things, and to the
various invisible forces of the world. One might say, in short, that they are more
disposed toward an attitude of *live and let live*. African philosophies provide the
intellectual support for this world-view. Within that world-view the distinction between plants, animals, and inanimate things, between the sacred and the profane,
matter and spirit, the communal and the individual, is a slim and flexible one. For
instance, the belief that humans, in certain circumstances, can transform into
animals and plants or into forces, such as the wind, is very prevalent within this
system and has very significant implications for the way nature is approached.

In like manner, metaphysical conceptions, ethics, customs, laws, and taboos form
a single unbroken chain within this African outlook. So much was this the case
that in the traditional past, it was not usual to separate them, at least from the
point of view of the ordinary members of the community.

The traditional world-view within which I was born (that of the Nso' of the
grassy highlands of Bamenda in Cameroon) recognizes the differences between
plants, animals, human beings, and super-human as well as sub-human spirits.
But it does not suppose that human beings have any mandate or special privilege,

God-given or otherwise, to subdue, dominate, and exploit the rest of creation, as is the case with the Western outlook. Because the Nso' attitude toward nature and the rest of creation is that of respectful coexistence, conciliation, and containment, there are frequent offerings of sacrifices to God, to the divine spirits, both benevolent and malevolent, to the departed ancestors and to the sundry invisible and inscrutable forces of nature. The Nso' Year (*Ya' Nso'*) always begins with fertility sacrifices. Through the course of the year, numerous other sacrifices are offered all over Nso' by the custodians of arable land (*ataangvën*), lineage heads (*ataala'*), and *agaashiv* who normally combine the functions of medical doctor, priest, psychiatrist, counselor, and exorcist.

Among the Nso' even something like the treatment of illness is basically a matter of appeasement and containment. The aim is never to eradicate, eliminate, or exterminate illness, but rather to coax and plead with it to leave its innocent victim alone. Otherwise, there is no insistence that illness, in itself, should not exist. If illness did not exist, how would people die? In Nso' thinking, death, as an inevitable end, is not considered necessarily a bad thing, especially when it is timely and relatively painless and neither premature nor overdue (Tangwa 1996: 195).

The general point about this African background is that it is only consistent with cautious and piecemeal use of technology.

Western Outlook

Among the catalysts of change in the Western world, the Industrial Revolution of the eighteenth and nineteenth centuries has pride of place. The Industrial Revolution drew its impetus from the slogan that "knowledge is power" and from the belief that knowledge is convertible into commercial value. Associated with this were the assumptions that all knowledge is unqualifiedly good, that nature is, in principle at least, completely knowable and controllable, and that the universe was something that ought to be explored, subdued, dominated, and exploited. These ideas and attitudes had their origins and foundation in Judeo-Christianity; but they led, paradoxically, to the secularization, desacralization, and profanation of everything in the universe – which is the very antithesis of the Judeo-Christian ethic. The Industrial Revolution and the technologies resulting from it greatly assisted Western imperial nations in their voyages of exploration and discovery, and the subjugation, colonization, domination, and exploitation of other peoples. Today, Western culture is, indisputably, the dominant culture of the world in the domain of science and technology. Western culture is the acknowledged master at whose feet other cultures sit as apprentices. But this does not mean that others have to learn and accept all other things from Western culture. Science and technology, in themselves, do not determine, for example, how people conceive of, or worship, God or how they marry and bring up children. Nor do they instruct people as to how to organize their social system or, most importantly, as to the *uses* to which science and technology themselves may be put.

The issues in Western biomedical research and practice that have been most discussed recently include, randomly, the following: experimentation on human subjects, cruelty to animals (including using them in experimentation and killing and eating them), animal liberation, animal rights, informed consent, euthanasia, assisted suicide, the artificial prolongation of life, brain death, the transplantation of human organs, sale of human organs, cadaveric harvest, banking and sale of human eggs and sperm, surrogate motherhood, artificial insemination, in vitro fertilization, abortion, acquisition and use of genetic information, creation and release of genetically modified organisms, animal cloning, human cloning, etc. Apart from the issues in this list that concern non-humans, the rest could roughly be categorized into three groups: those relating to the beginnings of human life, i.e. birth; those connected with the duration of human life, i.e. living; and those concerning the end of human life, i.e. death.

Aside from the complications brought into these issues by overt and covert economic or commercial motives, the main underlying ethical issues involved here are connected with the mechanization of life and its natural processes. This mechanization process threatens to turn human reproduction, as we have known it, into mere production. It threatens also to convert life and death into similar processes, depending largely on mere technical calculations involving, *inter alia*, the reading of graphs, charts, balance sheets, insurance policies, patents, costs, and the turning on and off of machines. Western culture can be described as a technophile culture, although that is not to say that there are no technophobes in the Western world. Without being either technophilic or technophobic, African culture could, perhaps, show the way back to those natural human values that Western culture has sacrificed to the god of technology and industrialization and commerce, if, indeed, it ever had them.

Human Reproduction

Let me dwell a bit on human reproduction as an example. There is enormous interest in the Western world in reproductive technologies. This interest in artificial reproductive methods is, however, curiously out of tune with the increasing lack of interest in natural reproduction and reproductive methods. The accelerated decline in the birth rate in Western countries, thanks to contraception, abortion, family size reduction, and so on, is, prima facie, hard to square with the almost feverish interest in artificial methods of reproduction.

In Africa, there would be an equally great interest in artificial methods of reproduction (or assisted reproduction) among those unable to procreate through normal natural methods. But this can be explained by pointing to the high value placed by the culture on procreation and children. In African culture, children are highly valued; so highly valued that procreation is considered the main purpose of marriage. In Africa, marriage for mere companionship is rare, if not completely non-existent. In my natal language, Lamnso, we say: *Wan dze wan, a dze lim nyuy* (a child is a child, the handiwork of God). A child is always welcome, no matter how it was conceived (excepting through such a taboo as incest – Tangwa 1996: 197–8), and no matter how it is. Some parents would nearly beat their daughter to death for getting pregnant "in the house," that is, outside marriage. But, watch

391

them dancing with joy and celebrating when she eventually delivers her baby, and you would not believe they are the very same parents who nearly killed her for getting thus pregnant.

Within African culture, a child is accepted and loved unconditionally. It is, no doubt, to support this moral imperative that the culture bestows greater value on handicapped children. Within Nso' culture, for example, a handicapped child is considered *mbuhme*, a special gift (of God). Such children are generally believed to possess psychic powers and extraordinary "depth." They are also thought often to be messengers of God or disguises of spirits. For this reason, they are treated with great care and respect. However, this by no means implies that anybody would pray to have a handicapped child. On the contrary, the prayer is always that all the children should be healthy and elegant like the palm tree and robust and strong like the iroko. If there were a means of selecting the child before birth, surely no one would select a handicapped one. Just as, were it possible to choose one's personal destiny before birth, as in some fables, surely no one could conceivably choose to come into the world handicapped. But, once the handicapped child is already there as a fait accompli, it is accepted with unconditional love.

Within this sort of outlook, there would surely also be great interest in any technologies likely to assist the birth of healthy babies. However, it would be considered quite horrendous if such assistance were associated with trade and commerce or presented as a matter of seeking a child of a certain "quality" (Chadwick 1987). In Lamnso' it would be quite impossible to convey the idea that a certain procedure would help a couple to get a child of a higher quality. The spontaneous and unanswerable question would be: "How can one child be of a better quality than another?" Quality-talk in the domain of human reproduction is, perhaps, a case of adapting inappropriate concepts and vocabulary from the domain of positive economics and marketing propaganda under the influence of a calculative moral approach, such as utilitarianism.

The saying that a child is a child has a generalized version: a human being is a human being. All human beings are equal. Of course, each human being has a host of individuating physical and non-physical characteristics. Some are taller, others shorter; some are fatter, others slimmer; some intelligent, others less so; some highly educated, others quite ignorant; some rich, others poor, etc. But, despite all this, it makes no sense to claim that one human life is of better or higher quality than another. This not only implies that every human being must be treated as an end in herself (to adapt Kant's expression) but also that he or she must accept his or her finitude and limitations, including accepting mortality with calm and dignity. Within Nso' culture, timely death is accepted quite calmly, if not cheerfully.

Technology and the Environment

The Western world-view can be described as predominantly anthropocentric and individualistic, and contrasted with its African counterpart, which I have described as eco-bio-communitarian. However, these different outlooks do not have any automatic consequences for the environment. An anthropocentric ethic, even an individualistic one, if it were sufficiently rational, need not necessarily endanger the environment, just as an eco-bio-communal one may not necessarily forestall all dangers to the environment. It must also be noted that in Western discourse, as distinguished from practice, the entire spectrum of attitudes to technology and the environment are indeed to be found (Attfield and Dell 1996). The important question, then, has little to do with the existing variety of environmental ethical theories. It is, rather, a question of which of those theories have influenced the most the actual uses to which technology has been put and whether they have been compatible with the preservation of the environment.

Some of the most harmful effects of technology, effects that have now assumed the proportions of urgent global hazards, are the following: global pollution (of air, water, and soil); global warming and consequent erratic and unpredictable changes in global weather systems; massive risks to plants, animals, and humans from toxic industrial wastes and from sophisticated weapons (conventional, nuclear, chemical, and biological); risks of upsetting nature's ecological balance; risk of accidentally triggering the collapse of the very foundations of life via gene technology, etc. These hazards are urgent for all human beings in all parts of the world, irrespective of their responsibility or lack thereof in their causation. It would therefore be a great mistake to think that the solution to these problems should be left to the Western world or even just to Western science and technology, or, more specifically, to Western scientists and technologists (DeGeorge 1994: 9). Scientific and technological knowledge may be for the specialists, but the morality of their uses is certainly within everyone's competence to consider.

Poverty and Shame

The eco-bio-communitarianism of Africa had a social correlate in the form of a welfare dispensation more solicitous of the welfare of the individual than is dreamt of in the social welfare of liberalism. For example, the culture within which I was born and within which I grew up took great pains both to ensure that no one should die out of sheer poverty and to emphasize that material poverty is nothing to be ashamed of. In Lamnso', my mother tongue, we have the following common sayings and proverbs:

> A si vishong bong kitan (Better to be poor than to steal)
> Wir yo' yi kpuh kitan (No one dies of poverty)
> Kitan ki yo' dze lii wir (Poverty does not belong with blameworthy actions)
> Bong ke ngah kitan (The poor person is better off)

That culture took great pains to ensure that the most basic necessities of life were freely available to all and sundry. There were taboos against the commercialization of things such as the staple foods, water, housing, fuel, wood, etc. These were things one gave or received, or simply took, but which one never bought or sold. Furthermore, it was the general practice that fruits, such as avocado pears, kola nuts, oranges, mangoes, no matter to whom they belonged, were at the disposal of anybody so long as they had fallen down from the trees of their own accord. In the late 1950s and early '60s, my natal village, Shisong, used to flourish in all the fruits mentioned above, and I remember very clearly how large numbers of people with baskets, some coming from as far as 15 kilometers away, would join us in the very early hours of the morning to pick fruits which had fallen overnight all over the village.

Besides, the culture had a strong egalitarian impulse. This did not, of course, forbid or prevent some people from getting rich. There were many individuals generally recognized as rich people. However, the culture had many ways of encouraging rich individuals voluntarily to recycle and/or exchange some of their riches for honorific positions and titles. As Jimoh Omo-Fadaka has very rightly remarked, "poverty, as it is known today, was almost unknown in pre-colonial Africa" (1990: 180).

Conclusion

The process of globalization, which today has turned the world into a veritable global village, is increasingly bringing both the benefits and hazards of Western technology and, especially, biotechnology to all parts of the globe. Some of the most urgent hazards involve human health and the global physical environment. It is my considered view that there can be nothing wrong with technology in and of itself but only with the motivation for its development and the *uses* to which it is put. The motivation for the development of Western technology and the uses to which it has been put was driven by the will to possess and dominate the world. This motivation is, conceptually, quite separable from the disciplines themselves of science and technology, which may possibly be the best things that ever happened to humanity. The standpoint of these reflections is that a more humble motivation for the pursuit of science and technology based on the eco-bio-centric attitude of *live and let live* can be substituted for the aggressive motivation of domination to the immeasurable advantage of the whole of humankind.

Note

I thankfully acknowledge the support of the Alexander von Humboldt Foundation for this work.

References

Attfield, Robin and Bell, Katharine (eds.) (1996) *Values, Conflict and the Environment* (Aldershot: Ashgate).

Beck, Ulrich (1995) *Ecological Politics in an Age of Risk*, trans. Amos Weisz (Cambridge: Polity Press).

Chadwick, Ruth F. (1987) "The Perfect Baby: Introduction," in *Ethics, Reproduction and Genetic Control* (London and New York: Routledge).

DeGeorge, Richard T. (1994) "Modern Science, Environmental Ethics and the Anthropocentric Predicament," in H. Odera Oruka (ed.), *Philosophy, Humanity and Ecology: Philosophy of Nature and Environmental Ethics* (Nairobi, Kenya: ACTS Press).

Ferré, Frederick (1994) "Technology, Ethics and the End of Nature," in H. Odera Oruka (ed.), *Philosophy, Humanity and Ecology: Philosophy of Nature and Environmental Ethics* (Nairobi, Kenya: ACTS Press).

Kassiola, Joel Jay (1990) *The Death of Industrial Civilization* (Albany: State University of New York Press).

McKibben, Bill (1989) *The End of Nature* (New York: Random House).

McLaughlin, Andrew (1993) *Regarding Nature: Industrialism and Deep Ecology* (Albany: State University of New York Press).

Omo-Fadaka, Jimoh (1990) "Communalism: The Moral Factor in African Development," in J. Ronald Engel and Joan Gibb Engel (eds.), *Ethics of Environment and Development: Global Challenge and International Response* (London: Belhaven Press).

Tangwa, Godfrey B. (1996) "Bioethics: An African Perspective," *Bioethics*, 10(3): 183–200.

Further reading

Omoregbe, Joseph (1979) *Ethics: A Systematic and Historical Study* (London: Global Educational Services).

Rolston III, Holmes (1992) "Challenges in Environmental Ethics," in David E. Cooper and Jay A. Palmer (eds.), *The Environment in Question: Ethics and Global Issues* (London and New York: Routledge).

Singer, Peter (1975) *Animal Liberation* (New York: Random House).

Singer, Peter (1993) *Practical Ethics* (Cambridge: Cambridge University Press).

Tangwa, Godfrey B. (1992) "African Philosophy: Appraisal of a Recurrent Problematic. Part 2: What is African Philosophy and who is an African Philosopher?" *COGITO* (winter): 138–43.

Taylor, Paul W. (1986) *Respect for Nature: A Theory of Environmental Ethics* (Princeton, NJ: Princeton University Press).

Wiredu, Kwasi (1994) "Philosophy, Humankind and the Environment," in H. Odera Oruka (ed.), *Philosophy, Humanity and Ecology: Philosophy of Nature and Environmental Ethics* (Nairobi, Kenya: ACTS Press).

31

Ethics and Morality in Yoruba Culture

JOHN AYOTUNDE ISOLA BEWAJI

Ethics and Morality in Africa

Morality and ethics in Western and non-Western societies have similar importance in that human social and interpersonal behavior is under the necessity of the adjustment of interests among individuals for attaining the general well-being of the community. In all societies the concepts of right and wrong are determined by perceptions of what constitutes the good life for individuals, on the one hand, and the general good of society, on the other. Divergences of moral norms as between Western and non-Western societies are largely due to variations in cultural traditions and to ecological, sociological, and other existential differences. At the risk of being accused of ethnophilosophizing, I will attempt an account of the wellspring of morality in Africa (and parts thereof) for the purpose of facilitating the proper analysis and appreciation of the foundations of that morality.

In this regard, one can boldly affirm that the wellspring of morality and ethics in African societies is the pursuit of a balance of individual, with communal, well-being. It is not unusual to get the impression that African cultures extol the virtues of community, that moral obligations are primarily social rather than individual, and that communal factors often take precedence over individual rights or interests. The impression exists, furthermore, that morality is predicated on a religious foundation. When these suppositions are meant as derogatory commentaries on the moral universe in which Africans live, they are based on an improper understanding of the principles that fashion the moral and social fabric of African societies.

Consider the idea that each person is a representative of himself or herself as well as of his or her family. This has the implication that an individual has to consider not only how a course of action contemplated by him will affect him personally, but also how it will affect his family, either directly or in terms of the way in which they will be perceived in the society. For example, one is expected, even as one pursues one's own goals, to be careful not to tarnish any tradition of excellence in conduct established by one's lineage. But this does not diminish the responsibility that society has to the individual.

What is this responsibility? This is a very serious and all-important question. It may seem that morality is a personal thing, first and foremost. This is only partially true, from the African perspective. The artificial separation of individual moral responsibility from that of society is the result of superficial thinking. It is obvious that the context in which moral obligations arise is an interactive one. It is the social milieu in which competition for the scarce resources of the environment takes place. But it is not only the resources of the environment that are scarce. The human resources of love, patronage, recognition, compassion, companionship, etc. are also scarce, and require deliberate efforts in both their generation and equitable distribution. Here lies the crux of the moral responsibility of society to its members and to itself. And this fact is represented in numerous ideas in African moral thought.

Commenting on African ideas of community and individuality, Gbadegesin has written:

> From this it follows that there need not be any tension between individuality and community since it is possible for an individual to freely give up his/her own perceived interest for the survival of the community. But in giving up one's interests thus, one is also sure that the community will not disown one and that one's well being will be its concern.... The idea of individual rights, based on a conception of individuals as atoms, is therefore bound to be foreign to this system. For community is founded on notions of an intrinsic and enduring relationship among its members. (1991: 66–7)

If we shift gears a bit, we will immediately understand the full meaning of the above reflections. The suggestion that Africans are "in all things religious" and that religion is the basis of their morality misses the relationship between religion and morality. That view has been disseminated by such African theological scholars as Bolaji Idowu, John Mbiti, and J. O. Awolalu and their Western mentors, such as G. E. Parrinder, R. S. Rattray, and A. B. Ellis. These authors fail to understand what makes religion important in African life, namely, the welfare of the individual and that of society. This is why many reflective students of morality in Africa will easily recognize Wiredu's position that the basis of morality in Africa is human welfare. According to him (1997), the basis of morality is universal in all societies, though what is moral in concrete moral situations may not be universally the same in all societies. In *Philosophy and an African Culture*, Wiredu says:

> It has often been said that our traditional outlook was intensely humanistic. It seems to me that, as far as the basis of the traditional ethic is concerned, this claim is abundantly justified. Traditional thinking about the foundations of morality is refreshingly non-supernaturalistic. *Not that one can find in traditional sources elaborate theories of humanism.* But anyone who reflects on our traditional ways of speaking about morality is bound to be struck by the preoccupation with human welfare: What is morally good is what befits a human being; it is what is decent for a man – what brings dignity, respect, contentment, prosperity, joy, to man and his community. And what is morally bad is what brings misery, misfortune, and disgrace. Of course, immoral conduct is held to be hateful to God, the Supreme Being, and even to the lesser gods. But the thought is not that something is good because God approves of it, but rather that God approves of it because it is good in the first place – a distinction which, as Socrates noted in the context of a different culture, does not come easily to every pious mind. (1980: 6; my emphasis)

I might mention that I have italicized a sentence in the quote from Wiredu to bring attention to my dissent with it. Wiredu claims that traditional African sources will not show elaborate reflections on the humanistic foundations of ethics. This is inaccurate, as the Yoruba Ifa demonstrates serious efforts to show that the basis of morality lies in the concern for human welfare (see Gbadegesin 1991). This point is not considered a serious issue here and will not be pursued further. Instead, we will return to the question of the humanistic foundations of ethics in Africa.

Wole Soyinka (1988) laments the tendency toward a socially disintegrative individualism in American society. In a chapter entitled "Between Self and System" (ibid. 61–85), he pays attention to the dislocation between intellectual and artistic efforts in American thought. For him there can be little separation, if any at all, between the ends of art and the ends of ethics. This is not unexpected, as in Yoruba thought there is an inseparable integration between ethics and all aspects of life. In particular, there is often the characterization of that which is moral or ethical as that which is beautiful – that is, as that which is aesthetically pleasing. Roland Abiodun (1983) dilates this relationship between beauty and good character, concluding that both are inseparable in Yoruba ethics and aesthetics. Thus, Wiredu's views are in tandem with this conception. Wiredu says:

> There is an aesthetic strain in our traditional ethical thought that is worthy of special mention in this connection. As noted already, what is good is conceived to be what is fitting...what is fitting is what is beautiful.... There are, indeed, aesthetic analogies in the moral language of other cultures. But aesthetic analogies are taken much more seriously and have more extensive moral relevance in our traditional thought. (1980: 6)

Elaborating a little on the humanistic basis of indigenous morality, he later observes:

> The first axiom of all Akan axiological thinking is that man or woman is the measure of all value.... And every Akan maxim about the specifically moral values that I know, explicitly or implicitly, postulates the harmonization of interests as the means, and the securing of human well-being as the end, of all moral endeavour. (1996: 65)

> The circles of obligations, rights, and privileges which radiated from the center of household relations of kinship to the larger circumferences of lineage and clan affinities provided a natural school for training in the practice of sympathetic impartiality which, in its most generalized form, is the root of all moral virtue. (ibid. 71)

All the foregoing is contrary to the notion that the basis of African morality is to be found in religion. Still, there is some relationship between religion and conduct in African society, and we need to be clear about it. Briefly, in African society religion is both an instrument of cohesion and a factor of order, bringing to the fore the creative genius of members of society. In essence, it is being suggested here that religion developed out of human necessity and served the human need for knowledge and security. The injunctions of morality, insofar as they are related to religion in the African environment, will be found to be motivated by humanistic considerations. Thus the invocation of the Supreme Being, the divinities, the ancestors, and other forces in moral matters is mainly intended to lend legitimacy, through an already available reinforcement mechanism, to what is often taken for granted as morally obligatory in a humanistic sense. Being morally upright is not as much a matter of pleasing the supernatural forces as it is of promoting human welfare. It is in the light of this that the attitude of the Yoruba people pertaining to the place of religion and the supernatural forces in morality becomes easy to understand. Devotion to the deities is not as much in the interest of the deities as it is in the interest of the people; and when a deity fails to bring benefits to society, people feel free to sever the relationship.

Some Ethical Concepts in Yoruba Philosophy

To gain a more concrete idea of the substance of an African morality, let us consider a number of related concepts used in the assessment of behavior in Yoruba ethical reasoning. In Yoruba philosophical discourse, ethics relates to the norms that govern human behavior, on the one hand, and the behavior of the supernatural beings in their relationship with humans, on the other. As the above suggests, it is not only humans that have to be ethical: the gods too do.

In Yoruba language, ethical behavior and morally approved conduct is called, variously, *iwa rere*, *iwa pele*, *iwa irele*, *iwa tutu*, or *iwa omoluwabi*. A morally upright person, a person who exhibits such virtues as honesty, respect (for himself, the elders, and for others, in general), decency, benevolence, etc., is *oniwa rere*, *onirele*, *oniwa tutu*, *oniwa pele*, *Omoluwabi*. Such persons are highly valued and respected in Yoruba society, and are rewarded by society in various ways for their goodness.

The first concept that I want to examine here is *ese*, or sin. This concept has gained much currency in religious discourse because of the influence of Christian ethics in many African societies. This is not to suggest that it was absent originally from the lexicon of Yoruba people, contrary to Bolaji Idowu (1962: 148). But it is important to note a fundamental distinction between *ese* and the Christian concept of sin. In the Yoruba language *ese* refers not only to religious infractions against the Supreme Being, the deities, and the ancestors, but also to infractions against fellow human beings. Indeed, the religious cases are *ese* only because the infractions are ultimately against fellow human beings. Thus, while a person may have done wrong, it does not necessarily follow that the person has sinned, if sin is understood in the purely Christocentric sense. One may speculate that probably the disintegration of the moral fabric of the Nigerian polity is a consequence of the substitution of an alien concept of right and wrong for the indigenous ideas of morality. This substitution seems responsible for the apparent feeling that infractions against fellow humans are not so very grave, since they are no longer regarded as sins, which are now only possible against God, Allah, Olodumare, Chukwu, or Osanobuwa, depending on each person's religious terminology.

The Yoruba concept of sin (*ese*), then, defines a broad category covering infractions against persons as well as supernatural beings. But there are important subcategories of *ese* that are of use in the understanding of Yoruba ethics. This brings us to the concepts of *eewo*, *aimo*, *egbin*, *abuku*, *aleebu*, *ibaje*, *aidaa*, among others. It is only possible here to discuss a few of these briefly.

I begin with *eewo*. This concept has two aspects. It is often translated as *tabu* by theological writers on African religions in their attempt to understand Yoruba beliefs. *Tabu* or *eewo* in this sense relates to things prohibited by the Supreme Being, the divinities, and the ancestors. However, there is the more secular meaning of *eewo* or *tabu* which relates to morality *simpliciter*. *Eewo*, conceived in this sense, means things that are wrong to do and for which sanctions will be incurred. When one says "sanctions," this is not to be construed as meaning punishment formally enforced, as in legal punishment. It may be in the form of simply losing stature, status, or face in the community, whereas in the religious sense, some atonement or sacrifice has to be made to assuage the unseen forces that may have been offended.

Another important concept in Yoruba moral discourse is *abuku*. Literally, this concept translates as "blemish." In the Yoruba understanding of morality, to act against moral expectations is to exhibit a moral blemish on one's character. Human beings with moral blemishes are deformed by the blemish, and will, for instance, be shy, as a consequence, to raise their voice in public to participate in the discussion of community affairs. In fact, to have such a blemish is to be unworthy of communion with one's peers or of holding a responsible office in the community.

I come now to the concept of *aimo*. The word *aimo* has two meanings, one epistemic, the other moral. In the epistemic sense it means "lack of knowledge" or "absence of knowledge" (Hallen and Sodipo 1986). *Aimo* in this sense could lead to infractions in the ethical sense, for ignorance can be a liability in many ways. But our main concern is with the moral sense of the term. In this sense *aimo* is very close to the blemish of *abuku* discussed above. The difference is that *aimo* is a more episodic failure and is easier to expiate and be rid of. There are many things that may create *aimo* for a person, some of them small, others big. The significance of these acts of vice can be cumulative, and their destructive effect on one's image, as well even as on one's own self-conception, can be very real. Accordingly, Yoruba moralists are especially keen to urge all and sundry to be mindful lest one's personal integrity be overtaken by an accumulating *aimo*.

An equally interesting, though somewhat more striking, concept is that of *egbin*. The word *egbin*, with but a variation in tone marks, expresses two polar ideas. On the one hand, superlative beauty in a person or thing is characterized by comparing the person or thing to a beautiful animal by the name *egbin*. On the other hand, when an act is despicable and odious to the senses, capable, so to speak, of causing nausea, it is said to be *egbin*.

In the moral meaning of *egbin*, it is clear that the Yoruba have calibrated the degrees of moral decadence that members of the community are cautioned against. Children are brought up with a clear sense of the differentiation of all these degrees of defect of behavior or character, and they mature with the consciousness of the need to internalize the virtues of good behavior that are highlighted by the delineated polarities. If these imperatives are implemented in actual conduct, one result is that the subject wins the good opinion of his peers and, indeed, of the community at large, a consideration that is of the last consequence in a communalistic society.

Other concepts that space does not permit us to discuss here, but which we mentioned, are *aleebu*, *ibaje*, and *aidaa*. These three are related, in a variety of ways, to those that we have discussed above. *Aleebu* and *ibaje* are cognate to *abuku*, while *aidaa* is cognate to *aimo*, except that the latter is more easily detected in behavior, while *aidaa* may be concealed to the unwary, only to come to the surface when critical situations arise.

It may merit mentioning here that acts that are described in Yoruba ethical discourse as bad or less than good concern not only requirements to do various things, but also one's manner of carriage in society and such things as discretion and the ability to keep peer confidence. These are clearly factors that are seriously viewed in judgments of character and evaluation of conduct. And it would be strange to see an adult in Yoruba society who is not aware of all the aspects of personal and public morality noted here.

Concluding Remarks

Clearly it might be said that what we refer to as moral concepts reflect practical nuances of right and wrong conduct. This is true but incomplete. Morality in most civilized societies does not start and end with mere notions of right and wrong, dissociated from the emotions and feelings of members of society. What makes moral dictates so powerful is not the mere rationality of the grounds for their determination. What gives moral notions the imperativeness of their purport is the fact that persons and communities *feel* that infractions of the demands of morality constitute serious challenges to the survival of human life and culture.

Moral education consists in both prescriptions and proscriptions. The concepts discussed above form the basis of various proscriptions. Together they give a vivid, though incomplete, portrayal of Yoruba morality. In a more extended discussion one would not only cover more concepts for proscriptions but also treat of those concepts that motivate the prescriptions that help to define the Yoruba ethic. In some cases, however, as in the present one, the negative can be quite effective in highlighting the positive.

It has been suggested above that ethics in Africa may be described as humanistic. If care is not taken to clarify what is intended by this, it may be asked: "If so, why do we see so much human disaster in Africa?" The interlocutor may want to know why there is so much leadership disorientation and violent conflicts with their attendant socio-economic catastrophes. The proper understanding of the fundamental factors that have led to this situation is deeper than what a cursory glance can unravel. Suffice it to say that many of the leadership crises experienced today are consequences of a breakdown in the indigenous ethic. This has been the result of the adoption, in a largely adverse historical process, of various alien cultural elements. Thus, for example, the ethos of politics, law, and business operative in contemporary Africa is in many ways alien to her indigenous cultures. When this is taken account of, it becomes clear that the human disasters current on the continent are predictable and unavoidable.

Finally, the interplay of specific rules of behavior with general ideas about morality in this discussion is typical of traditional African life and thought. It signalizes

401

the integration of the concerns of the moral life with those of the philosophical understanding of the same.

References

Abiodun, R. (1983) "Identity and the Artistic Process in Yoruba Aesthetic Concept of *Iwa*," *Journal of Cultures and Ideas*, 1(1): 13–30.

Gbadegesin, S. (1991) *African Philosophy: Traditional Yoruba Philosophy and Contemporary Realities* (New York: Peter Lang).

Idowu, E. B. (1962) *Olodumare: God in Yoruba Belief* (London: Longman).

Hallen, B. and Sodopo, J. O. (1986) *Knowledge, Belief and Witchcraft: Analytic Experiments in African Philosophy* (London: Ethnographica).

Soyinka, W. (1988) *Art, Dialogue and Outrage* (Ibadan, Nigeria: New Horn Press).

Wiredu, K. (1980) *Philosophy and an African Culture* (Cambridge: Cambridge University Press).

Wiredu, K. (1996) *Cultural Universals and Particulars: An African Perspective* (Bloomington: Indiana University Press).

Further reading

Abanuka, B. (1989) "The Ultimate Origins of Moral Norms," *The Nigerian Journal of Philosophy*, 9(1 & 2): 61–8.

Abimbola, W. (1968) *Ijinle ohun enu Ifa – apa kiini* (Glasgow, UK: Collins).

Abimbola, W. (1977) *Awon oju odu mereerindinlogun* (Oxford: Oxford University Press).

Almeder, R. (1992) *Death and Personal Survival* (Lanham, MD: Rowman and Littlefield Publishers).

Almeder, R. (1992) *Harmless Naturalism* (Peru, IL: Open Court Publishing Co.).

Almeder, R. (2000) *Human Happiness and Morality* (Lanham, MD: Rowman and Littlefield Publishers).

Appiah, K. A. (1992) *In My Father's House: Africa in the Philosophy of Culture* (New York: Oxford University Press).

Ayer, A. J. (1936) *Language, Truth and Logic* (London: Penguin).

Balogun, O. A. (1998) "Moral Problems in Nigeria: Yoruba Ethics to the Rescue," in J. O. Oguejiofor (ed.), *Africa: Philosophy and Public Affairs* (Enugu, Nigeria: Delta), pp. 285–301.

Ebijuwa, T. (1995) "Conscience, Morality and Social Responsibility in an African Culture," *Quest: Philosophical Discussions*, IX(2): 87–100.

Gordon, L. R. (1997) *Her Majesty's Other Children* (New York: Rowman and Littlefield Publishers).

Gyekye, K. (1987) *An Essay on African Philosophical Thought* (Cambridge: Cambridge University Press).

Gyekye, K. (1995) "African Communalism," in G. Percesepe (ed.), *Introduction to Ethics* (Englewood Cliffs, NJ: Prentice-Hall), pp. 97–105.

Hare, R. M. (1952) *The Language of Morals* (Oxford: Oxford University Press).

Mackie, J. L. (1977) *Ethics: Inventing Right and Wrong* (London: Penguin).

Makinde, M. A. (1988) *African Philosophy, Culture and Traditional Medicine* (Athens, OH: Ohio University Monograph in International Studies).

Momoh, C. S. (1988) "On Cultural Philosophy," *Journal of African Philosophy and Studies*, 1(1&2): 25–38.

Momoh, C. S. (1989) "Can One Willingly do Wrong: A Re-examination of the Socratic Platonic Paradox," *The Nigerian Journal of Philosophy*, 9(1&2): 1–9.

Oladipo, O. (1992) *The Idea of African Philosophy* (Ibadan, Nigeria: Molecular Publishers).

Oladipo, O. (1996) *Philosophy and the African Experience* (Ibadan, Nigeria: Hope Publications).

Oluwole, S. B. (1984) "The Rational Basis of Yoruba Ethical Thinking," *The Nigerian Journal of Philosophy*, 4(1&2): 14–25.

Oluwole, S. B. (1988) "The Legislative Ought," *Oye: Ogun Journal of Arts*, 1: 82–97.

Omamor, A. (1986) "Some Taboo Expressions in the Western Delta of Nigeria," *Africa Notes*, X(1): 25–37.

Omoregbe, J. I. (1989) "Law and Morality," *Africa Notes*, X(1): 53–60.

Oseovo-Onibere, S. G. A. (1986) "Eto: A Retributive Principle in Owhe Society," *Africa Notes*, X(1): 38–44.

Otakpor, N. (1990) "The Architectonics of Secular Humanism," *The Nigerian Journal of Philosophy*, 10(1&2): 45–54.

Passmore, J. (1957) *A Hundred Years of Philosophy* (London: Penguin).

Rachels, J. (ed.) (1979) *Moral Problems* (New York: Harper Collins Publishers).

Singer, P. (ed.) (1986) *Applied Ethics* (Oxford: Oxford University Press).

Sodipo, J. O. (1972) *Philosophy and Culture* (Ile-Ife, Nigeria: Unife Press).

Williams, B. (1972) *Morality: An Introduction to Ethics* (Cambridge: Cambridge University Press).

403

32

Aesthetic Inquiry and the Music of Africa

KOFI AGAWU

"The aesthetics of music," writes Francis Sparshott, "normally designates attempts to explain what music means: the difference between what is and is not music; the place of music in human life and its relevance to an understanding of human nature and history; the fundamental principles of the interpretation and appreciation of music; the nature and ground of excellence and greatness in music; the relation of music to the rest of the fine arts and to other related practices; the place or places of music in the system of reality; and the nature of the musical work itself" (1980: 120). The student of European musical aesthetics – the tradition about which Sparshott writes – has at his disposal a large body of writings by philosophers and musicologists from which he can explore these issues. So whether he begins with Plato or Aristotle, proceeds in the manner of Enlightenment rationalists, or builds on insights from Hanslick, Schopenhauer, Nietzsche, Langer, or Dahlhaus, one thing is certain: the student does not operate in a vacuum; he is part of an intellectual tradition.[1] Nor does his legacy consist solely of philosophical texts. Musical texts in the form of published scores, multiple recordings of a good portion of the core repertory, and regular, live performances are readily available. The inquiry need not be framed historically either; it may be systematic and analytical. For example, Roger Scruton's *The Aesthetics of Music* (1997), the most comprehensive recent study of European musical aesthetics, forsakes the broad brush of history for a more direct engagement with such concepts as sound, tone, imagination and metaphor, ontology, representation, expression, language, understanding, tonality, form, content, value, analysis, performance, and culture.

A comparable body of philosophical, critical, or documentary work is not (yet) available to the student of African musical aesthetics. In the first place, scholarly study of African music is of comparatively recent origins. Consequently the pioneering contributions of German comparative musicologists from the early 1900s and of Africanist ethnomusicologists since the 1950s have had to establish the material as well as conceptual foundations upon which later philosophical reflection can be built.[2] Secondly, although Africa boasts a numerically significant heritage of field recordings, much of this sonic data is confined to specialized collections and so is not readily or commercially available. Its potential as a catalyst in research into African musical practice thus remains to be fully realized.[3] Thirdly, the nature of the ethnographic enterprise, the recurrence of an uncannily imperial impulse to possess bits of the African musical landscape, and the reluctance of scholars to engage one another's data directly – these are among the factors that have delayed the emergence of the sort of critical discourse of which aesthetic reflection would form a part.[4]

There may be some virtue in this state of affairs, however. Instead of seeking to formulate an aesthetics of African music in parallel with an aesthetics of European music, and thus risk reducing the unique problematic of African musical aesthetics to what can be fitted into a European frame, the researcher is challenged to begin the not inconsiderable task of imagining an aesthetics that takes its inspiration directly from the particularities of African life, thought, and expression. Framed this way, the task may be undertaken with some help from early writings by amateurs, recent ethnomusicological accounts, and, perhaps most significant of all, the implicit aesthetic discourse enshrined in indigenous talk about the activities of composing, listening, and performing. Amateur writings by colonial officers, leaders of scientific expeditions, travelers, and missionaries have the virtue of raising aesthetic issues directly and in language unburdened by jargon. At the same time, their ideological leanings are not hidden.[5] Detailed musical ethnographies of various African groups by professional ethnomusicologists provide a valuable framework for comparative study.[6] And analytical studies of musical structure, studies that unveil patterns of compositional choice among African musicians, help us to understand the nature of musical creativity and the basis of reception.[7] In drawing upon this body of work for the purposes of aesthetic inquiry, the student should not be under the illusion that a pristine aesthetic theory lies hidden somewhere awaiting discovery by a persistent Afrocentrist. Nor would one wish to deny the possibility that the very attempt to formulate a separate aesthetic discourse is already tinged with "European" influence. The purpose, rather, would be to take as given the complex historical reality of contemporary Africa, including its contradictory styles of intellectual inquiry, and to proceed to imagine the terms of an appropriate aesthetic discourse.

It is appropriate, therefore, that we say something at this point about the nature of the musical society. Contemporary Africa is marked by an astonishing variety of musics. These are perhaps best understood in terms of a three-tiered framework consisting of traditional, popular, and art music. Traditional music is music nurtured by traditional institutions. Examples include the ceremonial and ritual musics that are performed in and around the Asantehene's palace, at the courts of Benin, or in the kingdom of Baganda. Another prominent form is music associated with funerals, including dirges, laments, and various forms of sacred drumming. These musics originated in precolonial Africa and appear to have remained unchanged as long as the institutions that sponsor them have retained their essential structure. Those searching for authenticity in African music often turn to traditional music.[8] By contrast, popular music is a direct outcome of Africa's encounter with Europe since the end of the nineteenth century. The musical language of popular music typically fuses European with African elements, including diatonic or modal melody, hymn-like harmony, memorable rhythmic *topoi*, and verbal texts broaching topical matters and drawing on techniques of African oral poetry. Core instruments like guitars, saxophones, and trumpets combine with drums and rattles. Popular music includes genres like West African Highlife, Zairean Soukous, and Nigerian Jùjú. Widely available on records, cassettes, and CDs, popular music may be heard on most radio and TV stations on the continent; it also serves as entertainment music in dance halls, clubs, cafés, community centers, and schools.[9] Art music, the least prominent of the three genres of music, represents another response to colonialism. Here, however, and unlike popular music, the response is to the so-called high musical traditions of Europe epitomized in the canonical works of Bach, Mozart, Beethoven, and Brahms. Practitioners work essentially in a written tradition, producing scores in standard musical notation, or written directions in the case of improvised or semi-improvised works. Performances of art music in concert halls, churches, and private homes are relatively few. Audiences are generally small and each performance occasion is extreme in the sense that the audience quietly contemplates the music but does not normally dance or move to it as happens routinely at performances of traditional and popular music. Leading figures in this tradition include the Nigerians Fela Sowande, Akin Euba, and Joshua Uzoigwe, and the Ghanaian Ephraim Amu.[10]

The foregoing categorization is of course only a rough guide, for it hides certain connections and distorts others. A few qualifications need to be entered. In a contemporary African society like Ghana, the three genres of music exist in a kind of constellation. Composers of popular and art music often draw upon traditional music for inspiration and ideas. Although traditional music is perhaps most alive in rural communities, strands of popular music may be heard there too. Brass band music, for example, which began as part of Protestant church music-making, has now developed into a form of highlife-influenced popular music, and remains alive in some rural communities. Also interesting is the fact that, as a result of migration, a number of traditional musics have become urban phenomena. The Southern Ewe dances *Agbadza* and *Atsiagbekor*, for example, are regularly played by migrants in urban centers. Indeed, styles of playing away from "home" sometimes influence styles of playing at home. So the rural area is not simply a site of authenticity, while the urban acquires a mark of syncretism. The trade in stylistic practices between rural and urban populations goes in both directions and calls for a more nuanced understanding of such things as origins, influence, and authenticity.[11] Another qualification of our scheme stems from the fact that the dividing lines between genres are not always firm. From a historical point of view, traditional music represents Africa's earliest music, while popular and art musics developed out of the colonial experience. Yet, since recreational musics have always existed in African communities, it is likely that yesterday's popular music has become today's traditional music. This may be the case with another Southern Ewe dance, *Gahu*. Given its ensemble of performers (drums, rattle, bell, singers, and dancers) and its polyrhythmic texture, *Gahu* may be conveniently consigned to the traditional category; yet, as a frequently performed recreational musical type, it merits the designation "popular" as well.[12] Unlike highlife, soukous, or jùjú, however, it has no commercial standing. The Northern Ewe dance *Bobobo* may serve as another example of the blurring of categories. Invented as recently as the late 1950s in the town of Kpandu, *Bobobo* has become a staple of various Northern Ewe community

406

and school performances. It has thus won its authenticity and become part of the entertainment *tradition* of Ewe society.[13] In short, our three-tiered scheme is helpful in alerting us to the different genres of African music, but it needs to be refined if it is to be a useful analytical construct.

What, then, are the aesthetic issues raised by the traditional, popular, and art musics of Africa? We will focus here on two: the aesthetic object and the distinction between functional and utilitarian music. Perhaps the most fundamental issue concerns the nature of the aesthetic object itself: what is music, and what is the musical work? The patterns of indigenous discourse suggest that African conceptions of music involve entanglements rather than the neat separation into dimensions characteristic of European theory. In Ewe, as in a number of African languages, there is no single word for "music." There is, in other words, no word that would enable us to describe a funeral dirge, a children's play song, and a recreational dance as forms of "music." One possible equivalent is the word *vu*, which literally means drum. *Vu* also refers to the occasion on which drums are beaten. Since, with a few exceptions, the beating of drums elicits or accompanies dancing, *vu* may also denote the occasion of drumming and dancing. Occasions of drumming and dancing are invariably accompanied by song, so *vu*, or more properly *vutefe* (the place of the drum), may describe such occasions. The distinction between vocal and instrumental music does not register in Ewe discourse. The word for "song" is *ha*, and *ha* may be spoken or sung. Melody is *hagbe*, which translates as "the language or voice of the song." Melody is also rendered sometimes as *gbedidi*, meaning "the sounding of the voice." Rhythm is especially elusive. There is no single word for rhythm in Ewe. One possible equivalent, *vugbe*, means "the language of the drums" and allows the user to distinguish between different drum languages or dances. But *vugbe* is of no use to anyone who wishes to discuss the rhythm of song. For that, one would have to converse around the concept, broaching matters of speed and/or intensity.[14] This brief sampling may be enough to indicate the terms in which an indigenous aesthetic discourse may be couched. If one then places Northern Ewe conceptions of music and music-making in a comparative pool that includes the Tiv, Dan, Fon, Kpelle, Hausa, Vai, and Akan – to name only some of the groups that have been studied closely by ethnomusicologists – one obtains an even clearer view of patterns of African thought about music (see, respectively, Keil 1979, Zemp 1971, Rouget 1996, Stone 1982, Ames and King 1971, Monts 1990, and Nketia 1984: 10–12). It would seem that African conceptions of music are more holistic than modern European notions, closer perhaps to those of ancient Greece.

What about the musical work as aesthetic object? Since practically all music considered traditional or popular exists orally and aurally rather than in written form, the work as such exists as a memory. (It is true that some leaders of popular bands nowadays employ written notes or graphic symbols as aids to memory, but it is a rare jùjú or highlife band that plays regularly from notation.) The music sung by dirge groups, the ceremonial music played by court orchestras, and the ritual incantations that accompany healing are preserved in the memories of performers and recreated on each performance occasion. None of this is to imply any loss of recognition on the part of listeners. On the contrary, the first rhythmic strains of a dance like *Atsiagbekor* are enough to excite participating audiences, just as the recitative-style introduction to *Bobobo* or *Gbolo*, in which proverbs and wise sayings are offered for reflection (e.g. "Sponge and soap went to the river; sponge came back but not soap"), can immediately transform one's mood. Oral texts have a kind of expanded existence, one that encourages performers to explore a range of alternatives in realizing the work. The work, in other words, enshrines a set of possibilities; it is emphatically not a fixed text. Of course, even in written traditions, the existence of a range of readers ensures that no text can be said to be permanently fixed. The difference between oral and written musical texts is therefore one of degree, not of kind. In searching for the African aesthetic musical object, then, the student is better prepared if armed with flexible notions of process rather than fixed ones of product. A product such as a scholar's transcription or field recording is best understood as the record of a form fixed for a particular occasion by particular creative minds. A different occasion with different performers will produce a recognizable work marked by difference.

Implicit in the discourse surrounding the enactment of certain rituals are aesthetic considerations that bear on the nature of the musical work. A case in point is the funeral, one of the most stable of traditional institutions. Consider an Akpafu example. The dirges that mark various stages of an Akpafu funeral may be variable or fixed. During the bathing of the corpse, for example, singers may choose from a repertory of three or four dirges which one to sing on the particular occasion. Thus "Who will not be bathed by the death sponge?" or "Bathing, women of the village, bathe him/her for me" are interchangeable. Although their rhythmic and melodic profiles differ, so that they *sound* different, they are said to be "the same." In this case, ritual function is what determines identity. By contrast, the dirges that begin and end the period of mourning are fixed. "Who laid a mat for him so that he slept so soundly?" is the dirge with which every death is announced, while "Peace! They said it and said it but they didn't really say it" is sung immediately after the body has been buried or "hidden," as the Akpafu say. No other dirge may be substituted for these beginning and ending ones.[15] In rehearsing individual dirges – rehearsals, incidentally, are not necessarily separate from performances – singers frequently interpolate words and phrases that imply a dynamic conception of beginnings and endings and thus of a song's ontology. "Raise the song" or "fetch the song" refers to the lead singer's Call, while "Receive it," "Catch it," or "Love it" are ways of responding to the Call. "Cut the song" and "It is finished" refer to closure, as does the more colorful "The throwing-away place," used to describe the end of a musical phrase. These tiny examples should be sufficient to show that a comprehensive study of indigenous vocabulary can provide a valuable aid to understanding African conceptions of the nature of the musical work.

The other basic issue in formulating an aesthetic inquiry derives from the common designation of African music as *functional* (or *utilitarian*) as opposed to *contemplative*.[16] Functional music is made in response to specific social imperatives; the music thus bears traces of the social or extra-musical impulse. To understand it properly, one must factor the morphology of its social function into the analysis. An example of functional music is the genre of work songs in which the nature of the work activity (e.g. farmers hoeing, carpenters nailing, fishermen paddling) motivates certain patterns of, say, metrical organization. Thus the duple meter of fisher-men's work songs is not chosen abstractly or without motivation; rather, it responds directly to the left-right left-right action of paddling. Similarly, the long silences between the sung phrases of an Akpafu funeral dirge allow mourners to supplement the sung with the spoken. Sung lines are fixed, generalized in expres-sion, and carve out an experience of time that departs from the ordinary. Spoken interjections, on the other hand, are spontaneous, allow mourners to thematize the specific death, and recreate for us the lived and painful reality threatened by the intermittent moments of singing. An analysis of the Akpafu dirge that ignores this contextual information and focuses exclusively on the patterns of musical organiza-tion fails to grasp the functional basis of the dirge. Contemplative music, by con-trast, is music whose *raison d'être* is to be listened to. This is art for art's sake and demands nothing but "mere" contemplation of its inner workings. The listener benefits from this experience not by being incited to dance or move to the work – behavior that is discouraged in concert performances – but by achieving a kind of emotional catharsis, or by admiring the composer's artistic prowess. The canon of European classical music is a good example of contemplative music. Its equivalent in Africa, the emerging body of works of art music, is also essentially contemplative.

Although the distinction between functional and contemplative seems useful at first sight, it turns out to be hugely problematic when examined closely. First and most obviously, all music is functional if by that we mean that the music serves a particular purpose, fulfills a certain social function. Thus a funeral dirge for mourning is not categorically different from a funeral march incorporated into a symphony. While their contexts of performance differ, and while the nature of the interaction between performers and audiences differs also, the two kinds of music are created for specific functional purposes. Secondly, the distinction overlooks the fact that there is a contemplative element in functional music, while contemplative music also has its functional elements. Let us dwell for a moment on how Africans contemplate some ostensibly functional music. Below are the words of a Northern Ewe dirge in which the word *alele*, an exclamation expressing the singer's desper-ation, is repeated many times:

1   Alele, alele! Dzeno deke mele du ke me o za, neva ho ha nam dzro?
    Alele, alele! Is there not a lead singer in this town to come and receive my song for me?
2   Alele, alele, alele, alele, Tsalele, alele, alele, alele, alele!

Extensive repetition serves to defamiliarize the word *alele* and to open up a contem-plative dimension for the singer/listener. Because we have all known sorrow, we are invited to contemplate it directly in those spaces of the song in which semantic information is frozen so that the underlying musical processes can be savored for themselves or used as grounds for speculation. Whether or not one reads such moments as invitations to active contemplation, it is obvious that the category "functional music" cannot possibly exclude opportunities for contemplation.

It is obvious, too, that practically every musical genre is meant to be heard in the first instance. A lullaby has a specifically musical appeal in its words, rhythm, and melody. Its work of lulling a child to sleep depends on the child's contemplation of the elements of structure. Lullabies are therefore not merely functional. Similarly, the greatly feared *Adabatram* drumming of the Northern Ewe, even though it achieves its effect by means of symbolic coding, is nevertheless effective only when heard. And the allure of popular recreational musics like *Kpanlogo* and *Bobobo* owes everything to their being first heard. To say that some music is functional while other music is contemplative is not useful; all music is contemplative. When John Miller Chernoff, attempting to improve our understanding of African music, states that "[t]he reason why it is a mistake 'to listen' to African music is that African music is not set apart from its social and cultural context" (1979: 33), he means to dissuade us from *merely listening* to African music, that is, listening to song or drumming on audio recordings without the benefit of their choreographic components. Yet, there is much to be gained from even this partial exercise for it brings us face to face with the naked musical elements. A provisional bracketing off of external or extramusical props may serve a valuable purpose in aesthetic inquiry in that it may facilitate a more intense engagement with concrete creative procedures. In any case, the full meaning of African music, held up as an ideal, is never accessible to him who has not listened.

There is other evidence of the role of listening in African musical traditions. A wordless music called *Gogodze* performed by the people of Ve in the Volta Region of Ghana has no other purpose than to be listened to. Similarly, there is a genre of "songs for thinking" that has been brought to light among the Gbaya of the Central African Republic (Dehoux 1986). Even the vocabulary with which Northern Ewe discuss music is replete with expressions that must have originated in close listening. Awareness of pitch, for example, is evident in expressions like "The song is too high," "The song has fallen," "The song has caught their throats," and "The voice with which you caught the song is not good." Similarly, aesthetic evaluation is often based on things heard: "The song is sweet," "The song is pleasant to listen to," "The song has really gone inside for me (i.e. moved me)," "The singer has done it too much (or in excess)," "The singer has put salt into the song," "The song is beautiful," and "The singer changes the voice."

On the other side, contemplative music like opera is shot through with functional elements. Recall, for example, the moment toward the end of Act 2 of Puccini's *Tosca* when Scarpia consents to give Tosca a safe conduct in return for a carnal favor so that she and Cavaradossi can leave the country. While Scarpia sits at his desk writing the note, the musical narrative continues. Puccini provides functional, time-killing music. But because opera is musical drama – because, in other words, the foundation of discourse is music rather than words – the functional aspect of this moment never eclipses its contemplative dimension. More subtle is the inclusion of material in musical works whose primary purpose is to meet the requirements of a strict precompositional plan. One finds this sort of thing in Bartok, especially in works in which the desire to bring the proportions of the Golden Section or Fibonacci series into operation impels the use of certain kinds of repetition. The music in bars 22 and 23 of the eighth improvisation for piano, op. 20, may be an example of this kind of motivated repetition. Although these stretches of repetition meet a functional need, at no point does the music cease to be music for contemplation.

To insist on an irreducible contemplative element in all African functional art may strike some as an over-zealous attempt to construe African music in European, specifically Hanslickian terms. After all, many Europeans turn to the music of Africa not to find parallels with their own tradition but to discover difference – difference that they can savor and from which they can derive a kind of spiritual supplement to their overly technologized modes of existence. The things to stress about the African musical landscape, according to this view, are the complete integration of music and society, the musicality of all people and not just of a few, the naturalness and spontaneity of music-making, dance as a common experience linking whole communities, the use of music in healing ceremonies, the correction of anti-social practices through music, and so on. These are indeed the themes found in standard accounts of African music. Yet, although they are consistent with some aspects of traditional African practice, emphasis on them can become an excuse for not engaging directly with the musical elements. Unlike the great masterpieces of European music, which are often analyzed as repositories of styles, structures, and techniques, the generic "works" of African traditional and popular music are too often interpreted in terms of emotional effects and sociological significance rather than in terms of structural organization. It is time to embrace without apology the rigorous technical study of African music in order to establish accurately what the African creative genius actually produces. Without this knowledge, the discourse of African musical aesthetics will not have proper foundations.

By way of illustration, I cite an example of careful musical analysis that might aid an interpretation of the aesthetic truth in one dimension of African music. I refer to African rhythm. It is commonly believed that African music is essentially a rhythmic phenomenon, and that rhythms are elaborated in very complex ways. Instead of attempting to specify the nature of this complexity, some writers are more likely to seek to mystify this aspect of African music by declaring it incomprehensible or – more deviously – incomprehensible in European terms. Thanks, however, to the research of scholars like David Locke, Simha Arom, and Gerhard Kubik, we need not speak solely in mystical terms. Locke's detailed study (1987) of the Southern Ewe dance *Gahu* is a case in point. *Gahu*'s fully activated texture features four or five contrasting rhythmic layers unfolding within a polyrhythmic matrix. The bell provides a referential pulse for the whole ensemble within its own distinctive pattern. A rattle reinforces this pattern as well as the pattern of hand-clapping that invariably accompanies ensemble musics that involve dancing, singing, and drumming. Smaller drums respond to and contrast with the bell, trade motifs with the lead drummer, or articulate a consistent off-beat pattern that never migrates on to the beat. Stylistic choices such as the preference for asymmetric time lines, the assumption of a downbeat rather than its external articulation, and the preference for musical patterns that seem to originate and terminate within metrical units rather than at their beginnings or endings – these and other choices emerge clearly from Locke's copious transcriptions. Armed with such concrete knowledge, we can begin to understand African musical sensibilities across a wider range of repertoires. We should, however, not overestimate the auxiliary function of technical analysis, for as the work of a figure like Adorno (1984) makes clear, aesthetic inquiry may be framed in such a way as to render superfluous a good bit of the technical data

411

that theoretically-inclined analysts produce. Whether and how this conceptual diffi-culty applies to African aesthetics remains to be seen.[17]

We began this brief survey by noting that Africa, unlike Europe, is not (yet) in possession of a large body of aesthetical writings. There is, however, an implicit aesthetics in the African-language oral discourses employed by musicians. Carefully analyzed, these discourses can serve to orient us to indigenous conceptions of music and music-making, compositional procedure, the bases of reception, and the elem-ents of structure. While the terms mentioned in this chapter refer mainly to trad-itional music, they can be easily adapted to the critical discussion of more recent popular and art musics. In their extraordinary diversity and structural sophistica-tion, the musics of Africa constitute a rich site for the cultivation of aesthetic inquiry.

Notes

1 Beardsley (1966) provides a concise introduction to the general field of aesthetics. An excellent short introduction is Dahlhaus (1982). Two valuable anthologies in English are Peter le Huray and James Day (1981) and Bujic (1988).

2 On the traditions of African music scholarship, see Nketia (1998), Waterman (1991), and Agawu (2003).

3 On recordings of African music, see Merriam (1970) and Tracey (1973).

4 For a comprehensive bibliography of African music, see Gray (1991). For a valuable videography, see Lems-Dworkin (1996). For an indication of the current state of scholar-ship, see Stone (1998).

5 For samples, see McCall (1998).

6 Outstanding musical ethnographies include Nketia (1963), Blacking (1995), Zemp (1971), Fiagbedzi (1977), Keil (1979), Rouget (1996), and Friedson (1996).

7 See Arom (1985), Locke (1987), Euba (1990), Agawu (1995), and Nzewi (1997).

8 A straightforward introduction to African music may be found in Nketia (1974). See also Bebey (1975).

9 A good introduction to popular music in Africa may be found in Graham (1989).

10 For a list of works by these and other composers of art music, see Euba (1993).

11 On rural–urban migration, see Avorgbedor (1992).

12 On the origins of *Gahu*, see Ladzekpo and Eder (1992). A systematic study of rhythmic procedure may be found in Locke (1987).

13 For a detailed study of *Bobobo*, see Bareis (1991).

14 Further discussion of Northern Ewe musical terminology may be found in Agawu (1995: 5–7).

15 For more on the Akpafu funeral dirge, see Agawu (1988).

16 The distinction is made, for example, by Euba (1972).

17 For a related discussion, see Nketia (1984).

References

Adorno, Theodor (1984) *Aesthetic Theory*, trans. C. Lenhardt, ed. Gretel Adorno and Rolf Tiedemann (London: Routledge).

Agawu, Kofi (1988) "Music in the Funeral Traditions of the Akpafu," *Ethnomusicology*, 32(1): 75–105.

Agawu, Kofi (1995) *African Rhythm: A Northern Ewe Perspective* (Cambridge: Cambridge University Press).

Agawu, Kofi (2003) *Representing African Music: Postcolonial Notes, Queries, Positions* (New York: Routledge).

Ames, David W. and King, Anthony V. (1971) *Glossary of Hausa Music and Its Social Contexts* (Evanston, IL: Northwestern University Press).

Arom, Simha (1991) *African Polyphony and Polyrhythm: Musical Structure and Methodology*, trans. Martin Thom, Barbara Tuckett, and Raymond Boyd (Cambridge: Cambridge University Press). Orig. French edn.: *Polyphonies et polyrythmies instrumentales d'Afrique Centrale: structure et méthodologie* (Paris: Selaf, 1985).

Avorgbedor, Daniel Kodzo (1992) "The Impact of Rural-Urban Migration on a Village Music Culture: Some Implications for Applied Ethnomusicology," *African Music*, 7(2): 45–57.

Bareis, Urban (1991) "Formen neo-traditioneller Musik in Kpando, Ghana," in Veit Erlmann (ed.), *Populäre Musik in Afrika* (Berlin: Staatliche Museen Preussischer Kulturbesitz), pp. 59–108.

Beardsley, Monroe (1966) *Aesthetics from Classical Greece to the Present: A Short History* (Tuscaloosa: The University of Alabama Press).

Bebey, Francis (1975) *African Music: A People's Art*, trans. Josephine Bennett (New York: Lawrence Hill; orig. pub. as *Musique de l'Afrique* (Paris: Horizons de France, 1969)).

Blacking, John (1995) *Venda Children's Songs: A Study in Ethnomusicological Analysis* (Chicago: University of Chicago Press; orig. pub. Johannesburg: Witwatersrand University Press, 1967).

Bujic, Bojan (ed.) (1988) *Music in European Thought, 1851–1912*. Cambridge Readings in the Literature of Music (Cambridge: Cambridge University Press).

Chernoff, John Miller (1979) *African Rhythm and African Sensibility: Aesthetics and Social Action in African Musical Idioms* (Chicago: University of Chicago Press).

Dahlhaus, Carl (1982) *Esthetics of Music*, trans. William Austin (Cambridge: Cambridge University Press).

Dehoux, Vincent (1986) *Les "chants à penser" des Gbaya (Centrafrique)* (Paris: SELAF).

Euba, Akin (1972) "Creative Potential and Propagation of African Traditional Music," in *African Music: Meeting in Yaoundé (Cameroon) 23–27 February 1970*, organized by UNESCO (Paris: La Revue musicale), pp. 119–25.

Euba, Akin (1990) *Yoruba Drumming: The Dùndún Tradition* (Lagos and Bayreuth: Elekoto Music Centre and Bayreuth African Studies Series).

Euba, Akin (1993) *Modern African Music: A Catalogue of Selected Archival Materials at Iwalewa-Haus, University of Bayreuth, Germany* (Iwalewa-Haus: University of Bayreuth).

Fiagbedzi, Nissio (1977) "The Music of the Anlo: Its Historical Background, Cultural Matrix and Style." Ph.D. dissertation, University of California at Los Angeles.

Freidson, Steven (1996) *Dancing Prophets: Musical Experience in Tumbuka Healing* (Chicago: University of Chicago Press).

Graham, Ronnie (1988) *Stern's Guide to Contemporary African Music* (London: Zwan Publications and Off the Record Press).

Gray, John (1991) *African Music: A Bibliographical Guide to the Traditional, Popular, Art, and Liturgical Musics of Sub-Saharan Africa* (Westport, CT: Greenwood Press).

Keil, Charles (1979) *Tiv Song: The Sociology of Art in a Classless Society* (Chicago: University of Chicago Press).

Kubik, Gerhard (1994) *Theory of African Music*, vol. 1 (Wilhelmshaven: Florian Noetzel Verlag).

413

Ladzekpo, Kobla and Eder, Alan (1992) "*Agahu*: Music Across Many Nations," in Jacqueline Cogdell Djedje (ed.), *African Musicology: Current Trends*, vol. 2 (Los Angeles: University of California, African Studies Center), pp. 181–90.

Le Huray, Peter and Day, James (eds.) (1981) *Music and Aesthetics in the Eighteenth and Early Nineteenth Centuries*. Cambridge Readings in the Literature of Music (Cambridge: Cambridge University Press).

Lems-Dworkin, Carol (1996) *Videos of African and African-Related Performance: An Annotated Bibliography* (Evanston, IL: Carol Lems-Dworkin Publishers).

Locke, David (1987) *Drum Gahu: A Systematic Method for an African Percussion Piece* (Crown Point, Indiana: White Cliffs Media Company).

McCall, John (1998) "The Representation of African Music in Early Documents," in Ruth M. Stone (ed.), *The Garland Encyclopedia of World Music: Africa* (New York and London: Garland Publishing), pp. 74–99.

Merriam, Alan P. (1970) *African Music on LP: An Annotated Discography* (Evanston: Northwestern University Press).

Monts, Lester P. (1990) *An Annotated Glossary of Vai Musical Language and Its Social Contexts* (Paris: Peters-SELAF).

Nketia, J. H. Kwabena (1963) *Drumming in the Akan Communities of Ghana* (Edinburgh: Thomas Nelson and Sons Ltd.).

Nketia, J. H. Kwabena (1974) *The Music of Africa* (New York: Norton).

Nketia, J. H. Kwabena (1984) "The Aesthetic Dimension in Ethnomusicological Studies," *World of Music*, 26(1): 3–28.

Nketia, J. H. Kwabena (1998) "The Scholarly Study of African Music: A Historical Review," in Ruth M. Stone (ed.), *Africa: The Garland Encyclopedia of World Music* (New York and London: Garland Publishing), pp. 13–73.

Nzewi, Meki (1997) *African Music: Theoretical Content and Creative Continuum: The Culture-Exponent's Definitions* (Olderhausen, Germany: Institut für populärer Musik).

Rouget, Gilbert (1996) *Un Roi africain et sa musique de cour: Chants et danses du palais à Porto-Novo sous le règne de Gbèfa (1948–76)* (Paris: CNRS Editions).

Roger Scruton (1997) *The Aesthetics of Music* (Oxford: Clarendon Press).

Sparshott, Francis E. (1980) "Aesthetics of Music," in Stanley Sadie (ed.), *The New Grove Dictionary of Music and Musicians*, vol. 1 (London: Macmillan).

Stone, Ruth M. (1982) *Let the Inside Be Sweet: The Interpretation of Music Event among the Kpelle of Liberia* (Bloomington: Indiana University Press).

Stone, Ruth M. (ed.) (1998) *Africa: The Garland Encyclopedia of World Music* (New York and London: Garland Publishing).

Tracey, Hugh (1973) *Catalogue: The Sound of Africa Series*. 210 Playing Records of Music and Songs from Central, Eastern, and Southern Africa, 2 vols (Roodeport, Transvaal, South Africa: International Library of African Music).

Waterman, Christopher (1991) "The Uneven Development of Africanist Ethnomusicology: Three Issues and a Critique," in Bruno Nettl and Philip V. Bohlman (eds.), *Comparative Musicology and Anthropology of Music: Essays on the History of Ethnomusicology* (Chicago: University of Chicago Press), pp. 169–86.

Zemp, Hugo (1971) *Musique Dan: La Musique dans la pensée et la vie sociale d'une société africaine* (Paris: La Haye, Mouton).

33

Art and Community: A Social Conception of Beauty and Individuality

NKIRU NZEGWU

A philosophical examination of the conventions governing the creation of some traditional African art reveals profound issues about a conception of art that is molded by the assumptions of a unitary framework. On this scheme, art is conceived as intricately interwoven with other aspects of life. It is community focused. Owing to this relational quality, the critical question in creativity is no longer what constitutes a work of art, but what is the relationship between creative objects and social life in a given society. In this chapter, I examine the relation between objects of artistic expression and Igbo community interests, through the social meaning of two figural statues: *ugolochamma* and *ikenga*. The genre of *ugolochamma* statues consists of minimally clad, standing female paragons of beauty that glorify the state of *agbo* (puberty and maidenhood). They are tangible symbols of *mma* (beauty) understood as morally mediated. By contrast, the genre of *ikenga* statues symbolizes individuality, assertiveness, and the self, and they underscore the importance of personal success and achievement.

Statues of *Ugolochomma*

Statues of *ugolochomma* represent nubile maidens who, in localities along the Niger, Nkisi, and Omambala rivers, are admired as *ugolo mma* (beautiful maiden). "*Ugolo*" is another term for pubescent girls and "*mma*" means beauty. The sculptures portray girls in their post-*nkpu* finery,[1] and hence may be seen simultaneously as portraits of girls' rite of passage from puberty to full social maturity and as historical documents of fashion styles. In the pre-1960 language of female beautification in rural areas, to assert that a maiden "*na cho mma*" (literally, "is seeking beauty") is to proclaim that she is engaged in her toilette; indeed, that she is making-up, grooming her hair, or decorating her body with *uli* designs. These acts of beautification translate as "*i cho mma*," explicitly naming a subset of acts whose goal is to create *mma* (beauty). The lexical emphasis on *cho mma* (past tense) rather than *na cho mma* (present continuous) highlights the fact that the statues depict maidens who are fully adorned and made-up. However, when *ugolochomma* statues are referred to as *ugolochamma* ("maiden who washed her beauty"), evaluators critically

415

dwell on the fact that making-up is metaphorically an act of washing or cleansing that amplifies the brilliance of beauty. This shift alerts us that "make-up" is metaphorically an act of culturalizing the body to local taste. In the audience's mind, human beauty is never to be left in its natural state, but has to be tweaked and shaped to socialize it. In this enhanced state of "washed beauty" or "culturalized beauty," *ugolochamma* statues are schematic portraits of select post-*nkpu* belles.

The basic form of *ugolochamma* statues is a standing female figure with firm upright conical breasts, with a hint of corpulence that reflects a post-*nkpu* stage of maturity. In a setting where "formal wear" means minimal clothing, elaborate hairstyles, and profuse, intricately patterned indigo *uli* body designs, the statues are formally decorated with sensitively designed *uli* patterns applied with precision and flourish. In some statues, *uli* patterns carefully define the cheekbones and the almond shape of the eye, enhancing the aquiline sharpness of the nose. Neat precise patterns on the forehead visually pull the eye to the hairstyle. Crowning the head is a variety of dramatic coiffures that mirror the popular fashion styles of the day. In some statues, the hair is decorated with numerous small flat disks the size of quarters; in others, wigs are used that are studded with intricately carved wood evoking metal hair pins; and, in still others, small circular disks are fastened to the crested plume of the helmet-shaped hairstyle. Immediately below the base of the puffed-up plume, the hair is sculpted into wavy lines that tightly mold the head like a cap.

On the torso, tiny intricate patterns of scarification or *mbubu* (keloid marks) run right down the abdomen extending the visual tactile appeal of physical beauty. The carvers also depict valuables borrowed from mother and grandmother's trinket box. These include agate beads with leopard claw pendants, multicolored circular or rectangular mirrors (*ugogbe*) in wooden frames, which were usually held aloft in one hand, and small *nzali* (small whisk of horse's hair). Double armlets of bone or copper were often worn on either arm, and thick wide ivory bracelets (*odu aka*) circled the wrists. The use of ivory bracelets indicates the affluent status of the model's family. A girdle of *jigida* (waist beads) wraps the lower waist and discreetly shields the pubic region. Stretching from the ankles to the knees are spiral coils of brass, *nja*, which were removed immediately after marriage to signal the end of *agbo* (puberty and maidenhood).

Entirely secular, *ugolochamma* statues lack religious or ancestral significance. The creation of these statues was initiated in two main ways: by individual families and by male dancing associations. Parents and suitors, who maintained the maidens during the *nkpu* pre-nuptial seclusion, sometimes commissioned the statue for the post-*nkpu* ceremony of either their daughter or bride as flamboyant proclamations of their wealth. Depending on its size, these display sculptures were carried around the town by the male members of the bride's entourage. Monumental statues, four feet high and over, were displayed at a clearly designated spot in the family compounds where they would be evaluated and appraised by relatives and friends. The statues were public statements of the family's affection for their daughter or bride, and of their satisfaction with the marriage alliance. Although *ugolochamma* statues are usually female figures, occasionally, male figures have been carved when the objective has been to produce images of couples. This occurs when a suitor chooses to make public his affection for his prospective bride, thereby revealing the passion-

416

ate basis of the marriage. Such public declarations, which normally would occur in love (*ifu naya*) matches, position the wife as *obi di ye* (the heart of the husband).

The second path to the production of *ugolochamma* statues is when male associations commission the statues of village paragons for their *agbogho mmuo* (maiden spirit) dancing group. The dance routines of these male groups impersonate girls who have recently passed through *nkpu*. In a photograph in a book by G. T. Basden, we see a group of men dancing behind a man carrying an *ugolochamma* sculpture as display emblem (1966: 353a). This is another occasion when female and male *ugolochamma* couples are carved as part of the *agbogho mmuo* (maiden spirit) dance-drama routine. In this production of couples and single female figures, the paramount aim was to dramatize aspects of human experience through the eyes and lives of women in "competitive and festive dance displays of age-grades" (ibid. 108). Although women invented the original body art and form which male carvers later copied, *ugolochamma* statues are increasingly being contextualized within male artistic conventions, and presented as forms invented by men. This appropriation has resulted in making women peripheral to the artistic conceptualization of these sculptures, and has illegitimately reversed male dependency on women's creative vision for artistic inspiration.

In theoretical contexts, where sculpting is portrayed as male creative expressions, and women are typically incorporated into analysis as passive objects, women are stripped of their initiative and inventiveness in producing the original models. The basis for this erasure is a set of disciplinary assumptions about art, and about gender relations. By emphasizing sculpture as art and disregarding the body as an art medium, women's ingenuity in inventing the form and fashion styles of *ugolochamma is* missed. Disciplinarily, art history privileges physical objects as art over art forms created with the human body. Since men sculpted the inanimate objects and women worked with their bodies, creative initiative was credited to men. Additionally, in intellectual contexts where men are hierarchically privileged and women are presented as subordinate, the implicit gender logic of art discourse automatically disqualifies females from occupying a position of creative prominence. All these factors converged to effectively shift attention away from the institution of *nkpu*, the concept of *agbo* and from females who, in the first place, had created the images that were the referent of the statues.

The concept of agbo

Agbo, the concept of maidenhood, provided an occasion of female artistic inventiveness in which the body became a medium for creative expression. The institution of *nkpu* celebrates maidenhood and marks important social and physiological rites of maturation that are involved in the life of Igbo females. *Agbo* defines the biological period of puberty in which girls undergo extensive hormonal changes, starting from about age 14 to age 16 or 17 when marriage takes place. Socially, it marks the period of impending marriage.

The prenuptial rites of *nkpu* validate the nubile pubescent development of girls. By age 16, girls were at the height of *agbo* and almost all were betrothed. Up until the beginning of the Nigerian/Biafran war (1967–70) girls in some rural Igbo

417

communities prepared for marriage and for their future state of motherhood by going through *nkpu*. During this period of seclusion, which lasts from one to six lunar months, they were prohibited from working, pampered, and sumptuously fed three times a day. The enforced inactivity expedited weight gain as the girls only engaged in body grooming, beautification, and dancing. They passed the time grooming their hair, shaping it into spectacular forms, preparing camwood dye, massaging and smoothing their body with oil and camwood, and liberally painting their body with indigo *uli* designs. The brass spiral rings known as *nja*, which were fitted on their legs by a blacksmith at the onset of puberty, were regularly polished to a high sheen. Shortly before emerging from confinement, the girls received *mbubu* cicatrization cuts. Typically, these are three rows of small round scarification keloids that run right down the chest, abdomen, and waist in intricate formation.

At the end of the confinement, the maidens turned their bodies into works of art. They emerged elaborately groomed, to parade the town with an entourage of singing and dancing friends and well-wishers. Not only was the focus of the parade on the beauty of the corpulent brides-to-be, it was also on the special gifts and presents provided by the suitor and the girl's family to mark the occasion (Leith-Ross 1965: 99). Northcote W. Thomas's account (1913) of this event in Awka is important, since it reveals the display-oriented nature of the "coming out" parade and the gender character of the event. His description shows that the central actors in the post-*nkpu* festivities at the turn of the century were both young men and women (ibid. 64), not just girls. This information accords with present-day practices in which unmarried male members of the family, lineage, and *ogbe* (ward) participate in the festivities and closing rites of this phase of female development. In this "coming-out" ceremony, post-*nkpu* maidens were decked out in their finery and became the models that gave the male carvers their inspiration. During these parades the body art creations of maidens were scrupulously observed and aesthetically evaluated. The praise names of *"agbogho ugo"* (regal maiden), *"ugo mma"* (beautiful maiden), and family-specific honorific names were showered on the belles who displayed regal carriage, poise, self-assurance, and assertiveness. Evaluations of female beauty opened up further discussions on the beautification skills of the maidens and body designers.

The concept of mma

Because *mma* (beauty) is a recurring theme in the evaluation of post-*nkpu* maidens and *ugolochamma* statues, it is important to determine how it is construed. Public discourse on female beauty inevitably established a linkage between the beautiful and certain cultural imperatives. One example of a saying that captures this kernel of aesthetic truth is *Enenebe eje olu*, literally, "Looking admiringly (at the object of attention) prevents one from going to work." In a 1970s song that, significantly, used this maxim as title, the highly popular female vocalist, Nellie Uchendu, spells out some of the time-honored ingredients of the Igbo criterion of beauty. The foil she used was a specific maiden, Chinwe Ude, whose transfixing beauty was acclaimed far and wide, and whom the community had aptly renamed *Enenebe eje olu*. As the superlative lyrics celebrate, Ude is tall, supple, and slender; she has good

418

healthy skin, gleaming dark complexion, well-defined facial features, great physiognomy, and poise. In short, she is an *oyoyo* (a peerless beauty). However, as the song goes on to reveal, Ude's physical beauty is greatly amplified by the fact that she is *ezigbo nwa* (the good child). She is hardworking, strong, and immensely generous, hence is free from both physical and moral defects (*olusi*).

In fables and songs, used primarily as instructional tools, one finds that the socially approved notion of beauty has a moral basis. Although this reading seems to derive from the society's need to provide guidance to children and the youth, it brings to attention a critical ambiguity about beauty that explains Igbo ambivalence about it. The phrase *"enenebe eje olu"* does this in complex ways. At the denotative level, *"enenebe"* underscores that the specified act of perceiving is extensively prolonged in space and time. Connotatively, it captures the idea of admiration that is triggered by a beautiful form. But the clause *"eje olu,"* which literally means "fails to go to work," highlights the potential social problem of peerless beauty and the negative social effect admiration might occasion. It problematizes the transfixing quality of physical beauty and cautions viewers about the state of idleness that "continuous looking" could cause. In a relational scheme in which one thing affects another, the effect of beauty toward social good is carefully considered. When beauty is seen as lacking constructive social consequences, there is tension between the idea of "beauty as wondrous" and "beauty as socially incapacitating." This tension highlights Igbo ambivalence with respect to the idea of morally unmediated beauty. Because greater social premium is placed on *idi uchu* (industry), *olu* (work), and *ezigbo omume* (good character), beauty is valued only if it embodies positive behavioral traits and transcends the potentially distracting elements that may impede social utility and function.

Consequently, in the Igbo conceptual scheme, the idea of beauty is intricately intertwined with morality, since societal well-being and progress set the standard for the good life. As a result of this moral basis, individuals routinely stress the importance of inner beauty (character) over outer epidermal beauty. They insist too that one need not be physically beautiful to be included in the category of attractive people. One with a pleasant personality and good character is beautiful. This attitude is enshrined in statements such as: *Oji nlecha ba na mma* (One can use vivacity to enter the category of beauty). This construal of beauty as a category that anyone could enter given certain redeeming qualities readily clears a space for the introduction of socially approved varieties of beauty. On this conceptual scheme, vivacious females, women with wonderful personality, good-natured females with good character, and women with great physiognomy are all beautiful and desirable, even if, visually, they may not be all that striking. Once beauty is linked to social relevance and is channeled into character-building, a physically beautiful female who is utterly vain, lacks good character, or is lazy is viewed as socially unattractive and is said to have *olusi* (a defect). Thus the rhetorical question, *Ene eli mma eli?* (Is beauty eaten?) simultaneously underwrites the idea that epidermal beauty requires morality for completeness, and it reconceptualizes *mma* (beauty) as a vital glue for societal cohesion.

419

Ikenga and Notions of Self

After examining the relations between beauty and morality, it is now time to turn our attention to the relation between art and self-identity. With the *ikenga* we see how art objects are used in reinforcing self and cultivating assertiveness.[2] Standard art historical descriptions present the *ikenga* as a wooden sculpture, a symbol of personal success and individual achievement. Visually, *ikenga* are usually between six inches and six feet high and there are three stylistic types: the architectonic, the anthropomorphic, and the abstract cylindrical. Of the three, the most interesting to art historians have been the architectonic and anthropomorphic types, while the small portable type, generally favored by constantly traveling *dibias* (diviners and herbalists), attracts little attention.

The basic sculptural form of miniature and modest-sized *ikenga* consists of a cylindrical block of wood, between six inches and two feet in height. Projecting from the top section is an abstractly carved head with a pair of horns. Carved out of hardwood, the cylindrical mid-section may be incised with vertically stacked elaborate motifs and patterns. Sometimes simple geometric designs are gouged out to create neat parallel rows of ridges and channels around the cylindrical block. Most times, the *ikenga* may be shaped simply like a thread spool with minimal incisions of cross-hatchet designs.

The style of representation of the anthropomorphic *ikenga* is idealized, involving a schematic treatment of a seated human form. The basic form is a human figure seated on a stool with a pair of long, sometimes coiled or vertical horns sprouting from the head. Some of the seated figures may have complex architectonic head-dresses of birds, pythons, and leopards intertwined in interesting formations (Boston 1977). On some, the headdress may be a tableau symbolizing a mounted personality of importance with an entourage of followers. On others, the tableau may consist of antelope-heads or human-heads, with leopards or pythons at the crest. In many of the anthropomorphic *ikenga*, the seated forms are extensively covered with dark colored *uli* body designs. Breasts or the male genitalia may be visibly displayed. Still, a number of *ikenga* are not sexually marked even though the human form may be socially marked with *uli* body designs. Typically, the seated figure either carries a machete, a gun, an *abana* (ceremonial sword), or an *otulaka* (small elephant tusk) in the left hand, and either a human skull (symbol of prowess), a full-size elephant tusk (symbol of wealth), or *akpa ego* (a bag of money) in the right hand. Depending on the requirements of clients, the anthropomorphic *ikenga* may be monumental and elaborately adorned with achievement and status-related symbols like *ichi* (linear scarifications running down the length of the seated figure's face), *uli* body decorations, elephant tusk, ceremonial sword, eagle feathers, coral beads, and cloth.

In the Anambra valley region, the architectonic *ikenga* have a corpus of colorful tiered figures. Symbols and motifs are usually community owned, and the immense sizes of the sculptures represent this collective ownership (Cole and Aniakor 1984: 31–2). These impressive wood sculptures tower over six feet high and may function as the principal object in a shrine in which there are a number of subsidiary sculptures. Or, they may have an entirely secular role, functioning as aesthetic symbols of splendor and affluence. During *Ogbalido* or *olili ikenga* (i.e. feast of *ikenga*) these secular architectonic sculptures may be ceremoniously paraded through the village (ibid. 32), but if they are monumental in size they may be stationed at a public site for display. The features that make up the building block of both the architectonic and anthropomorphic *ikenga* are an assortment of animal and human referents. The horns are the most critical feature and the focal point of attention of *ikenga* sculptures. The formal treatment of these horns, which may be either realistic or schematic, is always exaggerated and pronounced. They may shoot upwards like two jagged peaks; or they may sweep backwards in a tight curl. The curl may be located at the end tip of vertical upright horns, or they may sweep sideways encircling the ears in neat curls. Modifications of this curl abound, depending on the type of wood utilized by carvers.

The overall meaning of the seated figure derives from the collection of symbols portrayed. On the Igbo referent scheme, the horn is assigned the attribute of will power. It evokes a purposive force that cuts a swathe through life. Horns connote assertiveness, strength, daring, and persistence. Icons such as leopards, pythons, and antelopes that proliferate on the *ikenga* have socially assigned attributes. The leopard motif symbolizes power and fearlessness; the elephant connotes strength and immensity; and the python, a totemic symbol of veneration, "owns" the pathways as well as symbolizing the rainbow. The machete, sword, or gun that is carried in the right hand represents the tool or instrument utilized by individuals in changing their material condition.

Ikenga, *chi, and individuality*

So what are the conceptual boundaries of *ikenga* and its connection with the self? How do we understand the concept of "self" and the concept of "individuality"? What does *ikenga* tell us about personhood?

Ikenga possesses multiple roles: it is simultaneously a spirit or psychic force, a sculptured piece, an icon for meditation, and a "text" of psychological principles in which "utilization" of the "text" unravels encoded knowledge. At the core, an *ikenga* is a part of the spirit in us. Each person is essentially a *mmuo* (spirit or vitalizing force that may have reincarnated many times with possibly a different sex in each existence), and each *mmuo* embodies a *chi*. *Ikenga* sculpture reflects the traits defined by the *ikenga* (the spirit element) that is an aspect or a constituent part of the *chi*. Each person has a *chi* that is conceived as a personal guardian spirit (*mmuo*) or personality essence that controls one's destiny. The *ikenga*, as an aspect of the *chi*, is understood as the force that facilitates personal achievement and propels individuals to success.

The theory is that preparatory to incarnation, a sentient earth-bound spirit or *mmuo* chooses its biological sex, type, and the length of its life on earth. This decision is made in conjunction with the ancestral spirits of the lineage into which the earth-bound spirit will incarnate. The choices are then affirmed in the presence of Chukwu (the Supreme Being). A strong metaphysical and sociological case is made for independence and agency. A sense of individual agency and autonomy is inculcated through presenting individuality as something that also transcends

421

earthly life. Fate is not something that is foisted on an individual, but a set of choices that are freely made by her spirit as a necessary condition of earthly development. It is pertinent, however, to point out that this idea of individuality does not conform to the notion of atomistically autonomous individuals one finds in the liberal democratic tradition and also in Christian thought. Implicit in the Igbo outlook is the idea that life begins in the context of family, and that, therefore, personhood necessarily evolves in the nexus of family. The idea of an individual is intelligible only as a member of a family.[3] In other words, a person cannot be an agent capable of self-defined and self-defining choices without family situatedness.

Ogbalido: *mapping a self*

Because Igbo culture values social mobility, individual initiative and resourcefulness are highly valued in its social arrangements. The concept of *ikenga* is used to strike a balance between family obligations and individuality, and between free will and fate, by making an individual responsible for his or her successes or failures in life. A person's *ikenga* functions satisfactorily when it facilitates the individual's progress in accordance with her pre-birth life choices. The *chi* is good if one is successful in life. But if one's choices are bad, provision is made for one to transcend the seemingly inexorable laws of fate and to improve one's lot. It is here that the *ikenga* assumes the vital role in breaking the finality of fate. Individuality is preserved as the *ikenga* works to direct the individual through life, provided one activates that force and works in harmony with it.

One is in a dialectical relationship with one's *chi*, using the sculpted *ikenga* as a physical medium for fixing one's attention on specific goals and matters in hand. At a psychological level, the sculpture, as a tool of meditation, is used for strengthening one's will, and for raising individual consciousness. The sculpture, a work of art, is therefore also a pragmatic tool for promoting the ideals of individuality and initiative. Socially mature individuals do this by entering into a dialogue with the spiritual dimension of their *chi* and *ikenga*. Owners clearly visualize and state their goals; they affirm their objectives, and then activate them through vocalization in a prayer. Intently articulating personal goals and focusing on what is willed aligns one's thoughts with one's will. The fusion of the two generates intense psychic energy, heightens one's commitment, and results in the release of one's creative powers. Articulating one's goal and meticulously working toward its realization transfigures the self and one's surroundings, through fostering inner strength, confidence, self-assurance, initiative, and strength of character.

When one succeeds in one's ventures, one validates *ikenga* (the spirit force) using the sculpture as a visual interface with the inner. One gives it "food" and "drink" to thank it for being "awake." On escaping from danger one does the same; and if ill luck befalls one, one "communes" and prods one's *ikenga* (spirit force) to drive away the bad luck. The symbolic act of feeding and communing with *ikenga* (spirit force) is an affirmation of the efficacy of the underlying psychological principle that one can strengthen one's will and inner strength to overcome existential problems and transcend ungainful pre-life choices. The underlying idea of the concept of *ikenga* is that one can make of life what one wants. Individuals are not necessarily bound by fate. Thus, failure is not seen exclusively as the result of fate, but as one's inability to effectively take charge of one's life. To this end, the anthropomorphic *ikenga* are made in such a way that the seated figure assumes an alert and watchful pose. The sword or knife must be turned upward, ready to strike and neutralize whatever negative forces may come the way of the individual. A downward pointing sword suggests a passive, inattentive pose, in which one's guard has been dropped.

A posture of inattention is the very antithesis of *ikenga*, which must always be poised to act positively. Accordingly, Ibo culture motivates individuals against accepting adversity with equanimity. Thus, should misfortune befall one, or should one not be satisfied with his or her progress in life, one is expected to enter into a conversation with one's *ikenga* to find a way out of the morass. If, after working hard, one still meets with failure, one must first cajole one's *ikenga*. But if progress continues to be elusive, one may threaten not to "feed" it, unless it works harder. If these threats prove futile and misfortune persists, one can destroy the *ikenga* (sculpture), the outer representation of the *ikenga* (spirit force). Because *ikenga* are normally destroyed four days after a deceased individual's burial,[4] the willful destruction of the physical object while one is alive is perceived as the death of the spirit force. This act ritually "kills" the *ikenga* without an individual having to go through earthly death. A new *ikenga* is then carved to replace the old one in a process that results in the creation and fashioning of a new spirit/force. It is worthwhile to note that this enactment of the death and resurrection of *ikenga* shows that human individuals are endowed with divine creative powers. The fact that individuals can recreate new *ikenga* (spirit force) – in other words, recreate aspects of their spirit selves – vests in them the ultimate mark of individuality and individual autonomy: the responsibility to fashion their lives and change their social environment. In each one's hands lie the powers of success or the possibility of failure.

Given this notion of the *ikenga* as a redemptive force, the Igbo conception of destiny is seen not to be antithetical to change. The power to think positively and to act decisively is built into the very relationship of fate and free will. Individuals are not slaves to destiny, and the fact that they can refashion their destiny is proof that the material conditions of life are changeable. *Onye kwe chi ya ekwe* tells us that "when one affirms (with an active *ikenga*), one's *chi* (or overarching spirit) affirms," and "if one affirms strongly, one's *chi* affirms strongly."

Conclusion

As we have seen, a conceptual relocation into the artistic universe of Igbos reveals the complex relationship of art and life, and the role of works of art in mapping out ethical and psychological principles about human nature and social life. Ideas about psychology and individuality coalesce around the concept of *ikenga* and are given visible form in three types of sculptural forms: the miniaturist abstract, the anthropomorphic, and the architectonic. Equally too, ideas about puberty coalesce around the nubile form and are explicated by *ugolochamma*, a sculptural form that defines the relationship between morality and the beautiful, and eloquently testifies to the desirable place of young maidens in the society. Other traditional African art forms and symbols encode and sustain important sociological, metaphysical, and political ideas.

Notes

1 *Nkpu* is a socially mandated period of pre-marital seclusion, in which young girls are withdrawn from the family's labor force and are confined at home and pampered. During this period of social inactivity and rest, they are generously fed, groomed, and prepared for their marriage and future state of motherhood. Because the effect of this enforced inactivity and generous food portions result in a corpulent form, *nkpu* has wrongly been described by anthropologists as a fattening room process.

2 In a detailed study I have undertaken on the relations between *chi* and *ikenga*, I have argued that *ikenga* is not restricted to males. Evidence abounds that women had *ikenga* – some of this information had been documented. However, the overly masculine emphasis of many early anthropological studies has been drawn upon by many scholars, including Igbo men, to contend that *ikenga* is exclusively male.

3 This is why the four arms of the lineage – two paternal and two maternal *mmuo* – oversee the earth-bound spirit's choosing of its fate.

4 Bosah (1979: 131) presents the *ikenga* in the context of a life cycle. On the fourth day the deceased's relationship with the living is severed in a rite known as *ikpowa ikenga*. The *ikenga* is removed from the shrine of the deceased by members of the age-grade, who then proceed to split the object into two for burying.

References

Basden, G. T. (1966) *Niger Ibos* (New York: Barnes and Noble, Inc.; orig. pub. 1938).

Bosah, Nnayelugo S. I. (1979) *Groundwork of the History and Culture of Onitsha* (Apapa, Nigeria: Times Press Ltd.).

Boston, John (1977) *Ikenga Figures Among the Northwest Igbo and Igala* (Lagos: Ethnographica, in association with Federal Department of Antiquities, Nigeria).

Cole, Herbert and Aniakor, Chike (1984) *Igbo Arts: Community and Cosmos* (Los Angeles: University of California Press).

Leith-Ross, Sylvia (1965) *African Women: A Study of the Ibo of Nigeria* (London: Routledge & Kegan Paul Ltd.; orig. pub. 1938).

Thomas, Northcote W. (1913) *Anthropological Report on the Igbo-Speaking Peoples of Nigeria, Part I* (London: Harrison and Sons).

34

The Many-Layered Aesthetics of African Art

AJUME H. WINGO

Gracing a wall of my father's living-room was a vibrant, evocative, and prepossessing work of art depicting a forest inhabited by elephants and men. Early childhood lessons on *savoir-faire*, tolerance, and mutual respect were taught through this drawing. The work was charcoal on paper. One of the elephants, the largest, is positioned with its trunk wrapped around a man's body, lifting him about five meters high. The man's arms are held up; and his torso is bent away from the elephant's nose. Two men run away from the scene. Three run towards it. One man spears the leg of this elephant. One swats the trunk of another elephant.

This vivid imagery captured the attention of visitors to our compound. And there were many visitors. My father was a popular figure in town and our compound is centrally located in Kumbo, the capital town of the Fondom (kingdom) of Nso, an ethnic group in the North West Province of Cameroon. The drawing inspired myriad exegeses, critiques, and narratives from various visitors.

Intriguingly, my father's artwork also summoned a certain integrity, a certain grace from the onlookers. All behaved tolerantly. All waited for their turn to speak. Even our nextdoor neighbor, noted for imposing his will on others, would sit during his visits and listen calmly and respectfully. Somehow, the work precipitated a tacit sense of *savoir-vivre*.

In Africa, we have a flexible way of conceiving art and aesthetics. In this chapter, I present the conceptual factors that go into making an artwork and the sort of aesthetic ideas that underlie art. In other words, I pursue the questions: "What is the relation between art and aesthetics? Does the drawing in my father's house qualify as artwork in Africa? Why or why not?" I invite you to come back to this question after reading the rest of the chapter and decide for yourself.

In the West, for example, this question is answered by focusing on some assumptions about the relation between art and aesthetics. Three distinct assumptions may be noted. One is formal. Shape, color, and size are taken into consideration. We are called upon – by, for instance, Immanuel Kant and, even more urgently, by Clive Bell (1969) – to detach ourselves from the content of the art (or what is represented) and consider simply the representation. We are, that is, called upon to take on an "aesthetic attitude" of disinterestedness, distance, and detachment. In this perspective, what makes a work an artwork is primarily its invocation of this attitude, and what makes an aesthetic experience worthy is this "aesthetic" attitude itself that one adopts. All else can be a distraction.

In the second perspective, the content of an art object is what is of primary importance. The focus is on what is represented, not on the representation itself. From this standpoint, people can approve or disapprove of a piece of artwork based upon its moral worth. The fact that something has form and is made by an artist does not make it an artwork until the moral element has been assessed. According to this view, elephant dung on a representation of Jesus is ugly – nay, is non-art.

The third approach focuses on the efficient or institutional aspect. From this point of view, it matters who makes the artwork and how it is made. But the fact that matter and form have been imposed on something is not sufficient to make it art. The question is, did the right artist make it? Authentic art presupposes an artworld and a formal way of doing art business. There is a sort of checklist or script: is so-and-so artist a member of such-and-such an art organization? Did she attend an art school or obtain an apprenticeship from a venerated artist? Has she an MFA? Has her work been invited by a curator and displayed in the museum? Has she received any funding from the National Endowment for the Humanities? These are questions that presuppose an institution of art, a valorized world.[1]

I am not going to question or dwell on the three approaches to art noted above; rather, I would argue for an additional factor: a social dimension. This is an element of African communal art. In this conception of art, what makes a piece of work an artwork is not *merely* who made it, where it was made, and what it was made of, but, more importantly, whether it can invite people together. That is, more is required in Africa to give something the status of an artwork – a room full of people, for example, invited by an artwork. Art is an everyday thing, not a thing to be treasured away. As such, I will argue, art is a social affair.

I argue this claim in the following way. First, I define art and aesthetics. Second, I give three examples to illustrate the definition. Last, I conclude with a brief look at the utility of art as a magazine of African material life and of its eventful past, in other words, at art as art history.

By aesthetics, I mean human feeling and imagination as *shaped* and made conscious, scientious, and sententious by a created object, for example an artwork.[2] To explain what I mean by shaped feeling and imagination, consider the proposition that our sensuous feelings are potentials to be activated and made conscious by forms of stimulation that are external to the sensuous feelings themselves. What we mean by aesthetics in art is not the awakening of our sensuous feelings and imagination by just any form of visual, tactile, and olfactory experience. It is a particular form of external experience, namely, one that is awakened or stimulated by particular objects involving human creativity and volition. Thus a dragonfly that catches my sight and stimulates in my imagination imageries of an airplane does not count as a work of art. Nor do the feelings, no matter how pleasant, cathartic, and intense, count as aesthetic. As stated, the external object must involve human volition and creativity – it must be a product of art to count as a source of aesthetics experience.

The original raw material of art is purely amorphous, infinitely permeable, and capable of stimulating the imagination with various degrees of intensity. The imagination exists as a potential. The external world and the intellect are the main highways to our imagination. Human anxiety, yen, and the urge for self-expression can be the motivation for intentionally visiting one's imaginative world.[3]

An artist's creation constitutes, from the onset, a dialectical interaction between our faculty of the intellect and the imagination. To state the obvious, it is a process. The initial stage is imagined, shaped, or formed in a particular space and time. That product resides in the intellect. The second stage is the formal materialization of the already intellectually finished product. It is the pulling out of the self, by way of some raw material, the image, which can be in the form of melody, sculpture, painting, poetry, drawing, and so forth. This stage is more of a technical process and involves breathing life into amorphous material objects, such as in carving masks out of logs of wood, sculpting sonorous poetry out of a myriad of words, and so forth. The last stage is the presenting of the artistic experience, now an admixture of formal and material qualities, to the public, because the end of art is social. To this last claim I will return below.

The formal and material qualities should not be dichotomized; they reside together. Properly, they should be referred to as form-material, depicting the two qualities as one. Where there is the one, there is the other. We too are wholly beings of form and material. To the extent that everything around us is perceived as form and material together, art, by and large, is an imitation of nature's way. Nature's way is both formal and material. Hence the proverb in Nso: "*Mangkong bong veyeh*," that is "The world in itself is very beautiful." Note that a given material can also be looked upon as a form of significant content, as in poetry and song.

In short, art is shaped imagination made sententious. I insist that its proper and essential end is human pleasure. I must emphasize that what exists in the human imagination is useless until pulled out of the imaginative world and made into sententious, sensible, knowable objects. Raw sounds, for example, are useless unless given sensible shapes, that is, content and meaning. An instance of giving meaning to sounds is when they are made into a melody. We do not dance to a bird's sounds or to car noises unless we give them shape and, hence, meaning. It is the delicate selection, the blending and balancing of wild sounds that makes an artwork. Similarly, it is the delicate selection and balancing of wild smells that make good incense for our olfactory senses.

The number of people aesthetically affected by an artwork is the function of an artist's creative ability to select, blend, balance, and unite conflicting modes of imagination for public enjoyment out of the wild, wild universe of the imagination. It is the mark of a good artwork that it appeals not just to many people but to a diverse public, here and now and, perhaps, in the faraway future. The more creative the artwork, the more it allows us to share the artist's and our own experience of the invisible world.

Art attendants or the public are the ultimate judges of art. Though art-making is essentially the work of the intellect, the appreciation of art is an affair of the senses. Good art catches the senses not the intellect. I say this because good art does not give one a chance to intellectualize about it. If one tries to enjoy art by thinking about it, as, for example, by counting the musical notes or wondering when a song will come to an end, that is a sign that no beginning of real enjoyment has been made. When it comes to good art, reason is the last capacity to be awakened and brought into action.

What goes for art goes for the development of human capacities. Reason is normally the last of the human capacities to be awakened. So, the Kantian idea of an aesthetic attitude of disinterestedness, distance, and detachment is misplaced because it tells the story of art and aesthetics from only one side – the formal side.[4] My claim is different from Kant's. The other side is the material quality. I do not claim that we enjoy simply the material quality or the content of art, which would be the exact opposite of Kant's claim, but rather that the material and the formal qualities of art are inextricably glued together and can only be enjoyed as an organic whole.

I have witnessed masquerades with such elegant masks and theatrical display that they evoked tears from Nso onlookers. Good music can lead one to sing or hum and to tap one's foot to the beat. A good song can stick with a person and visit her memory quite frequently. It is a mark of good music to cause one to complain: "I can't get the song out of my head!" A good artwork in Nso is like a celestial flame; it can warm and set fire to the soul, as it cuts sharply to the nadir of one's heart.

To create an artwork that gives life to wood, paint, canvas, and sounds and enlivens attendants is not an easy task. It is a task for a specialized set of people and can be as difficult as thinking about God. People know this in Nso. It is not uncommon to hear people saying that only those who are inspired by the Supreme Being can make art. This is a way of acknowledging the artist's creativity. Nso artists undergo a lifelong apprenticeship. In fact, most artists come from families with a lineage of venerated traditions of art. Most Nso artists are born and raised within the ethos of art creativity. The effect of being brought up in such a family tradition should not be underestimated in the enterprise of art creation.

Good communal art is, first, abstract art in Nso and most of tropical Africa. By abstract art I mean a construct that does not immediately capture the particulars of our world. It calls on everyone alike. It levels out our experience and imagination, cleanses our palate and our palimpsest, and influences people in their diversity. The experience one gets at this level is universal and abstract. It is a morally innocent experience. To inflame and direct the passion, the artist adds another level of abstraction. This may be done by adding a feature like an eye or a nose to a mask without making the mask the face of a person or animal that we can specifically identify. Another layer results from adding particular but still generally abstract features such as gestures, posture, and facial features. These are the seasonings of the mask, as it is known in Nso.

What aesthetics in art means for us is not merely a checklist of qualities. An artwork evokes an interaction within and between a group of people. A good artwork alters people's dispositions. There are unarticulated lessons that people can discuss without fighting. This may sound mysterious, but this kind of experience exists in the West in jazz and classical music. Music as such is more abstract than visual art. That is why it can invite such a lot of people. The more abstract an artwork, the more the intensity and the duration of the experience of it. What is more interesting is that in Africa all art, plastic, painting, and dancing, take on this abstract quality.

428

Most African communal art is not museum-oriented art. A mask in Nso, for example, is made by artists to be used in association with a costume made with the same artistic configuration as the mask. It is made by the artist to be accompanied by music and a specific group of dancers. A mask alone may be elegant and moving. But what is more important is the creativity that is involved in bringing the mask together with xylophones, dancers, drums, flutes, songs, etc. to a high resolution, to a harmony. When it is done properly, when the heterogeneity of the parts is thus harmoniously resolved, we get what in Nso we describe as *kinsetti shuu ke ki nyo*, or the indescribable. As the masks, xylophones, songs, drums, and dancers burn the hearts of everyone participating in the drama with joy and delight like wild fire in the harmattan, one might well think that the gods are visiting us. This represents one of the highest forms of art, as diverse and at times conflicting and incommensurable elements of art are proactively given an organic unity by an artist. These aspects of the drama change the meaning of the mask looked upon as an entity in itself.[5]

Most masks in West Africa are made by artists to be worn on the faces of people for public entertainment or for ritualistic purposes such as the invocation of our ancestral spirits.[6] Some masks are created specifically for use in Regulatory Societies, what Western anthropologists refer to as secret societies. In Nso, for instance, Regulatory Societies use masks to serve the civilly pedagogical function of enhancing a sense of cohesion, participation, solidarity, continuity, tolerance, and mutual respect among the Nso as well as non-Nso peoples. Respect for non-Nso people is considered necessary because human beings, irrespective of their origin, social stations, or their conceptions of the good, are conceived as having in themselves a "speck" of the divine substance of supreme creator and are, therefore, deserving of respect. In this way, function hides behind art, not the other way round, as many historians of African art have thought.[7]

For a regulatory society in Nso to perform its pedagogic function well, secrecy must be broadcast. As I have argued elsewhere, the claim that a secret can be broadcast is merely an apparent oxymoron. The fact that there is a secret is broadcast, the secret is not; it is only known to members of the regulatory societies. Masks perform the function of broadcasting secrecy. Artists make masks to capture the imagination of diverse sets of individuals in Nso's society, which is a multicultural setting. This is not an easy task for the artist. Masks must be evocative, provocative, lovely, and lovable so as to be loved and enjoyed by a diverse laity. I emphasize diversity because the masks must capture and maintain the imagination even of people who may know little or nothing about Nso culture. The artists lavish on masks the most elegant of abstract designs. Since they must appeal to diverse groups of people, features must have a universal appeal. For example, masks have eyes, mouth, and nose irrespective of their shapes, sizes, and decorations. They at once embody perspicuity, simplicity, and universality.

Masks must also be interactive. That is why they are made abstract with complex arabesque. Those patternations one finds on most African masks are intended by the artists to be decoded or encoded by viewers. In other words, the masks entice the imagination. Thus some of the most attractive and prepossessing masks are intended by the artists to be worn with the face facing away from the viewers. The intention is to cause viewers to long for a clear view of the face; it is to invite their interaction.

429

This is why I have termed this type of aesthetics, "the aesthetics of hiding and revealing." All this is without prejudice to the fact that, as I have pointed out elsewhere, these masks can be enjoyed independently of the masquerade ritual. That is why our masks can be enjoyed as such in museums all over the world (ibid.).

As noted earlier, masks in Nso are meant to perform civic pedagogic functions. This normally happens during important events like the death celebration of an elder. Such events bring various people and families together to celebrate and send off a deceased elder to the ancestral world.[8] This is a way that we have of not allowing death to have the last word. We aestheticize it.

A word about song and dance is in place here. Communal song and dance are, at one level, simple and, at another, complex. At the level of simplicity, communal songs are mainly onomatopoeic.[9] Onomatopoeia can please all; it is a form of leveling. At the level of complexity, we have the recounting of Nso history, which pleases some and informs others. Communal dances involve dulcet music as well as antiphonal singing. Communal dancing is obviously choreographed, and what goes for the making of masks goes also for the choreographing of dances and the composing of communal songs: there is resort to the aesthetics of hiding and revealing.

During dance, another form of aesthetic takes place. Communal dances, especially the celebration of an elder's death in Nso, are often accompanied by the sprinkling of substances on people's bodies by a person called *Taa Kiserve*, or sprinkler. The substance is carefully selected and put together. It chills the body upon contact. It is normally administered during the climax of dance rituals when people are wet with sweat. It is called *kiserve*, the blessing. This is a form of tactile-aesthetics.

Our remarks about Nso masks in the above discussion are, to a considerable extent, applicable to what are known as the Asante gold-weights. These are small figures or geometrical shapes, cast in brass, usually from wax originals that were used for weighing gold dust when that was the Asante currency (see Appiah 1997: 46). The gold-weights, once the medium of exchange among the Asante, are collected nowadays for their elegance of design, that is, for their aesthetic appeal. Appiah has expressed this idea in a passage that deserves to be quoted at length:

> The figurative gold-weights are wonderfully expressive: they depict people and animals, plants and tools, weapons and domestic utensils, often in arrangements that will remind an Asante who looks at them of a familiar proverb. And the *abstract* geometrical weights, their surfaces decorated with patterns...In short, the gold-weights of West Africa are richly embedded in significances...Anyone who has handled a decent number of the weights...*they cried out from the museum's vitrines to be touched* – will have noticed quite often among these elegant objects, *so obviously crafted with great skill and care*, one that has a lump of unworked metal stuffed into a crevice, in a way that seems completely to destroy its aesthetic unity; or, sometimes, a well-made figure had a limb completely hacked off. These amputations and excrescences are there because, after all, a weight is weight: and if it doesn't weigh the right amount, it can't serve its function. If a gold-weight, however finely crafted, has the wrong mass, then something needs to be added (or chopped off) to bring it to proper size. (ibid.; my emphasis)

The point is plain. The gold-weights can be enjoyed for their aesthetic elegance. The artists made them that way, to be enjoyed as such but also to perform a function.

The abstractness and the patternation are encoded into the pieces crying out for decoding. The functions of the Asante gold-weights were veiled by aesthetics because we are aesthetic beings.[10]

Obviously there is more to art and aesthetics in Africa than the above.[11] The objects I described above are parts of cultural artifacts of particular ethnic groups. As Appiah succinctly wrote:

> Africa's creative traditions are both various and particular. You will no more capture the essence of Africa's art in a single tradition than you can grasp the meaning of European art by examining the Tuscan painting of the fifteenth century. And what goes for art goes, even more, for life. Africa's forms of life are too diverse to capture in a single ideal type. (ibid.)

A thorough study of human creativity in Africa would cause the intellectual world to marvel. Her art and aesthetics are as diverse, multi-layered, and complex as the continent itself.

Western historians of a colonial mentality have claimed that most of sub-Saharan Africa had no history until the introduction of writing by the colonialists.[12] I submit that such claims are misplaced with dire consequences for the understanding of our human experience. Quite apart from our long-standing records, Africa's ancient history is chiseled in stones, cast in brass and bronze, carved in wood, painted on stones and walls of caves, and frozen in songs and stories waiting for the brave to decipher. Some are kept in magazines deep in the ground waiting to be excavated by archeologists. For those willing to look there is no lack of signs. Recent excavations in Tassili, North Africa, have much to tell us about the history of a people and the history of the earth. The paintings of cattle and elephants on walls dating back to the fifth millennium BC tell us that once upon a time what is today a desert was a dense, lush, and luxuriant forest (see Willet 1993: esp. ch. 2). The paintings and engravings of people on the walls of caves tell us a lot about the material life of the then Africans. The abstract engravings discovered in Tassili show that African abstract art has a long tradition. And so on. It is true that some parts of sub-Saharan Africa had no writing in recent history, but our ancestors certainly kept stock of our ancient history in artworks.

Notes

1 Art is valorized in the West. That means, nowadays, that we have, for instance, artists, art critics, art connoisseurs, art correspondents, art dealers, art lovers, art collectors, curators, art magazines, art schools, art students, art teachers, art departments in universities, art professors, degrees in art, art galleries, art museums, National Endowment for the Arts, Art Councils as in Great Britain, conferences on art, art journals, etc.

2 I define aesthetics non-restrictively in ways that may not match the definition of most theorists. For more on aesthetics in Africa, see Appiah 1997: 48.

3 This does not rule out financial and other motivations.

4 Clive Bell was even more wedded to the formal aspect of art than Kant. For more on this claim, see Bell 1969.

5   To say that this is among the highest forms of art does not deny short harmonious and sonorous poetry a place in that judgment.

6   My use of the phrase "most masks" is by design. I use the phrase to accommodate the variety of uses of masks in Africa. Not all masks are made by artists to be worn on the face. Consider the little masks that were used as an international passport in West Africa prior to colonialism. These were small masks that could fit into one's trouser pocket with a little difficulty. They were particularly common in what is now known as Benin as travelling identification objects. Other uses abound. "At the initiation rites of certain Dan secret societies, the path to the gathering place was strewn with these small masks, and initiates had to pay to get them removed. At circumcision, the knife blade might be wiped on a small mask; a tray of masks might represent a benevolent spirit of a region; they might be installed on personal altars. They are in fact small representations of a human face; what is done with them, what they are *for*, can be enormously various" (Appiah 1997: 47).

7   The moral innocence of art is often argued in the West. I submit that aesthetic elements are innocent all the way. But in the art of art-making, moral claims can be brought in behind the aesthetic elements. And that is what is important here. Since pure aesthetic elements, such as color and shape, are of little use to humans until acted upon by an artist, it matters how we represent color and shapes. They can have moral implications.

8   Certainly, there have to be venues and occasions for viewing artworks. Museums and theaters are some of the main venues to view art in the West. It is not at all clear to me what it is that motivates individuals to go to these museums. In most of traditional West Africa, death celebrations, naming ceremonies, and other communal occasions serve as communal analogues of museum visits in the West. They also serve as sources of motivation for viewing artworks. In contemporary West African societies more occasions are being found for the experiencing of art. But they are still usually communal, and the civic pedagogic functions are not lost sight of.

9   Some jazz and symphony music may fall into that category.

10   In most of West Africa it is understood by the tutored, the elders, that there are sources of aesthetic experience all around us. It is clearly understood that this includes our very selves and our products. Thus our artifacts are designed with aesthetics in mind. The same is true of our gestures, our locution, and, I am tempted to say, our everything.

11   I have said little or nothing about contemporary African art. That is a whole subject of its own and should be dealt with as such.

12   "Perhaps in the future, there will be some African history to teach. But at the present there is none: there is only the history of the European in Africa. The rest is darkness," insisted Hugh Trevor Roper among others ("The Rise of Christian Europe," *The Listener*, Nov. 28, 1963, p. 871; quoted in Appiah 1998).

References

Appiah, K. Anthony (1998) "The Hidden History," *New York Review of Books*, XLV (December).

Appiah, K. Anthony (1997) "The Art of Africa," *The New York Review of Books*, XLIV (April).

Bell, Clive (1969) "Significant Form," in John Hospers (ed.), *Introductory Readings in Aesthetics* (New York: Free Press), pp. 87–99.

Willet, Frank (1993) *African Art* (London: Thames and Hudson).

Wingo, Ajume H. (1998) "African Art and the Aesthetics of Hiding and Revealing," *British Journal of Aesthetics*, 38(3).

Part VI

POLITICS

35

Government by Consensus: An Analysis of a Traditional Form of Democracy

EDWARD WAMALA

Introduction

Is it possible to talk of democracy in a traditional African society that was clearly monarchical, in a social political set-up that had neither an elected parliament nor a people's representatives? Would we be using the concept of democracy in the commonly accepted sense when we apply it to social political organizations that seemingly did not have any ideas about the separation of powers and checks and balances, and, moreover, in a sociocultural milieu that lacked political parties in which there were no periodic elections? Could traditional African society have been democratic unconsciously, i.e. without elaborately worked out ideas of democracy? Below, I attempt to answer these and related questions by looking at the social political organization of traditional Ganda society with a view to showing how ideas we would consider crucial for democracy were operative, sometimes implicitly, sometimes explicitly, in traditional society.

Demography and Democracy

Demographic factors seem to have played a considerable part in the evolution of democracy in traditional society. One might recall that it was the smallness of the population in the ancient Greek *polis* that facilitated the participation of all free citizens in the running of its affairs. In traditional Ganda society, a similar demographic factor seems to have been central to the institution and regulation of social political life, and the creation of what we would call a democracy. But while the small population resulted in a democracy in the Greek *polis* at a time when monarchism had virtually died away, with the few vestigial kings being seen as merely ceremonial figures, in Ganda society a small population facilitated the evolution of a democracy that was situated in a rural setting, and, moreover, was under the reign and rule of a king. Since the Greek case is well known, we will not pursue it further. Rather, what we will do in the first part of this chapter is to attempt to show, by historical and structural analysis, how the demographic element was related to the social political culture of the Ganda people.

Prior to the development of a monarchical social political structure in Buganda, Ganda society was constituted by independent patrilineal totemic clans, each one headed by an *Omutaka* and sub-divided into a descending series of segments, starting at the top with the major lineages (*Masiga*), the minor lineages (*Mituba*), and going down through the minimal lineages (*Nyiriri*) to the sub-minimal lineages (*Olugya*) and finally to the household (*enda*). *Omutaka*, as the head of clan, presided over a cultural hierarchy in which the different descending segments were headed by *Bataka* (clan leaders) of descending social ranks. The monarchical structure of social organization emerged in Buganda when the more powerful *Bataka* out-competed the weaker ones in the struggle for power, with the more powerful becoming *Ssabataka* (leader of clan leaders), while the weaker ones remained in their original *Bataka* positions, a development which saw the centralization of power and the formation of the Ganda state.

In his newly acquired role, *Ssabataka* (also called *Kabaka*) was head of all patrilineal totemic clans brought together as a single unit. As head of all clan leaders, *Ssabataka* (*Kabaka*) was *primus inter pares*, an equal among equals, an arrangement which (as we shortly show) crucially influenced the political ethos of the times.

As head of totemic clans, *Kabaka* was also at the head of religious activity in the tribe. Note here that religion centered round the cults of gods (*Bakatonda*), ancestors (*emizimu*), and spirits (*emisambwa*). Whereas ordinary folks invoked those beings to solve personal problems, the *Kabaka* invoked them, on behalf of the state, to secure supernatural support in war, or to avert natural catastrophes.

Whether in the cultural or political realm, the fact of a small population, inhabiting abundant agricultural land, dictated the nature of social relations and the political ethos. In the cultural sphere where the *Ssabataka* was *primus inter pares* there was always a delicate and uneasy balance between him and the rest of the *Bataka*. Because the office of the *Ssabataka* grew in strength in proportion as that of the *Bataka* weakened, whenever the *Ssabataka* sought more power, of course, at the expense of the various *Bataka*, the latter resented it, creating a strained relationship or what sociologists have termed "an avoidance relationship." (The term "avoidance relationship" seems to have been coined by Fallers (1964: 76).)

The availability of open land (occupied by a scant population) made it possible for an individual chief (*Mutaka*) to secede from a harsh *Kabaka* and strengthen his own power among his clansmen. The avoidance relationship was crucial for the creation here of what we may call a democracy in the following way. The withdrawal of recognition and support by the *Bataka* was bound to create for the *Ssabataka* not only a legitimization crisis, but also a problem of power. This is clear from the fact that the very existence of his office depended on the recognition of the *Bataka*. There would be no *Ssabataka* without individual *Bataka*. In the actual or threatened withdrawal of their support and recognition was the implicit reminder that "government is best which governs least." As a rule, the further implication that government is best when it governs with the consent of all concerned was not lost on the *Ssabataka*.

The avoidance relationship also brought into sharp focus the importance of the democratic principle of subsidiarity, recognizable in Aristotle, and tersely expressed in the following Ganda proverbs:

1   *Obukulu Ndege, tezivugira mumazzi* (Authority is like ankle bells; they do not ring in water)

2   *Omukulu takulira mpya bbiri* (A master cannot rule two homesteads)

In both proverbs was an allusion to the idea of subsidiarity, the idea that the proper responsibility at the family level must not be taken away by the city, nor that of the city by the state. Inherent in the idea of subsidiarity was the principle that higher units had legitimate authority, but only to promote the well-being of the lower units, aiding them to realize their good and their potential. There was in the proverbs just cited an indication that interference from above in the affairs of smaller units was not welcome and that even the *Ssabataka*, who had overall authority over the tribe, was, nevertheless, supposed to recognize domains where others had authority. Indeed, there is a well-known saying which hints at the principle that no one, including the *Ssabataka*, is above the law: *Ekinene tekyetwala: Kabaka ayingira owa Kibale* (Nobody can be completely above the law; the king is in the power of Kibale – the official in charge of settling royal disputes).

The avoidance relationship not only tamed the *Ssabataka*'s use of power; it also forced the individual *Bataka*, that is, the clan leaders, to be democratic, because a chief who withdrew his recognition from the *Ssabataka*, if he were to survive that stand-off, needed the support of his own clansmen. To mobilize and maintain support, an individual *Mutaka* needed to behave in a manner that endeared him to his clansmen. But, in the converse, a *Ssabataka* who engaged in a stand-off with individual *Mutaka* also needed to endear himself to the rest of the *Bataka*. He too needed to behave justly, fairly, and with a sense of propriety, or risk alienating many *Bataka*, thereby facilitating military coalition against his rule. Ganda folklore is replete with stories of *Batakas* joining hands to send kings to exile. Seeking consensus was thus the rational way to govern.

The Epistemological Roots of Consensus in Traditional Society

But seeking consensus in traditional Ganda society seems to have been more than simply a political expedient to avoid legitimation crises; it seems to have been at the heart of social and political organization and the ethos of the people of Buganda. The dedication to consensus seems to have been rooted in the firm epistemological belief that knowledge is ultimately dialogical or social, and in the ethical belief in the collective responsibility of all for the welfare of the community.

Western theorists like Jürgen Habermas, who today talk of the social or dialogical nature of knowledge, are only restating an old truth long since discovered and lived in traditional Ganda society. Oral literature is replete with proverbs showing the dialogical nature of knowledge and the value of consultation. The following are a few.

1   *Magezi muliro, bwegukuggwako, ogunona wa munno* (Knowledge is like firewood in the hearth, if you have none you fetch it from your neighbor)

437

2   *Ndi mugezi nga muburile* (I am wise, only if others have informed you)
3   *Magezi gomu, galesa Magambo ku kubo* (Belief in his intellectual self-sufficiency resulted in Magambo's failure to reach home. Magambo, a blind man, failed to reach home because of his arrogance and unwillingness to consult others)

The link between belief in the dialogical nature of knowledge and the social emphasis on consensus is apparent. Nobody has a monopoly on knowledge; everybody is in need of the knowledge and opinions of others. Issues had to be looked at, cogitated over, and discussed until a general agreement was reached as to what was to be done. The frequent imputation of epistemological authoritarianism to the elders in traditional African society seems to ignore this fact. Traditional society could not have emphasized consensus amidst a confirmed habit of epistemological authoritarianism.

The dialogical conception of knowledge in Ganda society did not exempt even technical experts from the epistemic help of others, as may be seen from the following proverbs.

4   *Nasiwa mukange asiwa mukabukuku* (I will brew my beer in my own calabash even if it ends up brewing in a rotten one)
5   *Omuwesi ekyamuzimbya kukubo kulagirirwa* (The reason a blacksmith locates his workshop by the roadside is to have access to the views of others)

It is important to point out, however, that the dialogical conception of knowledge would not have led to the emphasis on consensus if it was not coupled with the equally important idea of collective social responsibility tersely expressed in the proverb *Ekyalo ddiba lya mbogo: terizingibwa bwomu* (A village is like a buffalo skin; one man cannot roll it up by himself). The point of the proverb is the centrality of political participation and social capital. Owing to the complexity of society, everyone was supposed to contribute his or her part, working alongside others.

Social capital, by which is meant "features of social networks, norms and trust...that enable participants to act together more effectively to pursue shared objectives" (Putnam 1996: 1), has only recently been rediscovered in contemporary social and political discourse. This is largely because, for a long time, it was taken for granted, and theorists only woke up to the fact when it became more noticeable, ironically, because of its increasing absence.

At the heart of social capital is the nature of traditional kinship relationships, where everybody in the tribe was a relative. In the immediate family, a brother to one's father was a father. Similarly, a sister to one's mother was a mother. At the larger tribal level, because of the cultural tradition never to marry into one's patrilineal clan, any family found itself related to several other clans, as the sons in that family married into those clans, and likewise the daughters married into clans other than those they were born in. What emerges, consequently, is a very strong sense of the "social" as opposed to the "individual" or the "personal" or even the "private." Such a frame of mind was doubtless conducive to a consensual approach to governance.

438

Okukiika

The attainment of consensus was facilitated by the custom of "paying homage to a chief's court," known as *Okukiika*. By this custom, anybody could, on his personal initiative, visit the court of a chief or even of the king to apprise himself of the latest developments in the community. The following two common sayings testify to the thinking behind the practice. The Ganda say: *Akiika embuga amanya ensonga* (Whoever pays homage to the court is apprised of the latest developments in society). Also they say: *Okweggala si magezi: emirembe give mbuga* (To isolate oneself is not wisdom, peace comes from the chief's court). (The reference to chief's court here, by the way, is not to a trial court but rather to his parliament.)

The custom in question did at least two things. It gave the citizens the opportunity to manifest their loyalty to the state while also providing them with the chance to learn about what was going on in the community. The first function was particularly important in the case of persons of position and influence from whom signs of loyalty were bound to be highly reassuring to the king. To ordinary citizens, on the other hand, the special importance of the practice was twofold. As noted, they could ask questions about matters of state; but also they could actually take part in proceedings at the ruler's court, contributing ideas and directly participating in the political process and minimizing thereby the problems that sometimes come with being represented by other people. Thus, in fact, the practice of paying homage to the king's court was one of paying a visitation. This openness to citizen input is certainly one of the hallmarks of a commitment to consensus.

Some scholars of traditional African societies have sometimes criticized the idea of consensus in tribal societies on the grounds that it posits a unanimity in tribal society which was never actually there. There is a kind of idealization of the past, so the criticism goes, which ignores and, in fact, obscures the deadly conflicts that Africa endured before colonialism. This criticism misses a very important point, namely, that consensus presupposes dissensus, and talking until people agreed points to the existence of opposed views which needed to be reconciled. The idea of political opposition was, therefore, not alien to traditional Ganda society, only it was not the formal and ossified opposition instituted for the sake of an adversarial form of political pluralism. Definitely there was political opposition. If that were not the case, it would have been superfluous to talk of reaching consensus. At times, indeed, that was never reached, and in such circumstances, certain courses of action were taken. We have already referred, for example, to kings whose subjects turned against them and sometimes forced them into exile. These were, however, the exceptions that proved the rule.

A Monarchical Democracy

As a rule, the traditional consensus system of government worked well. It was a monarchical system of a limited rather than an absolute sort. The monarch ruled through a council of heads of clans, and there were heads, sub-heads, and chiefs at the various levels of society. In any debate the aim was to reach a consensus. Consensus was thus central to the operation of democracy in Buganda society and, indeed, in many African societies. If after due deliberations the council reached a consensus, it was taboo for the monarch to oppose or reject it. This is why the monarchy was of the "limited" variety; it is also why the monarchical character of the system was compatible with its being democratic. It is true that the monarch had a semi-divine status, being thought of as a link between the ancestors and the living. But he was made to understand, as already indicated, that he was not welcome to be autocratic.

It should be pointed out that the king rarely took part in the deliberations himself, the rationale being that the monarch should not prejudice the proceedings. Democracy demanded that the king execute what was arrived at by the council. If the king had anything to contribute, he could get it across through one of his closest advisors, who would then pass it on for discussion. There is another thing we need to note. The quest for consensus was carried on at the highest level of governance as well as all the various levels in the structure of society down to the level of the household.

What has just been said discloses a remarkable difference between Ganda traditional democracy and some modern forms of democracy. There is no such thing as the veto in the Ganda system. Neither the king nor anybody else had a veto. The idea of a veto is defined as the constitutional right of a president to reject a decision of the legislature under certain conditions. Such an idea contradicts the idea of consensus and is alien to traditional Buganda concepts of legitimate governance.

The Evils of the Party System

Another contrast between the two types of democracy concerns the party system. Africa today is being encouraged to "democratize." Invariably, this has meant the introduction of party political pluralism. We note that the resulting "democratization process" is largely externally generated, and has not taken full cognizance of the internal cultural dynamics of societies in which these changes are being introduced. In fact, the multiparty system, as also the party system itself, is inhospitable to the consensual values of traditional Ganda society.

Political parties have come to the scene with many promises, but at the same time with many inherent problems. The party system destroys consensus by deemphasizing the role of the individual in political action. With the rise of the party system, the party replaces the "people." Thus the candidates proposed by a party no longer appear as individual men and women of flesh and blood. What you have are party members resplendent with party cards. With the massive help of the party machine, party members will try to win the people's votes by appealing to their basest instincts and sentiments. Driven to a frenzy, the electorate, in turn, is not so discriminative. Finally, those who are elected are representatives, not really of the people but of the party, which has become a power in itself. Party members do not really have loyalty to the people whom they are supposed to represent, as is understood by the principles of political delegation. Rather, their loyalty is to the party that ensured their success in the elections. The same being true of members of opposing parties, where is there room for consensus formation?

But political parties have come with yet another problem. Any party worth its name will try to come into power in order to implement its programs. In order to come to power or retain it, political parties have had to resort to Machiavellian strategies. Acting on the notorious principle that the end justifies the means, political parties in the modern state have drained political practice of all ethical considerations. Yet, such considerations had been a key feature of traditional political practice. As the traditional values that are thrown overboard were the guiding mechanism of consensus formation, so what we are left with are materialistic considerations that foster the welfare not of society at large, but of certain suitably aligned individuals and groups.

Admittedly, traditional Buganda politics was characterized by personal rule. The king knew personally all his senior officials and a great many other position holders besides. The situation was due to the small size of the ethnic group. Though supposedly rejected in the modern state on the grounds that such personal rule fosters corruption and nepotism, the phenomenon of personal rule remains very much a feature of contemporary society. Owing to the development of political parties, we find that in elections the electorate delegates its power to their alleged representatives. But not every party member has power in the party hierarchy. As only a few members at the top wield power, even the parties that command the majority and therefore form the government are really ruled by a handful of persons at the top of the party. The powerful party bosses, as a matter of fact, personalize power, and whoever wants favors will try to come under their wings. Thus, personal rule, after seeming to be eliminated, makes a return to the political arena of the modern state.

The cultural inappropriateness of the party system is, indeed, deep. In the cultural milieu of the Ganda, in which individualism was almost unknown, the idea of institutionalizing disagreement was alien. A way was always sought to reach a meeting point. In the contrary tendency of the multiparty system a deadly complication has ensued in Africa. Because the ethnic groups are apt to feel a mutual solidarity that makes them see themselves as one, multiparty politics easily becomes tribalized. The consequences to life and limb of the resulting struggles are there for all to see.

The upshot of all this is that multiparty politics, although conceivably good for alternative policy advancement in individualistic societies, has tended to be very problematic in communalistic societies. The challenge then is: how can societies, in which consensus was, traditionally, the preferred method of political decision-making, institutionalize democracy in the modern world? A creative answer to this kind of question can save contemporary Africa the headache otherwise caused when ideas are adopted without adequate consideration.

References

Fallers, L. A. (1964) "Social Stratification in Traditional Buganda," in L. A. Fallers (ed.), *The King's Men: Leadership and Status in Buganda on the Eve of Independence* (Oxford: Oxford University Press).

Putnam, Robert D. (1996) "Tuning in, Tuning Out: The Strange Disappearance of Social Capital in America Feature," *PPSP*: 1.

Further reading

Hoebbel, E. Adamson (1942) *Man in the Primitive World: An Introduction to Anthropology* (London: McGraw Hill Book Company).

Roscoe, John (1911) *The Buganda: An Account of their Native Customs and Beliefs* (London).

Southwoeld, Martin (1964) "Leadership, Authority and the Village Community," in L. A. Fallers (ed.), *The King's Men: Leadership and Status in Buganda on the Eve of Independence* (Oxford: Oxford University Press).

36

Democracy, Kingship, and Consensus:
A South African Perspective

JOE TEFFO

Introduction

The election of April 1994 in South Africa ushered in a new era that changed the face and history of the country in a very profound way. The founding document of the "new South Africa," that is The Constitution of the Republic of South Africa, Act 108 of 1996, created space and time for the recognition and flourishing of all the cultures within the nation. This constitution unequivocally recognizes the institution of traditional leadership and traditional authorities that exist side by side with other government structures, national, provincial, and local. Of course, this was not always so. Successive colonial authorities in apartheid times attempted to destroy indigenous African institutions, laws, and customs. That they did not quite succeed demonstrates the historical embeddedness and cultural vitality of those institutions.

Domesticated Democracy

Even under the new dispensation, however, the question has lingered on as to whether the traditional system is democratic. It is not in the nature of philosophical concepts to be susceptible to one conclusive definition. Democracy is one such concept. We will here invoke Abraham Lincoln's definition, but this is not so much because his is better than others as because it is the most quoted and apparently accepted one. Lincoln declared that "Democracy is government of the people, by the people, and for the people." Granted Lincoln's definition, one should nevertheless remain mindful of George Orwell's caution that "in the case of a word like democracy, not only is there no agreed definition but the attempt to make one is resisted from all sides.... The defenders of any kind of regime claim that it is a democracy." Present debates and existing scholarship seem to be comfortable with Lincoln's view, often paraphrased differently. In this connection, two levels of discourse present themselves: the level of conceptual analysis and the level of application or implementation. Thus the concept is applied differently by different states, at different levels of their historical development. I therefore align myself with Sindane when he avers that "the least we can expect from democracy is that it should be a process of decision-making which involves the people, especially those people who will be affected by the decisions" (1994: 2). Logically, therefore, democracy has to be representative, accountable, and participatory (Teffo 1995: 140).

Some contemporary societies manifest tendencies toward universal hegemony. Thus it is that the Western superpowers have sought to impose their brand of democracy as the only viable option for human survival and flourishing. Indeed, their brand of democracy seems to work for them. However, other societies need not mimic the West without taking cognizance of the cultures in which their democracy is located. Several systems that are not, by Western definitions, democratic are flourishing. So emphasis should be on the system not the name. In this connection, Finley cites G. Parry, who argues that "democracy" or "democratic" "have become the twentieth-century words by which to evince approval of the society or institution so described. This has necessarily meant that the words have become so debased they have almost ceased, without further definition, to be of any use in distinguishing one particular form of government from another" (1985: 9).

The question that flows from the last paragraph is whether there necessarily is one brand of democracy that is universally acceptable. Is there only one paradigm for the conceptualization of democracy? Perhaps it is against the backdrop of these questions that some contemporary African philosophers have begun scrutinizing the concept of democracy. Thus, for example, Wamba dia Wamba has written an article entitled "Beyond Elite Politics of Democracy in Africa." The central thesis of that article is that "the content of democratization is determined by modes of politics...its content is shaped by the dominant mode of politics. It must, therefore, [in Africa] be redefined in terms of the change from a mode of politics in crisis towards a new mode of politics" (1992). According to Ramose, who has written a response to Wamba dia Wamba's article, "the main reason for the thesis is to underline the necessity of 'emancipative politics'. Thus the theme of emancipation or liberation is the regulative principle on the basis of which Wamba assesses Africa's experience with imported 'democracy' and the prospects of a political praxis 'beyond elite politics of democracy'" (1992: 63). The reference, of course, is to multiparty democracy as transplanted to Africa from the West. An essential feature of that system is the institutionalization of conflict in the form of a governing party and an opposing one. This gives rise to what is aptly called adversarial politics. Ramose is explicit in this connection:

> The oddity of adversarial politics is emphasized even more by the fact that quite often this kind of politics degenerates into opposition for the sake of opposition. No doubt the protagonists of this system will retort that the aim of opposition is to accede to the position of political power by displacing the ruling party. Without denying this rather egoistic aim, I still argue that, understood in this way, adversarial politics undermines the principle of solidarity in traditional African political culture. (ibid. 75)

It should be stressed, pursuant to the argument of the philosophers just quoted, that the diversity of the cultures of the world suggests the reality of many "democracies." And my contention below is that there is a suitable tradition of democracy in indigenous African culture. It is, therefore, incumbent upon Africans to retrieve and preserve what is both logically sound and empirically justified from the African tradition and to try to perpetuate it. Certainly, the argument here is not for returning to the good old days. There is no question that some practices of the past are no longer consonant with modernity. Such practices must be discarded or adapted. After all, no culture is static. And all cultures, including those of the West, are subject to acculturation and enculturation. At the heart of this argument is the view that African tradition should remain, for Africans, the source of innovative reconstruction. In this connection, I endorse Wiredu's warning: "It would profit us little to gain all the technology in the world and lose the humanist essence of our culture" (1980: 21).

The need to be mindful of the connection between democracy and culture was captured by the Norwegian Minister for development cooperation in a speech to the Advisory Committee of the Global Coalition for Africa:

> We must not forget that democracy must grow from local roots, it cannot be imported, sold or paid for. It cannot be imposed from outside. The people of each nation must take their fate into their own hands and shape the form of government most suited to their national aspirations. Consequently, we must avoid imposing pre-defined models of democracy on African countries. (Grete Faremo, as quoted in *Human Rights Handbook 1992*, part II, p. xiii)

The Principle of Consensus as a Feature of Democracy

To come now to the indigenous system, we note that its centerpiece is the institution of kingship. Now a chief is born not elected. Where there is any simulacrum of election, the scope of choice is severely limited, for candidates must come from the royal family, or, more strictly, lineage. This non-elective character of chiefly office has been made a ground of objection. It is held to be anti-democratic. The critics argue that the only way kings and chiefs or anybody, for that matter, can attain political power legitimately is through being elected to political office. Short of election, kings and chiefs have no right to political power. This short-sighted argument forgets that history teaches that historical and even contemporary kings and queens all over the world have not, as a rule, acquired their constitutional status through elections. And yet, their status has not been seen as necessarily antithetical to a democratic polity. The Queen of England, for example, was not elected to that position, nor will that be the case with her successor, but British democracy is not felt to be in any jeopardy on that account. So it is possible, even in our times, to attain political and symbolic power without election. Of this, more below.

But first, let us note that African social organization is undergirded by the principle of solidarity. It is characterized by humane people-centeredness. Precisely because of this principle, adversarial politics, the hallmark of the Western-style multiparty system of democracy, is rather foreign to African political culture.

Second, and even more importantly, kingship, as a special manifestation of democracy in African society, embraces complete equal participation by the community.

445

Admittedly, in some communities, participation was restricted to adult males only – more specifically, to circumcised adult males. This was due to the belief entertained in those communities that an uncircumcised man is still a "boy," even when he is married. Thus, indeed, an uncircumcised adult male could become a junior to his own begotten son, if the latter is circumcised. Circumcision, then, is a rite of passage to adulthood that bestows on one the inalienable right to participate in all community affairs. Women also were under some restrictions based on various beliefs. Obviously, some comments are urgent regarding the restrictions just noted. It must be immediately pointed out that, if one can speak of ancient Athenian democracy, when women and slaves were excluded from participation, the same courtesy is warranted here. It is, however, more important to understand that the problem has to do not with the essential character of the traditional political system, but, rather, with some specific contingent beliefs. With the withering away of the beliefs, the practice is easily seen to be unsupported. This provides an illustration, by the way, of how some traditional practices and institutions can be reviewed in the light of modern belief habits without necessarily jettisoning them root and branch.

Third, and most importantly, consensus-seeking is the hallmark of traditional political decision-making in many African communities. Any system that gives such priority to consensus is quite clearly democratic in a far deeper sense than any system in which decision-making proceeds on the principle that the majority carries the day. In the African communities under discussion, kingship is an integral part of a communalistic social order. The special importance of kingship is seen in the fact that the institution symbolizes, inspires, and facilitates the unity and continuity of the community's culture and traditions. The system involving the kingship institution might be called a *communocracy*, insofar as it is a type of governance based on general community involvement and participation. Communocracy, then, might be said to be a form of democracy characteristic of many traditional African societies. One might mention in this connection the Zulu of South Africa, the Bugandans of Uganda, and the Akans of Ghana.

It should, thus, not be difficult for an unprejudiced mind to see signs of democracy in traditional African political life. Such an observer will be further aided by the principle expressed in local sayings such as: *Kgosi ke kgosi ka batho* (A chief is a chief through the people). It follows from this maxim that one cannot be a chief without the people. You become a king by consent of the people and you remain one as long as the consent is not withdrawn. This is not without some analogies to Rousseau's social contract theory in Western political thought. Effectively, the king is the king by the grace of the people and not by the grace of God, as medieval Western political thought held. This, it should be noted, is an important extenuation of the non-elective nature of kingship. Although the king is not elected in the way in which, for example, a British parliamentarian is elected, a royal cannot become a king unless he is acceptable to the people. Nor, if enthroned, can he remain a king except at the pleasure of the people. For every king, the possibility of being deposed by the people on grounds of unpopularity was always a live contingency that it was unwise to discount. But by far the most important consideration in favor of the democratic standing of the system of which kingship was a part is that it is not the individual king but a leadership unit that has the final say in the deliberations of the ruling council. Both in theory and practice the chief only pronounces the decision of the council. Decisions are never perceived as his, but as of all the members of the council. Any king given to trifling with council decisions was liable to lose his throne. In the light of this, it should be understood that the great respect that people have for chiefs or kings attaches to the institution and not the individual chief per se. Of course, individual chiefs may, through outstanding personal qualities, enjoy a special reverence from the community.

Following from the preceding thoughts, it can be concluded that the idea of a chief as an autocrat with absolute power is a misunderstanding of traditional African constitutional thought. Gyekye underscores the argument thus:

> It appears the most important injunction was that the chief should never ever act without the advice and full concurrence of his councilors, the representatives of the people. Acting without the concurrence and advice of his Council was a legitimate cause for his deposition. Thus the chief was bound by law to rule with the consent of the people. (1988: 11)

If we now revisit the analogy between African monarchy and the British variety, it is obvious that what they have in common is the fact that though they symbolize the power of the state, they do not exercise it. They only express or, more strictly, reflect the decisions of the ruling body. And that is why their position is not necessarily prejudicial to democracy. There is an important difference, however. The African king, but not his British counterpart, sits in the ruling council and participates in its deliberations. But this difference does not affect the main point.

In thinking about the traditional system in relation to the question of democracy, it needs to be emphasized that the ruling councils were representative within the canons of representation accepted within the culture. The councils were constituted by lineage heads chosen by their lineages on the combined grounds of seniority, wisdom, popularity, and vitality. These representatives were in close touch with their constituency, which consisted of their close kins, and remained in status so long as the desirable qualities remained intact. To this is to be added the important fact, hinted at above, that the councils worked by consensus. This means that they literally engaged in deliberation until a consensus was reached. This is what makes the system cooperative rather than adversarial. It also certainly strengthens its democratic standing.

In South Africa today, more than in any of the kingdoms of the so-called First World, the traditional leaders are crucial to any constitutional dispensation. The reason is that they remain in touch with the people who reside in the rural areas. Kingship still controls social relationships between people in the rural areas. It regulates and governs, inter alia, kinship behavior, customary rites, and marital contracts, and oversees the affairs not only of the living but also of the dead.

> Indeed, this sense of kingship binds together the entire life of the tribe, and is even extended to cover animals, plants and non-living objects through the totemic system. Almost all the concepts connected with human relationship can be understood and interpreted through the kingship system. It is this which largely governs the behavior,

thinking and whole life of the individual in the society of which he is a member. (Mbiti 1969: 104)

Let us now recall some questions raised earlier on. Is the multiparty political system, which is an integral element of the Western democratic culture, the panacea for Africa's political problems? Should African modes of social thought and organization be replaced wholesale with Western political philosophy and practice? If the answer is in the negative, as it should be, then there is a role for traditional leaders to play even in contemporary society.

There is also the need to abstain from the undue *absolutization* of the multiparty system. Rather, in their contemporary political culture, Africans should seek to reincarnate, among other things, the values of solidarity and consensus. Such an effort would give content and impetus to the African Renaissance Movement that is under way in South Africa.

Conclusion

This brief exposition should enable an open-minded reader to gain some understanding of the basic nature of the traditional political system and to appreciate the power and role of our chiefs and the valuable contribution they make and are capable of making. Indeed, frequently, they are the only link between the modern national government and the communities, and should not be seen to be in competition with it. The institution of kingship is one of the main traits that define African culture. It would therefore be a mistake for Africans to try to discard kingship in the name of modernity, especially modernity as perceived and conceived by foreigners. Since cultures are not static, I suggest that we seek a balance of the traditional and the modern, rather than a substitution of the one for the other.

I would like to stress that my thesis in this discussion has two parts. The first is that the traditional political system still has a contemporary vitality. This, as noted earlier on, is recognized in South Africa today by the national constitution. The role of the traditional system within the contemporary polity seems to be only supplementary to the latter. But even in that capacity, it may, as previously conceded, need some updating in some respects. But reflection on the values and decision procedures of the traditional system raises the philosophically challenging question of whether the notion of democracy entails a multiparty, or indeed any sort of party, arrangement at all. The second part of my thesis is that this is not the case, on the grounds that the traditional system was democratic, because consensual, but did not incorporate any sort of party system. And my suggestion has been that there is something to be learnt from this. The practical implication is that it should be feasible to devise a national system of government based on an institutionalized quest for consensus. Such a system cannot, logically, be a party system, whether it features one party or two parties or any number of them. Many subtle issues arise here that are worthy of the attention of philosophers, political scientists, and others. In exploring them, they will be advancing the cause of democracy in Africa (and possibly the world at large).

References

Finley, M. I. (1985) *Democracy, Ancient and Modern*, 2nd edn. (London: Hogarth Press).

Gyekye, Kwame (1988) *The Unexamined Life: Philosophy and the African Experience* (Accra: Ghana Universities Press).

Mbiti, J. S. (1969) *African Religions and Philosophy* (London: Heinemann).

Sindane, J. (1994) *Democracy and Political Tolerance* (Pretoria: HSRC).

Wamba dia Wamba, E. (1992) "Beyond Elite Politics of Democracy in Africa," *Quest*, 6(1) (June).

Wiredu, Kwasi (1980) *Philosophy and an African Culture* (London: Cambridge University Press).

Further reading

Achebe, C. (1966) *A Man of the People* (New York: Doubleday).

Achebe, C. (1984) *The Trouble with Nigeria* (Oxford: Heinemann).

Banana, C. (1987) *Towards a Socialist Ethos* (Harare: The College Press).

Gyekye, K. (1992) "Traditional Political Ideals, Their Relevance to Development in Contemporary Africa," in K. Wiredu and K. Gyekye (eds.), *Person and Community: Ghanaian Philosophical Studies I* (Washington DC: Council for Research in Values and Philosophy).

James, G. G. M. (1992) *Stolen Legacy* (New Jersey: Africa World Press).

Malan, J. S. (1998) *Cultural Anthropology: An African Perspective* (Pietersburg: University of the North).

Mojela, K. and Mabiletsa, M. (1997) "Good Governance, Traditional Law and Land Reform," in P. de Villiers and W. Critchley (eds.), *Rural Land Reform Issues in Southern Africa: Lessons for South Africa's Northern Province* (Pietersburg: Unin Press).

Potholm, C. P. (1979) *The Theory and Practice of African Politics* (New Jersey: Prentice-Hall).

Ramose, M. B. (1992) "African Democratic Tradition: Oneness, Consensus and Openness: A Reply to Wamba dia Wamba," *Quest*, 6(2) (December).

Simunyu, V. G. (1987) "The Democratic Myth in African Societies," in W. O. Ogugi and A. Gitonga (eds.), *Democratic Theory and Practice in Africa* (Nairobi: Heinemann).

Teffo, L. J. (1995) "Kingship and Democracy in South Africa," in J. Malherbe (ed.), *Decolonising the Mind* (Pretoria: UNISA).

Teffo, L. J. (1995) "Racism and Escapism: Who is the Victim?" *Maseno Journal of Education, Arts and Science* (Nairobi: Maseno University College).

Teffo, L. J. (1995) "The Hounded Black Intellectuals," *Pretoria*, CSD Bulletin, 2(4).

Thiongo, N. (1996) *Decolonizing the Mind: The Politics of Language in African Literature* (London: James Currey).

Wiredu, Kwasi (1997) "Democracy and Consensus in African Traditional Politics: A Plea for a Non-Party Policy," in Emmanuel Eze (ed.), *Postcolonial African Philosophy: A Critical Reader* (Oxford: Blackwell Publishers).

37

Fellowship Associations as a Foundation for Liberal Democracy in Africa

AJUME H. WINGO

The people are the Fon and the Fon is the people.
A Nso praise singer[1]

Introduction

There is no denial that our new African nation-states today, as yesteryear, face deep political and consequently economic and social pathologies such as a lack of trust, of democratic freedom, of rule of law, and of the accountability of the government to the governed. My contention is that African states stand, as it were, in the middle of two powerful forces. The first can be traced to traditional African ways of life and indigenous political cultures. Fluid as traditions and cultures in Africa are, some are carry-overs from the precolonial past and some came into existence or gained strength as a reaction to colonialism and postcolonial governments. The second force comes from the legacy of oppressive colonial regimes and a foreign version of democracy. So what we have in most African states is a myriad of indigenous systems of government with superimposed foreign structures. These mixed institutions evolved locally over time and sit, as it were, on the breast of Africa's peoples. Within the indigenous regimes, politics is a natural affair and, as Aristotle would have it, all are politicians. Then, there are contemporary African states faced with the task of governing the many separate ethnic groups within their states by means of contemporary political principles and processes, but they are miles away from the people they are supposed to be governing in the first place. Faced with this sorry state, some African political theorists take a fundamentalist stand: either a total return to the African past or a total unmitigated acceptance of Western political arrangements. One of those political fundamentalists is Mwangi S. Kimenyi, who has argued (1998) for the complete return to precolonial boundaries. A simple response is, let him give the date.

Neither of these approaches is viable. The real political problem is how pro-actively and non-coercively to achieve well-entrenched liberal democratic arrangements in the African states.[2] I will argue here that indigenous African political arrangements and fellowship associations are to a large extent alive and well and must be used to build trust and foster the virtues that a liberal democratic institution requires. In other words, a well-ordered liberal democracy should be built on deeply rooted African traditions. I particularly argue that the deeply rooted

450

traditions in African fellowship associations provide an avenue for fostering an overarching political culture within which other cultures can flourish. Put differently, I am offering an empirical analysis of existing local social organizations (some with liberal democratic and others with anti-liberal democratic impulses), as well as postulating a vision of how we are supposed to get to a well-connected liberal democracy from where we are. By a well-connected liberal democracy, I mean a liberal democracy with secure roots at the local (grassroots) level.

A Brief Definition of Liberal Democracy

Before I get into my main argument, I must first briefly define democracy and the term "liberal" which modifies it. The word "democracy" is a conceptually vague word and one that is emotively charged. As George Orwell puts it:

> a word like democracy not only [has] . . . no agreed definition, but the attempt to make one is resisted from all sides. It is almost universally felt that when we call a country democratic we are praising it: consequently the defender of every kind of regime claims that it is a democracy and fears that they might have to stop using the word if it were tied down to any one meaning. (1968: 132–3)

"Tie down," I will. Democracy – the noble term and concept provided by the ancient Athenians – bestows spirit and form on the peculiar experience of human and societal relations. As Lincoln reminded us, democracy – from the Greek *demos*, the people, and *kratos*, rule – in essence translates as "government of the people, by the people, for the people." That is, a government that is ultimately answerable and accountable to the people. In other words, the government is a proxy for the people. This occurs through the process of selecting public officials and deciding policy. The process is that of open and free elections and the principle of one and only one vote for each. Jane Mansbridge, a leading contemporary theorist of democracy and grassroot democratic practices, reminds us that democracy is also a way of deliberating and reaching consensus among people sharing similar interests.[3] She refers to such a process as "unitary democracy" as being distinguished from the mere process of elections, which she refers to as "adversary democracy." Democracy, then, is a process of selecting leaders and deciding policies when citizens' interests conflict as well as deliberating and arriving at a consensus.

Political liberalism refers to the rule of law, separation of powers, and the guarantee of the rights of individuals and groups to live life and pursue happiness as they deem worthy. In short, political liberalism refers to political freedom backed by the state. In the United States, as in many nations in Europe, liberalism and democracy are wedded together. Before the marriage there was skepticism as to whether the two were a good match, much less whether they could live peacefully together, "until death do us part." With concessions here and there, as happens in good marriages, the wedding took place about 200 years ago. Some of the concessions by democracy to political liberalism in the US included counter-majoritarian arrangements such as the Constitution, the Supreme Court, the demographically

451

unequal apportionment of Senators, federalism, and the Electoral College. And some concessions by liberalism to democracy included such things as the customary restrictions on speech. To the extent that the two are spouses, those concessions are welcome. Political liberalism and democracy in the US form an organic whole to such an extent that we do not even see the two as being distilled from different traditions and history. Reference to democracy in the Western world is a reference to the two ideas.

The history of the Western political system shows that the guarantee of human rights and rule of law (political liberalism) has sometimes preceded democracy. Put another way, democracy as a desirable form of government was taken seriously by political thinkers when it was connected to the framework of political liberalism. Liberalism regarded as rule by law is clearly present in the rule of enlightened despots such as Catherine the Great and Peter the Great of Russia, Emperor Franz Josef of Austria, Frederick the Great of Prussia, and Napoleon Bonaparte of France. Though there was rule of law, people were not given equal participatory rights. The system of government was "liberal autocracy" (see Zakaria 1997). In African states, by contrast, "democracy" is what there is. Since the fall of the Soviet Union, Africans have been participating (even if imperfectly) in elections more than ever before. Leaders are voted into offices. The principle of democratic legitimacy is fulfilled in virtue of the people's vote. But, what we end up with in African states are "illiberal democracies" (ibid.). The democratic conditions of legitimacy are fulfilled symbolically, formally, or superficially, but not the liberal conditions – conditions in which the governors are held accountable for their actions and behavior by the governed. Of course, this condition requires that democratic processes and arrangements must be carried on in ways that citizens can freely consent to. It is easier to fulfill the democratic than the liberal condition of legitimacy. Nowadays, television cameras can capture people in the process of voting. But what is difficult to capture on camera is the rule of law, the guarantee of equal opportunities and protection of similarly situated people so that they can pursue their happiness as they see fit. What we have in mind here, in short, is the existence and valorization of freedom, toleration, and equality.

I should explain what I mean by valorization. A state of affairs is valorized when it is enforced and taught in school as part of our overarching culture, and when it serves as a normative foundation for our institutions. For example, freedom is valorized in the United States. It is written into the Constitution, it is commemorated by the Statue of Liberty, people are willing to fight and die to defend it, and so forth. Rehearsing the history of liberal democracy can help us in many ways to understand the political pathologies in which African states wallow. Elections in Africa can mean nothing more than a symbolic gesture on the part of the governors as well as the governed. A well-connected liberal democratic state requires elections, deliberation, and much more. It requires holding public officials accountable for their actions and behavior.

Because liberal democratic governance is not a genetic endowment, people have to be taught how to conduct their lives within a liberal democracy. Part of the preparation for citizenship happens outside of the state, be it in families or in associations with other citizens. A legitimate liberal democratic government requires in its citizens trust, a sense of cohesion and solidarity, virtues such as reciprocity, accountability, and the inclination to actively participate in a system of civic pedagogy. Next, I will examine the vital African tradition of voluntary social organizations – or what are more appropriately called fellowship associations – as a legitimate avenue for cultivating and preparing a citizenry for well-connected liberal democracy for Africa. I will demonstrate that some of the organizations contain necessary tendencies for good government. I also show that they are the viable paedeia for liberal democratic governance.

Social Organizations: Definition and Taxonomy

Fellowship associations are part of a civil society. By civil society, I mean non-state administered and (even) non-state-regulated organizations.[4] Civil society can be distinguished from state-regulated and administered organizations like political parties and the US Peace Corps. Fellowship associations are formed and reside outside state apparatuses. People are held together in these organizations by an intrinsic shared pleasure of socialization. According to Michael Walzer:

> The picture here (civil society) is of people freely associating and communicating with one another, forming and reforming groups of all sorts, not for the sake of any particular formation . . . but for the sake of sociability itself. For we are by nature social before we are political or economic beings. (1995: 160–1)

Membership in such organizations is voluntary. However, a member can be forced to exit if he or she behaves in a manner that is deemed to be unacceptable. There is a horizontal base, as members are social equals. Local social organizations are prevalent and ubiquitous; they come in various types. There are the save-and-thrift, self-help, and rotating credit organizations. According to Robert Putnam:

> Rotating credit associations have been reported from Nigeria to Scotland, from Peru to Vietnam, from Japan to Egypt, from Indian immigrants in the eastern United States to Chicanos in the West, from illiterate Chinese villagers to bank managers and economic forecasters in Mexico City. Many U.S. Savings and Loans began life as rotating credit associations. (1993: 167)

An adult in a typical African traditional setting may belong to as many as five or more of these fellowship associations, and members form tightly woven networks of socialization. In indigenous African political systems, these associations occupy a large space and the state so small a space that at times one wonders if the indigenous states can be regarded as states in the contemporary sense of that word. The indigenous states are various. I will describe an indigenous state in Nso, a Fondom (approximately translated as Kingdom) in the North-West Province of Cameroon. Describing a Fondom could help my analysis in two ways. First, it can deepen our understanding of the wider customs that support fellowship associations and, second, it can demonstrate how local fellowship associations can further function as external agents of restraint and constraint on indigenous political power.

453

The complexities of Nso's (let alone Africa's) cultures could be detailed ad infinitum; however, a description of the overriding concept of *chu* in Nso society provides adequate cultural understanding for the purposes of this chapter. *Chu* comprises many principles that add up to a principle greater than the sum of its constituent parts. No comparable concept exists in Western culture – and thus no word or phrase in the English language fully captures its meaning. There is something like it in Chinese philosophy called "Li" (see Mote 1989). *Chu* is reverence, calm, assurance, patience, justice, reconciliation (or more precisely *ntangri*), impartiality, morality, courage, and passion. *Chu* tempers the power of leaders. It compels, persuades, and moves people without violence. *Chu* achieves harmony. *Chu* is embodied through rituals, symbols, and ceremonies conducted by the Fon and Yaa (male and female leaders of the Fondom), and Taawong and Yeewong – the chief priest and priestess (non-political roles). For example, *chu* allows for the criticism of the political system through a variety of institutionalized – yet flexible – means. Such criticism pacifies the people and enables an equanimous maintenance of the social structure. As Martin Luther King wrote: "A riot is at bottom the language of the unheard" (1967). *Chu*'s protest rites let the citizens voice their discontents – in a culturally relevant manner – to a listening government. These rites include, among many other things, the presentation of protest songs – which can be directly sung to government officials or even to the Fon or Yaa – and the performance of a comical, polyglot clown who dramatizes citizens' grievances, with the aid of an interpreter, to assembled political administrators. Also integral to *chu* is the reverential evocation of ancestors and the recognition of temporal infinitude. Veneration for the past entails thoughtfulness about one's actions in the present and consideration for the future.

Fellowship Associations as Paedeia for a Viable Liberal Democracy

Kwame Anthony Appiah writes:

> [I]f the state is ever to reverse recent history and expand the role it plays in the lives of its subjects, it will have to learn something about the surprising persistence of these "pre-modern" affiliations [what I call fellowship associations], the cultural and political fretwork of relations through which our very identity is conferred. (1992: 171)

The firm continuation of the multitude of fellowship associations in Africa despite modernization through exposure to the wider world, and the threat of eradication by contemporary governments warrant further examination. A categorization and description of Nso's fellowship associations follow. Their contents, functions, and methods can be considered, *mutatis mutandis*, similar to others in Cameroon and throughout Africa. In an attempt to give shape to the tapestry of associations I grew up with, I classify the Nso social organizations according to their membership initiations. Membership initiation can be classified as ascriptive, voluntary, or invited.

454

Birth or "adoption" into one of the families belonging to organizations in the ascriptive category grants immediate "potential" membership. Within each ascriptive organization (as many as seven), smaller organizations may exist. Prominent among the ascriptive social organizations are the Nwerong and Ngiri regulatory societies centrally located in Nso's palace. Membership in the Nwerong and Ngiri excludes women, but every adult male is a potential member. The Chong and La-lir ascriptive societies, also located in the palace, admit only women. Nwerong, Ngiri, Chong, and La-lir are not only private social organizations, but also a defining part of the indigenous polity. A group of long-deceased Nso residents, who believed that the Fon and Yaa should also be regulated, are credited with forming these societies, in particular the political wing of the Nwerong.[5] The Fon and Yaa may lead Nso; but the Nwerong regulatory society makes certain that they do not lead alone. The Ngiri societies, founded by families seeking an alternative to the Nwerong, are viewed as highly social. Ngiri entertainment, like that of the Nwerong, Chong, and La-lir, is performed for the public at large.

Any male member of the Fondom expressing an interest in the appropriate association is eventually invited to join within the "invited" category (minor restrictions may at times apply). Significant among such associations, and, as further testimony to the overlapping of voluntary organizations and the indigenous state, are the Manjong organizations or "warrior" social organizations. Core membership is confined to men (which is more than a minor restriction). Once a male youth proves himself to be mature by the standard of the elder members – he must be composed, courageous, alert, patient, etc. – he is invited to join. Proud to be recognized, a young man invariably accepts.

Voluntary membership of social organizations – as the name implies – means that entry is potentially open to all. In Cameroon as in many African countries, these organizations are widespread. They are termed *njangis*. *Njangis* have no hierarchy; they are horizontally structured. Affairs are managed democratically in a face-to-face manner using consensus.[6] The affairs of the *njangi* are conducted – as it is expressed in Nso – in "the fullest daylight"; that is, all processes are revealed, all are transparent. Any information pertaining to the *njangi*, including members' financial contributions, is announced or readily available to the interested. *Njangis* are further categorized into mutual aid, save-and-thrift, and rotating credit societies. (In Nso, they are referred to as *a-ngwah*: *ngwah* loosely translates as "contract"; *a* indicates plurality.) Mutual aid societies (the name is self-evident) are integral to a healthy Cameroonian society.

As a rule, the aforementioned societies, ascriptive, voluntary, and invited, variously encourage members to develop characteristics which coincide with the preconditions for a successful liberal democracy: individual autonomy and group cohesion, autarky, consensus through thoughtful deliberation and debate, honesty, tolerance, mutual respect, and organized, enthusiastic participation. Putnam describes the growth of another all-important value – trust: "Social networks allow trust to become transitive and spread: I trust you because I trust her and she assures me that she trusts you" (1993: 167).

In Nso as well as elsewhere in Africa the fabric of voluntary organizations is the foundation of morality. The basis of morality in most of Africa is humanistic. That means that ultimate moral values derive from humans, and human fellowship is to be preferred to all other.[7] Our moral understanding of the world is the last defense line we have in the humanly constructed world of liberal democratic politics.

Furthermore, the question of what we ought to do when interests, preferences, or conceptions of the good come into conflict is answered by the venerable African tradition of consensus at the nerve center of the fellowship associations. In this tradition of the adjustment of interests in pursuit of the common good, no one is left out. Discussion is open. This tradition of consensus, a tradition derived from the lineage ordering of human relations in traditional society, is prevalent in the fellowship associations.

When interests clash – and they often do – deliberation takes over until the voices of all have received a hearing and a reconciliation of interests has led to a consensus. Those from the West who are used to party politics – a gladiatorial system – may find this hard to imagine when the number of people involved is large. Any system requires familiarity as well as efficiency. This tradition of consensus is as efficient as, if not more efficient than, the non-consensual system, everything considered. Fellowship associations are like schools for consensus.

These fellowship associations are held together by aesthetic activities. These may include dances, music, and singing. Inconspicuously (even unconsciously) interwoven into the day's (and night's) fun are civic lessons, lessons that teach members of the community how to live peaceably and profitably with one another. Future liberal democracies must realize the inextricable import of these fellowship associations in African society so as to benefit from their ability to instruct people unobtrusively in principles that are important for the liberal democratic form of polity.

Local Fellowship Associations and Liberal Democracy

A well-ordered liberal democracy must be anchored in civic education. Civic pedagogy trains citizens to conduct their lives effectively within and in support of their polity. This education is particularly crucial because a liberal democratic state must foster in its citizenry character dispositions that allow them to be tolerant, self-governing, and both self-respecting and respectful of others. It also enhances the desire to participate effectively in democratic deliberation and to hold their public officials accountable for their actions and behavior. Such a demanding civic pedagogy goes far beyond the walls of a school classroom. Part – I am tempted to say most – of the character education for future full members of a liberal democracy takes place within family and social settings. In Africa, local fellowship associations should be valued as paedeia to build civic virtue, encourage cooperation, and foster trust, as well as promote political participation at the grassroots level. Such associations have been valued in America for the same reasons. My example of a typical local *Njangi* in Cameroon demonstrates certain virtues and values that a well-connected liberal democratic arrangement must possess. *Njangi* members are considered social equals irrespective of their economic, social, and political standing

456

outside of the social organizational setting. Power in local voluntary social organizations is isocratic. As such, the associations are spheres in which these social equals engage each other in free and open deliberations about matters of common interest. There, members learn to deliberate effectively and to arrive at a consensus. What is important to note is that these tendencies can be efficiently carried over to liberal democratic politics. Furthermore, trust is developed in these local associations. Almost all the fellowship associations involve some form of pecuniary dealings. Rotating credits are prominent. As I have said, the associations live their lives outside the state's coercive apparatuses. The rotating credit associations depend on the trust of their members to reciprocate in their financial dealings. As Putnam puts it, trust becomes transitive. Since members in these associations belong to more than one association, they are tied together via a dense network of trust which, more often than not, is multiethnic and crosses class lines. Stories about good people in one part of the country can be heard in other parts via these social networks. Furthermore, the organization is tied to familial relations at the grassroot level.

Following on the heels of trust is the ability of members to hold their elective officials and representatives accountable. This ability is contingent upon the open procedures of the associations as well as the well-known indices of duties and obligations of the elected officials available to everyone. Appiah speaks to the true meaning of duty in these organizations:

> In many of these organizations – whether it be sport club or an *association des origi-naires* or the Asante Kotoko Society – there is a remarkable degree of formality: Elections, rules of procedure (in the Anglophone world, sometimes even the Robert's Rules), and a considerable concern with the responsibility of leaders – those who manage the organization's day-to-day life and, in particular, its finances; a concern with constitutions and procedure is a key feature. (1992: 170–1)

In addition to deliberative discourse, there is an informal participation in the voluntary activities of the members, such as giving one another a helping hand in farming. This takes place when, for example, a member is ill or on maternity leave. A sense of cohesion and cooperation is a prime feature of the organizations in question.

At the local level voluntary social organizations are sources of constraint and restraint on the discretionary use of power by the indigenous political officials. That is, the network of local voluntary associations is like a panopticon insuring that indigenous governors act fairly, that is, according to the prescribed customs and the interests of the general public.

A Well-Connected Liberal Democracy with a Base at the Local Level

The first step on the road to a legitimate liberal democracy is to decentralize as many state functions as possible and reinsert them at the local level. There are at least two reasons for this. One is that the local level in Africa is made up (as I have shown) of a dense network of fellowship associations. There, responsibility, reciprocity, and accountability are more in evidence than restraints and constraints. Second, legitimate politics in Africa is largely a local affair. People are moved to participate on matters that are closest to them.

Active participation is a sine qua non of a liberal democracy. The commonest danger to good government lies not in wars from other states, nor in economic poverty, but in a citizenry that has exiled itself from active participation in politics. A sedentary citizenry is always the death of a liberal democracy.

In conclusion, I want to point out that a well-connected liberal democracy at the local level – that is, one that builds on the rock-solid traditions of voluntary social organization in Africa – is more likely to be legitimate, stable, and prosperous. I contend that people are often willing to die for principles they believe they created themselves. What I have tried to demonstrate is that it is not only possible but also legitimate to build a liberal democracy in Africa on grassroot resources that have liberal democratic impulses. If there are some with contrary impulses, I would hope that something radical could be done to bring them in line with good government.

A well-connected local liberal democracy is bound to have reverberations at the level of central government. According to Mill: "To recommend and advocate a particular institution or form of government, and set its advantages in the strongest light, is one of the modes, often the only mode within reach, of educating the minds of the nation not only for accepting or claiming, but also for working, the institution." The state can gain the trust of the people by connecting with civil society and thereby, among other things, demonstrating its accountability. Once the state is accountable to the people, the distance between them and the government would shrink to nothing and the national praise singer can sing, truly, "the government is the people and the people are the government."

Notes

1 In the North-West Province of Cameroon, the Fon is a leader of a group of people who live in a Fondom. Fon does not translate well into English but the English equivalent of Fon is king and Fondom is kingdom. I prefer to talk of Fondoms rather than ethnic groups when talking about groups of people in the North-West Province of Cameroon, because under a Fondom may be groups of people who may or may not share a language, ethnicity, familial ties – in short they may share nothing in common apart from the political culture inherent in a Fondom.

2 Our societies' inhabitants are culturally, ethnically, religiously, and economically diverse. The countries of Africa (excluding Lesotho, Somalia, and Swaziland whose nation-states correspond to precolonial monolingual societies) were indiscriminately demarcated at the Berlin Colonial Conference and are consequently composed of multiple groups speaking different languages. Cameroonians alone speak more than 200 languages. Most countries are multicultural, multiethnic, even multiracial (e.g., Zimbabwe, Kenya, and South Africa).

3 I must hasten to add that Mansbridge's conception of democracy goes far beyond the symbolic gestures in elections, etc. Hers is a much deeper conception than meets the eye. See Mansbridge 1980.

4   For difficulties in pinning down what a civil society means, see Schmidt 1998.
5   According to conversation with my uncle, now a family head with a title of Shu-Fai, one of the titles that is bestowed on family leaders. A family with a titled member may number anywhere from 100 members and above.
6   For details on face-to-face democracy ("Unitary Democracy"), see Mansbridge 1980.
7   For details, see Wiredu 1992.

References

Appiah, Kwame Anthony (1992) *In my Father's House* (Oxford: Oxford University Press).

Kimenyi, Mwangi S. (1998) *Ethnic Diversity, Liberty and State: The African Dilemma* (Northampton: Edward Elgar).

King, Martin Luther (1967) "Where Do We Go From Here?" in James Melvin Washington (ed.), *A Testament of Hope: The Essential Writings and Speeches of Martin Luther King Jr.* (San Francisco: Harper and Row)

Mansbridge, Jane (1980) *Beyond Adversary Democracy* (Chicago: Chicago University Press).

Mote, Frederick (1989) *Intellectual Foundations of China*, 2nd edn. (New York: McGraw Hill, Inc.).

Orwell, George (1968) *In Front of our Nose, 1945–1950: The Collected Essays, Journalism and Letters of George Orwell*, vol. 4 (New York: Harper and Row).

Putnam, Robert D., Leonardi, Robert, and Nanetti, Raffaella Y. (1993) *Making Democracy Work* (Princeton: Princeton University Press).

Schmidt, James (1998) "Civility, Enlightenment, and Society: Conceptual Confusion and Kantian Remedies," *American Political Science Review*, 92(2): 419–27.

Walzer, Michael (1995) "The Civil Society Argument," in Ronald Beiner (ed.), *Theorizing Citizenship* (New York: SUNY Press).

Wiredu, Kwasi (1992) "Moral Foundations of an African Culture," in Kwasi Wiredu and Kwame Gyekye (eds.), *Person and Community: Ghanaian Philosophical Studies*, I (Washington, DC: The Council for Research in Values and Philosophy).

Zakaria, Fareed (1997) "The Rise of Illiberal Democracy," *Foreign Affairs*, 76(6): 22–43.

38

Economic Globalism, Deliberative Democracy, and the State in Africa

GEORGE CAREW

Introduction

The dominant economic system in the world today is the capitalist economic system.[1] An economic system, broadly defined, is a particular pattern of behavior, a certain ordering of relationships among people and the institutions they create to meet the material needs of their society. An economic system is capitalist if it provides the following answer to the question: "How are we to organize ourselves to create and distribute what we need in order to live?" The answer is that a free market determines what people should create and the rewards or benefits they should receive. The word "free" implies that there will not be social and political pressures constraining how a capitalist operates. A global free market, then, is a market that functions according to the basic principles of supply and demand.[2]

From the foregoing perspective, it is argued that a free-market setting offers the best chance for democratic reforms and economic development. However, in practice global capitalism actually undermines democratic reforms and sustainability, because in its working out it limits the state's ability to be democratically accountable. The situation is particularly critical in states that exist at the margins of the capitalist global system.[3] Since such states have been rendered obsolete by economic globalism, can they really be expected to carry the burden of democratizing their respective polities?[4]

The broad purpose of this chapter is to explore the possibility of an alternative approach to the question of economic globalism and democratic transition and consolidation, one that would avoid the trap that capitalist democracy has created but seems unable to overcome. In particular, I shall focus on African states for the simple reason that they provide an excellent example of failed policies designed by defenders of economic globalism. Another reason why African states have been chosen for this analysis is that they are currently facing profound political and economic crises and are, or ought to be, looking for a way out that focuses not only on the domestic nature of their problems but also on their interconnectedness with global politics and economics. To all intents and purposes, that global system is one that has marginalized and "recolonized" the African polities.[5]

I defend the claim that deliberative democracy[6] is a suitable replacement for capitalist democracy. To make this case, I begin by showing that it is global capitalism not democracy that is in crisis. Then I show how deliberative politics is the best way to resolve the tension between global capitalism and national democracy. Finally, I apply this theory to the postcolonial African state. I begin with a brief statement of the problem.

An Analysis of the Problem

In a global context characterized by both economic inequality and a hegemonic hierarchy, the promise of democracy will likely remain an elusive goal for dependent states, such as those of Africa, because they occupy the margins of economic globalism.[7] As a nation-state, the African state is ostensibly an embodiment of its people's will and the sole representative of its interests in the interstate system. In fact, this involves a contradiction.[8] There is, on the one hand, the supposition that the African state is like the other sovereign states in the interstate system. But, on the other hand, there is at least the implicit understanding that dependent states are, by their very nature, incapable of providing the kind of leadership necessary for democratic change. It is obvious that these two views pull in opposite directions.

The point of this inquiry is to show how wrong capitalist democrats have been in believing that the democratic control of the global economy is neither desirable nor useful for the promotion and sustainability of democracy. Despite the steady decline of third world economies under the strict supervision of the World Bank and the International Monetary Fund (IMF), these capitalist institutions have yet to admit that their policies have not worked.[9] The nation-states of Africa are weaker today than at any other time since independence. By 1992, Africa's external debt had reached $290 billion, about 2.5 times greater than it was in 1980.[10] The record of the IMF/World Bank is equally grim in Latin America and Asian debtor countries. The net transfer of resources from the poor countries to service their external debts to the rich countries totaled $155 billion between 1984 and 1990. Susan George, a writer and civil society activist, expresses the view of the third world when she says that the economic policies of the IMF and the fund on debtor countries "have cured nothing at all. They have, rather, caused untold human suffering and widespread environmental destruction, emptying debtor countries of their resources and rendering them less able each year to service their debts, let alone invest in economic and human recovery" (1994: 30).

This is the prevailing sentiment in the poor states of the North/South divide. If true, the southern states have not been empowered through the economic policies of the IMF, as has been presumed. Far from being empowered, the marginal states have been rendered obsolete through policies that, in effect, have bypassed the state, compelling its citizens to adhere to programs no rich country dare impose on its people.[11]

Global capitalism has actually assigned fixed social positions to marginal states, and there is little those states can do on their own to improve their condition. This creates a dilemma for the African state. How can the African state democratize within a global context that undermines the very political conditions for democratic

461

transition? Once the policies of economic globalism render the state ungovernable, there can be little hope for any meaningful democratic reform. The critical issue at this point is: "How can we resolve this dilemma?" Will those people who take democracy seriously and are concerned to resolve the tension between global capitalism and democracy be willing to follow the path that leads to a solution?

I shall argue that the kind of democracy that has the potential to resolve capitalist democracy's dilemma is what has generally been referred to as deliberative or discursive democracy, and that only a democratic control of the global economy can ensure that the market remains free of the kind of influences that privilege some nations and their people at the expense of other nations. The real challenge, then, for political economy in the twenty-first century is not whether capitalist democracy will promote democratic freedoms and development, because it will not; but, rather, whether the threat posed by world capitalist domination and the obsolescence of the dependent states that it generates might be remedied in ways that would enhance global democratic freedom and economic development. In particular, what does this say about the chances of success in the negotiation of democratic transition in weak and dependent states? Can people in weak and dependent states change the quality of their lives by uprooting the global social hierarchy within the capitalist democratic process?[12] I shall pursue these and other issues in what follows. But, first, a brief description of deliberative democracy.

What is Deliberative Democracy?

There are various versions of deliberative democracy; however, there is a common thread that pulls all these different conceptions together. I shall describe the set of issues that define the common thread as the ideals of rational legislation, participatory politics, and civic governance.[13]

The ideal of rational deliberation is a crucial part of the meaning of deliberative democracy. It means that free and reasoned agreement among equals is necessary for democratic decision-making. The emphasis here on the connection between dialogue and political decision-making is not to be treated lightly. I offer the following three reasons why dialogue is vital for a deliberative conception of democracy:

1 It is a way of promoting common understanding and a shared sense of purpose.
2 It is also a means for clarifying issues and expanding social knowledge.
3 It is, more importantly, a way of safeguarding our cherished values of freedom and equality, thereby ensuring social justice in the polity.

The next ideal, the ideal of participation, amplifies further why rational dialogue is so important. The point to note about participation is that it makes possible not only the airing of all views, but also the acknowledging, in deliberative democracy, of the historical and concrete particularity of the diverse perspectives represented. This innovative approach to dialogue seeks to ensure that no voice is silenced or group excluded from the political process.

462

The third ideal, the ideal of civic governance, builds on the foregoing ideals and grounds political decision-making in the normative democratic principles of equality and freedom. This is the background context that is so indispensable to the creation of civic awareness in the polity. In short, the moralization of social relations is the crucial innovative quality that deliberative dialogue brings to bear on democratic decision-making.

Although the deliberative approach is a recent innovation in politics and certainly not without its own problems,[14] it is nonetheless a useful corrective to pure democratic proceduralism, which is incapable of guaranteeing a democratic outcome that might be described as just.[15] Thus, it is an important supplement to liberal democratic proceduralism. The question we must ask then is how and in what way is this to be accomplished? This brings us to a consideration of its method, which begins with civil society rather than the state as its starting point.

Civil Society and Deliberative Politics

The brief account of deliberative politics is a useful starting point in my defense of an alternative to state-led democratic reforms within the context of global capitalism. As I have argued, the internal logic of global capitalism renders the marginal state incapable of administering democratic reforms. That is to say, the very structure of global capitalism makes the state an unsuitable agent for democratic change. So, an alternative strategy that will bring about democratic reform by circumventing the state is required. Following John Dryzek, I will argue that we can derive the tools and resources necessary for challenging the global capitalist status quo from civil society. However, I shall take this argument one step further than Dryzek to show that the democratization of civil society along deliberative lines should be viewed not only as an alternative approach but also as a strategy in the pursuit of transformative politics. Indeed, it is only through transformative politics, I shall argue, that the institutions of global capitalism can be replaced with democratic ones. I shall then show how and in what way a transformed global democracy might provide an indispensable support for democratic transitions and sustainability in African states.

But what is transformative politics and how is it different, if at all, from deliberative politics? Deliberative politics, as I have argued, emphasizes dialogue and mutual consideration and respect as the base on which citizens can come to an understanding about the public good. Thus the practice of this form of politics would presuppose that transformation in a way has occurred in such attitudes as are envisaged by, say, liberal egoists, who hold that politics is only about self-interest and the market. But how exactly might such a transformation occur? What crucial move or moves could lead to the moralization of social relations? Theorizing this overlap is clearly the concern of transformative theory.[16] This requires a full-length essay by itself and ought not to detain us here. However, that which is certainly worth noting here is how a focus on the transformative process within deliberative politics might lead us to innovative institutional designs that can embody deliberative principles.

463

From this perspective, one is inclined to view the starting point in civil society as an opportunity to inject a spirit of solidarity and civic consciousness in not only the national but also the international community. Empirically minded theorists like John Dryzek[17] have argued that there is some solidarity among national and international non-governmental organizations (NGOs). Dryzek in particular advocates greater coordination among these groups to oppose the hegemonic drive of global capitalism. He did not, however, move his vision in the direction of institutional replacement as evidenced in his rejection of David Held's cosmopolitan design (see Held 1992). Held's bold proposal included democratic reforms to ensure democratic control over both global politics and the economy. Also, under Held's plan, international civil society would have a greater role than hitherto in the lives of the different peoples of the world. Under this dispensation, regional and national assemblies and the UN special agencies as well as the World Court will all be energized to validate substantive claims to human rights and human well-being.

In sum, one may agree with both Dryzek and Held albeit for different reasons. Dryzek is right to de-emphasize the state as the starting point for democratic reforms, but he failed to address the institutional questions which would have made sense of Held's effort. Held, for his part, was correct to anticipate the democratization of the state, but failed to show that this may come about through civil society, not the state, as the starting point in building a global civic community that is free of the domination of a market-oriented mind-set. In other words, Held's institutional innovation would succeed only if it was already grounded in a global deliberative political culture.

In the next section, I shall suggest deliberative democracy as an alternative solution to the current political and economic crises in contemporary African states.

The African State and Deliberative Democracy

The unraveling of the postcolonial state is a crisis the framers of constitutional decolonization did not anticipate. From their perspective, the postcolonial state had taken its place among the family of equal sovereign states and should discharge its obligations as a sovereign nation by simply adhering to the rules. That is to say, like the other states in the global economy, the postcolonial state was expected to promote a market economy. Yet in many respects, the postcolonial state was not like the metropolitan states it was modeled after. Internally, it was fragmented along ethnic and cultural lines, and externally it occupied a subordinate and dependent status in the global capitalist hierarchy (see Young 1994: ch. 9). All of these factors clearly escaped the narrow gaze of the decolonization mission.

As a result of this colonial presumption, democratic theorists focused exclusively on internal issues that were deemed to have produced the crisis in good governance. The role of external factors in this crisis consequently was underestimated and in some cases misrepresented. My aim is to correct this imbalance by refocusing on the role of external factors in shaping the crisis of governance and democracy in the African states. Then I shall show how a different global context could have produced quite different results.

After the second wave of unsuccessful attempts to democratize politics in Africa in the 1980s, the Western powers now openly acknowledged the precarious nature of the debt-ridden African state on the world stage.[18] But, encouraged by the collapse of communism in the Soviet Union and Eastern Europe, the international lending institutions, at the behest of the Western powers, took the bold step of linking democratic reforms to a market economy.

In other words, a market economy was now being viewed as a necessary condition for democratic transition in the successor states to colonialism. The IMF and the World Bank therefore devised strategies known as Structural Adjustment Programs (SAPs) ostensibly to assist those debt-ridden countries to improve their economic performance and hence create a politically friendly climate for democratic transition. SAPs basically consisted of the promotion of an export-oriented economy; the resort to devaluation to curb domestic inflation; and the removal of government subsidies and price controls on imported commodities.

Despite such innovations, the third wave of attempted democratic transition in Africa has also been declared a failure. So what went wrong this time? I think the problem can be formulated in this way: while the fiscal measures imposed on African states were generally sound monetarist policies, the conditions of their implementation have intrigued critics. As one critic, Davison Budhoo, expressed it:

> Removal of price controls domestically leads to sudden increases in the prices of commodities used by the poor. Big increases in interest rates cause bankruptcies in domestically owned small businesses and further unemployment. Removal almost overnight of trade restrictions throws domestic industries into disarray and liquidation and compounds unemployment. Dismantling foreign exchange restrictions allows the elite classes to export funds overseas, carte blanche, as capital flight, thus worsening the balance of payments. (1994: 21)

Budhoo's analysis is clear and useful. It explains why the seeds of democracy cannot be sown under the stringent conditionalities of the IMF and the World Bank. Monetarist policies and democratic and other reforms were being attempted simultaneously. But, in fact, these processes turned out to be not complementary but, rather, conflicting. The economic programs created grave instabilities that led to coups or military takeovers, despite the intended strengthening of democratic institutions.[19] Political unrest created by massive layoffs in the private and public sectors was too high a price to pay for democracy. How was it to be explained to a household of several sub-family units that the few breadwinners in the household should be laid off as part of an IMF-inspired downsizing of government bureaucracy? It is clear that SAP measures have had the effect of punishing the vulnerable and undermining the state. Because the states were powerless to alleviate the suffering of the masses, they became victims of the very policies that were meant to empower them.

The situation thus makes it necessary to rethink the African state within the context of a global system other than that of capitalist democracy. In order to clarify the issues we must address, it will be useful to state at this point what is at stake, especially with regard to the prospect for democratic transition. It is clear, from our earlier arguments, that there is an unresolved tension between democratic and market reforms. Assuming that both may be necessary for a robust democracy, how and in what way must we conceptualize their relation so that democratic reform connects with economic reform?

I shall address this question by focusing on how an alternative to capitalist democracy might respond to some of the implications of capitalism. The following are two such implications. (1) In its conception, the current interstate system implies that any interstate redistributive scheme will undermine a nation's sovereignty. (2) The structure of the United Nations has marginalized and rendered voiceless the weak and vulnerable states of the world. Simultaneously, the present policies of international lending institutions have turned out to be oppressive and geared mainly to profit making for the already rich countries.

The reason why any interstate redistributive scheme would, from the standpoint of capitalist democracy, be thought to undermine the ideal of national sovereignty is that trade between nations is presumed to be free and open to competition, so that any nation gets what it deserves. On this view, therefore, it would be unfair to require some nations to give some of what they have legitimately earned to others in the interstate system. States may give charity or offer aid to others, but they are under no obligation to share their wealth with poor states.

This argument, however, is valid in what it states but unsound in what it implies. Trade in a global system of capitalist domination is certainly not free. The presumption of sovereign equality in the interstate system is the basis of the belief that each state is solely responsible for the well-being of its citizens. Yet, given the substantive inequality between states, it is inevitable that some states will lose out in the competition for resources. Sovereign equality, it seems, is a myth and not a reality.

What are some of the consequences if sovereign equality is a myth? One possible consequence is that it raises the issue of the need for a mechanism of global intervention to regulate interstate relations in order to secure the autonomy of states. In an interstate system in which the gap between the rich and the poor has widened rather than narrowed, dependent states face the grim prospect of extinction without some such global intervention. There are factors, however, that might seem to make this problematic. Since autonomy is central to the conception of democracy, the implication seems to be that such global intervention might take away from the poorer states whatever is left of their autonomy after the abrogation of sovereign equality through unequal and unfair competition. The state, whether rich or poor, it might be argued, still has the right to conceive and act on its plans and interests. The poor state, in particular, expects to exercise that right to initiate actions that might lead, however modestly, to the alleviation of poverty. Thus, some states stand to lose their autonomy if the idea of global intervention should prevail. In any case, if a state is regulated from the outside it is denied not only the right to choose for itself but also the right to the ownership of rewards and benefits that are directly linked to its activities and decisions.

To put this problem in a nutshell, the question at issue here is not simply about the aims of global intervention, because it is laudable to ensure the survival of the poor. The problem, rather, is whether it is in the best interest of democracy to bypass the state for any reason whatsoever. If one takes this line of reasoning

466

seriously, it privileges autonomy over everything else. The clash between global intervention and sovereign autonomy at this point appears unresolvable.

Yet, the deplorable fact of global poverty is instructive with regard to the absence of autonomy in the poor and dependent states. A defense of autonomy in the face of powerlessness and oppression merely serves to obscure rather than illuminate the core issue, which is about the empowerment of dependent states in the interstate system.

Is there another way of looking at the problem of state empowerment in the context of a global intervention that does not give rise to the tension noted above? The misrepresentation of this possibility by capitalists, who are apt to portray the "developed" states as the future of the "underdeveloped" or "developing" states, is an attempt to conceal the hegemonic hierarchy underlying the current interstate system and its moral implications. The possibility of an alternative approach to the philosophical and moral issues of globalism, conceived on the model of capitalist democracy, lies, I suggest, in the idea of deliberative democracy.

From the perspective of deliberative democracy, the fundamental mistake of capitalist democracy lies in the way the problem is conceptualized. Sovereign autonomy and global intervention are opposing principles *within* capitalist democracy because of the manifest need to protect the independence of states against authoritarian or totalitarian corrosion. But, as I have argued, these principles need not be in conflict, because, according to the deliberative formulation of the problem, the two principles are in fact complementary. The crucial factor here is the democratization of the decision-making process at all levels, including the global. In this way, limitations on state sovereignty should make the state not vulnerable but responsible. A responsible use of the state's autonomy to protect the interests not of a few but of all its citizens is what a deliberative global democracy will guarantee. This analysis, despite its endorsement of limited sovereignty, empowers each state and the global community to face the political and moral challenges of our times.[20]

Given a commitment to global democracy, the claim that the resources of the world belong to everyone is plausible. This means that the attempt by a few to monopolize the world's resources is clearly not justified. It follows that the responsibility for the negative consequences of exploitative policies would be undeniably theirs. This represents a moral breakthrough because the new democratic world order may now be justified to expect the dominant states to cooperate in the removal of structures of domination as a precondition for free trade.

In the case of Africa, therefore, her right to an equitable share of resources may be only the first step in seeking redress for harm caused by a capitalist world order. Subsequent moves will require not only redistribution of resources but also reparations to correct the injustices of a previous world order. This might take many forms, including, for example, debt cancellation, and other forms of assistance aimed primarily not at poverty alleviation, as they now are, but its eradication.

At present, the UN system can hardly be characterized as democratic. It combines two contradictory principles, namely, the principle of equal sovereign states and the principle of differential rights for superpowers. The latter principle implies a form of global social hierarchy. The implication is that the interests of superpowers must never be sacrificed for democracy in the event of a clash. To illustrate this point: at a gathering in the late 1990s of world leaders at the UN to articulate a vision for the new millennium, the summit was noted more for its silences than for its accomplishments. There were clearly two narratives. The dominant story spoke of an age of prosperity unknown in the annals of human history, a prosperity that was driven, no doubt, by a capitalist world-view. The other narrative spoke of misery, war, disease, and utter despair going into the millennium. The gap between the narratives is practically unbridgeable within the global status quo. The media, one of the instruments of domination, in characteristic fashion ignored the voices of the poor and powerless. In the end, it was only the "voices" of the rich and powerful states that were heard.

The creation of a democratic global system of decision-making would put an end to the unfair and unjust process. In such a system, African states, like all other states, will participate in the decision-making that will directly affect their citizens. It is unlikely therefore that they would agree to policies harmful to their citizens. The devolution of power recommended by Held's cosmopolitan order would guarantee that regional and continental parliaments would exercise real but responsible authority over individual states, including those in Africa. Also, the present institutions which direct the activities of the world market (the IMF, WTO, and the World Bank) will need to be reinvented or, perhaps, replaced to reflect the deliberative ideal.

In sum, the present difficulties in the capitalist interstate system suggest that it might not be able to prepare the way for democratic transition in the postcolonial states of Africa. To rectify this situation, global deliberative politics requires the elimination of all structures of oppression and domination, in order that the democratic principles of equal freedom can be embraced by all. A deliberative international community will acknowledge the primary function of African governments, as of all governments, in the ordering of society. Law and government should embody deliberative principles. And citizens have a duty to abide by laws that are duly adopted by orderly and just processes of government. But in the deliberative system citizens have a right to appeal beyond the state, if they deem the actions of their governments unjust. Individuals and groups must feel secure in their right to live within an orderly society. This is only possible where there are international efforts to develop a more just international order in which the limited resources of the earth will be used to the maximum benefit of all peoples and nations.

Notes

1 The ascendancy of a single global market system has been made possible by the collapse of the Soviet Union and the East European communist nations. China also is on its way to creating a market-based economy.
2 This claim is an expression of the capitalist ideal. But, as the evidence suggests, no self-respecting liberal theorists would claim that social and cultural factors have no bearing on economic activities. Modern capitalist democracies, recognizing that social and cultural factors are implicated in economic processes, have applied constraints to limit their influence. At the international level, the GATT and WTO are, in fact, examples of a design, albeit woefully inadequate, to regulate international commerce in accordance with the free trade dictum.

468

3 David Held, a neo-liberal, approvingly comments that the structure of global capitalism imposes constraints on all states, but more so on marginal states. As he observes, the UN perhaps has a greater influence in marginal states than in the others. In other words, given the indebtedness of such states they lack the power to reject proposals that are imposed on them.

4 Because the marginal states are powerless in this way in the international context, no amount of internal democratization will empower them to take control over their own economic destiny. For an insightful study of this problem, see George 1992; see also Bandow and Vasquez 1993.

5 It is instructive to note the irony here, because those marginal states were former colonies, which received their independence only to be recolonized.

6 Deliberative democracy emphasizes a dimension of democracy that is often obscured in capitalist democracy, namely, the significance of dialogue or discussion in political decision-making. As I shall try to show, there is a significant difference between political decision-making based on the aggregation of pre-political interests and decisions which are the product of democratic dialogue. Note that the emphasis in deliberative democracy is less on the number of people who participate than on the different perspectives represented in the political dialogue. Any time a perspective is left out, a serious damage is done to the democratic process despite its commitment to the popular vote.

7 Neo-Marxists and progressive liberal theorists are agreed on one important point, namely, that capitalist democracy conceals a social hierarchy. How each group proposes to solve the issue is another matter altogether. For our purposes, a global hierarchy divides the world into two groups: the rich capitalist nations constitute the core of the system, while the poor, so-called third world states exist at the margins. Another name for this type of relationship is the North–South divide.

8 Sovereignty and democratic legitimacy inhere in the state in an interstate system that gives priority to states rather than individuals. For a useful discussion of the dilemma this generates, see Young 1994.

9 The World Bank and the International Monetary Fund (IMF) are commonly referred to as Bretton Woods Institutions. They were instituted after the Second World War to help in the recovery of a world devastated by war. A further aim was to introduce order and economic discipline in a chaotic capitalist system.

10 Source: World Bank Debt Tables, published annually by the UN Department of Public Information.

11 The rich nations of the North applied pressures on third world countries to remove subsidies from social services and agriculture. However, those very same countries were busy subsidizing agriculture and operating a welfare economy. Was it, as one economist, John Gershman, has claimed, a global project by the North to undermine Southern unity and to restructure the North–South relationship? This is plausible because, as Gershman suggests, "the 1970s saw increased Southern assertiveness, including demands for new international economic and information orders and a strengthening of UN agencies" (1994: 25). These things posed a threat to Northern hegemony.

12 It is easily argued, even by those who believe in capitalism, that the problem is not free trade but the undesirable consequences of the social hierarchy that free trade initially generates. The argument for free and fair trade, though the minority view, seeks to limit the influence of unequal economic opportunity in the global market.

13 For an interesting discussion of the different approaches to deliberative theory, see Bohman and Relig 1999.

469

14   The deliberative approach to politics is a fairly recent development in academic circles. Both John Rawls and Habermas have touched on it in various ways in their theories. The Rawlsian idea of *reflective equilibrium* implies some form of moral deliberation and so does Habermas's *ideals of free speech*. One possible weakness of deliberative theory is that it sometimes fails to produce a consensus, and even when there is a consensus, it cannot guarantee that it is the truth or the correct thing to follow.

15   Deliberation and democratic proceduralism vastly improve chances of a just political outcome.

16   This aspect of democratic transition has been underthematized. It is, in my view, the factor that, in the main, helps to explain whether or not democratic transition will take place. See recent attempts at theorizing this crucial process in Barber 1999 and Cohen 1999. My essay (Carew 2000) focuses much more specifically on the passage from non-democratic societies to democratic ones.

17   John Dryzek (1996: ch. 4) was perhaps the first to apply deliberative principles to the international context.

18   For a thought-provoking insight into the failures of subsequent waves, see Ihonvbere 1996 and Segal 1996. These essays are important not because of what they say, but rather because of what they leave unsaid. For even after the failure of the "Third Wave," empirically minded political theorists have continued to ignore the global context within which African states have been called upon to democratize.

19   There have been more than 70 coups and numerous civil wars in Africa since the 1960s.

20   Global deliberative democracy, unlike capitalist democracy, need not limit democracy within the boundary of the state. This explains why the limitation on state sovereignty is required in order to ensure accountability in the international community. The global commitment to human rights is an indication that individuals are now thought to have rights that predate the state.

References

Bandow, Doug and Vazquez, Ian (1993) *Perpetuating Poverty: The World Bank, the IMF and the Developing World* (Washington DC: Cato Institute).

Barber, Benjamin (1999) "Clansmen, Consumers, and Citizens: Three Takes on Civil Society," in Robert K. Fullinwider (ed.), *Civil Society, Democracy and Civic Renewal* (Lanham, MD: Rowman and Littlefield Publishers, Inc.).

Bohman, James and Relig, William (eds.) (1999) *Deliberative Democracy* (Cambridge, MA: MIT Press).

Budhoo, Davison (1994) "IMF/World Bank Wreak Havoc on Third World," in Kevin Danaher (ed.), *Fifty Years is Enough: The Case Against the World Bank and the International Monetary Fund* (Boston, MA: South End Press).

Carew, George (2000) "Transitional Democracy," in Yeager Hudson (ed.), *Studies in Social and Political Theory* (Lewiston, NY: The Edwin Mellen Press).

Cohen, Jean (1999) "American Civil Society Talk," in Robert K. Fullinwider (ed.), *Civil Society, Democracy and Civic Renewal* (Lanham, MD: Rowman and Littlefield Publishers, Inc.).

Dryzek, John (1996) *Democracy in Capitalist Times* (New York: Oxford University Press).

George, Susan (1992) *The Debt Boomerang: How Third World Debt Harms Us All* (London: Pluto Press).

George, Susan (1994) "The Debt Boomerang," in Kevin Danaher (ed.), *Fifty Years is Enough: The Case Against the World Bank and the International Monetary Fund* (Boston, MA: South End Press).

Gershman, John (1994) "The Free Trade Connection," in Kevin Danaher (ed.), *Fifty Years is Enough: The Case Against the World Bank and the International Monetary Fund* (Boston, MA: South End Press).

Held, David (1992) "Democracy: From City-States to a Cosmopolitan Order," *Political Studies*, 40 (special issue): 10–39.

Ihonvbere, Julius O. (1996) "Where is the Third Wave? A Critical Evaluation of Africa's Non-transition to Democracy," *Africa Today*, 43(4) (Oct–Dec).

Segal, Aaron (1996) "Can Democratic Transitions Tame Political Successions?" *Africa Today*, 43(4) (Oct–Dec).

Young, Crawford (1994) *The African Colonial State in Comparative Perspective* (New Haven, CT: Yale University Press).

39

Nationalism, Ethnicity, and Violence

ALI A. MAZRUI

What is Nationalism? A Comparative Analysis

Nationalism can be both an ideology with specific constituent ideas or a set of sentiments, loyalties, and emotional predispositions. Outside Africa, nationalism emerged in the course of the development and maturation of the European nation-state. For many European and later African nationalists, no distinction was made between loyalty to the state as a system of authority (vertical allegiance) and loyalty to the nation as a fellowship of community (horizontal allegiance). To most nationalists, one's own state or nation was entitled to supreme loyalty.

In the history of Europe, nationalism emerged with the decline of two earlier paramount allegiances – the erosion of more localized feudal fiefdoms, on the one hand, and the decline of the transnational influence of the Church in Christendom, on the other. Defeudalization and the beginnings of secularization left a fertile ground for new foci of fidelity. The Treaty of Westphalia of 1648 had been the midwife of the new nation-state. By the eighteenth century nationalism had become one of the ideological forces of Europe. In Africa, defeudalization sometimes took the form of detribalization – to be followed by wider allegiances.

The political thought of Jean-Jacques Rousseau was complex, but it did include a nationalist tendency. His distinction between "the general will" and "will of all" was a distinction between the inviolate will of the nation, on one side, and the will of all the citizens at any particular moment in time, on the other. The "general will" was superior to the "will of all." The nation was more enduring than its citizens. Rousseau's thought subsequently influenced nationalism in Francophone Africa.

In the eighteenth and early nineteenth centuries nationalism was often combined with liberal values. Prince Otto von Bismarck was among the first great European conservative nationalists and authoritarian unifiers. A much worse example of right-wing European nationalism combined with militant unification was, of course, Adolf Hitler in the twentieth century. In Africa one might identify Tutsiphobia among the Hutu in 1994 as the nearest African equivalent to genocidal Nazism.

The full internationalization of modern nationalism did not occur until the ideas and sensitivities manifested themselves in Asia and Africa under colonial domination. In the Arab world nationalism was often combined with transnational pan-Arabism. In Africa the anti-colonial struggle gave birth to both localized nationalisms and to pan-African movements.

A desire to build an empire can itself be a goal of nationalism. Rudyard Kipling was an imperial nationalist who glorified empire building by the white man:

Take up the White Man's burden
Send forth the best ye breed,
Go bind your sons to exile,
To serve your captives' need.

Take up the White Man's burden
– The savage wars of peace –
Fill full the mouth of famine
And bid the sickness cease.

The ports ye shall not enter,
The roads ye shall not tread,
Go make them with your living,
And mark them with your dead.

Kipling wrote the poem (1962 [1899]) partly as an appeal to American nationalism, encouraging white Americans to accept the burdens of an imperial power in the Philippines. He and Cecil Rhodes also often appealed to that side of British pride which was in effect *imperial nationalism*.

Nationalism can sometimes be preoccupied with the defense or revival of culture, rather than with fidelity to the state. Among the former European imperial powers the French are still pre-eminent cultural nationalists, though combined with fidelity to the French state. Cultural nationalism in France profoundly affected their colonial policies, and gave rise to such goals as the assimilation of the colonized. The defense of French cultural influence has also affected French foreign policy more broadly, complete with a readiness to invest considerable resources in the propagation and teaching of the French language from Senegal to Saigon.

Nationalism is sometimes a combination of culture as *identity* and culture as *communication*. When the nationalism and the language are either completely or substantially fused, what we get is linguistic nationalism. The focus of the nationalism is substantially pride in one's language.

Nationalism can also be inspired by race. In the Black world this includes movements like Negritude, Black Power, Mobutu Sese Seko's doctrine of authenticity, and certain schools of pan-Africanism. The Nation of Islam led by Louis Farrakhan in the United States combines nationalism with both religious and racial symbolism. The National Socialists (Nazis) under Adolf Hitler combined nationalism with militant racism. Afrikaner nationalism in South Africa included race-consciousness.

Nationalism can sometimes be sustained by political nostalgia – an idealized memory of the past, with a desire to revive it. The most successful nationalism of nostalgia was the Zionist movement, which did succeed in bringing into being a new Israel (with its citizens now called Israelis instead of Israelites). Was Liberia born out of Black Zionism – the return of African Americans to their ancestral continent?

But nationalism can also be sustained by particular negative memories of the past – especially a sense of martyrdom from a specific experience. Armenian nationalism has been partly sustained by the sense of martyrdom going back to the Armenian massacres under the Ottoman Empire in 1915. Certain schools of Jewish nationalism also draw inspiration from the Semitic martyrdom under the Nazi Holocaust. Afrikaner nationalism is partly inspired by a sense of martyrdom, especially under British colonial rule.

Recurrent nationalism can be sustained by rivalry for territory and by disputes over borders. Nationalism in both India and Pakistan has been influenced by the dispute over the fate of Kashmir. This is quite apart from the nationalism of the Kashmiri people themselves, in rebellion against forced integration with India. The twentieth century was coming to a close with Ethiopia and Eritrea at war over a border.

Nationalism may seek to reunite those who have been divided by history and imperialism – such as Somali nationalism and Kurdish nationalism. On the other hand, nationalism may want to pull out of an enforced territorial marriage – such as the separatist nationalism of Eritreans before 1992 to pull out of Ethiopia, or the nationalism of the Igbo to pull out of Nigeria in the Biafra war (1967–70).

The word "nationalism" has transcended its etymology. Nationalism is now much wider and more diverse than the unit of the "nation." As we have indicated, it is possible to have transnational nationalism (like that of the Arabs) or sub-national nationalism (like that of the Afrikaners). The term "nationalism" has come to be associated with certain forms of militant patriotism and with units of allegiance which are more diverse than merely the nation-state.

Anti-Colonial Wars: Who Benefits?

The most difficult moral category to assess is one in which armed struggle against imperialism turns out to be more advantageous to the imperial power than to the freedom fighter. It may be worth juxtaposing three very different visions in this regard – the vision of the black revolutionary writer from Martinique, Frantz Fanon (1925–61), the vision of the rather shy English poet, Oliver Goldsmith (1730–74), and the Christian concept of the crucifixion as a form of redemption.

Frantz (alias Omar) Fanon was convinced that anti-colonial violence was a healing experience for the colonial freedom fighter: "At the level of individuals, violence is a cleansing force. It frees the native from his inferiority complex, from his despair and inaction" (1968: 94). If the crucifixion of Jesus was an act of violence, and it was at the same time an act of atonement and redemption, there are moments when Fanon's thought has points in common with Christian doctrine. In Fanon's words: "Violence is thus seen as comparable to a royal pardon... The colonized man finds his freedom in and through violence" (ibid. 86). The crucifixion was violence as a royal pardon in the ultimate sense – redemption by the king of kings. The Son of God was killed – so that human beings might live.

474

With regard to Oliver Goldsmith, he enunciated a vision of a good man who was bitten by a mad dog. Under normal circumstances the man would have developed rabies or hydrophobia – and experienced one of the most painful forms of dying that a human being can experience. But the man's inoculation against rabies was his moral worth. His morality was his vaccination:

> That still a godly race he ran,
> Whenever he went to pray . . .
> The naked every day he clad,
> When he put on his clothes . . .

On the other hand, the mad dog had evil appetites when it bit the good man. The moral fiber of the man was not only a protection for the man; it turned out to be fatal to the dog:

> The dog, to gain some private ends,
> Went mad and bit the man . . .
> The man recovered of the bite,
> The dog it was that died.[1]

What really happened in the anti-colonial wars in places like Algeria, Mozambique, and Angola was a remarkable reversal of who gained from the violence. Frantz Fanon was wrong about who gained by violence. In the short run, the greater beneficiary of armed struggle in Algeria was not the Algerians but France. France was purified by the violence, not Algeria. The war in Algeria destroyed the Fourth French Republic and inaugurated the more stable Fifth Republic. The Algerian war brought Charles de Gaulle back to power in France and he helped to launch France into new European and global roles. France emerged stronger after losing Algeria than she was before. And yet Algeria itself continues to bleed in new forms of postcolonial trauma.

The anti-colonial wars in Angola, Mozambique, and Guinea-Bissau helped to destroy fascism and political lethargy in Portugal. Portugal had resisted every progressive formative European force in modern history – the Renaissance, the Enlightenment, the Reformation, the legacies of the American and French Revolutions and the Industrial Revolution. It took anti-colonial wars waged by Africans to dislodge Portugal from its age-old lethargy and reaction. In April 1974 a coup took place at last in Lisbon, Portugal, as a direct result of the colonial wars. The coup turned out to be the beginning of the modernization, democratization, and re-Europeanization of Portugal. And all this because African liberation fighters had challenged the Portuguese fascist state in its imperial role.

It is here that the paradox arises which contradicts Fanon and revises Oliver Goldsmith. It turns out that anti-colonial violence is a cleansing force not for the original victim but for the imperial villain. Angola and to a lesser extent Mozambique are still in a desperate condition – while Portugal is experimenting with modernization and democracy. Algeria is struggling with problems of instability and culture conflict – while the Fifth Republic in France remains relatively firm. Anti-colonial violence has helped the imperial villain – but has it helped the colonial victim? Fanon was right that anti-colonial violence led to moral rejuvenation. But who was rejuvenated – the colonized or the colonizer?

With regard to Oliver Goldsmith, let us assume that the mad dog was the imperial order and the morally upright man was Global Africa. When the mad dog bit Global Africa, what really followed? We have to amend Goldsmith as follows:

> The dog, to gain some private ends,
> Went mad and bit the man...
> The man *suffered* from the bite,
> The dog it was that *healed*!

This is very different from "the dog it was that *died*." In the imperial order the villain has been healed – while the victim still suffers.

It is in this context that the case for reparations becomes stronger than ever. Even when Africans fought for their independence, the short-term consequences were of greater benefit to the imperial order than to the former colonial subject:

> The man suffered from the bite,
> The dog it was that healed.

While a world war in the Northern hemisphere has been a midwife to decolonization in the South, wars of decolonization in the Southern hemisphere have played midwife to democratic modernization in the North. Northerners fighting each other have aided the decolonization of the South. Southerners fighting Northern colonialism have helped positive reforms in the North.

World War II, while devastating in the Northern hemisphere, did have some beneficial consequences in the Southern hemisphere. Imperial Great Britain was exhausted by the war, and was ready to concede independence to India and Pakistan within two years of the end of the war. The occupation of France by the Germans had destroyed in the colonies the myth of French invincibility and re-energized Francophone African aspirations.

The African soldiers who participated in the war discovered the human frailties of the white man – fear, cowardice, anxiety – and this helped to demote the image of the white man from demi-god to fellow human, potentially vulnerable.

In the wider African populations the war widened international horizons beyond distant battlegrounds in France, Burma, and North Africa. As they sought news about the war, ordinary Africans learnt about places they would never have known about but for the vicissitudes of conflict.

The rhetoric of the Allies emphasized freedom and opposition to tyranny. This approximated self-determination with the Atlantic Charter signed by Franklin D. Roosevelt and Winston Churchill. If it was wrong for Hitler to occupy Poland and Czechoslovakia, why should it not be wrong for Britain to occupy India and Nigeria? The rhetoric of World War II fed into the rhetoric of general anti-colonialism.

World War II also knocked out imperial Western Europe from the pinnacle of world hegemony – and substituted two superpowers, both ideologically anti-colonial to a certain extent. The United States and the Soviet Union in the second half of the twentieth century helped to pressure Western Europe toward rapid decolonization. The Soviet Union went to the extent of helping armed liberation in such colonies as Angola, Mozambique, and Zimbabwe. World War II also helped to give birth to the United Nations, which became in time one of the arenas of anti-colonialism. The Trusteeship Council of the world body, originally conceived as an instrument of collective imperialism, was transformed into an instrument of collective decolonization.

What all this has meant is that a world war originally ignited in the Northern hemisphere, and utterly devastating in the North, has had benign consequences in the Southern hemisphere, especially in the area of decolonization. Hitler, the ultimate racist, became by default the benefactor of Black peoples.

But while a primarily Northern war was beneficial to Southerners, we have sought to demonstrate that some Southern anti-colonial wars have been beneficial to Northerners. We have referred to the impact of the Algerian War of Independence (1954–62) on the birth of the Fifth Republic in France and the resulting political stability. We have also referred to the impact of the anti-colonial wars in the Portuguese colonies on the modernization, democratization, and re-Europeanization of Portugal following the military coup in Lisbon in April 1974.

Resistance: Primary and Secondary

In African studies a distinction has been made between primary resistance to colonialism and secondary resistance. This distinction was first made or popularized by what used to be called the Dar es Salaam school of African historiography, led by Professor Terence Ranger.

The sense of primary and secondary in the Dar es Salaam school of historiography was essentially chronological. Chronologically, primary resistance occurs when the colonial power first comes into a potential colony; secondary resistance is a rebellion by those who have already been colonized for some time. Primary resistance seeks to stop colonization from starting or from consolidating itself. Secondary resistance seeks to end colonialism when it is already well and truly established.

But there is a different sense of primary and secondary resistance, which the Dar es Salaam school did not fully explore. This is a cultural rather than a chronological distinction. *Culturally*, primary resistance is resistance rooted in *indigenous* culture and symbolism regardless of when during the colonial period it occurred. The Mau Mau war in Kenya (1952–60) occurred on the eve of Kenya's independence (1963) – yet the Mau Mau rebellion was primary resistance because it was rooted in indigenous Kikuyu culture and symbolism.

Secondary resistance in this cultural sense is resistance substantially rooted in the values and techniques of the *colonizer*. In Africa this meant resistance by Westernized Africans using Western ideologies, rhetoric, techniques, and sometimes methods of warfare.

Jomo Kenyatta in Kenya stood astride the cultural divide. In spite of the many years he had spent in England in his younger days, Jomo Kenyatta continued to

477

be ill at ease with Western culture. He seemed much more comfortable speaking Kiswahili or Ki-Kikuyu than speaking or reading something in English. Was he a founder of Mau Mau – or merely an inspiration behind it? Kenya historians are still debating Kenyatta's role.

Chronological primary resistance, because it occurs before colonization has fully established itself, is simultaneously cultural primary resistance. The Maji Maji war against the new German colonizers in Tanganyika at the beginning of the twentieth century was primary both chronologically and culturally.

On the other hand, chronological secondary resistance can be either culturally primary (as in the case of Mau Mau) or culturally secondary (as in the case of the African National Congress in South Africa). Mau Mau "went almost totally native," while the African National Congress was a Westernized nationalist response to the Western or white architects of apartheid.

The cultural primary resistance has certain characteristics. It is, first of all, *primary* because it is rooted in the indigenous values and symbolism of the resistance movement. There is a *strong supernatural and divine* component in this form of resistance, often rooted in African traditional religion. If it is male-led, there is a high equation between masculinity and combat – even a direct linkage between the spear and the penis. However, the combat can be female led, which emphasizes the supra-sexual and the supra-natural. Let us explore these dimensions.

The Gender of Cultural Resistance

One of the advantages of cultural primary resistance is that it could indeed actually be led by a woman as a military strategist or political rallying point. This history includes Yaa Asantewa of Asante, at the time when the British were trying to colonize Ghana. As the leader of the Asante people, Yaa Asantewa mobilized thousands of warriors, put the new British Resident under siege in his fortress for weeks, and gave British reinforcements a hard time before her army was defeated and she herself was captured and sent into exile. According to the British officer who arrested her, she resisted to the bitter end – and even spat in the face of the arresting officer as her last act of defiance (see Hall 1939: 9).

Another case of female-led primary resistance was Nyanda of the Shona of present-day Zimbabwe (sometimes called Nehanda as a spirit medium). Zimbabwe has two main ethnic groups – the Shona and the Ndebele. Cecil Rhodes, the British nationalist and adventurer, thought that the Shona were docile and a walkover. The Ndebele were the tougher fighters. It turned out that Cecil Rhodes underestimated the Shona women. In 1896 Nyanda called upon her spiritual followers in Northern Shonaland to get rid of the new white interlopers. Under her inspiration the Northern Shona were able to regain their lands in three or four months of fighting. They even captured the British Native Commissioner for Nyanda's area, a man called Pollard. The man used to flog "natives" to bleeding, occasionally flogging them to death. Nyanda sentenced Pollard first to a period of servitude as a domestic servant. Pollard was later executed.

The rebellion of the Shona and the Ndebele was finally suppressed by early 1898. Nyanda, or Nehanda, was sentenced to death by Cecil Rhodes and his gang. When invited to become a Christian before execution, she refused. She was hanged on April 27, 1898 – another African Joan of Arc paying with her life in the blaze of primary resistance.

Indigenous African culture continued to produce female leaders of resistance in Africa even after colonial rule. When the government being resisted is a postcolonial African regime, it has still been possible to see African "Maids of Orleans" leading men to battle.

In recent Ugandan history these have included Alice Lakwena, an Acholi opponent of the government of Yoweri Museveni. The Acholi were once regarded by the British Raj as a "martial tribe" – their men disproportionately tall, tough, and "macho." They came to constitute the largest single group in the Ugandan army. Yet macho men from this same "martial tribe" followed Alice Lakwena into battle – a warrior-priestess confronting the regular army of Yoweri Museveni. Like other Joans of Arc before her, Alice Lakwena was vanquished. But unlike some, she was imprisoned rather than executed or burnt at the stake. What is significant is that indigenous African culture has continued to be capable of producing warrior-priestesses right up to the present day.

While cultural primary resistance led by women has on the whole been asexual in its rituals, cultural primary resistance led by men has often linked the masculine with the martial, the spear with the phallus.

Some of the Mau Mau oath ceremonies involved holding the penis against the skin of a goat – the hide of the goat being later used to make a shield. Other Mau Mau oaths used menstrual blood as a symbol of the cleansing of the womb. War as a system of destruction, and sex as a process of reproduction were counterpoised. The symbolism of combat and the rituals of consummation were intertwined. Cultural primary resistance was digging deep into primordial culture.

Six Paradoxes of Postcolonial Violence

And then independence came to Africa, and most of the second half of the twentieth century revealed entirely new patterns of conflict, resistance, and violence. These patterns were often dialectical and paradoxical. Let us take a closer look at them.

As the twentieth century came to a close Africa consisted of some 54 countries. Since independence about a third of them have experienced large-scale political violence or war. This does not include those countries that have had relatively bloodless military coups or occasional assassinations. After all, even the United States has had presidential assassinations.

Countries differ in their levels of violence even when they are nextdoor neighbors. For example, Kenya shares borders with five other countries. Four of those other countries have experienced civil wars – Ethiopia, Somalia, Sudan, and Uganda. The fifth is Tanzania, which was partly born out of a revolution – the Zanzibar revolution of 1964. By comparison with its neighbors, Kenya has been spared large-scale civil conflict – so far!

Let us now explore the subject of conflict in Africa in terms of a series of dialectical propositions – sometimes ironies, sometimes paradoxes, sometimes outright contradictions. In the second half of the twentieth century more people died as a result of conflict between Black and Black than because of conflict between Black and White. This is the paradox of racial deficit. While anti-colonial wars did cost a lot of lives (especially in places like Algeria where more than a million perished at the hands of the French) postcolonial wars have been even more ruthless. And yet the seeds of the postcolonial wars themselves lie in the sociological mess which colonialism created in Africa by destroying old methods of conflict-resolution without creating effective substitute ones in their place.

Secondly, there is the paradox of fatal borders. While most African conflicts are partly caused by borders, those conflicts are not themselves *about* borders. The conflicts are partly caused by borders because those were created by colonial powers to enclose groups with no traditions of shared authority or shared systems of settling disputes. The human chemistry between those groups has not necessarily had time to become congenial.

On the other hand, African governments have tended to be possessive about colonial borders and have discouraged challenges to them. The borders generate conflicts *within* them, but have not been encouraged to generate conflict *across* them. The dispute between Ethiopia and Eritrea is more an exceptional interstate conflict than a rule.

Thirdly, there is the paradox of religion and ethnicity. While the worst conflicts in Arab Africa are religious, the worst conflicts in Black Africa are ethnic (so-called "tribal"). By the end of the century Algeria had the worst conflict in Arab Africa proper – a conflict between Islamists and military secularists. It has been one of the ugliest wars in the world. Egypt in Arab Africa also has a *religious* conflict. The worst conflict in Black Africa in the 1990s was between the Hutu and the Tutsi, especially with the genocide in Rwanda in 1994. This was an *ethnic* conflict.

Sudan has been caught in between: is the conflict between north and south primarily ethnic or primarily religious? You may take your pick. In Somalia the conflict was sub-ethnic – i.e. between clans rather than between tribes.

The fourth paradox is between identity and resources. While Black against White in Africa is a clash over resources, Black against Black is a clash of identities. The thesis here is that racial conflicts in Africa are ultimately *economic*, whereas tribal wars are ultimately *cultural*. White folks and Black folks fight each other about who owns what. Black folks and Black folks fight each other about who is who. Apartheid was ultimately an economic war. But Hutu against Tutsi has been a culture conflict.

The fifth paradox is between modern weapons and pre-modern armies. While African wars are fought with modern weapons, African armies are *not* yet modern armies. One of the destabilizing forces which colonialism bequeathed to independent Africa was a standing army with Western weapons. One of the few African countries to consider whether to do without a standing army was Tanzania. In 1964 Nyerere even had the opportunity to disband his entire army and consider whether to build an alternative one. He did disband the old one, but he did not follow Costa Rica's example and do without.

At independence the weapons were less modern but the armies were more disciplined and professional. Now the weapons are more modern and the armies are less disciplined and less professional.

The sixth paradox is between civil wars and interstate conflicts. While Africa should indeed celebrate that it has relatively few conflicts *between* states today, should Africa also lament that it did not have more such interstate wars in the past? In Africa has the balance between external conflict and internal conflict tilted too far on the side of internal? And as human history has repeated time and time again, civil wars often leave deeper scars, are often more indiscriminate and more ruthless than are interstate conflicts short of either a world war or a nuclear war. The United States, for example, lost more people in its own civil war in the 1860s than in any other single war in its more than 200-year history, including Vietnam and the two world wars.

Conclusion

In the study of nationalism we need to distinguish between the nationalism of the colonizer and that of the colonized. In studying resistance, a distinction has been made in African studies between primary resistance and secondary resistance to colonialism. Chronologically, primary resistance occurs when the colonial power first comes into a potential colony; secondary resistance is undertaken by those already colonized for a substantial period. Primary resistance seeks to stop colonialism from starting; secondary resistance seeks to end colonialism already established. But what are the *cultural* differences between these two forms of resistance? Do those cultural differences affect the methods of combat and the nature of the goals? There are times when "the dog it was that healed." And the former colonies carry the heavy burdens of six dialectics of violence. Primary violence is a contest about the boundaries of the political community; secondary violence is a contest about the goals of political community. Cultural primary resistance may link sexual symbolism with combat. Culture, chronology, and combat converge toward a new political equilibrium.

Note

This paper is indebted to the author's previous work on ethnic violence and the politics of armed resistance, including his Keynote Address at an international conference on the theme "Nationalism and War" held at the London School of Economics, University of London, March 25–26, 1999, and sponsored by the Association for the Study of Ethnicity and Nationalism (Ninth Annual Conference).

1   The relevant stanzas of the poem went as follows:

> This dog and man at first were friends;
> But when a pique began,
> The dog, to gain some private ends,
> Went mad and bit the man.

Around from all the neighboring streets
The wond'ring neighbors ran,
And swore the dog had lost his wits
To bite so good a man.

The wound it seem'd both sore and sad
To every Christian eye;
And while they swore the dog was mad,
They swore the man would die.

But soon a wonder came to light,
That show'd the rogues they lied:
The man recover'd of the bite,
The dog it was that died.

References

Fanon, Frantz (1968) *The Wretched of the Earth* (New York: Grove Press).
Goldsmith, Oliver (1966) "An Elegy on the Death of a Mad Dog."
Hall, W. M. (1939) *The Great Drama of Kumasi* (London: Putnam).
Kipling, Rudyard (1962) "The White Man's Burden" (1899), repr. in Louis L. Snyder (ed.), *The Imperialism Reader: Documents and Readings in Modern Expansionism* (Princeton, NJ: N. J. D. Van Nostrand), pp. 87–8.

40

Western and African Communitarianism: A Comparison

D. A. MASOLO

Introduction

Communitarianism is a fairly recent doctrine in social and moral philosophy. It is the antithesis of individualism, but its manifestations in intellectual traditions around the world reveal important regional modifications. In Euro-American philosophical traditions communitarianism still lacks a uniform and normative expression which can be said to unite all its exponents in either socio-political or moral theory, but it has become a fairly strong and important source of critique of the perceived excesses of the liberal ideology of individualism. It does not articulate a substantive theory of what a communitarian society ought to be, or of which specific aspirations are to be expected of the inhabitants of a communitarian order, but its adherents subscribe to the general view of the political and moral community as having rights which are not only independent of those of the individual but also important enough in some crucial ways to warrant the adjustment of the freedoms of the individual to the conditions of the good of the collective whole. Such a position may be considered to be largely a methodological rather than a substantive theory; its dominant image is that of a critique of liberalism.

Deriving from Hegel, Western communitarianism maintains that the rights of individuals are not basic, and that the collective can have rights that are independent of, and even opposed to, what liberals claim are the rights of individuals. As is evident from this characterization, communitarianism in this sense directly or indirectly follows in the path of a philosophical romanticism by which the state found a new definition and a mystical meaning in the hands of the nineteenth-century German historical school of which Hegel was part. Inspired to some extent by the patriotic instinct to resist the French emperor who had conquered and trampled over a disunited Germany, a new mood developed among German writers and poets, turning their interests inward upon their own nation, their people, their race. For them the people, the *Volk*, was endowed not merely with a history, which obviously every people possesses, but also with a sort of mystical essence and value transcending both the merits of the nation's present members and the external facts of its past. To this depersonalized but emotionally powerful entity Rousseau's idea of the *volonté générale* as something different from the mere opinion of the majority, something which rather subsumed majority and minority in an irresistible higher synthesis defying numerical analysis, supplied a further dimension. Among German scholars of the time, this mystical sense of the nation awakened a genuine historical sense and a genuine passion to penetrate and understand the German past. A whole constellation of intellectuals inspired by national feeling appeared, leading to the formation of the so-called "Heidelberger Romantik," the result of their nostalgic association of German cultural history with the destroyed streets of Heidelberg. Hegel was part of this historical school with Friedrich Carl von Savigny. The spirit of this generation of German intellectuals is encountered in the origins of Hegel's complex reliance on history, in his theory of the dialectic as the constitutive dynamic of reality. Indeed, the intellectuals in question believed that what Germany needed was not a rationalistic corpus of legal mechanisms, but a thorough insight into the history of her existing institutions. Only when this had been gained could a start be made of the systematic codification of the laws by which the mystical essence of the state could be realized in concrete fact.

The state, for Hegel, is not a simple, unitary entity, but one with three separately conceived characteristics, all interconnected because all operative amongst the same population on the same territory, but still all conceptually distinct. There is the state in the sense nearest to our own common usage, the "political" state, which can be described by pointing to its institutions of government and lawmaking. There is also the "civil" state, consisting of the mass of arrangements which individuals make with one another rather than have imposed upon them, such as contracts, marriages, the establishment of corporations; things perhaps which might have spontaneously evolved even if the political state did not exist. And then there is the state in a far wider and less concrete sense, the state as the sum of all the ethical values, all the shared experiences and responses, the consciousness of belonging together through history, reinforced by religious and cultural homogeneity. This "ethical" state is the one to which Hegel accords supreme value and importance. It is in this alone that the individual achieves freedom and self-fulfillment through participation in its transcendent life. The expressions Hegel used for conveying his ideas about the state in this very special sense can be found in his *Philosophy of Right* (1967: 279–80):

> The state in and by itself is the ethical whole, the actualization of freedom; and it is an absolute end of reason that freedom should be actual. The state is Mind on earth and consciously realizing itself there...The march of God in the world, that is what the state is. The basis of the state is the power of reason actualizing itself as will. In considering the Idea of the state, we must not have our eyes on particular states or on particular institutions. Instead we must consider the Idea, this actual God, by itself...
>
> What the state demands from us as a duty is, *eo ipso*, our right as individuals, since the state is nothing but the articulation of the concept of freedom. The determinations of the individual will are given an objective embodiment through the state and thereby they attain their truth and their actualization for the first time. The state is the one and only prerequisite of the attainment of particular ends and welfare.

In the same book, Hegel makes it clear that he genuinely believes in individual freedom and in the value of the individual, and deplores evil or oppressive states. The state, he says, "is no ideal work of art; it stands on earth and so in the sphere of caprice, chance, and error, and bad behavior may disfigure it in many respects" (ibid. 280). And he disapproves of the state as Plato had envisaged it, because, in it, "subjective freedom does not count" (ibid.), and subjective freedom must be respected, as, for example, by letting people choose their own calling in life.

Since Hegel, a thin layer of communitarianism has remained in Western thought. Contemporary Western communitarians, especially the Canadian philosopher Charles Taylor, claim to continue with this Hegelian idea of the individual as part of a larger whole within which she attains her freedom by way of the incarnation of an historically creative Mind. Other contemporary Western thinkers who are widely regarded as espousing communitarianism include Alasdair MacIntyre, Michael Sandel, and Michael Walzer. The moral philosopher John Kekes fits in this fold as well. These are, of course, by no means the only members of the club. It appears that in the light of its Hegelian beginnings, Western communitarianism has defined itself – at least so far – primarily as a critique and rejection of the images of the individual which it finds in "West European," meaning French and British, philosophy. The idea of community entertained by the "German" as opposed to the "West European" thinkers involved something akin to a *Weltanschauung*, or cosmology, a total view of the (natural and social) world, fundamentally in conflict with the essentially humanist and rationalist thought typical of the rest of Western civilization. Thus, in Steven Lukes's observation: "While the characteristically French sense of 'individualism' is negative, signifying individual isolation and social dissolution, the characteristically German sense is thus positive, signifying individual self-fulfillment and ... the organic unity of individual and society" (1973: 22). Georg Simmel captures this new conception of the individual in the following passage:

> [T]he total organism which has grown out of the individuals engaged in the division of labor and which includes and mediates their interrelated effects and counter-effects, shifts, so to speak, into a location high above them. The specificity of the individual thus requires a powerful political constitution which allocates his place to him, but in this fashion also becomes his master. It is for this reason that this individualism, which restricts freedom to a purely inward sense of the term, easily acquires an anti-liberal tendency. It thus is the complete antithesis of eighteenth-century individualism which, in full consistency with its notion of atomized and basically undifferentiated individuals, could not even conceive the idea of a collective as an organism that unifies heterogeneous elements. (1950: 82)

Nineteenth-century German social theory, it appears, was sharply opposed to the contractarian view of the evolution of the state and the role of law in it. It was opposed to the view of the state as a mere watchdog for the protection of the freedoms of the individual against the hostilities of others. In its place was envisaged a society in which individuals were metaphysically connected through a principle which made each one a significant element of the whole. Thus, to attain freedom, in this new conception of society, individuals were called upon to participate in a life of mutual dependency with others. State and society were seen as forces that emerged out of the relations of particular individuals and out of the intricacies of particular social and political institutions which embodied and incarnated the whole.

485

Commentators on the emergence of German Romanticism have observed that the use that Hegel made of the concept of individuality came to define a German variation of its previous French use. According to Steven Lukes:

> There is . . . quite distinct from [the] French use of the term, another use whose characteristic reference is German. This is the Romantic idea of "individuality" [*individualität*], the notion of individual uniqueness, originality, self-realization – what the Romantics called *Eigentümlichkeit* – in contrast to the rational, universal and uniform standards of the Enlightenment, which they saw as "quantitative," "abstract" and therefore sterile. (1973: 17–18)

Georg Simmel called it "the individualism of uniqueness [*Einzigkeit*] as against that of singleness [*Einzelheit*]" (Simmel 1950: 51). There had been other rival German expressions of individualism, some of which, like that of Max Stirner, embraced an extreme form of egoism.

Like their predecessors, contemporary Western communitarians strive to show that the individual has more interactive connections with the Whole than libertarians make of her. While not denying the autonomy of the individual, they emphasize the significance of her participation in as well as dependence on the community for her sense of self, for her freedom, and for her moral development and agency. According to this view, individuals are constituted by the institutions and practices of which they are part, and their rights and obligations derive from those same institutions. As Charles Taylor argues:

> [There is] a connection between four terms: not just (a) our notions of the good and (b) our understandings of the self, but also (c) the kinds of narrative in which we make sense of our lives, and (d) conceptions of society, i.e., conceptions of what it is to be a human agent among human agents . . . Our modern senses of the self not only are linked to and made possible by new understandings of good but also are accompanied by (i) new forms of narrativity and (ii) new understandings of social bonds and relations. (Taylor 1989: 105)

Taylor's position parallels MacIntyre's on the individual's construction of her self-identity and agency as a result of participation in specific social bonds and narratives of which they are part. In *After Virtue* MacIntyre writes:

> I can only answer the question "What am I to do?" if I can answer the prior question "Of what story or stories do I find myself a part?" We enter human society, that is, with one or more imputed characters – roles into which we have been drafted – and we have to learn what they are in order to be able to understand how others respond to us and how our responses to them are apt to be construed . . . I am someone's son or daughter, someone else's cousin or uncle; I am a citizen of this or that city, a member of this or that guild or profession; I belong to this or that clan, that tribe, this nation. Hence what is good for me has to be the good for one who inhabits these roles. As such I inherit from the past of my family, my city, my tribe, my nation, a variety of debts, inheritances, rightful expectations, and obligations. (1984: 216–20)

The above passages have prompted criticisms by some liberals, who infer that such a conception of social embeddedness attributes to individuals irrevocable obligations, such that a person cannot rationally choose to reject obligations assigned to them by virtue of their situation within a Whole. It is not clear that to claim that we develop our sense of the moral good through our experiences of relation with others implies the irrevocability of the roles by which our participation within such social bounds is defined.

Both Taylor and MacIntyre return, significantly, to Hegel. Even more significantly, they too, like their German predecessors, take on, and develop, their social-moral theory against the brand of individualism which owes its origin to the French and British traditions, deriving, MacIntyre says, "from two distinct tendencies, one chiefly, though not only, domesticated in analytical philosophy and one at home in both sociological theory and in existentialism. The former is the tendency to think atomistically about human action and to analyze complex actions and transactions in terms of simple components . . . [thus] the unity of a human life becomes invisible to us when a sharp separation is made between the individual and the roles that he or she plays" (ibid. 204). This remark from MacIntyre compares well with Simmel's observation about "eighteenth-century individualism which, in full consistency with its notion of atomized and basically undifferentiated individuals, could not even conceive the idea of a collective as an organism that unifies heterogeneous elements" (1950: 82).

In political terms, the individual envisaged in such atomistic individualism is a fairly abstract one, born and raised between the middle of the seventeenth and the beginning of the nineteenth century. The individual as thus conceived became the subject of the social contract arguments which start with the conception of man in the state of nature. Even Rousseau, as Hegel, and later Marx, observed, at times speaks in terms of abstract individuals. This is the case when he writes in *The Social Contract* (1913), for example, despite the social thrust of his thought, of the legislator transforming "each individual, who is by himself a complete and solitary whole, into part of a greater whole from which he in a manner receives his life and being." Rousseau's idea of the individual is also encountered in Kant whose individual subject, according to Simmel, was "abstract man, the individuality that is freed from all ties and specificities and is therefore always identical, the ultimate substance of personality and, thereby, the ultimate value of personality. However unholy man may be, Kant says, humanity in him is holy" (1950: 70). Thus the sovereignty of the individual was the ultimate and only source of group authority, and the community was only an aggregate – a mere union, whether close or loose – of the wills and powers of individual persons. All these thinkers agreed that all forms of social life were the creation of individuals, and could only be regarded as means to individual objectives. This is the individual revived recently by John Rawls as the beneficiary of "equal right to the most extensive basic liberty compatible with a similar liberty for others" as well as of wealth and social advantages accumulated under the umbrella of such an uncompromisable right. Against this view, the essentially social conception of the individual encountered in communitarianism claims that the real individual is one who is socially embedded, related to others in both history and tradition. The interconnectedness of the social individual extends his idea of the moral and political good beyond his own self. For him, actions are right or wrong depending on whether their consequences are assessed good or bad not just for him but also for the community within which he is located. While, then, the liberals tend to be deontologists in the Kantian mold, the communitarians tend to argue like consequentialists.

According to MacIntyre, the goods pursued by individuals cannot be comprehended outside the context of historical traditions. A living tradition, then, he says, "is an historically extended, socially embodied argument, and an argument precisely in part about the goods which constitute that tradition" (1984: 222). In other words, for MacIntyre, the criteria of rationality for justifying moral values and for accounting for what counts as, for example, justice and its practical instances, are grounded in tradition. As a result, there are different types of practical rationality. A tradition, he contends,

> is such a movement in the course of which those engaging in that movement become aware of it and of its direction and in self-aware fashion attempt to engage in its debates and to carry its enquiries forward. The relationships which can hold between individuals and a tradition are very various, ranging from unproblematic allegiance through attempts to amend or redirect the tradition to large opposition to what have hitherto been its central contentions. (1988: 326)

From this standpoint, MacIntyre argues, liberalism may be seen as part of a discourse located in the heart of a search for solutions to practical problems in a lived tradition. Western communitarianism is a similar kind of search. But because it arises in the context of a perceived incongruency between the values of liberalism, on the one hand, and, on the other, the reality of the deprivation of groups, which is viewed as contrary to the very values articulated by liberalism, it stands more as a watchdog for the common good than as a robust social theory.

Communitarianism in African Systems of Thought

By contrast, Africa's recent intellectual movements have tried to give communitarianism a robust and prescriptive status. Claims that the values of community override the freedoms and rights of the individual pervaded much of the nationalist rhetoric which was associated with independence movements in the 1960s. While much of this rhetoric was brought to light through the language of nationalist politics in the traditional sense of the term, it was committed to writing by those politicians who also often doubled as Africa's pioneer intelligentsia. Among these were celebrated leaders like Léopold Sédar Senghor of Senegal, Kwame Nkrumah of Ghana, and Julius Nyerere of Tanzania. Their difference from Western communitarians lies in the fact they could appeal to African traditional social and political orders as backing for their claims.

In the case of Nyerere, the traditional background led to a bold but grossly unwise decision to establish new political "villages" modeled after the traditional extended family homesteads. But the sharp differences between culture and politics soon ran Nyerere's political villagization program aground. There can be no doubt that these politicians-turned-public-intellectuals soon influenced a whole tradition

488

in African social theory. Committed to a new and radically different beginning for their respective countries, and driven by the nationalist ambition to create out of Africa something that was radically different from the political systems of her colonizers, these pioneers opted for a political program that would combine values from Africa's living indigenous histories and social structures with an anti-capitalist ideology such as had become familiar since the Bolshevik revolution. While making allowances for practical variations based on national diversities, the general trend of the program remained fairly common, precipitating what came to be popularly known as African socialism. But because of the national diversities, African socialism came to mean different things to different people, reflecting different configurations of Africa's indigenous traditions. While it meant, for some, a secular set of humane values based on altruism as the basis of social unity and cooperation, for others it reached into the heart of the Islamic outlook and built on the religious values of Islam, especially those which call for mutual respect among people, and for the practice of alms-giving.

For some Africans, African socialism meant a combination of African communitarianism with a hefty dose of Marxism. Senghor, for his part, while being quite intrigued by Marxism, argued that that Marxist ethic fell short of stressing the centrality of people and their freedom. Rather, it placed emphasis on the priority of the economic factor and the class struggle "to the detriment of man and his freedom . . . it is a terribly inhuman metaphysics in which mind is sacrificed to matter, freedom to the determined, man to things" (1964: 76–7). By contrast, he asserts, West African realities include the fact that "They are community [Fr. *communautaires*] countries where the group holds priority over the individual; they are, especially, religious countries, unselfish countries, where money is not King" (ibid. 77). Although he did not give it a clear definition, Senghor thought of African socialism as part of his humanism which, in turn, is a function of Africa's Negritude. (It is useful to note that his idea of Negro-Africans included the Berbers of the north.) He believed that there was a clear distinction between the Negro-African society and what he called "the collectivist European society":

> I would say that the latter is an *assembly of individuals*. The collectivist society inevitably places the emphasis on the individual, on his original activity and his needs. In this respect, the debate between "to each according to his labor" and "to each according to his needs" is significant. Negro-African society puts more stress on the group than on the individual, more on *solidarity* than on the activity and needs of the individual, more on the *communion* of persons than on their autonomy. Ours is a *community* society. This does not mean that it ignores the individual, or that collectivist society ignores solidarity, but the latter bases this solidarity on the activities of individuals, whereas the community society bases it on the general activity of the group. (ibid. 93–4)

In the discussion that follows the above passage Senghor traces the African's tendency toward communitarianism to a way of life rooted in his experience of the world. It is the way he feels and thinks, in union not only with all other people around him but "indeed with all other beings in the universe: God, animal, tree, or pebble." Senghor's earlier work, including his definition of Negritude, had addressed the naturalness with which Africans embrace and participate in nature rather than relating to it cognitively from a distance. In other words, for him, the communitarian habits of Africans are not acquired; rather, they are part of the African way of expressing being. On this idea he built what later would become a fashionable refrain for most of the essentialists among black intellectuals: "Black people are communitarian by nature." It is perhaps due to this assumption that Senghor, like most others who later espoused his idea, saw no need to give an analytical account of their claim that African societies were communitarian in their social-political ethic. Instead, it is merely asserted as an abiding truth that such was the case with African societies.

Self as a Metaphysical Collectivity

Ethnographical texts on African societies have sometimes reported African beliefs which appeared to confirm this view of community as a natural formation. In particular, for example, texts on African concepts of personhood – a metaphysical view of how persons are constituted – speak clearly of a general pattern of cultural articulation of the sources of self in African societies. Among the Dogon, for example, ethnographical data tell us that the selves of individuals are formed out of the spiritual forces of the ancestors (see Griaule 1965). Every individual self is constituted of a *nommo*, a *nyama*, and a *kikinu say*, all being spiritual forces from the Dogon metaphysical (ancestral) storage. According to their beliefs and teachings, these forces give humans their general characteristics as members of the human species as well as members of specific clans and families, and, finally, as unique individuals. Of the three, *kikinu say* is the seat of a person's capacity to exercise will and use their intelligence. In union with another element, *nani*, it is the individuating principle which makes every individual unique from every other. In other words, the uniqueness of individuals is manifested in and through their moral and intellectual dispositions which they, in turn, reveal through their public behavior.

The Luo of Kenya speak of the individual as made up of *del* (body), *obuongo* (brain, but also intelligence when used in an active sense), and *juok* (a spiritual element in which reside several human capacities, particularly what is rendered in English as "will"). The latter is particularly interesting and has been the topic of much debate, sometimes greatly discordant. One inherits a *juok* from an ancestor; in fact, it is an ancestor's "spirit" which, when inherited by a new-born, becomes its *juok*.

What this cosmology of life transmission tells us is that individuals depend on others (parents and ancestors) for their organic existence as well as for what really makes them humans in the real sense of the term, namely, their ability to communicate, that is, to acquire, use, and transmit ideas. Individuals acquire both *nani* and *kikinu say* from the generations of the past, and it is binding upon every member of the lineage to take care of and cultivate these endowments so as to pass them on to the next generations when their turn comes. The idea is that as individuals inherit these endowments, they become automatically inducted into the ranks of specific communities.

African theologians have theorized that Africans' sense of community forms a strong foundation for the very ideas of communion, unity, and participation around which the Christian Church is structured as a community or family writ large. The argument was that while the European Church was built out of traditions that have for long been accustomed to thinking of the individual person as the pillar of society, the African Church already had a fertile ground upon which a Christian communitarianism could flourish (see Mulago 1958, 1968, 1972).

According to Vincent Mulago, a Franciscan theologian from the Democratic Republic of Congo, the feeling of participation with others in a common life forms the basis of an essentially African contribution to Christian theology. The principle of common participation, of oneness – *Ubumwe* – explains Bantu solidarity and their belief in the vital communion existing between the members of a family, clan, or even an entire tribe. Each member of such an entity should strive toward the safety and preservation of the whole. God, as the real source of life, communicated it to the first ancestors of the group whose duty it is to perpetuate it in their own descendants. The ancestors constitute the invisible but not inactive part of the total community. All those who participate in this common life are said to be *Ntu* (Mulago 1972: 116). François-Marie Lufuluabo, the Cameroonian theologian, expresses similar views, illustrating them with the Bantu fable whose decoding unravels the Bantu expression of the social and spiritual unity of humankind as the basis of their nature and destiny (1962: 58).

Most African theologians believed strongly that the ideas touched upon above could produce a new theological synthesis in which Africanization and Christianization would merge to form a new Church in Africa built on an existing communitarian foundation (Hebga 1976: 76–8). The outcome, as Mudimbe (1997) notes, would, of course, be an institution *métisse*. It is no wonder, then, that African theologians considered African religions an important resource for today's civilizational values. After a pan-African theologians' colloquium held in Cotonou in August 1970, the participating African theologians published an interesting document entitled *Les religions africaines comme source des valeurs de civilisation* (Présence Africaine 1972), a perfect echo of Senghor's exhortation: "We must extend this [African] solidarity vertically to Europe and to America, the daughter of Europe; horizontally to all Africa, even to Asia. This will be our positive contribution to the construction of the Civilization of the Universal" (1964: 90).

The Cultivation of the Person: Culture as Education and Vice Versa

In African modes of thought, personhood is a concept closely related to the defining capacities of humans. As we saw earlier, the factors that determine personhood are believed to be acquired partly from the individual's socio-ontological beginnings, but its defining levels are only attained through an individual's learning to apply those capacities in ways considered socially appropriate. In this sense, being a person is attained through an educational process that intensifies at every stage in one's growth and development. Before their initiation, children are trained to carry messages across villages to kin and friends of the family. While appearing simple, especially to readers accustomed to largely mechanized modes of communication, the act of sending children as messengers across villages has a very central

491

communal benefit to their development. Apart from training them to sharpen their ability to listen carefully, understand, remember, and precisely transmit verbal messages, it also teaches them other virtues. The practice of taking and delivering messages also trains children – and adults alike – in the virtue of obedience and service to others while also bringing them to the knowledge of close and distant relatives, an obvious attempt to fit children into the larger social system of the extended family and beyond.

As they grow older, children go through more formalized processes for inculcating communal virtues. Moral education and the acquisition of the values which sustain the social order are part of initiation rituals in most African societies. These rituals, which are an important aspect of the rites of passage, create a person out of the untapped potentialities of a child. Cultural education typically includes a period of seclusion in the forest. Hence the rebuke to a person who misbehaves or reasons poorly: "Why do you act (or reason) as if you never went to the forest?" The period of seclusion gives society the opportunity to steep the person in the communal ethic, which includes the fundamentally altruistic impulses underlying social existence. Circumcision and other cultural practices physically and permanently symbolize the attainment of this stage of growth and development in a person's life. These symbols mark the shedding of childhood and, with the moral instruction gained at initiation, mark the birth of the person as a moral agent. Lessons in endurance and self-control instill in the person the ability to subdue personal impulses and hold firmly in the mind the greater ideal of the common good.

Communication and Communalism

While the contractarian theory of civil society places the credit for discovering the true basis of social order in the hands of eighteenth-century European philosophers, it does not take much effort of common sense to realize that sheer survival would be rare and a matter of chance without some regulation of conduct in a manner that calls on all to respect and honor the rights of others. But the workings of contract alone would not suffice to make human life comfortable and enjoyable without those values, which, though not describable as ethical in the strict sense, nevertheless account for much of what we appreciate about being with other people. Moral and customary teachings at initiation processes in African societies put great emphasis on the collective consequences of everyone's actions. It is emphasized also that no good society can come about without the efforts of every member of society. Similarly, no society can engender for its members a sense of safety and humane conditions of life unless everyone contributes to making them possible. Through these teachings it becomes easy for individuals to grasp that although every individual has, as the Luo say, "their own placenta," they would not be what they ought to be without the input of most others with whom they share a social space. Together with taboos, a sub-category of African moral systems, moral knowledge is closely monitored and tapped into for the everyday management of social order and human welfare, a process which is considerably stronger among traditional than among modern Africans (see Wiredu 1983). In this connection, compliance with custom (avoidance of social opprobrium) and with taboos (avoidance of spiritually sanctionable actions or inactions) is the aspiration of everyone desiring social respectability.

Wiredu alludes to another role of community in enhancing the mental development of the individual. This role, he argues, is played in the act of communication. Becoming truly a human member of a specific community occurs through communication which makes it possible for people to create coherent scenarios that articulate *shared* meanings. Wiredu (1996) has compellingly argued a physicalist position for the Akan according to which the human mind, conceived as the functional *capacity* of the brain to formulate ideas and concepts, is formed in social settings through communication with others. It grows and matures with the incremental change in the span of an individual's communicative world. In other words, human nature is community-based. Their cognitive and moral capacities are developed by and in the context of their sociality. They are formed, Wiredu argues, through a learning process:

> To possess a specific concept, an idea, entails some linguistic ability, however slight. But such an ability is the result of training. Human life is a learning process, which begins almost immediately on arrival in the world [regardless of where we place the point of arrival during the course of human biological beginning and development]. This learning has to be in the context of a society, starting with the narrow confines of mother or nurse and widening to larger and larger dimensions of community as time passes. This learning process, which at the start is nothing much more than a regime of conditioning, is, in fact, the making of mind. In this sense a new-born baby may be said to have a brain but no mind, a reflection that is in line with the traditional Akan view that a human creature is not a human person except as a member of a community. (1996: 19)

In all these examples, African scholars and ordinary African people appear to share the view about the individual as dependent on their social world for their organic needs as well as for their spiritual (moral and conceptual) growth. There is therefore an important difference between Wiredu's monistic (physicalist) view of the individual and the Dogon one which, at least in its appearance through ethnographic texts, is pluralist. Wiredu's position expresses only the basic point that knowledge is gained and shared through sociality. Another thing one can take note of at this point is that while the nationalist communitarians had been wrong in attributing to Africans community-dependence as their ontological (that is, essentialist) character, they were right in their recognition of the role of community in the making of the human world. Wiredu's position is that it is the universal order that conditions the nature of humans generally, not just Africans.

Communitarianism and Modern Society in Africa

In Africa, the theoretical beginnings of communitarianism, as noted earlier on, are due to the emancipatory politics of independence from European colonialism. But as an ethic of everyday life it precedes recent African political and intellectual movements. Its expression can be found in many local idioms among African communities. Among most Africans, communitarianism is not a doctrine, although most

Africans would be able to explain clearly why the social order related to its ethic would be a better way of living for humans than any other. "It is humans who sacrifice for each other" (literally, "it is among humans that one may decide to go hungry for a night so another person can eat" – *dhano ema nindo-niga wadgi kech*) is a common Luo saying used to exhort someone to help a needy relative. The saying points to the idea of interdependence as a characteristically human mode of life; it is part of human nature.

The above Luo saying also asserts that the promotion of human well-being is a collaborative and reciprocal endeavor where those more able in some domains ought to assist those less able. In its moral definition, communitarianism describes the belief in the principle of practical altruism as an important social virtue. It recognizes and encourages sharing with others as an important characteristic of human life. Like everywhere else in human societies, African communitarianism is a principle for guiding the practice of everyday life in ways that aim at creating a humane world in which, to quote from Wiredu, "individuals will have the chance of realizing their interests, conceived as being intrinsically bound up with the interests of others in society" (2000). It is expected that everyone should carry their share of the responsibility for creating humane conditions of life for everyone. In relation to the principles of production and distribution, African communitarianism has been cited as a significant economic factor in the regulation of the circulation of wealth.

People accustomed to regarding competitive access to the material goods of the modern economy as the ideal way of expressing and celebrating varying abilities of individuals are bound to find this social ethic to be very strange. They might even find it to be exploitative of those who work hard to build assets for themselves and their immediate families. The individualistic alternative, well articulated in Western liberal social theory since Locke, is that the individual has sole rights to the results of his or her labor, which, in turn, is the effect of his or her individualized capacities. Thus, the pursuit of goods is primarily geared toward the satisfactions of the individual self. Beyond this, one has duties only toward one's own spouse and children. Africans, on the other hand, appear to extend the boundaries of their duties well beyond spouse and offspring.

Some Africanist political economists (see, for example, Hyden 1983) have called the economic practice under this distributive ethic "the economy of affection." The phrase has a critical side to it, but it also suggests a key difference between communitarianism and liberalism. Some scholars of Africa's political economy have claimed that the African practice of the communalist ethic within the modern economy represents an anomaly. Their argument is that adapting the benefits of the modern economy to the communalist ethic contradicts one of the primary objectives of modern liberal economics, namely, the ability of individuals to increase and diversify the quality of their own life through access to modern consumer goods and benefits. Thus, while liberalism focuses on such things as the enactment of laws that protect the rights and freedoms of individuals and institutions and to promote and protect the rights of the individual to justly pursue their interests, communitarianism builds on empathy and other such altruistic feelings. But while the benefits of such feelings can be taught, their practice can neither be determined nor enforced beyond urging.

Communitarianism and Individual Rights

As previously noted, the early post-independence leaders in Africa, who often doubled as political visionaries, tried to crystallize the communitarian ethos of Africa into a political system. The different brands of "African socialism" claimed to offer a rationalized ideological basis for a socialist polity. These leaders seemed, by deed if not by words, to think that the stress on individual rights was not compatible with communitarianism. Like African theologians, African political leaders in the early days of independence tried to lift this communitarian wisdom and way of life into a political morality, that is, into a rationalized and organizing ideology for modern political institutions. The different brands of "African socialism" fit this description. Like the theologians before them, these political leaders – and the intellectuals who stood by their side – believed that the values of individual worth and freedom were incompatible with those of communitarianism.

I believe differently. I believe that communitarianism has its benefits as well as its burdens on individuals; and that these, if properly considered, are not as oppressive of the individual as is often believed. But they can be misunderstood or even abused, just as the liberties of the individual under liberalism have sometimes been. I believe that because it calls for mutual and reciprocal responsibility from everyone, communitarianism is based on an ineluctable fact of human life: that to exist as an individual within a social space is to differ, to be different. But communitarianism goes farther in involving the idea that being inscribed in a social space requires of everyone to realize that they cannot live in society and be indifferent. The ethics of participatory difference requires of everyone a responsibility toward those with whom they share a social space. Everyone is called upon to make a difference by contributing to the creation of the humane conditions which, at least, conduce to the reduction of unhappiness and suffering.

Kwame Gyekye, like Kwasi Wiredu, a Ghanaian philosopher, has recently defended African communitarianism (see Gyekye 1997: 35–76) as upholding rather than opposing the rights of individuals. While arguing that African communitarianism is not perfect, he believes that its shortcomings can be rectified and that improvements can be made, especially in the area of integrating some aspects of individual rights into the conception of the communal good. Wiredu (1996) argues that at least some of those rights, especially the rights that are concerned with basic human needs, are already clearly upheld in the traditional thought systems and practices of some African societies, like the Akan of Ghana. The very idea of a person in Akan thought entails the demonstration in conduct of a commitment to the social values of the community. Humans need family – and hence community – for their biological, cognitive, and moral growth. In response to these needs there is an extensive network of kinship relations, which generates, according to Wiredu (1996: 159), a thick system of rights and obligations.

The critique of liberal individualism latent in African communitarianism is, therefore, not a rejection of the value of individuality; rather, it merely envisages an alternative way of pursuing it in the human community. As a matter of fact, the criticisms of individualism in the African texts noted above compare well with

MacIntyre's (1984), Taylor's (1989), and Kekes' (1997) critiques of the Western liberal idea of autonomy as a failure and an escape from having to address the prevalence of evil.

Conclusion

Nearly every concept we have mentioned above has been the object of criticism in recent debates on the nature of the public sphere. Some have argued that commitment to any sort of collective is questionable. It has been contended that commitment to such abstractions as a nation, a caste, an ethnicity, and so on can lead to the oppression of other people, because it encourages a relativistic moral outlook (see, for example, Nussbaum 1996). Defenders of communitarianism have countered that identifying oneself with a collectivity – such as in our nationalist or patriotic proclamations in the struggle against colonialism – does not necessarily prevent us from being cosmopolitans at the same time (see, for example, Appiah 1996). I understand Nussbaum's fears, and they are well founded. But I side with the latter view. I see the dangers addressed by Nussbaum to relate particularly to the ontological construal of group identity. Once we think of ourselves as ontologically tied to one group to which we ought to be also morally committed, there is little doubt that our canons of moral judgment and aspirations will put what we identify as our primary group interests above the interests of all others, regardless of reason. In fact, just being our group's interests is often regarded as enough reason for our defense of them. The view I endorse, however, regards group identity as part of how we express our humanity. But there is no ontological determinism to it. Accordingly, social self-identity should be kept separate from our canons of moral thinking. In his widely debated work, Appiah (1992) argues against any supposed scientific basis of such ideas as, for example, race.

African social systems, as we have described them above, have been criticized as authoritarian. In particular, the communitarian ethic has been criticized as non-cognizant of the value and agency of the individual as the creator of knowledge. It has also been suggested that it calls for unquestioning conformism rather than encouraging critical discourse from members of society. But this too has been countered – again, by none other than Wiredu (1983). Oruka's study of the philosophical sagacity of certain indigenous sages of Kenya also showed that indigenous knowledge creation was carried on largely by critically-minded individuals whose discursive engagements influenced the content of cultural beliefs (see Oruka 1990). Thus, even within African philosophy, questions of the apparent opposition between liberalism and communitarianism have been raised. In particular, Wiredu argues, against the self-regarding inclinations perceptible in liberalism, that the very foundation of morality, which he calls the principle of sympathetic impartiality, is the ability to imagine ourselves empathetically in the shoes of others. This is what disposes us, in our better moments, not to desire for others what we would not desire for ourselves. Our cognitive and moral capacities start with the reality of others with whom we enter into association. For Wiredu, as for Gyekye, this association is part of the essence of being human.

References

Appiah, Kwame A. (1992) *In My Father's House: Africa in the Philosophies of Culture* (New York and Oxford: Oxford University Press).

Appiah, Kwame A. (1996) "Cosmopolitan Patriots," in Joshua Cohen (ed.), *For Love of Country: Debating the Limits of Patriotism, Martha C. Nussbaum with Respondents* (Boston: Beacon Press; repr. in Pheng Cheah and Bruce Robbins (eds.), *Cosmopolitics: Thinking and Feeling Beyond the Nation* (Minneapolis: University of Minnesota Press, 1998).

Griaule, Marcel (1965) *Conversations with Ogotemmêli: An Introduction to Dogon Religious Ideas* (London: Oxford University Press).

Gyekye, Kwame (1997) *Tradition and Modernity: Philosophical Reflections on the African Experience* (New York: Oxford University Press).

Hebga, Meinrad (1976) *Emancipation d'églises sous tutelle: essai sur l'ère post-missionaire* (Paris: Présence Africaine).

Hegel, G. W. F. (1967) *The Philosophy of Right*, trans. T. M. Knox (Oxford: Oxford University Press).

Hyden, Goran (1983) *No Shortcuts to Progress: African Development Management in Perspective* (Berkeley: University of California Press).

Kekes, John (1997) *Against Liberalism* (Ithaca, NY: Cornell University Press).

Lufuluabo, François-Marie (1962) "La Conception bantoue face au Christianisme," in *Personnalité Africaine et Catholicisme* (Paris: Présence Africaine), pp. 57–72.

Lukes, Steven (1973) *Individualism* (New York: Harper & Row).

MacIntyre, Alasdair (1984) *After Virtue: A Study in Moral Theory*, 2nd edn. (Notre Dame, IN: University of Notre Dame Press; 1st edn. 1981).

Mudimbe, V. Y. (1997) *Tales of Faith: Religion as Political Performance in Central Africa* (London and Atlantic Highlands, NJ: The Athlone Press).

Mulago, Vincent (1958) "Dialectique existentielle des Bantu et sacramentalisme," in *Aspects de la culture noire* (Paris: Librairie Arthème Fayard), pp. 146–71.

Mulago, Vincent (1968) "Christianisme et culture africaine: Apport africaine à la théologie," in C. G. Baeta (ed.), *Christianity in Tropical Africa*. Studies presented and discussed at the Seventh International African Seminar at the University of Ghana, April 1965, London (Oxford: Oxford University Press), pp. 308–17.

Mulago, Vincent (1972) "La Religion traditionnelle, élément central de la culture Bantu," in *Les religions africaines comme source des valeurs de civilisation, Colloque de Cotonou 16-22 August 1970* (Paris: Présence Africaine).

Nussbaum, Martha C. (1996) "Patriotism and Cosmopolitanism," in Joshua Cohen (ed.), *For Love of Country: Debating the Limits of Patriotism, Martha C. Nussbaum with Respondents* (Boston: Beacon Press).

Oruka, H. Odera (1990) *Sage Philosophy: Indigenous Thinkers and Modern Debate on African Philosophy* (Leiden: E. J. Brill; also Nairobi, Kenya: African Center for Technology Studies, 1991).

Senghor, Leopold S. (1964) *On African Socialism*, trans. with an introduction by Mercer Cook (New York: Frederick A. Praeger).

Simmel, Georg (1950) *The Sociology of Georg Simmel*, trans., ed. and with an introduction by Kurt H. Wolff (New York: The Free Press).

Taylor, Charles (1989) *Sources of the Self: The Making of the Modern Identity* (Cambridge, MA: Harvard University Press).

Wiredu, Kwasi (1983) "Morality and Religion in Akan Thought," in Henry O. Oruka and D. A. Masolo (eds.), *Philosophy and Cultures* (Nairobi: Bookwise Publishers), pp. 6–13.

Wiredu, Kwasi (1996) *Cultural Universals and Particulars: An African Perspective* (Bloomington: Indiana University Press).

Further reading

Beidelman, T. O. (1993) *Moral Imagination in Kaguru Modes of Thought* (Washington, DC: Smithsonian Institution Press).

Clinton, Hillary R. (1995) *It Takes a Village and Other Lessons Children Teach Us* (New York: Simon and Schuster).

Devisch, René (1996) "The Cosmology of Life Transmission," in Michael Jackson (ed.), *Things as They Are: New Directions in Phenomenological Anthropology* (Bloomington: Indiana University Press), pp. 94–114.

Gross, Michael L. (1997) *Ethics and Activism: The Theory and Practice of Political Morality* (Cambridge: Cambridge University Press).

Gyekye, Kwame (1992) "Person and Community in Akan Thought," in Kwasi Wiredu and Kwame Gyekye (eds.), *Person and Community: Ghanaian Philosophical Studies, I* (Washington, DC: The Council for Research in Values and Philosophy), pp. 101–22.

Jackson, Michael (1982) *Allegories of the Wilderness* (Bloomington: Indiana University Press).

Jackson, Michael (ed.) (1996) *Things as They Are: New Directions in Phenomenological Anthropology* (Bloomington: Indiana University Press).

Kratz, Corinne A. (1994) *Affecting Performance: Meaning, Movement, and Experience in Okiek Women's Initiation* (Washington, DC: Smithsonian Institution Press).

MacIntyre, Alasdair (1988) *Whose Justice? Which Rationality?* (Notre Dame, IN: University of Notre Dame Press).

MacIntyre, Alasdair (ed.) (1972) *Hegel: A Collection of Critical Essays* (Garden City, NY: Doubleday & Company Anchor Books).

Nkrumah, Kwame (1970) *Consciencism: Philosophy and Ideology for Decolonisation and Development with Particular Reference to the African Revolution* (London: Panaf Books).

Nozick, Robert (1974) *Anarchy, State, and Utopia* (New York: Basic Books).

Nyerere, Julius K. (1968) *Ujamaa: The Basis of African Socialism* (Oxford: Oxford University Press).

Sandel, Michael (1998) *Liberalism and the Limits of Justice*, 2nd edn. (Cambridge: Cambridge University Press; 1st edn. 1982).

Senghor, Leopold S. (1961) *Nation et voie africaine du socialisme* (Paris: Seuil).

Senghor, Leopold S. (1964) *Liberté I, Negritude et humanisme* (Paris: Seuil).

Senghor, Leopold S. (1971) *Liberté II, Nation et voie africaine du socialisme* (Paris: Seuil).

Taylor, Charles (1979) *Hegel and Modern Society* (Cambridge: Cambridge University Press).

Wiredu, Kwasi (1992) "The Moral Foundations of an African Culture," in Kwasi Wiredu and Kwame Gyekye (eds.), *Person and Community: Ghanaian Philosophical Studies, I* (Washington, DC: The Council for Research in Values and Philosophy), pp. 193–206.

41

Human Rights in the African Context

FRANCIS M. DENG

Introduction

Human rights is a concept of universal dignity which all human beings yearn for, irrespective of their race, ethnicity, nationality, religion, or culture. The issue of human rights protection in Africa can be approached from two interrelated perspectives. One has to do with the conventional perception of human rights as a Western concept and the extent to which it is familiar or alien to the African cultural heritage. The other is the degree to which African cultures have a distinctive contribution to make in legitimizing and reinforcing the universality of human rights with African values and practices. Specific examples in this regard are African indigenous notions of democratic participation in governance and socio-economic development.

Cross-Cultural Perspectives on Human Rights

The argument is often made that human rights emanate from the Judaic-Christian tradition and are therefore distinctively Western, although the values that underlie the principles of human rights are of universal validity. If what is meant by human rights is the set of normative standards enshrined in the International Bill of Rights, composed of the Universal Declaration of Human Rights, the International Covenant of Civil and Political Rights, and the International Covenant on Economic, Social, and Cultural Rights, together with the other human rights instruments, then this argument is, to a certain degree, justifiable, since the West played a leading role in their promulgation. But even from this specific perspective, the fact that these standards were adopted by the most inclusive international organization at the global level gives them a universal value. However, the more profound roots of the claim to universality lie in the fact that human rights reflect the universal quest for human dignity.

Although the formulation of human rights standards and their enforcement mechanisms and procedures are fraught with controversy, their basis in the universal concept of human dignity is not only inherent, but often explicit, in human rights instruments. The preamble of the United Nations charter refers to "the dignity and worth of the human person," while the Universal Declaration of Human rights stipulates "the recognition of the inherent dignity and of the equal and inalienable rights of all members of the human family." There is nothing particularly Western about these principles. While universalism seems self-evident, relativism, whether based on culture, religion, or differences in public policy priorities, is a reality dictated by conditions on the ground, and cannot be dismissed lightly. The challenge is to debate the arguments on both sides with a view to fostering understanding and narrowing the ideological gap toward an optimal or functional consensus.

Kwasi Wiredu, addressing the increasing tendency toward human rights violations in modern Africa, concludes that these cannot be "rationalized by appeal to any authentic aspect of African traditional politics.... How to devise a system of politics that, while being responsive to the developments of the modern world, will reflect the best traditional thinking about human rights (and other values) is one of the profoundest challenges facing modern Africa. A good beginning is to become informed about traditional life and thought" (1990: 257, 260). On the assumption that all cultures recognize the inherent dignity of the human person and postulate various norms and procedures for its pursuit, it would be useful, as Wiredu suggests, to understand how local cultures seek to achieve this otherwise global objective. Ultimately, it is possible to conceive relativism as a local reinforcement and enrichment of universalism that at the same time explores the sources of genuine conflicts between the local and the universal. Indeed, some of those who argue that international human rights, as now articulated, are Western in origin do not necessarily object to them on that account, but merely wish to underscore, as Makau wa Matua suggests, that what is at stake is "the opportunity for all major cultural blocs of the world to negotiate the normative content of human rights law and the purpose for which the discourse should be legitimately deployed" (1996: 642).

As Abdullahi Ahmed An-Na'im has argued (1990), to be legitimate, the universality of human rights must rely on the norms and institutions of particular cultures. If meaningful and lasting changes in local attitudes and practices are to be achieved, where necessary, any proposed modification has to be undertaken from within the given culture by people who, while promoting universal norms, are sensitive to the integrity and authenticity of the local cultures. Their arguments in favor of universal human rights standards need to be consistent with the internal logic of the culture. With such internal cultural legitimacy, those in power will not be able to argue that national sovereignty is demeaned when compliance with universal standards is demanded.

This approach is understandably suspect to universalists as providing potential grounds for justifying obstructionist policies or practices (see Howard 1990). To guard against potential abuses of the need for legitimization within indigenous cultural traditions, corresponding legitimization at the international level becomes particularly essential. To enable individuals and groups in a given country to assert their human rights against nationally dominant cultures or against the state, international recognition is a necessary condition. The critical issue then is whether cross-cultural analysis can be used to transform local notions of human dignity into

500

human rights principles on which there is universal agreement.[1] Unless certain standards are recognized as universal, serious violations may be condoned because they happen to be tolerated or sanctioned by the cultural tradition of the society or the community in question. Nevertheless, it is important that the values that underlie international standards of human rights be shown to be universal through internal reinterpretation and cross-cultural harmonization of any differences.[2]

The precise language employed in articulating these standards may, of course, differ from society to society, but the values that underlie the inherent dignity of the human being remain universal. Using vernacular language, a Dinka elder from the Sudan, referring to what he saw as the disdain the Arab-Muslim people of the North had toward his people of the Southern Sudan, invoked the inherent dignity of the human being and the right to be treated decently:

> If you see a man walking on his two legs, do not despise him, he is a human being. Bring him close to you and treat him like a human being. That is how you will secure your own life. But if you push him onto the ground and do not give him what he needs, things will spoil and even your big share, which you guard with care, will be destroyed.... Even the tree, which cannot speak, has the nature of a human being. It is a human being to God, the person who created it. Do not despise it. (Chief Thou Wai in Deng 1980: 172)

In Dinka thought, because God created all of humankind, every human being, no matter what his race or religion, has a sanctity and moral or spiritual value that must be respected. To wrong him is to wrong God himself and therefore invite a curse. What is striking about the Dinka view is that protecting the rights of one individual is ultimately in our collective interest. From another part of Africa, the Akan people say: "Every one is the offspring of God; no one is the offspring of the earth" (Wiredu 1990: 244). Implied in this formulation is the right of each person to the dignity bestowed upon him or her as God's creature.

To say that all societies strive to promote the dignity of the individual human being is not to say that human rights are fully protected in all societies. Quite the contrary, the concept of human rights represents an ideal that no society, nation, or culture has fully attained. Furthermore, in the process of pursuing that ideal, different cultures develop different emphases on different aspects of the universal human rights agenda. This should provide a basis for cross-cultural dialogue on how best to promote the ideals of human rights. Taking Africa as an example of a particular cultural approach, it is widely known that communal relationships are very important in African society, in part as a result of the vital role the family plays in society. Not only is the family perceived broadly to include members of the extended family, the lineage, and the clan, but also the same principles that govern family ties are applied to the wider community. Group solidarity is highly prized even as individuals and groups compete and sometimes conflict.

This is a system in which the protection of the individual is inherent in the solidarity of the group. No family or group based on family values would allow its members to be tortured or subjected to inhumane treatment with impunity. But it is also a system which imposes on the individual certain reciprocal obligations in the

501

mutual interest of the group. The dynamic relationship between the individual and the group or between rights and duties, in itself, provides a cross-cultural perspective that is potentially enriching for the promotion of human rights. While Western cultures place emphasis on individual rights, African traditional systems are likely to see individual rights in the context of group solidarity, with mutual support entailing rights and duties.

Another area that could produce cross-cultural comparisons is that of the distinction often drawn between civil and political rights, on the one hand, and economic, social, and cultural rights, on the other. Since African indigenous political systems were based on the autonomy of the component groups down to the local territorial units of villages and families, there was little or no room for political oppression or persecution. Rights tended to emphasize cooperative support in the social and economic spheres of life. With the centralization of power in the modern state system, the need to protect individuals and groups against human rights abuses became urgent. This gave rise to the high profile given to civil and political rights. But the modern state is also called upon to cater to the welfare of the citizens in the social and economic spheres. Drawing a *sharp* distinction between these sets of rights can therefore be misleading.

As long as the collective goal of promoting human rights universally is borne in mind, these issues still have cultural dimensions that call for a constructive dialogue aimed at a comprehensive approach to human rights. Such a dialogue must never be allowed to degenerate into a divisive debate based on a negative notion of relativism that tries to rationalize human rights violations in the name of cultural differences. The challenge for humanity is to enrich and not to impoverish human dignity as an overriding value for all humankind.

Democratic Participation in the Cultural Context

A concept that is closely associated with human rights is that of democracy, which advocates popular participation in the political, economic, social, and cultural processes of governance. Increasingly, African countries are facing a call for democracy as a fundamental human right. As with the human rights agenda in general, this raises questions of cultural legitimacy and, in any case, poses a challenge to pluralistic states that are acutely divided on ethnic, cultural, or religious grounds. Because democracy has become closely associated with elections in which Africans tend to vote on the basis of their politicized ethnic or religious identity, its literal application risks creating a dictatorship of numbers, with the majority imposing its will on the minority. For this reason, the suitability of democracy to the continent is being questioned, both within and outside it (see e.g. Kaplan 1997; Zakaria 1997). This increasing assault on democracy is based on a narrow definition that places overwhelming emphasis on its procedural aspects, as reflected, for example, in elections, and then uses the negative consequence of this narrow definition to question democracy as a normative concept. A balanced perspective should draw a distinction between the principles of democracy and the institutional practices for its implementation.

502

Given the tendency of Africans to vote according to their ethnic or "tribal" identities, democracy will have to mean more than voting at elections. In the context of ethnic diversity, devolution of power through decentralization down to the local level, combined with some method of ensuring the representation of those who would otherwise be excluded by the weight of electoral votes, is necessary. In any case, democracy, however defined or practiced, implies accommodation of differences and a special responsibility for the protection of minorities.

Given the fact that many African countries are still in the process of nation-building, groups that find themselves threatened with a permanent minority status and without adequate protection for their rights would rather resist affiliation with such a stratifying national framework. Such groups would exist, if they have the capacity for resistance. This would pose a serious challenge to the legitimacy of the regime, if not the state itself, calling either for secession or for a major restructuring of the constitutive system. But although the electoral system should make allowance for the protection and participation of minorities in the short run, the goal in the long run must be to transcend these differences and apply democracy on a non-racial, non-ethnic, and non-religious basis under a truly unifying concept of nationhood (Horowitz 1991: 100).

The main point is that while democracy, broadly defined in terms of normative ideals or principles, is universally valued, it needs to be contextualized, by putting into consideration the African reality and making effective use of indigenous values, institutions, and social mores to make it home-grown and sustainable. As already hinted, perhaps, one of the most outstanding characteristics of traditional African society is the autonomy of the component elements of the political and social order. Related to this is the devolution of power and of the decision-making process down to the local units, down, indeed, to the smallest territorial sub-divisions, such as the lineages and the extended families. Although African societies were characterized by significant differences in their political systems, they all shared this approach, which might be described as a participatory mode of governance (Fortes and Evans-Pritchard 1940; Middleton and Tait 1958).

It has been observed that, "Despite the hierarchical system of traditional governments, most of these entities were generally governed by consensus and broad participation ... through group representation at the central level and village councils at the local level" (Dia 1996: 39). In the deliberations of the Council, any adult could participate and decisions were reached by unanimity. According to Wiredu, "The chief had absolutely no right to impose his own wishes on the elders of the council.... The elders would keep on discussing an issue until consensus was reached" (1990: 250). When important decisions had to be made, chiefs tended to consult village councils (composed mainly of elder lineage heads) and to seek unanimity, even if doing so required very lengthy discussion. "Majority rule, winner-take-all, or other forms of zero sum games were not acceptable alternatives to consensus decision making" (Dia 1996: 41).

This process of sharing power at all levels of the social structure is particularly pronounced in stateless or acephalous societies in which the autonomy of the various components of the segmentary lineage system is emphasized down to the level of the family and even the individual. The Nilotic peoples of the Sudan, in

503

particular the Dinka and the Nuer, who are a typical example of "stateless societies," are well known for their egalitarianism and sense of independence. And yet, leadership is of critical importance to their value system. Chiefs of the Sacred Spears (their symbol of authority) among the Dinka or Chiefs of the Leopard Skin (their regalia) among the Nuer are indispensable to the maintenance of peace and public order. However, a chief among them is a spiritual leader whose power rests on his moral authority, divine enlightenment, and wisdom. In order to reconcile his people, the chief should be a model of virtue and righteousness, "a man with a cool heart," who must depend on persuasion and consensus-building rather than on coercion and dictation. Godfrey Lienhardt wrote:

> I suppose anyone would agree that one of the most decisive marks of a society we should call in a spiritual sense "civilized" is a highly developed sense of the practice of justice, and here, the Nilotics, with their intense respect for the personal independence and dignity of themselves and of others, may be superior to societies more civilized in the material sense.... The Dinka and Nuer are a warlike people, and have never been slow to assert their rights, as they see them, by physical force. Yet, if one sees Dinka trying to resolve a dispute, according to their own customary law, there is often a reasonableness and a gentleness in their demeanor, a courtesy and a quietness in the speech of those elder men superior in status and wisdom, an attempt to get at the whole truth of the situation before them. (1963: 828)

Evans-Pritchard observed of the Nuer settlement of disputes:

> The five important elements in a settlement of this kind by direct negotiation through a chief seem to be (1) the desire of the disputants to settle their dispute, (2) the sanctity of the chief's person and his traditional role of mediator, (3) full and free discussion leading to a high measure of agreement between all present, (4) the feeling that a man can give way to the chief and elders without loss of dignity where he would not have given way to his opponent, and (5) recognition by the losing party of the justice of the other side's case. (1977: 164; see also Deng 1995: 195)

To emphasize the peacemaking role of the chiefs and elders in Nilotic societies is not to imply that these societies were non-violent. Quite the contrary, despite the emphasis the chiefs and the elders placed on persuasion, the Nilotics, as Lienhardt noted, were warlike and prone to violence. It can indeed be argued that the emphasis placed on the ideals of peace, unity, mediation, and persuasion emanates from the pervasiveness of violence. Internal violence can in turn be attributed to the generational distribution of roles and functions and the exaggerated sense of dignity that young members of the warrior age-sets acquired, as defenders of the society from aggression, a function they overzealously carried out to excess, resorting to violence at the slightest provocation. Yet, by the same token, leaders, even when young, must disavow violence and be men of peace. One chief, reacting to the assertion that the Dinka were traditionally a people in whose society force was the deterrent behind the social order, articulated the delicate balance between the violence of youth and the peacemaking role of leaders:

504

[I]t is true, there was force. People killed one another and those who could defeat people in battle were avoided with respect. But people lived by the way God had given them. There were the Chiefs of the Sacred Spear. If anything went wrong, they would come to stop the...fighting...and settle the matter without blood.... Men [chiefs] of the [sacred] spear were against bloodshed. (Deng 1980: 58; quoted in Deng 1995: 196)

And in the words of another chief: "There was the power of words. It was a way of life with its great leaders...not a way of life of the power of the arm" (ibid. 42; quoted in Deng 1995: 197). It is clearly paradoxical but perhaps logical that a society in which violence was so pervasive would be almost equally preoccupied with persuasive strategies and peacemaking. It is particularly noteworthy that despite the lack of police or military forces, civil order was maintained with very low levels of crime other than those associated with honorable fighting.[3] It was what Evans-Pritchard described as "ordered anarchy" (1977: 168).[4]

In most African countries, the determination to preserve national unity following independence provided the motivation behind one-party rule, involving excessive centralization of power and an oppressive authoritarianism in which systematic violations of human rights and of fundamental liberties were common. The participatory and inclusive process of decision-making in traditional African society was later exploited by nationalist leaders to justify the one-party system, the rationale being that since Africans traditionally sat down and debated until they all agreed, the multiparty system was antithetic to African culture. The delicate balance between the interest of the individual and that of the community was also misconstrued to give undue emphasis to communalism at the expense of individualism. It was also used to justify the imported concept of socialism, euphemistically dubbed "African Socialism."

Development as a Process of Self-Enhancement from Within

The value system first introduced by colonial intervention, and vigorously pursued by postcolonial governments, undermined traditional self-confidence by injecting the concept of development as a goal that was outside the cultural purview of the Africans and had to be externally designed and given to them. At independence in the late 1950s and early 1960s the highest policy priority for Africa was economic development. "African leaders adopted the ideology of development to replace that of independence," wrote the late Claude Ake. "But as it turned out, what was adopted was not so much an ideology of development as a strategy of power that merely capitalized on the objective need for development" (1996: 8–9). To create preconditions for development, African leaders saw the political and civic aspects of human rights and related notions of democracy as luxuries to be sacrificed or postponed until Africans were sufficiently advanced. "The ideology of development was exploited as a means for reproducing political hegemony and served hardly any purposes as a framework for economic transformation" (ibid.).

Despite the fact that rhetorical references to tradition were used to justify imported political and economic ideologies, indigenous structures, values, institutions, and

505

patterns of behavior were fundamentally undermined, and often openly disavowed. In a more fundamental way than can be explained by aid dependency, Africa became, and remains, linked to the global structures and processes of interdependence, in which it occupies the lowest stratum. The process of state formation and nation-building has thus denied Africa's peoples the dignity of building their nations on their own indigenous identities, structures, values, institutions, and practices.

But, history cannot be remade; the colonial state has become an African reality that cannot be wished away. On the other hand, the issue of the role of indigenous values and institutions in the development of Africa remains a matter of grave concern. There is an increasing demand among some African and Africanist writers, development experts, and the donor community that indigenous institutions, values, and practices should be recognized as the motor of participatory development strategies from the grassroots. There is therefore a growing demand not only to utilize indigenous institutions, but also to rationalize and formalize them (Fred-Mensah 1992: 7; see also Cole and Huntington 1997; Deng 1984; Dia 1996; Serageldin and Tabaroff 1994).

Conclusion

In discussing human rights in the African cultural context, this chapter has highlighted three features: cross-cultural perspectives on human rights with a view to balancing universality with relativism; indigenous African notions of popular democratic participation in governance; and socio-economic development as a process of self-enhancement from within. These elements of the human rights agenda imply that the challenge of realizing human rights is primarily internal.

However, the principle of universality that must ultimately prevail means that, by definition, human rights enforcement is a shared responsibility between the state and the international community. As an item of domestic governance, the first line of accountability for such responsibility rests with the country in question and its people. Where there is democracy, the electorates can act as effective watchdogs domestically and, by extension, regionally and internationally. But when a people are oppressed and are powerless to hold their governments accountable, international action becomes necessary. This is particularly so where cleavages in national identity result in a vacuum of governmental responsibility and the authorities are unable or unwilling to provide comprehensive protection of human rights for all citizens without discrimination on grounds of race, national origin, religion, culture, or gender. While the international community is far from achieving this objective, the universal demand for respect for the human rights of all peoples has made considerable progress and appears irreversible.

Notes

1   For examples of how traditional African cultures both reinforce and fall short of international human rights standards, see Deng 1990; Silk 1990; and Wiredu 1990.

2   The issue of the universality and the cultural or contextual relativity of human rights was heavily debated at the 1993 Vienna World Conference on Human Rights. Although positions were initially sharply divided, a consensus emerged affirming the universality principle with the need for sensitivity to national and cultural contexts. General Assembly, World Conference on Human Rights, *Vienna Declaration and Program of Action*, A/Conf. 157/23 (United Nations, July 12, 1993).

3   Sir Gawain Bell, who served as District Commissioner among the Ngok Dinka and the Missirya Arabs, observed: "I can't remember that we ever had any serious crime in that part of the District. Among the Baggera of Missiriya...there was a good deal of serious crime: murders and so forth; and the same applied to the Hamar in the North.... The Ngok Dinka were a particularly law-abiding people." Quoted in Deng 1995: 282.

4   The introduction of the police, who often harassed alleged wrongdoers, and the prison system, was seen as a source of great indignity and humiliation against what the Dinka called *adheng*, best translatable as "gentleman." It was often a subject of songs of lamentation and protest. See for instance, Deng 1974.

References

Ake, Claude (1996) *Democracy and Development in Africa* (Washington, DC: Brookings Institution).

An-Na'im, Abdullahi Ahmed (1990) "Problems of Universal Cultural Legitimacy for Human Rights," in Abdullahi Ahmed An-Na'im and Francis M. Deng (eds.), *Human Rights in Africa: Cross-Cultural Perspectives* (Washington, DC: Brookings Institution).

Cole, David and Huntington, Richard (1997) *Between a Swamp and a Hard Place, Developmental Challenges in Remote Rural Africa* (Harvard Institute for International Development: Harvard University Press).

Deng, Francis M. (1984) *Crisis in African Development: A Social and Cultural Perspective* (New York: Annual Report, The Rockefeller Brothers' Fund).

Deng, Francis M. (1990) "A Cultural Approach to Human Rights Among the Dinka," in Abdullahi Ahmed An-Na'im and Francis M. Deng (eds.), *Human Rights in Africa: Cross-Cultural Perspectives* (Washington, DC: Brookings Institution).

Deng, Francis Mading (1974) *The Dinka and Their Songs* (Oxford: Oxford University Press).

Deng, Francis Mading (1980) *Dinka Cosmology* (London: Ithaca Press).

Deng, Francis M. (1995) *War of Visions: Conflict of Identities in the Sudan* (Washington, DC: Brookings Institution).

Dia, Mamadou (1996) *Africa's Management in the 1990s and Beyond: Reconciling Indigenous and Transplanted Institutions* (Washington DC: The World Bank).

Evans-Pritchard, Edward E. (1977) *The Nuer*, 9th printing (New York and Oxford: Oxford University Press; 1st edn. 1940).

Fortes, Meyer and Evans-Pritchard, Edward E. (eds.) (1940) *African Political Systems* (London International Institute of African Languages and Cultures: Oxford University Press).

Fred-Mensah, Ben Kwame (1992) "The Dilemma of Much-Needed Institutional Change in Africa," *Social Change and Development News*, 4(1) (Spring–Summer).

Horowitz, Donald (1991) *A Democratic South Africa: Constitutional Engineering in a Divided Society* (Berkeley, LA: Oxford University in California Press).

Howard, Rhoda (1990) "Group Versus Individual Identity in the African Debate," in Abdullahi Ahmed An-Na'im and Francis M. Deng (eds.), *Human Rights in Africa: Cross-Cultural Perspectives* (Washington, DC: Brookings Institution).

Kaplan, Robert D. (1997) "Was Democracy Just a Moment?" *The Atlantic Monthly* (December).

Lienhardt, Godfrey (1963) "The Dinka of the Nile Basin," *The Listener*, 69; quoted in Deng, *War of Visions: Conflict of Identities in the Sudan* (Washington, DC: Brookings Institution), pp. 194–5.

Middleton, John and Tait, David (eds.) (1958) *Tribes Without Rulers: Studies in African Segmentary Systems* (London: Routledge and Kegan Paul).

Mutua, Makau wa (1996) "The Ideology of Human Rights," *Virginia Journal of International Law*, 36 (Spring): 589–657.

Serageldin, Ismail and Tabaroff, June (eds.) (1994) *Culture and Development in Africa* (Washington, DC: The World Bank).

Silk, Jim (1990) "Traditional Culture and the Prospects for Human Rights in Africa," in Abdullahi Ahmed An-Na'im and Francis M. Deng (eds.), *Human Rights in Africa: Cross-Cultural Perspectives* (Washington, DC: Brookings Institution).

Wiredu, Kwasi (1990) "An Akan Perspective on Human Rights," in Abdullahi Ahmed An-Na'im and Francis M. Deng (eds.), *Human Rights in Africa: Cross-Cultural Perspectives* (Washington, DC: Brookings Institution).

Zakaria, Fareed (1997) "The Rise of Illiberal Democracy," *Foreign Affairs* (Nov–Dec).

42

The Politics of Memory and Forgetting After Apartheid

PIETER DUVENAGE

Can South Africa learn anything from Germany's past and, more specifically, Habermas's interventions in it? Reacting to Adam Michnik's contextualizing attempts, Habermas commented:

> The *Historians' Debate* was a dispute for Germans, not for Poles. It would be a negative form of nationalism if we were to claim that the positions arrived at in the course of the *Historians' Debate* should form part of the political culture of every nation. Adam Michnik has drawn the correct conclusions from this debate for the Poles. But it is not up to me to point them out. We simply have to distinguish between what we say at home and what we regard as valid in any setting. (1994: 26)

There are obvious differences between the histories and political systems of Germany and South Africa. It has been suggested that apartheid was not a systematic attempt at extermination of a single ethnic group by the state, but rather the result of paternalistic intergroup relations.[1] After the war, except for a short period of military administration, the Germans remained in power. In South Africa the white minority lost political power. There has also been no "Historians' Debate" in which philosophers and historians made it their intellectual, moral, and public task to wrestle with an evil past in order to secure a just future in a democracy.[2] Despite these qualifications, though, the name of Auschwitz as well as the word "apartheid" have registered a moral catastrophe deep down in the psyche of the twentieth century (Liebenberg 1992). Like post-war Germans, South Africans, especially the whites, must ask uncomfortable questions about their past.

In an essay on apartheid, "Racism's last word," Derrida uses "last," firstly, as meaning the worst, the most racist of racism, and secondly "last as one says also of the most recent, the last to date of the world's racisms, the oldest and the youngest" (1985: 291; see also Derrida 1986). At a time when all racisms on the face of the earth were condemned, it was in the world's face that the National Party dared to campaign for apartheid – the separate development of each race. Derrida writes:

> APARTHEID: by itself the word occupies the terrain like a concentration camp. System of partition, barbed wire, crowds of mapped out solitudes... At every point, like all racisms, it tends to pass segregation off as natural – and as the very law of origin...

Even though it offers the excuse of blood, color, birth...racism always betrays the perversion of a man, the "talking animal." It institutes, declares, writes, inscribes, prescribes. A system of marks, it outlines space in order to assign forced residence or to close off borders. It does not discern, it discriminates. (ibid. 292)

The interesting point here is that Derrida places apartheid within the "text" of Western logocentrism. Where Habermas wants to link Germany to the Western traditions of universality and constitutionalism, Derrida interprets apartheid, like Auschwitz, as a product of Western modernity. With the help of Foucault's insight into Western reason as one marked by *exclusions*, it is not difficult to see Auschwitz as well as apartheid in those terms. Only within the logic and economics of the "Western way of life" could these events have presented their grim faces. The theologico-political discourse and the defense of apartheid, for example, were linked in a perverse way to the West. It happened under a regime whose formal structures were those of a Western democracy, in the British style, with "universal" suffrage for whites, a relative freedom of the press and judiciary, and the guarantee of individual rights (ibid. 295–7). Although the very South African uniqueness of this catastrophe can be recognized, it will be unsound to deny the historical roots of white South Africans and their specific "European" way of life in Africa.

What, then, is the moral dimension of the past for present South Africans? What is the meaning of collective guilt, anamnestic solidarity, historical traditions, and retroactive justice in this context? First, one can hold that apartheid was not just – as some have relativized it – an abortive social experiment conceived with the best of intentions.[3] If this point is taken, as in Habermas's critique of historical relativization, the next step is more difficult. How do we deal with the moral obligation to the past? Antjie Krog (1994), poet and journalist, answers this question with reference to the 26,000 Boer women and children who perished in British concentration camps during the Anglo-Boer War (1899–1902). Instead of historical relativization, she ponders to what extent the veiling of the concentration camp atrocities contributed to the type of character that devised the apartheid laws. What might have happened if the English had acknowledged the atrocities and asked for forgiveness? Could it have been the start of a history of human rights, respect for the other, and public accountability in South Africa? In the face of this absence, the experiences of injustice never entered into a discourse of dealing with the other.[4] It became instead a mythical pathology allowing a specific "threatened group" to use any means, moral or immoral, to secure survival against the other of apartheid. Consequently, Krog argues that apartheid was successful in dividing South Africans to such an extent that all individuals and groups only have memories stemming from isolation, "half-memories," which could easily turn into some dangerous present-day identity. Memory is identity and identity, which contains distorted memories, could easily lead to new offenses.[5] Krog argues in favor of a space where memories can be shared and communicated at a very basic level. Victims and their families must be allowed to tell the stories of their experiences in a way that respects each individual's language, words, accent, and rhythm. It must not be presented as mere statistical, objective, factual, and formal chronicles. It must reflect the particularity of those who suffered.

The psychological need for the sharing of stories and memories can be expressed with the concept of mourning. Although mourning normally operates in psychological terms as a reaction to the loss of a loved one, it can also be in reaction, as Erikson and Adorno indicate, to a loss of self-respect. It can also be an expression of empathy with those who have suffered (Erikson 1980: pt. III; Adorno 1977). As Freud states, unless the labor of mourning has been successfully completed – that is, unless individuals have sincerely come to terms with the past – they exhibit a marked incapacity to live in the present (1957: 243–4). There are subtle differences between this perspective and Habermas's use of development psychology, post-conventional identity, and historical evolution. In social-psychological studies of the 1950s, Adorno noted that many of the character traits displayed by some Germans revealed highly neurotic attitudes: defense in the absence of attack; no show of emotion when faced with serious matters; and a repression of what was known or half-known (1977: 556–7). The Mitscherlichs write similarly about "a determining connection between the political and social immobilism and provincialism prevailing in West Germany [in the 1960s] and the stubbornly maintained rejection of memories . . . the blocking of any sense of involvement in the events of the Nazi past" (1967: 9). The concept of mourning is used here not as referring to a form of repentance but, almost like the concept of anamnestic solidarity, as a conceptualization of past suffering that may contribute to the healing of individual and collective identities. The danger is that neurotic symptom formations can be readily transmitted to the character-structures of future generations, which only intensifies the difficulty of confronting the historical trauma that wounded the collective ego. Thus the crimes of the past tend to fade into oblivion, unmourned, uncomprehended, and still present and alive as ghosts in the collective ego. The Mitscherlichs warn: "World-redeeming dreams of ancient greatness arise in peoples in whom the sense of having been left behind by history evokes feelings of impotence and rage" (ibid. 22). The important point here is that unless the historical reasons that have led to disaster have been examined – and it cannot be done exclusively in the language of rationality – one risks falling yet again into the same historical cycle.

If the need for the sharing of memories and the role of mourning is acknowledged, the question is how such a process should be institutionalized. Various options seem possible, such as the German example of the Nuremberg trials; formal legal processes; general or qualified amnesty; and moral tribunals (Liebenberg 1996: 129–30; see also 1997). As a result of the special nature of South Africa's negotiated settlement (1990–4) the choice fell on a combination of the last two – and, more specifically, the latter. This choice must also be seen against the background of other recent examples where nations had to deal with past atrocities and human rights abuses. The Truth Commission of Argentina is usually cited as a good example of a collective search for truth and justice during a political transition. While it succeeded commendably during the "truth phase" in unearthing and exposing the past, it fell short during the "justice phase" in dealing with the perpetrators and in providing restitution for victims. In the case of Uruguay the result was more unsatisfactory, and the exercise, on the whole, had only a minimal impact for the good. The Chilean case, though, was more successful. This was due to its bipartisan nature and to the fact that it operated with limited terms of reference (mostly tied to the issue of

511

"disappearances") and was of limited duration (it had to report in nine months). Besides, state resources were placed at its disposal and it had the support of the then newly elected civilian president. Finally, it had excellent data-gathering ability and a clear policy on restitution (Liebenberg 1996: 140–1, 143–4).

The South African Truth and Reconciliation Commission (TRC) was officially announced through The Promotion of the National Unity and Reconciliation Act 34 of 1995. Members were appointed and the Commission, which was given a specific timeframe to complete its work, started its proceedings in April 1996. It was structured to operate through three specialized committees – one dealing with the violations of human rights, one on amnesty, and another on reconciliation and reparation. In essence, the work of the TRC involved hearing the stories of victims of gross human rights violations. It was also charged with the duty of considering applications for amnesty from perpetrators of such violations; and making recommendations on reparation to the victims, as well as devising measures for ensuring that human rights abuses were not committed again (ibid. 133, 150). In this process the main objective of the TRC was to deal with the thorny issues of "historical truth," on the one hand, and amnesty, reconciliation, and reparation, on the other. The aim was, thus, not to prosecute political leaders for crimes against humanity, but to secure a public recognition of the breaching of human rights in the past within the framework of an agreement on political amnesty. As in the case of Chile, this implies a qualified concept of justice.[6] Because of the nature of the Commission, it is understandable that not everyone was convinced that it was going to succeed. An important question was: will the work of this institution, with all its shortcomings, be able to keep the memories of the victims alive as an integral part of South Africa's future public debate?

In dealing with the politics of memory and forgetting after apartheid, the TRC can be seen as a compromise in more ways than one. First, the Commission was the result of a *political compromise*, being part and parcel of the negotiated settlement which marked South Africa's transition. The end of apartheid and white minority rule did not lead to the seizure of state power by the representatives of the majority. This political compromise at least avoided a full-scale bloody revolution or civil war, and amounted to a process of national reconciliation. The TRC was intended to bring this process of political compromise to a conclusion by, *inter alia*, granting amnesty to those who had committed gross violations of human rights for political objectives in the context of the conflicts of the past. Secondly, the TRC served as a *moral compromise*, evading justice in a narrow sense by concentrating on truth and reconciliation. The objective was not to prosecute and punish the perpetrators of those atrocities so that justice can be done (Du Toit 1996: 8). This is similar to Krog's argument that justice in the exclusive form of amnesty, trials, and compensation will not exhaust the concept of truth. The challenge was rather to enlarge the concept of truth by including the perceptions, stories, myths, and experiences of individuals and groups. Violators of human rights must be named, but in a way that will not present them as devils. Past offenses must be recognized in such a way that it is clear why it was wrong. In this sense a historical landmark could be situated between the past and the present, for the first time since the encounter between White and Black (Krog 1994: 8).[7]

Thirdly, the compromise must be seen against the background of an *international shift* in policies regarding human rights abuses in the past. Unlike the message sent after the Second World War by the victors to perpetrators (at least those with high military ranking), "reconciliation" seems now to be the main objective of the international community. As noted above, both Argentina and Uruguay preferred to shift from trying and punishing to "forgiving and forgetting." These governments, with a great deal of international support, decided either to interrupt, or not to initiate legal procedures against those responsible for atrocious crimes. This change of heart in favor of the policy of pardon, forgetting, and amnesty also found resonance in academic circles (De Greiff 1996: 94).[8] Ackerman, for example, argues that the project of "corrective justice" – i.e. the attempt to punish former criminals – represents a major threat to constitutionalism. The problem with corrective justice is that it is past-oriented, individualistic, and divisive; while constitutional justice is future-oriented, systematic, and consolidatory. The argument is that in the early stages of democratic transition, when a new regime enjoys – or suffers – a special combination of high moral capital and low bureaucratic capacity, it would be unwise to divide the citizenry unnecessarily. Ackerman's solution is to forget the "mirage of corrective justice," to concentrate on the future, and to burn the "stinking carcasses" in official archives (in ibid. 94, 96). The desire to punish those responsible for human rights abuses is, thus, counterbalanced by the exigencies of the transition to democracy itself – as the Argentinian case illustrated.

Fourthly, a compromise is needed because of a lack of *capacity* in young democracies. The systematic attempt to investigate and prosecute many hundreds or thousands of cases on an individual basis will require massive resources that will surely bog down the courts for many years to come. The inevitable option for new regimes under such circumstances is selective prosecution. But even if this path is followed, it is difficult to prosecute high officials because of a dearth of evidence, while the problem with prosecuting low-ranking officials is that there will always be legitimate differences about the reach of due obedience (ibid. 96). On the other hand, even if the quest for justice by prosecution is indeed to be such a priority, there is still the question of what would actually be achieved. Some perpetrators would be convicted, but it is also likely that in many other cases prosecutions would not be feasible, while in some cases where prosecutions are started they might fail to achieve actual convictions. In a due trial victims or others must also be willing to be witnesses, to be cross-examined, and to have their testimony questioned and critically scrutinized in all sorts of ways. Bringing the matter to trial may well impose on them a second and public ordeal on top of the original personal trauma (Du Toit 1996: 11). Finally, one of the problems of retroactive justice is that the behavior for which the new regime wants to punish members of the old regime was not classified, in many cases, as crime.

Of all these compromises, the moral one is probably the most difficult to accept in the South African case. It might seem that forgetting would take precedence over memory and that the respect for legal procedure and justice, which is so critical for new democratic regimes, will be disregarded. It is quite understandable that the victims and their families would demand that the perpetrators of violence and human rights abuses be brought to justice. Others have also argued that if the

513

political atrocities of the past are to be addressed, then nothing less than justice will do. Moreover, the establishment of a culture of human rights in South Africa cannot allow known gross violations of human rights to go unpunished. However, as Du Toit correctly pointed out, the TRC's terms of reference did not categorically rule out the prospect of doing justice through prosecution and punishment. Unlike Chile and Uruguay, there was to be no general amnesty for the killers and torturers. Indemnities were granted on individual applications only, and only on the basis of full disclosure. Those disobeying were open to prosecution. Again, amnesty was not automatic and unqualified. The act that set up the Commission specified a set of criteria for acts with political objectives that might qualify for amnesty. Moreover, it is not quite true that perpetrators who were indemnified went entirely "unpunished." There is a sense in which the requirement of disclosure, and the public recording of the particular acts for which indemnities were granted, in themselves, amounted to a significant form of punishment (ibid. 9–10).

The interesting aspect of the TRC is that its qualified concept of justice must be read with its orientation toward the perspective and the plight of victims. Only the Amnesty Committee focuses on perpetrators, while the other two committees provide victims and others with a forum in which they can tell their own stories and consider appropriate ways and forms of reparation. The intention here was to restore the human and civic dignity of victims by acknowledging the injustices that were done to them and accepting responsibility for their plight. It follows that the investigation and procedures of these committees needed to be structured in a sympathetic way. In the absence of hostile cross-questioning of witnesses, for example, the investigative process could contribute to a healing rather than a traumatic experience (ibid. 11). The difficulties associated with the policy of trial and punishment should therefore not lead to a hasty move in the direction of pardon and forgetting. Morality itself implies a commitment to the past, which gives grounds to object to such a policy. In an imperfect world the best option, as De Greiff indicates, is possibly judgment and forgiveness versus punishment and forgetting. Rather than simply maintaining that in an imperfect world there are moral commands we cannot fulfill, such a policy is both implementable – unlike trial and punishment – *and* morally unobjectionable – unlike pardon and forgetting. In this process the commitment to the past doesn't follow from a single principle, but from a reflection upon the nature of moral experience and deliberation (De Greiff 1996: 94, 97). If this is what the aim of truth involves, then it is not correct to see it as something less than justice, in the sense of prosecution and punishment. On the contrary, it involves a different value, one oriented more to restoring the dignity of the victims than seeking punishment for perpetrators (Du Toit 1996: 12).

It should be clear that the TRC was established by the South African Parliament in an atmosphere yearning for understanding not vengeance, reparation not retaliation, *ubuntu* (humanness) not victimization. The TRC was also in many respects unique. It was not a Commission by presidential decree, but a "uniquely democratic commission," being the result of a multiparty negotiated settlement that went through an extended process of parliamentary hearings and a similar process of public debate and scrutiny (ibid. 6). The process was also officially open to encourage public debate and input, by acknowledging a "truth phase" (implying the uncarthing or opening up of the truth) and a "justice phase" (implying restitution to the aggrieved and the possibility of action against perpetrators of human rights abuses). The end result of the TRC on the national psyche is not yet clear at this stage – it might be national reconciliation and "healing," or frustration and dissatisfaction. But one thing is certain: South Africans have been confronted with a chilling exposé of what many knew was happening, others suspected, and yet others held could never have taken place (Liebenberg 1996: 152–3, 155). One can also safely assert that the reflection on the past did not end when the TRC completed its work. In this sense, writers, historians, and institutions (such as universities and research bodies) have a special responsibility to engage in a pluralistic debate on the past.[9] Such a critical dialogue will hopefully address, amongst other things, the very important issue of "historical consciousness" in a multicultural society and examine national memories for their accuracy and plausibility.[10] In short, the identity of the present South Africa will not escape a moral obligation to the past.

How, then, should the "reality" and "truth" about Auschwitz and apartheid be addressed critically? First, we should remember that there is always a moral obligation to the past. We do not show respect toward who we are, our present identities, by forgetting the past. If the past becomes a locus of evasion or forgetting, it also becomes an evasion of the complexities of the present and fear of the future. By escaping from the responsibility of the deeds of the past, the original sin of apartheid is evaded. Secondly, we must take Benjamin and Lyotard seriously in their non-determined and non-totalizing view of the past. This does not imply the naive acceptance of any tradition as a sufficient criterion of morality. On the contrary, there is more than one way to show our respect to the past.[11] De Greiff writes: "Although it may be true that the past is part of what we *are*, this does not, on its own, answer the question about who we *ought to be*" (1996: 101–3). A common deficiency in contemporary ethical theories, and this includes Habermas's discourse ethics, is that they begin too late. As Nussbaum and Sherman have argued, they concentrate so much on the formulation of a decision procedure that they ignore the processes of moral experience and moral perception that precede decision. In stressing the importance of an *education of sensibility* they want to explain how, before the moment of decision, the agent has already perceived the situation in such a way that he or she understands that the circumstances call for a moral decision. The memory of who we are, what we have done to others, is thus a *precondition* of the exercise of moral judgment. In this sense remembering *precedes* moral principles. It helps us recollect the phenomena on which we will pass (principled) judgment (Nussbaum 1986; Sherman 1989).

But, what becomes of the obligation to the past and of retroactive justice in the absence of a tradition of moral universalism? How should the South African TRC be interpreted in this regard? These difficult questions can be tamed by understanding punishment in terms that go beyond incarceration. Thus the object of punishment is not the individual's freedom of movement (like a prison sentence), but of association. As De Greiff indicates, a new democratic regime might choose to punish violators of human rights by prohibiting their renewed association for any purpose (De Greiff 1996: 104). Secondly, the TRC challenges the conventional understanding of trial. Trials in courts of law have individuals as targets and are adversarial by nature. The TRC, in contrast, provides a space for the telling of heterogeneous

515

stories by the victims. There are no guarantees that these stories will represent the truth and that reconciliation will follow automatically. Neither personal nor collective memory can undo a monstrous past. These difficulties, however, do not imply that our obligation to the past justifies a policy of pardon and forgetting. The solution in this predicament may lie, as hinted above, in a policy of judgment and forgiving rather than punishment and forgetting.

Notes

This contribution is an abridged version of an article published in *Philosophy and Social Criticism*, 1999, 25/3: 1–28. I want to thank the editor and publisher for permission to use it here. I also owe much to Kwasi Wiredu's suggestions in finalizing this version.

1   Heribert Adam writes that "South Africa differs from the Yugoslav atrocities and earlier European genocides in its paternalistic inter-group relations" (1992: 16). Mamdani argues that the Holocaust is an inappropriate and misleading political metaphor for South Africa: "it abstracts from the real problem: whites and blacks in South Africa are not akin to Germans and Jews, for Germans and Jews did not have to build a common society in the aftermath of the Holocaust. There was Israel. South African whites and blacks, however, do have to live together in the aftermath of apartheid. Here, as in Rwanda, yesterday's perpetrators and victims – today's survivors – have to confront the problem of how to live together" (1996: 3).

2   In reviewing an article of mine (see Duvenage 1994), Tom Lodge (1994: 77–8) pointed out: (1) that South Africa has had a similar debate to the *Historikerstreit*; (2) that Hitler's defeat "was ... followed by nearly five years of foreign military occupation"; (3) that I had made a specific language mistake. See also Duvenage 1995: 99; Meulenberg-Buskens 1995: 102. Leaving Lodge's mastery of the English language aside, the following response is relevant: (1) The South African liberal/revisionist debate of historians cannot be compared with the German Historians' Debate, because it was mainly an academic debate with little impact on the public sphere and daily press; (2) Lodge is correct about the "foreign military occupation" in Germany, but historically the intention was very clear: to allow German self-government as soon as possible. On the whole, Lodge's review is a good example of the state of criticism in South Africa today.

3   See the reference to the South African playwright, Athol Fugard, in Cochrane 1991: 63. Fugard argues passionately, against a former white cabinet minister, that there is a legacy to deal with: "Lives have been wasted, lives have been deeply hurt, lives have been mutilated, lives have been lost. No, we can't just sweep all of that away as if it doesn't matter."

4   Krog quotes the following lines from Totius to illustrate the point: "Die wonde word gesond weer / as die jare kom en gaan / maar daardie merk word groter / en groei maar aldeur aan." (The wounds are healing / as the years come and go / but that mark remains / and keeps growing – my translation.)

5   Krog 1994: 7. Similarly the South African theologian J. R. Cochrane writes: "There is no hope where the memory of suffering is silenced, leaving traces of suppressed dialogue" (1991: 63). This remark is similar to Kundera's famous quote: "the struggle of man against power is the struggle of memory against forgetting," and Brodsky's essays and poems recruiting "memory as a challenge to the rigidity and forward-marching of the totalitarian state." See Wood 1992.

6   See Du Toit 1994: 9. Du Toit indicates that the "balancing act" excluded the possibility of Nüremberg-type trials. The thorny issue of justice involved leads Du Toit to the following remark made by Huntington: "Recognize that on the issue of 'prosecute or punish vs forgive and forget' each alternative presents grave problems, and that the least unsatisfactory course may well be: do not prosecute, do not punish, do not forgive (*sic!*), and, above all, do not forget" (ibid. 15). On transitional justice, see Kritz 1995.

7   Kader Asmal writes: "We need a revival of moral consciousness if we are ever to build from out of our diversity a common citizenship and a common national consciousness." Quoted in Du Preez 1992: 5–6.

8   De Greiff refers to the works of Ackerman 1992; Heller 1993; and Malamud-Goti 1996.

9   Apart from the contributions of Du Toit, Krog, Liebenberg, and Mamdani, see also Botman and Petersen 1996; Conner 1998; Jeffrey 1999; Orr 2000; and Tutu 1999. More generally, see Pauw 1997; De Kock 1998; and Waldmeir 1998.

10 See Rüsen 1991: 1. Butler writes: "Abuse of cultural memory – the manipulation of long-invalid past grievances to obtain present-day advantages – rules the day in the war-torn lands of Yugoslavia. Deliberate misreadings and misrepresentations of history are destroying the future in the Balkans. The fundamental cause of Yugoslavia's terrible calamity is not just recent history, such as the infamous genocide at the Jasenovac concentration camp during World War II . . . All these elements play a role in the minds of those destroying Bosnia. They are sick from history – from half-truths and ethnic prejudices passed from one generation to the next, through religion, political demagoguery, inflammatory tracts, and even through abuse of folk songs and tales. More recently, the books of unscrupulous writers and the deliberately inaccurate speeches of unprincipled leaders have further contaminated the atmosphere . . . motivated by fear of contamination from within" (1992: 21).

11 See Duvenage 1999: 17–22.

References

Ackerman, A. (1992) *The Future of Liberal Revolution* (New Haven: Yale University Press).

Adam, Heribert (1992) "Will Ethnicity turn SA into Another Sarajevo?" *Die Suid-Afrikaan*, 41 (Oct/Nov).

Adorno, T. W. (1977) "Was bedeutet: Aufarbeitung der Vergangenheit," *Gesammelte Schriften*, 10(2) (Frankfurt: Suhrkamp).

Botman, R. and Petersen, R. M. (eds.) (1996) *To Remember and to Heal: Theological and Psychological Reflections on Truth and Reconciliation* (Cape Town: Human and Rousseau).

Butler, T. (1992) "Centuries of Grudges Behind Today's Balkans Calamity," *The Guardian Weekly*, September 11–17.

Cochrane, J. R. (1991) "Nation Building: A Socio-Theological View," in W. S. Vorster (ed.), *Building a New Nation* (Pretoria: Unisa Press).

Conner, B. (1998) *The Difficult Traverse: From Amnesty to Reconciliation* (Pietermaritzburg: Cluster Publications).

De Greiff, P. (1996) "Trial and Punishment: Pardon and Oblivion. On Two Inadequate Policies for the Treatment of Former Human Rights Abusers," *Philosophy and Social Criticism*, 22.

De Kock, E. (1998) *A Long Night's Damage: Working for the Apartheid State* (Johannesburg: Contra Press).

Derrida, Jacques (1985) "Racism's Last Word," *Critical Inquiry*, 12.

Derrida, Jacques (1986) "Debate with McClintock and Nixon," *Critical Inquiry*, 13: 140–70.

Du Preez, M. (1992) "Nee vir blanko-immuniteit, ja vir 'n Morele Tribunaal," *Vrye Weekblad*, 25 (September).

Du Toit, A. (1994) "Agtergrond tot die Waarheid en Versoeningskomitee," *Die Suid-Afrikaan*, 50 (October).

Du Toit, A. (1996) "Philosophical Perspectives on the Truth Commission? Some Preliminary Notes and Fragments," unpublished paper.

Duvenage, Pieter (1994) "Dealing with South Africa's History of Violence and Covert Operations," in A. Minnaar, I. Liebenberg, and C. Schutte (eds.), *The Hidden Hand* (Pretoria: HSRC Publishers).

Duvenage, Pieter (1995) "Correspondence," *Politikon*, 22(2).

Duvenage, Pieter (1999) "The Politics of Memory and Forgetting After Auschwitz and Apartheid," *Philosophy and Social Criticism*, 25(3): 1–28.

Erikson, H. (1980) *Identity and the Life Cycle* (New York: Norton).

Freud, Sigmund (1957) *Mourning and Melancholia. Complete Works*, vol. 14 (London: Hogarth Press).

Habermas, Jürgen (1994) "More Humility, Fewer Illusions – Interview," *New York Review*, 24 (March).

Heller, A. (1993) "The Limits of Natural Law and the Paradox of Evil," in *On Human Rights. The Oxford Amnesty Lectures, 1993* (New York: Basic Books).

Jeffrey, A. (1999) *The Truth about the Truth Commission* (Johannesburg: South African Institute of Race Relations).

Kritz, N. (ed.) (1995) *Transitional Justice: How Emerging Democracies reckon with former Regimes*, 3 vols (Washington: US Institute of Peace Press).

Krog, Antjie (1994) "Die onreg van die Boere-Oorlog," *Die Suid-Afrikaan* (October).

Liebenberg, I. (1992) "Apartheid, Guilt and Retribution. To Confess or not to Confess," *Prospects*, 1 (December).

Liebenberg, I. (1996) "The Truth and Reconciliation Commission in South Africa: Context, Future and Some Imponderables," *South African Journal of Public Law*, 11.

Liebenberg, I. (1997) "Die Waarheids- en Versoeningskommissie (WVK) in Suid-Afrika en die implikasies daarvan vir 'n Suid-Afrikaanse *Historikerstreit* en eietydse Geskiedskrywing," *Journal for Contemporary History/Tydskrif vir Eietydse Geskiedenis*, 22(1): 98–114.

Lodge, Tom (1994) "Review of A. Minnaar et al., *The Hidden Hand*," *Politikon*, 21(1).

Malamud-Goti, J. (1996) *The Game without End. State Terror and the Politics of Justice* (Norman: Oklahoma University Press).

Mamdani, M. (1996) "Reconciliation without Justice," *Southern African Review of Books*, 46 (Nov/Dec).

Meulenberg-Buskens, I. (1995) "Correspondence," *Politikon*, 22(1).

Mitscherlich, A. and Mitscherlich, M. (1967) *Die Unfähigkeit zu trauern* (München: Piper) (trans. here by R. Wolin).

Nussbaum, M. (1986) *Fragility of Goodness* (Cambridge: Cambridge University Press).

Orr, Wendy (2000) *Search For the Souls of South Africa as a Commissioner of the TRC* (Saxonwold: Contra Press).

Pauw, J. (1997) *Into the Heart of Darkness: Confessions of Apartheid's Assassins* (Johannesburg: Jonathan Ball).

Rüsen, J. (1991) "Historical Education in a Multicultural Society," *Gister en Vandag/Yesterday and Today*, 21.

Sherman, N. (1989) *The Fabric of Character* (Oxford: Clarendon Press).

Tutu, D. (1999) *No Future Without Forgiveness* (Johannesburg: Random House).

Waldmeir, P. (1998) *Anatomy of a Miracle* (London: Penguin Books).

Wood, J. (1992) "Review of Joseph Brodsky's *Watermark*," *Guardian Weekly*, July 3–9, p. 28.

43

The Question of an African Jurisprudence: Some Hermeneutic Reflections

JOHN MURUNGI

What is the province of African jurisprudence? In this question, the word "African" qualifies jurisprudence. The qualification implies that there are other provinces of jurisprudence. The further implication of this implication is that the province of African jurisprudence is what it is, in part, by its intersection with other provinces of jurisprudence. Adequately understood, African jurisprudence, like any other jurisprudence adequately understood, ought to lead us to such an intersection. It is tempting to think of this intersection as what constitutes the proper province of jurisprudence, and to think of the qualifications of jurisprudence as merely marginal. This is likely to seduce some universalists into thinking that jurisprudence should concern itself only with what is universal. Succumbing to this seduction may lead to another seduction, namely, that of being led to think of jurisprudential inquiry as an inquiry that exclusively investigates what the provinces of jurisprudence have in common. In this view, the inquiry into African jurisprudence would marginalize what is African about jurisprudence and concentrate on what is universal in it. To the extent that such an inquiry is philosophical, what is African about philosophy would be essentially inconsequential to the inquiry. To meet the task at hand adequately, philosophical method would be directed to what is universal, and the very substance of philosophy itself would have to be universal. One would have to assume that, as a branch of African philosophy, what is African about legal philosophy in Africa should not be the focus of the inquiry. What is African about legal philosophy would have to take a back seat as attention is focused on legal philosophy in general. The temptation to view matters this way should be resisted if only because the presupposed nature of jurisprudence, as in the case of the presupposed nature of philosophy, is contestable. Construing the Africanness of African jurisprudence as marginal to jurisprudence or construing the Africanness of African philosophy as marginal to African philosophy is equally contestable. To see why this may be contestable one can imagine the absurdity of construing what it is to be human in a manner that marginalizes individual human beings. If one were to try to turn away from individual human beings and try to focus attention on human being as such, one would be focusing on nothing. Unless one is a Buddhist of the kind who focuses attention not only on nothing, but also on the nothingness of his or her own being, one who is to study *human being* must focus attention on *individualized* human being. Similarly, to study jurisprudence or to study philosophy, attention must be focused on contextualized jurisprudence or on contextualized philosophy. Therefore, it is improper to marginalize the Africanness of African jurisprudence or the Africanness of African philosophy. In either case, Africanness centrally matters. Saying so, of course, does not imply that how Africanness matters, or what Africanness is, is self-evident. It is the task of those who concern themselves with African jurisprudence or with African philosophy to inquire and articulate how Africanness matters.

Every philosophical introduction to jurisprudence is also an introduction to philosophy. When African jurisprudence is investigated by philosophers, it should be expected that the investigator's understanding of philosophy will thereby be revealed. When investigated from the standpoint of African philosophy, the investigation should reveal the investigator's understanding of African philosophy. Thus, to ask what is the province of African jurisprudence in a philosophical sense is to place this question in the province of philosophical interrogation. Understanding the nature of this interrogation is essential if the question is to be adequately understood, and if it is to be adequately answered. A hasty attempt to determine the province of African jurisprudence may be an obstacle not only to an adequate understanding of the province of this jurisprudence, but also to an adequate understanding of the province of African philosophy.

In recent history of African philosophy, there has been an attempt to rescue African philosophy from what Paulin Hountondji, an African philosopher, has referred to as ethnophilosophy. Ethnophilosophy is a pseudo-philosophy, a fictitious philosophy that has been constructed and attributed to Africans by European missionaries or by European cultural anthropologists. Under ethnophilosophy, African jurisprudence turns out to be ethno-jurisprudence. Apparently, each of the so-called African tribes has its own jurisprudence that is to be given fuller articulation by Euro-Western missionaries or by Euro-Western cultural anthropologists. Hountondji finds the notion of ethnophilosophy thoroughly unphilosophical and seeks to replace it with a genuine African philosophy. However, in his earlier writings, though he has now refined his position, he seemed to construe genuine African philosophy as a scientific activity. Such a philosophy borrows little from the thinking that prevailed in precolonial indigenous African thinking, since, on this showing, such thinking was largely unscientific. Because, on that view, philosophy, like any other scientific discipline, is the same everywhere, jurisprudence, when taken up by philosophy, should be the same everywhere. African legal philosophy would, then, have to be scientific. The word "African" in the expression "African jurisprudence" would only be a geographical designation. Since, according to this way of looking at the matter, science is a recent phenomenon in Africa, it would appear to follow that philosophy is equally a recent phenomenon in Africa, which would make philosophical jurisprudence in Africa a recent phenomenon. Some African philosophers, such as the late Kenyan philosopher Odera Oruka, or the Ghanaian philosopher Kwasi Wiredu, have a different point of view. To them, African philosophy is not a recent phenomenon. They recognize that there is much that indigenous African thinking can contribute to African philosophy. Oruka's Sage Philosophy is an attempt to demonstrate that there is a philosophical component to indigenous

African philosophical thinking. If only by implication, much can be gained from his thought, and from the thought of those who share his view, in the construction of African jurisprudence.

An investigator of African jurisprudence does not exist in a historical vacuum. This is the case in regard to the investigator of any other jurisprudence. For example, when one looks at Euro-Western jurisprudence, one finds that it is unintelligible if it is not understood in the context of Euro-Western history. This jurisprudence reflects a working-out of issues that have occurred in the course of Euro-Western history. The collapse of the European feudal society, the rise of bourgeois Europe, the conflict between church and state, and the rise of capitalism have had enormous influence in the shaping of this jurisprudence. Similarly, African jurisprudence is only intelligible if it is put into a historical context.

In colonial times, wherever and whenever possible Euro-Western jurisprudence was applied to local African conditions. Indigenous African tribunals, "chiefs," "kings," "leaders," and councils of elders were used to facilitate the subjection of Africans to a Euro-Western jurisprudential regime. Where this subjection was resisted, or rejected, force was used to bring about compliance. It is in this context that the rise of the "police" force in modern Africa is to be understood. Colonial jurisprudence in Africa, as in other colonized parts of the world, was largely the jurisprudence of subjugation. Violence was an essential feature of this jurisprudence. In the eyes of Africans, colonial law was a concrete manifestation of this violence. It was a coercive power in its raw sense. Jurisprudence was the justification or validation of this violence. It was the gunman situation writ large. It is precisely this kind of jurisprudence that is so well captured in Frantz Fanon's book, *The Wretched of the Earth*, the classic text on European colonialist violence in Africa.

In addition to the imposition of Euro-Western jurisprudence, Africans have also suffered from the imposition of Islamic jurisprudence. In Islamic thought, true jurisprudence is founded on Allah and His Messenger. The Quran and the Prophet's Sunna have had a central place in the constitution and interpretation of Islamic jurisprudence. According to the Muslim faith, there is one and only one true God, and that God is Allah. Hence, from the very beginning of the introduction of Islam in Africa, it was assumed that the African's gods were false gods, and that the worship of these gods by Africans was pure idolatry and had to be violently eradicated. Since the introduction of Islam in Africa centuries ago, an attempt has been going on to impose Sharia (the law that governs Muslims) on Africans. Today, millions of Africans are Muslims and live under this law. Among millions of Africans, Sharia and, hence, Islamic jurisprudence, has been embraced to a point where it can be said that it has been indigenized. It is also noteworthy that, since, for the most part, Islam in Africa is associated with Arabs, there has been significant Arabization of Africans. The process of Arabization has been so successful in some areas in Africa that there are now millions of Africans who are Africans and Arabs at the same time. Some have even discarded their African identity in favor of the Arab identity. To be sure, it can also be claimed that Africans have Africanized Islam, and that African Islam is not identical with Islam elsewhere. Nevertheless, in Islam, jurisprudence is so much tied to Islamic theology that an African who embraces it must renounce indigenous African theologies and African religions. For

521

Muslim believers, there is only one true religion and that religion is Islam. And since Islamic religion is at the core of Islamic jurisprudence, for the believers, Islamic jurisprudence is the only true jurisprudence. Thus, as previously indicated, in the eyes of the followers of Islam, indigenous African jurisprudence would not qualify as a true jurisprudence.

Much attention has been paid to what European colonialism has done to Africa and to Africans. Because the propagators of Islam have also not fared well at the hands of Europeans, their negative impact on Africans is yet to be fully investigated. These propagators may have thought of themselves as beyond savagery and barbarism, but in the eyes of Europeans they have mostly been seen as savages and barbarians. They have not been spared the Euro-Western violence that has been perpetrated in the name of law. Nor have they been spared the European version of jurisprudence that justifies this violence. Nevertheless, in thinking about African jurisprudence, we need to take into account the negative influence that Islamic jurisprudence has had in Africa.

Although formal colonialism has come to an end, it is not to be assumed that the anti-colonial process is anachronistic. Genuine decolonization must take into account the difficult process of decolonizing the African mind. The mind to be decolonized is not that proverbial mind that Descartes constructed. Rather, it is the African self-consciousness as it is exhibited in African culture. This decolonizing process is an essential element of African jurisprudence. This phase of African jurisprudence has no analog in the history of Euro-Western jurisprudence. In constituting their jurisprudence, Euro-Westerners did not have to undergo the process of decolonization. As previously indicated, the dynamics of Euro-Western history have given shape to the evolution of Euro-Western jurisprudence. Similarly, any other cultural tradition will have its jurisprudence shaped by its historical situation.

African jurisprudence is not solely a reaction to European colonialism or to the Islamic incursion into Africa. If it were no more than such a reaction, it would only confirm the colonialist/Islamic thesis held by Europeans and by Muslims that in precolonial Africa there was no African jurisprudence. Moreover, it would obscure the objective that motivates the anti-colonial and decolonizing processes. That objective was not implanted in the African by Europeans. What lies behind these processes, and what is the telos of these processes, is inherent in Africans as Africans. It is already found in precolonial Africa in Africans. It is a part of the substance of African jurisprudence. It is self-affirmation of the African people. It is precisely such an affirmation that colonialism sought to erase or deny, and it is precisely what anti-colonial and decolonizing processes seek to reaffirm and protect. Also, what must be taken into account is that self-affirmation does not mean the affirmation of an isolated self. Such a self can only be an expression of a mad person or of a person who is not conscious of his or her personhood. To the extent that African customary law recognizes the communal connotation of being a person, embeddedness in a community must play an important role in the construction of African jurisprudence.

Certainly, in Africa, but not only in Africa, personhood is social. African jurisprudence is a part of African social anthropology. Social cohesion is an essential element of African jurisprudence. Areas of jurisprudence such as criminology and penology, law of inheritance, and land law, for example, focus on the preservation and promotion of social cohesion. This cohesion is a cohesion that is tempered by justice. Justice defines a human being as a human being. Thus, injustice in Africa is not simply a matter of an individual breaking a law that is imposed on him or her by other individuals, or by a collection of individuals who act in the name of the state. It is a violation of the individual's duty to him or herself, a violation of the duty of the individual to be him or herself – the duty to be a social being. A human being is a human being as a social being. The view that jurisprudence takes a person in her or his social situation is precisely the same view that the Ancient Greeks expressed when they claimed that man is a social and political animal. Apart from social and political contexts, jurisprudence, African or non-African, is without meaning. As indicated, these contexts are the contexts of what is human. What is human from an African perspective is the province of African jurisprudence. It is precisely for this reason that the conventional modern Euro-Western literature on jurisprudence does not fully address what is at stake in juris-prudence. For the most part, jurisprudence in this literature concerns itself with the nature of law, the validity of law, the nature of legal obligation, the sources of law, the hermeneutics of law, the administration of law, the types of legal regimes, and so on. In this context, jurisprudence turns out to be an investigation of legal rules (substantive and procedural), and, on occasion, an investigation of the principles or policies that render them meaningful. This conception of jurisprudence is derivative. What is elemental in every jurisprudence is the conception of being human that is presupposed. It is precisely for this reason that it is herein claimed that African jurisprudence is what is at stake in being human for Africans. If jurisprudence is to be understood as a science, it is to be understood, in its African context, as a science of being human as understood by Africans.

As indicated above, African jurisprudence takes human beings in their social setting. Contrary to the claims of Western modernity, such a setting is not a social construction. Human beings are not social beings because they socialize with one another. They socialize with one another because they are social beings. The claim that human beings are social beings is not to be taken as denying individuality. That is, it is not to be taken as denying individual rights or individual autonomy. Individual rights or individual autonomy in a social vacuum are theoretical con-structions that are removed from human reality. In Africa, legality is not a social construction. It is a natural social setting in which the African has her or his being. This setting should not necessarily be linked with social tyranny. It should not necessarily be linked to communistic or totalitarian social systems. It is not an expression of an essentialism that dispenses with historicity or with temporality.

The portrayal of the precolonial African societies as societies in which individual rights or individual autonomy were suppressed is a misconception. This is not to deny that there were instances of such suppression. There is no society that is totally immune to such suppression. However, the overcoming of such suppression should not lead to a situation where human society is reduced to a mere aggregate of individuals. Such an aggregation can only lead to the individual becoming alien-ated from his or her humanness. Instead of construing the requirements of commu-nality as attenuations of the individual's autonomy, they must be seen as instruments for securing the humanity of the individual. Today, it is especially important to bear this in mind as we attempt to assert and protect human rights. The protection of communal rights is not antithetical to the protection of the human rights of the individual. Contrary to what appears to be the case in modern Euro-Western jurisprudence, communal rights are human rights, just like individual rights. Communal rights do not have priority over individual rights, and, conversely, individual rights do not have priority over communal rights. They do not exist in a hierarchy of importance. Moreover, they are, as noted above, not mutually exclusive. They implicate each other. They are both essential not only for human dignity but also for the very meaning of being human.

It is the forgetfulness of these last considerations that has led, for example, to the confusion in the perception and interpretation of such things as disputes in burial cases in Kenya. In one of these cases, the nationally famous Otieno case (1987), a wife contested the custody of her dead husband's body and the right to bury it at a place of her choice. Representatives of the ethnic group to which the husband belonged claimed the custody of the body and the right to bury it at an ancestral ground selected by them. During litigation, the wife asserted her right as an individual to bury her husband and claimed that her nuclear family had definitively severed ties with the husband's ethnic group. Ultimately, when the Court of Appeal ruled against her, she claimed that her individual rights as well as her human rights were violated. She objected to the subordination of her individual rights to communal requirements. She took the view that communal rights were not only spurious but also incompatible with individual rights. Throughout the litigation, she emphasized that her family was modern and cosmopolitan, and that it was not subject to African customary law. To demonstrate that her family was modern and cosmopolitan, she asserted that before marriage she and her husband had received Christian education, and that their marriage had taken place in a Christian ceremony. She pointed out that most of their married life was spent in an urban setting and that in the course of their marriage they, as a family, never practiced the so-called tribal customs. A part of what she ignored or failed to see is that being "modernized," "Christianized," "educated," or "urbanized" in the context of contemporary African history amounts, for the most part, to just being Europeanized. Indeed, it was brought out in the course of that litigation that one of the pieces of evidence brought forward to show that the dead husband was educated and modern, and had severed ties to "tribal" customs, was that he was fond of quoting Shakespeare. Moreover, by asking the Court to recognize the priority of her nuclear family rights over community rights, she was asking the Court to give legal legitimacy to the dismantling of the community and its reduction to an aggregate of nuclear families. Since it was in the Euro-Western world that such a thing would make legal sense, she was asking that an African judiciary should adopt foreign legal canons. In her eyes, this was the course that the correct administration of justice should take. But in doing this, she was asking the Court to do away with the institution of the African communitarian family and with the African communitarian self. Ironically, what she was asking a postcolonial Court to do was to further the mission of European colonialism – a mission whose objective was to break down the organic African communities and to transform them into aggregates of nuclear families for a more effective colonial administration.

524

Although it may strike one as obvious, an African is an African in the context of other Africans, and, as a human being, he or she is a human being in the context of other human beings. What African jurisprudence calls for is an ongoing dialogue among Africans on being human, a dialogue that of necessity leads to dialogue with other human beings. This dialogue is not an end in itself. It is a dialogue with an existential implication. It aims at living in accordance with what one is, which implies living in accordance with what one ought to be. Although one is what one is, one is what one is dialogically. To be dialogical, which necessarily is to engage others, leaves open what one is, and calls for dwelling in this openness.

In the African context, the other is not just the living other. The other is also the departed (the ancestor), and is also the one who is to come. Moreover, the other is not solely the human other. It is also all that is animate and even that which is inanimate. In other words, African jurisprudence is not solely a humanism. A human being, for the African, is more than a human being. She or he is a part of what is. For this reason, environmental law for Africans is not an extraneous component of African jurisprudence. It is a matter of the recognition and affirmation of the kinship of what is not human with what is human. Thinking of oneself as a part of what is, is extraordinary thinking. It is extra-ordinary thinking because, whereas ordinary thinking is made possible by a distance between the thinker and what is thought, in extra-ordinary thinking such distance does not exist. Accordingly, in Africa, for the most part, what matters is expressed proverbially, or in a cryptic manner. What is presented in such formulations usually has an enigmatic aspect. It is a representation in which the representer is implicated in the presentation and in which the presentation is implicated in the representer. That to whom the representation is made is also implicated in the representation and in the representer. The uncanniness of what transpires may strike one as a source of confusion; but, properly grasped, there is a translucency in this "confusion." One cannot get rid of this "confusion" without getting rid of what is essential about existence. A part of what Europeans have termed superstitious in African self-experience may yet throw light on what matters not only in African jurisprudence but also in that location where the various provinces of jurisprudence intersect. As for African jurisprudence, if it is granted that its focus is on what Africans understand and experience as law or as having a bearing on law, such an understanding and experience is fundamentally accessible only if an African's understanding and experience of being in the world is fundamentally accessible. What the Greeks in ancient times named physis, or what the Chinese in ancient times named Tao, is, perhaps, not so different from that which announces itself to the African under the guise of law in indigenous African thinking. Here, the "perhaps" is intended to remind any serious student of African jurisprudence that the path to African jurisprudence, adequately understood, intersects with the paths of jurisprudence in other traditions, if they are adequately understood. Each path of jurisprudence represents an attempt by human beings to tell a story about being human. Unless one discounts the humanity of others, one must admit that one has something in common with all other human beings. To discount what one has in common with other human beings is to discount oneself as a human being. What is essential to law is what secures human beings in their being. The pursuit and the preservation of what is human and what is implicated in being human are what, in a particular understanding, is signified by African jurisprudence. Being African is a sign of being African, and being African is a sign of being human. African jurisprudence is a signature. In this signature lies not only what is essential about African jurisprudence, but also what is essential about the Africanness of African jurisprudence. To learn how to decipher it, which, in a sense, implies learning how to decipher oneself, paves the way to genuine understanding.

Further reading

Abdullahi, Ahmednasir (1999) *Burial Disputes in Modern Kenya* (Nairobi Faculty of Law: University of Nairobi).

Allot, Antony (1970) *New Essays in African Law* (London: Butterworth).

Fanon, Frantz (1963) *The Wretched of the Earth* (New York: Grove Press).

Hountondji, Paulin (1996) *African Philosophy Myth and Reality*, trans. Henri Evans (Bloomington: Indiana University Press).

Ojwang, J. B. and Mugambi, J. N. K. (eds.) (1989) *The S.M Otieno Case* (Nairobi: Nairobi University Press).

Shivji, Isa G. (1989) *The Concept of Human Rights in Africa* (London: Codeseria Book series).

Wiredu, Kwasi (1980) *Philosophy and an African Culture* (Cambridge: Cambridge University Press).

Part VII

SPECIAL TOPICS

44

Knowledge as a Development Issue

PAULIN J. HOUNTONDJI

Introduction

The critique of ethnophilosophy, as developed by a number of African philosophers, including myself, for almost 30 years now, has been in many ways misunderstood and misinterpreted. What I want to do here is, first, to restate in a few words and in the most straightforward way the core argument of this critique and, second, to show what is ultimately at stake in this critique. This takes us well beyond the specific issue of the nature and requirements of philosophy as a discipline to the issue of the conditions of a self-reliant and sustainable economic growth and of development in general, whether in Africa or any other human society today.

The Critique of Ethnophilosophy

Not so long ago, there was a widespread belief that the only way for Africans to do philosophy was to philosophize about Africa. More exactly put, it was believed, first, that all Africans (or at a lower level of generalization, all the Wolof or Yorubas or Bantus, etc.) share a collective world-view; second, that these collective world-views may be called philosophies; and, third, that all we have to do today is to rediscover these collective philosophies, to study them as accurately as possible, and display them for the use and intellectual delectation of the external world.

Thousands of writings of all sizes, including books, articles, theses, doctoral dissertations, and conference papers, have been trying for 100 years or more – and especially since World War II – to describe African philosophy in that sense. I took it that this kind of investigation had been first launched in the West at a given point in the development of Western ethnography. What I accepted least, however, was the way African scholars themselves took up this project uncritically as handed down to them by this tradition. They too started writing about such topics as the Rwanda philosophy of being, the Luba notion of being, the dialectics of the Burundi, the idea of old age among the Fulbe, the sense of honor among the Wolof, the conception of life among the Yoruba, the African concept of time, African metaphysical clearings, etc. They did this without asking themselves what was the use of such investigations, what could be their significance for themselves, and whether such investigations were suitable for anything other than feeding the curiosity and other intellectual and even non-intellectual needs of Western readership.

I did not accept, either, the way in which this tradition implicitly defined the task of the African philosopher today. To make it clear that this way of doing philosophy was not the standard one, I described it as ethnophilosophy, i.e. a branch of ethnology mistaken for philosophy. More exactly put, I wanted to make it clear that this kind of investigation amounted to creating a new standard of philosophical practice specific to Africa and such other areas as are traditionally considered research fields for ethnographers and anthropologists. This new standard was one that was bound to hinder the African philosopher or, for that matter, the so-called primitive or semi-primitive philosopher from tackling issues of a universal meaning and significance (Tempels 1949; Hountondji 1970).

It so happened that my colleague from Cameroon, Marcien Towa, coincidentally used the same word with the same derogatory meaning in a booklet published in 1971, one year after my article on this issue. More specifically, he used the term to describe what he also called "la philosophie africaine dans le sillage de la négritude" (African philosophy in the wake of Negritude). Thus, his focus was on African ethnophilosophy rather than on ethnophilosophy as a whole (Towa 1971).

Starting from this point, my concern was about questions of the following sort. In what conditions did ethnophilosophy emerge in the West as a sub-discipline of ethnology or anthropology? What are the relations of ethnophilosophy to such disciplines as ethnobotany, ethnozoology, and ethnoscience as a whole? What are the origins of anthropology itself? What happens when scholars from societies hitherto considered as *terrains* for anthropological study undertake to do anthropology themselves? How have these scholars operated so far vis-à-vis the methodological standards, the epistemological paradigms, and the overall political, social, economic, cultural, and other assumptions handed down to them by the Western anthropological tradition? How have they, in short, generally operated and how should they now operate? What is the situation in other disciplines? What happens, for instance, when African scholars do research in the humanities or in the social sciences, including sociology, economics, political science, law, geography, history, psychology, linguistics, or the classics? What happens when they do mathematics, physics, chemistry, biology, computer science, astronomy, or any other so-called "hard science"?

To some of these questions, I had tentative answers or, at least, hypotheses. Reflection about ethnophilosophy had led me to the conclusion that this kind of approach was based on at least one misconception, which I called *unanimism*. This consists in the overvaluation of unanimity at the expense of debate among the people studied by anthropology. This attitude, in fact, went so far as to almost assume that in so-called "primitive," "archaic," "traditional," or "simpler" cultures everyone agrees with everyone. Unanimism,[1] understood in that way, seemed to me a sophisticated form of one of the original sins of anthropology, i.e. the oversimplification of non-Western societies and cultures. To me, the alternative to unanimism was pluralism. As far as anthropology is concerned, a pluralistic approach would consist in, first, acknowledging the fact of diversity, including diversity of

530

opinion and belief, in every human society, and, second, valuing diversity as a sign of cultural health, or wealth, and as a condition for more intense creativity even in non-Western societies, instead of viewing it as a cultural disease or a form of spiritual poverty.

However, another flaw of ethnophilosophy and, by extension, of anthropology seemed more serious to me. It has no longer to do with a misconception; it has to do with the social insertion of this kind of discourse. Who does it address? To whom is it intended? Obviously, the addressees are not the people talked about. The anthropologist's work is intended for the scientific community, and it is assumed that no member of the society talked about belongs to this community. Moreover, it is secretly expected that no member of this society would ever belong to the scientific community. Some authors express this expectation in the most naive and straightforward manner. For instance:

> Let us not expect the first Black-in-the-street (especially if he is young) to give us a systematic account of his ontological system. Nevertheless, this ontology exists; it penetrates and informs all the primitive's thinking and dominates all his behavior. Using the methods of analysis and synthesis of our own intellectual disciplines, we can and therefore must do the "primitive" the service of looking for, classifying and systematizing the elements of his ontological system.
>
> We do not claim that the Bantus are capable of presenting us with a philosophical treatise complete with an adequate vocabulary. It is our own intellectual training that enables us to effect its systematic development. It is up to us to provide them with an accurate account of their conception of entities, in such a way that they will recognize themselves in our words and will agree, saying: "You have understood us, you know us now completely, you 'know' in the same way we 'know.'" (Tempels 1959: 15 and 24)

I suggested therefore that Western anthropological discourse was based on some kind of exclusion, the exclusion of the people talked about, from the discussion about them. Now, when anthropology is taken up by scholars from the "talked-abouts," this circumstance does not really affect the nature, status, and mode of functioning of the anthropological discourse. The rank-and-file of the people remain excluded, the non-Western anthropologist being simply *co-opted* into a Western, or West-centered discussion. His or her discourse is therefore, I said, *extroverted*, that is, externally oriented, dependent on the questions posed by the West, and intended to feed theoretical and eventually practical needs expressed by the West (Hountondji 1976).

In the course of the discussion that developed in and outside Africa about ethnophilosophy, I came to qualify my critique of unanimism. I acknowledged clearly that any human group could live on a set of assumptions shared by all its members, whether or not this set of assumptions is systematic enough to be considered, as it often is, as a "system of thought." I still rejected, however, the hasty way in which ethnologists and some philosophers tended to label such sets of assumptions as "philosophies." To me, these assumptions represented instead the initial material *in relation to which* philosophy could develop as a critical, personal, body of thought (Hountondji 1982).

531

On the other hand, I have never renounced the concept of extroversion as a polemical or critical concept. Instead it has become, beyond the specific case of ethnophilosophy, more and more instrumental in my attempts at a critical diagnosis of scientific practice in Africa or, as I have sometimes put it, of intellectual work at the periphery (Hountondji 1988).

I will not expand on this point. Let me just mention that, as this diagnosis developed, my descriptive and very simple concept of extroversion appeared to me more and more clearly as a special case of the wider notion of economic extroversion, as used by neo-Marxist theorists of development. The Core/Periphery model became instrumental for me as a conceptual tool to account not only for the so-called economic underdevelopment of the Third World, as usually is done, but also for the North/South relationships in the field of scholarship and learning. In other words, I used the model in the analysis of the scientific and intellectual relations of production on a world scale. Based on this hypothesis, detailed description allowed me to show the many aspects and manifestations of "scientific dependence in Africa today," bringing out the weaknesses and shortcomings of knowledge production at the periphery (Hountondji 1990).

The Origins of Ethnophilosophy and Ethnoscience

Based on this analysis, a number of questions became inevitable. First, I wanted to know more about the origins of ethnophilosophy. Contrary to what many people still believe – and contrary to what Towa and myself, each on his own, certainly believed – the word "ethnophilosophy" was not coined in the early 1970s but much earlier. I quickly realized this upon rereading *Ghana: The autobiography of Kwame Nkrumah*, published in 1957 by the first head of state of independent Ghana. Nkrumah tells anecdotally of how, after obtaining his MA in philosophy in February 1943 at the University of Pennsylvania, he immediately registered for a PhD in "ethnophilosophy" at the same university. The word was uttered without further explanation. "Ethnophilosophy" appeared therefore to be the name of a subject, the name of a recognizable and recognized discipline in academia. Nkrumah mentions, however, that he did not have time to complete and defend his dissertation before he left in 1945 for Britain. We know he became assistant secretary of the fifth Pan-African Congress held in Manchester in October the same year under the chairmanship of W. E. B. Du Bois (Nkrumah 1957).

I wanted, therefore, to know, among other things, in what conditions Nkrumah undertook this PhD work; and, more specifically, whether the word was coined by him or by somebody else. I also wondered what was the subject and topic of his MA thesis, if any.

Secondly, I wanted to know more about the origins and development of ethnoscience. I assumed that ethnophilosophy, as practiced by Nkrumah in the early 1940s, was designed after such disciplines as ethnobotany and ethnozoology, which I knew were older. Ethnobotany is the study of the views and conceptions about plants in oral cultures, and ethnozoology is the study of the views and conceptions about animals. Similarly, ethnophilosophy appeared to be the study of the most general ideas and views in these cultures. There was a need, therefore, to find out the historical and intellectual context in which ethnobotany, ethnozoology, and other ethno-disciplines, if any, were conceived, and whether they show any evidence of the same kind of unanimism, exclusion, and/or extroversion. One needed also to examine the later developments of ethnoscience, its place and role today as a specific branch of ethnology or anthropology, and its overall contribution, if any, to the improvement of the quality of life among the "talked-abouts" of ethnology and anthropology.

While these questions were in my mind, I came to find out that Nkrumah not only started work on a PhD dissertation, but actually did complete at least a draft dissertation under the title "Mind and Thought in Primitive Society: A Study in Ethno-Philosophy with Special Reference to the Akan Peoples of the Gold Coast, West Africa." I also found out that at the University of Pennsylvania at that time, MA candidates could take a number of seminars instead of writing a thesis. The latter seems to have been what Nkrumah did. I am still not sure whether he coined the word "ethno-philosophy," or found it in the existing literature. He uses it at the end of his preface, without referring to any past usage but without presenting it as a neologism either. All we learn is that he postulates "a synthetic ethno-philosophy" by which anthropology, beyond its traditional questions, would "endeavor to go . . . into the basic and fundamental meanings underlying all cultures so as to arrive at a basic cultural *Weltanschauung* by which mankind may realize that even though race, language and culture may be separate and distinct entities yet they are *one* in the sense that there is but one race: *The Homo Sapiens*" (Nkrumah n.d.).

It would be interesting to compare Nkrumah's idea and practice of ethnophilosophy in America with those developed independently in the French-speaking areas of Africa shortly after he wrote this thesis. But I will resist this temptation here. One thing I would like to mention, however, is that during my visit to the University of Pennsylvania I was reminded that another African, Nnamdi Azikiwe, who was also later to become one of the first modern statesmen of his country, Nigeria, received his MA at the same university eight or nine years before Nkrumah. I hold a copy, graciously offered to me by the African Studies Center of the University of Pennsylvania, of Azikiwe's thesis in anthropology on "Mythology in Onitsha Culture."

Beyond these two specific cases, however, it would be interesting to explore the explanation for the fascination exercised by America over the minds of early intellectual and political elites in Anglophone Africa during the twentieth century, and the overall role of the African-American elites and of America as a whole in shaping modern continental Africa. Here again, however, I will resist going further.

As far as ethnoscience is concerned, it so happened that the formal creation of the relevant disciplines also took place in America. Botany seems to have been the first of the natural sciences to be given the prefix "ethno." This happened as early as 1895, and the author was an American agronomist and botanist named J. W. Harshberger. Zoology was to follow, around 1914. The generic term "ethnoscience" was coined much later, in the third edition of George Peter Murdock's *Outline of Cultural Materials* in 1950. It was used, in fact, as a synonym for "folk-science" or "popular knowledge," as understood by a group of young ethnographers, especially at Yale University, who wanted in the same period to launch a "new ethnography." The discipline ethnolinguistics was said to have been instrumental in this exploration of "folk science" (Murdock 1950; Revel 1990; Scheps 1993).

So far, I do not know much more on the origins and early developments of ethnoscience in America. What I know for sure, however, is that these developments in the US were but the American side of a long story that began much earlier in Europe. To understand the origins of ethnophilosophy, ethnolinguistics, and the ethno-disciplines as a whole, one has to get back at least to German Romanticism. Ideas about the *Volksgeist*, the spirit of the people, or of the nation, date back to this period. Works by Johann Herder in the eighteenth century and Wilhelm von Humboldt in the early nineteenth, including the latter's detailed empirical studies of Kavi and other languages and cultures, are obviously part of the theoretical background of what is known today as the Sapir-Whorf hypothesis (Herder 1772, 1879; Humboldt 1836–9).

Research into Endogenous Knowledge versus Ethnoscience

Today, there is increasing interest, both in Europe and America, in the study of so-called "indigenous" or "local" knowledge. An impressive bibliography was published in 1972 by Harold Conklin. Many new works have been published ever since, including those by Clifford Geertz (1973, 1983), Paul Richards (1985, 1986, 1996), Pieter Schmidt (1996), to give just a few examples (see also Conklin 1972; Brokensha et al. 1980).[2] It should be noted, however, and this will be my last point, that there are good and not so good reasons for this kind of study, good and not so good methods of approach, good and not so good theoretical assumptions, and good and not so good goals and objectives.

My colleagues at the National University of Benin and myself published a book some years ago under the title *Les Savoirs endogènes: pistes pour une recherche*, an outcome of a multidisciplinary seminar which I organized. An English version of the book was released a few years later under the title *Endogenous Knowledge: Research Trails*. Contributions were about, among other things, rainmaking and rainmakers, traditional iron-metallurgy in West Africa, *Fa* or *Ifa*, a divination system widespread among the Yoruba and the Yoruba-related peoples of West Africa, including the Fon, the Gun, and the Mahi of Benin. Other chapters were about traditional models of mental health and illness, herbal medicine, foreign objects in human bodies, traditional number systems and modern arithmetic, animal names in the Hausa language, a tentative psychosomatic interpretation of sorcery and witchcraft, graphic systems in precolonial Africa, writing and oral tradition in the transmission of knowledge, and food technology. My own introduction was translated under the title "Re-Centering Africa," which, in fact, is an interpretation of my French title: "Démarginaliser." I assume that the translator, who happens to be the well-known Ghanaian novelist, Ayi Kwei Armah, felt that a literal translation of this one-word title "Demarginalizing" would not make much sense to the Anglophone reader. But what I meant was that in Africa today what is often called traditional knowledge is still marginalized, and that an important step forward would be to integrate it into the mainstream of ongoing research for the benefit of Africa (Hountondji 1994).

This is where our approach differs from that of ethnoscience. We are not studying the "indigenous knowledge," "local knowledge," or "folk-science" for its own sake, from an aesthetic point of view, as if they were just products of fancy. We are asking how true they are, how valid they are. We are looking for ways and means to test them in order to validate whatever in them can be validated, and make contemporary science take them into account in a reciprocal process of updating. That makes a huge difference. Ethnoscience does not ask any question about the *truth* of local knowledge systems. It just describes them and leaves them as they are.

More exactly put, ethnoscience is part of anthropology, i.e. the study of "other cultures" (to use John Beattie's phrase). As such, it is part and parcel of a process of knowledge capitalization in the West for the benefit of Western societies. But we know that knowledge is power. It is not surprising, therefore, that part of the knowledge accumulated in that way should be processed afterwards by the natural scientists and other Western researchers, and sometimes developed into new devices and products. Such products are eventually patented, for instance, in pharmaceutical industries, by the laboratories where the "indigenous" devices were analyzed and processed. This, of course, raises an enormous issue as to who is the legitimate owner (Beattie 1964).

Knowledge and Development

In the past 20 or 30 years there have been some interesting developments.[3] Development experts and agencies have come to realize how inappropriate was the Western know-how, which they used to apply to developing countries. They, therefore, have come to value indigenous usages and practices, especially in the field of agriculture. Anthropologists have followed this trend. Some of them at least no longer study "local knowledge" for its own sake, as if it was an end in itself, but as a path to socioeconomic development. They have started doing what I would term applied ethnoscience. This new approach may be considered a step forward, in comparison to traditional ethnoscience (Brokensha et al. 1980).

Something is still missing, however. Applied ethnoscience also considers local knowledge as it is, without questioning its status and mode of existence within the original culture. Its only demand is that this knowledge should be made operational. My own view is different. Before being applied, and in order to be better applied, "traditional" knowledge should be tested again and again by the people themselves, reappropriated in a way that makes it possible to make the indispensable linkage with ongoing scientific and technological research. What is needed in Africa today is not just to apply traditional know-how in agriculture while continuing at the same time to import from the West, whether in agriculture or in other fields, technologies which are poorly understood by local users. What is needed, instead, is to help the people and their elites to master and capitalize on the existing knowledge. This is necessary whether the knowledge is indigenous or not. The rationale is to enable the people to develop new knowledge in a continual process of uninterrupted creativity, while applying the findings in a systematic and responsible way to improve their own quality of life.

535

Notes

1 I made it clear elsewhere where I borrowed this word from. The French writer Jules Romains advocated, at the beginning of the twentieth century, the spirit of solidarity with all humans, in a way very similar to the social lyricism of Walt Whitman. He called this sense of solidarity "unanimous life" and his doctrine was soon known as "unanimism." While borrowing the word, however, I turned it into a derogatory, instead of a laudatory term (Hountondji 1997a: 140; Romains 1908).

2 Pieter Schmidt, University of Florida, edited an impressive book published in 1996, *The Culture and Technology of Iron-Production in Africa*. My colleague Alexis Adandé of the National University of Benin could not have known of this book when he described " 'Traditional' iron-production in West Africa" in a lecture given at my seminar in Cotonou in 1987–8, which was to be published in 1994. Knowledge about this age-old technology is of paramount importance for a reassessment of the so-called technological inferiority of Africa. Adandé recalls in passing how this wrong argument was used to oppose the idea of political independence during the campaign before the De Gaulle referendum of September 1956 in the French African colonies: "You don't even know how to make a needle, and you want independence!" (Adandé 1994; Schmidt 1996).

3 A good landmark is the publication date of *Indigenous Knowledge-Systems and Development*. The editors themselves draw attention to the novelty of their approach, compared to traditional ethnoscience (Brokensha et al. 1980).

References

Adandé, Alexis (1994) "La Métallurgie 'traditionnelle' du fer en Afrique occidentale," in P. Hountondji (ed.), *Les Savoirs endogènes: pistes pour une recherche* (Dakar: Codesria; English translation: *Endogenous Knowledge: Research Trails*, Dakar: Codesria, 1997).

Beattie, John (1964) *Other Cultures: Aims, Methods and Achievements in Social Anthropology* (London: Cohen and West).

Brokensha, D., Warren, D. M., and Werner, O. (eds.) (1980) *Indigenous Knowledge-Systems and Development* (New York: University Press of America).

Conklin, Harold (1972) *Folk Classification: A Topically Arranged Bibliography of Contemporary and Background References Through 1971* (New Haven, Department of Anthropology, Yale University; rev. repr. with author index, 1980).

Geertz, Clifford (1973) *The Interpretation of Cultures: Selected Essays* (New York: Basic Books).

Geertz, Clifford (1983) *Local Knowledge: Further Essays in Interpretive Anthropology* (New York: Basic Books).

Herder, Johann Gottfried von (1772) *Abhandlung über den Ursprung der Sprache* (Berlin: C. F. Voss).

Herder, Johann Gottfried von (1879) *Ideen zur Philosophie der Geschichte der Menschheit* (Berlin: G. Hempel; trans. as *Outlines of a Philosophy of the History of Man*, London, 1800).

Hountondji, Paulin J. (1970) "Comments on Contemporary African Philosophy," *Diogenes*, 71.

Hountondji, Paulin J. (1976) *Sur la "philosophie africaine": critique de l'ethnophilosophie* (Paris: Maspero; trans. as *African Philosophy, Myth and Reality*, 2nd edn., Bloomington: Indiana University Press, 1996).

Hountondji, Paulin J. (1982) "Langues africaines et philosophie: l'hypothèse relativiste," *Les Etudes Philosophiques* (Paris), 4: 393–406.

Hountondji, Paulin J. (1988) "Situation de l'anthropologue africain: note critique sur une forme d'extraversion scientifique," in Gabriel Gosselin (ed.), *Les Nouveaux Enjeux de l'anthropologie: autour de Georges Balandier* (*Revue de l'Institut de Sociologie*, 3–4), Bruxelles: 99–108.

Hountondji, Paulin J. (1990) "Scientific Dependence in Africa Today," *Research in African Literatures* (Bloomington), 21(3): 5–15.

Hountondji, Paulin J. (1994) *Les Savoirs endogènes: pistes pour une recherche* (Dakar: Codesria; trans. as *Endogenous Knowledge: Research Trails*, Dakar, Codesria, 1997).

Hountondji, Paulin J. (1997a) *Combats pour le sens: un itinéraire africain* (Cotonou: Flamboyant).

Hountondji, Paulin J. (1997b) "From the Ethnosciences to Ethnophilosophy: Kwame Nkrumah's Thesis Project," *Research in African Literatures* (Bloomington), 28(4): 112–20.

Humboldt, Wilhelm von (1836–9), *Ueber die Kawi-sprache auf der Insel Java, nebst einer Einleitung über die Verschiedenheit des menschlichen Sprachbaues und ihren Einfluss auf die geistige Entwickelung des Menschengeschlechts* (Berlin: Druckerei der königlichen Akademie der Wissenschaften). The full-length introduction has been translated as *On Language: The Diversity of Human Language-Structure and its Influence on the Mental Development of Mankind* (New York: Cambridge University Press, 1988).

Murdock, Peter (1950) *Outline of Cultural Materials* (New Haven: Human Relations Area Files).

Nkrumah, Kwame (1943–5) "Mind and Thought in Primitive Society. A Study in Ethno-Philosophy with Special Reference to the Akan Peoples of the Gold Coast, West Africa," unpublished. National Archives of Ghana, # P.129/63–4.

Nkrumah, Kwame (1957) *Ghana. The Autobiography of Kwame Nkrumah* (New York: Nelson).

Revel, Nicole (1990) *Fleurs de paroles: histoire naturelle palawan. I: Les dons de Naqsalad* (Paris: Peeters-SELAF, "Ethnoscience").

Richards, Paul (1985) *Indigenous Agricultural Revolution: Ecology and Food Production in West Africa* (London: Hutchinson and Boulder: Westview Press).

Richards, Paul (1986) *Coping with Hunger: Hazard and Experiment in an African Rice-farming System* (London and Boston: Allen and Unwin).

Richards, Paul (1996) *Fighting the Rainforest: War, Youth and Resources in Sierra Leone* (Portsmouth: Heinemann).

Romains, Jules (1908) *La Vie unanime* (Paris: Gallimard).

Scheps, Ruth (ed.) (1993) *La Science sauvage: des savoirs populaires aux ethnosciences* (Paris: Seuil).

Schmidt, Pieter (ed.) (1996) *The Culture and Technology of Iron-making in Africa* (Gainsville: University of Florida Press).

Tempels, Placide (1949) *La Philosophie bantoue* (Paris: Présence Africaine; trans. as *Bantu Philosophy*, Paris, Présence Africaine, 1959).

Towa, Marcien (1971) *Essai sur la problématique philosophique dans l'Afrique actuelle* (Yaoundé: Clé).

45

African Philosophy and African Literature

ANTHONY KWAME APPIAH

> I'm an Ibo writer, because this is my basic culture; Nigerian, African and a
> writer ... no, black first, then a writer. Each of these identities does call for a
> certain kind of commitment on my part. I must see what it is to be black – and
> this means being sufficiently intelligent to know how the world is moving and
> how the black people fare in the world. This is what it means to be black. Or an
> African – the same: what does Africa mean to the world? When you see an
> African what does it mean to a white man?
>
> Chinua Achebe[1]

A central culture of philosophical questions that faces every contemporary African
of a reflective disposition centers on questions of identity. A great deal of ethical and
political weight is borne by many identities – ethnic, national, racial, and continental – in the life of modern Africa. And a great deal of modern African literature has
naturally had these questions at its heart. Chinua Achebe has put the matter characteristically concisely:

> It is, of course, true that the African identity is still in the making. There isn't a final
> identity that is African. But, at the same time, there *is* an identity coming into existence.
> And it has a certain context and a certain meaning. Because if somebody meets me, say, in
> a shop in Cambridge [England], he says "Are you from Africa?" Which means that Africa
> means something to some people. Each of these tags has a meaning, and a penalty and a
> responsibility. All these tags, unfortunately for the black man, are tags of disability. ...
>   I think it is part of the writer's role to encourage the creation of an African identity.
> (1982)

It is natural, therefore, that one way in which philosophy and literature are closely
related in Africa today is in their shared reflection on these questions; and these will
be the focus of this chapter.

Nevertheless, it is important to insist at the start that literature has an autonomous interest, and that mining it for its ethical, political, or identitarian messages,
while, as I shall suggest, quite fruitful, is, in the end, not to treat it as literature. The
point of identifying a written text as literary is, at heart, to insist that it does more
than it says: its paraphrasable content, its messages, may or may not be truthful or
important, but its status as literature depends, in part, on how it communicates, not
just on what. It is the specificity of the mode of expression, its particularity, that
makes it profitable to attend to a piece of writing as literary.

Here, however, I shall, as I say, attend to some literary writings as philosophical.
There is nothing inconsistent in supposing that both forms of attention – literary

538

and philosophical – can be rewarding. And, in fact, in my view, there is no better point of entry to the issue of the African intellectuals' articulation of an African identity than through the reflections of our most powerful creative writers: and of these, none, I believe, has been a more powerful literary, cultural, and political force, at least in anglophone Africa, than the Nigerian writer, Wole Soyinka.

Wole Soyinka writes in English. But this, like many obvious facts, is one whose obviousness may lead us to underrate its importance and its obscurities. For if it is obvious that Soyinka's language is English, it is a hard question whose English he writes. Amos Tutuola accustomed the Western ear to "Nigerian English"; Soyinka's English is only "Nigerian" when he is listening to Nigerians, and then his ear is exact. But with the same precision he captures the language of the colonial, matter and manner: only someone who *listened* would have the British District Officer's wife say, as her husband goes off to deal with "the natives" in *Death and the King's Horseman*: "Be careful, Simon, I mean, be clever" (Soyinka 1975: 49). Yet the very same text recalls, on occasions, the English of Gilbert Murray's translations from the Greek – Soyinka, we remind ourselves, has translated (or, we had better say, transformed) *The Bacchae* – as here in the first recital of the play:

Death came calling.
Who does not know the rasp of reeds?
A twilight whisper in the leaves before
The great araba falls. (Ibid. 11)

The resonance is one among a multitude. In reading Soyinka, we hear a voice that has ransacked the treasuries of English literary and vernacular diction, with an eclecticism that dazzles without disconcerting, and has found a language that is indisputably his own. For – and this is what matters – however many resonances we hear, Soyinka writes in a way that no contemporary English or American writer could. It is important to understand why this is. For the answer lies at the root of Soyinka's intellectual and literary project.

Though he writes in a European language, Soyinka is not writing, cannot be writing, with the purposes of English writers of the present. And it is for this reason above all that Soyinka's language may mislead. It is exactly because they can have little difficulty in understanding what Soyinka says that Europeans and Americans must learn to be careful in attending to his purposes in saying it. For there is a profound difference between the projects of contemporary European and African writers: a difference I shall summarize, for the sake of a slogan, as the difference between the search for the self and the search for a culture or, equivalently, as the difference between the search for authenticity and the search for identity.

For Africa, by and large, the search for authenticity is a curiosity: though trained in Europe or in schools and universities dominated by European culture, the African writers' concern is not with the discovery of a self that is the object of an inner voyage of discovery. Their problem – though not, of course, their subject – is finding a public role, not a private self. If European intellectuals, though comfortable inside their culture and its traditions, have an image of themselves as outsiders, African intellectuals are uncomfortable outsiders, seeking to develop their cultures in directions that will give them a role.

For the relation of African writers to the African past is a web of delicate ambiguities. If they have learned neither to despise it nor to try to ignore it – and there are many witnesses to the difficulty of this decolonization of the mind – they have still to learn how to assimilate and transcend it. They have grown up in families for which the past is, if not present, at least not far below the surface. That past and their people's myths of the past are not things they can ignore. When Ngugi wa Thiong'o says that "the novelist, at his best, must feel himself heir to a continuous tradition," he does not mean, as the Westerner might suppose, a literary tradition: he means, as any African would know, "the mainstream of his people's historical drama" (1972: 39). It is this fundamentally social-historical perspective that makes the European problem of authenticity something distant and unengaging for most African writers.

We must not overstate the distance from London to Lagos: the concept of authenticity, though often dissociated from its roots in the relation of reader or writer to society, is one that can only be understood against the social background. It is the fact that we are social beings, after all, that raises the problem of authenticity. The problem of who I really am is raised by the facts of what I appear to be: and though it is essential to the mythology of authenticity that this fact should be obscured by its prophets, what I appear to be is fundamentally how I appear to others and only derivatively how I appear to myself. Robinson Crusoe before Friday could hardly have had the problem of sincerity; but we can reasonably doubt that he would have faced issues of authenticity either.

Yet, and here is the crux, for European writers these others who define the problem are "my people," and they can feel that they know who these people are, what they are worth. For African writers the answer is not so easy. They are Asante, Yoruba, Kikuyu – but what does this now mean? They are Ghanaian, Nigerian, Kenyan – but does this yet mean anything? They are black – and what is the worth of the black person? They are bound, that is, to face the questions articulated in my epigraph by Achebe. So that though the European may feel that the problem of who he or she is can be a private problem, the African asks always not "who am I?" but "who are we?", and "my" problem is not mine alone, but "ours."

This particular constellation of problems and projects is not often found outside Africa: a recent colonial history, a multiplicity of diverse subnational indigenous traditions, a foreign language whose metropolitan culture has traditionally defined the "natives" by their race as inferior, a literary culture still very much in the making. It is because they share this set of problems that it makes sense to speak of a Nigerian writer as an African writer, with the problems of an African writer: and it is because he has attempted with subtlety and intelligence to face some of these common problems that Soyinka deserves the attention of Africans.

I want to try to identify a problem in Soyinka's account of his cultural situation: a problem with the account he offers of what it is to be an African writer in our day, a problem that appears in the tension between what his plays show and what he says about them.

540

We could start in many places in his dramatic oeuvre; I have chosen *Death and the King's Horseman*. "The play," Soyinka says, "is based on events which took place in Oyo, ancient Yoruba city of Nigeria, in 1946. That year, the lives of Elesin (Olori Elesin), his son, and the Colonial District Officer intertwined with the disastrous results set out in the play" (1975: author's note). The first scene opens with a praise-singer and drummers pursuing Elesin Oba as he marches through the marketplace. We gradually discover that he is the "King's Horseman" – whose pride and duty is to follow the dead King to ride with him to the "abode of the gods" (ibid. 62). In the words of Joseph, the "houseboy" of the British District Officer: "It is native law and custom. The King died last month. Tonight is his burial. But before they can bury him, the Elesin must die so as to accompany him to heaven" (ibid. 28). When a colonial official intervenes to stop Elesin Oba's "ritual suicide," his son, newly returned from England for the King's funeral, dies for him: and the Elesin responds by strangling himself in his cell with the chain with which the colonial police have bound his hands. The District Officer's intervention to save one life ends with the loss of two: and, as the people of Oyo believe, with a threat to the cosmic order.

The issue is complicated by the fact that Elesin Oba has chosen to marry on the eve of his death – so that, as he puts it, "My vital flow, the last from this flesh, is intermingled with the promise of future life" (ibid. 40). We are aware from the very first scene that this act raises doubts – expressed by Iyaloja, Mother of the market – about the Elesin's preparedness for his task. When the Elesin fails, he himself addresses this issue, as he speaks to his young bride:

> First I blamed the white man, then I blamed my gods for deserting me. Now I feel I want to blame you for the mystery of the sapping of my will. But blame is a strange peace offering for a man to bring a world he has deeply wronged, and to its innocent dwellers. Oh little mother, I have taken countless women in my life, but you were more than a desire of the flesh. I needed you as the abyss across which my body must be drawn, I filled it with earth and dropped my seed in it at the moment of preparedness for my crossing.... I confess to you, daughter, my weakness came not merely from the abomination of the white man who came violently into my fading presence, there was also a weight of longing on my earth-held limbs. I would have shaken it off, already my foot had begun to lift but then, the white ghost entered and all was defiled. (ibid. 65)

There are so many possibilities for readings here: and the Elesin's uncertainties as to the meaning of his own failure leave us scope to wonder whether the intervention of the colonizer provides only a pretext. But what is Soyinka's own reading?

In his author's note to the play Soyinka writes:

> The bane of themes of this genre is that they are no sooner employed creatively than they acquire the facile tag of "clash of cultures," a prejudicial label, which, quite apart from its frequent misapplication, presupposes a potential equality *in every given situation* of the alien culture and the indigenous, on the actual soil of the latter. (In the area of misapplication, the overseas prize for illiteracy and mental conditioning undoubtedly goes to the blurb-writer for the American edition of my novel *Season Of Anomy* who

unblushingly declares that this work portrays the "clash between the old values and new ways, between Western methods and African traditions"!)...I find it necessary to caution the would-be producer of this play against a sadly familiar reductionist tendency, and to direct his vision instead to the far more difficult and risky task of eliciting the play's threnodic essence....

The Colonial Factor is an incident, a catalytic incident merely... The confrontation in the play is largely metaphysical. (ibid. author's note)

I find the tone of this passage strained, the claim disingenuous. We may, of course, make distinctions more carefully than blurb-writers and scribblers of facile tags: Soyinka feels that talk of the clash of cultures suggests that colonizer and colonized meet on culturally equal terms. We may reject the implication. There is, as Soyinka says, something so over-simple as to be thoroughly misleading in the claim that the novel is "about," that it "portrays," the relation between European methods and African traditions.

Still, it is absurd to deny that novel and play have something to say about that relationship. The "Colonial Factor" is not a catalytic incident merely; it is a profound assault on the consciousness of the African intellectual, on the consciousness that guides this play. And it would be irresponsible, which Soyinka is not, to assert that novel and play do not imply a complex (and non-reductionist) set of attitudes to the problem. It is one thing to say (as I think correctly) that the drama in Oyo is driven ultimately by the logic of Yoruba cosmology, another to deny the existence of a dimension of power in which it is the colonial state that forms the action.

So that after all the distinctions have been drawn, we still need to ask why Soyinka feels the need to conceal his purposes. Is it perhaps because he has not resolved the tension between the desire which arises from his roots in the European tradition of authorship to see his literary work as, so to speak, authentic, "metaphysical," and the desire which he must feel as an African in a once colonized and merely notionally decolonized culture to face up to and reflect the problem at the level of ideology? Is it, to put it briskly, because Soyinka is torn between the demands of a private authenticity and a public commitment? Between individual self-discovery and what he elsewhere calls the "social vision"?

It is this problem, central to Soyinka's situation as the archetypical African writer, that I wish to go on to discuss.

The "social vision" is, of course, the theme of two of the lectures in Soyinka's *Myth, Literature and the African World*, and it was in this work that the tensions I have mentioned first caught my attention. Soyinka's essays are clearly not directed particularly to an African audience (hardly surprising when we remember that they are based on lectures given in England at Cambridge University). References to Peter Brook and Brecht, to Robbe-Grillet and Lorca, are intended to help locate the Western reader. Indeed, the introduction of Lorca is glossed with the observation that it is "for ease of reference" (1976: 50). And it is clear from the way in which the first chapter (on Yoruba theology and its transformations in African and African-American drama) tells us much that it would be absurd to tell to any Yoruba, and a certain amount that it would be gratuitous to mention for almost any African readership.

Yet, it is intended (and to a large extent this intention is achieved) that *Myth, Literature and the African World* should be a work which, like Soyinka's plays (and unlike, say, Achebe's novels), takes its African – its Yoruba – background utterly for granted. Soyinka is not arguing that modern African writers should be free to draw on African and, in his case, Yoruba mythology; rather, he is simply showing us how this process can and does take place. He tells us in his preface, for example, that the literature of the "secular social vision" reveals that the "universal verities" of "the new ideologue" can be "elicited from the world-view and social structures of his own [African] people" (ibid. xii). I have every sympathy with the way Soyinka tries to take the fact of Africa for granted. But this taking-for-granted is doubly paradoxical.

First, his readership as the author of dramatic texts and as a theoretician – *unlike* the audience for his performances – is largely not African. *Myth, Literature and the African World* is largely to be read by people who see Soyinka as a guide into what remains for them from a literary point of view (and this is, of course, a reflection of political realities) the Dark Continent. How can we ask people who are not African, do not know Africa, to take us for granted? And, more importantly, why *should* we? (Observe how odd it would be to praise Norman Mailer – to take a name entirely at random – for taking America for granted.)

It is part of the curious situation of the African intellectual that taking one's culture for granted – as politics, as history, as culture, and, more abstractly yet, as mind – is, absurdly, something that does require an effort. So that, inevitably – and this is the second layer of paradox – what Soyinka does is to take Africa for granted in reaction to a series of self-misunderstandings in Africa that are a product of colonial history and the European imagination: and this despite Soyinka's knowledge that it is Europe's fictions of Africa that we need to forget. In escaping Europe's Africa, the one fiction that Soyinka as theorist cannot escape is that Africans can only take their cultural traditions for granted by an effort of mind.

Yet in Soyinka's plays, Yoruba mythology and theology and Yoruba custom and tradition *are* taken for granted. They may be reworked, as Shakespeare reworked English or Wagner reworked German traditions, but there is never any hesitation, when, as in *Death and the King's Horseman*, Soyinka draws confidently on the resources of his tradition. We outsiders need surely have no more difficulty in understanding Soyinka's dramas because they draw on Yoruba culture than we have in understanding Shakespeare because he speaks from within what used to be called the "Elizabethan world-picture"; and Soyinka's dramas show that he knows this.

I think we should ask what leads Soyinka astray when it comes to his accounting for his cultural situation. And part of the answer must be that he is answering the wrong question. For what he needs to do is not to take an *African* world for granted, but to take for granted his own culture – to speak freely not as an African but as a Yoruba and a Nigerian. The right question, then, is not "Why shouldn't Africa take its traditions for granted?" but "Why shouldn't I take mine?" The reason that Africa cannot take an African cultural or political or intellectual life for granted is that there is no such thing: there are only so many traditions with their complex relationships – and, as often, their lack of any relationship – to each other.

543

For this reason, Soyinka's situation is even more complex than it is likely to appear to the Westerner – or to the African enmeshed in unanimist mythologies. For even if his writing were addressed solely to other Africans, Soyinka could not presuppose a knowledge of Yoruba traditions: and these are precisely what we need to understand if we are to follow the arguments of his first lecture. Even when addressing other Africans, that is, he can only take for granted an interest in his situation, and a shared assumption that he has the right to speak from within a Yoruba cultural world. He cannot take for granted a common stock of cultural knowledge.

These issues are important for my own project in these essays. As I have already said, it is simply a mistake to suppose that Africa's cultures are an open book to each other. That is one reason why the fact that I explain this or that Asante custom or belief does not by itself show that I am talking for the West. We cannot, therefore, infer a Western audience for Soyinka's – brilliant and original – exposition of Yoruba cosmology. What shows that Soyinka's audience is Western is the sorts of references he makes, the sorts of Yoruba customs he chooses to explain.

Now, of course, the only way that the misunderstandings I have been discussing can be overcome is by acknowledging and transcending them; nothing is to be achieved by ignoring them. And, despite the remarks in the preface I cited earlier, Soyinka knows this well. What I want to argue, however, is that the "African World" that Soyinka counterposes as *his* fiction of Africa is one against which we should revolt – and that we should do so, to return to my earlier argument, because it presupposes a false account of the proper relationships between private "metaphysical" authenticity and ideology; a false account of the relations between literature, on the one hand, and the African world on the other.

We can approach Soyinka's presuppositions by asking ourselves a question: what has Yoruba cosmology, the preoccupation of the first lecture of *Myth, Literature and the African World*, to do with African literature? It is not enough to answer that Yoruba cosmology provides both the characters and the mythic resonances of some African drama – notably, of course, Soyinka's – as it does of some of the Afro-Caribbean and African-American drama that Soyinka himself discusses in *Myth, Literature and the African World*. For this is no answer for the Akan writer or reader who is more familiar with Ananse than Esu-Elegba as trickster, and who has no more obligations to Ogun than he does to Vishnu. "Africa minus the Sahara North" – and this is an observation of Soyinka's – "is still a very large continent, populated by myriad races and cultures" (ibid. 97).

It is natural, after reading the first lecture of *Myth, Literature and the African World*, to suppose that Soyinka's answer to our question must be this: "Yoruba mythology is taken by way of example because, as a Yoruba, it happens to be what I know about." In his interesting discussion of the differences (and similarities) between Greek myth and drama and Yoruba, for example, he says "that Greek religion shows persuasive parallels with, *to stick to our example*, the Yoruba, is by no means denied" (ibid. 14; my emphasis) – as if the Yoruba case is discussed as an example of – what else? – the African case. Many other passages would support this interpretation.

Now if this is Soyinka's presupposition – and if it is not, it is certainly a presupposition of his text – then it is one that we must question. For, I would suggest, the assumption that this system of Yoruba ideas is – that it *could* be – typical is too direct a reaction to the European conception of Africa as what Soyinka elsewhere nicely terms a "metaphysical vacuum" (ibid. 97): and the correct response to this absurdity is not to claim that what appears to Europe as a vacuum is in fact populated with certain typical metaphysical notions, of which Yoruba conceptions would be one particularization, but rather to insist that it is richly populated with the diverse metaphysical thought-worlds of (in his own harmless hyperbole) "myriad races and cultures."

I do not want to represent Soyinka's apparent position as a kind of Yoruba imperialism of the thought-world. The motive is nobler, and I think it is this: Soyinka recognizes that, despite the differences between the histories of British, French, and Portuguese ex-colonies, there is a deep and deeply self-conscious continuity between the problems and projects of decolonized Africans, a continuity which has, as he shows, literary manifestations; and he wants to give an account of that continuity that is both metaphysical and endogenous. The desire to give an account that is endogenous is, I think, primary. There is something disconcerting for a pan-Africanist in the thesis (which I here state at its most extreme) that what Africans have in common is fundamentally that European racism failed to take them seriously, that European imperialism exploited them. Soyinka will not admit the presupposition of Achebe's question – "When you see an African what does it mean to a white man?"; the presupposition that the African identity is – in part – the product of a European gaze.

I had better insist once more that I do not think that this *is* all that Africans have culturally in common. It is obvious that, like Europe before the Renaissance and much of the modern Third World, African cultures are formed in important ways by the fact that they had until recently no high technology and relatively low levels of literacy. And, despite the introduction of high technology and the rapid growth of literacy, these facts of the recent past are still reflected in the conceptions even of those of us who are most affected by economic development and cultural exposure to the West. But even if these economic and technical similarities were to be found only in Africa – and they aren't – they would not, even with the similarities in colonial history, justify the assumption of metaphysical or mythic unity, except on the most horrifyingly determinist assumptions.

In denying a metaphysical and mythic unity to African conceptions, then, I have *not* denied that "African literature" is a useful category. I have insisted from the very beginning that the social-historical situation of African writers generates a common set of problems. But notice that it is precisely not a metaphysical consensus that creates this shared situation. It is, *inter alia*, the transition from traditional to modern loyalties; the experience of colonialism; the racial theories and prejudices of Europe, which provide both the language and the text of literary experience; the growth of both literacy and the modern economy. And it is, as I say, because these are changes which were to a large extent thrust upon African peoples by European imperialism, precisely because they are exogenous, that Soyinka, in my view, revolts against seeing them as the major determinants of the situation of the African writer.

545

Once he is committed to an endogenous account of this situation, what is left but unity in metaphysics? Shaka and Osei Tutu – founders, respectively, of the Zulu and the Asante nations – do not belong in the same narrative, they spoke different languages, their conceptions of kinship (to bow to an ethnographer's idol) were centrally patrilineal and matrilineal respectively. Soyinka could have given an account of what they had in common that was racial: but, as I have argued and Soyinka knows well, we have passed the time when black racism is possible as an intelligent reaction to white racism. So, as I say, we are left with common metaphysical conceptions.

Though I think that the appeal of the myth of Africa's metaphysical solidarity is largely due to Soyinka's wish for an endogenous account, there is, I suspect, another reason why he is tempted by this story. Soyinka, the man of European letters, is familiar with the literature of authenticity; and the account of it as an exploration of the metaphysics of the individual self; and he is tempted, by one of those rhetorical oppositions that appeal to abstract thinkers, to play against this theme an African exploration of the metaphysics of the community.

But in accepting such an account Soyinka is once more enmeshed in Europe's myth of Africa. Because he cannot see either Christianity or Islam as endogenous (even in their more syncretic forms) he is left to reflect on African traditional religions: and these have always seemed from Europe's point of view to be much of a muchness.

Some threads need tying together. I began by asserting that the central project of that pan-African literary culture to which Soyinka belongs could be characterized as the search for a culture – a search for the relation of the author to the social world. I then suggested that we could detect in a preface of Soyinka's a tension between a private "metaphysical" account of his play *Death and the King's Horseman* and its obvious ideological implications. Soyinka, I went on to claim, rejects any obviously "political" account of his literary work, because he wishes to show how an African writer can take Africa for granted in his work, drawing on "the world-view...of his own people," and because he wishes to represent what is *African* about his and other African writing as arising endogenously out of Africa's shared metaphysical resources. Most recently I have argued that we cannot accept a central presupposition of this view, namely the presupposition that there is, even at quite a high level of abstraction, *an* African world-view.

My argument will be complete when I have shown why Soyinka's view of African metaphysical solidarity is an answer to the search for a culture, and what, since we must reject his answer, should replace it. To this latter question, I can offer only the beginnings of an answer here.

African writers share, as I have said, both a social-historical situation and a social-historical perspective. One aspect of the situation is the growth both of literacy and of the availability of printing. This generates the now familiar problem of the transition from fundamentally oral to literary cultures: and in doing so it gives rise to that peculiar privacy which is associated with the written text, a privacy associated with a new kind of property in texts, a new kind of authorial authority, a new kind of creative persona. It is easy to see now that, in generating the

546

category of the individual in the new world of the public – *published* – text, in creating the private "metaphysical" interiority of the author, this social-historical situation tears the writer out of his social-historical perspective; the authorial "I" struggles to displace the "we" of the oral narration.

This struggle is as central to Soyinka's situation as it is to that of African writers generally. At the same time, and again typically, Soyinka, the individual, a Nigerian outside the traditional, more certain world of his Yoruba ancestors, struggles with the Soyinka who experiences the loss of that world, of these gods of whom he speaks with such love and longing in the first lecture. Once again the "I" seeks to escape the persistent and engulfing "we."

And with this dialectic of self-as-whole and self-as-part, we reach the core: for this struggle is, I suggest, the source of the tension in his author's note – the tension between Soyinka's account of his drama and the drama itself. But it is also at the root of the project of *Myth, Literature, and the African World*.

For Soyinka's search for a culture has led him, as the title of the book indicates, away from the possibility of a Yoruba or a Nigerian "we" to an African, a continental community. His solution to the problem of what it is that individuates African culture (which he senses as a problem because he realizes that Africans have so much in common) is that African literature is united in its drawing on the resources of an African conception of community growing out of an African metaphysics. The tension in *Myth, Literature and the African World* is between this thesis and the Soyinka of the dramas, implicit in his account of Yoruba cosmology in the first lecture, the Soyinka whose account of Yoruba cosmology is precisely not the Yoruba account; who has taken sometimes Yoruba mythology, but sometimes the world of a long-dead Greek, and demythologized them to his own purposes, making of them something new, more "metaphysical," and, above all, more private and individual.

Once we see that Soyinka's account of his literary project is in tension with his literary corpus we can see why he has to conceal, as I have suggested he does, the ideological role that he sees for the writer. If African writers were to play their social role in creating a new African literature of the "secular social vision" drawing on an African metaphysics, then the colonial experience *would* be a "catalytic incident merely" – it could only be the impetus to uncover this metaphysical solidarity. Furthermore, his own work, viewed as an examination of the "abyss of transition," serves its ideological purpose just by a *metaphysical* examination, and loses this point when it is reduced to an account of the colonial experience. Paradoxically, its political purpose – in the creation of an African literary culture, the declaration of independence of the African mind – is served only by concealing its political interpretation.

We cannot, then, accept Soyinka's understanding of the purposes of Africa's literatures today. And yet his oeuvre embodies, perhaps more than any other body of modern African writing, the challenge of a new mode of individuality in African intellectual life. In taking up so passionately the heritage of the printed word, he has entered inevitably into the new kind of literary self that comes with print, a self that is the product, surely, of changes in social life as well as in the technology of the word. This novel self is more individualist and atomic than the self of precapitalist societies; it is a creature of modern economic relations. I do not know that this new conception of the self was inevitable, but it is no longer something that we in Africa could escape even if we wanted to. And if we cannot escape it, let us celebrate it – there is surely a Yoruba proverb with this moral? – and celebrate it in the work of Wole Soyinka, who has provided in his plays a literary experience whose individuality is an endless source of insight and pleasure.[2]

I have tried to exemplify the ways in which close attention to literature can help us approach philosophical questions of the first importance for African philosophy: in particular questions about African identity. Other texts and writers would allow us to explore other such questions: Yambo Ouologuem's *Bound to Violence*, for example, allows us to explore questions about modernity and postmodernity (see Appiah 1999). But I should like to end, as I began, by insisting both that a philosophical reading of a literary text can be worthwhile, and that is far from being the only kind of reading that is fruitful.

Notes

This chapter is based on chapter 4 of *In My Father's House: Africa in the Philosophy of Culture* (1992).

1 See Achebe 1982. Some passages cited in the text are from my own unpublished transcription of the full interview which was edited for this briefer published version.
2 My discussion of *Death and the King's Horseman* is much influenced by Soyinka's production at Lincoln Center in early 1987.

References

Achebe, Chinua (1982) Interview with Anthony Appiah, D. A. N. Jones, and John Ryle in *Times Literary Supplement*, February 26.

Appiah, Anthony Kwame (1992) *In My Father's House: Africa in the Philosophy of Culture* (New York: Oxford University Press).

Appiah, Anthony Kwame (1999) "Yambo Ouologuem and the Meaning of Postcoloniality," in Christopher Wise (ed.), *Yambo Ouologuem: Postcolonial Writer, Islamic Militant* (Boulder, CO: Lynne Rienner Publishers), pp. 55–63.

Soyinka, Wole (1975) *Death and the King's Horseman* (London: Methuen).

Soyinka, Wole (1976) *Myth, Literature and the African World* (Cambridge: Cambridge University Press).

Thiong'o, Ngugi wa (1972) *Homecoming* (New York: Lawrence Hill and Company).

46

Philosophy and Literature in Francophone Africa

JEAN-GODEFROY BIDIMA
(TRANSLATED BY NICOLAS DE WARREN)

Even if the ultimate definition or final goal of philosophy still eludes us, philosophy is, at the very least, a form of expression that unites the art of living to that of writing. In this regard, textuality is an essential aspect of the development of philosophy since, in setting philosophy into narrative, philosophy puts to the test those difficulties connected with, on the one hand, interpretation and, on the other, communicability. If textualization is a crucial factor in philosophy, one must add that it does not represent all of philosophy. Nevertheless, philosophical problems are indeed similar to those encountered by another reflective and imaginative activity – literature. Much like literature, philosophy deals with problems regarding the nature of texts, their creation, their texture, their reception, and the interpretative criteria for their evaluation. The poetical activity that characterizes literature is, as with philosophy, reflective and auto-reflexive. In other words, philosophy shares with literature the task of critically investigating the great anthropological categories, such as time, space, subjectivity, action, and movement. In the case of African philosophy, the question naturally arises, where do philosophical and literary reflection intersect to reveal new horizons of problems?

Limiting our discussion here to francophone Africa, we note that two sorts of issue are at stake in the question just raised. First, there is, at the intersection of philosophy and literature, the epistemological question about the conditions of the possibility of an interdisciplinary African philosophical discourse. Second, there is the poetical issue of how the two types of discourse, which often deal with the same topics, can fertilize each other. In order to understand the cross-fertilization between philosophy and literature, two axes may be distinguished. The first axis deals with the general relations between philosophy and literature in francophone Africa. This section will take up (a) francophone African writers who have addressed philosophy, (b) philosophers who have concerned themselves with African writers and literature, and (c) philosophers who have dealt with general problems in aesthetics and who have been engaged with literature by way of a general reflection on art. The second axis has to do with transversal themes that have, in some form, preoccupied philosophers and writers. We will find that sometimes it is a case of one group influencing the other and sometimes a case of affinities without influence.

Our focus will be on (1) the theme of femininity (as explored by the Senegalese philosopher Awa Thiam and other novelists); (2) the relation between the work of writer Edouard Glissant (Antilles) and that of the philosopher Tshiamalenga Ntumba (Congo); (3) the medium of poetry, where we will discuss Senghor and the Congolese philosopher Kä Mana; (4) the genre of autobiography, where we will examine the works of Mariama Bâ and Paulin Hountondji; and (5) the theme of emancipation in the face of violence, where we will encounter Frantz Fanon and the Congolese novelist Ngandu. (Authors of the black Diaspora, such as Césaire, Fanon, and Glissant, will be considered here to the extent to which they themselves were engaged with Africa in their writings.)

The Relationship Between Philosophy and Literature

African writers and philosophy

Our discussion in this section will focus on three authors: L. S. Senghor (Senegal), Y. V. Mudimbe, and G. Ngal (Congo).[1] Senghor's notion of Negritude was shaped in the context of his study of the writings of various philosophers. Senghor is intellectually equally at home with Karl Marx or Teilhard de Chardin as with Gaston Berger or Emmanuel Mounier. However, it is important to note that it was Sartre's existentialism, Mounier's personalism, and Chardin's Christian spiritualism that provided the basis of his conception of philosophy. Senghor's exploration of Marx comes in his conception of African socialism and his critique of mechanical materialism in favor of Marxian humanism (Senghor 1947: 43). This particular understanding of Marx elevates humanity, rather than the mode of production, to the highest importance. A second prominent aspect of Senghor's thinking relates to the debate between infrastructure and superstructure. Following Engels, Senghor argues that both cultural and economic forces determine consciousness (1976: 13–15). He cites Althusser, who, for his part, saw an "epistemological break" between, on the one hand, an idealist and humanist Marx (in his pre-1845 writings) and, on the other, the scientific Marx of *Das Kapital*. In his own reading of Marx, Senghor rejects Marx's theory of class conflict and replaces it with a "suppression of inequality at the international level" (ibid. 49). In this way, Marx's theory of alienation is transformed into a critique of colonial alienation.

Senghor has also addressed the work of Teilhard de Chardin. From Chardin, he appropriates the idea that "man is a cosmic phenomenon" (1962: 34). Humankind, in all its complexity, represents the curious phenomenon of life (ibid. 56). To Marx and Chardin is added Gaston Berger, a Franco-Senegalese philosopher who specializes in characterology. From Berger, Senghor draws a philosophy of time and action. Concrete time becomes significant if, following Berger, we distinguish existential time (the time characterized by existential poets and by philosophers as angst) from the operative time of action. On the basis of Berger's distinction, Senghor arrives at the concept of the "prospective," which corresponds to the time dimension of the political party in connection with which he propounded his African socialism (1964: 390).

550

Senghor has also written about philosophy in a preface to a book about Alassane Ndaw (1982: 32). In this lengthy introduction, Senghor combats the primacy that rationalism has given to discursive reason to the detriment of intuition and emotion. He finds in Ndaw's thinking the legacy of Tempels and Kagamé to the extent that Ndaw places at the center of his investigations the notion of life that emerges from the concept of the vital force (*force vitale*) (see Ngal 1998). Senghor's itinerary through the landscape of philosophy enables him to place Negritude on a solid theoretical base. On this basis, Marx's notion of emancipation, Sartre's notion of existence, Chardin's notion of cosmo-homocentricism, Berger's notion of temporality, and the notions of life and vital force (Tempels, Kagamé, Ndaw) all play an important role in the development of Senghor's literary corpus.

The novelist Ngal's writings freely borrow and engage philosophical themes such as the nature of discourse, errancy, creation, and the time and space of movement and action (Ngal 1994, 2000; see also Mudimbe 1994a). Philosophy is, however, most specifically explored in connection with the question of style (Mudimbe 1994b). Taking inspiration from Deleuze's notion of difference (Mudimbe 1973), Derrida's notion of *différance* (Mudimbe 1988), and Merleau-Ponty's reflections on signs (Towa 1971), Ngal (1983) suggests that style poses substantial questions about linguistic ineffability, artistic creativity, expressive individuality, and literary theatricality. Ngal's philosophical reflections blaze, for African philosophy, a promising path of inquiry about its own diverse ways of textual exposition.

The essayist and novelist Mudimbe also takes up philosophical themes in his work. His treatment of the question of the subject and the dispersion of her identity is greatly influenced by Lacan's psychoanalysis. Some of his other concerns have been with the problem of time, Foucault's analysis of domination, and, most importantly, the question of unconscious processes that are sedimentated in the understanding of alterity. What Mudimbe gives to African philosophy, aside from his critique of ethnophilosophy, is an archaeology of philosophical discourse that, as a form of knowledge, is also an articulation of power.

Philosophers and literature

One of the first francophone African philosophers to write on literature in a university thesis was Marcien Towa from Cameroon. Towa (1971) attempts a critique of Senghorian Negritude by calling into question Senghor's appeal to intuition. Towa develops his criticism by calling into question the rampant biologism in Senghor's notion of Negritude and its espousal of a "black race" which is accompanied by a philosophical vitalism based on Bergson and Père Tempels. Towa opposes Senghor's "static" Negritude with the "dynamic" negritude of Césaire. It is important to note that Towa uses Lucien Goldmann's method of "genetic structuralism" in his analysis of Senghor's writings.

A second Cameroonian writer, Bernard Nanga, who received his degree in the Philosophy of Science from the University of Strasbourg, is the author of two novels: *Les Chauves-souris* (1980) and *La Trahison de Marianne* (1984). In the first, Nanga describes corruption and tackles the problem of alienation as a function of the depossession of the self and of the other (*l'autrui*). In the second, Nanga undertakes a critique of the *petit bourgeois* mentality that is embedded in French family life. For both Towa and Nanga, literature is the place where the philosophical idea of alienation (in its Marxian sense) can be examined in francophone African writing.

Philosophers and the general problem of literature

Up to now, we have been dealing with written literature. The theme and aesthetic problem of oral literature have been of central concern to my own work (Cameroon) and to that of Nkombe Oleko (Congo). Oleko (1972) has studied the proverb in its relationship to philosophy and has arrived at the conclusion that there is much to think about when literature is considered from the viewpoint of proverbs. He uses hermeneutic methods to try to understand the meaning of proverbs and their place in literature. For my part, I have also been engaged in the topic of proverbs. My approach has been to extricate the category of proverb from ethnophilosophy and examine the subject from the standpoint of what I call *trace*: "the proverb is in the nature of a trace" (Bidima 1998). Its economy mobilizes an emotional, pedagogical, and aesthetic program. As a trace, the inscription of a proverb already involves the effacing, or at least the blurring, of its own tracks. The texture of a proverb is both enriched and erased in the same gesture. The proverb is thus, strictly, not a *trace*, but a *path*. In other words, as a form of discourse, its significance does not lie simply in its origins or in an established meaning, but in its effects and in its variability.

More than simply a reflection on the proverb, my account is a study of the "orality of silence" (ibid. 816). Silence is part and parcel of oral literature, insofar as it displaces the phatic function of language. Saying everything by not saying anything at all, retaining everything by giving away everything, silence speaks the impossible; it is expressed inexpressibility.

Regarding general questions of aesthetics, I have studied two important notions in literary creation: *distance* and *utopia*. For literary creation, the idea of distance implies that of *return*. Literary writing is metaphoric in two senses: it is *diaphoretic* (sending the visible to the invisible) and *epiphonic* (returning the invisible to the visible) (see Bidima 1997). Metaphor always implies a return that indicates a distance between two poles. It is this distance that allows for the conceiving of a utopia. A utopia is, in this regard, a separation between life as actually lived and life as a future to be lived. A literature, written or oral, that cannot speak of its own utopia, of its own distance, coagulates into an eternal pseudo-construct that imposes immobility on becoming. Some pertinent questions are: how does utopia find expression in francophone African literature? And how does it express itself through the composition of texts that connect characters to the thematic of utopia?

Intersecting Themes

Femininity

It is important to raise the question of the condition of women in a francophone African philosophy that rarely speaks of sex and women, as if femininity were not also a philosophical problem.[2] How have African novelists conceived of female characters and what portraits of femininity have been drawn by francophone African philosophers? Among novelists, femininity is first of all productive. According to these writers, the traditional African woman has a procreative and nourishing role. Ahmadou Kourouma (Ivory Coast) affirms: "Allah has said that a woman gains entry to paradise by fulfilling her duties towards her husband" (1970: 177). Camara Laye recounts how once, having returned to his village after a period of study, his grandmother touched his face and looked at him to see if he had rosy cheeks, so as to check whether he was well nourished (1976: 42–3). In certain African societies a woman's imperative duty is to achieve self-fulfillment through motherhood. Mongo Beti (Cameroon) criticizes the fate in store for the sterile women of Niam. Victims of mistreatment, they abandon their homes (1977: 24–5).

But a woman also serves as a mediator who guarantees social solidarity. Ferdinand Oyono (1975) (Cameroon) has shown how Kelara, the wife of Meka and recipient of a medal which elevated her social status during the colonial period, mobilized around her, for emancipatory purposes, a whole network of relationships from Meka's ethnic group as well as from others. Woman is also a symbol of resistance against the rape of the colonialism, as in the case of Matali who refused to submit to the physical abuses of a white commander: "That evening, Matali was escorted to the camp of the colonial commander. Things took an ugly turn when her under-garments were torn off. Matali resisted, fought, and escaped the guards through a door and fled, disappearing into the jungle" (Kourouma 1970: 111).

There is a strong critique of patriarchal society among some African writers, as, for example, that of Paul Hazoumé (Benin): "There still exists between men and women a struggle. Men, who are very egotistical, only want to recognize one law: the passive submission of women to their sensual appetites" (1935: 480). Precisely this exploitation is denounced by Seydou Badian (Senegal): "This situation which we impose on women puts us forever in an inferior position vis-à-vis other people . . . we must liberate women if we aspire to live" (1957: 59–60). Other novelists have underlined the role of women and especially the status of femininity. On what basis does African femininity stand? With the beauty of the black woman (as in Senghor)? With maternity? Marriage? Is femininity definable outside of the functions that a woman must fulfill?

These questions lead us to the Senegalese philosopher Awa Thiam. In her PhD dissertation, published under the title *Continents noirs*, Awa returns to the question of femininity in terms that intersect with that of Hazoumé, Mongo Beti, and Kourouma. She uses an archaeological method of investigation that focuses on how femininity has been trifled with in the history of both Africa and the West. Furthermore, she establishes a parallel between the situation of women and that of blacks in the Euro-American world, and notes the double situation of black women. She challenges the equation "woman = sex," as well as the equivalence "womanhood = maternity." That is to say, "phallocratic discourse is to women, what colonial and neo-colonial discourse is to Africa and black people" (1987: 8). The current challenge consists in tackling the unconscious roots of the forgetfulness of the question of femininity in francophone African philosophy. Is this obliviousness a duplication of the Christian theological sense of guilt about sexual life or does it derive from a contempt of the body inherited from Platonism?[3]

Relationships

Relationships are the making of connections. They are the *frame* by which the determination of the self breaks away from solitude and integrates itself into the game of losing one's self-sufficiency and gaining a supplementary determination. The relationship is the *game* that mediates the known and the unknown, the same and the other. The same and the other, as Sartre would say, is what gives the thinking subject its place as a being in the world and, more specifically, as being in a "context." Being in the world means being in sync with my environment (*Umwelt*), and being in a context means entering into a relation with *an other* (*autrui*) only by means of language and action. The relationship shows that the subject is nothing without dialogue and without the intersubjectivity, which is itself the condition for language. At the cultural level, a historical culture can only become rich and enriched if, being deeply rooted, it extends its branches towards an encounter with "a somewhere else" (*un ailleurs*).

This is the basic thesis of the novelist and poet Edouard Glissant. Every determination is a relation with *an other* (which could be another culture or another person). The primacy of plurality over *ipseity* can also be found in the work of Tschiamalenga Ntumba (Zaire/Congo). Glissant begins with a critique of the notion of cultural identity from the perspective of his own ancestry from slaves and his own existence at the end of the twentieth century, which is marked by the resurgence of nationalism and racism. For Glissant, to conceive of an identity in terms of a unique root appears dangerous and is the source of fundamentalism: "As long as we persist with the idea of an identity based on a unique root, there will be Bosnias, Rwandas, Burundis" (1966: 90). Glissant borrows the notion of "rhizome" from *Thousand Plateaus* by the philosopher Deleuze and the psychoanalyst Guattari: "They established a perspective . . . of thinking, a thinking of the root and of the rhizome. The unique root is one which kills its surroundings whereas the rhizome is a root that extends towards an encounter with other roots" (ibid. 54). On the basis of this distinction, Glissant challenges atavistic notions of cultures that define their identity in terms of territory, origin, and ancestry. He opposes to this the idea of *composite cultures*, which, in the image of a rhizome, disregards territories and de-emphasizes genealogies and unilinear affiliation, thus giving rein to pluralities. Glissant criticizes other West Indian authors like Césaire, who insist on the pre-eminence of the African roots of their identity. Cultural identity is not an assertive identity; it is, rather, an inquiring identity in which relation to *the other* is determinative without being tyrannical (1981: 283). This fragmented and uncertain identity can only be defined "in relation to the other" (1990: 23).

The primacy of relationship is brought to the fore in Ntumba's studies of "*Bisoïté*."[4] For Ntumba, Western philosophy has placed too much value on the "I–Thou" relation at the expense of the dialogical community where intersubjectivity is the foundation.[5] The "we" (*Biso*) has a logical and ontological priority over the "I" of "I–Thou." Ntumba connects the notion of "we" to the notion of relation, as it is developed in Glissant. The challenge is to understand how to articulate the notion of relationships along with that of a dialogical community and diagnose the misunderstandings and divisions that inevitably emerge in any human society.

The poetic imagination

In Senghor's writings, we can follow the course of a creativity that sets the imaginary into motion. The flourishing of the imaginary begins with an elaborate exploitation of language and moves on through myth, images, and colors to meditations on time.

The development of Senghor's poetical language draws on myths of origin in which childhood imaginatively interacts with death. By the magic of the word, but also by that of an imagination that exults in the mysterious shadow of a floating song, the wandering imagination of the poet undertakes a journey to the kingdom of childhood. This journey arrives at the kingdom of death.[6] The peculiar language of death's kingdom is *silence*. Senghorian poetics magnifies rhythm and musicality, but it is also instructed by silence: "The role of silence is active. Silence is sonorous" (1990a).

Words naturally give birth to myths. Senghor rekindles these myths by the evocation of the magical names of queens and heroes. It should be noted, though, that Senghor's myths are not exclusively African; he borrows from other mythologies. Senghor cites the name of one of the founders of an African kingdom, Sidra Badral, but also Belborg from Northern European mythology (1990b: 33, 136). As for his imagery, Senghor insists not only on its mystical significance but also on its roots in the heart of the sensible (1990a: 164). The image is also a separation of the visible and the invisible. The image recalls color, which, for Senghor, is a melody: "Rhythm does not only have forms, it also has colors" (ibid. 292). Time is not thought of in a linear fashion but in terms of regeneration and becoming. Senghor in his multifaceted poetry privileges what he calls "image-analogy," which favors "figures of signification" over "figures of construction."

Senghor's influence in poetry is especially apparent in the writings of the philosopher Kä Mana (Congo). In Mana's work (1986), the tension between concept and image is continually evoked. For Mana, both concept and image complement each other, since neither can be excluded when studying meaning. Mana is also interested in understanding what constitutes the "virtuality" of poetry. What guarantees a poem's fecundity? It must be its evocative power. But an evocation is not a call from a hidden world or a nostalgic remembrance. What is evoked is something that is situated ahead of us. Mana's evocative poetry recalls the role played by Senghor's "figures of signification." The challenge today resides in establishing an association between this kind of study of meaning and a strategy of creation (in the sense of *poiēsis*). The question is: what does it mean to create something of significance? What are today's modes of creation?

Autobiography

Writing about the self is difficult because before starting, the constitution of the self must be understood. How does objectivity play a role in the narrative of

555

the self? How does the self duplicate itself in the attempt to speak of itself? These are questions that are posed to philosophers of the Cartesian tradition who have considered the subject of autobiography. The same questions can be found, in African literature, in the genre of autobiography. Often passed over in silence, one of the first francophone African novels was in fact a "writing about the self" – an autobiography. Bakary Diallo (Senegal) published in 1926 the novel *Force Bonté*. This novel is an autobiographical narrative that tells the story of the author's conscription into the French Army during the First World War. We read in this novel of Diallo's glorious feats of courage and of the glory of French "humanism." In this novel, autobiography is an instrument for the self-glorification of the author and of France. But we find a more social-critical use of autobiographical narrative in the work of Mariama Bâ (Senegal). In her novel, *Une si longue lettre*, Bâ criticizes polygamy and defends the institution of schooling and its mission of "allowing us to escape the quicksand of traditions and superstitions... allowing us to appreciate various civilizations without renouncing ours" (1980).

Autobiographical narrative also possesses a historical value; it tells, records, and transmits. In *Cette Afrique-là* (1963), Jean-Ikellé Matiba (Cameroon), through the character Mômha, recounts life in Cameroon before German colonization. The narrative of Mômha is a historical account of "cette Afrique-là," which has long since disappeared.

Autobiography also can be found, to be sure rather rarely, among certain francophone African philosophers. The French philosophical tradition in which these African philosophers were trained only rarely encourages the use of autobiographical narrative. One exception is Paulin Hountondji (Benin), whose most recent work is called *Combats pour le sens: un itinéraire africain*. In this work of previously published essays, Hountondji recounts the story of his intellectual development, beginning in Porto Novo in Benin until his stay in Paris. He then goes on to recount his intellectual interests in Husserl, Althusser, the critique of ethnophilosophy, and, finally, his foray into politics. He speaks of "My passage into government... as minister of national education during the transition, to be followed by an appointment as minister of culture and communication... with the foolish hope that my services would eventually be of some use until I finally wrote my letter of resignation on October 28, 1994" (1997: 252). This autobiography demonstrates, as in every autobiography, a "juridical mentality" (Adorno) that looks for self-justification and that rereads history *post factum*. The autobiographical writings of philosophers, poets, and novelists pose for francophone African philosophy a number of new challenges. How are we to describe the unity of the person and the diversity of itineraries within the same existential adventure in which the "I" is itself "played" by the subject who recounts? How is one to analyze the "intricacies of narrative" (Ricoeur) in the "mises en scène" of the self? How can the "autobiographical contract" (Lejeune) hide its latent justification and narcissism?

Emancipation and violence

Violence has many causes, such as the diversity of desires that is at the heart of every social group. In Africa, violence also has an infinite variety of manifestations and numerous points of entry into African history. Here are a few examples of the sorts of violence just alluded to: slavery, colonization, violent crime in the cities, the use of force in party propaganda, the deliberate destruction of intellectual spaces, pillaging, famine, etc. Novelists have often described violence in their writings. A critique of colonial violence is given by Mongo Beti in her novels, *Le pauvre Christ de Bomba* and *Ville cruelle* (Beti was still writing under the pseudonym Eza Boto). In these novels, colonization is attacked for its shameful exploitation of human beings, the arrogance of the colonizers, the inferiority complex it caused in colonized peoples, the introduction of a hypocritical form of Christianity, the creation of incongruous neocolonial elites, and, most of all, the new myths it caused Africans themselves to invent.

In this last respect, Beti's criticism is similar to that of Frantz Fanon. Fanon, the psychiatrist from Martinique, who was nourished intellectually on Parisian existentialism at its height during the 1960s, never ceased to fight colonial domination and the mental alienation it produced. His critique takes issue with the colonial's truncated sense of identity: "I begin to suffer from not being white to the extent that the white man discriminates against me" (1952: 99). Under the influence of Hegel's master–slave dialectic, Fanon attempts to reverse domination and comes to believe in the redemptive value of violence. With this view of violence, he places a special emphasis on the subjective side of revolution (the emergence of consciousness): "for the colonized peoples, life can only flow forth from the cadavre and decomposition of the colony" (1961). The violence of colonized peoples is a counter-violence of emancipation.

Fanon's notion of violence has been taken up by novelists and essayists such as Ngindu Nkashama (Congo-Zaire), notably in his novel *Vie et moeurs d'un primitif en Essone quatre-vingt-onze* (1987) and in his essay *Ruptures et écritures de violence* (1997). Both these texts raise the question of violence as a means of emancipation, and thus reflect Fanon's own analysis of violence. The richness of Fanon's thought makes it possible for African francophone philosophy to examine anew the relationship between emancipation and violence. The challenge consists in thinking anew the transformations of violence today: how can violence become transformed by adopting more subtle means?

Both literature and philosophy have a number of intertextual relationships, particularly as regards three domains: namely, political philosophy, philosophy of history, and aesthetics. One illustrative fact in particular should be emphasized. The political tendency of the critique of ethnophilosophy among African francophone philosophers (Towa and Hountondji) owes a great deal to numerous passages in *Discours sur le colonialisme* (1950) by the poet Aime Césaire; which is yet another confirmation of the extent to which philosophy and literature both journey along similar paths.

Notes

1   Our choice of these three authors is, admittedly, arbitrary.
2   For my own critique of African philosophers who have neglected the philosophical topic of women and sexuality, cf. Bidima 1993, 1995.

3 See my critique of the phallocentric tendency in Bidima 1995: 83–90.
4 Ntumba coins the term from the word "Biso" which means "we" in Lingala, the language of Congo.
5 Refer to Ntumba's critique of the Erlangen School. Ntumba's critique is influenced by the transcendental pragmatism of Karl Otto Apel. Cf. Ntumba 1985.
6 See Senghor's preface to "Ethiopiques" (1990b).

References

Awa Thiam, Ndeye (1987) *Continents noirs* (Paris: Éditions Tierce).
Bâ, Mariama (1980) *Une si longue lettre* (Dakar: NEA).
Badian, Seydou (1973) *Sous l'Orage* (Paris: Présence Africaine).
Beti, Mongo (1977) *Mission terminée* (Paris: Buchet-Chastel).
Bidima, Jean-Godefroy (1993) *Théorie critique et modernité négro-africaine: de l'École de Francfort à la "Docta spes africana"* (Paris: Publications de la Sorbonne).
Bidima, Jean-Godefroy (1995) *La Philosophie Négro-africaine* (Paris: PUF).
Bidima, Jean-Godefroy (1997) *L'Art négro-africain* (Paris: PUF).
Bidima, Jean-Godefroy (1998) "Présentation des cultures orales," in *Encyclopédie Philosophique Universelle*, vol. 4 (Paris: PUF).
Césaire, Aimé (1950) *Discours sur le colonialisme* (Paris: Éditions Réclame; 2nd edn. Présence Africaine, 1954).
Diallo, Bakary (1926) *Force Bonté* (Paris: Rieder).
Fanon, Frantz (1952) *Peaux noires, masques blancs* (Paris: Seuil).
Fanon, Frantz (1961) *Les Damnés de la terre* (Paris: Maspéro).
Glissant, Édouard (1966) *Introduction à une poétique du divers* (Paris: Gallimard).
Glissant, Édouard (1981) *Le Discours antillais* (Paris: Gallimard).
Glissant, Édouard (1990) *Poétique de la relation* (Paris: Gallimard).
Hazoumé, Paul (1938) *Doguicimi* (Paris: Larose).
Hountondji, Paulin J. (1997) *Combats pour le sens: un itinéraire africain* (Cotonou: Éditions Le Flamboyant).
Ikelle-Matiba, Jean (1963) *Cette Afrique-là* (Yaoundé: Clé).
Kourouma, Ahmadou (1970) *Les soleils des indépendances* (Paris: Seuil).
Laye, Camara (1976) *L'Enfant noir* (Paris: Plon).
Mana, Kä, *Une Poétique philosophique: De l'anthropologie de l'imaginaire à une esthétique évocative* (Ottignies/Louvain-La-Neuve: NORAF).
Mudimbe, Valentin Yves (1973) *L'autre face du royaume* (Lausanne: L'Âge d'homme).
Mudimbe, Valentin Yves (1988) *The Invention of Africa* (Illinois: Indiana University Press).
Mudimbe, Valentin Yves (1994a) *Les corps glorieux des mots et des êtres* (Paris: Présence Africaine).
Mudimbe, Valentin Yves (1994b) *Entre les eaux* (Paris: Présence Africaine).
Nanga, Bernard (1980) *Les Chauve-souris* (Paris: Présence Africaine).
Nanga, Bernard (1984) *La Trahison de Marianne* (Dakar: NEA).
Ngal, Georges (1983) *Poésie de la négritude. Approche structuraliste* (Sherbrooke: Editions Naaman).
Ngal, Georges (1994) *Lire le discours sur le colonialisme* (Paris: Présence Africaine).
Ngal, Georges (1998) *L'errance* (Paris: Présence Africaine).
Ngal, Georges (2000) *La philosophie du style* (Paris: Éditions Tanawa).
Ngandu, Pius (1987) *Vie et moeurs d'un primitif en Essonne quatre-vingt-onze* (Paris: l'Harmattan).
Ngandu, Pius (1997) *Ruptures et écritures de violence* (Paris: l'Harmattan).

Ntumba, Tshiamalenga (1985) "Y a-t-il un mythe du mythe?" *Diogène*, 132.

Oléko, Nkombe (1972) *Métaphore et métonymie* (Kinshasa: FTCK).

Oyono, Ferdinand (1975) *Le Vieux Nègre et la médaille* (Paris: Christian Bourgois).

Senghor Léopold Sedar (1962) *Pierre Teilhard de Chardin et la politique africaine* (Paris: Seuil).

Senghor Léopold Sedar (1964) *Liberté I* (Paris: Seuil).

Senghor Léopold Sedar (1971) *Liberté II* (Paris: Seuil).

Senghor Léopold Sedar (1976) *Pour une lecture africaine de Marx et d'Engels* (Dakar: NEA).

Senghor Léopold Sedar (1982) Preface: *La Pensée africaine d'Alassane Ndaw* (Dakar: NEA).

Senghor Léopold Sedar (1990a) *Liberté III* (Paris: Seuil).

Senghor Léopold Sedar (1990b) Preface: "*Éthiopiques,*" in *Œuvres Poétiques* (Paris: Seuil).

Towa, Marcien (1971) *Léopold Sedar Senghor: Négritude ou Servitude?* (Yaoundé: Clé).

47

Feminism and Africa: Impact and Limits of the Metaphysics of Gender

NKIRU NZEGWU

For the most part, prevailing definitions of gender in African studies have come from disciplines located within the Western body of knowledge. Scholars are often unaware how much these definitions are steeped in the mores and norms of the Judeo-Christian tradition, and the social conventions of European and European American cultures. These intellectual understandings of gender embody the political, social, and imperialist histories of the birth cultures. They reflect as well the binary opposition underlying Western epistemology in which women are defined in opposition to men, that is, are assigned converse attributes. "Gender," Susan Moller Okin, a feminist political scientist, declares, is *"the deeply entrenched institutionalization of sexual difference"* (her emphasis); it maps the culture of discrimination against women (1989: 2). This construal of gender, as implying male domination of women, owes its logic to the character of the original social context of discourse in which sex differentiation equals sex discrimination. The logical grammar of the concept exposes the inequality principle that lies at the heart of male–female relationships in that conceptual framework. Much more significantly, it reveals that the analytic category of gender is cognate with the category of woman.

Here I examine two ways in which the metaphysical implications of the concept of gender affect theoretical analyses and erode the cultural specificity and the historicity of societies, such as Igbo society. I start by examining the strategies employed in the false universalization of the Western concept of woman. I will then show how the theorization of a Nigerian female scholar achieves a similar objective even as she strives to produce a culturally grounded account of the position of woman in Igboland. My objective is not necessarily to invalidate the concept of gender per se, but rather to highlight the intrusive nature of the Western metaphysics of gender on theoretical formulations in and about other cultures.

This impact begins in innocuous ways in cross-cultural philosophical analysis. The white female US philosopher, Martha Nussbaum (1995), presents a picture of emotion in Igbo culture that she uses to validate the thesis that emotion is universally viewed as female, and passivity as womanish. She opens her article with a conflicted soliloquy by Okonkwo, the protagonist in Chinua Achebe's *Things Fall Apart* (1958). In it Okonkwo agonizes over his killing of Ikemefuna, who had clung to him as a son. He chastises himself for falling to pieces over this killing, especially since he had previously killed five men in battle. He worries that he has "become a shivering old woman." The excerpt ends with the following self-chastisement: "Okonkwo, you have become a woman indeed." Without questioning whether or not this fictional account of emotion has sociological accuracy, or whether the imagery of "shivering old woman" is correctly understood, Nussbaum deploys the soliloquy to represent Igbo culture as sexist. On this reading, emotion is relegated to the female side of the divide, a move that allows Nussbaum to globalize the social implication of sexism and to state that, on this showing, "Women are emotional, emotions are female." According to her, "this view, *familiar in Western and non-Western traditions alike*, has for thousands of years been used in various ways to exclude women from full membership in the human community" (1995: 360; emphasis mine). This opening strategy might well obscure the fact that Nussbaum is unproblematically treating Achebe's novel as a veridical sociological-cum-philosophical document, and is omitting examination of the specific sociologies and philosophies of the cultures in question.

The slide from fictional narrative to sociological truths may be symptomatic of the tendency to suppose that all societies – Western and non-Western alike – have the same ethical values, and that there is nothing complex or different in the conceptual categories of non-Western societies (including Igbo society). While it is important to see that this homogenization of the Western and non-Western worlds obstructs serious cross-cultural examination, it is more crucial to highlight the ways in which the false homogenization obscures contextual specificities and social complexities of a vast array of non-Western traditions. This homogenization makes them all seem unworthy of theoretical reflection. It needs to be reiterated that such appropriations of Africa legitimize, for example, the misreading of Igbo endogenous categories even when a scholar, such as Nussbaum, may be sympathetically trying to draw the cultures of Africa, China, and Micronesia into serious philosophical inquiry.

Though most commentaries on *Things Fall Apart* tend to focus on the novel's historical plot, notably, the colonial incursion and the Christianization of Igboland, readers focus less on Achebe's complex psychological study of a dysfunctional character in an achievement-oriented society. Caught in the restraining web of his obsessive fear, Okonkwo charges through life to self-destruction. The strength of the storyline is the completely believable way in which this insecure, frightened, frightful man represents a normal, well-adjusted Igbo man. The rich cultural data which Achebe skillfully marshals underwrite the plausibility of this picture. Completely absorbed with the protagonist's achievement, readers miss Okonkwo's periodic deviation from acceptable social norms. An example of this is Okonkwo's participation in the killing of Ikemefuna, the young sacrificial victim who had taken to him as a father, and the inability of his male social peers to make sense of some of his fears.

That Okonkwo's fears were not seen as normal is evident in Obierika's revulsion at Okonkwo's role in the death of Ikemefuna: "It is the kind of action for which the goddess wipes out whole families" (1958: 46). The gravity of Obierika's disapproval is, indeed, proof that Okonkwo, a male, was *expected to show emotion*. The existence of this expectation, and the expressed distaste of Obierika, clearly reinforce the view that males' expression of emotion was not perceived as a sign of weakness in Igbo

561

cultural logic. From the community's point of view, as conveyed by Obierika, human-ness rather than weakness is implicit in a father's expression of love for a child who has cleaved to him as a son. Such a demonstration of emotion is appropriate for fathers since this is precisely what it means to be a father; just as Okonkwo's emotional upset at his daughter's sickness would be viewed as an appropriate response rather than a sign of weakness. That Okonkwo missed this point and misinterpreted a socially approved behavior and its corresponding psychological state as weakness is a sign of his dysfunction rather than a revelation of Igbo cultural logic.

The problem is that in the haste to universalize a specific culture's reading of emotion, Nussbaum read the passage too literally. She thus came away with a warped interpretation of the Igbo conception of emotion.

Contextual Differences

While some may want Nussbaum to show good reason why she should treat a fictive account of emotion as a sociological account, I am more concerned with the fundamental assumption implicit in her argument that the category of women is unproblematic and that it truly captures female identities in all cultures and in all contexts. I will start by asking a seemingly obvious question: are there women in Igbo society?

An automatic response would be, "Yes, there are." However, shifting to the cultural logic of Onitsha (Igbo) society leads us to the word "*nwanyi*," the singular of "*umunwanyi*," which means offspring who are female. *Umunwanyi* is a category that distinguishes female human beings from *nwoke* (male human beings). Its primary and dominant function is to mark the biological sex of a child. Quite unlike the Western category "woman," *nwanyi* marks physiological differentiation without ranking or defining females in relation to males. In the translation of Igbo concepts to English, *nwanyi* has most regularly been treated as synonymous with "woman," even though they do not share the same attributes or conceptual scope. For instance, *nwanyi* does not exclusively refer to an adult female person; it refers to both children and adults. It does not imply that females are psychologically passive beings who are or ought to be submissive and subordinate to men. No social attribution is made about women's state of being or capabilities at this stage. In fact, there is no meaningful way to determine the social standing and what the temperaments of individuals in this generic category are, since their social identities still have to be independently fleshed out.

Western feminist analyses of the condition of women under patriarchy reveal, regardless of the social class or status of women, that the category "woman" defines women as the negative image of men. The ideology of masculinity underlying this patriarchal vision cast women as not just physiologically different, but as opposites. Men are strong and taciturn, women are weak and emotional; men are masters, women are subordinates. As feminist scholar Sheila Ruth succinctly puts it: "[t]hey all say that women as human beings are substandard: less intelligent; less moral; less competent; less able physically, psychologically, and spiritually;

small of body, mind, and character" (1990: 89). It is this masculist framework of the Western philosophical tradition that Nussbaum identifies as "typical in public life" when "it is claimed that women, on account of their emotional 'nature,' are incapable of full deliberative rationality, and should not perform various social roles in which rationality is required" (1995: 363–4).

As a concept of sex differentiation, *nwanyi* does not perform a similar function. This is because gender identity is a flexible, fluid state of being, and is tied to social roles and functions that demand deliberative rationality from females. Given their multiple social roles, Igbo females do not have one gender identity. The Igbo word that most closely approximates the meaning of "woman" in the Western imagination is *agbala*. It defines a category of self-assured, assertive females, who may or may not be married, and whose identity is not defined in relation to men. In sum, *nwanyi* and *agbala* refer to the female sex, but they do not ascribe specific social attributes, roles, or identities to them.

Meaningful social identity ascriptions take place at another level. In traditional times, and even today, within different communities, the first meaningful basis of identity is the lineage, where power is diffuse. Basic social differentiation occurs in the following categories: *umuada* (lineage daughters), *okpala* (lineage sons), and *inyemedi* (lineage wives). The principle of organization within each of these socially significant categories is seniority. Complications arise for the idea of a unitary social status for females if we examine the categories of *umuada* and *inyemedi*. Even though both refer to adult females, there are clear differences in identity and consciousness. The social nature of the relationship between *umuada* and *inyemedi* is a "husband"/"wife" relationship. As daughters of the lineage, *umuada* are in the social role of husbands to *inyemedi* or wives of the lineage. Consequently, *inyemedi* relate to *umuada* as wives. This husband/wife relationship of *umuada* and *inyemedi* is exactly the same that holds between *okpala* (lineage sons) and *inyemedi* (lineage wives). Under the lineage system, *umuada* (females, daughters) and *okpala* (males, sons) share the same dominant social role of "husband" to another group of females who are outsiders to the lineage. As outsiders, *inyemedi* or wives are socially subordinate to both lineage daughters and sons, whom they have to treat as "husbands." The effect on the consciousness of females relating to another group of females on the basis of a dominant/subordinate, "husband"/"wife" relationship means that solidarity cannot be built on biology. This fact must be grasped before any meaningful discussion of women's capabilities can begin.

The question of capabilities cannot even be addressed without considering a still further complication. Most *umuada* (lineage daughters) who inhabit a dominant location in their natal family also belong to the subordinate category of *inyemedi* (wives). Unlike the Western marriage structure that eliminates the rights of a married daughter in her natal family, *umuada* are ever-present forces in their natal families. They assume juridical and peacekeeping roles, and regularly perform purification duties as well as funerary rites for deceased members of the lineage. By virtue of the social importance of these roles, the question of being incapable of full deliberative rationality or of being unfit "to perform social roles in which rationality is required" never arises for *umuada*. This is because *umuada* never occupy an inferior, subordinate position in their lineage. They are never viewed as "less intelligent; less moral; less competent; less able physically, psychologically, and spiritually; small of body, mind, and character." A dominant influence in their lineages, while still maintaining permanent residence in their marital homes, *umunwanyi* (females) routinely develop at least two different identities between which they constantly switch back and forth.

By virtue of constantly shifting identity locations, females in western Igboland are never in either a permanently subordinate or dominant situation. Though the *inye-medi* (lineage wives) is a subordinate category within a lineage, no psychological or social attributions of the sort identified by Ruth are made about their emotional being. Further mitigating the effect of the formal subordinate status are the twin categories of motherhood and seniority that effectively transform the position of *nwuye* (wife) to one of formidable importance. Additionally, in a context where, historically, females could and did marry wives, "being a husband" or "being a wife" is not open to easy physiological interpretation as it is in Western culture. (*Di*, the term that is construed to mean "husband," merely refers to members of the family into which a female is married.)

Females can be both wives and husbands at the same time. Some can actually marry their own wife or wives (with no sexual relationship involved), and they can do so even when they are in a conjugal marital relationship with a male. Clearly, what this reveals are the deep conceptual differences between Igbo and US cultures, and the important sociological differences in the two cultures' conception of marriage that cannot be ignored in any determination of the intercultural relevance of the Western concept of "woman." As a matter of routine, all Igbo females are husbands, given the fact that there inevitably are some females who are wives in the family lineage. Females-as-daughters always stand in a husband relationship to the females who are wives in their family lineage. Because of this relational principle, and the entailed flexibility of identities, there is no absolute female identity outside of relational ties. No Igbo female is simply a wife; the daughter identity remains in force and is never erased by the wife identity. The term "husband" is not equivalent to a male designation, and what a female is cannot be sorted out without determining the governing relation between the individual and others.

Western Igboland is an achievement-oriented society, and in such a society individuals (both females and males) are expected to be industrious and to excel. Consequently, a social classification that subordinates women to men, or vice versa for that matter, cannot work. The question of reserving a negative set of psychological attributes for women and positive ones for men does not arise. Females are expected to succeed too, which is why honorific expressions like *agwu* (tiger), *odogu* (the brave), *o gbatulu enyi* (one who felled an elephant) are applied across sex lines to daring, shrewd, successful individuals of both sexes. Despite contemporary modifications of Igbo culture wrought by Christianity and modern social living, the existence of such ascriptions undermines the legitimacy of Nussbaum's claim that non-Western traditions (including the Igbo) share the passive view of women. The problem with Nussbaum's account, as with many feminists' accounts too, is the utilization of European American social histories, cultural values, and norms to frame her concept of woman and then use it to interpret Igbo social practice. This illicit method of interpretation generates stereotypical conceptions of patriarchal domination in Igbo culture at the expense of more compelling accounts.

A Sticky Metaphysics

The second major, and more subtle, way in which the metaphysics of gender generates distortions occurs primarily in the writings of African women scholars. Because the concept of gender has become such an important analytic tool, many African women scholars instinctively employ it without considering its cultural nuances. For many, the impressive thesis of oppression offers a powerful analytical tool that provides a neat overarching explanation for women's obvious disadvantages in societies. We see this in Amadiume's latest book, *Reinventing Africa: Matriarchy, Religion, and Culture* (1997), where she utilizes the concept of gender (a) to argue that, historically, matriarchy was the dominant ethos of sociopolitical organization and moral life in Africa, and (b) to try to establish a historical basis for the empowerment of modern African women.

According to Amadiume, in Nnobi (Igbo) society, "the ideology of gender has its basis in the binary opposition between the *mkpuke*, the female mother-focused matricentric unit and the *obi*, the male-focused ancestral house" (ibid. 18). This opposition of male and female and of father and mother invokes from the onset the conceptual scheme of patriarchy on which is based "the ideology of gender." Amadiume's deployment of the concept of gender involves an entrenched logic which construes sex differentiation as equivalent to sex discrimination. It endows it with ontological status through treating it as "a fundamental principle of social organization...that predates class and is carried over into class formations" (ibid. 113). Faced with the fluidity of the male and female roles in the society in question, which violates the sex discrimination logic of her category, Amadiume manufactures a "neuter gender construct" (a "third classificatory system"), to deal with the occasions when "men and women share the same status and play the same roles without social stigma" (ibid. 129). In other words, she tries to bypass the internal inconsistency of supposing that men and women who are by her theory intrinsically and definitively gendered can, at the same time, be neuter gendered.

But what does it mean to be gendered and neuter gendered at the same time? If gender is foundational, as Amadiume maintains, then the neuter construct is redundant given that only gendered bodies will share that role, and map their gender status upon it. On the other hand, if the corpus of social roles and statuses transcends the logic and politics of gender ascription, so that "monolithic masculinization of power was eliminated" (ibid.), then it must be that the category of gender is not really foundational. Because the shared status and roles existed historically in Igbo society, and no "social stigma" was attached to them, gender could not have been the operative category.

This suggests that it was the major social changes instituted during colonial rule that created some of the male-privileging traditions which today are being represented as "customary" or "indigenous." We are led to believe that these male-privileging traditions have historically been part of a culture that is supposed to be fundamentally patriarchal, even though "daughters were *classified as male* in relation to wives and had authority *just like their brothers*" (ibid. 148; emphasis mine). The point is not that Amadiume does not acknowledge these historical events that transformed Igbo society, which she does; the point is rather that she is unaware of the displacement of Igbo social history and conceptual schemes by the patriarchal force implicit in her categories of interpretation. For this reason, her acknowledgment of the historical changes wrought by colonialism does not go far enough.

A clear sign that Amadiume's acknowledgment falls short is seen in the fact that the male-privileging features of the concept of gender overwrite aspects of her descriptions of Igbo culture. Because she is committed to a gender frame of analysis, she fails to see the incompatibility between the gendered frame and the Igbo social frame. Thus, despite her brilliant insight that the flexibility of Igbo categories marks an important difference between Igbo society and European patriarchal societies, she undermines this insight by insisting on the gendered description of the surrounding culture.

Matters are substantially complicated by Amadiume's language of gender in that it produces cultural distortions in the Igbo context. It does this in the following ways. First, it injects the metaphysics of patriarchy into the cultures of western Igboland, where it positions the patriarchal scheme at the conceptual background. Second, it initiates a gender-based discourse that entrenches this scheme by making it a foil to the matriarchal scheme in the foreground. Third, it artificially opposes the *mkpuke* to the *obi* and presents this opposition as an accurate analysis of the relationship between the two units. And, fourth, it collapses sex differentiation into sex discrimination, so that all instances of difference are then made to imply discrimination. These steps, of course, guarantee her gender-mediated interpretation.

In fact, it is the conceptual complexity of Igbo culture at the foundational level that explains Amadiume's need to introduce a third category to circumvent, as it seems, the distorting effects of the constructed patriarchal structure that she had inserted into the culture. The neuter category, thus introduced, injects a false flexibility into the culture, and makes the gender-empowerment significance of the three examples she offers as proof of this flexibility problematic. These are that (1) daughters can become "male"; (2) females can marry and become husbands; and (3) wealthy women can buy access into male associations (ibid. 149).

Given that the direction of mobility in each case is toward the male roles and status, and rarely in the female direction, these examples of social flexibility and female empowerment are hardly convincing. They preserve intact the normative status of men, men's roles, and men's relationship to women. Whatever is "male" is privileged and constitutes the social space of worthiness. The existence of this concealed yardstick tells us that, contrary to Amadiume's objective, her account of matriarchy succeeds paradoxically in presenting Igbo society as patriarchal, one in which women were structurally disadvantaged on the basis of sex. Interestingly, her thesis of gender flexibility reinforces this structural disadvantage by exceptionalizing the efforts of successful women. It suggests that only a few wealthy women and a few audacious females could use the "neuter roles" to negotiate themselves out of the unfavorable situations of inferiority she had created. In short, her observation that the Igbo social "system was not monolithic and not rigid because gender-bending and gender-crossing were practised" (ibid. 149) is deployed in ways that ultimately reinforce the existence of a patriarchal classificatory scheme in which males occupy privileged positions.

Chasing Shadows: Getting our Analysis Right

The theoretical difficulties in Amadiume's analyses show that there is a disjunction between her interpretation of Igbo culture and society and the reality on the ground. If the third classificatory scheme is illusory, as I contend, what does this say for the roles and status she identified as "neuter"? Do they exist? Are there such roles and status in societies of western Igboland?

For all its claimed capacity to explain the flexibility of Igbo social structure, Amadiume's neuter category obscures the social logic of the roles it is deployed to explain. Basically, this is because it is a response to an artificial dilemma created by an interpretive scheme. Consider the "male-daughter" phenomenon that she represents as a neuter role. There is no such linguistic or cultural expression as *nwoke-ada*, which *is* the accurate translation of Amadiume's "male daughter." This is not to say that the social institution alluded to is imaginary, but rather that her representation of it misses the mark. There used to be (and there may still be in some communities) a widespread formal institution of considerable import known as *idigbe*, *idegbe*, or *mgba*. This institution enables a daughter to remain in, or to dissolve, her marriage and return to her natal home to have, with a paramour, children who are assimilated into her own lineage.

There are two senses in which *idigbe* or *mgba* is understood. The first sense describes a situation in which a female is in a consensual relationship with a paramour. She retains her primary identity as daughter and never becomes his wife. Because no bridewealth is exchanged, *ada no na iba* (literally, the daughter in the patrilineal sanctuary) or *ada di na obi* (literally, the daughter in the patricentric unit) has sole custody of the children of the union. The children of a female in such circumstances derive their name, identity, and rights from her lineage or *obi*. In this sense, *adiba*, or *adaobi*, formally describes this status of a daughter within the lineage, and informs the community of her role. It also indicates that her children have the same status in the lineage as those of her brothers. The second sense, which is the one Amadiume constantly alludes to, is also expressed by *adiba* or *adaobi*. It designates a daughter who formally occupies the ancestral family sanctuary of fathers. This occurs on the rare occasion that there is no male successor to pass on the family name, and there is no wife of a childbearing age in the compound to produce a male child. A daughter either foregoes marriage, or ends her marriage to uphold the family sanctuary and to prevent the obliteration of the family name.

Social roles have specific purposes and their meanings and interpretations have to be sought in the relevant sociocultural context of practice. Because Amadiume did not closely attend to the cultural parameters of the roles and status she classifies as neuter, her interpretation of the *mgba* and *adaobi* institution produces fictional meanings in which the gender-loaded imagery of "male daughter" is invoked to explain a social phenomenon whose meaning lies elsewhere. This chosen imagery is conceptually problematic for a variety of reasons. It conflicts with the logic of *adaobi* as "daughter in the patricentric unit." It problematizes the presence of this daughter exercising her responsibilities in the natal residence. Also, it implausibly

567

suggests that this daughter's presence is intelligible only if she is transformed into a male, a logic that casts the female presence as socially and ontologically deviant. The idea of *adaobi* implying the transformation of daughters into males wreaks havoc on Igbo cultural logic. It suggests that membership in an *obi* is predicated on "being male" rather than on "being a child"; it casts daughters as less worthy than sons; and it confers value on them only if they can somehow become sons. Not only does this state of affairs misconstrue the principle of family-as-lineage formation and what it means to be a father, it also arbitrarily nullifies a daughter's membership in her own *obi*.

In concluding, it is worth reiterating that other examples abound of misinterpretations of the cultural ethos of African societies, in which the deployed concept of gender invents false bridges to explain social roles, statuses, processes, and the logic of various practices. In my analysis of the works of Nussbaum and Amadiume, historicity is revealed as the critical constraint that would have limited the free-ranging effect of the metaphysics of the concept of gender. Historicity is not the mere recitation of "facts" and events, it involves confronting historical events, historicizing interpretations, and using an appropriate yardstick. The combination of these three ensures that timeframes are not illicitly collapsed, that societal formations are not redefined, and that conceptual frames of different cultures are not illicitly switched. Some of the principal shortcomings in feminist analyses come from inattentiveness to historicity. Nussbaum is oblivious to it, and though Amadiume is familiar with Nigeria's colonial and contemporary history, she underestimates the impact of change, the depth of cultural distortions wrought by the categories (e.g. generic man, woman, wife) and concepts (e.g. work, domesticity, and marriage) borrowed from Britain. Because of these limitations, both scholars adopted uncritically the European and American construal of gender and its implicit thesis of female subordination. In the particular case of Amadiume, this adoption propels her toward interpretive directions that are incompatible with the reasonable, historically sound aspects of her claim that a "monolithic masculinization of power was eliminated" in Igboland.

References

Achebe, Chinua (1958) *Things Fall Apart* (London: Heinemann Educational Books).

Amadiume, Ifi (1997) *Reinventing Africa: Matriarchy, Religion, and Culture* (London: Zed Books Ltd.).

Nussbaum, Martha (1995) "Emotions and Women's Capabilities," in Martha Nussbaum and Jonathan Glover (eds.), *Women, Culture Development* (Oxford: Clarendon Press).

Okin, Susan Moller (1989) *Justice, Gender and Family* (New York: Basic Books, Inc.).

Further reading

Adewoye, Omoniyi (1977) *The Judicial System in Southern Nigeria, 1854–1954* (London: Longman).

Amadiume, Ifi (1987) *Male Daughters, Female Husbands* (London: Zed Books Ltd.).

Appiah, Kwame Anthony (1992) *In My Father's House* (New York: Oxford University Press).

Boserup, Ester (1970) *Women's Role in Economic Development* (London: George Allen and Unwin).

Ekejiuba, Felicia (1995) "Down to Fundamentals: Women-centered Hearthholds in Rural West Africa," in Deborah Fahy Bryceson (ed.), *Women Wielding the Hoe* (Oxford: Oxford University Press).

Henderson, Richard (1972) *The King in Every Man* (New Haven: Yale University Press).

Mba, Nina (1982) *Nigeria Women Mobilized* (Berkeley: International and Area Studies University of Berkeley).

Musisi, Nakanyike B. (1992) "Colonial and Missionary Education: Women and Domesticity in Uganda, 1900–1945," in Karen Tranberg Hansen (ed.), *African Encounters with Domesticity* (New Brunswick, NJ: Rutgers University Press).

Nzegwu, Nkiru (1996) "Philosophers' Intellectual Responsibility to African Females," *American Philosophical Association's (APA) Newsletter*, 90(I): 130–5.

Nzegwu, Nkiru (1996) "Questions of Identity and Inheritance: A Critical Review of Anthony Appiah's *In My Father's House*," *HYPATIA: A Journal of Feminist Philosophy*, Special Issue on Feminist Theory and the Family, 2(1): 176–99.

Nzegwu, Nkiru (1999) "Colonial Racism: Sweeping Out Africa with Europe's Broom," in Susan Babbitt and Sue Campbell (eds.), *Philosophy and Racism* (Ithaca: Cornell University Press).

Okonjo, Kamen (1976) "The Dual-Sex Political System in Operation: Igbo Women and Community Politics in Midwestern Nigeria," in Nancy Hafkin and Edna Bay (eds.), *Women in Africa* (Stanford, CA: Stanford University Press).

Oyewumi, Oyeronke (1997) *Invention of Women: Making an African Sense of Western Gender Discourses* (Minnesota: University of Minnesota Press).

Ruth, Sheila (1990) "Images of Women in Patriarchy: The Masculist-Defined Woman," in Ruth (ed.), *Issues in Feminism* (Mountain View, CA: Mayfield Publishing Company).

569

Index

570

Ahmes, scribe 34
aimo (lack of knowledge/failure) 400
Akan culture: Abraham 101, 370;
communitarianism 495; community 493;
communocracy 446; cosmology 105; *creatio ex
nihilo* 267–8; destiny 318–19; drums 8;
dualism 347; evil 318–19; God 346;
Gyekye 110–11, 318–19, 347, 360; human
beings 501; immortality 348; mind 346, 347,
349–50; morality 112, 360; *Onyame* (Supreme
being) 357; personhood 332–3, 347, 350;
philosophy 111, 360; proverbs 112, 139n28;
sensation 204–5; shadow 341; soul 333, 347;
sunsum 341; time 10; truth 107–8, 264, 266,
271; Wiredu 347
Akan language 7–8, 16, 17, 271
Ake, Claude 131, 505
al-Akhdarî, Abd ar-Rahmân 70
Akoko, Mbuya 279
Akpafu culture 408, 409
akunlegba (destiny) 315
akunleyan (destiny) 315–16
Al Ma'mun, Caliph 67–8
Alain Locke Conference 91
Alan, John 213
Albert the Great 162
Alexandria 51
Alexandrian School 52
Alfa, Samuel Audu 9
Algeria: anti-colonialism 475; FNL 216;
France 216, 475, 477; *El Moudjahid* 217; religious
conflict 480; revolution 230n4; *see also* Fanon,
Frantz
'Ali Al Mazrui, *'alim* al-Amîn bin 73
Allies, World War II 476–7
Althusser, Louis 550
altruism 494
Amadiume, Ifi: gender 565–6, 568; male
daughters 567–8
Ambrose, St 60
American Philosophical Association 91
Amin, Osman 164, 165–6
Amin, Samir 131
Amo, Anton Wilhelm 24; as African
philosopher 205–6; *The Apatheia of the Human
Mind* 200–6; childhood 191, 200; Descartes 195,
200–6; dissertation 192–3; education 192;
Leibniz 195; Loescher 193–4; Nzima
language 198–9; spirit 200–1; university 192,
195–6; Winkelman 198; works 200
Amon 43, 49
Amon-Ra 40
Amselie, Jean-Loup 66
Amu, Ephraim 406
An-Na'im, Abdullahi Ahmed 500
Anambra valley region 420–1
ancestorhood 327–9, 379; *chu* 454; Islam 381,
382n10; Luo culture 490; poetry 378–9;
Wiredu 327, 380–1
Anderson, A. R. 291

Andryanos, Emperor 189
angels 53–4
anger 212
Anglo-Boer War 510
Anglophone African philosophers 6, 22, 99, 102,
124–5
Angola 475, 477
anima (force) 196
animals/human beings 180, 339
animism 355, 368
Anselm, St 58
Antel, inscription of 35
anthropocentrism 392–3
anthropology 2, 3, 530–1; classical 278;
culture 104–5; religion 355; tradition 127
anti-colonialism 20, 475–7
anti-ethnophilosophy 4, 5
Antun, Farah 164
apartheid 149–50, 154; aftermath 516n1;
defenders 153–4; Derrida 509–10;
dissidents 153–4; Mbiti 155; neutralists 153–4;
phenomenology 153; philosophy 149, 151–8;
reality/truth 515; violence 207
apatheia thesis 204–5
apokatastasis 54, 55
apostasy 191–2
Appiah, Anthony Kwame 119–22; fellowship
associations 454, 457; folk philosophy 120;
Islam 67; literature and philosophy 22;
modernity/postmodernity 548; progress 9;
race 120; self-identity 496; works 119–20
Aqît, Ahmad 'Umar Muhammad 72
Aquinas, St Thomas 61, 162, 238
ara (body) 320, 334
Arab culture 24, 67–8, 71–2, 171
Arabization 521–2
Argentina 511, 513
Aristotle: Bantu philosophy 239–40; being 235–6;
Islamic scholars/logic 67, 70; metaphysics 234;
Organon 68; politics 450; reason 41;
subsidiarity 436
Arkoun, M. 170
Armah, Ayi Kwei 534
Armenian massacres 474
Armstrong, D. M. 348
Arnauld, Robert 376
Arnobius 52
Arom, Simha 411
Aronson, Ronald 154, 157
art 22; abstraction 428; aesthetics 425; appreciation
of 427–8; authenticity 426; colonialism 431;
communalism 426, 428–9; community 415;
experiencing of 432n8; history 431;
imagination 426–7; institutions 426;
knowledge 271; moral element 426, 432n7;
onlookers 425; pleasure 427; reason 428; self-
identity 420–1; senses 427–8; society 426;
Supreme being 428; Western tradition 431n1
Arusha Declaration 256–7
Asante, Molefi 92

580

Mudimbe, V. Y. 118–19, 140n41, 231, 491, 550, 551
Muhammad, Askia 69, 70, 73, 75n10
Muhammad, Prophet 375–6, 377
Mulago, Vincent 491
muntu (human person) 326, 336
Murdock, George Peter 533–4
Murray, Gilbert 539
Mûsâ, 'Iyâd ibn 70
Museveni, Yoweri 479
music 405, 407–8; aesthetics 404–5, 410, 412; art 406; ceremonial 405; contemplative 409, 410; Ewe language 407; functional 408–9; funeral 405, 408–9; role of listening 410, 428; lullabies 409–10; Northern Ewe 407; popular 405–6, 410; religion 406; society 411; songs for thinking 410; traditional 405; vocabulary 407, 410; *see also* drumming
musical instruments 405–6, 411
musicality 411
musicology 404, 405
Muslim Brotherhood 164
Mutaka (chief) 436
muzimu (soul) 236
mythology 100, 543, 544–5, 555

Nairobi World Conference of Philosophy 388
naming 339, 340, 367
Nanga, Bernard 551–2
Nash, Andrew 151
Nation of Islam 473
National Action Campaign, ANC 209
national unity 505
nationalism 472–4; Afrikaans 150, 473, 474; colonization 481; cultural 358, 473; Kaunda 250–2; Zambia 250–2
nationalist-ideological philosophy 207, 263
natural law theory 132–4
Nazism 472, 473, 474, 477, 511
Ndaw, Alassane 551
Ndebele people 478–9
negation 287–8
Negritude 473; Blyden 80; Francophone African philosophers 99; identity 6; Senghor 5, 6, 99, 141n54, 156, 296, 489–90, 550, 551; Towa 551
The Negro 79–80
Negro-Berber humanism 246, 255
neo-Calvinism 151, 153
neocolonialism 115, 131
neo-Fichteanism 151, 153–4
neo-Marxism 469n7, 532
Neoplatonism 36, 51, 60, 161
neo-Thomism 164–5
nepotism 441
Nestorius 161
Newton, Sir Isaac 10, 348
Ngal, G. 550, 551
Ngandu, Pius 550
Nicol, G. G. M. 83
Nigeria 254, 406, 474

Nilotic peoples 503–4
njangis (fellowship associations) 455, 456–7
Nkashama, Ngindu 557
nkpu (prenuptial rites) 415–19, 424n1
Nkrumah, Kwame 18–19, 23, 99, 200; African socialism 245; communalism 252; communitarianism 488–90; conscientism 141n54, 157, 255; ethnophilosophy 532, 533; Fanon 216; human nature 244; leadership 243; Marxism-Leninism 245; one-party system 252; philosophy/social milieu 149
Nobel Peace Prize 207, 209
Nolutshungu, S. C. 213
non-existence 36–7
non-governmental organizations 464
non-violence 208; 213–14
North/South divide 461, 469n7, n11, 476
Northern Elements Progressive Union 254
Northern Ewe 407, 410
Northern People's Congress 254
nostalgia 473–4
Nso culture: art 425; *chu* 454; creativity 428, 429; death 392, 430; fellowship associations 454–6; Fondom 453–4; masks 428, 429, 430; praise singer 450; world-view 389–90
Ntumba, Tshiamalenga 550, 554
Nun (primordial waters) 40, 43
Nuremberg trials 511
Nussbaum, Martha C.: collectives 496; discourse ethics 515; emotion 561–2, 563; gender 568; Igbo culture 560–2; women's passivity 564
Nut (sky) 43
Nwala, T. U. 357–8
nwanyi (female offspring) 562, 563
Nyanda, Zimbabwe 478–9
Nyerere, Julius 18–19, 99; African socialism 245; army disbanded 480; communitarianism 488–90; one-party system 252–3; socialism 243, 245, 255–7; villages 488–9
Nzima language 198–9

Obatala, god 313
obi (male ancestral house) 565, 566
obligation 35, 185–6, 501–2
Ockham, William of 345, 346
Odu Corpus 313–14
Odu Ifa 266
Oedipus story 189
O'Fahey, Rex Sean 24, 74
Ogbegunda 313
Ogot, B. A. 372
Ogotemmeli: Dogon peoples 275, 276–7, 278; Griaule 2–3, 100, 140n46, 274, 275, 276, 278
Ogunda Meji, Ifa Corpus 313–14
okan (heart/mind) 313, 334
Okere, Theophilus 126–7
Okin, Susan Moller 560
Okolo, Okanda 127–8
okpala (lineage sons) 563–4

581